One Race, One Gospel, One Task

One Race
One Gospel
One Task

VOLUME II

WORLD CONGRESS ON EVANGELISM • BERLIN 1966

OFFICIAL REFERENCE VOLUMES: Papers and Reports

Edited by Carl F. H. Henry and W. Stanley Mooneyham

WORLD WIDE PUBLICATIONS

MINNEAPOLIS, MINNESOTA

Published by World Wide Publications, 1313 Hennepin Avenue,
Minneapolis, Minnesota 55403 U.S.A.

Library of Congress Catalog Card Number: 67–22479
Manufactured in the United States of America

TABLE OF CONTENTS

PAGE

INTRODUCTION TO VOLUME II   xiii

Section I

THE AUTHORITY FOR EVANGELISM • *Johannes Schneider*   1

The Teaching of the Bible

THE BIBLE AND THE EVANGELISTIC TASK • *Paul Schmidt*   11

THE USE OF SCRIPTURE
IN EVANGELISM • *Herbert M. Arrowsmith*   14

EVANGELISM AND THE TEACHING OF ACTS • *Philip Teng*   17

COMMISSIONED TO COMMUNICATE • *Bob Pierce*   20

REPORT OF GROUP DISCUSSION • *Harold B. Kuhn*   24

The Lord's Command

GO AND TELL • *Michael Kyriakakis*   25

THE GREAT COMMISSION • *Kenneth L. Chafin*   28

NEW TESTAMENT EVANGELISM • *Tom Rees*   31

CALLED TO OBEY • *Justin Mabiala*   35

REPORT OF GROUP DISCUSSION • *J. D. Douglas*   37

The Spirit's Constraint

THE CONFLICT OF THE SPIRITS • *V. Raymond Edman*   38

CHRIST AND THE SPIRIT • *J. Dwight Wadsworth*   40

THE STIRRING OF THE SPIRIT • *Alfred Stanway*   43

NO EVANGELICAL MONOPOLY • *Juan M. Isais*   47

REPORT OF GROUP DISCUSSION • *James M. Boice*   49

The Destiny of the Lost

THE WAY OF THE LOST • *Subodh K. Sahu*   51

LOST HUMANITY REQUIRES RESCUE • *Mervin E. Rosell*   54

THE PLIGHT OF THE LOST • *Suteichi Oye*   59

UNREACHED BY THE GOSPEL • *Percival W. Gibson*   62

REPORT OF GROUP DISCUSSION • *A. Morgan Derham*   64

The Return of Christ

EVANGELISM AND ESCHATOLOGICAL
IMPERATIVES • *Thomas F. Zimmerman*   65

EVANGELISM AND THE SECOND COMING • *Ian W. Thomas*   68

EVANGELISM AND THE LORD'S
IMMINENT RETURN • *Raghuel P. Chavan*   72

MOTIVATED BY THE FORWARD LOOK • *Ernst Schrupp*   74

REPORT OF GROUP DISCUSSION • *Stuart Barton Babbage*   76

The Church's Tradition and Practice

THE CHURCH'S FIRST FIVE CENTURIES • *Ezra Gebremedhin*   77

THE REFORMATION AND
EVANGELISM • *A. Skevington Wood*   81

MAJOR REVIVALS AND EVANGELISM • *Ian S. Rennie*   84

CONTEMPORARY EVANGELISTIC
TECHNIQUES • *J. Christy Wilson, Jr.*   87

REPORT OF GROUP DISCUSSION • *Dwight L. Baker*   91

Section II

THE BASIC THEOLOGY OF EVANGELISM •
Harold John Ockenga   95

The Fallenness of Man

AFFIRMATION AND PRACTICE • *Harold O. J. Brown*   104

THE FALL OF MAN • *Stuart Barton Babbage*   108

CONTEMPORARY SYMPTOMS
OF MAN'S FALL • *Samuel J. Mikolaski*   111

MODERN MAN AND HIS NEEDS • *Hans Rohrbach*   114

REPORT OF GROUP DISCUSSION • *Leon Morris*   119

Sin and the Moral Law

SIN IN BIBLICAL PERSPECTIVE • *Saphir P. Athyal*   120

EVANGELISM AND THE
REALITY OF SIN • *Samuel A. Benétreau*   122

THE NEED FOR BIBLICAL MORALITY • *A. Morgan Derham*   125

THE NEW MORALITY • *Leslie Hunt*   128

The Ground of Forgiveness

BASIC PREACHING
OF THE ATONEMENT • *John C. Winston, Jr.*   131

CHRIST THE MEDIATOR • *Theodore Williams*   134

REPORT OF GROUP DISCUSSION • *Jack Stowell*   136

The Nature of Faith

FAITH AND THE GOSPEL • *George R. Beasley-Murray*   137

A TRINITARIAN FAITH • *Jarl Wahlström*   140

A NEW LIFE PRINCIPLE • *Addison H. Leitch*   143

REPORT OF GROUP DISCUSSION • *Ted W. Engstrom*   146

Justification and Sanctification

ASPECTS OF CHRIST'S
REDEEMING WORK • *Jean-Paul Benoit*   147

SANCTIFICATION, THE FRUIT
OF JUSTIFICATION • *W. Stanford Reid*   150

CHRIST IN US • *Paul S. Rees*   153

REPORT OF GROUP DISCUSSION • *Ian Rennie*   156

The Regenerating Work of the Spirit

THE THEOLOGY OF REGENERATION • *J. Wayte Fulton, Jr.*   157

THE HOLY SPIRIT'S
REGENERATING WORK • *Maurice A. P. Wood*   160

REGENERATION AND THE
BELIEVER • *Theodore J. Stanley*   164

THE RESULTS OF REGENERATION • *Corrie ten Boom*   167

REPORT OF GROUP DISCUSSION • *Donald E. Hoke*   169

Section III

HINDRANCES TO EVANGELISM IN THE CHURCH •
                                Walter Künneth   173

Universalism

THE NEW TESTAMENT TEACHING • *Leon Morris* 180

UNIVERSALISM AND EVANGELISM • *James I. Packer* 182

A MANIFESTATION OF THE
NEW UNIVERSALISM • *Arthur M. Climenhaga* 185

JEWISH MISSIONS IN
RELATION TO UNIVERSALISM • *Jakob Jocz* 188

REPORT OF GROUP DISCUSSION • *Calvin Thielman* 191

Self-Containment, Parochialism and Isolation

THE CHURCH AND THE WORLD • *A. J. Dain* 194

THE GREATEST ENEMY IS WITHIN • *Samuel H. Moffett* 197

MAINTAINING A DELICATE BALANCE • *Everett L. Cattell* 201

SOME MODERN TEMPTATIONS • *C. Stacey Woods* 203

REPORT OF GROUP DISCUSSION • *Kenneth L. Downing* 205

Spiritual Indifference and Non-Expectation

LOSING GOD AT THE CENTER • *Festo Kivengere* 207

AS THE WORLD SEES THE CHURCH • *Robert E. Coleman* 210

THE POPE OF SELF • *Robert P. Evans* 213

SOME IMPORTANT FLAWS • *Augustus B. Marwieh* 216

REPORT OF GROUP DISCUSSION • *I. Ben Wati* 218

Doctrinal Unbelief and Heresy

PRESERVING THE TRUTH OF THE BIBLE • *Hermann Sasse* 219

THE UNIQUE CONTENT
OF THE GOSPEL • *Jules-Marcel Nicole* 222

PREACHING AN
AUTHORITATIVE MESSAGE • *Wayne Dehoney* 227

SOME OVERLOOKED HINDRANCES • *Pieter J. Mietes* 230

Infant Baptism and Sacerdotalism

BAPTISM AS A GATEWAY • *Richard Møller Petersen* 233

A PLEA FOR BELIEVER'S BAPTISM • *Duke K. McCall* 237

BAPTISM AS A RITE
OF INITIATION • *A. W. Goodwin Hudson* 240

BAPTISM IN REFORMATION
PERSPECTIVE • *C. Darby Fulton*   244

REPORT OF GROUP DISCUSSION • *Hans Bürki-Fillenz*   246

Section IV

OBSTACLES TO EVANGELISM IN THE WORLD •
                            Harold B. Kuhn   251

Materialism, Prosperity and Social Standing

ACHIEVING GREAT THINGS FOR GOD • *W. Maxey Jarman* 263

THE IMPACT OF MATERIALISM IN AFRICA • *Howard Jones* 268

THE GRIP OF MATERIAL COMFORTS • *Florentino Santana*   272

REPORT OF GROUP DISCUSSION • *C. Ralston Smith*   272

Renascent World Religions

ATTITUDES TOWARD NON-CHRISTIAN
RELIGIONS • *Hideo Aoki*   273

MAN'S UPREACH AND
GOD'S REVELATION • *Akbar Abdul-Haqq, Jr.*   276

OBSTACLES IN THE MUSLIM WORLD • *J. N. D. Anderson* 281

THE RELIGIONS OF ASIA • *Chandu Ray*   285

REPORT OF GROUP DISCUSSION • *Warren Webster*   286

Totalitarianism and Collectivism

THE TOTALITARIAN CLIMATE • *Samuel Escobar*   288

COMMUNIST OPPOSITION TO EVANGELISM • *Helen Kim*   291

COMMUNISM AND CHRISTIANITY • *Andrew Ben Loo*   294

THE U.S.S.R. AND EASTERN EUROPE • *Arthur F. Glasser* 298

REPORT OF GROUP DISCUSSION • *Duke K. McCall*   301

Political Nationalism

NATIONALISM AND EVANGELISM • *Hudson T. Armerding* 302

NATIONALISM AND THE GOSPEL • *Heini Germann-Edey*   305

BREAKING THE BARRIER
OF NATIONALISM • *Augustine G. Jebaraj*   309

THE ETHICS OF POLITICAL NATIONALISM •
                         Michael Cassidy   312

REPORT OF GROUP DISCUSSION • *Samuel H. Moffett*   316

Religious Cults

CONFRONTING THE CULTS • *William Culbertson*   318

MODERN RELIGIONS AND
PERSONAL NEEDS • *J. Stafford Wright*   321

REPORT OF GROUP DISCUSSION • *Arthur M. Climenhaga*   323

THE ZEAL OF THE CULTS • *Stephen Slocum, Jr.*   324

STRANGE AFRICAN CULTS • *Ernest K. Martin*   327

Discriminations and Intolerance

TRUTH BY FORCE • *Ernest H. Trenchard*   330

ECCLESIASTICAL TOTALITARIANISM • *Argos Zodhiates*   333

RELIGIOUS PERSECUTION • *Benjamin E. Fernando*   336

REPORT OF GROUP DISCUSSION • *J. Graham Miller*   338

Section V

METHODS OF PERSONAL EVANGELISM •
                      Richard C. Halverson   343

DISCIPLE MAKERS: KEY TO EVANGELISM • *Lorne C. Sanny*   354

REACHING THE ADOLESCENT • *Winnie Bonner*   357

THE "PHILIPPIAN METHOD" • *John W. Alexander*   359

FRANCE AS A MISSION FIELD • *Marcel Saltzmann*   362

REPORT OF GROUP DISCUSSION • *James M. Boice*   363

THE CONFRONTATION OF IDEOLOGY • *Hans Bürki-Fillenz*   364

AN HOUR FOR MOBILIZATION • *Muri Thompson*   367

TRAINING IN PERSONAL EVANGELISM • *William R. Bright*   370

WORKERS TOGETHER WITH GOD • *W. F. Batt*   373

REPORT OF GROUP DISCUSSION • *Sergio Garcia*   375

SPIRITUAL NEEDS OF THE NEGRO • *William E. Pannell*   376

NO STEREOTYPED APPROACHES • *Daniel Bakhsh*   381

CAUTION IN THE USE OF TECHNIQUES • *Ross F. Hidy*   384

MAN-TO-MAN EVANGELISM
BY BUSINESSMEN • *Dirk van Katwijk*   388

REPORT OF GROUP DISCUSSION • *Michael Cassidy*   390

COMPASSION IN PERSONAL
EVANGELISM • *Isaac H. A. Ababio*   391

EVANGELISM AND THE HOME • *Mogens Larsen*   394

FISHING PATIENTLY WITH A ROD • *Josip Horak*   397

THE MINISTRY OF LETTERS AND TRACTS • *Doan van Mieng*   399

REPORT OF GROUP DISCUSSION • *Samuel Wolgemuth*   402

WIN THEM BY FAMILIES • *Roy N. Oshiro*   403

EMPOWERED BY THE HOLY SPIRIT • *Thomas Cosmades*   406

THE SOUL-WINNER'S PRAYER LIFE • *Peter van Woerden*   409

FOREIGN MISSIONS EVANGELISM • *James R. Graham*   412

REPORT OF GROUP DISCUSSION • *David Foster*   414

PHILOSOPHY AND METHODS
OF EVANGELISM • *Samuel K. Arai*   416

NOT METHOD, BUT MESSAGE • *Hisashi Ariga*   418

VISITATION EVANGELISM IN JAPAN • *Shuichi Matsumura*   421

THE WORLD OF A SINGLE SOUL • *Takesaburo Uzaki*   424

REPORT OF GROUP DISCUSSION • *Akira Hatori*   426

Section VI

THE METHODS OF GROUP EVANGELISM •
A. W. Goodwin Hudson   431

AVOID CANONIZING ANY METHOD • *Oswald C. J. Hoffman*   441

PLANNING A GRAHAM CRUSADE • *Walter H. Smyth*   445

GROUP EVANGELISM IN ASIA • *Gregorio Tingson*   448

REPORT OF GROUP DISCUSSION • *Roy Fish*   450

THE PRACTICE OF TRUTH • *Francis A. Schaeffer*   452

THE EVANGELIST TODAY • *Stephen F. Olford*   456

LIKE A MIGHTY ARMY • *Horace L. Fenton, Jr.*   459

LESSONS FROM MASS EVANGELISM • *John Wesley White*   462

REPORT OF GROUP DISCUSSION • *Enos Zimmerman*   465

THE GIFT OF THE EVANGELIST • *Leighton F. S. Ford*   466

ASPECTS OF GROUP EVANGELISM • *Anton Schulte*   469

SOUTHERN BAPTIST EVANGELISM • *C. E. Autrey*   472

REPORT OF GROUP DISCUSSION • *Carl Lundquist*   474

TWENTIETH CENTURY EVANGELISM • *Oral Roberts*   475

NEW CONCEPTS OF EVANGELISM • *Harold John Ockenga*   478

A TIME FOR ACTION • *Efrain Santiago*   481

PREPARATION, PRESENTATION,
PRESERVATION • *Leo E. Janz*   485

REPORT OF GROUP DISCUSSION • *James M. Boice*   488

THE LOCAL CHURCH AND EVANGELISM • *José M. Martínez*   489

EVANGELIZATION BY GROUPS • *José Maria Rico*   492

EVANGELISM-IN-DEPTH • *Ruben Lores*   495

THE SOCIAL PROGRAM OF THE CHURCH • *José D. Fajardo*   498

REPORT OF GROUP DISCUSSION • *Herbert Money*   501

EVANGELISM IN FRENCH-SPEAKING LANDS • *Maurice Ray* 503

MASS EVANGELISM IN THE
IVORY COAST • *Joseph Diéké Koffi*   506

REPORT OF GROUP DISCUSSION • *David Barnes*   508

Section VII Supplementary Discussion Groups

LITERATURE EVANGELISM • *Jack McAlister*   513

REPORT OF GROUP DISCUSSION • *Kenneth McVety*   516

STUDENT EVANGELISM • *David Adeney*   518

REPORT OF GROUP DISCUSSION • *Isaac Ababio*   521

REPORT OF GROUP DISCUSSION ON EDUCATION
IN RELATION TO EVANGELISM • *James M. Boice*   522

REPORT OF GROUP DISCUSSION ON
MASS EVANGELISM • *Werner Bürklin*   523

REPORT OF GROUP DISCUSSION ON
EVANGELISM AND RACE • *Dana Minnaar*   523

REPORT OF GROUP DISCUSSION ON
EVANGELISM-IN-DEPTH • *Roger J. Voke*   524

REPORT OF GROUP DISCUSSION
ON YOUTH EVANGELISM • *Bill Yoder*   525

REPORT OF GROUP DISCUSSION
ON MISSIONS AND TECHNOLOGY • *David A. Hubbard*   525

REPORT OF GROUP DISCUSSION ON
FOLLOW-UP TECHNIQUES • *Angel B. Taglucop*   526

REPORT OF GROUP DISCUSSION ON
THE ETHICS OF THE EVANGELIST • *Gregorio Tingson*   526

REPORT OF GROUP DISCUSSION ON
EVANGELISM AND REVIVAL • *Norman Cook*   527

INTRODUCTION TO VOLUME II

The World Congress on Evangelism provided not only an opportunity to hear addresses by some of the world's best informed and most outstanding leaders in the field of evangelism but also time to study and discuss together some of the major related themes. These studies were presented in major papers to the entire Congress followed by group studies and discussions.

Volume II includes six of the major papers plus one hundred thirty brief addresses dealing with twenty-three related subjects. The papers, born out of a wide variety of cultures and backgrounds, bring an unmistakable challenge to face the scriptural mandate to "Go ye into all the world, and preach the gospel" (Mark 16:15).

As these studies brought many of those in attendance to a serious re-evaluation of their commitment, so may the study of these papers bring the readers a clearer concept of the Gospel and a sense of urgency for its dissemination into every part of the world.

SECTION I

INTRODUCTION TO VOLUME II   xiii

THE AUTHORITY FOR EVANGELISM •
Johannes Schneider   1

The Teaching of the Bible

THE BIBLE AND THE EVANGELISTIC TASK • *Paul Schmidt*   11

THE USE OF SCRIPTURE
IN EVANGELISM • *Herbert M. Arrowsmith*   14

EVANGELISM AND THE TEACHING OF ACTS • *Philip Teng*   17

COMMISSIONED TO COMMUNICATE • *Bob Pierce*   20

REPORT OF GROUP DISCUSSION • *Harold B. Kuhn*   24

The Lord's Command

GO AND TELL • *Michael Kyriakakis*   25

THE GREAT COMMISSION • *Kenneth L. Chafin*   28

NEW TESTAMENT EVANGELISM • *Tom Rees*   31

CALLED TO OBEY • *Justin Mabiala*   35

REPORT OF GROUP DISCUSSION • *J. D. Douglas*   37

The Spirit's Constraint

THE CONFLICT OF THE SPIRITS • *V. Raymond Edman*   38

CHRIST AND THE SPIRIT • *J. Dwight Wadsworth*   40

THE STIRRING OF THE SPIRIT • *Alfred Stanway*   43

NO EVANGELICAL MONOPOLY • *Juan M. Isais*   47

REPORT OF GROUP DISCUSSION • *James M. Boice*   49

The Destiny of the Lost

THE WAY OF THE LOST • *Subodh K. Sahu*   51

LOST HUMANITY REQUIRES RESCUE • *Mervin E. Rosell*   54

THE PLIGHT OF THE LOST • *Suteichi Oye*   59

UNREACHED BY THE GOSPEL • *Percival W. Gibson*   62

REPORT OF GROUP DISCUSSION • *A. Morgan Derham*   64

The Return of Christ

EVANGELISM AND ESCHATOLOGICAL
IMPERATIVES • *Thomas F. Zimmerman* 65

EVANGELISM AND THE SECOND COMING • *Ian W. Thomas* 68

EVANGELISM AND THE LORD'S
IMMINENT RETURN • *Raghuel P. Chavan* 72

MOTIVATED BY THE FORWARD LOOK • *Ernst Schrupp* 74

REPORT OF GROUP DISCUSSION • *Stuart Barton Babbage* 76

The Church's Tradition and Practice

THE CHURCH'S FIRST FIVE CENTURIES • *Ezra Gebremedhin* 77

THE REFORMATION AND
EVANGELISM • *A. Skevington Wood* 81

MAJOR REVIVALS AND EVANGELISM • *Ian S. Rennie* 84

CONTEMPORARY EVANGELISTIC
TECHNIQUES • *J. Christy Wilson, Jr.* 87

REPORT OF GROUP DISCUSSION • *Dwight L. Baker* 91

THE AUTHORITY FOR EVANGELISM
Johannes Schneider

1. The Basis of Authority

a. Authority for evangelism is grounded most deeply and finally in the risen Lord's Great Commission (Matthew 28:19). He himself commanded the disciples to proclaim the Gospel to all nations and upon baptism to receive those who believe on him into the redeemed fellowship of the new covenant. He thus gave a comprehensive charge which bound not only them, but all others as well who stand in his service, to win the world for Christ! This is the great objective he has placed before us. And he himself lends dignity to this command, for to him is given all power in heaven and in earth (Matt. 28:18). Through his disciples and messengers he is still continuing his earthly ministry: "As the Father hath sent me," he says, "even so send I you" (John 20:21, ASV; see also John 17:18). This indicates that evangelism is intrinsic and essential to God's plan of redemption. It is through evangelism that Jesus' great prophetic vision is being realized: "And this gospel of the kingdom shall be preached in all the world for a witness unto all nations; and then shall the end come" (Matt. 24:14).

b. In his lifetime Jesus shared with chosen men the tasks committed to him by God, first with the twelve, then with the seventy: they were to proclaim the Gospel, heal the sick, and cast out demons as a sign that God's kingdom had dawned.

The ministry of the disciples was confined first of all to Jesus' promise: "Ye shall receive power, after that the Holy Ghost is come upon you: and ye shall be witnesses unto me both in Jerusalem, and in all Judea, and in Samaria, and unto the uttermost part of the earth" (Acts 1:8). Thus was clearly set forth the plan for spreading the Gospel. This procedure was not born of human genius, nor was it the product of some deliberate far-flung missions strategy. No, it was the Lord himself who determined the manner and purpose of world-wide evangelism.

c. Through the outpouring of the Holy Spirit, the disciples were granted power to carry out their commission. Peter's mighty ministry on the Day of Pentecost is the first example of large-scale evangelism, and the miracle of tongues documents the beginning of world-wide missions, for representatives of all nations heard the message of salvation in their own language. The Spirit-filled message, in which God's mighty works were proclaimed, brought about repentance, conversion, faith in Christ and further building up of his church. The scattered seed of the Word yielded much fruit. The Gospel began its triumphal march throughout the world.

DR. SCHNEIDER is professor emeritus of theology, Humboldt University, East Berlin.

d. Then Antioch became the second great missionary center. Here, too, the Church placed itself completely under the effectual power of the Holy Spirit who commanded: "Separate me Barnabas and Saul for the work whereunto I have called them" (Acts 13:2). As the two accordingly embarked upon their ministry among the heathen, the Scriptures emphasize once again that they were sent out by the Holy Ghost (Acts 13:4).

e. Special blessing, moreover, attended the evangelistic and missionary labors of the Apostle Paul to whom the risen Lord had appeared on the road to Damascus. The Lord had set him apart as a chosen vessel and had authorized him to declare his Name to heathen nations, to kings, and to the children of Israel (Acts 9:15). This commission was of unprecedented breadth and ecumenical importance, an entrustment which until his martyrdom Paul fulfilled with indefatigable faithfulness, holy passion, and sacrificial dedication. He was gripped by a constraint that he could not shake. "Woe is unto me, if I preach not the Gospel" (I Corinthians 9:16). Paul speaks of the incomparable greatness and indescribable glory of his service (II Cor. 3:10) through which the bright light of the salvation message should illumine the hearts of men (II Cor. 4:4). In proclaiming the Gospel he does not limit himself to but one fixed method — he is anything but a man of narrow vision — instead, he adapts himself to the spiritual and religious condition of his listeners, yet never loses sight of the determinative objective, namely, to win as many as possible to Jesus Christ (I Cor. 9:19-23). His strongly emphasized self-identification with the Jews and with the heathen is but a point of contact for witnessing to the one and only truth that is equally valid for all men.

The Apostle considers his apostolic office a priestly service; the heathen are, as it were, to be an offering well pleasing unto God and sanctified through the Holy Ghost (Romans 15:16). He knows, too, that the results granted in his evangelistic work are not due to his own prowess, but are to be credited rather to the Lord who has achieved them through him (II Cor. 3:5). This is true not only concerning the authoritative message that he proclaims, but also concerning the power of the signs and wonders that accompany his proclamation. Thus through him and in most exemplary fashion, Jesus' promise that the Gospel will be made known to all the world began to be fulfilled.

f. Besides Paul there are other favored men of early Christianity whom Christ set apart as apostles, prophets, evangelists, pastors, and teachers (Ephesians 4:11). They know that the Christ of whom they bear witness is Lord not only of his Church, but Lord also of the cosmos, the one who fills all the universe (Eph. 4:10), the heavenly omnipotent One (*Pantokrator*) whose servants and messengers do his bidding.

g. Throughout the centuries and up to the present day the Great Commission has retained its power to constrain and engage the Church of Jesus Christ. In him, and in him alone, we, too, find our authority for evangelism.

2. Spiritual Essentials for an Authoritative Gospel Ministry

a. The same spiritual requisites pertain to evangelists as to anyone who acknowledges Jesus Christ as Savior and Lord. In conversion and regeneration they must have had a personal experience of salvation effected by the grace of God; they must believe on Jesus Christ with their whole being; must be in constant fellowship with him, by the power of the Holy Spirit; must live a life dedicated to the Lord; and in word and deed must show themselves to be living members of the body of Christ. Certainly every Christian has the responsibility of being a Gospel witness; this, however, does not make him an evangelist in the true sense of the word. For this he must have a special call.

b. Evangelism is a charisma, a gift of grace bestowed by the Holy Spirit. No one can determine to become an evangelist simply on the basis of his oratorical gifts. Fleshly ambition is absolutely out of place, so is even the desire to assume a leading role in the Church of Jesus Christ. Moreover, even a winning personality, or the ability to fascinate people and to spellbind them does not make an evangelist. Assuredly, God uses a person's natural gifts and puts them into service. But woe to him who boasts of these gifts! They are meaningful to evangelism only if they are sanctified by God, for it is God himself who by his own free choice calls those who are to proclaim his Word and by the Holy Spirit equips them with the unique gift to become authoritative ministers of the Gospel.

No doubt Apollos had the gift of evangelism. He was a highly endowed man who had outstanding ability in public speaking, was well educated, and was also apt in expounding the Scriptures. His preaching left a deep impression on Corinth. He represents that kind of evangelist in whom strong natural propensities are combined with God's special gift of grace. And yet it was the oratorically less gifted Paul who became the outstanding charismatic personality of early Christianity. Characteristic of him was an apostolic consciousness of being sent and a full awareness of the meaning of the spiritual office entrusted to him; Paul was freely the lord of all things, yet like no other he was a servant of Jesus Christ. Paul was humble and regal at one and the same time, a man who never boasted of his privileges and advantages; once when it was necessary he even called himself a fool (II Cor. 11:1-12, 16). He was a man of Christ who felt responsibility only to the Lord (*Kyrios*) of heaven and followed his instructions. He was accountable to no "missionary committee." He was no charming speaker who captivated the hearts of his listeners, nor was he a forceful evangelist by natural disposition. His enemies, while they probably exaggerated the situation and spoke in spite, said of Paul: "He's no speaker in any sense of the word! (His speech is contemptible)" (cf. II Cor. 10:10, and also II Cor. 11:6). At times his mien was far from impressive and his bearing lacked self-confidence. In I Cor. 2:1-4 Paul confesses openly and in all modesty that he had come to Corinth, that famous metropolis of the East, with no intention whatever of proclaiming the Gospel with overwhelming eloquence or show of human wisdom. This educated theologian who had been thoroughly trained in the School of the Torah at Jerusalem, and besides this was well-versed in Hellenistic culture, deliberately made no use at Corinth of this extensive knowledge; his one and only concern was to bear witness to Jesus Christ and him crucified. Unlike the wandering philosophers of that day, Paul did not try to strike an impressive pose; he came, rather, "in weakness," yes, even "in fear" and "much trembling." But he bore a message that surpassed all the wisdom of the world, and proclaimed it in demonstration of the Spirit and of power. Thus the Gospel and its indwelling power was fully vindicated and actively manifested. Paul knew the danger that threatens an evangelist who seeks personal prominence; to do so undermines the authority of the message.

c. Paul teaches us that our evangelistic preaching must be Christo-centric. Obviously we will treat many and diverse themes, for after all, we must be aware of our times and preach accordingly. That is, we must know people's questions, problems, and needs and must come to grips with them. Any evangelist who evades or ignores the current, concrete world in which he lives has failed his calling. He must be ready for questions and answers. This he can do only if he is thoroughly trained, possesses broad knowledge and is sensitive to and aware of every facet of people's lives. This concern is also essential for authoritative preaching. But evangelism which does not make Christ and his salvation central, that does not press for conversion and definite decision has fallen short of its purpose. Evangelism without commitment is no evangelism at all, but only a kind of religious activity.

d. Paul taught us also *how* we are to evangelize. What words and concepts we use is no matter of indifference. Repeatedly the apostle warned against language prompted by human wisdom; philosophical speech, after all, cannot properly delineate the content of the Gospel. Paul therefore emphasizes and stresses that in "comparing spiritual things with spiritual" (I Cor. 2:13) we must use words given us by the Holy Spirit. By this he means that the manner of our proclamation, yes, even our choice of words is not a matter of personal determination. It derives, rather, and is pressed in upon us from *what* we are to proclaim. Paul was the first to recognize today's very real problem of "theological communication" (Sprachtheologie) and met it in the only correct way. This, too, belongs to authoritative preaching. Otherwise it becomes very simple to adulterate the Gospel. For our day this simply means that in presenting the redemptive message we cannot take up the modern mode of existential philosophy and theology whose anthropological purpose limits or obscures the Gospel. Where this sort of approach leads is seen with frightening clarity in Bishop Robinson's book *Honest to God*. German theologian W. Künneth, who believes in revelation, points out in his publication, *Von Gott Reden?* (R. Brockhaus,

Wuppertal 1965, p. 78) that while Robinson has purported to bring the Gospel to "modern" man, in reality he has destroyed the Gospel.

e. Let us cite a concrete example from today's evangelistic scene. Dr. E. Bieneck is a leading German businessman who is also president of the German YMCA and has an excellent overall view of the present situation and of the church's impact in Germany. In "Bibel und Evangelische Kirche" (1956) he states: "I can only say, that in the course of my life I have verified time and again that the more simply the message of the cross is proclaimed, the greater are the results; this is true also today." Billy Graham's work is the best proof of this fact.

Dr. Bieneck also mentions a very enlightening experience he had during an evangelistic campaign in one of Germany's larger cities. The evangelist preached simply, almost in "Sunday School style." His preaching culminated in the message of the Cross and with an invitation that all who wanted to put their lives right with God should come to the front for personal conversation concerning spiritual things. Bieneck had invited a well-educated man to the meeting, a man who was a leading figure in the industrial world. This man had indeed come, and Bieneck was greatly concerned about how he would receive the simple, yet Christ-centered message. He then tells the following: "When I saw him again several days later, he told me to my amazement, that for years he had been well aware of great pulpiteers; in fact when traveling he always stopped to hear them here and there. Never in his life, however, had he been so personally confronted with the message of Christ; he could do nothing else but accept the call to come to the front. The following day he felt constrained to fetch the grown children of his first marriage in order to go forward again with them." This is what happened in the life of a very modern person who was saved not through an existentially philosophical sermon, but through the message of the Cross, a salvation proclaimed in the power of the Spirit.

f. If the evangelical sermon is essentially Christo-centric, then it will be properly related to all of Holy Scripture. From this center it will encompass the entire wealth of divine revelation and the fulness of redemption. From this centrality, too, it will derive its authoritative judgment of man and his entire godless, salvationless and sinful existence. At the same time, Christo-centric preaching will appropriate scientific findings concerning man which are very noteworthy indeed, findings which give a kind of insight as well as a measure of practical help. This benefit is undeniable, but redemption — redemption in Christ — these findings cannot provide.

3. The Purpose of Authoritative Evangelism

a. Proclamation of the Gospel begins with the idea that there is only one salvation for all mankind, namely, salvation in Christ. For "neither is there salvation in any other" (Acts 4:12). This basic statement establishes the purpose of evangelism once and for all: to win men for Christ. Evangelism therefore is the determinative saving action for a lost world. Through evangelism God offers the world the salvation that in his fathomless love he has prepared in Christ Jesus. But the Gospel is more than an offer of love; it has a mysterious unique dynamic — for to everyone who believes the message of the Cross it becomes the power of God (I Cor. 1:18). Since the Gospel contains God's entire plan of salvation, it demands obedience (Rom. 10:16). It comes with a universal appeal: God desires that all men be helped and that they come to awareness of the truth (I Timothy 2:4). Man's fate in time and eternity depends on his acceptance or rejection of the offer of redemption (II Thessalonians 1:8ff.). There is no other way of salvation.

   b. Evangelism is an imperatively essential task, for opposition to the Gospel grows apace in a most frightening manner.

   Today we are experiencing a constantly ongoing process of secularization. The world, as it has been rightly said, is becoming ever more worldly. This state is due to both secret and open revolt from God that culminates in political ideologies and world-views tied up with atheism to the very point of enmity toward God and Christ and persecution of the Church. Without yielding the battle in so many words, faith in God is abandoned even in so-called Christian countries. For many people, God no longer has any practical significance. People live without him and, apparently, make out very well without him. After all, it is said, God hinders man's free development. In truth, however, when man surrenders his ties to God, he does not become really free, but plunges all the more deeply rather into the grip of satanic-demonic powers. He loses every moral norm and creates his own rules for living, rules which are often his very undoing. Deification of power, of money, of material possessions, of sex does not bring him salvation, but rather destruction. He falls prey to lusts, passions and desires and becomes enmeshed in sins and guilt. Our so-called pluralistic society no longer has any determinative life core or centrality; it is subservient rather to the spirit of this world, that spirit by whom are ruled the sons of disobedience (Eph. 2:2, ASV). While the world indeed mobilizes spiritual and moral forces in opposition, it cannot delay or vanquish the doom that has broken upon mankind in all areas of life.

   c. In this situation, the Church of Jesus Christ must rally its powers all the more to proclaim the message of salvation with every possible means. It will not become discouraged even if its witness brings suffering and martyrdom, for at its side stands the Lord who has promised: "I am with you always, even unto the end of the world" (Matt. 28:20). Moreover, the apostle Paul's declaration will always be valid: "The word of God is not bound" (II Tim. 2:9; compare II Thess. 3:1). Christ himself gathers together his Church through the Word that declares him to be the crucified, risen one who lives forevermore.

4. *The Biblical-Theological Basis for Authoritative Practice of Evangelism*

Now we come to a very real problem. Because of certain impacts upon present day theology (by Bultmann and others), the matter of proper and currently relevant proclamation confronts us anew. This matter is of determinative significance not only for preaching in the churches, but also for evangelism.

We have already touched on the question briefly, but must now consider it more extensively. In doing so, we do not wish to deal in detail with the problem identified by the key word "demythologizing," but will limit ourselves rather to intensive discussion of that phase which relates directly to our topic. This actually concerns the matter of method and practical execution of evangelism; in the last vital analysis, it concerns the Gospel itself. This matter is so tremendously vital because preaching today already contains so much that is different from what, in obedience to the clear witness of the Word of God, we can subscribe to.

The best approach to the problem is from the vantage point of a passage in one of Paul's letters, II Cor. 5:19-21, because it plays a big part in helping us orient ourselves about the question under consideration and brings opposing viewpoints to light. Paul's exposition is dominated by three declarations:

a. The first states: "God was in Christ reconciling the world unto himself."

This is the basic statement of the Christian doctrine of salvation as presented by Paul. He announces an historical event of revelation accomplished by God which eliminates any and all human initiative and activity. By free decree according to the riches of his grace, God gave his Son to die as atoning sacrifice for the sins of the world; and in obedience to God's will, Christ took upon himself the sacrifice that has brought redemption to lost mankind. This is the unique, once-for-all and unrepeatable fact valid for all time. Although witnessed to throughout the entire New Testament, this event is dimmed in modern existential theology, robbed of its worth, or even denied. To deny the reality of redemption facts, is to pull the very foundation out from Christian faith. For Bultmann, the Cross of Christ has meaning only as it serves man's existential self-realization: I must decide to take up the Cross of Christ as my own. Robinson spoke similarly. He does not see a redemptive provision of God in the Cross of Christ, puts aside the fact of the atonement; and his theology comes to the conclusion accordingly that the Cross of Christ is only evidence of Jesus' selflessness, of a love that gives itself to and unites itself with the ground of being (Seinsgrund). To do this is to rob the Cross of Christ of its determinative substance. The statements of the New Testament are falsified to benefit an unbiblically oriented Christology.

The redemptive historical event of Jesus' resurrection is closely related to the salvation fact of Christ's death; for if Christ had not risen, then the saving and redemptive work of God would lose its meaning. Therefore Paul declares in I Cor. 15:17, that if there were no resurrected Christ then we should still be in our sins. But the apostles do indeed witness, and in full agreement, that *God* raised his Son from among the dead. That there has been no resurrection of Jesus as an historical event is another item of contention among representatives of existentialist theology. This, they say, is mythological speech; to them, the concept of an historical resurrection is irreconcilable with today's scientific view of the universe. This concept must therefore be given up. Only the appearances of the "Resurrected One" are historically ascertainable, they say, but no one can say with certainty of what kind they were and just how they took place among the disciples. It is presumed impossible to speak of an immediate intervention of God; to do so would contradict our modern concept of God in which the fact of God's transcendence and personal being have become irrelevant. Nonetheless — and this is what is so corrupt and deceiving — existential theology does maintain a concept of the resurrection. Christ, so the new interpretation says, was not raised to a new, glorified being, but — says Bultmann — was resurrected into Kerygma. That is, Christ does not continue to live as a person in a changed form, but is everpresent in the proclaimed Word. But how can he be active in proclamation if he does not actually exist, inasmuch as his death ended everything? This "kerygmatic Christ" has no reality whatsoever, nor is he identified with the historical Jesus of Nazareth; rather he is a fictitious greatness of some kind with which there is no fellowship, and to which one cannot pray. That is not the Lord to whom is given all power in heaven and on earth. Bultmann explicitly declares: "I must admit that I consider any talk about the personal aspect of Christ as mythology" (*Kerygma and Mythos I* — 1960 — 4, p. 127). Thus here, too, the redemptive-historical foundation of Proclamation is removed. The biblical message is totally falsified. An evangelism that falls for this sort of talk is totally without authority.

  b. The apostle's *second* declaration states: "God has set up among us the Word of reconciliation" (cf II Cor. 5:19, KJV).

  This indicates, further, that God himself has done something also in reference to the proclamation: in that *he* has established the Word of reconciliation, *he* has determined the content of the message. He who proclaims, whether he be preacher or evangelist, therefore has no freedom to dispense the divine Word as he will. He is bound to firm instructions. As a messenger in Christ's place he, like any ambassador, has his orders to carry out in the manner he has been instructed. That is, he is not permitted to project his own religious ideas, concoct more or less clever speculations, or engage in philosophical conjecture. In reference to our discussion this means: he has no right to interpret the soteriological statements of the New Testament in merely anthropological or existential terms. To do this is to destroy them, for what is "meant" is only that which is there recorded, not that which is read into or out of the texts with the help of a certain exegetical method. Proclamation's task first of all is to witness to the great acts of God; it must tell the world what God has fulfilled in Christ for the redemption of the world.

Only when proclamation has presented the basic events of the incarnation, of the cross, and of the resurrection of Christ can preaching say what these facts mean for us. Most certainly that which has occurred *extra nos* (totally independent of us) has occurred *pro nobis* (for our good). But it is impossible to speak of the "significance" of the salvation facts, that is, of the meaning they have for us, if they themselves are disregarded or even denied. If this happens, the Kerygma becomes a "free-floating" word. When the Kerygma is stripped of its revelational-historical foundation it simply dangles in thin air.

That to which everything tends, in the last analysis, becomes clear in today's well-loved, and in modern German theology's much used, concept of *Wortgeschehen*. What is questionable about this? At first glance, nothing. Like many theological slogans of our time, the term, "das Wortgeschehen," is not a particularly happy expression; one could accept it, however, if it indicated that proclamation of the Word is an event brought about by the Holy Ghost; an event that brings about the decisive turning point in the life of someone who accepts it by faith. But in existential theology much more than this is meant. The "Wortgeschehen" becomes the central and our only valid salvation event. This has logical consequences. For if the Cross and resurrection of Christ are declared unimportant for us or made totally devoid of value, then only that proclamation which confronts me relevantly here and now in my concrete existence can have decisive importance. Past history, that has lost its redemptive-historical nature by virtue of this new concept of historicity, at best is considered but a "redeeming moment" for the present. Because of this interpretation, Bultmann rejects any return to history behind the kerygma.

In the New Testament, by contrast, kerygma means message, proclamation, solemn impartation of *facts that have occurred*. So Paul understood the message of the Cross. It announced that act of God, through which he reconciled the world unto himself. For this very reason it is the power of God (I Cor. 1:18) which brings redemption and salvation to all who believe (Rom. 1:16). At the same time it is the total sum and substance of divine wisdom (I Cor. 1:24) which appears as foolishness to unbelievers, but which in truth is wiser than all human wisdom (I Cor. 1:25). Consequently the apostle tirelessly and zealously proclaims the crucified Christ (I Cor. 1:23) in whom we have redemption through his blood, the forgiveness of sins (Eph. 1:7). Beyond this, Paul witnesses to the unfathomable riches in Christ (Eph. 3:8, NEB) in whom dwells the entire fullness of God (Col. 2:9) – that Christ who is the likeness of God, the firstborn of all creation and the firstborn of the dead (Col. 1:14-20); the Lord of all and of the Church, that Lord who at his return in power and glory will usher in the fulfillment of redemption. If evangelism is to be authoritative, it must carry forward this true message of Christ.

c. Paul's *third* declaration states: "Be ye reconciled to God." This is an invitation; it is also a mighty summons to an unregenerate, lost world. It personally addresses each one who hears the Word of reconciliation. Authoritative evangelism would not fulfill its task completely unless it confronted men with a final, inescapable decision.

Existential theology likewise knows a concept of decision and takes it most seriously. Its aim is to lead man to "reality," to a proper understanding of himself, to a true God-willed existence. It speaks, too, of the sin-pardoning grace of God which gives man access to a new future. There is no word, however, of Christ's atonement as the redemptive-historical foundation of God's forgiving activity.

Paul does not ask *man* to reconcile himself to God; man is in no position to do this. In Christ, God has accomplished everything needful for man's salvation. Lost in his sin and guilt, man needs only to accept the completed reconciliation and apply it to himself. Through conversion which leads him to living faith in God and Christ, a new existence — life in Christ — is given him by grace. Zinzendorf's watchword is still valid for the evangelist today: "My joy until I die: to win souls for the Lamb."

If properly understood and not existentially misconstrued, Paul's three statements in II Corinthians contain all that belongs to the nature and realization of authoritative evangelism.

THE BIBLE
AND THE EVANGELISTIC TASK
Paul Schmidt

The best-known, God-called evangelist on the face of the earth today, Billy Graham, very often uses in his messages and appeals the statement: "The Bible says . . ." For every genuine Christian evangelistic effort, the first and last substantiation even in the twentieth century is that it must clearly have the Bible as its basis. This applies to all older and newer nations and cultures on all continents — to those which have known the Bible for hundreds of years, as well as to cultures and peoples to whom God's message of salvation in Jesus Christ is just being brought.

The Bible tells us who we are. It reveals to us who God is, who Jesus Christ is, what he offers us, and how he interprets our life.

It is clear and absolute when it proclaims: "Neither is there salvation in any other: for there is none other name under heaven given among men, whereby we must be saved" (Acts 4:12). This is said absolutely and totally, and it applies from the first preaching of the apostles down to the present day.

The Bible speaks in the same absolute and all-inclusive manner concerning the meaning of God's salvation for the individual man, when it declares: "Except a man be born of water and of the Spirit, he cannot enter into the kingdom of God" (John 3:5). "Forasmuch as ye know that ye were . . . redeemed with the precious blood of Christ, as of a lamb without blemish and without spot" (I Peter 1:18-19).

With the same clarity it tells man who he is and that he unconditionally needs redemption from the law of sin and death. "For all have sinned, and come short of the glory of God; Being justified freely by his grace through the redemption that is in Christ Jesus" (Romans 3:23-24). Thus the Bible speaks clearly of the reality of sin, which separates us from God and destroys our lives, and of how Christ Jesus redeems us and makes us God's children.

The Apostle Paul confesses, as it were, for himself and for all men: "O wretched man that I am! who shall deliver me from the body of this death?" He can thereupon immediately testify: "For the wages of sin is death; but the gift of God is eternal life through Jesus Christ our Lord" (Rom. 7:24, 6:23).

Because it is a fact that sin holds man in death under the reign of Satan, and that Jesus Christ has come to destroy the works of Satan, therefore, Jesus himself says to his disciples: "All power is given unto me in

DIREKTOR SCHMIDT is president of the European Evangelical Alliance in Berlin, Germany.

heaven and in earth. Go ye therefore, and teach all nations, baptizing them in the name of the Father, and of the Son, and of the Holy Ghost: teaching them to observe all things whatsoever I have commanded you" (Matthew 28:18-20). On the basis of this fact the Lord Jesus sends his disciples into the world and says to that end at his departure from the earth: "Ye shall receive power, after that the Holy Ghost is come upon you: and ye shall be witnesses unto me . . . unto the uttermost part of the earth" (Acts 1:8).

In this same passage, the Bible also speaks clearly of the evangelization of the entire world through his called and spirit-filled witnesses. Therefore we must neither overlook nor ignore the fact that this task can only be accomplished by his called and spirit-filled witnesses. Nor dare we ignore what the Lord Jesus says in addition to this: "Behold, I send you forth as sheep in the midst of wolves: be ye therefore wise as serpents, and harmless as doves" (Matt. 10:16). Herewith he suggests a wisdom in missions, which can be received from the Holy Spirit.

The Lord of missions and also of evangelism among the nations reserves to himself a very high estimate of this task of witnessing. Also concerning the success of these services Jesus does not leave his messengers in the dark. He says explicitly: "Strait is the gate, and narrow is the way, which leadeth unto life, and few there be that find it" (Matt. 7:14).

There is also another basic biblical principle to be applied here: "The disciple is not above his master, nor the servant above his lord. . . . If they have called the master of the house Beelzebub, how much more shall they call them of his household?" (Matt. 10:24-25). Even today in all of our genuine biblical evangelism we must reckon with misunderstanding, slander (or calumny) and malicious harassment. The Bible speaks very plainly, providing basic guiding principles for every situation, for each period of time and for every area of the world.

Also concerning the ultimate goal of evangelism, the Bible sets forth some very clear teaching. The aim of calling everyone to Jesus Christ is that his Church on earth may live as redeemed ones, and that the Church be strong in the love and in the life contained in this redemption. In addition to this, the words of Jesus refer to eternal life as follows: "Father, I will that they also, whom thou hast given me, be with me where I am" (John 17:24). According to the Bible, evangelism must be concerned with this eternal goal: from redemption, renewal of life and relationship to Christ, into maturity and full fellowship with Christ after the resurrection from the dead. The teaching of the Bible is comprehensive for proclamation. It acknowledges the miracles of God and does not end at the border of perception of the natural mind. It also knows of mysteries, speaks of them and permits them to exist. The Apostle Paul says clearly and distinctly in I Corinthians 4:1: "Let a man so account of us, as of the ministers of Christ, and stewards of the mysteries of God." To the Gospel of God belong his mysteries, also those concerning the consummation, Jesus' way of redemption, and of his resurrection from the dead and the promises of his return. If these miracles of God were to be deleted from the Gospel, then God's plan of salvation would be destroyed and man would lose his own worth. But the hand of man can neither delete nor destroy. God alone can do this.

When our theme says: "The Bible and the Evangelistic Task" then we are to understand this Bible as the Word of God. Therefore, it cannot in its totality and absoluteness be drawn simply into competition with any other philosophical or religious teaching. It stands above all limited human wisdom. Were this not the case, there would exist no ultimate certainties concerning us as human beings, concerning the purpose of our lives, and concerning death and our existence in general.

THE USE OF SCRIPTURE IN EVANGELISM
Herbert M. Arrowsmith

We submit a strong plea to this Congress, that in all areas of their influence its members will consider the role of the Scriptures as an instrument of evangelism.

There are four aspects to this general question:

1. The need for calling the corporate Church and individual Christians back to the authority and integrity of Scripture

This Congress was summoned, in part, because the missionary and evangelistic impulse has slackened at home and abroad, and because of a conviction that the decline of evangelistic passion is the most crucial matter facing Christendom today.

But this, in turn, is the result of a blunted conviction concerning Holy Scripture — its integrity, its authority and its infallibility.

The momentum of Bible use throughout the world is suffering retardation because of this lack of conviction. The trumpet is giving an uncertain sound. Consequently the spirit of worship and dedication has lost much of its dynamic and motivation. The lack of conviction *about* the Bible has led to inertia in the Christian mission *with* the Bible and failure to accept responsibility for distribution *of* the Bible. There is urgent need for certainty concerning the imperishable Word of God entrusted to us.

2. The need for advocating anew the authority of Scripture

The Bible has been under attack now for over 100 years. But it still stands supreme! It is time to stop apologizing for Holy Scripture, and to return to an unashamed affirmation of its authority, reliability and integrity. Our forefathers did not live in an age when the authority of the Bible was questioned. But we most surely do.

In our responsibility toward millions of people, particularly adolescents and university undergraduates, it is essential to emphasize the truth, and the reliability and also the relevance of Holy Scripture. The evangelical witness in the world today could profitably engage in a "tractarian" movement. We have the scholars for such a venture and the scientific expertise with which to present it. I should like to see millions of copies published, and persuasively issued, of ad hoc pamphlets such as chapter four of Austin Farrer's *A Science of God* and the last chapter of A. Cressy Morrison's *Man Does Not Stand Alone*. Other suggestions could enlarge this list.

CANON ARROWSMITH is General Secretary in Australia of The British and Foreign Bible Society.

3. The need for evangelicals to return to a greater use of the expository ministry

My limited experience has convinced me that *exposition* is the best *evangelism*. It is still true that the Spirit of God takes the Word of God to make a child of God. This needs to be explained to men and women.

All of this can be presented by *exposition* once we solve the tremendous question of how to get the ear of the world's millions. But this, of course, is God's problem too — if God can only get our ear, he has a message for each of us.

We are not making the best use of television and radio opportunities. Our general technique is one of harangue rather than of explanation and exposition. I should like to see:

1. Bible study on television
2. Bible study on radio
3. The use of, e.g., John's Gospel in the "One Way" format (American Bible Society) presentations similar to Campbell Morgan's *Great Physician*. This Gospel is rich in the record of Christ's encounter with *persons*.
4. Production of individual books of the Bible by the Bible Society movement in a modern translation and *interleaved* with blank pages, to permit people in the pew to make their own notes on Bible expositions they hear.
5. Placement of Bibles in the pews — since most people no longer carry their Bibles to public worship — to permit an effective and informed participation by the congregation when the Word of God is read and when the Word of God is expounded.

4. The need for rallying evangelicals throughout the world for a ministry of Scripture distribution

I would be the last one to deny the value of *any* distribution of the Holy Scriptures. But much of the present method of distributing complete New Testaments and complete Gospels is not as effective nor as economical as it could be. Much could be done by way of a guided distribution of smaller portions of the Bible to particular groups in specific situations. Let me illustrate. There is as yet no effective production and distribution of Scripture portions for *new literates*. For them we need smaller 4, 8, or 16 page portions in large type, with suitable line drawings or photographs of local interest and significance. It is not enough for the Church to talk about scores of millions of new literates; we must do something to evangelize this segment of the world's population.

Moreover, we need a simple translation in other languages of the New Testament for *children, similar* to that of the modern English Version. True, there is some danger in the proliferation of translations of the Scriptures. There are probably too many translations of the Bible in certain languages. This matter of new translations needs to be approached with caution lest the Word of God become debased and lest young people become confused when they hear one version read in church, but read another translation at school or at home. Nevertheless there is a need for presenting the Scriptures in a language that is more idiomatic and thus more suitable for primary age children. Particular sections of Scripture might also be produced for adolescents in secondary schools, due regard being given to any syllabus which may be used in this area.

Of particular concern today is the need to place the Scriptures persuasively into the hands of university students. Even a casual study of the international scene shows that university students are the center of unrest, frustration, despair and revolt. While experts would differ as to its contents, I am persuaded that the Church generally, in cooperation with the Bible Society, should produce — in the major languages of the world — a volume for university students in *Readers Digest* format. It might include, for example, Genesis, the book of beginnings; Amos, with its emphasis on social justice; the Gospel of John, presenting the intervention of the incarnation, and the life of our Lord and Savior and Master; and the epistle to the Romans that tells how God in Christ deals with sin.

Other specific editions could be published, the Christmas story, among other things (Luke 1:26-35, Luke 2:1-32); the Easter story (incorporating the crucifixion); Pentecost (Acts 2 or a portion thereof); the ascension; the parables of Christ; the Beatitudes, and so on. There is no end to the possibilities.

Through the various Bible societies and constituent members, the Bible Society movement offers the Church at large its maximum cooperation in using the Scriptures in an evangelistic thrust. Whatever requests are made for Scriptures in new formats, special type-faces, and special editions are given the utmost consideration for implementation by the Bible societies.

EVANGELISM AND THE TEACHING OF ACTS

Philip Teng

Ten years ago it would have seemed superfluous to try to prove to the Christian churches that evangelism is supported by the teaching of the Bible. "Of course it is," one would say. It was all taken for granted. If there were sermons on evangelism, they were preached only to arouse Christians to take up their responsibilities in evangelism. But the situation today is becoming different, even in the younger churches, because of the spread of Neo-Evangelism, Neo-Universalism and Neo-Syncretism. Every fundamental truth must be restated and restudied for reorientation.

We declare and confirm that evangelism is supported by the Bible. Since the Great Commission and the constraint of the Holy Spirit are being dealt with in other panel groups today, I will confine my remarks to what the book of Acts teaches about evangelism. To be more specific, I will deal with the practice, experience and teaching of the Apostles in regard to evangelism, as recorded in Acts.

One would not be exaggerating to say that the Acts of the Apostles is evangelism. Indeed, an apostle is actually "one who is sent" to evangelize. Apostleship consists mainly in witnessing and evangelizing, terms that are used synonymously in Acts. The office of an apostle would be devoid of significance if evangelism were removed from this connotation.

1. The Apostles' Commission to Evangelize

a. The empowerment and scope of the Commission

"Ye shall receive power after that the Holy [Spirit] is come upon you: and ye shall be witnesses unto me both in Jerusalem, and in all Judea, and in Samaria, and unto the uttermost part of the earth" (Acts 1:8).

The empowerment is "The Holy Spirit who is come upon you." No other power is sufficient for evangelism. A fresh seeking after the empowerment of the Holy Spirit is absolutely necessary in all evangelistic efforts today. For true success in evangelism, Christian churches must be awakened to a new sense of utter dependence on the power of the Holy Spirit.

The scope is "Jerusalem . . . unto the uttermost part of the earth." There is no stopping short of world evangelization!

b. The constraining knowledge in the Commission

First, the apostles knew that they were commissioned by the Lord to preach the only way of salvation: "There is none other name under heaven

MR. TENG is President of the Alliance Church Union, Hong Kong, and pastor of the North Point Alliance Church in Hong Kong.

given among men, whereby we must be saved" (Acts 4:12). This knowledge constrained them to proclaim the Gospel in season and out of season.

Second, the apostles knew that they were witnessing about something of which they were absolutely sure: "We cannot but speak the things which we have seen and heard" (Acts 4:20). Conviction of the reality of their message made them so bold that even their enemies were amazed.

Third, the apostles knew that they were commissioned by the Lord to pass on "the Word of life," "Go, stand and speak in the temple to the people all the word of this life" (Acts 5:20). The knowledge that what they preached would bring eternal life, as well as new life, to those who believed would certainly spur their efforts to fulfill their sacred commission.

Fourth, the apostles knew that to evangelize was to obey God: "Peter and the other apostles answered and said, We ought to obey God rather than men. . . . We are his witnesses of these things" (Acts 5:29-32).

c. Commission in face of persecution

At Damascus, Ananias was informed by the Lord of Paul's commission to send the light of the Gospel to many people and suffer for His sake: "He is a chosen vessel unto me, to bear my name before the Gentiles, and kings, and the children of Israel: For I will show him how great things he must suffer for my name's sake" (Acts 9:15, 16).

Concerning Paul's work at Corinth, we read: "Then spake the Lord to Paul in the night by a vision, Be not afraid, but speak, and hold not thy peace: For I am with thee, and no man shall set on thee to hurt thee: for I have much people in this city" (Acts 18:9, 10).

And at Jerusalem "the Lord stood by [Paul] and said, Be of good cheer, Paul: for as thou hast testified of me in Jerusalem, so must thou bear witness also at Rome" (Acts 23:11).

d. Commission to evangelize all classes of people

Paul sometimes selected a certain group of people as the object of his evangelistic labor. He worked for two years, for instance, among the scholars of the school of Tyrannus. He never worked so long at a time among any other class of people. He knew that there was wisdom in reaching the intelligentsia for the Lord. The result of this endeavor was that "all they that dwelt in Asia heard the word of the Lord, both Jews and Greeks" (Acts 19:10, ASV). Another example is Paul's work with the deputy of the Island of Cyprus whom he led to Christ, and thereby made an impact for the Christian faith throughout the area.

But Paul used this method only in order to reach all classes of people, for the Lord had commissioned him to be his witness unto "all men" (Acts 22:15), including Gentiles, "kings," and the children of Israel (Acts 9:15).

e. The commissioned message

It is very important to know what message the Lord commanded his apostles to preach.

"And he commanded us to preach unto the people, and to testify that it is he which was ordained of God to be the Judge of quick and dead. To him give all the prophets witness, that through his name whosoever believeth in him shall receive remission of sins" (Acts 10:42, 43). This passage makes it very clear that two important points in our proclamation are the coming judgment and the remission of sins through the Savior who is ordained of God. If we omit this in our preaching, we are not doing what we are commissioned to do.

f. Commission to reach the regions beyond

"And after he had seen the vision, immediately we endeavored to go into Macedonia, assuredly gathering that the Lord had called us for to preach the Gospel unto them" (Acts 16:10). Probably Paul never intended going to Europe with the Gospel. This was a real missionary call — to reach the regions beyond — and Paul was certain that it came from God. I believe that this is a call from God today for the younger churches in Asia, Africa and South America. The time has come for us to answer the Macedonian call.

g. Collective and personal evangelism

"And daily in the temple, and in every house, they ceased not to teach and preach Jesus Christ" (Acts 5:42).

"In every house" — this is personal evangelism. "In the Temple" — this is collective evangelism. Both are necessary. The apostles left us an excellent pattern of what is absolutely essential for fruitful evangelism.

2. *Followers in the Footsteps of the Apostles*

It is heartening to see from the book of Acts how the early Christians followed in the footsteps of the apostles in evangelism. Again and again we read: "They that were scattered abroad went every where preaching the word" (Acts 8:4), "They which were scattered abroad upon the persecution that arose about Stephen travelled as far as Phenice, and Cyprus, and Antioch, preaching the word. . . . (Acts 11:19, 20).

Witnessing apostles, plus witnessing Christians, wonderfully fulfilled the sacred commission for evangelism. This is the Divine Pattern. This was God's will not only for the Early Church but is his will also for the Church today.

COMMISSIONED TO COMMUNICATE
Bob Pierce

Nearly 20 years ago Dr. J. H. Bavinck made this observation in his book, *The Impact of Christianity on the Neo-Christian World:*

"There was a time — and it does not lie so far behind us — when men dared to think and speak quite optimistically with respect to the missionary task. That was the period in which men talked of 'the evangelization of the world in this generation.' That time is now past. The last decades have taught us that missionary work is infinitely more difficult and complicated than was formerly thought."

There is validity in Bavinck's emphasis on the complexity of the task. The longer I walk this world with God, the more I realize how complex the problem of world evangelism really is. I see men struggling to integrate their faith with their cultural heritage, their loyalties, their nationalistic attitudes and their responsibilities to self and family and community — and I see how infinitely deep and involved this problem is.

But Jesus would not settle for anything less than a whole world. That is one of the great differences between Jesus and most of his followers. He faced the task in its entirety, while most of us settle down with one little chunk of the job. Jesus told his disciples to go "into *all* the world and preach the gospel to *every* creature." What would it mean if the Church today took this commission seriously and faced the job in its entirety?

I for one believe that the critical moment is upon us when Christians must accept *world evangelism* as the task committed to us for our generation. Let me add, too, that I believe that the Church today has the resources to do the job. If scientists can dream of a manned landing on the moon, how can the Church do less than dream of winning a world? We need to get on with the business of realizing our dreams.

Although Jesus' followers were commissioned to communicate — his parting words bear this out — Christians today are doing a very poor job of communicating. All too often we simply voice our own orthodoxy amid the rushing traffic of a world jammed with other issues. Much of the time we are out of touch with the key issues that have captured the thinking of the world around us. And we soon discover that we don't get an audience by telling the world it is occupied with the wrong questions. Jesus can teach us to communicate better than that.

To communicate the Gospel effectively to the world around us we must begin by ridding ourselves of certain false assumptions — mistaken notions

DR. PIERCE is president of World Vision, Inc., in Monrovia, California.

that have often unwittingly become a part of our outlook. Let me be more specific.

1. We are deluding ourselves if we think that most of the world is waiting eagerly for our Christian message.

The world couldn't care less if the message is never preached. To recognize this gives us a better idea of our starting point. We must use every possible means to demonstrate that our message today is needed — that it answers the issues of our times.

2. We are deluding ourselves if we think that witness is all talk.

Talk is useless unless saturated with understanding of the people we are trying to reach and set aflame with Christian love. This requires a great deal both of doing and talking. We must show people that we care not only about their eternal destiny but that we care about them also here and now. Evangelism involves the whole man.

Said an old farmer who was visited each year at the time of the evangelistic campaign: "Every year during revival meetings you people come and talk to me about my soul. But between one revival and the next I never see you. I wish you cared less about my soul and more about me."

3. We are deluding ourselves if we think that Western missionaries and the Western cultural encrustations of the Christian Church will be accepted without question in the rest of the world.

Surely I do not question the wisdom of God, but for the sake of the Gospel I often wish that Jesus Christ could go directly from Jerusalem to Asia, Africa and Latin America, without being routed by his followers through Great Britain and the United States.

Most Orientals today are not really rejecting Jesus Christ. They are rejecting the Western interpretation of Jesus — the Western trappings of most of contemporary Christianity. We need to give these people a chance to confront Jesus himself.

4. We are deluding ourselves if we think that our responsibility ends when our words of witness have been spoken, that it is then up to the other fellow to understand, appreciate and accept what we say.

Too often we act as if we have made our one and final pronouncement; if the listener doesn't understand it, let him go to hell. But the fact that a man may be prejudiced against Christianity does not mean we are free of our responsibility. We must answer the questions his prejudice raises.

At what point, we may ask, have we successfully communicated with the Muslim, the Buddhist, the Communist? When does a man know enough to make an honest decision?

We must come to grips with people's indisposition to listen and treat it on its own grounds. We must meet people where they really are. A Japanese, for example, will say "yes" because he feels it is impolite to say "no." Awareness of this must become a part of our equation in communicating. We must help him understand, not change his language.

5. *We are deluding ourselves if we think that the pressing issues of our day are best understood and described in an exclusively theological frame of reference.* Our world has little time for theological abstractions.

From the point of view of the people we must reach, we are too often building straw men. Our language is not the language of the street. In this we have again missed a cue from Jesus. He spoke the language of the people. He was earthy, colorful, vivid in his speech. Why is it so difficult for us to be equally direct and simple?

6. *We are deluding ourselves if we think that heroic missionary and evangelistic efforts of the past will stir the young people of today.*

The Westerner has been too arrogant about his heroes. Missionary heroes of the past fail to stir the imagination of young people today. "So what," they say. "It takes courage to walk through Mississippi today, too." They look at the missionary and ask, "What are you running away from?"

In all this, we must recognize that our stability lies in a clearcut commitment to the Gospel of Jesus Christ. But jeopardy lurks in our easy clichés and unwarranted assumptions.

Let's not be so lofty that we cannot accept the best help available from disciplined scientists in communications, human relations, anthropology, sociology and other related fields. In addition to everything else, I believe that Jesus Christ was the very best sociologist of his times. How else can we explain the insights in his conversation with the woman at the well of Sychar? The well was a point of contact for Jesus just as Mars Hill was a point of contact for Paul. Today's point of contact has changed. It is more apt to be Time Magazine or the Reader's Digest rather than the well of Sychar.

I think it tragic that there is little communication among the hundreds of missionary societies working throughout the world, very little knowledge of what is being done, scant detail on the successes or failures being experienced. No doubt the funds are available in the Christian community to evangelize the present generation; from a business viewpoint, however, it is perhaps just as well that they have not been made available. If any large corporation deployed its people and its finances in the manner that Protestant missions have done, the stockholders might well question the company's management.

I am grateful to be able to report, however, that a project is now under way to help meet this problem and to grapple with the huge task of communicating the Gospel more effectively throughout the world. We have tried to combine the very best in management and scientific skills with persons of foresight from the missionary and theological community. Involved in the project are key men who have proved themselves in the Apollo program to put man on the moon, the Surveyor moon program and other similar ventures. Teamed with them are experienced missionaries and specialists in the study of church growth.

The approach has been to apply the *Program Evaluation and Review Technique* (PERT), originally developed for the Polaris missile program, that has subsequently become a valuable tool in other government, industry and engineering tasks. It has been used successfully in political campaigns and in other enterprises for promoting ideas or products. In applying this approach to the evangelization of the world the question arises: "What must take place before the goal is reached?" In other words, sooner or later we must face the question of the best use of our resources in the task to which we are committed. Hit-or-miss methods will no longer suffice.

The *scientific community* brings three things to this project:

1. Organizational and management ability to define, plan and administer a wide variety of projects, both centralized and decentralized.

2. Scientific knowledge about the world in which we live and about its people.

3. Modern machines in the form of high speed computers that can handle and interpret large masses of data and that therefore permit accurate consideration of this data and consequent improvement in decision making.

The *missionary community* brings three things to this study:

1. A history of past failures and successes.

2. Concepts of what might be successful if the resources were mobilized.

3. A knowledge of the theological basis of missions and means to evaluate whatever concepts are brought forth in terms of God's work.

We must not forget our dependence on the Holy Spirit. We must continue to increase our emphasis on prayer. God's formula is still "by my Spirit." But God will hold us responsible if we do not apply the very best tools available to our task.

Is it too much to believe that these very tools, now being used to put man on the moon, could have their ultimate purpose in bringing the Gospel to every creature? With all my heart I believe that these tools have come to the kingdom for such a time as this. How can we dare to have less vision than those who are involved in the great scientific exploits of our times? This is a time for faith that proves itself. Faith has been described as a "blind leap into the hands of God." We must take that leap rather than shrink from the challenge of our times.

Report of Group Discussion

Taken as a whole, the central concern of the papers was a renewed emphasis upon the integrity and vitality of Holy Scripture that might be combined with our evangelical thrust so as to implement and revitalize a program of world evangelism. Adherence to the historic view of the full inspiration and consequent authority of Scripture was assumed. With this as a point of departure, questions were raised at the following points:

1. To what extent should we rely upon tried and tested methods and approaches in evangelism, and to what extent should we be willing to accept the element of risk, and of possible failure in techniques?

2. What new application of the Word might be projected as a cutting-edge for evangelism which might lead to significant advance in evangelistic effectiveness?

3. To what extent should we be *avant garde* in adopting, adapting, and utilizing the techniques which are proving successful in such scientific projects as the Apollo program, or the PERT techniques developed in connection with the Polaris Missile Program, as a means to deploying our evangelistic resources?

4. At what points should an aggressive evangelistic movement within evangelical Christianity pioneer in the production and placement of religious literature, especially of the Holy Scriptures, whether whole or in part?

5. What can and should be done to penetrate such fields for evangelism as the university, or the expanding numbers of new literates?

More questions were posed than answers supplied. One participant sought to cut through the fabric of our self-delusions and our misunderstandings with respect to our task and/or our successes. Another presented criteria by which the permanent and the universal elements in the projection of the Gospel could be isolated and identified, as a guide to the separation of the Gospel from its trappings of regionalism and acculturation.

The final emphasis was upon the categorical and the unequivocal aspects of our witness, as opposed to the time- and space-conditioned factors which are peripheral to the Gospel and irrelevant to its world-thrust.

Reporter: *Harold B. Kuhn*

GO AND TELL
Michael Kyriakakis

The minister of the Old Testament dispensation was responsible for teaching and guiding those who came to him. He waited at the sanctuary for the people to come. He performed all the prescribed sacrifices and rites on behalf of the people.

The New Testament minister, on the other hand, is commanded to go out to the people. He is not expected to offer sacrifices, but to sacrifice himself in proclaiming the unique sacrifice of God's Son. Since worship in the Old Testament was centered in the temple, people went regularly to Jerusalem. Such a pilgrimage to the holy city was the climax of their spiritual experience. Ministry according to the New Testament has no fixed place. It is not carried out in one particular sacred spot. We are called to serve wherever there are people who must hear the Good News. We are not asked to stay where we are. We are commanded instead to go forth with the one purpose of communicating the Gospel.

This is the main reason why God allowed the apostolic Church at Jerusalem to be spread abroad in all directions. Although believers fled from Jerusalem in order to escape persecution, at the same time they were scattered in order to witness and to preach. While they did not avoid persecution, nevertheless they fulfilled their mission to become the means of transmitting the Gospel.

The pattern, then, of the New Testament witness is not to ring the church bells and wait for people to come. In the instructions for the Old Testament priesthood we find a very vivid picture of the evangelistic task of the New Testament Church and the command to evangelize. It is found in a statement concerning the Feast of the Trumpets:

"In the day of atonement shall ye make the trumpet sound throughout all your land. And ye shall . . . proclaim liberty throughout all the land unto all the inhabitants thereof." (Lev. 25:9-10).

Through the years of its history, Israel from time to time heard the trumpet call. But on this occasion it was the special feature of the day, and universally sounded throughout the land. Its special purpose was to announce the day of atonement, and the gathering in of the people.

We live in the day of the true atonement, made once for all. We are also commanded to make the trumpet sound throughout the land. And since the eschatological note is dominant in the New Testament, our sounding of the trumpet becomes an alarm. It is this note of urgency, in particular, that we must emphasize in our time.

THE REV. MR. KYRIAKAKIS is a pastor and moderator of the Greek Evangelical Church (Presbyterian) in Athens, Greece.

Christ's command, then, and his plan for evangelism, is that we should "Go and tell." We became God's children, not because we decided to follow Christ, but rather because Christ the Lord chose us to be his disciples.

He has chosen us to go and to witness for him. This makes it quite clear that unless we have an experience and a real conviction of what Christ has done, and is doing, we can do nothing in evangelism. Our only real argument is that the Spirit has convicted us. Anyone engaged in witnessing should be able to say, "I know whom I have believed." The command to go is the same command we received to come to Christ. The impulse to tell others is inherent in what I have experienced in Christ. If you should ask me, "Why have you left your old life?" my answer would be, "I cannot tell you why. I would rather explain how I found a new life. As to the *why*, though there are many answers, the final one is beyond my comprehension. The situation is simply this: I faced a challenge too strong to be resisted, a love too great to be rejected." And when you ask me why I left my business and my career in the bank to become one of God's heralds, my answer is the same: "I could not help it." This, I suppose, is how the Lord's command comes to every one of us. "Go!" he says, and we go. How can we do otherwise? Therefore the essential thing is not what we are doing for Christ, but what Christ is doing within us. What we do for him is determined by what the Spirit does in us.

The more we "go," the more we realize that of all man's many needs, his spiritual need is greatest. This spiritual need is met only by one, the Savior Jesus Christ, the Crucified and Risen Son of God. When we go, we go to a world divided between those who propagate false hopes, and those who have no hope at all. We find men and women who cry for something they know not what. They cry for bread, yet bread does not satisfy them. They cry for amusement and for excitement and the more they taste these things the more they plunge into despair. Both in the East and in the West, in highly developed countries as much as in underdeveloped areas, people cry for peace and justice and progress without realizing that behind all this unrest is a craving for the living God, a longing that constitutes the deepest need of the human soul. This is true even in our congregations, in world organizations, in the ecumenicity which is the fashion of the day. Nonetheless the command is plain: Go and tell. Tell them that Christ can satisfy, that only he has the power to make all men one in him.

The command to evangelize, then, springs from the nature of the Gospel, and also from the cry of needy hearts. We betray both the Lord and people when we do not do justice to the Gospel. There can be no true evangelism if we preach Christianity without Christ, if we are satisfied with a minimum of moral standards. There are those who say, "If we can only get rid of some metaphysics of heaven and hell, of worship, prayer — of all that is irrelevant to modern man, then we can approach him." If we approach modern man in this way — and there are those who do — we approach him without the Gospel, without the Evangel. This new approach becomes merely a new version of man's anthropocentric tendencies. Such an approach says: "Let us make our God not only in the image of man, let us make him in the image of Modern Man!"

The Lord's command is irresistible. There is no power in the universe that can stop its implementation. History has proved this fact. It is clear in the experience of the New Testament Church. Authorities, both ecclesiastical and secular, tried to silence the heralds of the Gospel. But they, conscious of their authority, and under the compulsion of their Lord's command, could not be silent.

"And they called them, and commanded them not to speak at all nor teach in the name of Jesus. But Peter and John answered and said unto them, Whether it be right in the sight of God to hearken unto you more than unto God, judge ye. For we cannot but speak the things which we have seen and heard" (Acts 4:18-20).

We cannot but speak! There are countries where we are forbidden to speak. There are other countries where we are allowed to speak but under restrictions. We are not entirely free to spread the Good News. Secular or ecclesiastical authorities may try to stop or harass the herald. There are countries where in every way freedom is enjoyed and valued more than life itself, yet so far as the evangelical witness is concerned, the right to speak freely and openly is in jeopardy. We have no access to the airwaves to broadcast the witness by radio. We cannot open a church without the permit of an ecclesiastical authority. Yet this does not mean that we shall not fulfill our commission. The command is as imperative as ever: "Go and tell!"

Therefore we go. "We cannot but speak. . . ."

THE GREAT COMMISSION
Kenneth L. Chafin

Dr. Schneider has said: "Authority for evangelism is grounded most deeply and finally in the risen Lord's Great Commission." My comments relate to this command of Christ.

We must remember the perspective from which the Early Church viewed the command of Christ. First, they viewed the command through the fact of the resurrection. This event authenticated his life and teachings, gave meaning to his death, gave dynamic to the Church, and was the center of its worship and witness. Second, they interpreted the command in the light of the experience of Pentecost. The power of the Holy Spirit had brought unity and boldness to the believers so that they actually became examples of the Gospel which they proclaimed. Third, they had to grow spiritually before they began to fathom the full implications of the command. Though Christ made it quite clear that the Gospel was for all men, the early disciples were so conditioned by their background and culture that they tried to limit their message to the Jews. The book of Acts is the record of the Holy Spirit's effort to break down all barriers so that the Church would preach the Gospel to all men without reservation. Let me present several implications that I see in the command of Christ.

1. The command to "Disciple all nations" reaffirms God's interest in all men.

At one time Christ was criticized because of his interest in and association with sinners. He answered his critics with three parables that are recorded for us in Luke 15. In the story of the lost sheep, the lost coin and the rebellious son, Christ tells us that God reaches out to the shepherdless, the wasted, and the estranged to forgive and cleanse and reconcile. Jesus demonstrated this concern as his personal ministry took him across social, racial, and religious barriers to reveal the Father to man.

If the Church today is to take seriously the command of Christ, it must find within its heart the same compassion for the peoples of the world as its Lord has. The Church must establish the same posture of outreach toward men which characterizes the Father. The Church must be willing to allow its love for men to cross every man-made barrier, whether social, racial, educational, or national. The world needs to sense that the Church is as interested in them as God is.

DR. CHAFIN is associate professor of the Billy Graham Chair of Evangelism at The Southern Baptist Theological Seminary in Louisville, Kentucky, USA.

2. The command of Christ assumes that evangelism will be done in a context of history.

The Gospel is the story of how God involved himself in history through his Son. The early disciples assumed that they were to disciple all nations in their day. Note the Gospel of John. John knew God through Christ. He was witness to his life and death and resurrection.

John was also very sensitive to his day. He knew its mood, its thought patterns, its schools of thought and its religions. The Gospel of John is a matchless example of an inspired effort to interpret the meaning of Christ to the First Century.

The implication for our day is this: those who do the work of evangelism in this century must have not only a thorough understanding of the Gospel it preaches but also an awareness of the world in which it is to be communicated. Evangelism is never done in a vacuum nor is it done in the past tense. Evangelism is done in the nowness of time. Those who make a diligent effort to bring together their knowledge of God with the age in which they live will be blessed for their efforts. Twentieth-century man, buffeted about by the processes of urbanization and secularization, desperately needs Christ to be presented to him in a way he can understand and to which he can respond.

3. The dimensions of the command make it necessary for the Church to call upon all of its resources.

First, all the people of God must be involved. During this century theologians have rediscovered the doctrine of the laity. It was always the intention of Christ that evangelism should be the work of all "the people of God." One of the primary tasks of the Church today is to equip the laity to be witnesses in all areas of life. Second, every possible means should be used. The imperative in the commission was "make disciples." Christ's followers used every means available to communicate the Gospel. As various discoveries and inventions came, the Church made them servants to their task. Today with almost unbelievable advances in the methods of communication, the Church has an obligation to make these marvels servants of evangelism.

4. The command of Christ is filled with hope.

When he commissioned the Church with what seemed like an impossible task he gave the promise of his presence and of the inevitable triumph of the Church. This hope permeated the Early Church as it moved into a hostile world with a message of love and forgiveness.

Too often the Church today acts and talks as if it were going to lose the battle. The "God is dead" theologians have given way to "The Church is dead" Christians. Some view the Church as having a terminal illness, and plan to sit with her until her death. Others see the Church as already dead, and feel called to bury her. Much of this despair stems from those who have turned aside from evangelism to an understanding of the mission of the Church that involves only social and political action.

The Church which lives with integrity and responsibility in the world can live with hope. It has a Gospel which has power. It has the promise of the presence of God in the proclaiming of his Word. As it carries out the command of Christ, it is time for the Church to move from the "Post-despair" era to one of triumphant hope.

NEW TESTAMENT EVANGELISM
Tom Rees

Scripture reading: Acts 11:19-30

The Mission to Antioch was an event of outstanding importance in Church history. Antioch was no mean city. It was surpassed in size and importance only by Rome and Alexandria. It was the new capital of Syria, and had a considerable population of Romans, Greeks and Jews. It was during this mission in Antioch that for the first time the Gentiles in large numbers heard the Gospel. It was during the follow-up work of the Antioch Mission that the apostle Paul commenced his ministry to the Gentiles. It was here in Antioch, after the Mission, that the disciples were first called Christians. It was from this city that Paul was sent forth by the Holy Spirit on his first missionary journey.

Luke tells us that these lay evangelists, some of whom were men of Cyprus and Cyrene (N. Africa) travelled as far as Phenice. From here some took ships and sailed to Cyprus, while others continued northwards toward Antioch, preaching the Word to none but the Jews. "(But) when they were come to Antioch, (they) spake unto the Grecians (Greeks – Gentiles), preaching the Lord Jesus" (Acts 11:20).

1. The message they preached

What a wonderful message they had: preaching the Lord Jesus! This was the message of the apostles: "And daily in the temple, and in every house, they ceased not to teach and preach Jesus Christ" (Acts 5:42). This was the message that Philip proclaimed in Samaria: "When Philip went down to the city of Samaria, and preached Christ unto them" (Acts 8:5). This was the message that Philip preached to the man of Ethiopia: "Then Philip opened his mouth, and began at the same Scripture, and preached unto him Jesus" (Acts 8:35).

It is tragically possible to preach the Church instead of Christ, the sacraments instead of the Savior, the creed instead of the Christ, the Scriptures instead of the Son of God. These things, the Church, the sacraments, the creed, the Scriptures, vital and important as they are, were never intended to be an end in themselves. They are to be a means to an end. The Church is to point men to Christ. The sacraments are to speak of the Savior. The Scriptures are to testify to the Son. The creed is to point us to Christ. They came preaching the Lord Jesus. Their object was to bring the men of Antioch into a living, vital, personal relationship with the Son of God; to introduce them one by one to a personal knowledge of Jesus Christ,

MR. REES is an evangelist and honorary general director of the Hildenborough Hall Evangelism Centre in Sevenoaks, Kent, England.

that each man deep in his soul might have a personal encounter with God in Christ. They came preaching the Lord Jesus. This, the vital message of the New Testament, has not altered one iota in the last two thousand years. Our message and our emphasis must always be the same: the Lord Jesus.

2. The power with which they preached

"And the hand of the Lord was with them" (Acts 11:21). What power! This phrase: "The hand of the Lord" occurs quite often in the Scriptures. When a man wants to work he generally uses his hand.

The prophet Isaiah heard the people of his day sighing for what no doubt they called the good old days. "In the olden days the hand of the Lord was not shortened as it is now. In those days he would shew his hand and save men, but things are not the same now." And their friends would reply, "Yes, and in the good old days the ear of the Lord was not heavy as it is today. God was wide awake then." Then came the message of Isaiah: "Behold, the Lord's hand is not shortened, that it cannot save; neither his ear heavy, that it cannot hear: But your iniquities have separated between you and your God, and your sins have hid his face from you, that he will not hear" (Isa. 59:1-2).

We do not know very much about these lay evangelists from Cyprus and Cyrene, but I am certain that they were men of prayer, for when they came preaching the Lord Jesus, the hand of the Lord was with them. Mark uses a similar expression in the closing sentence of his Gospel: "And they went forth, and preached every where, the Lord working with them, and confirming the word with signs following" (Mark 16:20).

And when Luke says that they came preaching the Lord Jesus and that the hand of the Lord was with them, he means that they were not preaching or working in their own power. They were not working for God, but they were working with God. And that is the only way to do Christian service, to be a worker together with God; not working for him, but cooperating with him in that which he is seeking to do. The hand of the Lord was with them.

3. The result of their preaching

"And a great number believed, and turned unto the Lord" (Acts 11:21b). We do not read that a great number of the people reformed, or made decisions, or were changed. We read that a great number believed and turned unto the Lord. This, and nothing short of this, is true saving faith, this is New Testament conversion. What does it mean to believe? The word "believe" is one of the most common words in the New Testament, and yet it is often one of the most misunderstood. "Believe" means simply "commit". In the closing paragraph of the second chapter of his Gospel, John tells us: "Now when he (Jesus) was in Jerusalem at the passover, in the feast day, many believed in his name, when they saw the miracles which he did. But Jesus did not commit himself unto them, because he knew all men" (John 2:23, 24).

The Greek word translated "believed" in v. 23 is exactly the same word translated "commit" in v. 24. Moreover the same word is translated more than 90 times elsewhere in John's Gospel as "believe." Remember what the Apostle Paul said? "I know whom I have believed, and am persuaded that he is able to keep that which I have committed unto him against that day" (2 Tim. 1:12).

4. Their counseling of the converts

"Then tidings of these things came unto the ears of the church which was in Jerusalem: and they sent forth Barnabas, that he should go as far as Antioch. Who, when he came, and had seen the grace of God, was glad, and exhorted them all, that with purpose of heart they would cleave unto the Lord. For he was a good man, and full of the Holy Ghost and of faith" (Acts 11:22-24).

The church which was in Jerusalem kept a very close eye on the spread of the Gospel. When the apostles heard of Philip's Mission in Samaria they sent Peter and John to investigate. When Peter himself did the unorthodox thing and went into a Gentile home and preached Christ to Cornelius and his family, it is clear he was sent for and had to give an account of his behavior to the brethren in Jerusalem. And when tidings of the conversion of many Greeks in Antioch reached the church in Jerusalem they said at once, "We must investigate; we must send a delegation; we must send a committee to look into the matter. It is most irregular. Laymen preaching! And that not to Jews, but to Gentiles!" Then the problem arose, whom should they send? And there in the midst was the very man, Barnabas. "Why," they said, "of course. These laymen who are in Antioch preaching to the Greeks are Cypriots, and Barnabas, too, is a Cypriot, a man of Cyprus," and they decided that they would send him. Who could have been better than he? "He was a good man, and full of the Holy Ghost and of faith."

Luke tells us that when he came, and had seen the grace of God he was not critical, but glad. Barnabas must have met many of the converts, people who had turned to the Lord from heathendom, immorality and pleasure-seeking, and in their faces he saw the grace and likeness of our Lord Jesus Christ. True to his name "exhortation" he gathered the missioners and converts round him, and: "Exhorted them all, that with purpose of heart they would cleave unto the Lord" (Acts 11:23b).

5. The result of their counseling

"And much people was added unto the Lord" (Acts 11:24b). Now, of course, they had not only the help of the evangelists who preached the Gospel to them but also that of Barnabas who exhorted them to cleave unto the Lord. With their hearts on fire with love for their new-found Savior, walking in the fear of the Lord and comfort of the Lord, and the comfort of the Holy Ghost, they went throughout the city of Antioch telling men and women about the Lord Jesus. The result was that much people was added unto the Lord.

But Barnabas soon realized that what the new converts really needed was a teacher. How desperately they needed to be taught the things of God! But all he could do was to speak a word of exhortation. They wanted far more than a word of encouragement, and so: "Then departed Barnabas to Tarsus, for to seek Saul: And when he had found him, he brought him unto Antioch. And it came to pass, that a whole year they assembled themselves with the church, and taught much people (Acts 11:25-26).

6. The disciples called Christians

"And the disciples were called Christians first in Antioch" (Acts 11:26b). Have you ever wondered why the disciples were called Christians — Christ's ones? Because they were living for Christ, loving Christ, serving Christ, and talking of Christ morning, noon, and night. Because they loved him so deeply and spoke of him so often that their fellow-citizens in Antioch gave them the nickname, Christ's ones — Christians.

The *message* of the evangelists was this: They came "preaching the Lord Jesus" (v. 20).

The *power* with which they preached was this: "The hand of the Lord was with them" (v. 21).

The *result* of their preaching was this: "A great number believed, and turned unto the Lord" (v. 21).

The *exhortation* to the new converts was this: "that with purpose of heart they would cleave unto the Lord" (v. 23).

The *outcome* of the follow-up was this: "Much people was added unto the Lord" (v. 24).

CALLED TO OBEY
Justin Mabiala

1. We must obey

Every born-again Christian must determine in his heart to obey God and to do whatever he commands.

No man can please God without wholehearted obedience to his commands. "To obey," wrote Samuel, "is better than sacrifice" (1 Sam. 15:22).

The Lord Jesus himself was obedient even unto death. In Hebrews 5:8 and 9 we read "Though he were a Son, yet learned he obedience by the things which he suffered; And being made perfect, he became the author of eternal salvation unto all them that obey him."

The success of the Christian Church depends on this full obedience. If Christians are obedient, the Church will stand and advance. This obedience must be to the vital, unchanging command, "Go ye into all the world, and preach the Gospel to every creature" (Mark 16:15). This command will last as long as this Church age continues. Time cannot kill it. Our worldly way of life does not change it. As Dr. Schneider pointed out, "The risen Lord *himself* commanded the disciples to proclaim the Gospel."

But obedience to the Lord's command is not a grim, cheerless task. The believer who is committed to the will of God will realize that evangelization of the lost is an expression of his thanks to the Lord for the wonderful salvation he himself received by the grace of God.

The Church of Christ in Africa is the result of fulfilling the Lord's command. Through missionaries many Africans living in terrible darkness saw the great light of the Gospel. And these early Christians in turn moved their people to believe on the one true God and to follow him. In this way the early African believers obeyed the Lord's command.

But today many of our African Christians have forgotten this example set by the first believers. We have come to think that we must first make our national church prosperous. We think that once we are prosperous in strong pastors, in money, in big churches, then we will move out into other areas of our country and into other countries of the world which lack the Gospel.

This failure to share the Gospel has dried up the Church in many parts of Africa. We should let the four lepers described in the book of II Kings teach us. When they found an abundance of food in the deserted enemy camp they began to gorge themselves with meat and drink. But then they remembered the starving city they had left behind. "Then they said one to another, We do not well: this day is a day of good tidings, and we hold our

THE REV. MR. MABIALA is director of the Bible Institute Kinkonzi of the Christian Missionary and Alliance Mission in Kinkonzi via Boma, Congo, Africa.

peace . . . now therefore come, that we may go and tell the king's household" (II Kings 7:9).

2. We must go now

"Evangelism is an imperatively essential task, for opposition to the Gospel grows apace in a most frightening manner," said Dr. Schneider. In all areas of life we see the world moving ever more swiftly toward that time described by the prophet when "darkness shall cover the earth and gross darkness the people" (Isa. 60:2).

In a paper on missionary activity, the Rev. L. L. King pointed out that one of the compelling reasons to evangelize the world is that while its population is ever increasing the Church of Jesus Christ is growing smaller. The world's population is growing by 5,000 persons every hour or about 50,000,000 a year. All these millions are "altogether born in sin."

If the Church does not do something now, how will these millions know the saving power of God? Today is the time to evangelize, today more than ever. As I heard Dr. Graham say in a radio message, "God's time is today." This is as true for the witnessing Christian as it is for the lost sinner. The apostle Paul's insistence that "now is the accepted time . . . now is the day of salvation" has as much meaning for the Church in its search for souls as it does for the sinner in search of a Savior.

3. We must obey together

How can we increase our efforts to rescue people from the slavery of sin? We must work together, work in collaboration. This thought is emphasized in the Great Commission as expressed in my mother tongue. The command, "Go ye," is stated in the plural: "Go, all of you." Every child of God should be willing to work together with his Christian brethren to evangelize the world.

There are many ways in which we can work together. One method is known as "Evangelism-in-Depth," a method in which many Christians collaborate in saturating a specific area with the Gospel witness. This method of evangelism is already in operation in different parts of the world.

Another method is radio. With God's help, the Church of Christ must add more transmitters and must broadcast more programs in the vernacular, in the language of everyday speech. It is safe to say that the radio is to my country what the newspaper is to a European country. And this is true in most developing countries of Africa. Even in villages far off in the bush, one can hear radios playing.

Literature, too, plays an important part. Although literature is no longer a totally foreign enterprise in the national Church program, we will need all the overseas help we can get for years to come. One of the newest and most encouraging examples of this working together in literature is the Africa Christian Press. Its recent publication, *Mr. Mee Escapes*, is a model of joint foreign and national effort in bringing a relevant witness to Africa's lost.

The missionary program is another way we can work together now to evangelize the world. Do not think that the day of the missionary evangelist is over. This missionary program, however, must also be the effort of the younger churches. They now support over 260 foreign missionaries of their own. This is a good beginning.

Evangelism-in-Depth, radio, literature, the missionary program — these and other methods are ours to use cooperatively in obeying God's command.

What would happen if we 1,200 delegates from many different countries went back to our work and literally rolled up our sleeves and obeyed the Lord's command? Christ said, "Go, all of you." We must obey now. We must obey together.

Report of Group Discussion

Delegates noted as a common fallacy the view that the Church is a man-made and therefore dispensable institution, while at the same time they were disturbed because evangelical Christianity in the U.S. is predominantly a secular type of Christianity.

They stressed that the ultimate issues of life are not to be settled only in the fields of social and political action. "I intend to ask for personal commitment to Christ," said one professor, "and I intend also to use my vote in my own home state."

The discussion at this point became somewhat disjointed until John Stott (England) changed its course. "How can we identify with the people we are called to serve?" Stott asked. "It is extremely difficult to penetrate into secular society. I am worried about the increasing emphasis on mass media. It involves the danger of our living in society at a distance, and not associating with publicans and sinners."

A consensus emerged that we do not identify because we do not have enough fellowship with Christ. It was suggested that we need cell-group penetration into the neighborhood. It was also suggested that we need to train converted laity to be evangelists where they are.

Reporter: *J.D. Douglas*

THE CONFLICT OF THE SPIRITS
V. Raymond Edman

The Bible makes plain that ever since that age in the distant past known as "the beginning" there has been continual struggle between light and darkness, between the Almighty and the Adversary who rebelled against him. Since early in the beginning there has been this clash of two great personalities: the Spirit of Light and the Spirit of Darkness.

From the inchoate chaos of the creation in the beginning of time, through the spiritual warfare of the centuries in the heavenlies and here on earth, until the ultimate triumph of the King of Kings, there continues the constant strife between the Spirit of God and the Spirit of Wickedness.

There continues the contest between the God of the universe who is light, for in Him is no darkness, and the god of this world who blinds the unbelieving, for in him or in them is no light. There continues the clash between the Savior and Satan, between the Anointed One and the Adversary. Always there is the hostility of the evil one, a murderer from the beginning, against the Messiah, with an implacable and insatiable hatred. Always there is the contention between the Word of God which brings salvation by grace through faith in the Savior, and the works of the wicked one with his substitute gospel of self-improvement and self-sufficiency. In the encounter between the divine Evangel and the diabolical enemy, God provides the opportunity for men to receive the Savior, despite the opposition of the cruel one.

In this spiritual warfare those who choose Christ are called to be soldiers with that clear word of command: "Thou therefore endure hardness as a good soldier of Jesus Christ." It is an individual warfare, as well as worldwide, marked by frequent skirmishes, bitter and brutal battles and long campaigns with dangers of imminent destruction. But the final victory is secure.

There is an Enemy. The Savior knew him and told us much about him. The Lord Jesus knew the stern realities of spiritual warfare. It was after his anointing by the Holy Spirit at his baptism by John that he was driven into the wilderness alone to face the foe. He knew deep testings of the soul and likewise triumph by the Word of God. The Scriptures indicate what is told by secular historians of the day, that there was great increase of demonic activity in the Near East at the time of our Lord's appearance there. It would seem that in these days there is also increased activity on the part of Satan and his hordes as though something of cosmic significance is about to take place. Missionaries, and not only they, can tell us that the dark places of the earth, unenlightened by the Word of God, are indeed full of the habitations of cruel and cunning demonic beings.

DR. EDMAN is the chancellor of Wheaton College in Wheaton, Illinois.

For this conflict between the Spirit of God which indwells us, and the principalities and powers of darkness, we have been provided with adequate equipment. We are instructed to take "the whole armour of God" so that we may be able to withstand the evil one and to stand triumphantly at the close of the evil day.

Bunyan's description of Christian's encounter with Apollyon is not some idle fancy or fiction. To every believer in every age the evil one has raged, saying, "I am an enemy to this Prince; I hate his person, his laws and people: I am come out on purpose to withstand thee." It was only after grievous combat and triumph by the Word of God that Christian learned that "in all these things we are more than conquerors through him that loved us."

To go uninformed and unarmed with the Gospel into all the world is to invite the onslaught of the wicked one, and to be defeated. Many are the casualties among those who respond to the Great Commission. They may know the love of God and the lost condition of the heathen, but they have not been taught the rudiments and stern realities of spiritual warfare.

On our part we are to be good soldiers of Jesus Christ. We are to be aware of our enemy and not ignorant of his devices. We are to be unafraid, in nothing terrified by our adversary, remembering that as we resist him he flees from us. We are to be fully armed and completely prepared in heart and head. Disciplined by the Captain of our salvation we are to follow him, to trust and to obey him who leads his people in triumph. We are to know the dynamic of the indwelling Holy Spirit and with him enter into the conflict against the powers of darkness to deliver treasures from the domain of the strong one.

The Acts of the Apostles gives us much instruction and encouragement in this warfare of the Spirit for the souls of men. We have the same message as had the apostles and the same power of the Holy Spirit. We face the same human needs and opportunities and likewise the same opposition that they encountered.

In the constraint of the Holy Spirit in the life of each believer, individually and corporately in the Church of the living God, there is always the conflict of the Spirit of truth and light against the spirit of error and darkness. It is by the indwelling Spirit of God that we can and should be more than conquerors in the name of the Savior. For effectiveness and victory in the warfare of the Spirit every believer is to be Spirit-filled, Spirit-armed and empowered, Spirit-taught and made bold. It is by Spirit authority that we win the lost to the Savior. Then in the hour of triumph in his presence we shall join in that song, "Thou art worthy to take the book, and to open the seals thereof: for thou wast slain, and hast redeemed us to God by thy blood out of every kindred, and tongue, and people, and nation; And hast made us unto our God kings and priests: and we shall reign on the earth" (Rev. 5:9, 10).

CHRIST AND THE SPIRIT

J. Dwight Wadsworth

Jesus' thorough preparation of his disciples for the coming of the Spirit is entirely consistent with the emphasis of John's prophecy, "Upon whom thou shalt see the Spirit descending, and remaining on him, the same is he which baptizeth with the Holy Ghost" (John 1:33). That this versatile Person who witnesses of Christ, indwells, convicts, empowers, enlightens, revives, bears fruit and bestows gifts should be especially identified with the evangelistic commission: "Ye shall receive power . . . go ye therefore" must have immense significance.

It is necessary to understand the identification of Jesus with the Holy Spirit in order to appreciate in what sense the Holy Spirit constrains toward evangelism. After all our best efforts to define and classify it, the Trinity remains a challenge to human logic; but since the Spirit is so vital to the functioning of Christ's Body we need an understandable, useable definition and need to state it often. Our incoherence and theological jargon concerning this heart-truth of Christianity has exposed us to abysmal weakness. One need only hear an average Christian try to convince a Muslim that we do not believe in three gods and one quickly understands why the evangelistic impact of Christ's Church has been so ineffective in some countries. God the Father is the almighty, unlimited, invisible, incomprehensible God. God the Son is this almighty God made understandable to finite minds. God the Spirit is this almighty God made comprehensible through the Word, made available to the now enlightened but persistently corrupt human nature for regeneration and equipment for service.

Paul was obviously not encumbered by complicated theological concepts of the Trinity in such passages as Rom. 8:9-11 where he uses the terms "Spirit of God," "Spirit of Christ," "Christ," "The Spirit," "the Spirit of him that raised up Jesus from the dead," and "his Spirit," almost interchangeably. Jesus used a unique demonstration to make clear how closely the Spirit was identified with the Son. In John 20:22 we read, ". . . he breathed on them and saith unto them, Receive ye the Holy Ghost." Even as his breath could not exist without him so the Spirit depends upon the Son. His breath extended the sphere of his personal influence and could be detected as a reality without actually being seen. Jesus obviously wanted his disciples to see the closest possible link between the two persons.

That Jesus should have stood and cried saying, "If any man thirst let him come unto me and drink . . ." and that John should have been inspired to explain the living waters, released by believing on Jesus as being ". . . the

DR. WADSWORTH is European Director of the Torchbearers, and president of their German laymen's Bible school in Obernhof, Germany.

Spirit, which they that believe on him should receive:" (John 7:39) has tremendous implications. It is not extreme to define the Holy Spirit as the now available, immediately accessible Jesus. One of the most illuminating parts of the ever-reiterated theme expounded during his final days on earth, found in John 14, 15, and 16, is the passage in 14:16-18. The disciples are to receive "another Comforter" who is to abide with them forever. This suggests that they have already had a Paraclete, or standby, or helper. Their Christian lives thus far had been totally dependent upon Jesus. They knew what a "standby" could mean and thus "another Comforter" could be understood only in terms of the one they had known. The first one could not abide with them continually in the physical sense because he had to die, and because it would soon be necessary, after Pentecost, for him to be in many places at one time if believers were to continue to enjoy his presence. This could be done only by his Spirit, who can be in a million places simultaneously. In case the disciples did not comprehend, Jesus put it very plainly, "I will not leave you orphans, I will come back to you" (v. 18). This makes it clear that when he used artesian water as a symbol, he was referring to the future possibility of his own indwelling by means of the Spirit.

In the hot climate of the East, water speaks in a special way of life and it is in this sense that the water of the Holy Spirit constrains to evangelism. It is characteristic of life to reproduce itself. This natural tendency toward regeneration is the urge, the constraint of the Holy Spirit. The same thought is expressed in the beautiful illustration Jesus uses in John 15. The vine lives and carries the responsibility for fruit-bearing, but the real goal of any fruit is reproduction. Fruit is the attractive package that guarantees the dissemination of life. In yet another picture, Jesus stresses reproductive activity; in John 4 after reminding the disciples that in God's eyes the harvest is always ready no matter what men may think, he tells them that he sent them forth to reap. One may be sure that the Holy Spirit reacts to unsaved masses exactly as Jesus did.

While the expression "constraint of the Holy Spirit" is used nowhere in the Bible there is a close parallel in II Cor. 5:14, "the love of Christ constraineth us." The context makes it clear that Paul is saying, "Knowing his love as we do, we are dominated by the urge to tell men how to be new creatures." It is this urge that is the constraint of the Spirit. He moves us, directs us, persuades us of the urgency to share his life. He can do this only in surrendered hearts however. This does not happen automatically. Moreover, the Holy Spirit can be quenched or resisted. But in him who willingly is a branch in the vine, who gladly lets refreshing waters flow through him to thirsting hearts, who submits to the Lord of the harvest in the work of gathering in unregenerate people, in such a one the Holy Spirit is doing his constraining work. All the fruit of the Spirit, so perfectly embodied in Jesus — beginning with love and continuing through long-suffering — will inevitably result in the impartation of new life.

It should be stressed that this constraint is not *necessarily* toward great activity. In contemplating Jesus' life as recorded in the Gospels one inevitably arrives at something serene, unhurried, and naturally relaxed. Jesus did not try to speak to every person in Palestine. He had only one commission: "the sustenance of my life is to do the pleasure of Him Who sent me and to completely finish His work" (cf. John 4:34, Berkeley). Inasmuch as Paul writes similarly in Eph. 2:10, "For we are his workmanship, created in Christ Jesus unto good works, which God hath before ordained that we should walk in them," it would appear that all Christians may enjoy the same sustenance. The only logical response to this truth is an attitude of complete reliance, unquenchable expectancy, and unhurried availability. This mood must result in consistent reproduction because God's Spirit, being aware of the desperate urgency of an over-ripe harvest field, and knowing how best to reap it with the available human instruments, and indwelling those very instruments, is persistent in his fulfillment of God's loving purpose. It is this life-imparting Spirit of Jesus who constrains all Spirit-born people toward world evangelism.

THE STIRRING OF THE SPIRIT
Alfred Stanway

To discover how the Spirit constrains men we turn to see first what they believed about the Spirit and his work, and then see its effect on their life and ministry. I intend to confine myself to the missionary aspect of the constraint of the Spirit and we shall go first to the New Testament and then more specifically to that greatest of all missionaries, Paul the Apostle. It is true that the world today is one vast mission field. There are, however, real differences. There are places where the Gospel is preached and rejected, places where it is preached and ignored, and places where it has not yet been preached. The obligation to take the Gospel, without delay, to those who have not yet heard, is part of our obedience. The long delay of the Church in fulfilling our Lord's command only intensifies this obligation.

One cannot read the Acts of the Apostles without noticing the tremendous place given to the work of the Holy Spirit. In Acts 1:2 the command to wait for the endowment of power is regarded as having been given by the Lord through the Holy Spirit. Pentecost was spoken of as fulfilling the Word spoken by the Holy Spirit through the prophets. The Apostles preached faith and repentance, and the people who responded were spoken of as having been given forgiveness and the Holy Spirit. From then on, nobody ever thought of a Christian apart from the work of the Holy Spirit. Christians were born of the Spirit and enabled by the Spirit to receive spiritual truth which an ordinary man could not understand. Through the Spirit the love of God was shed abroad in their hearts, which gave them the same deep concern for the souls of men that was manifested so completely in our Lord. The Spirit, by filling a man, gave him an immediate desire to fulfill our Lord's command to be his witness. This is clearly seen on the day of Pentecost. It is a compelling force, and the result of the filling was an immediate burst of Apostolic preaching, with power, which brought conviction and a turning to the Lord. Paul says, "We believe and therefore we must speak." In I Cor. 9:16, he says, "For necessity is laid upon me. Woe to me if I do not preach the Gospel! For if I do this of my own will, I have a reward, but if not of my own will, I am entrusted with a commission" (RSV). The content of his message was Christ. "We preach not ourselves but Jesus as Lord."

When the Spirit stirred the East African Church and the Revival Movement was born, even in the days of its immaturity certain things were evident. Men were compelled to witness. It was a deep obligation, and to deny it was to suffer loss spiritually. The witness was to Christ a crucified Savior, his Cross and his victory. Our Lord's all-sufficiency for the Christian life was

THE RT. REV. MR. STANWAY is Bishop (Anglican) of Central Tanganyika in Dodoma, Tanzania, East Africa.

an ever-occurring theme. It was noticeable that many who felt constrained to witness suddenly found that God through the Spirit had given them the gift of being an evangelist.

The compulsion of the Spirit to witness brought with it the guidance of the Spirit, to those who were his witnesses. In the Acts of the Apostles this guidance was continually constraining men to take the message to the Gentile world. The Church is ordered by the Spirit to set apart Barnabas and Paul. It is obvious from Galatians that Paul knew from the beginning that he was ultimately to take the Gospel to the Gentiles, and this sending forth by the Church through the Holy Spirit of these two missionaries meant the Gospel going to the Gentiles.

Perhaps the most significant evidence of the constraint of the Spirit in both its positive and negative sides is seen in Acts 16. The Apostles were moved by the Holy Spirit not to speak the Word in Asia. The Spirit of Jesus did not allow them to go to Bithynia, but the vision of the man of Macedonia was regarded as a clear direction and they set out to go "concluding that God had called us to preach the Gospel to them," a conclusion amply justified by events. From these and other passages, it is impossible to escape the conviction that the constraint of the Spirit was ever to widen the sphere in which the Gospel was preached; and the Spirit took special action so that the natural barriers that existed between the early Christians, the Samaritans, and the Gentile world should be broken down.

Let us now turn to some of the many things which Paul taught about the Spirit, for it is what he believed about the Spirit and the way he was led by the Spirit that made him the man that he was. Paul taught that all Christians were born of the Spirit. It is the Spirit that restrains the Christian from anxiety and doubt because he came to bear witness with their spirits that they were the children of God. Their bodies became the temple of the Holy Spirit. The Spirit indwelt them and the Spirit was regarded as the earnest of their inheritance, and they were sealed by the same Spirit. When we come to Romans 8 the whole of this chapter is based upon the fact that it is the Spirit that brings life. "If the Spirit of him who raised Jesus from the dead dwells in you, he who raised Christ Jesus from the dead will give life to your mortal bodies also through his Spirit . . ." (Romans 8:11). He teaches that those who live according to the Spirit set their minds on the things of the Spirit.

The Spirit helps us in our weakness and helps us in our prayers, and intercedes for us. Paul urges the Ephesians to be filled with the Spirit. In I Cor. 2, he speaks of the Spirit imparting a secret and hidden wisdom which has been revealed to us through the Spirit. He speaks of the Spirit as comprehending the thoughts of God, and therefore the Spirit which is from God makes it possible for us to understand the gifts bestowed upon us by God. "And we impart this in words not taught by human wisdom but taught by the Spirit, interpreting spiritual truths to those who possess the Spirit" (I Cor.

2:13, RSV). In II Cor. 3:2 the Spirit is the ink with which Christ writes when he impresses his mind on the hearts of men in characters which all can read. In II Cor. 3:7, 8 he speaks of the ministry of the Spirit being attended with greater splendor than that of Moses. In the same epistle he is commended as God's minister in many ways, including the Holy Spirit. Paul teaches that the list of Christian graces is the fruit of the Spirit, and thus the Spirit is related to our everyday living. Paul expects Timothy to "guard the truth that has been entrusted to you by the Holy Spirit who dwells within you."

Paul's beliefs are very important today when the very hub of the certainty of the Christian message is being attacked, not only as being irrelevant to our age but as being no longer true. Against such opposition we, like the Apostle Paul, must turn to the dominating power of the Holy Spirit to govern us, to command us and direct us; and in obedience to that direction we will find a message that is not only true but relevant in any situation.

These truths which the Apostle Paul held produced the following results:

1. They made him unashamed of the Gospel. Everywhere through his writings there breathes a deep conviction that men need the Gospel and are lost without the Gospel, and that the Gospel is the answer to their deepest needs.

2. It made him a debtor to all mankind. This sense of deep obligation is seen as the constraining work of the Spirit. Necessity was laid upon him to preach. The same constraint has been felt by missionaries in every age, and it has been one of the greatest factors in causing people to take the Gospel to every place.

3. It made him aware that he was a chosen vessel. God told Ananias that Paul had a special mission of suffering and of bearing the message to kings and Gentiles. Paul himself was well aware of this. He wanted to proclaim everywhere the unsearchable riches of Christ. He longed "that I might lay hold of that for which Christ laid hold of me."

4. It made a tremendous claim upon him. It made him want so to live that Christ should have the preeminence in all things. He was willing to count all things as loss for the sake of his Master.

5. It made him tremendously concerned with the quality of life of his converts. His aim was "every man perfect in Christ Jesus." He was concerned that they understand the Gospel, as his letter to the Galatians shows. He wants them to possess the full Spirit that is in Christ Jesus. His letter to the Ephesians is concerned with the quality of their life and their behavior. He wants them to be strong through the Spirit, to know the full range of Christ's love, to walk worthy of their calling, to be humble, forbearing, to keep the unity of the Spirit. He wants them to recognize their gifts and exercise them for the benefit of all. He wants them to come to full maturity — all in contrast to the Gentile world around them. On the negative side he wants them to put away falsehood, anger, stealing, corrupt speech, grieving

the Spirit, bitterness, wrath, clamor, an unforgiving spirit. Fornication, uncleanness, and covetousness are not to be named among them, and so on. He goes on to deal with the relationship of husband and wife, of parents and children, of masters and servants. All this points to an overwhelming concern for the spiritual state of the flock of Christ. A concern so deep, so all-embracing, is surely a concern that must have been born in him by the constraint of the Spirit. It was the natural outcome of the deep truths he believed about the Holy Spirit of God.

6. It made him aware of the gifts that God had given through the Spirit to the Christian for the benefit of the Church. How certain he is of this! "Each . . . has been given his gift, his due portion of Christ's bounty" (Eph. 4:7, NEB). The gifts are "to equip God's people for work in his service to the building up of the body of Christ."

7. Like the Apostle John, he came to see the supreme place of love in the Christian life. He saw it as part of the fruit of the Spirit, as God's love shed abroad in our hearts by the Spirit, as the better way, and the greatest of all the things that abide. He urges people to seek after it and he wants men to know its full range.

8. Finally it made him the great expositor of the Cross of Christ. By the Spirit, he was enabled to set forth its meaning, its centrality, its glory. This led Paul to see that man without Christ is lost, a doctrine which is despised today; but where it is not held, there is a loss of the compelling power of the Spirit, not only to preach but to seek out those who are without Christ and without hope in the world.

Without in any way ceasing to be men of the age in which we dwell and while making use of every good gift that God has given to the world, surely the contemplation of the way in which this man was constrained by the Spirit constitutes in itself a call to consider carefully our priorities so that the Spirit's leading, the Spirit's direction and the message which the Spirit has given should ever be our concern.

With such a deep assurance given by the Spirit, with such deep promises, with such divine equipment, with such a message so clearly set forth in the Scriptures, with our aim so clearly before us, such a glorious inheritance in front of us, let us dedicate ourselves afresh to him of whom the Spirit always speaks, our Lord Jesus Christ, our Head and Redeemer.

NO EVANGELICAL MONOPOLY
Juan M. Isais

Some people, to judge by their words and actions, think that the Holy Spirit — his ministry, collective work, and all that he is — has for many years been a special monopoly of evangelicals who emphasize the intervention and operation of the Holy Ghost. On the other hand, there are those who degrade the work of the Spirit of God, and refuse to take his ministry into account.

Throughout all of Holy Scripture every man and every movement that has been used, has been used because of the constraint of the Holy Spirit. Constraint is definite guidance to do those things with which God in his divine purpose has seen fit to entrust us.

We live in a badly-oriented world that is tormented by uncertainty and dazzled by science. There are educators and also a number of religious leaders who have ignored the Great Commission and have shut themselves off in their little niches; they believe that Christ died only for them and that they alone are the salt of the earth in our day. Faced with this kind of situation, we must accept our total responsibility toward a world that is dying without Christ, without God, and without hope.

Unfortunately, we have tried to hide our sin of unbelief, and our lack of evangelistic activity, by emphasizing our apparent differences and even our identification tags. Anyone who is genuinely constrained by the Holy Spirit cannot deny that only under God's constraint can evangelism in general, and personal evangelism in particular, be carried on with effectiveness, certainty and vision.

When a person is constrained by the Holy Spirit, social, organizational and administrative problems represent no real obstacles, but rather become a challenge to true faith — to the faith that Paul speaks of as calling "those things which be not, as though they were." When a man is constrained by the Holy Spirit, he thinks and works even against all hope, and does a supernatural work in a natural way.

If each of us here could understand the significance of being constrained by the Holy Spirit, we would spare no effort, today, tomorrow, or any time, to direct all our resources into an evangelistic activity that is multi-faceted and, above all, constant.

It was the Holy Spirit who constrained the mother of Moses to put him in a basket in the river Nile. It was also the Holy Spirit who constrained Pharaoh's daughter to rescue him. Later it was the same Spirit of God who constrained Moses to refuse to be called the son of Pharaoh's daughter, who constrained him to deny himself the joys of temporal things in order

THE REV. MR. ISÁIS is director of the Northern Zone of the division of evangelism of the Latin America Mission, in Mexico City, Mexico.

to become a leader who was sustained by looking to the Invisible One and by bearing the reproach of Christ.

It was the Holy Spirit who removed Philip from an obviously and definitely blessed activity to dedicate him to answering the quest of a truth-tormented soul on the way to Ethiopia. It was the Holy Spirit who constrained Peter to renounce his exclusivistic spirit, to go to the house of Cornelius with the message of Good News for those who long had agonized in prayer and good works for the answer to their spiritual restlessness. It was the Holy Spirit who constrained Paul to say, "I stand at Caesar's judgment seat." And the same Spirit constrained the leaders of the Jerusalem Council to reject a restrictive philosophy and to accept a new one that received both Jews and Gentiles into one body, the Church of Christ.

The marvel is that Peter himself says in Acts 2:39: "For the promise is unto you, and to your children, and to all that are afar off, even as many as the Lord our God shall call." The work of the Holy Spirit, as we can see, is many-faceted. It is not circumscribed or determined by circumstances, time or people. Rather it is the definite answer to a contrite, humble, and above all, obedient, heart.

It is not sufficient to know theoretically that the Holy Spirit can constrain us; it is absolutely necessary to accept by faith that he will do so.

The apparent absence of concrete manifestations of the Holy Spirit today is due not to the lack of modern apostles, nor to any scarcity of information about him, but rather to a negligent and unbelieving spirit on the part of leaders who proclaim the Good News of the Gospel even while they refuse to give liberty to the Holy Spirit, and who compensate for this lack by a mechanization of the faith.

Unconditional surrender to God is not only advisable, but desirable and imperative, in every member of the body of Christ (Psalm 51). Personal surrender to the Holy Spirit by leaders responsible for the work today is indispensable for the good health of the evangelical Church in the twentieth century. We can never create ministers. Our task is limited to discovering those who, constrained by the Holy Spirit, deny themselves — those who have lost their lives to find themselves.

When the divine call becomes something mechanical, then we obtain professional ministers "prepared unto every good work" but who have no consuming passion for their fellowmen. We cannot successfully develop permanent evangelistic enterprises unless the Spirit of God has absolute liberty in them. We cannot plant or develop churches as long as we insist on patterns of thought that deny the Holy Spirit a time to meet and abide in believers; or that deny believers the opportunity to have lips, mind, and personality touched, cleansed and pardoned as did Isaiah of old.

The Holy Spirit has the last word in regard to missionary work. Undeniably there are many mysteries, such as the absence of extensive missionary work for more than ten centuries. Nevertheless, some facts are obvious and it is well to consider them. The missionary philosophy of today tends constantly toward labor that implies neither faith nor sacrifice, neither self-abnegation nor the guidance of the Spirit. God has always been opposed to honoring methods that lack total surrender. The Holy Spirit is not restricted to using only people of a certain class; on the contrary, he uses anyone and everyone who, like Gideon, will challenge the God of the impossible.

Of course, good administrative sense requires organizational association with other agencies having similar purposes. The Holy Spirit should be taken very much into account in making our plans, in recruiting personnel, and in choosing places; we are to seek the Holy Spirit's guidance and not simply his accompaniment.

The Apostle Paul asked the Ephesians whether they had really taken the Holy Spirit into account in their plans, whether they had invited him to cast light on the solution of their problems. Must we perhaps confess that we have acted impiously deciding first, choosing first, and then saying, "Now, Lord, carry on!" The natural consequence of such a spiritual farce is discouragement, frustration, a desire to mechanize, and automatize our faith

The words of Paul should be our exhortation: "Be not drunk with wine, wherein is excess; but be filled with the Spirit" (Eph. 5:18). Note that the Apostle's invitation is closely related to life in the home, to the life of work, to the relationships between parents and children, between masters and servants. In a word, if the Church is truly to be the Church, it must be filled and guided constantly by God.

As we return to our countries may we not be constrained by those who, knowing more than we, have been able to impress us. But may we be constrained to love and serve others by the Spirit himself who will not betray us, and who, if we obey him fully and constantly, will honor our ministry, whatever may be the circumstances, place, or people, with supernatural power.

Report of Group Discussion

The five questions asked by the delegates dealt largely with the traditional problems of the theology of the Spirit or with practical matters of teaching or church order: such as the laying on of hands, the activity of the Spirit in exorcising demons, and the difficulty of Trinitarian apologetics.

A closing comment by Dr. Edman in reference to Colossians 1:18 was suggestive of the general orientation. Stressing that in all things Christ must have preeminence, Dr. Edman warned against an unwholesome concentration on the Spirit in theology and in the Church.

The discussion group did nothing to dispel the old and perceptive complaint that the doctrine of the Spirit is the Achilles' heel of Protestantism. Papers on the topic of "The Spirit's Constraint," tended to agree on the reality of the Spirit's compulsion to evangelism, without actually defining it. They stressed the diversity of the Spirit's gifts without attempting to link them to the specific needs of evangelistic enterprise. Dr. Wadsworth identified the constraint of the Spirit with the love of Christ. Mr. Isais stressed the necessity of obedience to the Spirit in contrast to an ecclesiastical or programmatic loyality.

Reporter: *James M. Boice*

THE WAY OF THE LOST
Subodh K. Sahu

1. Definition of the lost

God is holy love. Therefore he is revealed as personal in the Bible and in his creation. He created man in his own image. Man has personality. Man was created for the express purpose of enjoying God in loving worship and obedience. This God expected from man in response to his great love. Yet man chose to reject this privilege of fellowship and worship. He listened to the enemy and nursed the evil suggestions in his mind. He put himself in the place of God. He became hostile in his mind toward God. He sought freedom in "self-worship," but in doing so merely followed the desires of his body and mind, and made himself a slave to sin. He is lost to God. He has lost himself in bondage to sin. His communion with God is lost. He is so "lost," that he hates the one true God and is filled with all manner of wickedness and pride. He knowingly mocks at the just decree of God that those who reject him deserve to die. He takes pleasure, moreover, in the estrangement of others. In this way the lost not only practice evil but are also inventors of many kinds of evil.

2. The way of the lost

The whole life of the lost can be described as "obedience to wickedness." The inner evil or bias toward sin and self-centeredness that is enthroned in their personality shows its ugly face in various ways. They indulge in the lusts of defiling passions. They despise authority. They are bold and willful in their wickedness. Some commit evil publicly with no feeling of shame whatever, boasting in their cleverness and ingenuity.

But there are others, however, who obey wickedness under the guise of religion and philosophy, and all this in the name of God. They profess to know God, but deny him by their deeds. Their minds and consciences are corrupted. They think nothing of blaspheming the name of God through their hypocrisy.

The tragedy is that thereby their hearts become hard and impenitent. Their minds become base and darkened. In the name of liberty they give themselves to license, living in the passions of the flesh, having no hope and being without God in this world. This is seen in their attitude of "Eat, drink, and be merry, for tomorrow we die." Of course they do so-called good works before men in order to smother the pricks of conscience, saying their good deeds cancel their evil indulgences. They place their hopes in uncertain

THE REV. MR. SAHU is the secretary for evangelism of the Utkal Christian Council in Orissa, India.

riches. Evil craving for money makes them haughty, drives them to many an evil snare and hurtful desire which plunge them into ruin and destruction.

They strongly oppose the message of the grace of our Lord Jesus. Some even try to present another gospel, devoid of the stigma of the crucified Christ.

They are driven and obsessed by a sense of restlessness. Like wild waves of the sea they cast up the foam of their own shame. They defy the person of Christ and his will. They speak evil and harsh things against him.

3. Destiny of the lost

In keeping with his holy nature, God is continually revealing his wrath against the lost. God's holy law declares that the wages of sin is death. The prospect is extremely grim. The lost will die eternally in the next world. They will miss the destiny for which God made them. They are vessels of wrath fitted unto destruction. They ignore the fact that even though the wheels of God grind slowly, they grind exceedingly small.

A final day of judgment is appointed. None of the lost will escape it. Even the sea and the grave will surrender their dead. All the lost will be made to stand before God's judgment throne. His records will uncover their accounts and they will be judged according to their deeds, words, and thoughts. On that day the Lawgiver will execute his wrath in justice. The Stone will fall on the rejecters of the Christ of God, and scatter them to dust. He will inflict full punishment and execute his wrath to the uttermost. Nahum declares, "Who can stand before his indignation? And who can abide in the fierceness of his anger?" God is and will be a consuming fire! The punishment of eternal destruction and exclusion from the presence of the Lord and from the glory of his might will overtake them without exception.

4. God's plan for restoration of the lost

In his everlasting love, God yearns for the lost. Therefore the Son of Man came to seek and to save the lost. Though he was in the form of God, he did not count equality with God a thing to be grasped, but emptied himself, taking the form of a servant, being born in the likeness of men; and found in human form, he humbled himself and became obedient unto death. It was a substitutionary death for each lost person that he died on Calvary's hill outside the city-gates of Jerusalem — death on a cruel Roman Cross. There he paid the full ransom, once for all, according to the just demands of the law of God. There is now no reason why the lost should remain in the slavery of sin and away from God. God yearns and waits to forgive all who come and to restore them to full fellowship with himself. The only conditions for this restoration are repentance and faith in the Lord Jesus Christ.

5. Conclusion

If this compassionate, unchanging and ever-wooing Christ lives in our hearts, this one who saw the multitudes harrassed and helpless like sheep without a shepherd and had compassion upon them, if this Christ fills our hearts with his own compassion for the lost, we will walk in his footsteps to seek and save the lost. He will make us burdened for the lost, and will arouse his dedication in us to do his work. He will shake us from our self-centeredness so that we will bring the lost to full restoration with him. Then we will know that our lives are lived in union and communion with him. We will daily know that we are in the Spirit, and endued with his power. His great sorrow and unceasing anguish for the lost will be the motivation that drives us to evangelize even unto the ends of the earth.

LOST HUMANITY REQUIRES RESCUE
Mervin E. Rosell

Man, so evidently "lost," needs the thrust of Christian evangelism to be "rescued" and redeemed.

1. Man is "Lost"

Man as an individual is the microcosm that must be carefully examined in order to understand (in a measure) the otherwise inexplicable plight of humanity as a whole.

a. Outward evidences of man's "lostness"

To prepare a complete historical record of man's overwhelming confusion and admitted bewilderment would require the calculation of all the most advanced "electronic computers" of modern science.

The outward evidences alone are staggering! War, lust, crime, selfishness, greed, and rebellion against all authority produce the vast imbalance caused by sin, namely, inequity and inequality; poverty and famine; ignorance and idolatry; and finally, disease and death!

The war-zones, famine areas and rioting cities around us all give evidence of how far man has lost his way.

b. Documentary evidences of man's "lostness"

The Scriptures are our prime document. As the Bible says, "No one is good" — no one in all the world. "They have all gone *out of the way.*" Everyone has sinned; all are worthless to God. No one anywhere has kept on doing what is right, not one. Then, the Apostle Paul adds: "Not one of them has any excuse; in fact, all the world stands hushed and guilty before Almighty God" (Rom. 3:10-19, paraphrase from *Living Letters*, Tyndale House, Wheaton, Illinois).

Webster's definition of the word "Lost: Ruined . . . destroyed . . . having wandered from or unable to find the way," is matched by biblical writers like Isaiah: "All we like sheep have gone astray; we have turned every one to his own way." Throughout the pages of his Book, God delineates man's dilemma.

c. Personal, internal evidences of man's "lostness"

Far more profound than all the external evidences of humanity's consummate bewilderment — social, political, economic and so on — is man's personal sense of spiritual failure. The deep roots of his fear, frustration and guilt cannot be understood apart from the historical and biblical background, apart from Adam's rebellion and his expulsion from the security of God's presence into the "lostness" outside of God's presence.

DR. ROSELL is an independent evangelist and president of The American Crusade, in Tujunga, California, USA.

The Westminister Confession puts it this way: "They (Adam and Eve) being the root of all mankind, the guilt of this sin was imputed, and the same death in sin and corrupted nature conveyed to all their posterity, descending from them by ordinary generation. From this original corruption, whereby we are utterly indisposed, disabled and made opposite to all good, and wholly inclined to all evil, do proceed all actual transgressions" (Chap. 6:3, 4).

The doctrine of man's depravity, depredation and consequent debauchery is involved. As Charles Hodge has said: ". . . this corruption of nature affects the whole soul . . . it consists in the *loss* or absence of original righteousness, and consequent entire moral depravity of our nature, including, or manifesting itself in, an aversion from all spiritual good, or from God, and an inclination to all evil . . . it is truly and properly of the nature of sin, involving both guilt and pollution . . . it retains its character as sin even in the regenerated . . . it renders the soul spiritually dead, so that the natural or unrenewed man is entirely unable of himself to do anything good in the sight of God. This doctrine therefore stands opposed, — (1) To that which teaches that the race of man is uninjured by the fall of Adam. (2) To that which teaches that the evils consequent on the fall are merely physical. (3) To the doctrine which makes original sin entirely negative, consisting in the want of original righteousness. (4) To the doctrine which admits a hereditary depravity of nature, and makes it consist in an inclination to sin, but denies that it is itself sinful" (Charles Hodge, *Systematic Theology*, Vol. II, Grand Rapids, Wm. B. Eerdmans Publishing Company, Chapter 8, page 230).

While we analyze the universe and explore the problems of society, God's evidence explains: "The trouble is not there, but with me, because I am too sinful to obey it (the law). . . . I know I am rotten through and through so far as my old sinful nature is concerned. . . . Who will free me from my slavery to this deadly lower nature?" (Rom. 7:14 ff. paraphrase from *Living Letters*).

2. Lost Man Needs to be "Rescued"

a. Man's rescue demands bedrock reality

The emergency rescue of man cannot be undertaken without awareness of the amazing acceleration of danger in this thermonuclear age. Only apocryphal language can describe the possibilities of proliferation that lead to the indescribable holocaust.

Dare we even "theorize" about man's rescue? Surely we cannot "phase him out of his dilemma." Nor can we "phrase him into some philosophical scheme of human redemption." Thinking men do not "toy" with the emergency needs of a man who has "cancer of the soul" who, "lost in the dense fog," needs to be rescued and healed. (Cf. Gal. 1:9: "If any man preach any other gospel . . . let him be accursed.)

Christ claimed, "I am *the* Way, *the* Truth, *the* Life." We must acknowledge Christ's unique place in redemption. The new apostles of neo-universalism reiterate the same responsibility-relieving precepts that their fathers used a generation ago, when we observed the great decline in evangelism. Thirty years ago, I was often told as a young evangelist that urgency of mission and commission was "unnecessary" since God "somehow" would "save the lost." To theorize that God (in opposition to the direct commands of his Christ) can *not* judge because this is "simply unthinkable" would, if this attitude is true, relieve the church of its total obligation to evangelize.

Neo-evangelism has a compromise answer. For the traditional apostolic concept of Christian evangelism, it substitutes a type of "corporate redemption" that reaches entire segments of humanity with an "accommodating gospel." In an age of "the group" . . . the "society" . . . the "establishment" . . . we must be frank enough to state that God has never promised salvation "on the Family Plan."

b. *Man's rescue demands divine dynamic*

"The cause of evangelism to which I have dedicated my life," said Billy Graham, "is now suffering from confusion. There is confusion about evangelism both among its enemies and its friends. . . . The greatest definition of evangelism I have ever read is one written by the Archbishop's Committee in the Church of England. It says: 'To evangelize is so to present Christ Jesus in the power of the Holy Spirit that men shall come to put their trust in God through him, to accept him as their Savior and to serve him as their King in the fellowship of his church' " ("My Hope for the World Congress on Evangelism," by Billy Graham, World Vision Magazine, September, 1966).

Only God can meet man's sin problem. Christ alone became the "one mediator between God and men" . . . reconciling men unto God . . . "not by works of righteousness which we have done, but according to his mercy he saved us, by the washing of regeneration, and renewing of the Holy Ghost" (Titus 3:5).

3. *This Rescue of the Lost Requires Thrust*

In his omniscience God has devised a total and sufficient plan for rescuing lost man. But despite his omnipotence, he has chosen to use "thrusters" to project the message of his plan ("by the foolishness of preaching"). God commissioned these "thrusters" in the Person of his Son ("Go ye into all the world . . . to disciple") and empowered them by indwelling them in the Person of the Holy Ghost ("Lo, I am with you alway . . . even unto the end of the age"). By some glorious heavenly alchemy, the Omnipresent God involves yielded men in the thrust of evangelism!

a. *The thrust of direction in evangelism*

The word "cybernetics" comes from an old Greek word meaning

"steersman." It is often used in describing the guidance systems that deal with electronic computers in the realm of astrophysics.

Although God's eternal "rescue plan" for man is complete, an ever-changing race of men (growing overwhelmingly with the population explosion) demands the multiplication of the most refined processes of thrust. To coin a phrase, perhaps a "system of spiritual cybernetics" can be developed to delineate "goal-thrusts," to "trigger into action" an entirely fresh "complex of methods" in evangelism for Christ (I Cor. 9:22 "By *all* means.").

b. *The thrust of command in evangelism*

The authority of Christ's command should be sufficient to move every Christian into "rescue action." Even gentler souls must realize there is *motion* in devotion. However much compromisers have muted its militant note, the mandate still reads: "Go . . . teaching them to observe all things whatsoever I have commanded you . . ." (Matt. 28:19-20). *No new redemptive message is necessary!*

c. *The thrust of fulfillment in evangelism*

The lost man will *not* be rejected (John 6:37). The cancer of his lostness *must* yield to the touch of the Great Physician ("He healed them all"). The lost man *will* be redeemed (John 3:16).

"So, there is no condemnation awaiting those who belong to Christ Jesus. For the power of the life-giving Spirit — and this power is mine through Christ Jesus — has freed me from the vicious circle of sin and death" (Rom. 8:1-2, *Living Letters*). "For God was in Christ, restoring the world to Himself, no longer counting men's sins against them but blotting them out. He has given us this wonderful message to tell others. We are Christ's ambassadors. God is using us to speak to you: we beg you, as though Christ Himself were here pleading with you, receive the love he offers you" (II Cor. 5:19-20 *Living Letters*).

Now let me return to the fulfillment verse that climaxes the struggle of Paul described earlier. The answer to "Who will free me?" is simply, "Thank God! It has been done through Jesus Christ our Lord. He has set me free" (Rom. 7:25, *Living Letters*).

It was Voltaire who said, speaking of philosophers, "We never cared to enlighten cobblers and maidservants. That is the work of apostles."

"Thank God it is!" continues G. Campbell Morgan. "There is the supreme difference between all philosophy apart from Christ and the Christian evangel. Paul, just between midnight and the first flush of dawn upon the sky, took time to teach that brutalized jailer, the man who came in unworthy panic saying, "What must I do to be saved?" The answer came quick and sharp and vibrant with the music that the listening man knew not of: 'Believe on the Lord Jesus Christ.' "

We would join Campbell Morgan in saying: "It is a picture for all time.

Philosophers do not care to enlighten cobblers and maidservants; but apostles never speak of cobblers and maidservants. They speak of men and women in the image and likeness of God and it is always worthwhile to spend time with them, to explain to them the mightiest things of the universe. That is the picture of Christianity" (G. Campbell Morgan, *The Acts of the Apostles*, pp. 393, 394, New York, Fleming H. Revell, n.d.).

God grant that by the power of the Holy Spirit, we may so seek and speak to his praise, and to the salvation of the lost.

THE PLIGHT OF THE LOST
Suteichi Oye

Jesus said, "The son of man is come to seek and to save that which is lost." God's purpose in the incarnation was to save man from this lost state. There are two aspects to the problem: first, the fact of the reality of being lost; and second, the plight of the lost before salvation is experienced.

In Luke 15, the Lord gives a picture of the first aspect. He speaks of that which is lost, and of the one who has lost something. We can conclude that to be lost is to be cut off from the original relationship which we had with God, the creator of heaven and earth. This Father-son relationship has been severed because of man's sin. Man has shut God out of his heart. Therefore man reveals the fact of being lost by showing no response to God's heart of love.

Although we as Christians are aware of man's lost condition, man himself is not conscious of the fact that he is separated from God and in a lost state. Because of modern thought and knowledge, man thinks his condition is normal. He evaluates himself on the basis of existing conditions and laughs when he is told, "You are a lost soul." To the Japanese the concept that man is lost is complete nonsense.

Although lost man considers himself a normal person, he struggles with two problems: restlessness, and the pathetic fear of loneliness. If man were truly normal he would be contented. Originally created for fellowship with God, man is restless until this fellowship is restored.

Now let us consider the general situation among the Japanese people. We can divide this topic into two parts: first, the religious background of Japanese life; and second, the self-life or ego.

The religious background of Japan is very complex. Romans 1:21 is an apt picture: "[They] became vain in their imaginations and their foolish heart was darkened." To the original polytheistic system already present in Japan was added Confucianism from China. To this was added Buddhism. This syncretism of Buddhism and Shintoism has produced a really strange situation. For birth and marriage, for example, the rites of Shintoism are observed. But when a person dies he is given a Buddhist funeral. Every Japanese home has a Buddhist shrine where memorial services are held for the family ancestors. In the same home there is also a Shinto god-shelf where the family worships.

In this complex situation, how is man to satisfy the longings of his heart? Shintoism seeks to dispel loneliness by keeping people in close contact with the shrines. In every locality the inhabitants are considered children

THE REV. MR. OYE is pastor of the Hiroshima Alliance Church and president of the Japan Alliance Church in Hiroshima, Japan.

of the shrine. This attitude provides a sense of group-solidarity or togetherness by which loneliness is somewhat mitigated.

Anxiety about the future can be numbed by the whatever-happens-is-all-right teaching of Buddhism. Buddhism teaches that all things are constantly changing. There are no eternal verities: there is no peace . . . there is no god . . . there is no soul — and happy is the man who understands this.

To these various concepts, Western thinking was added. Materialism and evolutionistic theology were introduced. Economically the country developed rapidly. All these factors contributed to a sense of security. As a result, the need for religion practically vanished from Japanese society.

What then in this kind of society is the spiritual state of the individual ego? Mr. Akira Hatori has aptly described it by saying "The Japanese ego is imprisoned; it is not free."

Shintoism with its shrine-parishioner, local-society system has a firm hold on the people. When I was engaged in evangelistic work in the city of Nara, I was nearly expelled from the arena because I refused to contribute to a local shrine festival. And this happened even though our constitution guarantees freedom of religion.

Religion is thought of as culture or refinement. It is not a confrontation with God or eternal issues, but only a game of ideas.

Rather than aiding in an understanding of the Gospel, these forces become a hindrance. In Christianity we have the concept of denial of self, and Jesus' command to bear our cross. To the Japanese, these concepts are identical with their feudalistic morals. The average Japanese can incorporate Christian teachings into the fabric of his life without altering the original pattern. God, or Buddha, or what have you — anything, any god can be worshiped without this being thought the least bit strange. Every December accordingly we have the startling paradox of holding Christmas celebrations in Buddhist-sponsored kindergartens.

The Japanese ego is emasculated and essentially emotional. Rather than acting from reason, it is impulsive. It is especially prone to negative reaction. It is essential to the nature of the captured Japanese ego to oppose the members of another group. Japanese Communists, for example, are always looking for something to be against. And the average Japanese instinctively dislikes religions and concepts of other countries.

In this spiritual situation, we could not expect to find a consciousness of sin committed against a holy God. And indeed, such is the case. Buddhism, by teaching that good and evil are one, has clouded man's God-given conscience. There is fear of "losing face" but no fear of a holy God. There is no consciousness of sin, so consequently, no need for the Gospel.

In Japan, a country of nearly one hundred million people, only one-half of one percent are Christians, and this after more than 100 years of Protestant church work. These statistics help us understand how difficult it is to reach the Japanese.

This ground — the hard hearts of the Japanese people — has been trodden and packed down by many religions and philosophies. However before the Spirit of the Lord, and before the power of the Gospel, a harvest of good fruit shall yet come forth. Let us believe that he that goeth forth weeping, bearing seed for sowing, shall return to the place of the Father with shouts of joy and bringing his sheaves with him.

UNREACHED BY THE GOSPEL
Percival W. Gibson

The classical story describing the plight of the lost is that of the Prodigal Son. The plight of the younger son in the far-off country resulted from his desire to have his own way. But having his own way eventually brought hunger and isolation. Then the lad came to himself, to his true self, repented and sought forgiveness. The son in beggary is spoken of as "lost," and in repentance is referred to as "found."

While it is true that everyone in unrepented sin is "lost," in our present world situation two categories of persons stand out notably as rejecting, or as untouched by, the saving power of the Gospel. These are the men and women of higher education and the masses who have only a vague idea of Christianity.

The issues involved, therefore, are twofold. First, we must be able to meet the educated on common ground, and this common ground is that we are all sinners; and second, we must be able so to present the Gospel to the masses that a response may be possible. The crux of our situation is the absence of a sense of sin. The sinner is lost if, because he has no sense of sin, he has no sense of need for forgiveness.

What man needs, then, is a radical reformation; and this radical reformation is the essence of the Christian Gospel. The intellectuals need the child-like spirit and the sense of sin equally with the masses.

Because teachers exert such tremendous influence upon their students, the Gospel must be presented to them not only for their own souls' good, but for the good of the community, and ultimately for the good of all.

Christianity is a world-religion not only because of its world-wide missions, but because our Lord Jesus Christ intended it to be so. In what sense, then, do we expect Christianity to be universal in the future? Consider certain facts:

1. There is a slowing up of Christian missions in this century, as compared with the last century, due to the spread of Communism and scientific achievement.

2. The traditional religious bodies have in large measure become static, and have lost the allegiance of the working-man, while new groups and religious bodies, such as the Pentecostalists in Brazil, are making headway.

3. Modern prophetic voices are few and far between.

Offsetting these facts we note:

1. The new movements of the Spirit are making for greater unity and

THE RT. REV. BISHOP GIBSON is the Bishop of Jamaica (Anglican) in Kingston, Jamaica, West Indies.

devotion in the Christian Church. But, we should note, all these are within the Church.

2. Pope John XXIII's outlook and the Second Vatican Council have had a significant effect.

The Gospel must be presented to every creature for a testimony unto the nations. But salvation depends on the conditions laid down by our Lord as Head of the Messianic Kingdom. These conditions are repentance and faith. One of the reasons for the failure of the Church in the present age is the preaching of essay-sermons that lack the prophetic ring of a call to repentance and faith. According to St. Luke's Gospel, the Risen Christ said to the Apostles: "Thus it is written, that the Christ should suffer, and rise again from the dead the third day; and that repentance and remission of sins should be preached in his name unto all the nations, beginning from Jerusalem. Ye are witnesses of these things. And behold, I send forth the promise of my Father upon you: but tarry ye in the city, until ye be clothed with power from on high" (Luke 24:46-49, ASV).

Repentance means a change of mind, or as we generally say, a change of heart. We become God-centered and not self-centered. Faith in Christ is necessary first because Christ "bore our sins in his body on the tree" and so made a perfect atonement for the sins of the world, and secondly because faith (with Paul) involves such a commitment to Christ that we become united with him. The Philippian jailor realizing his own need said to Paul and Silas, "Sirs, what must I do to be saved?" And the answer came immediately, "Believe on the Lord Jesus Christ and thou shalt be saved." This belief is more than intellectual trust, it is a commitment of the whole life to Jesus as Lord and Christ.

If this Gospel is to be preached to the whole world, "How shall they hear without a preacher?" What we need in the present day is inspired preachers, not men who expound a text as best they can with a commentary, delving into a little psychology, a little philosophy, and adding a little of their own opinions. Prophets are "born" like Jeremiah or "called" like Isaiah; they are not *made* by mere book-learning and elocution lessons. Because, then, true preachers of the Word are called by God, we must pray that the "Lord of the harvest will send forth more laborers into his harvest." But the New Testament shows that the ministry of the Word is not confined to the clergy. Every Christian has a Gospel to proclaim.

Today, however, the laity in many Churches regard themselves as "receivers" and not as "givers." They seek their own salvation, but are not concerned with the larger cause of Christ. The truth is, the modern Church generally speaking has lost its sense of mission because it has lost the experience of the Holy Spirit. "Ye shall receive power, when the Holy Spirit is come upon you," said our Lord. And notice the result, "Ye shall be my witnesses. . . . unto the uttermost part of the earth" (Acts 1:8).

Report of Group Discussion

Comment soon settled on the non-Christian reactions to a doctrine of final condemnation. A representative from Turkey explained that many Muslims take a fatalistic attitude. From Brazil came a report that universalism is making headway; from Thailand, a note that Buddhists readily accept the concept of annihilation.

Three key questions were formulated by Nicholls (India):

1. Is there any essential difference between the lostness of 600 million in China who have never heard of Christ and those who have heard?

2. What do we mean by "eternal," and how do we reconcile eternal punishment with the love of God (cp. Colossians 1)?

3. What do we mean by hell? Is it a place or state? And what do we mean by the resurrection of the body as against immortality?

Little (USA) and Burki (Switzerland) spoke to the final question from their background of student work, Burki distinguishing the *biblical doctrine* of hell to which he submits from the *psychological concept* which he finds intolerable. The latter can only be contemplated with tears and compassion. "We cannot ever be happy with this doctrine," Burki said.

A follow up meeting was held that afternoon.

Reporter: *A. Morgan Derham*

EVANGELISM AND
ESCHATOLOGICAL IMPERATIVES
Thomas F. Zimmerman

Evangelism — the Church's active response to the total program outlined in the Great Commission — constitutes the greatest task man has ever been allowed to share with God. The span of this evangelism is bounded by Pentecost and the Parousia of Christ. He will come again to consummate redemption and to bring judgment upon those who "obey not the gospel" (II Thess. 1:8). Therefore the return of Christ serves as the orienting factor that compels the Church to make human history the history of world-wide evangelization.

The fact that eternity is always crowding time makes the prospect of his coming a genuine one in every generation. Whatever differences evangelicals may express concerning the temporal relationship of Christ's return to the millennium, we can all agree that the sure fact of his coming takes precedence over all other pertinent considerations. With Christians of all time we eagerly anticipate his appearance (Luke 12:36-40; I Cor. 1:7; Phil. 3:20; I Thess. 1:9, 10; Titus 2:12, 13; James 5:7, 8; Rev. 16:15) and announce its import for the world just as did the apostolic Church (Acts 2:20; 3:19-21; 10:42; 17:30, 31; 24:15, 21).

It is the anticipation of the End found in the uniqueness of Christ's resurrection, and re-enforced by the ascension (which supplies the pattern for his Parousia — Acts 1:11), that causes the Christian to know with certainty the inevitability of Christ's Second Coming. Of immense concern is the meaning of this sure event for evangelism. *What factors arising out of eschatology make evangelism imperative today?* How should the truth of the imminent appearing of Christ direct contemporary evangelism?

The first inexorable imperative is this: *Our generation must be confronted with the fact that God's judgment stands over this wicked world to be meted out when Christ returns to take vengeance on the unevangelized and the Gospel-rejectors, both living and dead.*

Whatever our problems in understanding the plan for imposing Christ's judgment "when [He] shall be revealed from heaven with his mighty angels, in flaming fire dealing out retribution . . ." (cf. II Thess. 1:7, 8, Berkeley), the central fact remains that his judgment will be *universal* and *final* (Matt. 25:31-41; II Tim. 4:1; Rev. 20:11-15).

The early Church had no qualms about preaching the "fixed . . . day" (cf. Acts 17:31, Berkeley) of judgment as well as the Gospel of grace.

DR. ZIMMERMAN is general superintendent of the General Council of the Assemblies of God in Springfield, Missouri, USA.

Indeed, there is only one alternative to the Gospel — and men must be told! Christ's final judgment is as certain as his resurrection. His verdict will be absolute. At his word men will "depart . . . into the eternal fire which [has been] prepared for the devil and his angels" (Matt. 25:41, ASV) or into the kingdom prepared for the righteous.

There is nothing more repugnant to modern mentality than the preaching of judgment and genuine repentance. Some argue that since the Gospel means "good news" by definition, this should be the whole of the message we give to the world. A "doomsday" doctrine is decried as hindering man from accepting the idea that he is reconciled to God just as he is without his sensing the condemnation of God (Rom. 7:24) or without experiencing eschatological alarm.

Often side by side with this creeping universalism is the subtle denial of all eschatology under the subterfuge of "realized eschatology." Thus the end-time events of the New Testament, viz., the resurrection of Jesus Christ, his Parousia, and his judgment are denied objective realization in concrete human history. They are conceived as "realized" existentially and exclusively in one's own present experience. Such revisions of New Testament doctrine will never stand the scrutiny of Scripture and must be stoutly rejected in favor of the whole counsel of God.

A further caution needs to be given evangelists intent upon obeying the imperative implicit in the imminent judgment of the world. Two kinds of preaching of eschatological truth must be avoided: (1) rehearsing merely the fear aspect in judgment, unloading only the emotional cargo of the subject without giving instruction in repentance and faith in the Gospel; (2) reduction of eschatology to an "exact science," alleging a detailed knowledge of future events and personalities in such a way as to pander to the curious rather than to present them with Christ as Lord and Savior.

The awesome anticipation of the Church's standing before Christ's judgment seat serves as the basis for the second major imperative: *Because Christ commissioned the Church to evangelize the world, we must faithfully and concertedly carry out his Word, if we are to receive him with joy when he returns!* No reason for evangelism is more compelling than the earnest desire to please him.

A sure sign that one will be ashamed at his coming is a reticence now about confessing the Gospel before men. The penalty for being ashamed of the Lord Jesus and his words will be unbearable (Mark 8:38).

The parables of our Lord relative to his coming and to the Church's intervening activity admonish us to constant alertness for service in his kingdom (Luke 12:35-48; Matt. 24:45-51), to preparedness for a long wait if necessary (Matt. 25:1-13), and to individual responsibility in terms of resources committed to us (Matt. 25:14-30). Argumentation about eschatological issues ("Lord, and what about this man?" — John 21:21, 22; "Lord is it at this time you are restoring the kingdom to Israel?" — Acts 1:6) constitutes no substitute for evangelism.

The prevalence of apostasy before the End (II Thess. 2:3) must not deter the true Church from her propagation of the true Gospel. Let her increase her efforts correspondingly in order to counteract the contagion of counterfeit Christianity.

For the Church as well as for all men the Second Coming will be "the moment of truth" (cf. II Cor. 5:10, I Cor. 13:12). Some will receive praise from God (I Cor. 4:5), but others "saved" though they be, will suffer loss (I Cor. 3:11-15). Paul was jubilant about the Parousia because of his converts (I Thess. 2:19). To the extent that the Church evangelizes will she "love his appearing" (II Tim. 4:8)!

EVANGELISM AND
THE SECOND COMING
W. Ian Thomas

We are participating in a Congress on Evangelism, not Eschatology. I will be careful, therefore, to relate the Second Coming to the main issue of the morning, namely, to the Authority for Evangelism.

1. The Second Coming is the Great Confirmation of the Gospel.

Only biblical theology will survive the Second Coming of Jesus Christ; philosophical conjecture about his birth, life, death and resurrection will be silenced at his coming. Uninspired theological empires that propagate man's views about God will tumble on that day when God reveals by Jesus Christ at his appearing what are his views about man.

Authoritative evangelism derives its message from biblical theology, but biblical theology has its climax in "the day of Christ," referred to constantly in the New Testament in the context of his Second Coming (I Corinthians 1:7, 8; Philippians 1:6, 2:16). Biblical theology stands as much upon the "Future Historicity" of Christ's return, as upon the "Past Historicity" of his resurrection. ". . . now is Christ risen from the dead." ". . . as in Adam all die, even so in Christ shall all be made alive." "Christ the first fruits; afterward they that are Christ's at his coming. Then cometh the end . . ." (I Corinthians 15:20, 22-24).

Historicity is only past or future in terms of human experience; God declares the end from the beginning, and from ancient times the things that are not yet done, saying: "My counsel shall stand, and I will do all my pleasure: . . . I have purposed it, I will also do it" (Isaiah 46:10, 11).

Christ said: "Before Abraham was" — in the past tense of human history — "I am" — in the eternal present tense of deity (John 8:58). With God the only difference between the future and the past is that certain truths which are as eternal as God himself, have not yet become part of human history.

The Old Testament recorded in advance the history of Christ's first appearing; the Old and New Testaments record in advance the history of Christ's second appearing, which is as certain now as was his first coming then. Our preaching derives as much authority from what by revelation we know is yet to be, as from what by fulfillment has already been. Both are

MAJOR THOMAS is the founder and general director of the Capernwray Missionary Fellowship of Torchbearers in Lancashire, England.

as certain as the Truth is in Jesus, the eternal I AM, and to this Truth the Holy Spirit bears witness (Acts 5:32). This constitutes our authority.

The bodily resurrection and the Second Coming of Jesus Christ are indivisibly inter-related. The past and future historicity of these two events makes redemption through his death both authoritative and meaningful.

(a) The Resurrection Constitutes God's Declaration of Intent.

Note Paul's apostolic affirmation at Athens: "[God] . . . commandeth all men every where to repent: Because he hath appointed a day, in the which he will judge the world in righteousness by that man whom he hath or-dained; whereof he hath given assurance unto all men, in that he hath raised him from the dead" (Acts 17:30, 31). God's specific intention to judge the world by Jesus Christ is as certain as the fact that he is risen, alive and coming again.

If "Christ be not risen, then is our preaching vain, and your faith is also vain. Yea, and we are found false witnesses of God" (I Corinthians 15:14, 15). Our Gospel is destitute of substance; God's warnings to the wicked are a hollow threat, and the Cross is sentimental foolishness.

(b) The Second Coming Constitutes God's Declaration of Integrity.

In the last days scoffers shall come, ". . . walking after their own lusts, And saying, Where is the promise of his coming? . . . all things continue as they were from the creation" (2 Pet. 3:3, 4). This is the "willing ignorance", Peter explains, "of ungodly men" — ignorant of the timelessness of God, and of the fact that the Second Coming and authoritative evangelism are mutually inter-dependent. Almost paradoxically, the return of Jesus Christ is being delayed to allow evangelism to hasten his coming, for "The Lord is not slack concerning his promise as some men count slackness; but is long-suffering to us-ward, not willing that any should perish, but that all should come to repentance" (2 Pet. 3:9). Evangelism calls men to this repentance.

Note Peter's apostolic affirmation in Caesarea: "Him God raised up the third day, and showed him openly: . . . And he commanded us to preach unto the people, and to testify that it is he which was ordained of God to be the Judge of [the living] and dead" (Acts 10:40, 42). In his second epistle, Peter categorically identifies himself with Paul's apostolic teaching on the subject, declares that "the day of the Lord *will* come" and exhorts the be-liever to hasten its coming (2 Pet. 3:10, 12).

Jude urgently exhorts us to contend for the faith which God delivered to his people once for all (Jude 3), and adds terrible warnings against all unrighteousness, and especially against those who corrupt the unchanging Truth. In harmony with the other apostles, he cites the prophecy of Enoch to support the fact that the Second Coming will end this age of grace: "Behold, the Lord cometh with ten thousands of his saints, To execute judgment upon all, and to convince all that are ungodly among them of all their ungodly deeds which they have ungodly committed, and of all their hard speeches which ungodly sinners have spoken against him" (Jude 14, 15). The imminence of Christ's return makes the task of world-wide evangelism imperative.

2. The Second Coming is the Great Consolation of the Gospel.

At Christ's return, God will avenge those who are troubled and have suffered for his kingdom. "The Lord Jesus shall be revealed from heaven with his mighty angels, In flaming fire taking vengeance on them that know not God, and that obey not the Gospel of our Lord Jesus Christ" but at the same time, he will come ". . . to be glorified in his saints, and to be admired in all them that believe" (2 Thess. 1:7, 8, 10).

We may confidently rejoice in Christ's wonderful promise: "I go to prepare a place for you. And if I go and prepare a place for you, I will come again, and receive you unto myself; that where I am, there ye may be also" (John 14:2, 3). This is the glorious hope of the Church, without which evangelism would be meaningless. Paul wrote to the Thessalonians: ". . . as we were allowed of God to be put in trust with the gospel, even so we speak; not as pleasing men, but God . . . For what is our hope, or joy, or crown of rejoicing? Are not even ye in the presence of our Lord Jesus Christ at his coming?" (I Thess. 2:4, 19).

If Christ is dead, then the hope of the Church was buried with him! We are of all men most miserable! But on the contrary, we serve "the living and true God" and we ". . . wait for his Son from heaven, whom he raised from the dead, even Jesus, who delivered us from the wrath to come" (I Thess. 1:9, 10). This is the Great Consolation of the Gospel.

3. The Second Coming is the Great Consummation of the Gospel.

God's remedy for sin involves:
  (a) The Redemptive Act
  (b) The Regenerative Purpose
  (c) The Consummating Climax

The Redemptive Act was not an end in itself, but the means to an end. Forgiveness has a regenerative purpose — the restoration of the Life of God to the soul of man. Fallen from the image of God in which he was created, the forgiven sinner is to "put on the new nature" (the regenerate self) "created in God's image" (Eph. 4:24 ANT). A new creation in Christ (2 Cor. 5:17) and a "partaker of the divine nature" (2 Peter 1:4), he is to be "strengthened with might by [God's] Spirit in the inner man" (Eph. 3:16) and be progressively "conformed to the image of his Son" (Rom. 8:29).

Holiness of life — the restored image of God in the life of the redeemed —must always be the aim and end of authoritative evangelism. We will never know till Jesus comes, this aim equated with the end, nor fully apprehend that for which we have been apprehended, but this we *do* know: "When he shall appear, we shall be like him" (I John 3:2).

This is the Consummating Climax, and the final consummation of the

Gospel. Reconciled to God by the death of his Son, and saved by his life, (Rom. 5:10) "I reckon that the sufferings of this present time are not worthy to be compared with the glory which shall be revealed in us" (Rom. 8:18).

Restored to LIKENESS! Restored to GLORY! HIS likeness and HIS glory — for we shall be LIKE HIM! We shall be *like* him, and we shall SEE Him — *as he is*! Amen — even so, come, Lord Jesus (Rev. 22:20).

EVANGELISM AND
THE LORD'S IMMINENT RETURN
Raghuel P. Chavan

The Lord's return is strategically significant in evangelical teaching, for the return of Christ and evangelism are clearly part and parcel of the same pattern in Scripture. World evangelization and the return of Christ are closely related. Our Lord left a distinct program for his Church to carry out during his absence, and is coming again when the task is completed.

We look forward to the day when he shall come again "in a cloud with power and great glory" (Luke 21:27). Until that time comes, there is work to be done. The Gospel of grace must be preached to every person (Mark 16:15), and must be heralded as a witness and testimony to the nations (Matt. 28:19, 20).

We are not to stand idly by but are to be his witnesses in the world — at home and abroad, nearby and afar off. We must hurry in our task. The time is short. Christ is at the door, and his coming is at hand.

The Good News must be proclaimed to the ends of the earth and the commission be fulfilled; then Christ shall come. The blessed hope of his imminent, personal, visible return is the strongest possible incentive to evangelism. Through the ages the great Church theologians, pioneer missionaries and ardent evangelists, realizing the imminence of Christ's coming, have sacrificed their time, money and lives for this cause. Several of the great missionary movements founded at the end of the last century were motivated by the expectation of the Lord's return. Efforts were made to reach the last tribe in order to bring back the King.

We do not know when the Lord will come again and so do not know how much time remains to carry out his program. We do know that with each passing day the time grows shorter. We must utilize every opportunity to make Christ known. We should not indulge in sentimentality or in idle speculation regarding the time of the Lord's return but rather should be faithful in our task, expecting him at any moment.

All signs point to the imminence of Christ's second advent. There are crises, revolutions, coups, cold wars and hot wars, population explosions, theological unbelief and false doctrine. Yet few are ready for his coming. All outside of Christ are under God's judgment. They need a Savior. We must tell them of the mighty Savior, Jesus Christ, who is the only hope for a world in upheaval and turmoil.

Effective evangelism must begin in the Church. There must be renewal

THE REV. MR. CHAVAN is a pastor and moderator of the General Assembly of the Christian and Missionary Alliance of India in Akola, Maharashtra, India.

within before there can be witness without to a restless and depraved world. Spiritual awakening and a return to holy living will result in effective evangelism.

The Early Church expected the Lord to return at any moment. Its members were so concerned that others be ready for his coming that through prayer and power from above they heralded the message with boldness and turned the world upside down. But today, lukewarmness, worldliness, lack of love, prayerlessness, carelessness and false doctrine make many in the Church unconcerned and powerless. Too many have forgotten that the Lord is coming again. Nothing will awaken the Church as much as hearing this truth preached over and over again.

The moment a man grasps the truth that Jesus Christ is coming again to receive his followers unto himself, that moment the world loses its hold on him. Those who look eagerly for Christ's return are eager to complete the unfinished task of evangelism. It is not enough simply to know Jesus. It is not enough to study the Word of God, to search out the deep things of providence and prophecy. We must join heart and hand in winning others to the Lord so they too can know him and be ready for his appearing.

This truth became real to me a number of years ago. I was converted at the age of fourteen, but for some years this doctrine had little significance for me. But after the death of two dear members of my family, I began to read about the Lord's second coming and to hope for his soon return.

I have turned my back upon earthly things and have dedicated my life to preaching the message of our crucified, resurrected and coming King. At first, I did not particularly preach about the return of Christ, but very soon realized that this was the most timely message for calling men to repentance. Many tremble upon hearing the Word and are converted.

My church is now putting forth effort, time and money to hasten the Lord's coming. It has sent four evangelists to work in the villages. It also helps support our Indian foreign missionary. Two thirds of its annual income is given to our coming King for the extension of his kingdom.

We must do everything to seek and save the lost. Waiting and winning souls go together. We must work for "the night cometh when no man can work." The hope of his coming will keep us busy at our Father's business.

The Lord is coming again. It may be soon. This will be the crisis of all human history and its final consummation. Before he returns, let us obey his orders and take the message of salvation in Christ to all men everywhere.

The departing Lord left us pounds and talents and told us to occupy until he should come. This time he is coming to reckon, to judge, to reward and to rule. He will determine if we have sensed the urgency of our task and been faithful to our stewardship.

Although this is the darkest period of human history, there is hope and cheer in looking for the personal return of the Lord Jesus Christ. It is not enough that we should recognize and accept this doctrine. We must prepare for his coming by continuous evangelism.

MOTIVATED BY THE FORWARD LOOK

Ernst Schrupp

In the New Testament the second coming of Christ is mentioned not merely in passing but forms an essential part of the Gospel message. Belief in the Cross and resurrection of Jesus Christ includes also hope in his second coming. This hope calls us to decision and urges us to activity. And in anticipating Christ's future we experience his sustaining and transforming power.

1. Evangelistic activity is brought about by consideration of Christ's second coming.

    a. God is still patient and still wants souls to be saved — for this reason Jesus Christ has not yet returned (II Pet. 3:9-15; I Tim. 2:4). For this reason God still calls men to conversion "because he has fixed a day on which he will judge the world in righteousness" (Acts 17:30 ff.). This warning must resound in a world which, despite the transitoriness of all earthly power and glory, repeatedly clings to visible, tangible things. This message of Christ's second coming must rouse the Church itself, so that she recognizes her duty as a watchman in these days and neither finds false security by conforming to the world, nor stands aloof from the world in pharisaical arrogance. Neither a Church conformed to the world, nor a Church ignorant of the world can fulfill her mission in the world.

    b. The Church and her mission stand under the divine "must": "Before" the Lord returns the Gospel *must* be preached throughout the whole world as a testimony to all nations, and "then" the end will come (Matt. 24:14; cf. Rom. 11:25). The *evangelistic urgency* of the last days is determined not by the closing doors of our day, not by the technical possibilities of evangelizing the world in this generation, but by the fact that God is still offering the Gospel to the world inasmuch as Christ has not yet returned.

    c. During this time the world is to be filled with the message of Christ. This does not mean that the world therefore will become "Christian;" on the contrary, the spirit of *Anti-Christ* will rise up more and more. The power of the evil one will culminate and manifest itself finally in one of several distinct ways (I John 2:18; Rev. 13:2; II Thess. 2). But just these things will point the believer to the Lord's imminent return. We may also take *Israel's* regathering in her own land as a valid sign and as a tangible indication "that God has remained faithful to his people" (Karl Barth; see Rom. 11:2).

    d. To fill the world with this message requires more than evangelistic specialization or concentration; and more is involved than the strength of individual congregations and churches. In view of Christ's second coming

MR. SCHRUPP is director of the Mission House and Bible School in Wiedenest, Germany.

the mission of the Church must become the fulfillment of the *essential purpose of the whole Church* and of its members. In doing this the Church anticipates its coming Lord.

2. *In our forward look we experience the sustaining and transforming power of the coming Lord.*

a. For us the world is not suspended in nothingness but is centered in Christ who has reconciled the world to God (II Cor. 5:19) and will redeem it (Rom. 8, etc.). We have not been left alone and without hope in the world (Eph. 2:12). We experience the power of the Lord who *sustains* us during the present time, and will also do so *during the crises of the last days.* We await the future not as some blind and awful fate but as the completion of God's plan of salvation. The afflictions and torments of the last days do not seem meaningless to us and do not drive us to rebellion or despair. We perceive them rather as "birthpangs" of what shall be new (Matt. 24:8; cf. I Thess. 5:3), and may therefore stand erect because our redemption is drawing nigh (Luke 21:28). Each day and each hour will bring the last day and the last hour even closer. Knowing this fact, yet not knowing its precise day and hour, brings us each day, brings us today to decision and calls us to vigilance and service (Rom. 13:11 ff.).

b. It is quite valid in our thinking to move repeatedly from our today to the tomorrow of Christ and back again and thus experience *eschatological* strength. For "we know that when he appears we shall be like him, for we shall see him as he is. And everyone who thus hopes in him purifies himself as he is pure" (I John 3:2, 3, RSV; cf. I Pet. 1:3). By his resurrection Jesus Christ thrust open the prison house of our dead selves. We can now complete the turnabout from orientation to what is past to orientation to what lies in the future. For the future no longer seems empty, but we see it as Christ's future. No longer do we rest in the security of our inadequate experience and usual self-assurance. But we seek "a city which is to come," and let the Scriptures move us forward to further possibilities (cf. Heb. 13:14 ff.). Thus we too in our generation shall realize a contribution to the Church that embraces all generations. Through our own incapabilities we move right on to the capacity of the returning Christ.

c. This forward look has a transforming effect upon the local church and, beyond that, upon the Church universal. We overcome the internal conflicts of congregations which cause so much loss of strength and call in question our task in the world. No matter how different and perhaps difficult our backgrounds may be, in the light of Christ's second coming we can all accept one another even "as Christ has accepted us;" we can love one another and bear each other's burdens (Rom. 15:7; I John 3:14; Gal. 6:2). Thus personality problems, racial and national traits, creedal difficulties, and the problems between generations will find their solution. For they are only temporary; they are never the final state of affairs. So on the basis of

Christ's future we have the present possibility of knowing one another "not after the flesh" but of being "a new creation in Christ" (II Cor. 5:16ff.).

The forward look saves us from quick and prejudiced judgments. "Therefore do not pronounce judgment before the time, before the Lord comes" (I Cor. 4:5, RSV). Our many prejudgments are a heavy burden from the past and a great obstacle among people. Better to make no judgment at all than to prejudge something or someone. The congregation which in keeping with Scripture continually keeps in mind Christ's return will anticipate the fulfillment of God's promises for today and tomorrow.

We may hope in the hope of the returning Lord for ourselves, for others and for Christ's entire Church. The hope of the second coming is also our responsibility for the world as we testify concerning the future in Christ, and as the world already sees the coming Lord in us and in the Church.

Report of Group Discussion

Discussion centered on the meaning of Matthew 24:14 ("This gospel of the kingdom shall be preached in all the world for a *witness* unto all nations") and led to the question whether a witness will have been given to all nations when the Scriptures have been translated into the remaining languages of the world. Bishop Jack Dain (Australia) cautioned against this comforting conclusion: " 'Of that day and that hour knoweth no man.' In this matter as in all others God remains sovereign and will himself determine the end. Furthermore *witnessing* means something more than *translating*."

Chairman W. Ian Thomas (England) suggested two points in closing: 1) there is a sense in which the Lord in mercy delays his return, and 2) there is a sense in which we can hasten the Lord's return by our faithful preaching of the Gospel.

Reporter: *Stuart Barton Babbage*

THE CHURCH'S FIRST FIVE CENTURIES
Ezra Gebremedhin

The missionary expansion of the Church in the early centuries was a result of the Great Commission (Matt. 28:19, 20) and no less of the joyful constraint created in believers' hearts on and following Pentecost. This great event was such a transforming experience that believers did not need to refer to a prior command for their missionary activities. They were spontaneously moved to proclaim the Gospel.

If we grant that one of the marks of authoritative evangelism is charismatic endowment, it becomes evident that the initiation and growth of the early Church resulted from authoritative evangelism in the purest sense of the term. The birth and expansion of the Church in the early centuries were thoroughly charismatic enterprises — made evident in preaching (Acts 2), signs (numerous instances in the book of the Acts), the selection and commissioning of different persons for the task of evangelism (Acts 13:2), and the distribution of different spiritual gifts to believers (I Cor. 12:7-11).

In the words of Roland Allen in his book *Missionary Methods*, "In little more than ten years St. Paul established the Church in four provinces of the Empire, Galatia, Macedonia, Achaia, and Asia. Before A.D. 47, there were no churches in these provinces; in A.D. 57 St. Paul could speak as if his work there was done, and could plan extensive tours into the far west without anxiety lest the churches which he had founded might perish in his absence for want of his guidance and support."

Such speed and thoroughness in the establishment of churches cannot be explained apart from the operation of the Holy Spirit.

The propagation of the faith was to continue beyond the apostolic age not only through the labors of renowned missionaries but also through the unassuming but dedicated lives of the faithful. The commissioning of missionaries, the proclamation of the Gospel by professional missionaries and lay people, the demonstration of the presence of the Spirit through signs and wonders, as well as the inevitable accompaniment of the Christian life — persecution — continued to mark the missionary expansion of the Church in the post-apostolic period.

The missionary responsibility was interwoven into the most important offices of the early Church. Each bishop was expected to be a missionary and to encourage the evangelization of pagans in his own diocese. Some of the renowned missionaries of the post-apostolic period were Gregory Thaumaturgos of Pontus who became bishop in 240 A.D., and carried on successful missionary work in his diocese; Gregory the Illuminator, of Ar-

THE REV. MR. GEBREMEDHIN is executive secretary of the Ethiopian Evangelical Church (Lutheran) Mekane Yesus in Addis Ababa, Ethiopia.

menia, under whom a mass conversion took place; Ulfilas (b. 311) who eventually preached to the Goths; the enthusiastic Martin of Tours (b. 316); Ambrose of Milan (b. 337); Augustine of Hippo (b. 354); and Patrick, the apostle of Ireland (b. 389).

Almost all these people were converts to Christianity and propagated their newly found faith with a Spirit-filled zeal that was reminiscent of the apostolic age.

In regard to the post-apostolic period Professor Latourette describes the missionary role of the faithful as follows: "The chief agents in the expansion of Christianity appear not to have been those who made it a profession or a major part of their occupation, but men and women who carried on their livelihood in some purely secular manner and spoke of their faith to those whom they met in this natural fashion. Thus when Celsus denounces a religion which spreads through workers in wool and leather and fullers and uneducated persons who get hold of children privately and of ignorant women and teach them, Origen does not deny that this occurs . . . Involuntary travellers such as slaves and Christians deported for their faith were also agents."[1]

The same Spirit who had blessed the labors of St. Paul blessed the labors of the Christians in the post-apostolic period and confirmed their preachings with signs. In a world that was keenly conscious of the presence of demons, the power of exorcism became almost a distinguishing mark of Christians and a sign of the divine approval of their teachings.

Through the same divine paradox which had originally created an irresistible Church out of twelve frightened disciples, a Church battered by years of persecution survived the stranglehold of a powerful empire. No wonder that one of the faithful was led to say: "The more men multiply our sufferings the more does the number of faithful grow." With the granting of the so-called Edict of Milan in 313 A.D. during the reign of Constantine, the Church could look forward to missionary work under very favorable conditions.

The early Church's persistence under persecution could have resulted only from a charismatically endowed missionary movement. In this respect both the apostolic and the post-apostolic Church were closely related. They were results of an authoritative evangelism.

One of the marks of an authoritative Gospel ministry is Christo-centric preaching. A cursory review of sermons in the book of Acts reveals a remarkable conformity to this principle (Acts 2, 7, 13, etc.). In these sermons the story of Jesus is neatly incorporated into Jewish religious history, in the context of which the preachers identified Jesus as the Messiah.

Paul had a definite reason for giving his sermons in the context of Jewish religious history. This method was part of his apologetic device and as such was essential for the propagation of the faith among Jews, and among Gentiles who had been influenced by Jews.

The early Church's intense preoccupation with the nature and function of Christ (exemplified in the heated Christological controversies and the various theories of the atonement) shows that its thinking, was strongly Christo-centric. Whether this Christo-centricity was as evident in its preaching is questionable.

The great apologies for the Christian faith, though lacking the directness of Paul's sermons, were intended to prepare the way for a favorable study of the Christian faith by non-Christians. They were chivalric attempts to defend the cause of Christ. Thus in their basic intentions, they were Christo-centric.

An essential mark of authoritative evangelism is credence of Holy Scripture in its entirety. The Church's eagerness to define the canon of Scripture partly indicates that it wanted the Bible to determine the content of, and the basic methods for, its evangelistic enterprise.

Except for Marcion who found large parts of the Bible unpalatable and therefore embarked upon a drastic amputation of the Scriptures, no churchman of any note is reported to have handled the content of the Bible arbitrarily.

The most virile type of Christianity flowed along the channels of the biblical canon and was propounded by men who accepted the Bible in its entirety. Even the Arian controversy which shook the Church to its foundations was based not on outright rejection but on different interpretations of biblical texts.

Admittedly, exegetes of the early Church were sometimes guilty of reveling in fantastic allegorical interpretations of biblical texts (e.g. the School of Alexandria). Nevertheless these exegetes did not consider incredible the biblical texts with which they worked.

Among the heathen, the fact that the Church possessed its own set of sacred Scriptures gave Christianity recognition as a bona fide religion.

It was to the Church's great advantage to give credence to the entire Bible, for some of its greatest converts (e.g. Justin Martyr, Tatian, Theophilus of Antioch, Augustine) found their way to the Church by reading the Bible.

Authoritative evangelism takes for granted that there is only one salvation for mankind. The early Church's refusal to be identified with Judaism, to place Jesus beside the gods of the Pantheon or to sacrifice to the gods of Rome was proof that it recognized this basic principle.

Persistence in the face of opposition and a clear stand against secularism which the early Church clearly displayed are marks of authoritative evangelism. The steadfastness shown by thousands of Christians under persecution and their refusal to keep silent about their faith was cause for admiration even among the pagans. The institution of monasticism, as well as the courage of Christians in the face of death, clearly indicates the stand taken, by and large, by the early church against secularism.

Authoritative evangelism uses all possible methods for spreading the Gospel. Public address systems, private disputations, miracles, exorcism, the itinerant ministry, catechetical schools (at Alexandria, Antioch, Edessa, Rome), the writing of hymns and translating of the Scriptures, all of which were utilized in the first five centuries, show that the early Church realized fully the need for many methods to carry out its Gospel ministry.

Recognition of the historicity of the Gospel accounts is another basic mark of authoritative evangelism. Throughout the history of the Christian Church, attempts have been made to revise the Gospel accounts, to make them rational and thus conformable to current world views and philosophical outlooks.

The apologists, the leading theologians of the early Church, attempted to validate doctrinal points by showing their necessity, their rationality and their supernatural possibility. Few questioned the historicity or the historical possibility of the Gospel accounts.

For the early Church, both the tangible and the supernatural were very credible realities. Not credibility but faith was their link with the supernatural.

The early Church believed the Pauline statements that God was in Christ reconciling the world unto himself — that God had given this message of reconciliation to the Church and that the Church should plead with men to be reconciled to God. Because the Church placed its evangelistic enterprise solidly on these facts, it carried on its missionary work with the assurance that its mandate originated not in questionable human suppositions but in God's eternal decrees.

Not everything was happy and unblemished, however, in the missionary enterprise of the early Church. Moralizations far removed from the basic teachings of the Gospel, humanly engineered or enforced "conversions," lapses from the faith, secularism, doubt as to the authenticity and credibility of the Scriptures — all these were operative. Nevertheless, the unique advance of the Gospel within the first five centuries against enormous odds, in itself makes the history of the early Church a legitimate hunting ground for the basic principles of authoritative evangelism. These basic principles appear to be:

a. A charismatically endowed missionary program,

b. Christo-centric preaching,

c. Credence of Holy Scripture in its entirety,

d. Persistence in the face of opposition and a clear stand against secularism,

e. Recognition that there is only one salvation for mankind,

f. Use of all possible methods for the spread of the Gospel,

g. Recognition of the historicity of the Gospel accounts.

[1] Kenneth Scott Latourette. *The First Five Centuries* (A History of the Expansion of Christianity). New York: Harper & Brothers Publishers, p. 117.

THE REFORMATION AND EVANGELISM
A. Skevington Wood

In enquiring as to the validity of tradition according to evangelical principles, a reconsideration of the Reformers' attitude may prove helpful. The
pioneers of Protestantism never claimed that what they taught was an innovation but insisted that it was a return to apostolic doctrine and catholic
(i.e. universal) tradition. *Sola Scriptura* was their slogan but they saw this
as reflected in the purest tradition of the Church.

Now that Rome seems to have abandoned the two-source theory of
revelation (Scripture and tradition), is it possible for Protestants to consider
Scripture as governing tradition rather than tradition governing Scripture?
Can we recognize the precedents of the Church's attitudes and actions in
history when these have been plainly under the control of the Word? Unless
we can, this subsection has no significance with reference to evangelism.
Surely there is a continuing ministry of the Holy Spirit in applying the sanc-
tions of Scripture to the contemporary situation. It was against "the traditions of *men*" that our Lord warned his disciples (Mark 7:8; cf. 13). The
apostle Paul received the true Gospel tradition, which was "in accordance
with the Scriptures" (I Cor. 15:3, NEB).

The Reformation is being discussed today as never before since its
inception. By some it is regarded as a regrettable mistake, and even as a sin
against charity. Evangelicals, on the other hand, are being compelled by the
very pressures of the times to reexamine and reaffirm the basic tenets of
Protestantism. They see the Reformation not as a revolt, but as a revival.
Its significance was not primarily political or social or ecclesiastical. It was
essentially a theological reorientation. It led to a new understanding of the
Gospel which in its turn brought about a renewed concern for mission. The
Reformation, it may be said, represents the most decisive turning-point in
the history of evangelism since the Church began.

After noting the work of the Lollards, we recognize Martin Luther as
first and foremost an evangelist. This is how he thought of himself, rather
than as a national prophet or an ecclesiastical statesman. He was content
to be a plain preacher of the Gospel. He had a mission from God to evangelize the people. Luther fully realized that evangelism is a *charisma*. It was
God himself who did the work. "I have done nothing: the Word has done
and accomplished everything," he said. Evangelism is not a human enterprise, it is a divine operation.

This being so, the evangelist is prepared to leave the results to God.
He has discharged his commission once he has declared the unsearchable

DR. WOOD is a minister-at-large with the Movement for World Evangelization in York, England.

riches of Christ. He cannot himself manipulate the outcome. Luther said, "I can get no further than men's ears: their hearts I cannot reach. And, since I cannot pour faith into their hearts, I cannot, nor should I, force anyone to have faith. . . . We have the right to speak, but not the power to do." Luther's doctrine of the Church was determinative in his conception of evangelism. He believed that the obligation to lead others to Christ is laid on all Christians, since they belong to the New Testament priesthood. This is not to deny the distinctive gift of the evangelist, however (Eph. 4:11).

The evangelistic responsibility of the Church was equally realized by John Calvin. "The whole world is assigned to be reduced under the obedience of Christ," he wrote concerning the apostles' commission, "that by spreading the Gospel as widely as they could, they might everywhere erect his kingdom." Calvin regarded evangelists as ranking next to the apostles. He believed, however, that like apostles and prophets they were not intended to be permanent, but were instituted merely for the purpose of establishing churches. But he conceded that God does still raise up evangelists as at the time of the Reformation.

Calvin taught that the work of the evangelist is more generally taken over by the pastor of the congregation, whose vocation is to preach the Gospel as well as to administer the sacraments. The Gospel was described by Calvin as "the clear manifestation of the mystery of Christ." Its content was defined as declaring "nothing more than that sinners, without any merit of their own, are justified by the paternal indulgence of God." It is summed up in Christ. In him is the whole stuff of our salvation. The believer's response to the Gospel lies in repentance. The benefit he receives is the remission of sins. Repentance follows faith and is indeed produced by it. Faith, according to Calvin, is that obedience to the Gospel which God himself makes possible. The efficient cause of salvation is the mercy and love of the Father; the material cause is Christ, with the redemption he purchased on the Cross; the formal cause is faith and the final cause is the righteousness of God. Each of these four excludes the possibility of salvation by works. Like Luther, Calvin interpreted the priesthood of all believers as a call to each Christian to be a witness for Christ.

Calvin put his convictions into practice as he directed a general mission through much of Europe. He sent evangelists not only into France, but also to England, Scotland, the Netherlands, Denmark, Germany and Italy. A mission to the New World was also considered in connection with Coligny's plan to colonize Brazil. It is too uncritically assumed that the Reformation afforded little stimulus to missionary endeavor, but this is not altogether the case. Later the Moravians, direct heirs of the Reformation, pioneered the modern missionary awakening.

We can barely mention the third man of the Reformation, Ulrich Zwingli. Zurich was second only to Geneva as a center of evangelism. Zwingli's market-day sermons reached the masses of the people who were strangers to the Gospel. "Ulrich aimed essentially at producing in his hearers a change of heart," notes Jean Rilliet, who comments on Zwingli's extreme clarity in presenting the Gospel.

Epitomizing the penetrating effects of the Reformation, Professor Pauck repudiates the charge of subjectivism. He speaks rather about the response of the individual "to the objective act of God through Jesus Christ, the Gospel of forgiveness." This surely is the goal of evangelism.

MAJOR REVIVALS AND EVANGELISM

Ian S. Rennie

The purpose of this paper is to examine the major post-Reformation Protestant revivals in their relation to evangelism. Because of the exigencies of the situation, we will restrict our observations, however, to the famous revivals in the British Isles and North America. Since this discussion takes place under the general theme of "The Authority for Evangelism," we must first ask whether the Church's tradition and practice of evangelism, in the singularly fruitful days of revival, are in any sense authoritative for the work of Gospel proclamation in our own day, or any other.

The question of tradition is very much in the fore in theological and ecumenical circles today. Although no generally acceptable statement of the authority of tradition has been reached, we surely must be mindful of the fact that in practice every church develops its own tradition. Moreover, those Christian groups which believe they have most successfully excluded tradition are those which are most oblivious to it in their midst, and are soon stifled by its dead weight. Tradition also illustrates Scripture, buttressing and elucidating it, and giving encouragement that throughout history God is faithful to his promises.

If the post-Reformation revivals run from the early seventeenth century to the late nineteenth, then the content of the message displays a remarkable apostolic correlation and continuity. The Men of the Covenant in Scotland, and the Puritan giants of England, preached a message that would have been readily recognized by the Apostle Paul as his own. Jonathan Edwards, in so many ways the key point of contact between the revivals of the seventeenth and eighteenth centuries, continued the emphasis on a crucified Savior who was to be received by faith.

Bishop Ryle, that most worthy successor of the Evangelical Revival, has outlined the preaching of the eighteenth-century evangelists in his own pithy way: the sufficiency and supremacy of Holy Scripture; the total corruption of human nature; Christ's death upon the cross . . . the only satisfaction for man's sin; justification by faith; universal necessity of heart conversion and a new creation by the Holy Spirit; inseparable connection between true faith and personal holiness; God's eternal hatred against sin and God's love towards sinners. Calvinist though he was, Ryle asserts this outline to have been as true for Wesley as it was for Whitefield. And this could be said as well of Charles Simeon and Thomas Chalmers, and of Brownlow North and the evangelists of the revival of 1859.

Although Charles Finney preached the traditional evangelical scheme,

DR. RENNIE is minister of Fairview Presbyterian Church in Vancouver, British Columbia, Canada.

there was one area of thought, particularly in his early years, where he differed. He emphasized that sin did not consist in disposition but in action. With this radical restructuring of depravity, prevenient grace gave place to free will. And with free will came a decline in emphasis on the objectivity of the atonement. It is to this objectivity of the atonement that some of the more biblical of the neo-orthodox brethren have been calling us. Although we deplore the practical universalism into which their inadequate view of Scripture has allowed the actual accomplishments of Christ's death and resurrection to slide, nonetheless we must not allow ourselves to overlook or sidestep the important question they are raising. And we must ask evangelical scholarship to help us in our evangelistic preaching at this point.

When we turn to the question of evangelistic method, we find in history, as well as in Scripture, an attempt to give articulate witness in a variety of ways to Jesus Christ as Savior and Lord. The men of the seventeenth century were parochial evangelists, who did not allow their restricted sphere to dull their concern, but who pressed forward with new methods. In his classic work, *The Reformed Pastor*, Richard Baxter sketches the plan of catechetical evangelism, and gives indications of its unusual effectiveness. In the next century, there were those who found ample evangelistic opportunity within the church order of the National Churches, while others turned to field preaching and itinerant evangelism in order to reach those in growing centers of population, or those who they felt were being ministered to by hirelings, rather than shepherds.

Finney and the frontier evangelists again adopted new methods. Protracted meetings, the anxious bench and anxious meetings, and all-night prayer meetings were utilized as effective ways of reaching early nineteenth century America. The new departure with Finney was to exalt methods to the level of abiding principles. Just as God would bless the right message, he felt, so God would accompany the right methods with his power. Method guaranteed success. Although Finney undoubtedly hoped that evangelism would be raised to the level of continuous revival, in actual fact revival was reduced to continuous evangelism, with the accompanying sense of frustration that God had apparently not been faithful. If the history of revival emphasizes anything, it is that God is sovereignly free in giving times of refreshing, and that when they are given, it is not merely through the "Christian presence," but through the Word.

In closing, we come to the evangelists themselves, men who communicated in a singular way with their day and generation. They were men of God and also men of their day. They did not become sharers of the contemporary mind by vast programs of study which so absorbed their time, energies and interest that they were neither able nor inclined to engage in active Gospel proclamation, but because God made them so. God knew what the *Zeitgeist* would be, and prepared men for it. They did not present an acculturated Gospel, but shared the pathos and aspirations of their fellows at the deepest levels, believing that in Jesus Christ was God's answer. Perkins, the eminent university evangelist of Cambridge, who, with his converts and friends, is so often derided as a representative of sterile seventeenth century scholasticism, represents much rather merely the spirit and mind of his day. Although Wesley was a far cry from the Enlightenment in doctrine and morals, he wrestled with some of the very same problems. Finney almost perfectly embodied the spirit of the Age of Jackson and the Era of the Common Man, while Moody, with his down-to-earth optimism, gained the ear of burgeoning America.

Such men usually do not come from evangelical homes where the ethos, and quite rightly so, is opposed to the spirit of the age. Nor do they come through the normal channels of evangelical training. They are *sui generis*, raised up and anointed by God to speak to a given age or generation. We cannot produce them, but we can pray God that he will (Matt. 9:37, 38).

CONTEMPORARY EVANGELISTIC TECHNIQUES

J. Christy Wilson, Jr.

Our Lord told us to "go . . . into all the world and preach the Gospel to every creature." But the question is, "How?" To answer this we need to explore the development of contemporary techniques in evangelism.

Our authority for evangelism comes from God himself. When Christ was questioned as to his authority, he replied by asking where John the Baptist received his right to preach and baptize — "from Heaven or of men?" The sanction for both Christ and John came from God. Martin Luther also appealed to this Divine authority as have countless others throughout the Church's history.

Much biblical revelation dealing with evangelism is directly linked to God himself. Our Commission, for example, could be described as follows:

1. The presentation of *"the Christ of God"* (Luke 9:20),
2. According to the revealed *"will of God"* (I Cor. 1:1),
3. Through the life and lips of *"the men of God"* (cf. II Tim. 3:16, 17),
4. Who are motivated by *"the love of God"* (Romans 5:5),
5. To preach to the lost *"the gospel of God"* (I Thess. 2:8),
6. That they may repent and receive *"the salvation of God"* (Luke 3:6),
7. In order to be built up in *"the church of God"* (cf. Acts 20:28),
8. Through the power of *"the Spirit of God"* (cf. Isaiah 61:1),
9. For *"the glory of God* the Father" (cf. Philippians 2:11).

Let us examine the contemporary techniques these points portray more closely.

1. The Presentation of "The Christ of God."

"Whom say ye that I am?" asked Jesus. "The Christ of God," replied Peter (Luke 9:20).

Some time ago I started on an airplane trip. The door was closed, seat belts were fastened, and all seemed ready for take off. Through the window, I then noticed a man running toward the aircraft and thought perhaps he was a tardy passenger. He began knocking on the door of the plane, but the steward who saw it was time to take off decided not to open the door. The man knocked louder and louder. When the door was finally opened there stood none other than our pilot! We had left out our pilot.

Contemporary techniques in evangelism that are successful present Christ as the living, personal Savior who longs to enter the heart of any repentant sinner who opens the door by faith (Rev. 3:20).

DR. WILSON is pastor of the Community Christian Church of Kabul, Afghanistan.

2. *According to the revealed "will of God."*

"Called to be an apostle of Jesus Christ through the will of God" (I Cor. 1:1).

Today despite large closed areas, there are probably more missionaries for Christ around the world than ever before. Because world-wide evangelism is the revealed will of God, thousands who themselves have been saved by the Gospel have heeded his call to go to "the uttermost parts," and like their Lord are establishing churches through preaching, teaching, and healing.

Also used of God today are Christian laymen whose regular vocations scatter them throughout the world and who witness for Christ as self-supporting "tentmakers." For example, it is through Christian teachers, engineers, diplomats, technicians, and others that the Lord is opening a country like Afghanistan to the Gospel, where missionaries have not been allowed. And we thank God that this summer official permission was just granted by the Government to build the first Protestant church ever to be in that land.

3. *Through the life and lips of "the man of God."*

"All Scripture is given by inspiration of God . . . that the man of God may be [complete], thoroughly furnished unto all good works" (II Tim. 3:16, 17).

The Greek word for "complete" also means "up-to-date," "fresh." In other words, the man of God is to evangelize the world with "up-to-date," "fresh" techniques. God's methods are men, but these men must be quick to follow the Lord's leading as to the most effective ways of evangelizing.

In Afghanistan I have held services in tough construction camps. While the men have always been very cordial and have gone to great pains to provide a temporary chapel, only two or three would actually come to the services. Most of them were afraid of being ridiculed. So I determined to go to them instead. While eating with them in the dining hall, I stood up between courses and preached the Gospel. The response was the best I had ever had in a construction camp, and all the men were present without personal embarrassment.

Ezekiel knew this technique for he says, "I sat where they sat" (Ezekiel 3:15). And Wesley, when he was locked out of Anglican churches went where the common people were and preached in cemeteries, mines and market places. Billy Graham calls this "sinner contact." We need to take the Gospel beyond our formal places of worship. We need to witness by lip and life in our homes, on our streets, at prayer breakfasts in secular hotels, and in our places of work. Bible studies, even in non-Christian homes, are being blessed to the salvation of souls. Jesus referring to such outreach to humanity said, "As ye go, preach." (Matthew 10:7).

4. Who is motivated by "the love of God" (Romans 5:5).

A drug addict threatened David Wilkerson with a long switchblade and asked him how long he thought it would take to cut him into a thousand pieces. David said he didn't know how long it would take, but he did know that every one of those thousand pieces if it could talk would say, "I love you!" This love melted the heart of his would-be assailant and instead of attacking him, he surrendered the switchblade. The only way to reach hardened, rebellious teen-age addicts, says Wilkerson, is through the love imparted by God the Holy Spirit.

As Paul, the greatest of all evangelists, put it: "The love of Christ controls us, because we are convinced that one has died for all" (II Cor. 5:14, RSV).

5. To preach to the lost "the gospel of God."

"We preached to you the gospel of God" (I Thessalonians 2:9 RSV).

Contemporary techniques that succeed in bringing about conversions rely on faithful presentation of God's Word. Moody told of a personal worker who continued quoting the Bible to a man who maintained he didn't believe the Bible. Finally the message got through, however, and the man was wonderfully converted. He then asked the personal worker why he had persisted in quoting the Bible. The worker answered that since he knew the Word of God is the sword of the Spirit and a wonderful weapon, he refused to throw it away during battle because the enemy objected to it.

God is blessing efforts to communicate his Word, be it through Bible translations, Christian literature, or audio-visual techniques.

Another modern and richly blessed method is Scripture memorization, a special emphasis of the Navigators. Learning verses by heart has often made the difference between converts becoming backsliders or going on with the Lord.

6. That they may repent and receive "the salvation of God" (Luke 3:6).

The reason groups like Youth for Christ have led so many people to the Lord is that they have clearly presented the finished work of redemption on the Cross, have preached salvation as a free gift and have called for decisions to accept Christ as Savior, "Ye shall know them by their fruits," said Christ (Matthew 7:16).

7. In order to be built up in "the church of God."

"Feed the church of God which he hath purchased with his own blood" (Acts 20:28).

Dr. Nevius and Dr. Soltau have shown how the Great Commission includes also the establishing of self-supporting, self-governing and self-propagating churches. Evangelistic efforts are more greatly blessed when churches cooperate. This was the late Kenneth Strachan's passion for Latin

America that resulted in development and implementation of the "Evangelism in Depth" technique, which starts with small prayer groups and works up to nation-wide rallies and campaigns, through the cooperation of as many churches as possible.

8. Through the power of "the Spirit of God."

"The Spirit of the Lord God is upon me; because the Lord hath anointed me to preach" (Isaiah 61:1).

In his paper on "The Authority for Evangelism," Dr. Johannes Schneider says, "Evangelism is charisma, a gift of grace bestowed by the Holy Spirit." Many feel that the charismatic renewal we are seeing today is a fulfillment of Joel's prophecy which Peter quotes in Acts 2:17, 18: "And it shall come to pass in the last days, saith God, I will pour out of my Spirit upon all flesh: and your sons and your daughters shall prophesy, and your young men shall see visions, and your old men shall dream dreams . . ." In both Joel and Acts, this passage moves on to an evangelistic consummation, "And it shall come to pass, that whosoever shall call on the name of the Lord shall be saved" (Joel 2:32, Acts 2:21). Is this charismatic renewal perhaps the beginning of the worldwide revival for which we have longed and prayed? In spite of acknowledged misuses and excesses, physical healings and exorcisms in the name of our Lord Jesus Christ are taking place today; and many testify that these have been the "signs following" which have confirmed the Word (Mark 16:20) and have brought them to saving faith.

9. For "the glory of God the Father."

"Every tongue should confess that Jesus Christ is Lord, to the glory of God the Father" (Philippians 2:11).

What a joy it is to turn on the radio in Afghanistan and to hear the Gospel in the language of the people! Truly today "the heavens declare the glory of God" (Psalms 19:1) in a new way as evangelistic broadcasts and telecasts penetrate many parts of the world. The supreme purpose of evangelism and of all its legitimate techniques is to manifest God's glory on earth and in the lives of the redeemed both now and through eternity "that God may be all in all" (I Corinthians 15:28). To this end may the Holy Spirit increase the efforts being made to bring individuals to a saving knowledge of Christ. May he continue to lead and bless in the evangelistic techniques he desires us to use for the glory of the Father. And may he enable us to carry out our Lord's commission to "preach the Gospel to every creature" in this our generation!

Report of Group Discussion

Questions turned upon the personal experience and opinions of the delegates. There was general agreement that the divine initiative of God in evangelism must be emphasized, a number of delegates (Dr. A. Skevington Wood, Dr. Ian Rennie and a delegate from Spain) taking this position. At the same time, however, two speakers (one from South Africa and one from the United States) wished to call attention to the divine conditions without which God's power will be lacking in human efforts. II Chronicles 7:14 was listed as containing such conditions.

Early in the discussion period a delegate from India expressed his view that God is blessing in his area. "There are many who say that the Lord is appearing to them in visions, especially after attending evangelistic meetings or after extended prayer meetings. Wherever meetings are held, people respond and real conversions and real transformations result. Many who are coming are Hindus, and usually these are baptized by national pastors within four or five days of their conversions. In many places recently converted Hindus make up half the congregations."

Reporter: *Dwight L. Baker*

SECTION II

PAGE

THE BASIC THEOLOGY OF EVANGELISM •
Harold John Ockenga   95

The Fallenness of Man

AFFIRMATION AND PRACTICE • *Harold O. J. Brown*   104

THE FALL OF MAN • *Stuart Barton Babbage*   108

CONTEMPORARY SYMPTOMS
OF MAN'S FALL • *Samuel J. Mikolaski*   111

MODERN MAN AND HIS NEEDS • *Hans Rohrbach*   114

REPORT OF GROUP DISCUSSION • *Leon Morris*   119

Sin and the Moral Law

SIN IN BIBLICAL PERSPECTIVE • *Saphir P. Athyal*   120

EVANGELISM AND THE
REALITY OF SIN • *Samuel A. Benétreau*   122

THE NEED FOR BIBLICAL MORALITY • *A. Morgan Derham*   125

THE NEW MORALITY • *Leslie Hunt*   128

The Ground of Forgiveness

BASIC PREACHING
OF THE ATONEMENT • *John C. Winston, Jr.*   131

CHRIST THE MEDIATOR • *Theodore Williams*   134

REPORT OF GROUP DISCUSSION • *Jack Stowell*   136

The Nature of Faith

FAITH AND THE GOSPEL • *George R. Beasley-Murray*   137

A TRINITARIAN FAITH • *Jarl Wahlström*   140

A NEW LIFE PRINCIPLE • *Addison H. Leitch*   143

REPORT OF GROUP DISCUSSION • *Ted W. Engstrom*   146

Justification and Sanctification

ASPECTS OF CHRIST'S
REDEEMING WORK • *Jean-Paul Benoit*   147

PAGE

SANCTIFICATION, THE FRUIT
OF JUSTIFICATION • *W. Stanford Reid* 150

CHRIST IN US • *Paul S. Rees* 153

REPORT OF GROUP DISCUSSION • *Ian Rennie* 156

The Regenerating Work of the Spirit

THE THEOLOGY OF REGENERATION • *J. Wayte Fulton, Jr.* 157

THE HOLY SPIRIT'S
REGENERATING WORK • *Maurice A. P. Wood* 160

REGENERATION AND THE
BELIEVER • *Theodore J. Stanley* 164

THE RESULTS OF REGENERATION • *Corrie ten Boom* 167

REPORT OF GROUP DISCUSSION • *Donald E. Hoke* 169

THE BASIC THEOLOGY OF EVANGELISM
Harold John Ockenga

"All power is given unto me in heaven and in earth. Go ye therefore, and teach all nations, baptizing them in the name of the Father, and of the Son, and of the Holy Ghost: teaching them to observe all things whatsoever I have commanded you; and lo, I am with you alway, even unto the end of the world" — *Matthew 28:18-20*

Evangelism must be Trinitarian if it is to be biblical. The Great Commission defines the program of the Church for this age by the authority of the Triune God. The Great Commission is one of the earliest statements of Trinitarian creedalism; along with the apostolic benediction of Second Corinthians 13:14, it is the basis of the so-called Apostles' Creed, which is so clearly Trinitarian.

The Bible is our authority. A Bible which is the infallible rule of faith and practice is the reason for the existence of Protestantism. The Reformation rediscovered three major truths that established Protestantism as a return to New Testament Christianity. The first truth, called the formal cause of the Reformation, is that the Bible is the final and infallible authority in matters of faith and practice. This is the principle of *sola scriptura*. The second truth is justification by faith, called the material cause of the Reformation. This is the principle of *sola fide*. The third truth is the priesthood of the believer. It is a corollary of the other two. The doctrine of the priesthood of the believer proclaims the freedom of the Christian man, expressing his deliverance from priestly mediation, sacerdotalism, and ecclesiastical control.

The principle of *sola scriptura* has been rejected by liberal Protestantism. For the liberal, the Bible is not authoritative, not dependable, and not authentic. This dismissal of the Bible has resulted from the acceptance of evolutionary naturalism and higher criticism. Evolutionary naturalism applied to religion, necessitated a view that the Hebrew people evolved religiously from polytheism to henotheism to monotheism, to ethical monotheism. In accordance with this presupposition, the Bible is viewed as the record of the evolving of religious experiences of the Hebrew people and the books of the Bible are re-dated on this premise. Higher criticism joins hands with evolutionary naturalism to bring about this result. Thus Karl Barth, speaking at the University of Chicago, could say, "The Bible is full of errors," and Emil Brunner could make the Bible a shambles in his *Revelation and Reason*. The removal of the Bible from the central place of authority in Protestantism has debilitated its power to evangelize. A liberal Protestantism cannot meet the com-

DR. OCKENGA is minister of Park Street Church, Boston, Massachusetts.

petition of the Roman Church. In order to build a power structure comparable to the Roman Church, it has embraced the activities of the ecumenical movement. This movement not only intends to unite the various Protestant churches, but also to circumvent the Reformation in order to find a basis of theology and tradition for reunion with Rome. The 1963 Montreal Conference on Faith and Order of the World Council of Churches spent much time seeking to discover and express the tradition which will bring together the various traditions of the individual branches of Christianity and will supply a basis for dialogue in the areas of reform and reunion.

The necessity for a return to biblical authority is the reason for our gathering. We are under the Word. Let us therefore give proper place to the Word of God in all of our deliberations. Otherwise, only two alternatives exist: the first is to go on to left-wing rationalism in which the human mind is the supreme authority in religious matters; the second is to return to Rome, where the church is the final authority in Christian doctrine and ethics.

Biblical evangelism is Trinitarian. The Bible honors each member of the Trinity in the theology of evangelism. The New Testament makes it clear that the Father elects, which is predestination; that the Son redeems, which is atonement; and that the Holy Spirit regenerates, which is salvation. Heresies arise from the neglect of one aspect of this Trinitarian theology or from an overemphasis upon one particular facet. Historic Christianity has maintained the elements of Trinitarian redemption in balance as it has occupied the central stream of orthodoxy.

A biblical foundation supports all great movements of evangelism. The Reformation, in a literal sense, was a revival. The leaders of the Reformation embraced the truths of the New Testament and sought to reform the existing church in accordance with these truths. They discovered that the church was unreformable and they themselves were excluded by excommunication from its membership and benefits. Therefore, Martin Luther, John Calvin, Ulrich Zwingli and their colaborers returned to New Testament Christianity though it meant separation from the Roman Catholic Church of the day. Upon his deathbed in Eisleben, Luther was asked, "Reverend father, do you die in the faith which you have preached and which you have proclaimed?" He replied, "Yes." The Reformation freed men from the intellectual bondage of scholasticism, from the economic thralldom of feudalism, and from the spiritual slavery to the priesthood. The movement swept the masses into a new sense of freedom. For a time the revival promised to engulf all of Europe.

The Evangelical Revival under the Wesleys and George Whitefield occurred two centuries later in the recovery of wide areas of Christian experience that had been obscured. From the Puritans, they inherited the emphasis on the indwelling of the Holy Spirit. From the Lutherans, they received the truth of justification by faith. They rediscovered the truth of the witness of the Holy Spirit and of personal assurance. They preached on the witness of the Spirit more than on any other subject. George Whitefield's favorite text was, "The Spirit of the Lord is upon me," (Luke 4:18). From this emphasis a revival influence spread throughout England to counteract deadness in the Anglican Church and the moral corruption of the masses. The result is known as the Evangelical Revival.

The Finney revival of the mid-nineteenth century came from the emphasis upon the Law and the Gospel. Charles G. Finney's preaching of the law produced conviction, and his offering of the Gospel brought comfort to the hearts of convicted men. Finney's emphasis was in accord with such great confessions as the Westminster Confession of Faith and the Heidelberg catechism wherein the law is given its proper place in Christian life.

Today, the Billy Graham evangelistic meetings emphasize the Bible as the sword of the Spirit. Dr. Graham's oft-repeated clause, "the Bible says," is characteristic of this evangelistic emphasis. Hence, in these various movements we see that evangelism was based upon biblical theology. If we examine this theology we will find that it is Trinitarian, for each person of the Trinity bears an important role in evangelism.

1. God the Father in Evangelism

In speaking of the role attributed to God the Father in evangelism, we emphasize the decrees of God, the election of God, and predestination by God. The divine decrees constitute the plan of salvation. This redemption expresses the divine attributes of love, justice, and wisdom. The Bible makes it plain that redemption originated in divine love, that "God so loved the world that he gave his only begotten Son," (John 3:16), that "God sent his Son to be the propitiation for our sins," (1 John 4:10), and that "that God was in Christ reconciling the world unto himself" (II Cor. 5:19). Grace then is God's love in motion toward our sins. However God is just, and justice must be satisfied. The Governor of the universe must do right and God could not forgive sin without satisfaction. The eternal Father in infinite wisdom devised the means of salvation which is called the plan of redemption. This plan is expressed in the eternal covenant of redemption. In this covenant the Father agreed to give to the Son a people; the Son covenanted to represent this people by substitution in a life of obedience and in a death of suffering; the Spirit covenanted to apply this efficaciously to men so that there would be a redeemed people belonging to the Son. This we know from the biblical texts that declare there is a "kingdom prepared for you from the foundation of the world" (Matthew 25:34), that there is a "lamb without blemish and without spot: who verily was foreordained before the foundation of the world" (I Peter 1:19, 20), and that there is a people "chosen . . . in him before the foundation of the world" (Ephesians 1:4). For this reason, Isaiah could say that Jesus Christ "shall see of the travail of his soul and shall be satisfied" (Isaiah 53:11). Christ endured his sufferings with joy because of the people that were given to him. Jesus Christ on the cross got a glimpse of the countless multitudes who were redeemed by his suffering and he was satisfied.

The decrees of God thus established the end from the beginning and the steps along the way. These embrace the fall of man, the atonement made for sinful man through the incarnation and crucifixion of Jesus Christ (all prophesied in detail), the offer of salvation through universal preaching, and the salvation of those who believe or respond affirmatively to this preaching.

God's part in redemption is called election. Here there are competing theories. The five points of Calvinism speak of the sovereignty of God, the depravity of man, a limited atonement, irresistible grace, and the perseverance of the believer. Not all Christians share this formulation, but in accordance with it those who do, hold that God elected some and passed by others. Calvinism declares that the Gospel must be preached in all the world and that those who are elected will accept the Gospel, believe on Jesus Christ, and will persevere in good works unto the end. It also teaches that no one can know who is elect except by the fact that he continues in good works and perseveres unto the end.

An illustration of this is found in the Huguenot piety and perseverance in the face of the terrible suffering which these people underwent for a century and a half. The Huguenot movement began under the preaching of Stapulensis in 1524 and was most successful. Calvin had to flee from France and settled in Geneva from whence he directed the Reformation in France. For a time it seemed as if all France would be won to the Reformation, but then reaction set in under the leadership of the Guise family and the Spanish inquisition. The Huguenots were persecuted economically, socially, and physically. Numerous massacres occurred, not the least of which was that of St. Bartholomew's Day. Six wars of religion occurred which ended in the defeat of the Huguenots and in their emigration to the Netherlands, to Germany, to England, and to America. These Calvinists were inspired by this stern faith to maintain their spirit through the most terrible suffering.

The second view is that named after Arminius, who taught in the University of Leyden from 1604 until his death. Arminius returned to the pre-Augustinian view of conditional election. By his eternal and immutable decree, God ordained in Jesus Christ to save those who by the grace of the Holy Spirit believe in Jesus Christ and persevere in that faith and obedience. Christ died for all and each so that he gained reconciliation and remission of sins on the condition that believers remain faithful. Those grafted into Christ by faith have the means to fight Satan, to win the victory, and to persevere by the Holy Spirit. God foreknew this faith and elected believers unto salvation.

The view which one adopts is of great importance to his evangelistic fervor. The matter of election is no mere question of semantics. The resolution of the matter rests in giving proper place to each biblical emphasis. We must not neglect either emphasis. For my part, I approve a practical synergism of affirming prevenient grace, the responsibility of each individual, and of election in Christ of all who believe. Thus I say that salvation is all of God, reprobation in all of man. I cannot throw the responsibility of man's reprobation upon God.

This raises the question of predestination by God and the invitation to accept Christ. The Bible makes it plain that the Holy Spirit attends the preaching of the Word and enables a sinner to accept Jesus Christ as Savior. The offer of salvation is real, and God does not mock us. It is the Spirit's work to attend that offer with life-giving power. Yet we witness two attitudes toward the giving of an invitation.

Some ministers, much used of God, have never given an invitation to accept Jesus Christ and will not permit such an invitation to be given from their pulpits. I refer to men like the late Dr. A. W. Tozer, the late Dr. Donald Gray Barnhouse, and Dr. Martyn Lloyd-Jones. On the other hand, invitations extended in the ministry of Billy Graham and others have found thousands responding affirmatively to the opportunity to accept Christ. In both instances there have been valid and permanent conversions: I have personally known many of them. We must conclude that we cannot be exclusive in our methodology, nor can we sit in judgment upon those who use a different methodology in evangelism from our own. God is sovereign. God honors his Word when it is preached. He attends it by the ministry of the Holy Spirit, although it may be done in different ways.

2. God the Son in Evangelism

Evangelism must center in the offer of the person of Christ. It pleased God by the foolishness of the kerygma, or the message preached, to save those who believe (I Cor. 1:21). The kerygma centers in the incarnation, the crucifixion, the resurrection, and the ascension of Jesus Christ. In the early centuries of the Church, doctrinal controversy centered upon the person of Christ — whether he possessed one will or two wills, whether he had one nature or two natures, whether he was a man upon whom the Christ descended at his baptism and from whom he ascended before his death, whether he was eternal or a demiurge or first creation above all creation. Finally at the Council of Chalcedon, the orthodox view of the person of Christ stated that he possesses a full Divine nature and a full human nature, in one person, and so will continue to be forever. He is very God of very God, and very man of very man. There is one mediator between God and man, the man Christ Jesus, who gave his life "a ransom for all, to be testified in due time" (I Timothy 2:6).

This is the orthodox view — the view of the Scripture, of the creeds and of the confessions of Christendom. Christ was pre-existent, co-eternal and co-equal with the Father, became incarnate, lived a perfect life, worked miracles, atoned for sin by his death on the Cross, arose from the dead, ascended into heaven, exercises the priestly ministry of intercession, and will come again to reign over his eternal kingdom.

The high view of Christ has always been accepted by evangelical Protestantism and is a prerequisite of evangelism. If we are to have a doctrine of salvation, the full deity of our Lord Jesus Christ and the real humanity of Jesus must be preached. The low view of Christ taken by liberalism cuts the nerve of evangelism and missions. The Revised Standard Version of the Bible unquestionably is a better translation than the King James Version and is more faithful to the manuscripts. My personal objection to it, however, is that wherever the manuscript evidence permitted the translators to present either a high or low view of Christ, as in Isaiah 7:14, or in Micah 5:2, the translators chose the lower view. This does not impinge upon their ability as translators, but it does reflect their presuppositions in the translation. Liberalism has always taken the low view of the person of Christ. As the Word of the crucifixion, resurrection and coming again is preached, we are confronted with the necessity of a decision which results in salvation or reprobation. It is only by preaching the Christ of the Bible that converts may be won spiritually.

Evangelism centers in the offer of the propitiation of Calvary. The Bible statements of this fact are many (Romans 3:25; II Cor. 5:21; I Peter 2:24; 3:17). Three words are used in these statements. One is *peri* (translated *for*), meaning concerning; another is *anti* (translated *instead of*), meaning in the place of; and another is *huper* (translated *in behalf of*), meaning for the sake of. The Bible teaches that Christ died for us, in the place of us, and in behalf of us. Various theories concerning the atonement have been taught, such as the governmental view, the exemplary view, the piacular view, the view of vicarious repentance, and so on.

Dr. Joseph Sizoo illustrated these theories by the use of four houses. First, there is the courthouse, which represents the governmental view; second, there is the playhouse, which represents the exemplary view, or the view of moral influence; third, there is the counting house, which represents the vicarious view; and fourth, there is the home, which represents God's loving sacrifice. All these emphases are to be found in the Scripture, but they are found as manifestations of the basic teaching that Jesus Christ satisfied the demands of Divine righteousness, substituted for us in his act of passive obedience to justice, and thus demonstrated in his life and death a Divine justice and love. From this derived the governmental, the moral, and the exemplary views of the atonement. It is this gospel of redemption which is able to affect the will; nothing will move men to repentance and faith as does the preaching of the propitiation of Calvary.

Evangelism must emphasize the particularism of the Christian faith. In the teaching of the liberal wing of contemporary theology, we have a universalism which declares that all men are redeemed by Christ and reconciled to God so that all which remains is to publicize this to them. In an article on universalism, Harold Lindsell says: "Now the idea of some non-Christians being 'in Christ' has yielded to the conclusion that all men everywhere are 'in Christ,' even though they may not be conscious of him; men need only to be made aware of this truth." In support of his affirmation he quotes from W. Norman Pittenger, Bishop James Pike, Dr. Nels Ferré, Dr. T. D. Niles, and Dr. W. O. Johnson, to show that they are universalists in the above sense.

Such universalism is hardly compatible with biblical teaching. The Bible declares that the Gospel must be preached universally, that the death of Christ is sufficient and applicable for all, but is efficacious only to those who believe. The Bible emphasizes the responsibility of acceptance of Christ. The plain alternative to this is the state of being lost and of suffering eternal torment. The Bible doctrine of torment and hell has thrust some into the belief in ultimate restorationism after a period of punishment, and others into the belief in universalism of atonement and of the application of the atonement. We must remember that the greatest emphasis upon hell and suffering as the alternative to salvation was made by the Lord Jesus Christ. If we give the proper emphasis to the responsibility of man, we have no problem with the doctrine of hell.

3. God the Holy Spirit in Evangelism

Evangelism is dependent upon the ministry of the Holy Spirit. Contemporary theology discloses a new interest in an emphasis upon the Holy Spirit's ministry. This does not so much apply to the Spirit's ministry in common grace, but rather to the ministry of the Holy Spirit in special grace. The Holy Spirit restrains the destructive processes of sin and thus enables humanity to maintain an orderly life. The Holy Spirit also is the source of the renewing processes in the churches and in society. The emphasis upon spiritual renewal in the Roman Catholic church and the various branches of Protestantism is directly attributable to the work of the Holy Spirit. The Spirit has had a part in every stage of redemption, in creation, in revelation, in inspiration, in the incarnation, in the atonement, in the resurrection, in the formation of the Church, in the missionary undertaking, in the prayer life of the believer, in the transformation of the believer into the image of Christ, and so on. His work is a prerequisite to effective evangelism.

Evangelism may be equated with the public proclamation of the Good News of the Gospel, or the private witnessing to the Good News of the Gospel, with the purpose of bringing individuals to faith in and confession of Christ as Savior. This is called conversion, and conversion has two meanings. It may be the active turning on the part of an individual as a response to the Gospel. This is the lesser sense of conversion and is within the ability of the individual. The New Testament uses the word "epistrepho" in the active tense. Theologically, conversion is often used in the larger sense of being equated with regeneration. This is the work of the Holy Spirit. It is the Holy Spirit who convicts, converts, and transforms the life of the individual. There is no possibility of an evangelistic outreach without the ministry of the Holy Spirit. The twentieth century has seen the growth of the so-called "third force," which is the Christian movement emphasizing the person and work of the Holy Spirit.

Regeneration, or the new birth by water and the Spirit (John 3:5) is the requirement for any spiritual and evangelistic movement. Jesus said, "Except a man be born again he cannot see the kingdom of God" (John 3:3). Too much religion omits the necessity of the new birth. Some theology minimized the place of evangelism in regeneration. Some Lutherans and Anglicans teach baptismal regeneration. Some reformed theologians teach that regeneration by the Holy Spirit precedes conversion. The evangelical position is that regeneration is conditioned upon repentance, confession and faith. This alone stimulates evangelism.

The new emphasis upon the Holy Spirit is centered in the modern charismatic movement as it is seen in all of the established denominations, especially the Episcopal, Presbyterian, and the Congregational. We must examine the validity of this movement. Some preclude the possibility of such validity by adopting the position that God withdrew these gifts after the apostolic days so that they have not been the possession and the experience of the Church since. Historically, it is evident that the gifts were withdrawn and ceased to be manifested and practiced for a thousand years. But there is no biblical evidence requiring us to believe that God has withdrawn these gifts. If the curtain came down on the supernatural manifestations of the Holy Spirit with the close of the apostolic era, there is nothing in the Scripture to indicate this. It is a conclusion drawn from history. On that same basis, we would have to retract the theory if gifts of the Spirit were historically manifested in these latter days.

It is irrefutable that the spiritual gifts were a part of the New Testament Christian experience (I Cor. 12:4-31; 14:1-40; Eph. 4:7-16; Rom. 12:3-8). The manifestation of these gifts was experienced by those who were baptized with and filled with the Holy Spirit in the New Testament age. The claim is made today that these gifts are reappearing in the charismatic movement. Small groups of people are meeting for fellowship, worship, and the expression of these gifts in many areas of the world. Intelligent and responsible individuals have testified to receiving the gifts. Great evangelistic zeal and devotion have been manifested by those who claim to possess these gifts. This has created what is called "the third force."

I believe that we cannot limit God by some pre-conceived theory that declares that he cannot manifest the gifts of the Spirit in this age. I, personally, have not seen the manifestations of these gifts, especially the gift of healing and gift of speaking in tongues. Should this movement prove valid and a modern manifestation of the supernatural, it could be an answer to the rationalists in the church who accept no argument for the biblical faith and who even go so far as to proclaim "God is dead" in the name of Christianity. God may be giving a supernatural demonstration that will confound unbelief.

A visitation of the Holy Spirit is the greatest need of the Church and of Christians today. Revival in the Church is contingent upon the visitation of the Spirit. We are encouraged to believe that the new emphasis upon the Holy Spirit's person and ministry may very well be the prelude to revival. My understanding of the Bible is that revival can occur at any time up until the second advent of our Lord Jesus Christ (Acts 3:19-21). If we are to have this revival we must not wait on the divine sovereignty, placing responsibility for the absence of spiritual visitation and quickening upon God. God uses means to bring about his purposes, and our dedication is not the least of these.

Is there any formula for us to fulfill in order to bring revival to reality? An analysis of New Testament experience and of historical revivals would suggest these prerequisites. First, united confession. It is essential that evangelicals confess their fragmentization, their divisions, their suspicions, their impotencies, their faithlessness, and their quarreling. Nothing will break down barriers faster than this. Second, we must have united prayer. The promises of Scripture are based upon such spiritual unity in prayer (Matthew 18:18-20; Isaiah 45:11). Third, there must be united believing (Mark 11:24; Matthew 21:21, 22). Fourth, there must be united witnessing (Acts 2:1, 11). All these conditions were fulfilled in the pre-Pentecostal prayer meetings of the apostles and disciples. In the proportion in which we fulfill them today, we may experience revival visitation.

As the early and latter rains were promised in Ancient Israel (Hosea 6:3), and as God promised to pour out his spirit upon all flesh (Joel 2:28), we believe that we may experience times of refreshing in this age. Let us have faith in the promise of God, for with God nothing is impossible. Let us act upon this promise, depending upon the Holy Spirit to attend the Good News with quickening power.

AFFIRMATION AND PRACTICE
Harold O. J. Brown

The presentation by Dr. Ockenga contains a minor proposition, a major proposition, and several suggestions for constructive action. The minor proposition is that the Bible is our sufficient and fundamental authority. When the authority, sufficiency, and clarity of Scripture are not acknowledged, the result is spiritual blindness or apostasy (Rom. 1:18, II Tim. 3:13, 14 and 4:4, II Peter 1:16-21, Titus 1:9). If one is unwilling to accept biblical authority, Dr. Ockenga sees only two alternatives: (a) Roman Catholicism, and (b) what he calls left-wing rationalism, which makes the human mind the supreme authority. We should also consider a third alternative, namely, (c) irrationality. It involves a rejection of reason and an unwillingness to use the mind and the tools of logic in religious inquiry, discussion, and proclamation. There is even some danger that evangelicals will make the mistake of turning to irrationalism to support their position of "belief in spite of all the evidence." If the historic faith is ever reduced to the level of something held in spite of fact and reason, it will not be a "greater faith" as existentialist theologians might put it; it will be an absurdity and a perversion of the Gospel of Jesus Christ.

We agree that it is important to acknowledge the soundness of and the necessary for, the proposition. The full authority of the Word of God, "able to make thee wise unto salvation," (II Tim. 3:15) must be affirmed and reaffirmed today. Half-way positions are inadequate, for they ultimately result in uncertainty or in mysticism — neither of which is a satisfactory substitute for the reliability of the God who reveals himself in an authoritative Word.

I would amplify Dr. Ockenga's presentation by stressing the clarity and understandability of Scripture. The Holy Spirit must help us if we are to understand Scripture, not because Scripture is obscure, but because our own minds are dark and obscure (II Cor. 3:15).

A major question remains: is this affirmation enough to build an effective foundation for evangelism in today's world? We are called upon to show *in practice* that the God whom we worship and proclaim makes a difference — in other words, that we worship a living God. It may appear increasingly necessary, if our evangelism is to succeed, that we exhibit lives changed by the power of God and that we become more and more conformed to the image of Christ, so that people find our witness to the living God more credible (cf. Matt. 5:16).

To sum up: the authority of Scripture is a necessary presupposition

DR. BROWN is theological secretary of The International Fellowship of Evangelical Students in Lausanne, Switzerland.

for evangelism, but may not be a sufficient basis for an effective witness. People may demand to see more of a demonstration in terms of consistent Christian living and of trust in the Lord in the affairs of daily living. We denigrate the liberal emphasis on ethics first – the Gospel only later, if at all. But sometimes we act as though we put 'Gospel *theory* first, and take the moral and ethical consequences only later (if at all).

The major proposition is that biblical evangelism is and must be trinitarian. In this analysis, Dr. Ockenga develops a theology of evangelism that follows traditional theological teaching in attributing specific actions to particular Persons of the Trinity. He points out that in evangelism we are carrying out the tasks assigned by the whole Trinity and we witness to the whole plan of God; we are not to overemphasize one Person over another.

Dr. Ockenga thus introduces an element of fundamental theological doctrine into a realm where it is often lacking, namely, into evangelism. In this trinitarian emphasis, he stands firmly on historic ground. The Athanasian Creed, or *Quicumque Vult*, states that belief in the Holy Trinity is necessary for salvation. This strikes against two modern prejudices. First of all, it opposes universalism: "whosoever will be saved, must . . ."; it lays down a condition. For many churches and theologians, it is unpleasant to suggest that the Gospel promise of salvation is limited to a particular class of people – as the *Quicumque Vult* says – to those people who actually believe. It goes on to specify a distinctly trinitarian belief, which by virtue of its doctrinal content becomes unpalatable to those who see faith only as an attitude and not as something with content. One has the impression of being asked to hold it to be true ("für wahr halten"); but our proclamation must, in fact, have content.

Like the Athanasian Creed, Dr. Ockenga's major proposition with its strong trinitarian emphasis stands over against certain trends in today's evangelism as well as in certain theologies which we reject. They may concentrate exclusively on the Son, on Jesus Christ. Many do this in evangelism, by "looking only to Jesus", or seeking to "know Christ only." In some contexts, these statements are wonderful mottoes. In others, they can lead to preaching a Christ isolated from the context of the Trinity, and thus to a kind of "unitarianism of the Son." The result can be a loss of the full context of the revelation, and ultimately of God himself. Our access to God in Christ depends on Christ's being the incarnate Son.

A non-trinitarian approach to evangelism can be dangerous if it appeals to people to accept Christ as personal Savior without making clear who God is. This, too, like classical liberalism, is a form of reductionism. We are upset at the blasphemy inherent in the so-called "death-of-God" school of theology, which talks about the possibility of Christian atheism. But some winds of evangelism also approach this, when they see only Christ; when they leave out the Father and the Holy Spirit, or underemphasize them. It is against such a mistake that Dr. Ockenga warns us.

After having established the trinitarian nature of evangelism, he deals with the work of the individual Persons of the Trinity: election by the Father, redemption by the Son, and regeneration by the Holy Spirit. Dr. Ockenga touches upon the question of predestination, notes that it is important, but passes over rather quickly to the statement, "The offer of salvation is real, and God does not mock us." It seems to be a question for which there is no possible theoretical answer, only the practical one of teaching the Gospel to all nations, in the confidence that whoever believes will be saved (Matt. 28:19, John 3:16). I would suggest the rubric of obedience to and trust in God's Words of command and promise, and prefer to avoid the semi-Pelagian implications of the term synergism.

That evangelism must center in the offer of propitiation is an over-specialization. Prior to the crucifixion Jesus and his disciples often *evangelized* without being specific about his approaching sacrificial death. The offer of new life in the Gospel is possible only because of the *eph-apax* work of Christ at Calvary, but does not necessarily include a full theology. For many, true conviction of sin and repentance comes only after an acquaintance with Christ that is arrived at in an oblique way.

The emphasis on the gifts of the Holy Spirit which one finds in some circles may lead either toward or away from Christ. The charismatic movement, like certain other unrelated phenomena — occultism, extra-sensory perception, and psychedelic drugs — all point to the reality of a spiritual dimension which the modern world often likes to deny. Unfortunately, like the other three phenomena, even the charismatic movement can have very negative features as well as strongly positive ones. Manifestations of the Spirit, especially speaking in tongues, can be duplicated in other religions or under circumstances where it is difficult to believe that the Holy Spirit is at work. Here, as in all emotional experience, we must not ask merely about the intensity of the experience but about its content; moreover, the Holy Scriptures themselves offer us the only reliable guide for distinguishing between an experience that exalts the Lord Jesus Christ and serves to further his Kingdom, and one which is of legitimate significance only for an individual, or which may be seriously detrimental to the work of the Church of Jesus Christ.

In his concluding recommendations, Dr. Ockenga calls for human dedication and sense of purpose. I question the priorities which may be implicit in the final four points where united believing comes third, and might more properly come first. Confession in the Scripture has a positive meaning (e.g. Rom. 10:9, 10, confessing Christ as Lord) as well as the negative one of confession of sins. A weakness of current evangelistic efforts is the lack of clarity concerning confession in the sense of Romans 10:10; it may even vary among the participants.

The most serious criticism of the presentation is that it touches on some crucial points, viz. divine election, the charismatic movement, and united belief, without being explicit enough, a difficult task indeed in the time allowed. Christians may have legitimate differences on all these issues and we must admit this fact. Can a conference such as this do something toward clarifying and resolving these differences? This is the difficult task we face if we want to have a united theology of evangelism. Humility and a willingness to hear and bear with others, as Dr. Ockenga suggests, is vital. A biblical foundation and a full trinitarian theology, as he shows, are essential prerequisites.

THE FALL OF MAN
Stuart Barton Babbage

Fallen man exists in a state of deprivation and depravity. In the words of *The Thirty-Nine Articles of Religion* (Article IX), "man is very far gone from original righteousness and is of his own nature inclined to evil, so that the flesh lusteth always contrary to the spirit . . ." *Negatively* stated, man no longer possesses that original righteousness with which he was endowed. *Positively* stated, man has a perpetual bias toward evil.

Thus, as the result of the Fall, man is in a state of moral inability, unable to do that which is good. He is also in a state of moral corruption, turned in on himself, as Luther put it.

The doctrine of total depravity does not mean, however, that man is totally corrupt and unable to do anything that is good. It means that man is corrupt in the totality of his being, and that there is no part of his being that is untouched by sin. It does not mean that every man is as bad as he can be, destitute of every vestige of good; it means that no part of his being is unaffected and uncontaminated. Every part of man's being has been infected by the fatal virus of sin. His body, his mind, his will, all have been corrupted by man's fall. Sin, Luther insists, is rooted not only "in 'the flesh,' that is . . . 'the inferior and grosser affections,' but in the most exalted and most noble powers of man . . . that is, in the reason and in the will." Calvin says the same. "Everything in man, the understanding and will, the soul and body, is polluted."

The Bible bears clear testimony to a radical corruption of man's being. "The heart," Jeremiah testifies, "is deceitful above all things, and desperately corrupt" (17:9, RSV). Our Lord Jesus Christ, who knew what was in man (John 2:25), said "Out of the heart come evil thoughts, murder, adultery, fornication, theft, false witness, slander . . ." (Matthew 15:19).

The life of fallen man is characterized by perversity and disobedience. The hallmark of sin is lawlessness (I John 3:4). The mind of the unregenerate man "is hostile to God; it does not submit to God's law, indeed it cannot; and those who are in the flesh cannot please God" (Rom 8:7, 8, RSV).

Fallen man is not only an alien — "separated from Christ, alienated from the commonwealth of Israel . . . having no hope and without God in the world" (Eph. 2:12) — but is also a slave. "Everyone who commits sin," Jesus explains, "is a slave to sin" (John 8:34, RSV).

But how is a sinner to escape from the bitter bondage of sin into the glorious liberty of the sons of God? Man, in his fallen state, can neither will nor do that which is good (Phil. 2:13). His will is bound; his feet are

DR. BABBAGE is Visiting Professor of Practical Apologetics at Columbia Theological Seminary in Decatur, Georgia.

fast bound in misery and iron; every imagination of the thoughts of his heart is only evil continually (Gen. 6:5). This is not to deny that he enjoys a certain freedom: he is free to be himself, that is, to follow the inclinations and desires of his own sinful nature. Because he is an evil tree he can bear nothing but evil fruit (Matt. 7:17). To bear good fruit he must be transplanted from the wild olive tree and be grafted into new stock.

Pelagius, in opposition to Augustine, taught the unconditional freedom of the human will. Augustine knew better; he had a deeper understanding of "the abysmal depths of the human personality," a more profound awareness of the impotence of the human will.

No man, Augustine insists, has the power of self-recovery or self-determination. The gift of life is the work of grace. Through the gift of grace the will is renewed so that man is able both to desire and to do that which is good.

The controversy was renewed by Erasmus when, at the urgent instigation of the pope, he wrote against Luther. Man has the ability, Erasmus confidently affirmed, either to accept or reject the proffered grace of God. Luther contradicted him: "A man cannot be thoroughly humbled until he comes to know that his salvation is utterly beyond his own powers, counsel, endeavors, will and works and absolutely dependent upon the will, counsel, and pleasure of another." "God," Luther repeated, "does nothing by contingency, but he foreknows, purposes and does all things according to his immutable, eternal and infallible will." All is of grace.

Luther was delighted that Erasmus had raised the important issue of the freedom of the human will. "I cannot praise you enough," he wrote, "that you alone have attacked the central thing, the really knotty problem; instead of pestering me with tiresome trifles about the papacy, purgatory, indulgences, and other futilities of the same order; you have truly seized me by the throat." Calvin agreed: "Here is the greatest difference which we have with the papists."

This issue is still of paramount importance in relation to the evangelization of fallen man. Do we really believe that it is God alone who can kill and make alive (I Sam. 2:6)? Is man spiritually dead, dead in trespasses and sins, or has he a little life? Is sin a radical infection of our being, or is it only an imperfection? Are we to think in terms of guilt or of weakness?

"What ails us," says P. T. Forsyth finely, "is not limitation but transgression, not poverty but alienation. It is the breach of communion that is the trouble — the separation, the hostility. We are not his counterparts but his antagonists . . . As a race we are not even stray sheep, or wandering prodigals merely, we are rebels with weapons in our hands. Our supreme need from God, therefore, is not the education of our conscience . . . but our redemption. It is not cheer that we need but salvation, not help but rescue."

It is a humanist delusion to imagine that man's deep hurt can be healed by simple exhortations of a helpful kind. It is not sufficient to say, with Coué, "Day by day, in every way, I'm getting better and better." What the humanist conveniently forgets is that, beneath the surface veneer of our accomplishments, there are volcanic depths of lawless desire. The tragic truth is that man is a creature not only of ambiguity but of perversity, not only of duality but of depravity, not only of contradiction but of corruption. That is why, as true servants of God, we are precluded from joining the company of those who seek to heal the wound of the people lightly, saying: "Peace, peace, when there is no peace" (Jer. 6:14).

Our judgment of the human problem will determine our understanding of the Gospel. Norman Vincent Peale finds a remedy for all our ills in the magic potency of positive thinking; Ella Wheeler Wilcox suggests that "Just the art of being kind/Is all the sad world needs."

Now, as always, accurate diagnosis is a necessary prerequisite to effective prescription.

If we would interpret the Gospel aright, we must be ruthless and realistic in our analysis of man's malady and of the corruption with which he is infected. What the Bible affirms, with blunt incisiveness, is that "the imagination of man's heart is evil from his youth" (Gen. 8:21), and that what man needs, to be saved, is a new heart as the consequence of a new birth.

Hugh Thompson Kerr, in a series of alliterative antitheses, reminds us of the nature of our task: "We are sent, not to preach sociology but salvation; not economics but evangelism; not reform but redemption; not culture but conversion; not progress but pardon; not the new social order but the new birth; not resuscitation but resurrection; not a new organization but a new creation; not democracy but the Gospel; not civilization but Christ. We are ambassadors, not diplomats." In relation to the fallenness of man, our entrusted responsibility is to proclaim that God has made peace through the blood of the Cross so that man might be delivered from the bondage of corruption into the glorious liberty of the children of God (Rom. 8:21).

CONTEMPORARY SYMPTOMS
OF MAN'S FALL
Samuel J. Mikolaski

Let us turn to modern man's recourses for an index of his sinfulness. Examination of that to which men turn in the critical areas of their lives may
prove a useful indicator of the human spiritual condition. Let us look at
human recourses in the intellectual, emotional, political, economic and religious realms. I speak out of my experience in Canada, in the United
States, in Britain, and in western Europe, though I believe these comments
should stimulate reflection on man's sinfulness wherever he is found. To
reflect on these recourses is not to say that they are distinctly sinful in
themselves, but that within these realms many modern people seek a life
independent of God. Contemporary man seldom thinks of taking God into
account in his life.

1. Intellectual recourse

Our age is characterized by a massive demonstration of unbelief, in
man's attempts to show what he can accomplish without any traditional
belief in God at all. This is not due to science as such, but more to "scientism,"
which especially marks student reaction to religion. It is a skeptical outlook
on ethical and religious values. This attitude also conveys the impression
that unbelief is solidly grounded in the assured results of experimental
science. In the United States such beliefs are often based on the philosophy
of naturalism. Recently, as in the work of Arthur Koestler, behaviorism, the
ally of naturalism, has again come under heavy fire.

Such attacks on the spiritual nature of man are paralleled by a wave
of the animalization of human behavior, especially with regard to sex mores.
In the name of freedom and natural pleasure, it is now felt by many that
a new standard of sex mores is actually in force which, it is claimed, makes
the views of religious people not only anachronistic but dishonest. Pronouncements by some clergy and theologians have also tended to encourage
thinking youth to discount the supernatural basis of true religion and the
divine sanction of moral standards. At issue are the spiritual nature of man
and his moral responsibility to his Creator. It is evident that similar trends
are present in Britain and western Europe.

2. Emotional recourse

Indulgence of the passions in the terms of modern hedonism is thought
by some to be a landmark of modern man's right to freedom and his chief

DR. MIKOLASKI is professor of systematic theology at New Orleans Baptist Theological Seminary in Louisiana.

end. An incongruous aspect of modern hedonism is the tension between its egoism and its altruism. It is difficult to see how the highly subjective need-satisfaction activity of human organisms can be translated, or why it ought to be translated, into altruistic behavior. A considerable section of modern psychological and sociological teaching is based on the theory of selfish behavior of the organism.

Selfishness and restlessness characterize modern man, especially middle-class, well-to-do man. The issue of selfish living is frustration. The symptoms and diseases of frustration are many, including drug addiction, alcoholism, mental breakdown, obsession with sex, criminal activity, and cruelty. The final outlet of frustration is often suicide. Absorption with sex has assumed public epidemic proportions. Entertainment commonly features sadism and violence. A bitter harvest of such influences is now being reaped. Unbridled lust and violence characterize the large, troubled cities of the western world, and one cannot discount the intellectual and emotional environment of the present generation as important causes of these, as well as the economic factors. Freedom has been interpreted as liberation from an over-sensitive conscience, but new voices are calling for reconsideration of the traditional biblical doctrines of sin, guilt, and forgiveness.

3. Political and economic recourses

Pressure to conform is enormous in all societies. The guarding of basic human needs by society seems to have carried with this achievement the radical impersonalization of life. The increasing use of conditioning and propaganda techniques is universally apparent. Truth in the market place is shockingly absent in a broad fringe of the business world.

Socially, discrimination against color groups and ethnic groups is a common feature of modern life. No nation is exempt from this charge. An economic malaise of the modern world is the wasteful exploitation, some-times involuntary, of natural resources and the senseless destruction of wildlife. The exploiting tendencies of man in relation to the creatures that furnish his livelihood and food are now being brought under moral scrutiny and judgment. The political disillusionments of the past generation com-prise a sort of quiet revolution. The failure of recent political ideals has been a dramatic feature of contemporary political life.

4. Religious recourse

It is likely that the fallenness of man is exhibited with astonishing clarity in institutionalized religion, including the Christian religion. While the Church intrudes into public affairs by way of pronouncement more and more, many see it to be in retreat on the need of godliness in its own life, on the need of morality, and on the need of a concerted effort to get the Gospel to the common man, especially at the central urban level. Appearing to be religious may be simply a way of conforming to accepted mores.

The life of the Church has been petrified into social strata which parallel divisions in society. Dominant religions often tend to paralyze nations socially and economically, to say nothing of spiritually. War is justified in the name of religion. People are excluded from churches on grounds of poverty, lack of education, color, or nationality. This is true of churches of all theological persuasions. To play little religious games in church with those of one's own kind may well be a prime index of man's fallenness.

Ignorance, intolerance, and religious persecution form an astonishing team. They continue to characterize countries where certain religions and denominations are dominant. In religion, history attests to the fact that the fall is the greater because the claim is higher. The Church can never be at peace with society but must always have its own life and the life of the world under the judgment of God's Word. World-wide revival is possible in our time. Let men seek the God who redeemed them, who as Father, Son, and Holy Spirit is worthy of all praise now and ever.

MODERN MAN AND HIS NEEDS
Hans Rohrbach

1. Modern man's situation and needs

What characterizes "modern man?" What particular traits do we have in mind when we speak of "modern man?"

I think of at least three factors.

One is his triumphant advance in science, with its vast extension of knowledge, culminating in man's entrance into outer space and his utilization of atomic energy. The mysterious universe, in both its largest and its smallest dimensions, is increasingly being grasped and revealed by man's *own* power, by *his* spirit and abilities. The underlying motivation here is the desire to be free and independent, to be autonomous.

Paralleling this effort to gain freedom from the outer world is a strong tendency toward an inner, mutual independency, attested by emphasis on a "pluralistic society." Everyone must tolerate everyone else and integrate himself fully into the community, not subject to any authority or principle or conscience — yet willing to do what is expected of him. The underlying trait here is the desire to be accepted and acknowledged, to fit into society but without question and being questioned.

In addition there is a third aspect which may seem contradictory, but which, nevertheless, is decisive for shaping the whole behavior of modern man. This is the fact that consciously or unconsciously, man has become aware of his aloneness and separateness. By himself, he is helpless against the forces of nature and society; this fact makes him feel anxious and imprisoned. This awareness stimulates the desire for liberation, the desire to reach out and to unite himself in one way or another with other people and with the universe.

On the basis of this short psychological sketch, the question arises how modern man in this desperate situation can best be helped. Of course, for someone who believes in the personal God revealed in Jesus Christ the answer is clear and simple. The separateness and aloneness of modern man — as well as of any man — is due solely to the fallenness of man, and for this reason can be overcome only by man's reunion with God. Such a reunion *is* possible, but it is to be gained only through the redemption accomplished for us in Jesus Christ on the Cross of Golgotha.

2. The wrong way to meet modern man's needs

The problem, then, is how to inform modern man about this possibility of reunion. Many contemporary theologians think that people today

DR. ROHRBACH is president (rektor) of the University of Mainz, Germany.

are no longer moved by religious language, especially not by that of the Bible. They imply that, because of the technical environment to which he is accustomed, modern man can be impressed only by scientific, i.e., empirical categories. Therefore the aim of theology, they say, should be to transform the biblical message in such a way that secular man can accept it. According to Carl F. H. Henry's inspiring book, *Frontiers in Modern Theology* (Moody Press, Chicago, 1964, Christian Forum Books edition, p. 151), they believe and declare: "Christian faith is gone; Christian hope is gone; all that is left is Christian love – but that is enough."

In the course of this modern conviction, therefore, the correct biblical statement "God is love" (I John 4:8) is inverted into "love is God." And the meaning of this – according to certain European radical theologians – is: God does not exist as a personal God but only as an existential event that takes place every time two persons encounter each other in a friendly, loving way. To them love is nothing more than the realization of that which "God" stands for in themselves.

Against this attitude C. F. H. Henry states and rightly so (*loc. cit.*, p. 151): "Because theological renegades ask the wrong question – How transform Christianity to enlist secular man? – they come up with the perverse answer: Restructure the Gospel! rather than: Regenerate the sinner!" But how does it happen that theologians ask the wrong question? Their analysis of modern man's situation and outlook is absolutely correct! But their point of departure is definitely wrong, for their own thinking still rests upon the scientific view of the world projected by classical physics in the nineteenth century, and they therefore believe they must reject all biblical statements that involve science. They feel that what they call "intellectual honesty" demands this rejection, and it is this attitude which gives rise to their theological treatment of modern man. But no man-made remedies can rescue modern man from his fallenness.

3. The paradox of science and the Bible

In my opinion, the most important fact theologians should realize – and this applies to theologians of every school, evangelicals as well as liberals or rationalists – is the paradox of science and the Bible.

Thesis 1. The so-called modern scientific view of the world is not actually the view of the Bible.

Thesis 2. The so-called biblical view of the world is not actually the view of the Bible.

Although I cannot go into detail here, I wish to emphasize that the nineteenth century view of the world as an everlasting universe that extends into infinity, with space, time, and matter as absolutes and in which eternal, unalterable laws of nature rule everything – once called a scientific view – has more recently been scientifically refuted. That is, all categories of absoluteness or eternality are now stripped away from space, time, matter, and the laws of nature. These were not really scientific facts, but were metaphysical interpretations which man superimposed upon the universe.

One of the main results of this important change in scientific thinking should be to eliminate the conviction held by many theologians (1) that there is only *one* reality, namely, the visible world; and (2) that there cannot be a personal God who acts in history as well as in nature. So much by way of a short comment on Thesis 1.

But perhaps Thesis 2 is even more striking. For nearly everyone who refers to the biblical view today, whether sympathetically or critically, has the notion that the naïve three-storied picture of heaven and earth is the genuine biblical view.

Here I wish first of all to give a short historical account. About 350 B.C., the Greek philosopher and scientist Aristotle developed the geocentric view of the universe with crystal spheres bearing the sun, moon, planets, and stars moving around the earth as their common center. About 250 B.C. the Greek astronomer Aristarchus of Lamos came to the embarrassing opinion — which since Copernicus we call "the heliocentric view" of the universe — that the sun forms the center, and that the planets, one of which is the earth, move around the sun, and that the moon moves around the earth. In addition, he knew of the vast expanse of the universe with the stars therein. But because of this theory, Aristarchus was accused of blasphemy, and in about 150 B.C. the scientists of that time, scholars of the Academy of Alexandria, declared it to be a false doctrine. Obviously the views of Aristotle had already become authoritative for the scientific and public opinion of the second century B.C. When Jesus of Nazareth was born, the geocentric view of the universe was generally accepted.

The real view of the world is that which revelation presents us.

4. The two realities of which the Bible speaks

In my opinion, every evangelical theologian and layman should emphasize the fact that the Bible points to *two* realities. These are, of course, God's world and man's world, but what really matters is their mutual relationship, namely the fact that man's world, i.e., the universe, is always viewed as *incorporated* into God's world. His world existed long before he brought the universe into being by his Word. When he said: "Let there be . . ." his dynamic word was transformed by his will into physical energy, i.e., into that stretched-out medium of electric, magnetic, and gravitational forces which in some way manifest matter. Every scientist knows about these forces from which came whatever fills the universe. But none can discover by scientific means from whence these forces come. According to the Bible this whole *visible* world is embedded in God's *invisible* world in a way that can only be described as a kind of unperceivable "within-each-other." Through this mutual penetration — two realities in one unity, to be clearly distinguished but not separated from each other — the visible constantly gains its energy from the invisible (Heb. 11:3; Col. 1:15, 16; II Cor. 4:18).

Even fundamentalists need to emphasize that the biblical revelation does not teach an evident three-storied world as is generally assumed. From the biblical account of creation we can gather that by his Word God placed the visible into the already existing invisible. When he did so he did not push aside the invisible — as if to make room for the visible — but let the visible become permeated by the invisible. Thus an interpenetration of the two worlds took place that, in its own way, is just as paradoxical as what our fathers expressed in the Chalcedonian Creed of 451 A.D. concerning the two natures of Jesus Christ: *together* but *distinct* in the one person Jesus of Nazareth are the true divine and the true human natures. In the same way, the scientist would say in the same complementary way, the visible and the invisible are *together* (i.e., truly joined) yet *distinct* (i.e., truly separated); we may say then that Jesus was truly and totally man in the visible, truly and totally God in the supernatural — and yet one person.

5. The correct way of addressing modern man

Despite his glorious achievements and endeavors from the viewpoint of mankind, modern man is a fallen man from God's viewpoint. But since he is not fully aware of his situation, he must be told about it. For God desires that all men be saved and come to the knowledge of the truth (I Tim. 2:4). Therefore modern man must know that he is mistaken in assuming that there is only one reality. He must be taught about the existence of the invisible in addition to the visible, and about their mutual relationship. And he must learn that the so-called three-storied world is neither the view nor the doctrine of biblical revelation. He must be taught about the complementary within-each-otherness of the two realities.

Modern man must also be taught that the invisible God can act and does act in the visible world; that, in fact, he did so in creation and still does so in keeping the visible world according to his will; that in the invisible all events have their origin — the daily, ordinary, comprehensible happenings that follow pattern and laws, as well as the unique and miraculous events, especially God's deeds in the history of salvation.

But modern man needs not only to be taught. He must also be challenged. Important as it is to clear his mind of traditional mistakes, it is even more important to recognize the hardness of his heart. Besides being taught of the *existence* of the invisible, modern man must be led to *experience the reality* of the invisible.

6. The meaning and task of evangelism

The condition of modern man as fallen man would be hopeless if God had not promised to change man's heart: "A new heart I will give you, and a new spirit I will put within you; and I will take out of your flesh the heart of stone and give you a heart of flesh (i.e., a living heart). And I will put my spirit within you, and cause you to walk in my statutes and be careful to observe my ordinances" (Ezek. 36:26, 27, RSV). Only God's spirit can work in man's heart, and he can fill it only if the hardened heart is renewed. This therefore, is the task and the meaning of evangelism: to prepare co-workers for God in Jesus' name, to fill them with knowledge of and love for modern man's needs, and then to send them with the unabridged message of the Cross and resurrection under the sure expectation that God by his Holy Spirit will use their proclamation to accomplish the marvel of quickening man's spiritually dead heart.

Actually, God allows no man to call in question his right to quicken him. Herein lies the grace of God. The quickening takes place without, usually against, man's unregenerate will. Our heart is not quickened because the natural man desires God. On the contrary, man as sinner makes it very difficult for God to rouse him. But in grace he confronts us without asking us. This does not mean that God ever forces a person to be converted. Quickening, rousing the heart is not conversion. Quickening means simply that the heart, i.e., conscience, can speak again or more clearly than before. *How* God accomplishes the marvel of quickening is his secret. But the quickened one *experiences* the invisible, and God's greatness and holiness begin to dawn upon him. For as soon as conscience makes itself known, it speaks unremittingly of God's will and man's sin. It brings man under the judgment of the divine Word and to a place of decision. Quickening thus has reached its goal, namely, to present the *possibility* of conversion to the quickened person. If he stumbles at God's Word and at the truth presented to his conscience he will seek to subdue this awareness, either by force or by self-deception. If he submits to the truth, he will deliver himself up to God's judgment and grace. If this occurs, he has made his decision for Christ and will experience God's grace, namely, acceptance by God and consequently his own conversion.

If the quickened person reaches this point, then evangelism has reached its goal as far as he is concerned. Conversion does not, however, reinstate man to the position he once occupied before the fall. He does indeed obtain peace with God and access to grace (Rom. 5:1, 2), but only by faith and not by sight (II Cor. 5:7). Even the redeemed person remains imprisoned in the fallen world. For this reason evangelism requires follow-up. The new convert needs guidance and counsel — at least for a time — and needs to be brought into Christian circles where God's Word is read and lived. He is to prove himself in the liberty to which Christ has made him free (Gal. 5:1). This requires pastoral care in such matters as discussion, confession, and forgiveness of sins. The new convert needs the environment of a biblically-grounded Church where he can grow up spiritually to bear his witness for Jesus Christ.

Report of Group Discussion

Discussion reflected doctrinal questions in the minds of the delegates. Can Pelagianism and Augustinianism coexist? What is meant by the "bondage of the will"? Is there not a danger of softening the Gospel by minimizing our doctrine of sin? These questions received predictable answers. A French delegate called attention to a lack of serious discussion of Genesis 3.

The paper presented by Dr. Rohrbach was not predictable however, and the stimulating German professor returned to it in amplifying upon his thesis. He spoke of the Trinity and of the fall in reference to visible and invisible realities. In both cases there is interpenetration. As the unity of the Trinity is stressed, so must we also stress the unity of decision and of God's election. We must hold both. In no case may such facts be separated. Seen against the background of the visible and invisible realm suggested in Scripture, decision is both God-given and man-caused.

A French delegate stressed the need for a well-grounded consciousness of sin, intellectual as well as moral. A German speaker added that the lostness of man is nowhere better seen than in the Cross.

In evangelism the Church must face man's intellectual questions. But the time can come for us to say, "Stop asking questions. These are only evasions. Tell me instead what you are unable to cope with. Business? Sex? Your wife? Ask God to solve your problems, and the intellectual problems will take care of themselves."

Reporter: *Leon Morris*

SIN IN BIBLICAL PERSPECTIVE
Saphir P. Athyal

Any sound theology of evangelism can be understood only in the general framework of a serious view of sin and its power.

The primary biblical teaching concerning sin is that it is directed against God. The most commonly used words for sin in the Old and New Testaments characterize sin as opposition to or movement away from God. "Your iniquities have made a separation between you and your God, and your sins have hid his face from you" (Isa. 59:2, RSV). Even in instances where sin is a direct offence against one's fellowman, its going contrary to God is what makes it a matter of concern (Gen. 39:9, Ps. 51:4, Hos. 4:1-2). Sin as opposition to God is seen clearly in man's very first sin. Here the main issue is not so much man's act of disobedience or his selfishness as his doubt of God's veracity and of the validity of his commandment. The first couple took the tempter's word at its face value but not God's (Gen. 3:4). Eating the forbidden fruit was but the result of the sin of repudiating God's authority and deliberately rejecting his demands.

God reacts to sin in anger and in judgment. If sin is man's contradiction of God and his expressed will, God cannot be complacent about sin and still be God. Just as man's sin is a personal, real fact and not an abstract principle, so God's wrath or reaction to sin is very real and personal. The common saying, "God hates sin but loves the sinner," is anything but biblical. God hates the sinner with a perfect hatred but loves him with a perfect love.

If the claims of God upon man may be summarized in the word "law" then sin is lawlessness (I John 3:4). Paul in the early chapters of his epistle to the Romans explains the relationship between sin and law. It was not law that occasioned the consequences of sin. Law but defined the terribleness of sin and made it sharp and clear. Because of law, sin becomes a conscious act and a deliberate breach of conduct (Rom. 7:8).

How then shall we understand law and specifically moral law? Law is the expression of the will of a holy and perfect God. It is the expressed pattern of behavior that he has set for his creation, and not man's consensus about his conduct nor a summary of his observations concerning the consistencies of nature. Except for man, the rest of creation conforms to God's rule non-volitionally. But with man, the exercise of his will or his choice of right and wrong is involved in his actions.

Thus God's will with regard to man's conduct may be understood as moral law. Its demands come to man through the workings of his conscience,

DR. ATHYAL is professor of Old Testament and chairman of the department of Biblical studies at Union Biblical Seminary in Yeotmal, Maharashtra, India.

through his sense of "ought," or through his rationality. Since man is created in the image of God he has imbedded within him the wishes of his Creator concerning him. We read in Rom. 2:14-15, "When Gentiles who have not the law do by nature what the law requires, they are a law unto themselves, even though they do not have the law. They show that what the law requires is written on their hearts" (RSV). God as the maker of man has a right to command man. His laws are perfect and altogether binding on man. Often the laws in the Old Testament are made imperative by the phrase, "I am the Lord."

In understanding sin in relation to moral law, there is a clear distinction between the biblical and non-biblical concepts. In Hinduism, sin is not understood in terms of moral evil. Sins are primarily ritual offences. In philosophic Hinduism, sin is not a fact but an illusion and may supposedly be overcome by denying its reality. Then again law is obeyed not necessarily because it leads to morally right action nor because it reflects the will of a supreme and holy God for man's life, but because it is prescribed. Law is not thought of in terms of the lawgiver but as an end in itself. The distinctive thing about Christian teaching in this matter is that man is directly responsible to the supreme God in all his conduct.

If "through the law comes knowledge of sin" (Rom. 3:20, RSV) and apart from the knowledge of sin there could be no conviction of sin (cf. James 2:9), then law becomes instrumental in one's coming to Christ. Thus law is not contrary to grace but complementary to it.

In the minds of many today, there is no clear distinction between right and wrong and consequently society has undergone widespread moral decay. Men generally hold that moral law is fluid, flexible and relative, and to be viewed as founded on man's varied circumstances and training.

It is in the context of this kind of thinking that we are reminded by the Word that man in all his conduct is answerable to his sovereign God, concerning whose personal demands upon him man is in no doubt whatever. Any departure by man from what he knows he ought to do, however small his offence may be, slaps the very face of God. Sin is sin under any circumstances and is always an expression of man's disregard for God's rule over him. Return to a high view of moral law, and thus to a serious view of sin, is imperative today.

EVANGELISM AND THE REALITY OF SIN
Samuel A. Benétreau

"All great movements of evangelism are planted firmly on a biblical foundation" declared Dr. H. J. Ockenga in his study on "The Basic Theology of Evangelism." Each period of evangelical expansion corresponds to the rediscovery of a scriptural truth, or of several. We ought, therefore, seriously to ask ourselves the following question: *Is the Christianity of our time neglecting or minimizing some important aspect of biblical teaching*, thus inevitably harnessing itself to a weakness in its witness?

We must answer in the affirmative. There are grave weaknesses, even in the most orthodox churches, and one of the gravest weaknesses concerns the *teaching about sin*. It is hard to find a strong conception and a strong personal and sharp consciousness of sin. Even when our definitions are exact, we have difficulty in grasping the vigorous character of that which Scripture designates as sin.

In spite of themselves, Christians are influenced by the spirit of their age. Modern man does not admit the idea of sin; he does not even understand it. Not that he pretends to be perfect or that he has illusions about his own virtues. Twentieth century man is not seeking so much to affirm his personal righteousness before divinity or before his fellowmen, but rather he is filled with complacency concerning his weaknesses and faults. He considers them inherent in the human condition; he thinks that education, culture, and the scientific knowledge of man and of the universe can, within a certain measure, surmount these weaknesses or diminish their consequences for society.

On the one hand this particular context explains the difficulty which Christians have in hating sin and in measuring its seriousness; on the other, it explains the problems of evangelism in our time.

This raises a very important question: *Is it possible to evangelize men who have lost the idea of sin?* Evangelists often have the painful impression that they are teaching without being heard. Their message does not get to the listener. What, for example, can the Good News of the Redeemer mean to those who are ignorant of what sin is? A deliverer on the social plan or on the psychological plan may interest them, but to speak about deliverance from the curse and the power of sin is to propose a solution to a problem that is neither felt nor recognized. To have a high idea of the person of Christ it is also necessary to have a strong idea of sin.

What, therefore, is sin? It is not an illusion, as Christian Science teaches. It is not merely something passive which man undergoes, a kind of constitutional weakness. Nor is it the residue of out-of-date mythical thinking, as

THE REV. MR. BENÉTREAU is pastor of the Free Evangelical Church of Paris, France.

certain recent champions of the "new morality" would affirm. These theologians refuse to believe that there is a supernatural God and reject the idea of God-given absolutes. Modern man, they think, can accept only a relativistic morality tied to the particular circumstances of his existence.

For the humble Christian who wants to keep not the mentality of an age, but biblical revelation as his criterion, sin ought to be understood in terms of the Creator God and the Redeemer, who has absolute rights over his beloved creatures. *Sin is the refusal of divine lordship, and disobedience to God's will.*

From the first pages of the Bible, the benevolent God gave ordinances, and it is when man rebelled with respect to these ordinances that sin appeared. The God of the Covenant also made his will known to his chosen people, Israel. In the law he declares who he is and how he should be served. Jesus, in the Sermon on the Mount, in extending the lines of the Mosaic law, manifested all the demands of God's holiness: "Be ye therefore perfect, even as your Father which is in heaven is perfect" (Matt. 5:48). This moral law has kept its full validity (cf. Matt. 5:18, James 2:10-11, etc.).

In preaching salvation by faith without the works of the law, Paul rejects the law as a way of salvation accessible to man, but maintains it as a norm and goal. The moral law brings into evidence and establishes the sin of man as rebellion against his God (Rom. 7:7-13). *Sin, therefore, may be called "the transgression of the law"* (I John 3:4).

But we must go still further. Sin is not only a state of disobedience; it is also *a state of slavery* (Rom. 6:6). The sinner is subject to evil powers which enslave his intelligence, his will, and his emotions.

Sin is accompanied by the most tragic consequences: "The wages of sin is death" (Rom. 6:23). The sinner is not only *a guilty being* who must pay for his crime, he is also *a cursed being*; the wrath of God is upon him (Rom. 2:8-9).

In a world which tends to permit or to excuse everything, how can we Christians preserve and maintain a sensitivity to sin? Not by remaining attached to the law, for we would constantly be hampered by the danger of legalism and self-justification. No, we will be sensitive to sin through Christ, who in living out the total divine exigencies, manifested the beauty of holiness, and who on the Cross suffered all the consequences of sin, and thus showed its horror. By remaining closely united to him who became both the victim and conqueror of sin, we will truly see ourselves and the world in the right light. He gives us the Holy Spirit who searches our hearts and cleanses our conscience from sin.

But we must not forget that God has given us a total, complete revelation. In order to keep a proper perspective, we need all Scripture, and must see it from the point of view of the salvation accomplished in Jesus Christ. We need the Ten Commandments, the teachings of the Sermon on the Mount, the apostolic exhortations. A clear, balanced and complete idea of sin necessitates the assimilation of the total teaching of the Word.

In our work of evangelism, how then shall we create a consciousness of sin in those whom we wish to lead to the Lord? Is it necessary to preach law and judgment before preaching the Gospel of Grace? Must we establish the fact of sin before presenting the Savior, as certain evangelists did in the past, who addressed essentially religious people who were theoretically instructed in Christian truths? To reach the profoundly de-Christianized man of the twentieth century, it is better to preach the Gospel directly, but the complete Gospel that includes the law. The Apostles preached Jesus Christ without beginning with the law, as shown by the book of Acts and by the Epistles. All we need is found in Jesus Christ. The law is "our schoolmaster to bring us unto Christ" (Gal. 3:24). But it is wholly through Christ that this can be accomplished.

Let us enthusiastically proclaim the Good News of the holy, just Christ of the Scriptures, who so loved the world that he became sin for us. Let us envelop our message in fervent prayer, asking for the powerful working of the Holy Spirit. Then we will see miracles, eyes will be opened, the power of Satan will be broken, the Holy Spirit will convict hearts of sin and will enable them to find the Savior.

THE NEED FOR BIBLICAL MORALITY
A. Morgan Derham

The Puritans used to speak of the "law work" as an essential preparation for the Gospel, stating the truth about sin before going on to proclaim the Good News of salvation. This can be likened to the need in medicine for sound diagnosis before beginning any kind of treatment. Intention to heal is not enough; accurate diagnosis is basic to everything else.

The biblical diagnosis of man's situation is clear: he is under judgment because of sin. And if we ask how sin reveals itself, we are quickly enlightened: sin is seen in the breaking of the moral law, the revealed will of God for human living, summed up in the Ten Commandments and in the teaching of Christ, and expressed in full detail in the Scriptures as a whole.

At this point we are now meeting a direct and serious challenge in our day, a challenge that is coming not so much from *outside* the Christian Church as from *within*, from some who rank high in historic denominations. This challenge is all the more important because it has direct bearing upon evangelism. We know that sin is fundamentally a broken relationship between man and God at the personal level. But obviously the functioning of sin as a breach of moral law is a basic element in defining that shattered relationship. And if it is to be replaced by a different concept, largely subjective and emotional; and if we are to substitute the phrase "in a state of existential despair" for "under condemnation," we must make fundamental changes both in message and method, something that advocates of the New Morality seem to demand.

We find an example of this kind of thing in a book by Canon D. Rhymes of Southwark Cathedral. He says:

"It seems to me that if Christians approached people with the attitude of Christ rather than with the laws of the Church and the moral code, they should be able to reach those who take no notice of the laws of the Church."

This sentence neatly states the heart of the matter from the point of view of the New Morality: it assumes a contrast, if not a contradiction, between "the attitude of Christ" and "the moral code;" it assumes that barriers of resistance to the Gospel are created by the preaching of the concept of a fixed morality.

Such assumptions are not secondary or marginal to our evangelistic concern; they are primary and central, for they question our message *and* our methods; they throw down a gauntlet to traditional evangelism and declare that they have arrived at a better solution to the problem of bringing mod-

MR. DERHAM is the general secretary of The Evangelical Alliance in London, England.

ern man to Christ. We assert that this way of thinking results in hopeless and dangerous confusion. In particular:

1. It confuses the situation as between regenerate and unregenerate man.

The "Law of Christ," to which the believer is bound, is inseparable from life lived in the strength of the indwelling spirit of Christ. Christian morality ought not to be preached in isolation (and very rarely is, surely). It is part of what may be called a "package deal," and the package includes the promise of the very spirit of Christ to those who have been born again into the family of God.

The basic moral code outlined in the creation ordinances of Genesis 1-3 and in the commandments of Exodus and Deuteronomy is certainly binding on the human race — though we should note that even the Ten Commandments were not given in isolation; they were given to a Covenant people at a time of Covenant renewal and in association with a sacrificial system which made provision for the forgiveness of sin. But no evangelist worthy of the name preaches a bare moral code.

In their attacks on a perverted legalism, the teachers of New Morality are, in fact, creating a totally false impression of the situation, and giving to many impenitent and unregenerate men and women a solace which is in the true succession of Amos's vivid word-picture, "It will be as if a man . . . leaned with his hand against the wall, and a serpent bit him" (Amos 5:19, RSV).

2. It confuses primary and secondary causes.

The new antinomianism seems to see the primary cause of modern man's resistance to the Gospel in terms of resistance to legalism and external authority. Thus, to quote Rhymes again, "This long standing traditional morality, based upon authoritarian law and suspicion of the flesh, is today being rejected on all sides, and especially among the younger generation. . . ." He says further, "Today the moral duty of the individual seems to lie less in conforming to such generally accepted standards than in realizing his potentialities as an individual." But the primary cause of man's resistance to the grace of God is not the existence of moral law nor the failure of some Christians to live up to their beliefs. It is the twist in the core of man's being, the corruption we call sin. "These antinomians who say our whole problem is the Law are quite wrong. Our real problem is sin, not the Law. It is thus indwelling sin, our flesh or fallen nature, which explains the weakness of the Law to save us. The Law cannot save us for the simple reason that we cannot keep it; we cannot keep it because of indwelling sin" (John Stott).

It is this fact that makes tragic nonsense of the underlying claim of the New Moralists that the answer lies in new patterns of behavior based on the principle of self-expression rather than of self-discipline. It is like saying that all the owner of a car needs to do is to tune up his vehicle so that it gives the highest performance possible. This is very good, of course, but when the vehicle goes out on the road, its driver must obey the rule of the road and the laws of the country. If he does not, then the higher the car's performance the greater the menace he creates.

It is not enough, however, for orthodox Christians to expose the inconsistencies and errors of false teachers. We must keep up a counter offensive, and there is no reason why we should hesitate to do so. There is no need to apologize for biblical morality. We are bound to see before long in the Western world a reaction against the moral libertinism and license and relativism of our time. Men cannot forever go on playing musical beds to music played by Eros, the great god of our day, the world's most unpredictable performer, who calls the tune in so much of our Western culture.

Man must have boundaries if life is to be tolerable. *Time* is one such boundary. There was a period when the boundary of *space*, shutting man in on what was for him the all-important earth, helped to this end. But now this boundary has disappeared and we find ourselves orbiting in incomprehensible space on our own space-ship, with only a frail atmospheric shield between us and extinction. No wonder we live in a lost generation! But this is our *opportunity*. The *ultimate* boundaries stand as always — God himself, our Creator, Judge and Redeemer; and his pattern of living revealed in the moral law, exemplified in the life of his Son, and brought within range by his sacrifice on the Cross and the outpouring of his Spirit on all flesh. Within this framework man can yet find meaning and purpose; aided by the Spirit, the Christian here finds a quality of fulfillment that outdoes all rivals and competitors.

THE NEW MORALITY
Leslie Hunt

Evangelism has always met opposition from without the Christian Church, but today it faces grave opposition from within, in the form of the widespread movement called the New Theology. This movement strikes at the very core of evangelism — its theology — and challenges its reason for existence. The New Theology which repudiates the objective view of God and the biblical concept of sin; and its close associate, the New Morality which dismisses the moral law as an outmoded system of moral legalism, clash with evangelism and its proclamation that in the Cross of Jesus Christ there is the needed salvation for sinful man.

What is so serious is that the New Morality is finding its leadership and thrust in persons of academic competence who occupy high places within the church. Moreover, the movement is beaming its alleged gospel at the impressionable minds of the younger generation. Modern youth is fertile ground, for they are deluged from all sides with the assertions that the old standards of their parents are worn out and finished, and that they must be freed from the absurd restrictions and complex legalism of the Christian moral law. A wide hearing and ready approval are being given to the tenets of this New Morality, which declares that what was formerly regarded as sin may not necessarily be wrong at all. Any act, it is claimed, even including such evils as murder, rape, incest and adultery, is morally right if the situation is right. Morality may now be reduced to a simple formula, namely, "do the loving thing in every situation." We are witnessing a general breakdown of moral standards which is not by any means confined to the youth of our day. Modern man in all levels of society is relegating the Christian moral law to the limbo of outmoded relics and justifying any act he does as right.

What has happened to bring about this drastic change in the view of sin and the moral law? Modern man, it is claimed, has come of age; and the moral law as a basic idea of truth is hopelessly out-dated, is irrevelant to the modern situation, and does not touch the masses. Indeed, Christianity with its doctrine of sin and insistence on the moral law is regarded by some as the cause of, not the answer to, man's problems. The psychological sciences, so popular today, in many cases have been a factor behind the prevailing distaste for morality. In a desperate pursuit of self-fulfillment, modern man has lost sight of his true destiny.

When God is reduced to the mere "ground of man's being" or declared "dead" and eliminated altogether, the moral law becomes simply the accumulated ethical wisdom of man and therefore there is no reason why it

THE REV. CANON HUNT is the principal of Wycliffe College in Toronto, Ontario, Canada.

should not be changed or abandoned. The New Morality presents what it calls "a new law" for man's conduct—the law of love. Love has formed the foundation stone of the Christian ethic since Jesus taught it. So the law of love has much to commend it, but can hardly be called new. As presented by the New Morality, it displays glaring fallacies. The directive for conduct resolves itself into the formula "when faced by any moral issue or perplexity one does in every case the most loving thing." The point seems to be overlooked that while the loving thing to do may involve just two people directly, very often indirectly it may involve a number of other persons; and what may be the loving thing for two people to do, may be the most unloving thing in terms of the others concerned. Another glaring weakness of this law of love which claims that any act is right in the right situation, is the indefinable nature of the right situation. It results in ethical relativism and makes the individual his own law-maker. From our experience of human nature, we know that he who is free to make his own rules can just as readily set them aside. In a world with no recognized moral law which is binding and where every individual is left to decide what is right and what is wrong, moral chaos would result. When pressed further, this approach could become the basis of operation for civil law. The protection of man's rights, for which civil law is designed, would be jeopardized if each person could decide for himself the issues of right and wrong. The claim of the New Morality to supersede the restrictions of the old moral law because of its depth of concern for the rights and freedom of the individual proves to be a gross fallacy.

The current moral crisis is due, not to the alleged irrelevancy of the moral law, but to the refusal of modern man to pay serious attention to it or even to the ethical code already existent in man's conscience. Conscience itself is not enough because, like cut flowers, it is severed from its sustaining roots, from the faith that every man is made in God's image. This faith places man's moral action where it ought to be, in a theocratic position. What man needs in order to rise above his human relativities is the vital relationship of obedience to the eternal God. Man rejects this condition because of sin which has made him a rebel. Only in Jesus Christ and his redeeming love can man become reconciled to God and become subject to his will. Only then can he clearly see the demonic nature of sin endemic in man which sets the creature over against the Creator and distorts man's true destiny.

It is in this new restored relationship to God that the redeemed man appreciates the force of the term New Humanity. This new order is composed not of those progressive souls who have outgrown their need for God and his laws, but of those who have accepted God's gift of forgiveness and have moved from alienation to sonship. They form the true New Humanity because they have become new creations in Christ. They discover a new quality of moral conduct expressed by the word "Agape." The fullest meaning of this word is discovered at the Cross and becomes alive for the Christian by reason of his relationship to his Lord. With the coming of Grace, the Law as a legal system whereby men sought to be justified was abolished, but not as an expression of the righteous will of God. This still stands, now fulfilled in Jesus Christ, as a guideline to the Christian but enriched by the fuller law of "Agape." By the power of the Holy Spirit, the Christian can now meet the demands made upon him by both the natural law of conscience and the codified moral law of God.

It cannot be denied that the New Morality in our day, with its claim to offer moral freedom to what it calls the New Humanity, presents a major frontier of concern and a continuing challenge to the moral imperatives of the Gospel of Jesus Christ. One of the primary tasks of evangelism must be to reaffirm with conviction the biblical concept of sin and the eternal nature of the moral law.

BASIC PREACHING OF THE ATONEMENT
John C. Winston, Jr.

To describe the many aspects of Christ's atonement, let alone to keep them in perspective, is a vast undertaking. In our position paper we read that all these emphases are found as manifestations of the *basic* teaching that Jesus substituted for us in satisfying the demands of divine justice. And "evangelism therefore *centers* in the offer of the propitiation of Calvary." Let us examine this hotly contested affirmation. A discussion of emphasis and perspective can usefully begin by recalling how the atonement was viewed in years gone by.

The Greek Fathers viewed all of redemption as a colossal struggle between God and Satan that culminated in the Cross. Plenty of texts in Barnabas, Ignatius, Justin Martyr and Irenaeus, however, develop the judicial aspect of Christ's sacrifice.

If in the patristic age God's victory over Satan was a leading interpretation of the meaning of the Cross, two others came into prominence during the Middle Ages. The legal and moral or psychological views have alternately won favor in Church circles right down to the present time. Anselm launched the first school of thought and Abelard the second. Anselm's great contributinon was to bring out the biblical emphasis on sin as an offense to God's Person and rights, and on Christ's voluntary substitution for guilty men. Unfortunately, less biblical considerations dominated the popular preaching which gave rise to the Crusades, and strengthened the widespread notions of penitence and good works.

By and large, the Reformers returned to Anselm's teaching on the atonement. Sensing that a legal conception of the atonement did not fully exhaust its meaning, Luther, unlike Melanchthon, brought back the dramatic patristic view in which God through Christ overcame death, Satan, and hell. Calvin's biblical studies led him to formulate a clear statement on the wrath of God. After grounding redemption in Christ's objective work of grace, the Reformers drew out the practical applications of his pardon in a host of effective sermons and tracts.

Unfortunately the creative writing and preaching of Reformation days which had brought new life to the Church, degenerated into the sterile controversies of a Protestant scholasticism. Seventeenth century German and Dutch theologians, in their own way, enlarged endlessly upon the judicial aspects of Christ's atoning work. A reaction was inevitable. Modern liberal thinking on the atonement had been established with Schleiermacher and Ritschl in the eighteenth century. With its emphasis on the moral value of

THE REV. MR. WINSTON is dean of students and administration at the new Free Theological Seminary in Vaux-sur-Seine, France.

Christ's work, it stands in direct line with its first great exponent, Abelard, who in the twelfth century opposed Anselm's legal view. Redemption, wrote Abelard, is the awakening in man of a love which like the Suffering Savior's, conquers all. Pursuing in this vein, Schleiermacher asserts there is no connection between the sufferings of Christ and divine punishment of sin. There is no question of appeasing God's wrath, affirmed Ritschl, Christ's death is an act of solidarity with the human race, not a substitution for it.

Another form of reaction to the seventeenth century caricature of Anselm's view, and more fruitful of evangelistic preaching, is that of the early German pietists, Franke, Spener, and Zinzendorf. Scorned for their evangelistic views at home, they turned abroad and sent missionaries overseas. The Wesleyan revival and the whole modern worldwide missionary and evangelistic movement can trace its ancestry back to the early pietistic preaching of the moral and personal effects of the atonement, based on the objective propitiation of Calvary.

It thus becomes evident how in attempting to grasp the meaning of the atonement, Church leaders in the past have so often stressed one or another of its aspects to the exclusion of the others. It would also appear that those who adopted a biblical harmony of the manifold aspects of Christ's redemptive work unleashed their energies in productive preaching and writing rather than in needless discussions. Only the New Testament which revealed the atonement to us in the first place can give the proper perspective for viewing its component parts.

The interpretation of the meaning of the Cross was a major concern of the first Christians. To the ancients the word "cross" was inevitably associated with the deepest guilt and shame, and for the Jew, the curse of God; for a hanged man is accursed of God (Deut. 21:23). While persecuting Christians, Paul must have frequently led other Pharisees in anathematizing Jesus. But when he met the risen Christ, he gave a new dimension to the curse by adding the words "for us." The theme of this hanged Man who was accursed of God for us became basic to Paul's preaching.

In the Gospels the Savior foretells his death and gives its meaning. In the words "Father, forgive them, for they know not what they do," Christ gives an implicit meaning to his death. This remarkable prayer, says Jeremias, took the place of the expiatory vow which a condemned man had to say before his execution. Jesus applies the atoning virtue of his death not to himself, but to his executioners. This prayer, and the eucharistic words of him who came to give his life a ransom for many, imparted a basic orientation to the disciples' thinking about Calvary.

This interpretation of his death finds confirmation and perspective in the teaching on the Mount. In fulfilling the law, Jesus raises the Old Testament themes of justice and love to new heights. The Matthew 5 passage seems to indicate that if God condemns man for his unholiness and grieves over his lovelessness, he does so deeply concerned with man himself. Do not the two virtues of love and holiness in God, or the lack of them in men, complement rather than contradict each other, each giving perspective and also meaning to the other?

How God both judges and cares for the sinner is finally revealed at the Cross. As both the Condemner and the Condemned in his Son, God the Father at the Cross fully revealed the indignation and love which fill his heart. The human heart, of course, tends to emphasize God's love and minimize his wrath. In our century, the horrors of two world wars have helped bring back sin and judgment into religious vocabularies. C. H. Dodd says that Paul constantly uses "wrath" or "the wrath" in a curiously impersonal way, and that he retains the term "the wrath of God" not to describe the attitude of God to man, but to describe the inevitable process of cause and effect in a moral universe. After systematically defending impersonal wrath in his book, "The Wrath of the Lamb," A. T. Hanson makes this revealing comment: "If we once allow ourselves to be led into thinking that a reference to the wrath of God in the New Testament means that God is conceived of as angry, we cannot avoid some sort of theory of expiation; we cannot avoid maintaining that in some sense the son endured the wrath of the Father; we cannot avoid thinking in forensic terms."

All this falls in with the thinking of our times, when many of life's relationships have been de-personalized and thereby weakened. But one may ask, is it possible to remove the personal element from wrath in the Bible and not from love? Are not both revealed as intensely personal? Can a sinner be convicted of sin on any other basis? The repentant sinner realizes that Christ endured the Cross for him, thereby satisfying God's outraged holiness and providing the only objective ground for his personal forgiveness. That is why nothing else will move men to repentance and faith, and why evangelism must center in the propitiation of Calvary.

CHRIST THE MEDIATOR
Theodore Williams

Evangelism is basically the offer of forgiveness to man who is estranged from God. Human pride has always rebelled against the doctrine of forgiveness. George Bernard Shaw wrote, "Forgiveness is a beggar's refuge; we must pay our debts." However, this does not alter the fact that forgiveness of sin is one of the basic needs of man. In the Apostles' Creed we affirm, "I believe in the forgiveness of sins." St. Ambrose said in the fourth century, "I will not glory because I am righteous, but because I am redeemed; not because I am clear of sin, but because my sins are forgiven." How true it is! Ours is the religion of the forgiven.

Forgiveness and Atonement

It may be asked on what ground does God forgive? There is a doctrine of cheap grace which says that there can be no other ground of forgiveness than the very nature of God which is love. The Hindu religion has a doctrine of grace which makes room for forgiveness of sins on this basis. To repeat with fervor the name of a particular deity, or to fulfill certain religious duties, is thus thought to bring divine favor and forgiveness.

But, according to the Bible, forgiveness is costly. The Levitical sacrifices reveal that the process of reconciliation of a sinner is not easy. "Without shedding of blood is no remission [of sin]" (Heb. 9:22). The same idea is brought out in New Testament passages which speak of the price of redemption (I Cor. 6:20 and I Pet. 1:18).

The New Testament teaching is that forgiveness cannot be taken for granted. It is free only as it is mediated to sinners through the death of Christ. God cannot forgive except in consistency with his whole character. He is just and at the same time he is also the justifier (Rom. 3:26). To do justice to his character, he must forgive in such a way that sin is not treated lightly. The reality of his love, as well as the reality of the awfulness of sin in his sight, must be demonstrated. This was what necessitated the Cross.

Atonement Explained

The law of *Karma* makes it difficult for the Hindu to accept the Christian doctrine of atonement. According to this irrevocable law, each man must bear the consequences of his own action and no one can interfere with the lot of another. There is assertedly no such thing as vicarious suffering. All suffering is traced ultimately to the sufferer's own evil deeds in this life

MR. WILLIAMS is evangelist-at-large for the Emmanuel Methodist Church of Madras, and teacher-cum-evangelist associated with the South India Bible Institute, Bangarapet, Mysore State, India.

or in the past life. Thus an impersonal law of cause and effect is thought to be at work in the moral order of this universe. But the Gospel declares that Christ has taken our *Karma* (i.e. the total effects and consequences of our sin) upon himself and thereby broken its power and made us free from it. But it does not stop here. While admitting the presence of the law of retribution in the moral order, we relate its working to the personal activity of God. The atonement delivers not only from the effects and consequences of sin but also from divine wrath.

The word *propitiation* is used in the New Testament (Rom. 3:25 and I John 2:2) to describe the work of Christ. Propitation, in the biblical sense, is the turning away of divine wrath and not the mere expiation of sin. We cannot truly understand the forgiveness of sin in the Christian sense unless we accept the biblical concept of the wrath of God. The wrath of God is not the same as the capricious and vindictive anger of pagan deities. In the Old Testament, it is seen as "the stern reaction of the nature to evil in man." In the New Testament also, it is associated with the personal activity of God. It is not just an impersonal "inevitable process of cause and effect in a moral universe." "The wrath of God is the wrath of divine personality." The death of Christ removed this divine wrath for all who put their trust in him.

The idea of *reconciliation* is also used to indicate the work of Christ on the Cross. Sin has caused a state of enmity between man and God. Christ's death removed this enmity and brought about reconciliation between God and man. Christ died *instead of* us as our *Substitute*, as well as *on behalf of* us as our *Representative*.

Justification is another great word portraying the forensic aspect of the work of Christ. Substitution and justification are closely linked. The sinner is acquitted because Christ bore the penalty of his sin according to the law. This judicial explanation of the atonement is sometimes criticised as "immoral." This is not true because "from first to last this has been the work of God" (I Corinthians 5:18, NEB). He is the judge and it is his laws that are broken. He himself has borne the penalty. He did not take our sins and lay them on another. So there is no break-down of principles of justice here.

It is also said that the relation of the judge to the criminal in a court is not intimate enough to represent the relationship of God to the sinner who is forgiven. In reply we must remember that God is not only the judge but also the substitute who identified himself with us and bore the penalty of our sin.

Some Important Facts

Evangelistic preaching on the Cross often ignores some important facts. First of all, it must be remembered that we are dealing throughout with the *work of God*. This does not mean that there is no divine reaction against sin which needs to be reconciled. Because it is all of God, it is *objective* to man. We must also note that it is the work of *the Triune God.* God the Father, God the Son and God the Holy Spirit were all involved in the atonement. It is not right to separate them in this activity.

There is no other *ground of forgiveness* except on the basis of what God has done for us in Christ. In these days of religious relativism, we need to declare with certainty the words of James Denney, "If God forgives at all, it must be in this way and in no other."

Though the atonement is universal in scope and in application, its efficacy is *conditioned* on its acceptance by faith. In his book *Upon the Earth*, Dr. D. T. Niles writes, "God made us. God loves us. Jesus died for us. Our trespasses are not counted. . . . These affirmations are true of all men and for all men whether they know them or not, like them or not, accept them or not." This universalism is not in accordance with the teaching of the Bible. The Bible makes a clear distinction between those who believe and those who do not believe.

In conclusion, it must be remembered that it is the Cross and not the crucifix which is the symbol of biblical Christianity. The Cross does not represent a Christ who died but a *Christ who died and rose again.* Forgiveness of sin is offered not through the crucified Savior, but through the living Savior who was crucified for our sins (Acts 10:39-43, 13:38). May we go forth in the power of the Holy Spirit offering the living Christ and his salvation to our generation.

Report of Group Discussion

Some attention was directed to the subject of man's part and God's part in salvation. Barry Moore (Canada) called attention to the linguistic distinction which exists in the New Testament itself: "except ye *be* converted" and "except ye repent." Ronald Ward (Canada) expressed the same distinction, in terms of the evangelical proclamation of the Gospel, between God's accomplished reconciliation of man to himself in the Cross and man's opportunity and obligation to repent and turn to God. "The gospel message must always be 'God has redeemed! Repent and believe!'," he said. A South African delegate attempted to express the difficult distinction between an eternal redemption accomplished in the mind of God "outside of time" and the actualizing and appropriating of that redemption in human history.

A number of delegates appealed for efforts to make the doctrine of redemption understandable to those theologically untrained. "People must see the relevancy of Christ's atonement for me today," said David Adeney (Hong Kong). "The atonement must be expressed in non-theological terms."

Reporter: *Jack Stowell*

FAITH AND THE GOSPEL

George R. Beasley-Murray

1. Christian faith is not simply belief in God. It is related to the Gospel.

Faith springs from hearing the message, and the message comes through the proclamation of the Christ (cf. Rom. 10:17). Faith is response to the Good News about the Christ.

This Good News revolves about two foci. On the one hand, Paul calls it "the word of the cross" (I Cor. 1:18, RSV). On the other hand, he epitomizes the Christian message as Christ raised from the dead (Rom. 10:9). Sometimes the early Gospel traditions bring these two together, e.g. Rom. 4:25, I Cor. 15:3-4. Observe that faith *believes* that these things are so, as in Rom. 10:9. Faith therefore has an intellectual content, and it consists of the Gospel proclamation of Christ crucified and risen as Lord and Savior.

To confess that Jesus is Lord goes beyond belief that he is Lord of all; it implies the confession, "Jesus is *my* Lord." This involves the will, as well as the intellect. Paul therefore frequently brings together faith and obedience, and sometimes equates them (consider Rom. 10:16 and his commission in Rom. 1:5).

Faith, however, goes beyond the intellect and the will. It includes trust. This is well illustrated in the fourth chapter of Romans.

Faith, then, involves acknowledgment of the truth of the Gospel, turning to the God revealed in Christ, trust in him who has opened the Kingdom of Heaven to all believers, and confidence in God's love and power in this and the coming ages. The whole man is engaged in the faith that turns to the Lord, even as the Lord redeems the whole man in spirit, soul and body (I Thess. 5:23).

2. To juxtapose faith and conversion calls to mind the relation between the human and the divine elements in faith, that is, the relation between faith and grace, or faith and the Spirit.

Here it should be noted that we hardly solve the problem by postulating conversion as man's work and regeneration as the Spirit's work (so Dr. Ockenga). Is there no activity of the Spirit in man's turning to God? Most theologians are prepared to answer "Yes." Some, however, wish to go further and assert that faith is *wholly* the product of grace. They call attention to Paul's habit of linking faith with the name of Christ in the genitive, as though he were referring to Christ as the author or subject of faith (see Gal.

DR. BEASLEY-MURRAY is the principal of Spurgeon's College in London, England.

2:20, "I live by the faith of the Son of God"). They urge that to lay down any condition for receiving salvation is to revert to a doctrine of works and to deny the Gospel. Viewing faith as the gift of God, they commonly regard regeneration as the *condition* for faith, rather than its consequence.

One can sympathize with the desire to glorify God by making every step of salvation to be wholly of grace. Yet this is not the whole story. The instances of Paul's speaking about "the faith of Jesus Christ" are capable of a different explanation. For example, while Gal. 2:16 could be translated, "No man is justified by doing what the law demands, but only through the faith of Jesus Christ," even a beginner in Greek knows that a genitive can express the object of the noun it qualifies; in this instance it means that a man is justified "through faith *directed to* Jesus Christ." The other examples of this construction should be similarly interpreted.

The claim that to regard faith as a condition for receiving salvation is a denial of the Gospel is to be rejected. The oppositions in Paul's writings are faith and works, or grace and works. The Apostle never opposes faith and grace, and he never classifies faith as a work of the law. Rather, he opposes the notion of salvation through deeds of the law by his Gospel of salvation by grace through faith.

The idea that faith is given *after* regeneration is equally inadmissible. A cardinal fault here is to assume that regeneration can be isolated from other aspects of salvation and from the Person who regenerates. Regeneration signifies entry into the "regeneration," which is the new age or the new world (Matthew 19:28). It takes place when the Holy Spirit unites a man with the Lord, who by his resurrection initiated the new creation. Paul expressed the thought without the word when he spoke about a man becoming a new creation in Christ (II Cor. 5:17). To assert that this can happen to a man before he believes, and in order that he may believe, is surely to set the Gospel on its head.

In this matter of the relationship of grace to faith we have a crucial intersecting point of divine sovereignty and human freedom; at this stage of history we ought to know better than to deny the reality of either element. It is difficult to improve on Adolf Schlatter's statement "In faith two characteristics are inherent: it is worked by God and willed by man."

3. A third feature of faith has become so controversial that some participants at this conference may hesitate to discuss it.

Modern evangelism proceeds on the assumption that faith should be confessed. This is right. Romans 10:9 shares this assumption. But every scholar knows that Rom. 10:9 reflects a confession of faith *made in baptism*. And there lies the problem. In the New Testament Church, faith was confessed in baptism, and baptism was the high point of conversion. In modern evangelism, baptism must never be mentioned.

The difficulties in attempting to remedy this state of affairs are obvious, but I wonder if perhaps we do not exaggerate them. The New Testament reflects a missionary situation in which the Church confronted a hostile world with a Gospel that was real news. But are we not rapidly moving into a comparable situation all over the world? In many areas the churches are tiny minorities — little islands in enormous oceans; in them the problem of rebaptism hardly arises, and surely in other areas an agreed policy (as distinct from theology!) ought to be possible.

The desirability of making this clear to those outside the Church is obvious. It is right biblically and it would bring clarity to the Gospel.

If we want apostolic mission, we should seek it in its totality, not in a choice of elements that suit a quiet life among sensitive ecclesiastics and theologians. Only the apostolic Gospel is good enough for sinners perishing for lack of it, and only that Gospel will bring the Church into the fullness of blessing for which it was created.

A TRINITARIAN FAITH
Jarl Wahlström

The disciples of Christ have always been a small minority. The Master referred to this when he said: "Ye are the salt of the earth" (Matt. 5:13). As long as this minority has possessed the right kind of faith, it has been a mighty power in the world. The first witnesses were only a handful, yet they turned the world upside down.

If we are to extend the Kingdom of God in these days, yes, if we are to keep the field, as far as evangelical Christianity is concerned, we need this kind of faith. We need a new vision of the omnipotence of God. In our consideration of the nature of faith we will discuss what it means to believe in an *Almighty God*. We will discuss faith in God the Father Almighty, in God the Son Almighty and in God the Holy Spirit Almighty.

It is necessary to consider two aspects of faith. Faith may be either in-tellectual — i.e. believing some*thing* with the understanding, or it may be heart faith, i.e. the act of trusting some *one*, or faith in action.

1. Faith in God the Father Almighty

"I believe in God the Father Almighty, maker of heaven and earth." The first article of the Apostles' Creed means faith in the Creator, in the Law-giver and in the Father.

"In the beginning God created the heavens and the earth." We fix our faith on this fact: God is the eternal source of the universe. This conviction has an important practical application. God is unchangeable; the Reason and Power that created the world are at our disposal. Faith in the Almighty Creator means security.

We believe in God as law-giver. Contrary to modern thinking, we are convinced that he has every right to lay down the standards of human behavior. The Ten Commandments can never become obsolete. This gives us courage to preach sin and judgment, and this is necessary if we are to proclaim the free gift of Grace.

Faith in God as the Father Almighty means a conviction that he is not only able to guide and help, but that he is also willing to do so. The Master's favorite name for God was "The Father." Faith in the Fatherhood of God implies complete surrender of everything into his strong, loving hands, complete committal of ourselves to his care.

In these days of fear and uncertainty, it is important that ministers of the Gospel possess and exhibit the serenity of heart and mind that is the

BRIGADIER WAHLSTRÖM is the principal of The Salvation Army Training College in Helsinki, Finland.

outcome of trust in God the Father. This faith will give us freedom to proclaim the Good News.

2. *Faith in God the Son Almighty*

"I believe in Jesus Christ his only Son our Lord . . ."

The results of our evangelical work will very largely depend on our faith in the truths contained in the second article, which occupies a central position in the Creed.

". . . conceived by the Holy Ghost, born of the Virgin Mary . . ."

I am convinced that if we do not believe literally in the supernatural birth of Christ, many other important things will collapse. "Who is he that overcometh the world, but he that believeth that Jesus is the Son of God" (I John 5:5).

". . . was crucified, dead and buried . . ."

The vicarious death of Christ was efficacious and universal. Our faith in such an atonement encourages us to offer forgiveness in his name to any one who truly repents of his sins. And forgiveness is what men and women need more than anything else.

". . . the third day He rose again from the dead . . ."

A professor of physics told me he could not believe in the supernatural resurrection of Jesus. His theory was that Jesus did not really die on the Cross, but was put into the tomb apparently dead and possessed enough strength to come to full life again and to gain his freedom. Many other theories have challenged this truth that is so vital to us. We are positive in our faith and declare with Paul: "But now is Christ risen from the dead . . ." (I Cor. 15:20). I feel that the resurrection ought to be emphasized much more than is usually the case in our evangelical preaching.

". . . ascended into heaven . . ."

Our faith in a living Christ, who stands before the Father interceding for us is a mighty impetus to pray, to preach and to work. Even as we here in Berlin are praying for a world revival, the Almighty Son is making intercession.

". . . from thence shall come . . ."

To put into action our faith in the Second Advent of our Lord means to "look eagerly for the coming of the Day of God and [to] work to hasten it" (II Pet. 3:12, NEB). We must not leave the preaching of this truth only to certain millennial movements.

3. Faith in God the Holy Spirit Almighty

"I believe in the Holy Ghost."

We believe intellectually in the omnipotence of the Spirit. Yet sometimes our religion is so very weak. Why? Perhaps our faith is too vague. We hear preachers speak of the Spirit as a mere influence or attribute of God instead of a person. But the main reason for our weakness is that we have not put our faith into action by opening the doors of our hearts and churches to the fullness of the Spirit.

It has been interesting to hear about the new emphasis upon the Holy Spirit and the modern charismatic movement. We have also heard amazing stories of reborn men in our day. There is the work among young drug-addicts in New York for example, related in the book "The Cross and the Switchblade." More could happen if our faith were more practical.

Hugh Redwood writes that the main reason why religion has lost its hold on the public mind is that religious leaders have "bucked the subject of holiness and bucked the subject of healing" (Hugh Redwood: Kingdom Come, pp. 109–110). There is much in what he says. Holiness is the fruit of the Spirit (Gal. 5:22, 23). And healing is among the gifts of the Spirit (I Cor. 12:28-31). A practical faith in the Almighty Spirit will give us both.

If the results of the work of the Spirit — regeneration, holiness and healing — abound in the Church, then revival will not be far away.

Faith in God means complete surrender of body, mind and soul to him and constant trust in his power to save, sanctify and keep, and, moreover, to use individuals and churches according to his good will.

A NEW LIFE PRINCIPLE
Addison H. Leitch

Hebrews 11:1 reads, "Now faith is the assurance of things hoped for, the conviction of things not seen" (RSV). This verse is, I suggest, the closest thing we have to a biblical definition of faith. It is a nice question, however, just how definitive this definition is. Translators and versions approach the Greek which underlies this definition in numerous ways. The King James Version "Faith is the substance of things hoped for, the evidence of things not seen." In the New English Bible, we read, "Faith gives substance (or assurance) to our hopes, and makes us certain of realities we do not see." The three definitions in these three versions (Revised Standard, King James, New English Bible) seem to turn on the question of how objective or subjective we want faith to be.

The problem rests on the interpretation of some very difficult Greek words. There is, first of all, the word *hupostasis* — our old friend out of the trinitarian controversies — which raises all kinds of questions about what anyone means when he is talking about substance or substantial. The word *elegkos* also is capable of wide interpretation, meaning, among other things, "a proof," or, again, "that by which something else is tested," or, more specifically, the way by which we prove invisible things, either by things that are visible or by a conviction of the mind. This is all by way of saying that if we are looking for a definition of the nature of faith, we are forced to run the gamut of a variety of versions and translations, which, in turn, rest on at least the two words, *hupostasis* and *elegkos*, both of which are difficult to define sharply, are capable of a wide variety of translations and are more open to interpretation and illustration than to definition. Any definition of faith, judging by the brief and simple one in Hebrews, soon becomes a paraphrase, or a paragraph, or a sermon, or a book!

Hupostasis means substance, but just how much substance can one put into that idea? Do we mean "stuff" or "matter"? Are we talking about a "thing," or the "thing-in-itself" that Kant thought necessarily lies behind sense experience? Anyone acquainted with the history of thought, East or West, or the history of Christian theology in the West, especially in the debates of the Early Church, knows how evasive this word can be. And yet faith is defined as a *hupostasis*. The same sort of thing can be said about the less-known word *elegkos*. Do we mean external evidence, or internal assurance, or conviction apart from any sense experience? When Job says, "I *know* that my Redeemer liveth," we are talking about inner con-

DR. LEITCH is assistant to the president of Tarkio College in Tarkio, Missouri, USA.

viction. When James says, "Faith without works is dead," the works are surely in the area of sense experience. When we participate in the Lord's Supper, the question of interpretation swings from the "trans-substance" of the Roman Catholics to the Real Presence of the Calvinists, and both talk about the visible signs of invisible realities. And both in some fashion discuss the Lord's body by the eyes of faith.

Personally, I like the blunt translation of the King James Version, which seems to throw the weight over on the side of physical evidence. Thus, our key words are translated *substance* and *evidence*. "Substance," at least in the English understanding of the word, means something one can lay hold of with the hand. And "evidence," at least in the English use of the word, means a something that is evident to the physical senses. If we hold to this substantial (i.e. physical, evidential) meaning of our key words, then faith can be understood best, it seems to me, as a two-world word. It operates in the area of that which is substance and that which is of the nature of evidence. And it operates also in the world of things unseen and still hoped for. Faith, then, gathers to itself the truth as well as the mystery of both worlds. Things that a man has faith in may be physically unseen and still hoped for in terms of future time. And yet these very unseen and hoped for realities give a set, a quality, a direction to his life, all of which are substance and evidence of the unseen world yet to be fulfilled in his life. It is indeed true that he "walks by faith," but he does walk. "One step enough for me" at least means that he takes the next step. And he takes the next step in substance and with evidence in terms of things hoped for and unseen. It is only as we swing back and forth between the world of substance and the unseen world that I think it is possible for us to understand the nature of faith.

Other Scripture verses jump to mind as illustrations of this particular approach to the understanding of Christian faith. "It is not yet evident what we shall be, but we shall be like him, for we shall see him as he is." Or, again, "I am the Alpha and the Omega, the Beginning and the End." "He that hath seen me hath seen the Father," and in another context, "Flesh and blood did not reveal this to you, but my Father."

What is being said in all this in Christian terms is that things hoped for and unseen are laid hold of by man or lay hold of him. What is a Christian? Perhaps we could say it this way in this context: A Christian is one who accepts Christ, but what does that mean? Christ is living and dynamic, infinite and eternal, personal and, of course, much more. Are we saying that someone who "accepts Christ" grasps and understands him in his person and in his eternal glory? To raise such an idea is to dismiss it. What does a person do when he accepts Christ? Not much more, it seems to me, than the taking of the first step, the one step open to him in terms of what he does grasp of the nature of Christ. He accepts, in effect, that from this time forward the clue to all reality, here and hereafter, lies in the Living

Word. Much is unseen. Very much is hoped for. But like the Apostle Paul, the new believer has no notion that he has "attained" but he presses on from this point. Christianity is not an attainment, but a relationship; not a point of arrival, but a sense of direction; not a success, but a commitment. The man who has accepted Christ begins to give substance and evidence in his daily walk of the things he hopes for and that are yet unseen. In some fashion the things of God are brought to bear on the affairs of man, and what we say about "new birth" or "a new creation in Christ" means at least that the new regenerative life principle of the new Christian is that he has laid hold on this reality, or, better, that this reality has laid hold on him. If we remind ourselves that faith is a gift, we must remember also that grace is a gift; that Christians do not have just another ideal or another vision, but they have a living Lord, who not only sets before them what ought to be or can be, but promises to walk with them toward the goal which is fulfilled in him. Thus he really is "the Alpha and the Omega, the Beginning and the End," the One toward whom we move and yet the starting place and the process. As Paul would say, "For me to live is Christ." This, I take it, is the nature of the Christian faith, the daily walk, constantly motivated, sustained, enhanced, and guided by the very One who is the goal of the whole process.

An old preacher once described faith for me as "a man plowing." Things unseen and hoped for are the crops that will grow next spring and summer. Meanwhile, the substance and evidence rest in the furrows which the man turns over. One would not guess, looking at plowed ground, what a wheat crop would look like, yet apart from the plowed ground, now in substance and evidence, things hoped for and unseen will not come to pass until next summer.

James makes clear to us that we show our faith by our works, and this idea is evident in all that we have tried to say here. For strong support for this whole thesis, continue in the eleventh chapter of Hebrews from which we have taken our definition. Once the definition has been established, the rest of the chapter is illustration. As we have already suggested, faith is more clear from illustration than from definition. Note how this famous chapter proceeds. By faith Noah *did* something. By faith Abraham *did* something. And finally, in the great summation, "and what shall we more say? . . ."

All the heroes of the faith put into action things unseen and hoped for, and yet, as the writer to the Hebrews so wonderfully expresses it, they would not reach their goal completely, because, in some strange fashion, they need our works of faith toward that same goal. "These all died," and we may too, unfulfilled in any perfection except the perfection of the One to whom we are committed. Thus, surrounded by this great "cloud of witnesses," we today run the race which is set before us, "looking unto Jesus, the Author and the Finisher of faith." And there it is again. We fix our eyes on Jesus, who is the goal, but who is also the Author, the Initiator, the File Leader, the Companion of every day's walk, through the days of our years.

Report of Group Discussion

To relate the theme of the session to *world* evangelism, three questions were posed:

1. Where does faith differ from mystical experience as it is stressed, for example, in Hinduism and Buddhism? How does faith meet the new (and old) emphasis of mysticism?

2. What is the relationship of faith to repentance? How do both relate to restitution?

3. What is the relationship of baptism to faith?

A general approach was made to these three questions by many who contrasted non-Christian with Christian mysticism. At its best, mysticism means union with God and, in one form at least, is at the heart of Paul's preaching. At the same time however, biblical mysticism is linked to the facts of Christianity (the Cross and Resurrection above all) and to the Scriptures. The mysticism of the non-Christian religions is far different, being for the most part a doctrine of human salvation by self-discipline.

One of the differences between Islam and Christianity lies in the object of faith peculiar to Christianity — Jesus Christ. It is not the degree of faith but the person which is important, many said.

Reporter: *Ted W. Engstrom*

ASPECTS OF CHRIST'S REDEEMING WORK
Jean-Paul Benoit

In the Bible the concepts of justification and sanctification express aspects of the redeeming work of Christ in man.

To justify means to make just, or to reckon as just. Only God is just, and the whole Bible insists on this righteousness of God which is expressed either by his holiness or by his abhorrence of all uncleanness. The Lord is too pure to allow evil to come into his presence. As for man who finds himself face to face with God (Isa. 6), he is thrown, because of his unrighteousness into the deepest fear; no one can see God and live! The drama of the Cross moreover reveals to the eyes of all — believers and unbelievers alike — the blind and cruel baseness of man who despises and kills the just.

One day God reckoned the cup was full and overflowing. His patience was at an end (Rom. 3:25). His righteous sword would fall, justice would be established and the guilty punished.

But because the poison of sin had invaded all mankind, and punishment might annihilate everything, God "invented" (Péguy) a new justice. He took the whole matter upon himself. His only Son, pure and just, offered himself in the culprits' place. The prophets had foretold this and Jesus took it up again: the only just wanted to be the only guilty. He was made sin for us. He became the serpent, the likeness of Satan and was "lifted up" for the salvation of all. Perfect righteousness was accomplished.

Now therefore the just God must forgive us. On the Cross God allowed the arms of his justice to be tied, in order that by opening his arms of mercy, he may "impute" to us the righteousness of the man Jesus. If I had to appear tonight in the presence of the holy God, what should I offer in my defense? If just now I am claiming God's help, who am I to dare to summon him? Nothing; I am nothing, and I have nothing to say but this: "Lord, Thy Son died for me." God has promised to receive all who come to him with the protection and covering of the white robe of the Righteous One. God looks upon them as righteous and justifies them because of Jesus Christ. Therefore I can stand before God "with my head up," said Luther. Should I doubt his Word? Should I refuse the Grace that he grants me? It is enough for me to accept it. This faith alone is sufficient. Besides, what else could I offer him except my praise?

Such Grace immediately impels me to humility and a vital interest and hope for any other human being, however wretched and worthless he may be. For him, for her, Christ died. In the name of Jesus I can stretch out a brotherly hand to him. It is the forgiveness which God grants me,

PASTOR BENOIT is the president of the French Evangelical Alliance in Paris, France.

that peace which his justice has signed with me in the blood of his Son, that justification which gives me confidence and compels me to despise no one, that becomes for that wretch as for myself the strength to lift him up from his drabness. He is no longer an outcast. The Son of God made himself his brother. The love of Christ constrains us and draws up both of us to him.

The redeeming work of a God of love cannot stop here. He cannot be content to rub out as with a stroke of a sponge (even if it was hard for him) the dark picture of my past iniquities. A new bright page must be written.

Moreover, if we consider the Cross where Jesus died, that Cross covered with our iniquities, we see that this Cross inspires Paul the apostle with the image not only of God's forgiveness by means of the final and all sufficient sacrifice accomplished by the silent Lamb, but also of the triumphal chariot (Col. 2:15; II Cor. 2:14), to which he binds his enemies with chains and makes a show of them to the world (an allusion to the Roman practice of the "triumph" which the Senate had power to grant to a general after a dazzling victory). Does not Jesus use a similar picture with Nicodemus who failed to grasp how he could be "born again." The Lord recalls the serpent, the image of Satan, which was lifted up in the desert by Moses: "If a serpent had bitten any man, when he beheld the serpent of brass, he lived" (Num. 21:8-9).

Here again the simple look of faith is enough. The victory over sin, won by Christ, is, as it were, infused or transmitted to us. And we rediscover John Calvin insisting on the grace of the law and obedience next to the grace of forgiveness. Like John Wesley and the Salvation Army, and so many others that call us to holiness in the name of the Bible, we will sing the work of "sanctification": already accomplished in the death of Jesus by his victory over "dominions and powers;" in his resurrection which allows us to live as being "risen;" and in the gift of his Spirit, whose fruits recall the radiance of Christ himself, who now is "living in our hearts by faith" (cf. Eph. 3:17, Phillips).

Today, many declare that it is no longer possible to offer to the non-Christian multitudes this proclamation of justification and sanctification. In the first place, the Church has not shown and does not show in her life these lovely fruits. And then, who today bothers himself with the forgiveness of God? Who admits sin, who believes in the devil and hell? The ambitions of modern man are efficiency, knowledge, freedom and social justice in the world.

Is this true? A famous psychiatrist tells us that in Paris many sick people today are fretting with anxiety, losing their reason, being haunted with feelings of "justice." We feel, we know ourselves to be guilty, and we are afraid that one day punishment will come. Such an obsession is all the more dangerous as man no longer believes in God and his forgiveness. How dare we, then, in this century where suicides and mental disease are on the increase, not proclaim: "If your conscience condemns you, God is greater than your conscience, and he knows all things and will forgive you"? Modern man needs this inward peace as much, and more than ever before.

As for man's regeneration, if our century has been able to see because of its very science and techniques the events of two world wars, gas chambers, and a recurrence of torture, is not, because of this accelerated power, the great problem of the hour that of man, his conscience, his moral ideal and the strength which will allow him to live up to it? Others may advocate their ideals and their methods. We offer as our model Jesus, and as our victorious strength for regeneration his work accomplished for us, and offered to each one.

SANCTIFICATION, THE FRUIT OF JUSTIFICATION

W. Stanford Reid

Although some Christians do not recognize the fact, justification and sanctification are two aspects or the two sides of the one coin of divine redemption. While they are related, they are quite different in character and in their purposes. At the same time, they do not conflict with, but rather complement each other. In fact, we may say that sanctification grows out of justification; it is the fruit of justification and fulfills the objective of justification. In true biblical evangelism, therefore, it is very necessary to remember this fact, inasmuch as confusing the two in time past has often disastrously beclouded men's understanding of the Gospel. One of the great accomplishments of Luther and of the other sixteenth century reformers was to make this difference absolutely clear.

Sanctification Differs from Justification

The essence of justification is to declare someone who is accused of a crime to be not guilty. It is a forensic term and comes from the law courts. It relates primarily to one's status before the law. In the case of the Christian, the term "justification" refers to his position before the law of God. God regards him as being without condemnation, and therefore free from the penalties and terrors of the law (Rom. 5:1; 8:1). At the same time justification has nothing to say concerning the Christian's inward spiritual condition (Rom. 4:5; 5:6); it deals only with his outward position before the righteous demands and standards of God's own holiness. The Christian being declared just, all his sins are passed over, are forgiven, so that he is no longer under judgment.

Sanctification, on the other hand, deals not with the matter of man's legal position, but rather with his actual spiritual condition. Furthermore, sanctification has no real parallel in the natural world, for it is a dynamic, even miraculous, act on the part of God. As the root meaning of the term indicates, sanctification refers to God's action in making man holy. God re-orients the Christian, in order that he may no longer seek his own way and will, but rather may endeavor to do the will of God. This comes about only because of a radical transformation in man himself, that brings about a changed outlook and changed principle of action. Man now seeks the holiness of God in all that he does, and spurns sin as that which is contrary to

DR. REID is a professor and head of the Department of History at Wellington College in the University of Guelph, Ontario, Canada.

his own nature. Not his legal status, but his inward state is the subject of man's sanctification.

Sanctification Results from Justification

The Christian is justified, not by his own works or character, but solely because Christ has paid the penalty for his sins (Rom. 5:6; Col. 2:13-15); it was to this end that Christ came into the world. Furthermore, in Christ's life, death and resurrection, the Christian — by God's sovereign design and decree — was united to him. Consequently, the Christian is counted as having suffered with Christ on the Cross (Rom. 5:10-21; Gal. 2:19, 20). He attains this justification, however, only by appropriating for himself the work of Christ on his behalf. By faith, he lays hold on that which God in Christ has done for him with the result that before God's law he is justified and forgiven all his sins (Eph. 2:1-9; Col. 1:20-23). Never again does he come under condemnation, for he is justified forever through faith in Christ (Rom. 8:1).

The Christian's faith, however, is not something which he himself creates, for he cannot originate his own faith from an evil and sinful heart. Faith is the gift of God (Eph. 2:1-10) that results from the regenerating action of the Holy Spirit (John 3:5). When a man is "born again," however, thus becoming "a new creation" (II Cor. 5:17), the Spirit does not then leave him to his own devices to achieve holiness by his own efforts. The Spirit continues to work within him, that he may grow in grace and in the likeness — into the image — of Jesus Christ (Phil. 2:12, 13; Gal. 3:1-5; I Cor. 2:11-16; Rom. 8:28 ff.). In this way the Christian is sanctified by the Spirit, his inward man being renewed day by day.

Sanctification Fulfills Justification

To what end is a man justified before God? The immediate answer is, that man may find forgiveness before God who acts always according to justice (Rom. 3:26). Forgiveness, however, involves more. He whom God forgives enters into the Kingdom of God, into the household of faith in order to become one of God's people upon earth. His citizenship in the heavenly Kingdom involves the concomitant duty of showing forth the glory of his King. Thus the ultimate purpose of the Christian's justification is the manifestation of God's glory in all things (Rom. 9:19 ff; I Cor. 10:31; Eph. 6).

The fulfillment of this ultimate purpose of justification comes in the Christian's sanctification. Christians can manifest the glory of God only as they become conformed to the Lord Jesus Christ. This is not a matter primarily of outward acts and deportment, but rather of inner conformity in spiritual life and character (Col. 3:4). Outward manifestation then results. But the Christian grows only as the Spirit works within him, so that he increasingly lays aside the weights and the sins which so easily beset him in order that he may grow into the fullness of his Lord (Heb. 12:1, 2). In this way, and by these means, his sanctification redounds to the glory of God.

As the Christian grows in his faith and sanctification, so his witness becomes stronger. But his witness is not merely something verbal, for words alone are not enough. True, the Spirit uses a man's words, but he uses the whole man. For this reason words must reflect life, and life bears its witness only as it becomes conformed to the image of Jesus Christ. Unfortunately, so many who would evangelize the world today present unattractive and even repulsive lives which tend to contradict their message of the love and grace of God in Christ. The proclamation of the Gospel requires not only the Word of divine forgiveness, but also the evidence of a sanctified life.

CHRIST IN US
Paul S. Rees

Martin Luther left the distinct impression that the ability to distinguish properly between the Law and the Gospel, and at the same time to relate them rightly to each other is just about the summit of theological art. Some would say that an equally admirable skill is that of drawing right distinctions between God's gracious *acceptance* of a sinner in justification and his equally gracious *assimilation* of a forgiven sinner to his holy will and service in sanctification.

To this concern we now add, in the context of the present discussion, another dimension of meaning. The question is raised: How are these two aspects of the Gospel related to evangelism?

1. First of all let us consider some historical perspectives that are useful to our purpose: (1) the Reformation perspective, (2) the pietist, and (3) the perfectionist.

a. The Lutheran *Small Catechism* gives the following simple summary of the Reformation view of justification: "We confess that we receive forgiveness of sins and are justified before God, not by our works, but by Grace, for Christ's sake, through faith."

But central as it was in the witness of the Reformers, justification by faith was never regarded by them as the whole of salvation. They saw, as we their heirs must see, that Jesus, the living, dying, rising Redeemer, came that we "might have *life*, and have it more abundantly."

But the moment we speak of the "new life" of the Christian we have left (although not abandoned) what is purely forensic and have invaded the realm of the experiential and evidential.

Thus, we may say that within the perspective of Reformed theology, allowing for differences of approach and stress, justification is seen as *Christ for us* in the virtue and value of his atonement, while sanctification is seen as *Christ in us* in the vitality of his Holy Spirit and in the vocation of Christian holiness, it being understood that we never leave the one in order to embrace the other.

b. The pietism of early nineteenth century European church history may be thought of as a protest against the barrenness of a justification that does not sanctify. That is, where the doctrine of Grace is one-sidedly stressed as assuring the sinner's renewal so as to walk in "newness of life," the Church will grow statistically fat and spiritually lean. Historically, pietism is the revolt against Christian nominalism.

DR. REES is Vice-President at Large of World Vision, Inc., in Monrovia, California, USA.

Pietism must likewise be seen as a protest against anti-nomianism. Both earlier and later pietists rightly objected to a misuse of Luther's bold cry to children of the Reformation to "sin boldly."

In our own day, a similar protest is lodged against Karl Barth and the dialectical theologians. Indeed Koberle notes that "the continual attacks on pietism" by the advocates of dialectical theology "are in themselves the most abominable Pharisaism."

To be sure, pietism has had its own perils. It has not always been aware of its own narrowness. It nevertheless must be understood in terms of those situations from which it sprang in protest and witness.

c. The third perspective from which we may view justification and sanctification is that of *perfectionism*.

Bishop Stephen Neill in *Christian Holiness* has some stringent remarks concerning those perfectionists who claim too much within the ample folds of the covenant of grace. He concludes by saying however, "And yet, when every possible exegetical deduction has been made, this exacting, perfectionist strain does remain in the pages of the New Testament."

Consider the definition of sanctification as given in the *Westminster Shorter Catechism*: "The work of God's free grace whereby we are renewed in the whole man after the image of God, and are enabled more and more to die unto sin, and live unto righteousness." It might be asked whether this gradualism is the *sole* category of meaning within which we are to understand the New Testament message of God's sanctifying work in the life of the Christian.

A common procedure is to quote St. Paul in support of a completely gradualistic concept of sanctification, or to use a related term, of perfection. We appeal to Philippians 3:12 (RSV), "Not that I have already obtained this or am already perfect," and note that the Apostle says this at the end of a long life of service. But to leave the matter there (as is usually the case) is hardly fair to Paul or to those seriously concerned with an important aspect of theological truth. Actually only three verses later the same Apostle declares: "Let those of us who are mature" (the revisers have chosen a variant rendering of the same Greek word as we have in verse 12) "be thus minded," that is, let them be characterized by a "this-one-thing-I-do" disposition.

Whether one prefers the word "maturity" or the word "perfection" the exegetical concern in this whole passage remains the same. It is too seldom realized, and too seldom expounded, that Paul was at once perfectionist and imperfectionist. The sanctification begun in regeneration and never finished as long as we are in this "vale of soul-making" admits, nevertheless, of a recognizable stage from which the immature pass to maturity — a maturity, it should be quickly added, that leads on to ever greater maturity.

To recapitulate, we need the Reformed perspective to keep clear the inseparable correlation between justification and sanctification; we need the pietist perspective to keep in focus the subjective work of the Holy Spirit, as the counterweight of the objective "finished" work of Christ in crucifixion and resurrection; and, guardedly, we need the perfectionist perspective to fix our eyes on the goal of Christlikeness, a goal that may be reached proximately in the single-mindedness of the mature but that remains, nevertheless, a "flying goal" whose further advances beckon us from whatever spiritual hilltop or valley we may be experiencing.

2. *But what, we may ask, is the bearing of all this on evangelism?*

a. Let us remember that both justification and sanctification, though each in a different way, have a "here and now" significance. There is an immediacy about them that partakes of the Evangel. This is owing to the fact that they are of Grace. They are by faith. They presuppose the initiative, the prevenience, the election, and the faithfulness of the triune God.

b. If our understanding of justification and sanctification is substantially what we have here indicated, it follows that evangelism must be carried on *within* the Christian community as well as beyond it. As Professor T. A. Kantonen has observed, "It is dangerous to presume that all church members are regenerate. Even a Lutheran or Anglican view of regeneration in infant baptism requires that provision be made for an experience of "conversion," (call it "confirmation" or whatever) which brings home to believers the assurance of Christ's forgiveness, acceptance and peace.

c. It must be seen that a Church of immature, static (rather than growing) Christians, is a poor and handicapped instrument for outreaching evangelism. We have yet to plumb the full depths of meaning and potency disclosed to the body of Christ on the Day of Pentecost. There remain, and always will, points of ambiguity and therefore differences of interpretation in the biblical record. But nothing can alter the fact that something happened to the disciples that transformed them from being units in an association to being components of a fellowship, from being self-seeking to being Christ-centered, from being stricken with fear to being dauntless in courage. The result was an evangelism that remains the marvel of the centuries.

If the Church today is to awake to the full authority and splendor of her evangelizing mission, she must realize that her evangelism consists as truly of what she *is* as it does of what she *says*. She is Christ's holy presence in the world of the unholy, different from the world because delivered from it, yet all the while redemptively linked with it. If the Pharisee's superior glint is in her eye, she is useless. If the slave's apron is wrapped about her for service, she is authentically fruitful.

Report of Group Discussion

It was striking in a congress on evangelism, in which justification is naturally a dominant theme, that when justification and sanctification were considered together the whole discussion period revolved around the latter. In the opinion of some observers, the delegates came with the conviction that the evangelist must live a sanctified life, the sanctified lives of his converts being the full proof of his ministry, and that the double threat of neo-paganism in the world and antinomianism in the church add urgency to the latter concept.

Again and again I Corinthians 1:30 was cited, "Christ Jesus who of God is made unto us . . . sanctification. . . ." Although growth in sanctification may confirm assurance, the Christian is not to trust in his sanctification. He is to trust in Christ alone.

Delegates also agreed that the sanctifying power of Jesus Christ operates in the believer by his Spirit through the Gospel; the Word of God therefore is the basis of growth in Christian maturity. More particularly, it is the message of Christ crucified and risen which provides the motivation and dynamic for a holy Christian life.

Most speakers felt that the redirecting of the Christian man is a lifelong process never completed in the temporal order. At the same time, however, several called attention to epochal events in the process of sanctification. J. Gilchrist Lawson's *Deeper Experiences of Famous Christians* was cited as a helpful description of these events in the lives of Christians of every age and from every section of the Church.

The relation of sanctification to evangelism drew concluding comments. The peripatetic, as over against the pastoral evangelist, cannot be expected to emphasize sanctification. At the same time, all his preaching must be in the context of the holiness of God. If this background is not present, evangelism may result only in a sentimental relationship with Jesus.

Reporter: *Ian Rennie*

THE THEOLOGY OF REGENERATION
J. Wayte Fulton, Jr.

"Jesus answered and said unto him, Verily, verily, I say unto thee, Except a man be born again, he cannot see the kingdom of God. . . . That which is born of the flesh is flesh; and that which is born of the Spirit is spirit. Marvel not that I said unto thee, Ye must be born again." (*John 3:3, 6, 7*).

1. Introduction

In stark simplicity Jesus said to Nicodemus, "Ye must be born again." Neither nobility of birth, nor degree of education, nor attainments in morality can bring us to the Kingdom of God. A new life is utterly essential to salvation and only by this gift of the Holy Spirit do we become "partakers of the heavenly calling," and "members of the general assembly and church of the first born whose names are written in heaven."

To evangelicals of whatever persuasion this has always been the teaching of the Word of God, and as such has been affirmed in one way or another in the classic creeds of Christendom.

2. The agency in regeneration

The Scriptures teach that the agency in regeneration is the Holy Spirit. To this third person of the blessed Trinity has been committed in the divine economy the application of the work of redemption so fully accomplished by Christ. Eternally proceeding from the Father and the Son, and possessing all of the attributes of deity, he is a true and holy Person, continually present in the life of the people of God, the strength and the honor and the power of the Church.

He perfects and consummates the work of the Father in creation and redemption. As the author of Scripture, he is the Spirit of Truth; as the Illuminator of the darkling mind, he is the Spirit of Light; as the divine energy at work in the world, he is the Spirit of Burning; as the vindicator of the majesty of God's law, he is the Spirit of Holiness; as the strength and sustainer of the family of the redeemed, he is the Spirit of Power, and as the voice that speaks in the act of resurrection, he is the Spirit of Life.

3. The nature of regeneration

With humility and gladness, let us turn to the mystery and the wonder of regeneration, the mighty act of the Holy Spirit. When we seek to define

DR. FULTON is the minister of Shenandoah Presbyterian Church in Miami, Florida.

regeneration, we need to remember that in the history of Christian doctrine, it has been considered both in the broad sense of the application of salvation to the whole man, and (in more modern times) in a narrow and restricted sense as the initial, instantaneous act of God's grace by which and in which the sinner is brought from the darkness of sin and death to the brightness and blessedness of the new life in Christ.

The Roman Catholic church seems historically to have regarded regeneration in the larger connotation as embracing the whole of man's salvation, and in doing so has confounded justification and sanctification. The early Reformers also generally conceived of regeneration and conversion in more or less synonymous terms. This was true of Calvin (Institutes: Book III, Chapter 3, Paragraph 9).

Shedd calls attention to the fact that this generalized concept of regeneration led to confusion in understanding the application of salvation to the heart of the believer. He properly notes that regeneration and conversion are two distinct words, and that two separate and distinct ideas are associated with them in the teaching of Scripture.

In more recent times, Hodge, Dabney, Strong, Warfield, Kuyper, Bavinck, and Shedd more or less adopt this proper distinction between conversion and regeneration. Regeneration is an act, conversion is an activity. Regeneration is an instantaneous change from spiritual death to spiritual life. It is an act of the Holy Spirit in which the disposition of the soul is made holy, and the believer is thereby enabled freely to embrace Christ as he is offered in the Gospel.

Since God in the Holy Spirit is the initiator of salvation in the act of regeneration, the "election" to eternal life is not conditioned upon any foreseen faith, merit, or good works on the part of the believer, but upon a sovereign act of free, unmerited grace on the part of God. Salvation is therefore wholly of grace. Hence, man does not "come and accept Christ;" he "accepts Christ" and comes.

In the act of regeneration man is necessarily passive and even unaware of the divine activity. He can no more recall the precise moment and the circumstances attending his spiritual birth than he can recall the circumstances of his physical birth. But the effects he will most surely know. Whether his conversion, as evidenced by godly repentance and saving faith, is dramatically sudden or quietly gradual, he will be able to say: "I know a man in Christ, he liveth in me."

Thus the order in the application of salvation would seem to be: election, effectual calling, regeneration, repentance, faith, justification, sanctification, glorification.

4. The necessity of regeneration

Why then is regeneration so necessary? Two reasons will suffice: first, the condition of man in his lost estate, and second, the character of God who is holy and just. If man is lost, and not able to do anything about his unregenerate condition, then only God can act and only God can save. And God does. Only as man gains God's perspective, will he be fitted for a life with God. To enjoy heaven as a place, man must possess heaven as a condition of life.

Man, like "all Gaul," is divided into three parts: he thinks, he feels, he acts. In the act of regeneration man's understanding is divinely illuminated, his heart is filled with a holy fire, his will is renewed so that he is able to appropriate Christ as Savior and Lord. Regeneration touches the whole of man.

Moreover, the character of God demands regeneration, for "without holiness, no man can see him." Sin is essentially lawlessness, and if ever we are to know the order and stability of the blameless family in heaven, we must be imbued with the Spirit of Christ and conformed to the image of Christ.

5. The results of regeneration

Consequences of great significance for the salvation of the individual, and for the hope of society will flow from the fountain of regeneration.

Usually we look upon births with little interest. They are tabulated as prosaic statistics of day to day occurrence, not too important except to the parents and relatives. But the birth of a baby may have tremendous significance.

Like the birth of a child, the coming of the Kingdom is never very dramatic nor ostentatious, but the Church which is to overcome all opposition and to be established as an everlasting dominion began and continues to grow with an act of birth—the new birth, the new life which by the power of the Holy Spirit is hid with Christ in God. Out of a moral and spiritual graveyard, he will continue to bring forth the flowers and the fruits of the Kingdom of Heaven.

We may know a great many things in this day which were hidden from our fathers. We may know all of the wonders of space age travel and cybernetic comfort; we may know all of the "isms" of philosophy and theology; we may know the "bench made" law of England, and the "bar made" law of Rome; we may be steeped in all the classics, and versed in all of the arts and sciences. But unless we know Him, whom to know aright is life eternal, we are poor, and wretched and deaf and dumb and blind.

Therefore, we cannot help but rejoice, in all of the freshness of new discovery, that our transgressions have been covered, that the stain which we have cast upon the holy law of God has been cleansed in the blood of infinite preciousness; and that from all the wells of salvation, whose common source springs from the Rock of Calvary, flows the stream that shall at last wash away the sin and the sorrow of our world.

THE HOLY SPIRIT'S REGENERATING WORK

Maurice A. P. Wood

Jesus Christ gave his infant Church her marching orders for spiritual warfare, without respite, when after his death and resurrection, he commanded that "repentance and remission of sins should be preached in his name among all nations," and each member was to be "endued with power" (the power of the promised Holy Spirit) for witness (Luke 24:47, 49).

At Earls Court in the Greater London Crusade of June, 1966, we saw the Holy Spirit gloriously at work convicting, illuminating, converting and establishing young Christians in the faith. It is this work of the Holy Spirit, however, that is the forgotten factor in the planned strategy of the Church's evangelism today, and what we saw in London in 1966 needs to be repeated throughout the world Church, and to be underscored in this great Congress.

In his masterly paper, Dr. Ockenga states, "There is no possibility of an evangelistic outreach without the ministry of the Holy Spirit."

Let us study this matter of the Holy Spirit in evangelism under three headings:

1. The Holy Spirit and Pre-Evangelism
2. The Holy Spirit and Conversion
3. The Holy Spirit and the New Convert

1. The Holy Spirit and Pre-Evangelism

As evangelists, we believe we are called to do God's work; we do not simply call God in to do our work. The Holy Spirit, the divine Author of Holy Scripture, reveals in the Bible the mind of God concerning evangelism: "God our Savior, who will have ALL men to be saved, and to come unto the knowledge of the truth" (I Tim. 2:3, 4). The same Holy Spirit reveals the all-sufficiency of our world message: "There is one God, and one mediator between God and men, the man Christ Jesus; Who gave himself a ransom for ALL" (I Tim. 2:5, 6). And here is our encouragement to obey Jesus Christ's unrepealed commission: "Go ye into ALL the world, and preach the gospel to *every* creature" (Mark 16:15). From the creation, the Holy Spirit hovers over God's world (the picture of a mighty eagle brooding over its young is suggested in the Hebrew word "Ruach" in Gen. 1:2). In all our preparation to win men for Christ, we may with confidence look for God's loving concern for his created beings. Moreover, man needs God and knows it by the Spirit's working.

THE REV. MR. WOOD is the principal of Oak Hill College in London, England.

Christ Jesus himself taught that in this day of grace the Holy Spirit would sharpen this general concern to a definite conviction concerning sin, righteousness and judgment. The Holy Spirit will "convict (or reprove) the world of sin, and of righteousness, and of judgment" (John 16:8).

Without ostentation, the Holy Spirit loves so to arrange men's circumstances that they are brought within the sphere of God's influence. Therefore, we should never decry the place of the Christian home, the God-given ordinances of baptism and the Lord's supper, the sphere of Church life and worship, and the reading, study and preaching of the Word of God as vital factors in the Holy Spirit's unceasing work of pre-evangelism. God's initiative prepares the seeker for the saving work of the Gospel. The Holy Spirit works in this threefold way of concern, conviction of sin, and personal circumstances. The story of Cornelius should encourage us to evangelize all, even nominal church members. "Cornelius," we read, "thy prayer is heard, and thine alms are had in remembrance in the sight of God" (Acts 10:31). Here is prevenient grace indeed!

2. The Holy Spirit and Conversion

Bishop Kenneth Kirk of Oxford used to say: "It is the Church's task to turn adherents to the Church into possessors of Christ." This, through Bible-based evangelism, the Holy Spirit delights to do in the following ways:

a. The Holy Spirit convicts of sin. A close study of John 16:7-11, John 3:16-21, Eph. 2:1-3 and Rom. 3:20-23, shows that this Spirit-given conviction reveals to man that he is a sinner by nature, by action, and by an attitude of not trusting in the crucified Savior who died to redeem him. Our evangelistic preaching should follow this direction.

b. The Holy Spirit reveals Christ and his Cross to the seeker. The Person of Christ and the meaning of his death were Jesus' primary lessons for his disciples (Mark 8:29, 31). They were revealed by God and not merely discovered by man (Matt. 16:17, Luke 24:44-46). So, in evangelism, we must pray for this work of the Holy Spirit who Jesus said would "glorify ME: for he shall receive of mine, and shall show it unto you" (John 16: 14). In evangelism we pray that the Holy Spirit, through the Word of God, may reveal Jesus as Lord to the enquirer and lead him in penitence to the foot of Christ's Cross, gently persuading him toward that repentance and faith which are the necessities of personal salvation (Acts 20:21).

c. The Holy Spirit gives new life to the believer. "Ye *must* be born again," was Christ's quiet bomb-shell that shattered Nicodemus' religious self-sufficiency (John 3:7). Church membership which does not become a stepping-stone to personal faith in Christ can become a blind alley that halts spiritual progress. In the 39 Articles of Religion, in the Church of England's Prayer Book, the Anglican Communion teaches this need of personal faith in Christ: "We are accounted righteous before God, only for the merit of our Lord and Saviour Jesus Christ by faith . . . wherefore we are justified by faith only" (Article XI). ". . . For Holy Scripture doth set out unto us only the Name of Jesus Christ, whereby men must be saved" (Article XVIII).

Even Dietrich Bonhoeffer says in his "Ethics," by which he desired to be most remembered: "Our foundation is the life, the death, and the resurrection of the Lord Jesus Christ. Faith means the finding and holding fast of this foundation. It means casting anchor upon it and being held fast by it. Faith means founding my life upon a foundation which is outside myself, upon an eternal and holy foundation, upon Christ. Faith means being held captive by the sight of Jesus Christ. Jesus Christ alone is the certainty of faith. My faith that my life is justified is faith in the Lord Jesus Christ."

When men repent of their sins and turn in faith to God through Christ, in accordance with the apostolic teaching (Acts 20:21) based on Christ's own words (Mark 1:15-17, Luke 24:46-47), their conversion leads to the Spirit's regeneration, and they are truly born again of God's Spirit. "If any man have *not* the Spirit of Christ, he is none of his" (Rom. 8:9).

To quote Dr. Ockenga again: "The evangelical position is that regeneration is conditioned upon repentance, confession and faith. This alone stimulates evangelism." Some of us have seen this mighty miracle-working activity of God the Holy Spirit in the recent Greater London Crusade. To God we give all the glory, and cry Hallelujah!

3. The Holy Spirit and the New Convert

Conversion and regeneration are not the end, but only the beginning of a whole range of new experiences for the young Christian. It has been my privilege to be closely associated in some small way with Dr. Billy Graham's various campaigns at Harringay, Wembley, the University of Cambridge, Glasgow, and recently at Earls Court, London, to name five crusades in the British Isles in the last 12 years. I vividly remember the first night of the All Scotland Crusade in March, 1955. Many young Scotsmen and Scots lassies, who are usually so reserved about their religious views, streamed forward as enquirers. I remember standing close to Dr. Graham, visibly moved in the land of his early forefathers, and hearing him say to these "babes in Christ": "Read your Bible. Pray every day. Tell someone you belong to Christ, and join the Church."

The continuing work of the Holy Spirit in implanting these new desires in the hearts of young converts is as important in post-evangelism as in pre-evangelism. Paul's prayer for spiritual maturity in young converts asks God that they may be "strengthened with might by his Spirit in the inner man; That Christ may dwell in your hearts by faith; that ye, being rooted and grounded in love, May be able to comprehend with all saints what is the breadth, and length, and depth, and height; And to know the love of Christ, which passeth knowledge, that ye might be filled with all the fullness of God" (Eph. 3:16-19).

The Holy Spirit who regenerates the convert *also* desires to sanctify and equip him for the service of his Lord and Master Jesus Christ in his own day and generation. Holy Ghost evangelism is never ending!

May the same Holy Spirit challenge the whole Church to present the whole Gospel to the whole world, till Christ our King returns in glory!

In this Congress *we* may be looking for better evangelistic methods. The Holy Spirit desires to cleanse and purify us to become better evangelists. May God grant this, to the glory of the name of Jesus!

REGENERATION AND THE BELIEVER
Theodore J. Stanley

The Bible teaches that man is a sinner not primarily because he commits bad actions but because he possesses a bad nature. The natural man, that is man apart from every divine influence, is bad because, in the final analysis, the motive of his heart is bad. As such, he is said to be "dead in sins," by which the Holy Scriptures mean that natural man is unable to respond to the Spirit of God and is powerless to free himself from the bondage of sin. Man's basic need, therefore, is not gradual improvement of character through education and cultural refinement, but rather a dramatic restoration to spiritual life.

Whereas humanism in all its forms, both inside and outside the organized church, considers man's salvation a mere extension of his own inherent goodness, Scripture despairs of his salvation upon any lesser principle than that of radical and revolutionary change. The apostle Paul defined man's need in the relevant alternatives of his day by saying: "Circumcision is nothing; uncircumcision is nothing: the only thing that counts is new creation" (cf. Galatians 6:15)! Even more explicit are the words of Jesus: "I tell you, unless a man is born over again from above, he cannot see the Kingdom of God. . . . Flesh can give birth only to flesh; it is the Spirit that gives birth to spirit. . . . You must be born over again from above" (cf. John 3:3, 6, 7).

As far as the individual is concerned, the unity and totality of the work of the Spirit may best be expressed by the word regeneration; for this one word best expresses the fact that the work of the Holy Spirit is one and indivisible. Redemption, as the work of the Spirit, means rebirth. The Holy Spirit, as that person of the divine trinity whose function it is to apply the redemptive work of Christ to the individual believer, is the very principle of new life. The Spirit is the life-giver, that is, he is God breathing the breath of life into man, both in creation and redemption.

The word regeneration points to the origin of rebirth. Accordingly, the origin and impulse of transition from death to life is not self-effort but exclusively the work of the Holy Spirit. Every attempt to ascribe the least function to human will — be it no more than a cooperation with divine influences — entails a denial of Scriptural insistence upon man's total depravity. Rebirth implies total inability and passivity, for no one can contribute to his birth; "Thus it does not depend on man's will or effort, but on God's mercy" (Rom. 9:16, NEB). "It is the Spirit (alone) that quickeneth. . . ." (John 6:63).

DR. STANLEY is a missionary teacher at the German Bible Institute, Seeheim/Darmstadt, Germany (Greater Europe Mission).

Secondly, the word regeneration points beyond the origin of rebirth to the goal of the Spirit's work in the individual, namely, perfect conformity with Christ. In regeneration, Christ through the Spirit becomes our life so that we are progressively changed into his image. More precisely, the goal of regeneration as conformity to Christ is properly the work of sanctification, by which expression the systematic theologian designates the believer's life-long growth in holiness, as different from the instantaneous act of justification.

Thirdly, the word regeneration points to the ministries and gifts of the Holy Spirit; for if regeneration comprises the unity and totality of the Spirit's work in the individual believer, then it follows that there is no aspect of Christian experience which lies outside of, and which does not derive from, that regenerating work. Accordingly, regeneration encompasses the filling of the Holy Spirit or, more precisely, the result of the filling as seen in the charismatic gifts. For according to I Cor. 12 through 14, every Christian is to receive a special gift from the Spirit for building up the body of Christ and for implementing its witness. The apostle Paul says, moreover, that every Christian is earnestly to desire the higher gifts of the Spirit.

In the book of Acts, Luke the historian describes the creation of the church as a breaking through of the Spirit at Pentecost and as a reiteration thereof at chronologically successive stages of its growth. Of four recorded episodes, two mention an interval after conversion; and one, the coming of the Holy Ghost upon the household of Cornelius, appears to be simultaneous with conversion. But in developing a normative conception for established churches, Paul the apostle never speaks of a second act or of an interval of time: to Paul, this third aspect of the regenerating work of the Holy Spirit belongs to justification and sanctification, and forms an inherent unity with them.

A complementary understanding of the Lukan and Pauline texts is readily apparent when we recognize the two writers' respective viewpoints as historian and missionary-theologian, and then concentrate upon that aspect of the Spirit's work which is common to both, namely, the emphasis upon the purpose of exercising charismatic gifts. When Luke therefore describes the outpouring of the Holy Spirit, he emphasizes not so much the accompanying phenomena as their purpose; he stresses not that believers experience something, but that they do something, namely, communicate the Gospel in power. Similarly, the Pauline standard for judging charismatic gifts in the Church is whether or not they are of use for the benefit of the Church and its witness to the world (I Cor. 14:23-25). According to the biblical writings of both Luke and Paul, therefore, to be filled with the Spirit means that the individual believer becomes so equipped by the Spirit that he becomes usable in the Spirit's outgoing ministry of edifying the body of Christ and of evangelizing the lost.

Thus the regenerating work of the Holy Spirit comprises the unity and totality of the Spirit's work in an individual, not only for the person's personal benefit in his justification and sanctification, but above all for implementing his share and responsibility in fulfilling the Church's great commission. In terms of missionary witness, then, through regeneration the sinner is freed from the sin of self-centeredness and changed into the likeness of the Son of God, who came "not to be ministered unto, but to minister, and to give his life a ransom for many." "Go ye therefore and teach all nations. . . ."

THE RESULTS OF REGENERATION
Corrie ten Boom

A woman who had accepted the Lord telephoned her lawyer and said, "I take back my request for a divorce. I have seen that my sins have caused the trouble in my marriage." The Holy Spirit had begun his regenerating work in her. "The fruit of the Spirit is love . . ." (Gal. 5:22). Perhaps one of the greatest miracles that the Holy Spirit performs, is to implant love for one's enemies.

We evangelists, too, need the renewing work of the Holy Spirit in our lives. When we give place to bitterness and unwillingness to forgive, we cannot preach forgiveness. "But all of us who are Christians are transfigured by the Spirit of the Lord in ever-increasing splendour into his own image" (cf. II Cor. 3:18, Phillips). During the war I learned that the Holy Spirit gives one love for his enemies. He used me to bring the betrayer who had caused the death of four members of my family to the Lord.

Perhaps we need a greater miracle to forgive fellow-Christians who hinder our work. Can you forgive people who have thrown you out of your own Church, because of a difference in vision of a certain truth in the Bible? Can you forgive the man who has stolen the love of your wife? The people who through their gossip and slander try to steal your good name? Are you not willing to forgive? Jesus says: "If you will not forgive other people, neither will your Heavenly Father forgive you your failures" (Matt. 6:14, Phillips). Don't try to "theologize" this away. Jesus said it. It has helped me remember how many sins the Lord has forgiven me in the 74 years of my life. You never so touch the ocean of God's love, as when you forgive and love your enemies.

We Christians are in training for higher service. An athlete does not complain when the training is hard, but thinks of the sports-day ahead. Revelation 2 and 3 tell us about overcomers. God is building up overcomers for these last days before Jesus' return. The enemy sometimes uses fellow-Christians to make our lives difficult. When "self" is enthroned in our heart, we are quickly offended. But when Jesus is on the throne, he makes us more than conquerors. Hallelujah!

The Holy Spirit opens our eyes to our own disability and grants dependence upon his ability. Sometimes my head hurts from the halo that Americans insist on giving me when they introduce me. The story of the woodpecker has helped me. While he was pecking at the trunk of a tree,

MISS TEN BOOM, an evangelist and author living in Soestdijk, Holland, has done evangelistic work in 55 countries.

lightning struck and destroyed the tree. Flying away, the woodpecker said: "I did not know I had such power in my beak!" When there is blessing in a meeting, it is not the power of our "beaks" but the work of the Holy Spirit that is responsible. An evangelist must learn to depend totally on him and not on his own ability.

I learned this in Tasmania, during the six days I had to give noon-day radio messages. Unexpectedly on the seventh day, the minister came and, although I was not prepared, insisted that I take the broadcast. We were late, and I hate being late for I am a Dutch woman and a watchmaker. And to be late at a radio station is a double blunder. I had only my Bible with me and no notebooks. I tried to remember what I had said before, but my head was a blank. To repeat a text is not wrong, but to repeat a story or an illustration is foolish especially in a radio message. I prayed: "Lord, you know I can't do it. I can't give that radio message." I received the same answer I always get when I say: "I can't do it." The Lord said: "I've known that for a long time, but I am glad that *you* know it, for that is why now you can let *me* do it." And he did.

I thought that my message was a bit incoherent. I even thought: "If I had prepared the message myself, I should have done a better job." That evening I asked a student: "Did you ever make a decision for Jesus Christ?" "Yes, I did it this afternoon," he said. "For three years I refused the Lord. This noon I turned the knob of my radio, and heard such queer English that I decided to find out from which country the lady speaker came. So I heard your talk. It was the very message I needed. I knelt before the radio and surrendered my life to the Lord."

After the meeting I left for Brisbane. The woman who sat next to me in the plane said: "I heard you speak in many meetings this week. God blessed me there, but it was that last talk over the radio that did the job." So the Holy Spirit had not done a bad job after all. "God, who first ordered light to shine in darkness, has flooded our hearts with his light. We now can enlighten men only because we can give them knowledge of the glory of God, as we see it in the face of Jesus Christ. This priceless treasure we hold, so to speak, in a common earthenware jar — to show that the splendid power of it belongs to God and not to us" (II Cor. 4:6 and 7, Phillips).

God has called me to work in Eastern Europe. Beginning in Russia, I knew that here was a work that was far beyond my ability to do. It is the "foolishness" of God to send Conny van Hoogstraten, my fellow-worker, and me to perform such a task. Nowhere else have I experienced the victory of Jesus Christ in such a way. God's power is demonstrated in our weakness. "God's foolishness" is wiser than men, and his "weakness" is stronger than men (I Cor. 1:25).

The world is in a chaotic state as never before. The Holy Spirit shows us God's plan for this world. "Where there is no vision, the people perish" (Prov. 29:18). In Communist countries, but not only there, people see things from an atheistic point of view. In the U.S.A. a journalist asked me: "Do you think that we are living in a post-Christian world?" I answered him: "No we live in a pre-Christian world. This earth will one day be covered with the knowledge of the glory of God, as the waters cover the sea (Hab. 2:14). Every knee will bow before Jesus. Every tongue will confess him, either as Savior, or as Judge" (Phil. 2:10, 11). I believe that in Eastern Europe, but elsewhere too, Christians need the encouragement that the Holy Spirit gives in showing them things from God's point of view, as it were, by granting spiritual insight and understanding (Col. 1:9, Phillips). Major Ian Thomas has said: "God has plans for this world, not problems. There is never a panic in heaven." The best is yet to be. Jesus will come soon, he who promised: "I [will] make all things new" (Rev. 21:5).

Report of Group Discussion

Discussion honed in on three key questions:

1. When is a person regenerated? Many agreed that although regeneration is an instantaneous work of God, there is a possibility that one may undergo a period of spiritual gestation — a person possibly being conceived in Christ for months or even years before coming to the new birth.

2. Should people be encouraged to come into the church before conversion?

3. What is the relation between the baptism of the Holy Spirit and regeneration? After a few helpful attempts to define the term "baptism of the Holy Spirit," the discussion lapsed into a presentation of proof texts pro and con relating to the descent of the Spirit upon men subsequent to the new birth.

Reporter: *Donald E. Hoke*

SECTION III

HINDRANCES TO
EVANGELISM IN THE CHURCH ·
Walter Künneth   173

Universalism

THE NEW TESTAMENT TEACHING · Leon Morris   180

UNIVERSALISM AND EVANGELISM · James I. Packer   182

A MANIFESTATION OF THE
NEW UNIVERSALISM · Arthur M. Climenhaga   185

JEWISH MISSIONS IN
RELATION TO UNIVERSALISM · Jakob Jocz   188

REPORT OF GROUP DISCUSSION · Calvin Thielman   191

Self-Containment, Parochialism and Isolation

THE CHURCH AND THE WORLD · A. J. Dain   194

THE GREATEST ENEMY IS WITHIN · Samuel H. Moffett   197

MAINTAINING A DELICATE BALANCE · Everett L. Cattell 201

SOME MODERN TEMPTATIONS · C. Stacey Woods   203

REPORT OF GROUP DISCUSSION · Kenneth L. Downing   205

Spiritual Indifference and Non-Expectation

LOSING GOD AT THE CENTER · Festo Kivengere   207

AS THE WORLD SEES THE CHURCH · Robert E. Coleman   210

THE POPE OF SELF · Robert P. Evans   213

SOME IMPORTANT FLAWS · Augustus B. Marwieh   216

REPORT OF GROUP DISCUSSION · I. Ben Wati   218

Doctrinal Unbelief and Heresy

PRESERVING THE TRUTH OF THE BIBLE · Hermann Sasse   219

THE UNIQUE CONTENT
OF THE GOSPEL · Jules-Marcel Nicole   222

PREACHING AN
AUTHORITATIVE MESSAGE · Wayne Dehoney   227

                                                                    PAGE
SOME OVERLOOKED HINDRANCES • *Pieter J. Mietes*   230

Infant Baptism and Sacerdotalism

BAPTISM AS A GATEWAY • *Richard Møller Petersen*   233

A PLEA FOR BELIEVER'S BAPTISM • *Duke K. McCall*   237

BAPTISM AS A RITE
OF INITIATION • *A. W. Goodwin Hudson*   240

BAPTISM IN REFORMATION
PERSPECTIVE • *C. Darby Fulton*   244

REPORT OF GROUP DISCUSSION • *Hans Bürki-Fillenz*   246

HINDRANCES TO EVANGELISM IN THE CHURCH

Walter Künneth

This theme, concerned with objections and hindrances to the Gospel in the Church, is a call to self-examination. It is certainly no matter of indifference, whether or not we are ready for such self-evaluation, whether we are willing to recognize the problems and requirements of Christian identification in the world, whether we are willing to investigate seriously the actual condition of the Church.

This matter involves a question of basic importance. What does it mean when we say that the Church — which by its nature and commission is to be the bearer of the Good News — may itself hinder the influence of the Gospel, that Christians themselves may be guilty when limitations and barriers prevent the spread of God's Word? Certainly such critical charges cannot be put aside lightly. It is only right that we take these important questions seriously. They deserve a full and thorough reply.

An intensive approach of this kind is possible, of course, only after we have clearly established the basic meaning of the concepts "Gospel" and "Church," and have determined what relationship "Gospel" and "Church" actually bear to each other.

This much is certain: "Gospel" and "Church" are not two giant entities that stand side by side in isolation, and that can be judged independently. Actually they stand in an indissoluble relationship. The Gospel points to the Church, and the Church derives from the Gospel. This statement will be understood properly only if we turn aside from what history has come to designate as "Church." We do well to guard against the many forms and differences, the misconceptions and contradictory statements given in various religious presentations. Likewise when we use the word "Gospel," we must remember that its meaning is not determined by some current concept, nor by subjective interpretation, nor this or that person's theology.

Moreover, in considering the determinative relationship between the Gospel and the Church, we must go back to the original setting of the New Testament record. We will gain the correct answer to our problem only if we ascertain the origin of the Gospel, and the beginnings of the "Christian Church." This source available to us is thoroughly enlightening. The judgments gained therefrom are of basic significance for our investigation.

DR. KÜNNETH is professor of Systematic Theology in Erlangen University, Germany.

We must keep three facts clearly in mind: first, we must understand that basic to every statement concerning the Gospel and the Church is a presupposition that, like a great railroad switch, turns everything in a specific direction. This presupposition is a fact, a reality that men have neither brought about, nor can they produce. This fact is the invasion of God's revelation into history. The fact that Almighty God descended into the earthly realm of his creatures, that the living God locked himself into the history of humanity, spoke and dealt in a unique way through a specific nation and then poured out the fullness of his deity and grace in Jesus Christ, manifests a reality that is totally new and beyond comparison. Therefore this reality of the God revealed in Jesus Christ cannot be measured in human terms. Human reason, the world's reasonableness, must shatter upon it. The definition of the Gospel now becomes signally clear. It is the "joyous news" that no man could ever have devised, the news that in Jesus Christ, God took pity on the world; that the Incarnate One, God's Son become flesh is Jesus of Nazareth; that the One who was crucified and died, the Resurrected One, he whom God raised from the dead, is the Redeemer of the world. This is the "joyous news": Jesus Christ died as a sacrifice for the world, he lives for us as the Risen One, he leads mankind toward its eternal goal.

This brings us to a second consideration: it was this Gospel that gathered together the body of Christ, that inspired the Christian Church. We fail to understand the meaning of the Church unless we marvel that, as the Easter message spread throughout the world, the Spirit of the living Lord opened the pathway of faith to humble hearts and enabled them to witness for Christ. The Church issued from this Gospel and not from some system of ethics. For this reason the Gospel and the Church stand in the closest of essential relationships. The Gospel is the means, the tool, the instrument through which Jesus Christ reveals himself as active and alive in the Church. Everything, accordingly, depends on whether or not this Gospel is preserved and carried forward unclouded and unabridged. This Gospel not only brings the Church into being, but also impresses upon it its nature and substance; the Gospel is the Church's life-stream which united it with Christ as its head and heart, as the very core of its being.

In the third place, it becomes evident from this origin of Christ's Church in the revelational event, that the Church has a task to do in the world, and that it is empowered to go throughout the world. If, as the body of the living Christ, the Church has become the beginning of a "new creation," then it is directed to proclaim its joyous news to the world. The overwhelming apostolic confession that "If any man be Christ he is a new creature" the Church does not wish to keep only for itself, but desires to proclaim as a promise to a weary, death-ridden world. As a Church of the Gospel, therefore, the Church is not called to flee and despise the world, not forced into a narrowminded isolation, not condemned to a ghetto existence; just the reverse is true: the Church is called to be on display before the world. The Church stands under its Lord's command: "Go ye into all the world," "Ye shall be my witnesses," "for God so loved the world that he gave his only begotten Son." The Gospel that the Church proclaims to the world is the very invitation extended by Christ himself: "Come unto me, all ye that labor and are heavy laden, and I will give you rest."

This relationship between the Gospel and the Church represents an extraordinary situation, an unusual authorization, a unique responsibility. What happens, however, when opposition is leveled at the Gospel in the Church itself, when hindrances stand in the way of the Gospel? This is a depressing thought. It is one that deserves our complete attention.

Everything pertaining to this matter centers around the basic question of what facts, what circumstances harm the Gospel in the Church, and that do so, in fact, from within. The first determinative principle can be summarized thus: anything, everything that bedims the message of the Gospel, that prevents the heart of the Gospel from shining through clear and true must be considered an obstacle and hindrance.

We must remind ourselves of what confronts us a thousand times over in the life of the Church. We think of Christians who are consciously identified with their churches, who attend and participate in the worship services according to custom, who are willing to give themselves to charitable works — all these things are worthy of note and of recognition. But a certain lack should not be overlooked. There are many who abide completely by and within the limits of the traditional patterns of the Church, who are satisfied with the "iron rations" of the confession of faith learned in childhood, whose Christianity is a matter of sentiment and who now and then succumb to a pious mood. Certainly we ought not to minimize this, but there are those whose faith has stopped growing, whose progress in the life of faith has been interrupted. They accordingly have stopped meditating personally on the Gospel in order to gain clarity concerning the meaning and significance of their faith. For them, Christian phrases and biblical terms are like old worn coins whose value is no longer discernible. Therefore their faith does not radiate, has no convicting power, and the Gospel appears lame and weak. If someone calls himself a Christian and does not himself understand the illuminating power of the Gospel, he is neither qualified nor in a position to bring the Gospel to those who are outside the Church and to make it plain. The New Testament was keenly aware of this dangerous possibility in the churches, and thus laid down the principle: "Be ready always to give an answer to every man that asketh you a reason for the hope that is in you." If Christians hesitate to give an accounting to themselves and to others concerning the what and wherefore of their faith, and step aside from essential exposition of questions of the faith, then the Gospel will become muddied and unclear.

Much more serious, certainly, is the hindrance to the Gospel that comes from the weak faith, the doubting faith, yes, even the unbelief of those who call themselves Christians. Among these, their church membership notwithstanding, an internal falling away from the Gospel has set in; among these, through the deception of non-Christian spiritual powers, deterioration has begun. In such a situation, the influence of all kinds of ideologies and world views, of religious speculation such as spread by the sects, of nihilistic skepticism even to the point of atheistic disputing of God, can spread stealthily through the Church. Suddenly the Christian who through baptism and confirmation was planted into fellowship with Christ succumbs to the whisperings of false spirits, yields to superstitions, and charts his life by horoscopes. The age-old doubt, "Hath God said?" only too often becomes linked with egoistic lovelessness that cares nothing for one's neighbor and says, "Am I my brother's keeper?"

This failure to trust the faith and this denial of neighbor love become a constant offense to the world round about. Because Christians appear so "unredeemed," and act as if they had no faith, the death sentence is passed upon the Church and thus upon the Gospel itself. The disfigured image that these false representatives give to the life of the Church makes the proclamation of the Gospel untrustworthy and counteracts the unfolding and outworking of the Gospel that would arouse men and women to faith.

With an eye to hindrances of the Gospel, we must be aware also of another fact: that in the course of history the difference between the form or structure of the Christian Church and its content or message is inescapably obvious. Of course, it would be a fanatical delusion to think that the Church of the Gospel could do away with all outward forms and still fulfill its tasks. The reality of revelation, that "the Logos, the Word of God, became flesh," shows the necessity for the historical, the bodily, earthly-human aspect of the Church. The first gatherings of the early Church show certain definite patterns, as seen by fellowship in the apostles' teaching and faith, the Lord's supper and prayer. The Christian Church in the midst of the world always needs some external form or structure. A glance at church history shows us an abundance of church institutions, large and small organizations of impressive and historically important church groups, as well as powerless church endeavors unnoticed by the world. Their names may be diverse, diverse also their external structure and inner organization; on the one hand is the hierarchical range of offices that stem from the Church; on the other, the multiplicity of functions.

For our discussion, the question is especially pertinent as to what importance form has had for the success of the Gospel. To what extent does the external structure and order of a church body, however indispensable and justified this form may be, constitute a hindrance to or obscuring of the Gospel?

A Church that bears a thankful sense of responsibility to its Reformation fathers will be concerned for maintaining the purity of the Gospel and its furtherance. It will therefore consider church forms, ceremonies, rites, and traditions of only relative value, and in no way necessary for salvation. The structure of the Church in itself is never "sacred," but, determined only on the basis of suitability, is oriented to implementing a purposeful proclamation of the Gospel.

This interpretation of church form immediately makes clear what danger for the Gospel may lurk in this historical institutional structure. It is possible to retain old religious forms, encrusted traditions which hinder and do not promote a new vital development of the Church, or there may be a revered language of the Church that as time passes no longer clearly communicates the meaning of the Gospel; there may be a jungle of religious bureaucracy that supersedes the principle of stated order, that assaults and controls the course of daily life and embitters people.

The need for church reform has been stated repeatedly in numerous ways in our time, at the Kirchentage (church conventions), for example. One ought not to be deceived into thinking, however, that much will be accomplished simply by changing external forms. On the contrary, modern accommodations to current tastes, or even the adoption of cheap gimmicks in the Church can pose hindrances to the Gospel, inasmuch as interest is shifted to secondary things and the centrality of proclamation is pushed aside.

The only valid consideration for the Church to realize at all times must be what serves the Gospel, its credibility, its deepening, its propagation. What forms, customs and ordinances must be removed, changed or avoided, lest the Church itself be a burden to faith in the Gospel? When it is under the control, under the lordship of the Gospel, the Church remains in vital operation, experiences constant proper reformation, and is self-critical in order that its entrusted Gospel can function in the world as "light" and "salt."

We find situations in still another area of the Church that hinder the Gospel, and in quite another way. Difficulties to proclaiming the Gospel that we have considered thus far have stemmed from man's wrong relationships, from the human weakness of church members, or from erroneous evaluation and inadequate ways and methods of presentation; now we confront hindrances that come from altering the Gospel itself. We have seen that correct doctrine and proper proclamation do not guarantee the penetrating power of the Gospel, since various personal and very real circumstances can hover over the Gospel like a dismal smoke screen and thus make its clarity difficult to understand. But what can be done when the very content of the Gospel is abused and changed, when its very essence is misunderstood and misinterpreted?

This decisive fact probes open wounds that particularly characterize the Christian Church today. The dire case would seem to be that man no longer subjects himself as a listener to and receiver of the testimony of the

Gospel, but instead puts himself under the norm of his own personal discoveries and experiences; and then according to his comprehension and rational promptings adjusts the Gospel message to suit his own needs, corrects them and manipulates them to his own purposes. In this manner, he at one stroke exalts himself above the authority of the Gospel, makes himself lord over the Word, over God's revelation.

Obviously, this change in the content of the Gospel has far-reaching implications, since the birth, maintenance or destruction of faith are at stake. Church history has demonstrated the many ways in which such diminution of content has expressed itself. Even in apostolic days such threats to the pure Gospel were acute. The early Church obviously was not sheltered and protected like some island in a sea of nations and peoples; rather, it stood in the very midst of countless religious ideas, mythological concepts, philosophical world views; in other words, the early Church was exposed to foreign influences of many kinds and degrees. The Apostle John accordingly found it necessary to warn against the spiritualism of the agnostics who denied the revelation of Christ come in the flesh. And at any and all ideas that would adulterate the Gospel he proclaimed into some new legalism, Paul hurls a severe, harsh "No!" He pronounces a passionate "Beware!" upon every perversion of the Gospel, upon the preaching of "another Gospel."

Like dark shadows, such death-dealing threats to the Gospel pursue the Church of Jesus Christ here on earth. Again and again voices are heard that offer their own ideas, their own piety, their own ethics in place of the Gospel's. On the one hand one hears claims that only by some particular way, and according to one particular method, only on the basis of some one specific experience may one become a true Christian; on the other hand, one sees all these statements of the Gospel silenced and pushed aside that are not in harmony with the particular convictions being propagated. Even today one finds a narrow-minded, rigid kind of Christianity that lays burdensome demands and duties on the Gospel, a Christian legalism that is neither winsome nor gladdening, but repels and makes being a Christian seem something joyless and depressing.

The face of a distorted Gospel is quite different however, a distorted Gospel that under the influence of some current philosophy and absolutely defined scientific arguments and hypotheses has undergone a content-changing revision. It has become apparent to many who discern the situation that today we are dealing with just such a profound threat.

The tendency here is not to burden "modern" man with a heavy package of what he must believe; rather the procedure is to avoid whatever he does not want, and whatever he does not consider rationally comprehensible or actually possible. The point of departure is total adaptation to a philosophical system in which the only valid reality is the here and now. This purely immanentistic thought system discards every suggestion or thought of a metaphysical other world, and any thought of transcendent reality.

Into these clichés that bear the imprint of certain presuppositions of present-day existentialism, the Gospel must then be fitted. The result, obviously, can only be a thorough-going transformation of the Gospel. One can then no longer speak of God as someone above and beyond the world who in sovereign majesty and power can step into the world as Creator and Redeemer. In the realm of causal relationships, no room then remains for miracles whose reality is indissolubly linked with the Gospel. Jesus Christ can be honored only as a man, not as the world's Redeemer who died on the Cross for mankind, not as the risen Lord in whose life rests the basis of eternal hope. In the last analysis, the Gospel itself becomes a mere symbol, a code to some new human understanding of the self, a thrust to help gain some anthropological meaning for existence.

The much-vaunted effort of modernistic theology to make practicable and to simplify Christian faith for today's man is purchased by changing the essential nature of the Gospel. Continued use of Christian-biblical concepts like Word and Faith, Christ and Redemption, Pardon and Eschatology, must not keep us from seeing that these terms have a new content, communicate an entirely different meaning. Perplexity of spirit, fogging of the battle lines, uncertainty of individual Christians in knowing what to believe are the fruit of this falling away from the Gospel. A Gospel that has become cheap is a defeated, emasculated Gospel that can no longer sound a clear trumpet call.

Obstacles and hindrances to the Gospel inside the Church? To be keenly aware of them and not to consider them harmless is the Church's responsibility, the task of her theology. This involves honest insight into the deepest needs of the Church and knowledge of how error develops within the Church. Such self-awareness is a form of true repentance.

What is needed? A return to the substance of the whole Gospel. Only if the Church stays with its task are fruitful conversation and meaningful encounter possible with a surrounding world that thinks differently. The large number of values and viewpoints today demands singleness of belief by the Church. Only the message of Christ, however unpopular and offensive it may be, can steady a tottering world. In the last analysis, man is unable to break down the barriers and overcome the hindrances; this only the Gospel itself can do, the Gospel that displays the presence and the power of God's Holy Spirit.

THE NEW TESTAMENT TEACHING
Leon Morris

If it is true that all men will ultimately be saved, there is no reason why we should inconvenience ourselves by trying to bring the Gospel to those who do not believe. Yet the Christian Church has always been evangelistic. How is it then that some Christians embrace a view that removes all the urgency from evangelism?

The reasons given for this view are partly scriptural. Universalists draw attention to passages in the New Testament which seem to them to teach that all people will eventually be saved. Thus "God has consigned all men to disobedience, that he may have mercy upon all" (Rom. 11:32, RSV). The fact that so many are disobedient to the divine call, it is urged, is not the significant thing. God has "consigned" all men to this state with a view to ultimate mercy on all. But this reasoning overlooks the fact that "all" does not necessarily mean "every single individual." The verse can mean, as Sanday and Headlam put it, "All the classes into which the world may be divided, Jew and Gentile alike, will be admitted into the Messianic Kingdom or God's Church. The reference is not here any more than elsewhere to the final salvation of every individual."

Similarly, when Jesus said, "I, when I am lifted up from the earth, will draw all men to myself" (John 12:32, RSV), he was telling us "by what death he was to die" (v. 33), and not how many people will be saved.

Other passages are cited, but they all come short of demonstrating the point of universal salvation. They show that there is a wideness in God's mercy so that his salvation is indeed not restricted to some narrow segment of mankind. But the critical point is that not one of the passages ever says in clear terms that every individual will be saved. There is not one unequivocal passage in the entire New Testament which assures us that in the end every individual in the race will be saved. If this conclusion is to be reached there must always be a jump in reasoning.

Moreover, many New Testament passages actually point in the opposite direction. Jesus spoke more often of hell than of heaven, and, for example, he said, "It is better for you to enter the kingdom of God with one eye than with two eyes to be thrown into hell, where their worm does not die, and the fire is not quenched" (Mark 9:47 ff., RSV). It is difficult to conclude from this that ultimately all will be saved, and that we therefore have nothing to fear.

Jesus constantly teaches that men divide themselves into two groups. Thus "the gate is wide and the way is easy, that leads to destruction, and those who enter by it are many. For the gate is narrow and the way is hard, that leads to life, and those who find it are few" (Matt. 7:13, RSV).

DR. MORRIS is the principal of Ridley College in Melbourne, Australia.

The concluding words in the judgment scene in Matthew 25 remind us that this division has eternal consequences: "they will go away into eternal punishment, but the righteous into eternal life" (Matt. 25:46, RSV). There is a "great chasm" fixed between those in Abraham's bosom and those in torment (Luke 16:26) and in the end many "will seek to enter and will not be able" (Luke 13:24, RSV).

The New Testament, then, does not teach universalism. In particular, Jesus makes it plain that men face an important choice. If in the end they reject God's way, then the consequences are serious and eternal.

The real reason for espousing universalism is not the teaching of the Bible; the reason rises rather, from the conviction that something in the nature of God ensures that he will save all men. Thus it is often said that God is a God of love and therefore could not allow any man to perish. But this kind of thinking does not reckon with God's justice which may affect the way love operates. Nor does it allow for the fact that love takes man's personality with full seriousness. God might theoretically have constrained men to be good, to do the things he chooses. But he has in fact made it possible for them to sin and they do sin. His purposes must be understood in the light of this reality.

We have no reason to think that in eternity God will depart from his practice hitherto and compel men to choose him. All the evidence we have points in the other direction. God has no need of marionettes. He pays men the compliment of allowing them to live without him if they so choose. But if they live without him in this life they must also live the next life without him. This is what makes the Gospel offer of salvation so serious. When Christians evangelize, they are not engaging in some harmless and pleasant pastime. They are engaging in a fearful struggle, the issues of which are eternal.

Continuance in sin leaves its mark. It makes man a sinner — proud, lustful, selfish or whatever else his particular brand of sin may be. It is unkind and unfair to let men think that the effects of unrepented sin can ever be wiped out. If men live and die in unrepented sin they make themselves unfit for heaven. Universalists must face the fact that eternal life means life with God and with God's people. Those who prefer to live apart from God would find this kind of life quite intolerable.

Sin is a grim reality, and its effects prevent the sinner from qualifying for heaven. The only way around it would seem to be for God to compel the sinner to be what he wills him to be. But to do this is to take away from man the right to be himself.

Modern man finds the universalist dogma attractive. But it is not well grounded, for neither is universalism taught in Scripture, nor is it compatible with God's loving respect for the personalities he has made. Universalism must not be allowed to hinder us from pressing on with the urgent task of evangelism. "Now is the day of salvation "

UNIVERSALISM AND EVANGELISM
James I. Packer

Universalism is the increasingly influential belief that every human being whom God has created, or will create, will eventually enter into the bliss prepared by God for them that love him. Over the past century, the status of this belief has advanced from that of an idiosyncrasy to that of a respectable theological option, favored by many leading scholars, and it continues to make great strides throughout the Protestant world. In its modern dress it is an optimism, not of nature, but of grace. Its key-thought is not that no one is bad enough to merit damnation, or that God is by nature too kind to inflict it. Its key-thought, rather, is that sovereign grace will not have triumphed fully or finally until every member of our hell-deserving race is safe in glory. Universalists are convinced that no position other than their own can do justice to the graciousness of God.

Universalism is a speculation, however, that goes beyond Scripture. Last-century attempts to find it explicitly stated in the New Testament failed. Three classes of texts were appealed to; one group was thought to predict the salvation of all men (e.g. Acts 3:21; John 12:32; Rom. 5:18), another to declare God's intention to save all (e.g. I Tim. 2:4; II Pet. 3:9), and a third group (e.g. II Cor. 5:19; Tit. 2:11; Col. 1:20; Heb. 2:9; I John 2:2) to show that because of the Cross all men were already objectively reconciled to God, and in due course would therefore enjoy full salvation. But the texts cited do not prove what they are invoked to prove, while other texts clearly envisage some finally perishing under divine judgment (compare John 12:32 with 5:29, for example; Acts 3:21 with verse 23; Rom. 5:18 with Rom. 2:5-13, etc.). As long ago as 1908 Robert Mackintosh wrote: "The question is generally argued as one of New Testament interpretation. The present writer does not think that hopeful. He sees no ground for challenging the old doctrine (sc., that some will perish) on exegetical lines."

Modern universalists mostly agree; hence they represent their thesis as an irresistible theological inference, based on the overall thrust of New Testament thinking about God, and not, therefore, invalidated by either lack of explicit Scriptural statement or the presence of explicit Scriptural denial. Thus Nels Ferré writes: "The total logic of the deepest message of the New Testament, namely, that God both can, and wants to, save all, is unanswerable." This is typical. Similarly, J. A. T. Robinson writes: "Christ, in Origen's old words, remains on the cross as long as one sinner remains in hell. This is not speculation; it is a statement grounded in the

DR. PACKER is the warden of Latimer House, an Anglican evangelical study centre, in Oxford, England.

very necessity of God's nature." But it is a speculation, of course; all statements about "the necessity of God's nature" which go beyond Scripture are speculative.

There is, in fact, a threefold speculation here. First, there is a speculative hermeneutic which not merely allows us, but actually directs us by appeal to a critical principle of theological development within the New Testament (its "total logic"), to formulate a system which at many points goes *beyond* the thoughts expressed by the apostolic writers to something supposedly "higher," something more moral, and more spiritual. Second, there is a speculation about God's purpose, namely, that the "necessity of his nature" as sovereign love obliges him to save all. But in the Bible the proclamation that God is King, and is love, stands alongside the lively expectation that some will finally perish through sin and unbelief; so the speculation is not cogent. Third, there is a speculation about the means whereby God's purpose of universal salvation will be fulfilled. Recognizing that there is no eternal life without repentance and faith in Christ, and that the New Testament threatens those who die in unbelief with hell, universalists develop a doctrine of hell as a means of grace. In hell, God in Christ will meet men again, and strive with them till their hearts are changed. Universalism is thus one of the group of "second-chance" theories, distinguished from others by its conviction that God's striving with unbelievers after their death will in every case succeed. But Scripture gives no hint of this. Instead, it pictures hell as an ultimate state — *inextinguishable* fire, an *undying* worm, *eternal* punishment and destruction. The hell of the New Testament has no exit door.

Though a rationalistic speculation, universalism is gaining ground among Protestants. Our knowledge of the size, and our sense of the oneness of the world community; the currency of subjective hermeneutical principles; emphasis in modern theology on the triumph of grace, and the racial inclusiveness of the atonement; recognition of the grace of God in non-Christian religions, together with a fatal obscuring of the distinction between common and saving grace — all these factors provide fertile soil in which universalism may grow. Yet it remains a heresy. It cannot make sense of the pervasive particularism of the biblical witness to election, redemption, effectual calling, and final glory; nor can it accept the pervasive insistence of the New Testament that this life is decisive for the settling of eternal destiny.

How does universalism affect evangelism? A universalist of the type described, who acknowledges repentance and faith as the only way into eternal life, will not lack interest in evangelism, or doubt the necessity of preaching the Gospel and calling for response. But differences between him and an orthodox evangelical will become evident at three points. First, he will feel free to argue that in particular situations other ways of loving one's neighbor are more important than seeking to win him to Christ. Second, he cannot help intellectualizing the Gospel, for his message is not "believe on the Lord Jesus Christ, and thou shalt be saved," but rather, "believe that the Lord Jesus Christ is your Savior already, and show your thanks." The thought of believing *on* (into, *eis*) Jesus, and coming *to* Jesus, is thus overshadowed. Third, since he does not believe that a decision against Christ is really decisive of anything, his evangelism will lack the urgency which marks New Testament evangelism. He will not preach or pray in terms of the prospect of unbelievers being finally lost.

Attractive though his tranquil Olympian optimism undoubtedly is, the universalist is notoriously not an outstanding evangelist; nor can we wonder. Universalism is the evangelist's "By-Path Meadow." We shall do well to stick to the road.

A MANIFESTATION OF THE NEW UNIVERSALISM

Arthur M. Climenhaga

People sometimes use terms because of a bent for new phrases, or to get away from platitudes, or because they are merely ignorant of the inner meaning or intent of words. Terms often have a way of becoming relative.

The problem of word relativity can be seen especially in theological terminology. Three decades ago the difference between a fundamental theological stance and liberal theological expression was evident from the definitions (e.g. Jesus Christ, the Redeeming Son of God over against Jesus the Man, a great Leader and Liberator). Today one must probe behind a term or title to ascertain what is really meant. For example, is the incarnation fact or the deity of Christ a concept of God the Logos become flesh in the virgin birth — or is it an alleged conjunction of the Logos, the Christ, with the human Jesus at some given point within the lifetime of Jesus?

Similarly, we can examine use of the term *mission* as applied to the life of the Church and the practice of evangelism. To many in the biblical framework the term "mission" refers to the inherent command of Matt. 28:19 and 20 and Rom. 10:8-18. To others, the term has become a kind of cliché, a new pet expression. Both may consider *mission* to embody the concept of the Great Commission just as definitively as the formerly used word *missions*.

Then again, mission may be used to emphasize the sense of total Church involvement in witness to a total world. Here it requires eliminating the seeming dichotomy between *foreign* and *home* missions or *missions* on the one hand and *service situations* on the other. The argument is that joining these terms connotes total involvement of the entire Church.

We certainly sympathize and agree with any desire to combine home missions, foreign missions, relief and welfare work, and service ministries where this is functional and administrative, and when it is based on theological motivation of world-wide concern to realize the Great Commission. Questions must be raised, however, when an ecumenical leader declares:

"At the same time we are forced to contemplate the prospect of a giant and increasing jumble of programs and relationships if these two streams of 'mission' and 'interchurch-aid-and-service' continue to run in separate channels.

. . . Unless we are to confine mission to verbal evangelism — which means largely ineffectual evangelism — there is no way of maintaining a

DR. CLIMENHAGA is the executive director of the National Association of Evangelicals in Wheaton, Illinois.

clear distinction between mission and services on either practical or theo-logical grounds." [1]

What is really meant here? Is this a movement for joining the two areas of missions and service on a functional basis, a basis which can be harmonized with Scripture? Or is it an attempt to get away from the di-chotomy felt to exist between what is termed *a rather narrow evangelistic sense* and *a wider area of service*? What is implied in alleging that *verbal evangelism* means largely *ineffectual evangelism*? What kind of evangelism, what kind of theology, what type of program is envisaged under the words "church in mission"?

If such joining of terms refers only to a *method of mission,* then a new theological direction is not necessarily involved. But where the infer-ence is drawn from a change in the message of mission that "verbal evan-gelism" is ineffectual or "evangelistic effort" is narrow, then the course is sharply set in a new direction. Such change can be seen in the suggestion, for example, that we need to eliminate traditional symbols such as heaven as the abode of saved souls and hell as the place of torment for the damned. To speak of evangelism in mission as "plucking brands from the burning" or to look upon the urgency of mission as inherent in the lostness of hu-manity without Christ is considered irrelevant to the life of modern man.

What then follows in "church mission" can be seen in at least six propositions deduced from a presentation by Dr. Pieter de Jong entitled, "The Difference the Gospel Makes." [2]

1. *Evangelism has cosmic implications.*

2. *Man under God is the master of nature.*

3. *Man is called to become co-creator with God and to help him in leading the world to its final goal.*

4. *The gospel with its concern for one's neighbor becomes a penetra-tion of this value into other cultures and religions.*

5. *The gospel is the impetus for a converging trend.*

6. *The Lord of the Church is the Lord of the world.*

Seen in this light, the mission of the church then is to inform men that they are in fact redeemed by Christ and should start to live accordingly. This perspective precludes any need first to win them to Christ.

How this new universalism moves into the program of "church mission" now becomes clearer. It communicates once again a sense of the brother-hood of man under the fatherhood of God and then suggests that service is the act of reconciliation by the "church in mission." In this approach, sin is not *an individual act* which must be dealt with by the message of reconciliation in personal redemption but is rather *the corporate deed* which alienates man from God. Corporate sin rends the human fabric

---

[1] Stowe, David M., *A New Look At An Old Subject,* pp. 3, 4, 5.

[2] de Jong, Pieter, "Evangelism in Contemporary Theology," chapter 3 in *Evangelism and Contemporary Issues,* Baker, Gordon Pratt (ed).

and makes peace a fugitive. To reweave this torn fabric and to restore peace there must be a reestablishment of a right relationship with God. But this reestablishment is on a corporate and not on an individual basis.[3]

As a further step of development in the concept of "church mission" it can then be held that the reconciling acts of God may be found in all religions. Dr. Niles asserts, "But what of those who already have 'faith' to whom this declaration is made? Are there not those who have not consciously accepted God in Christ, but who nevertheless in some measure respond truly to God's action on them? Are there not those who, being outside the Christian faith, still do the truth? (John 3:21). The answer is 'yes.'"[4]

From this position it is then but a short step to a new universalism of all religions and faiths—a veritable syncretism of universalistic Christianity, and of other ethnic faiths and animistic religious beliefs.[5]

It is here then that this particular meaning of the *mission of the church* comes to full universalistic syncretistic flower. There is no necessity to challenge men to flee to the Lord Jesus Christ from the city of destruction. There is no "Woe is me if I preach not the Gospel." There is no wishing one's self accursed for his kinsmen's sake because they are lost! Instead we find a concept of love and service which depends on dialogue with the various faiths and practices of the world to introduce them to what they already are by the grace of God and what they will be whether they accept it in this life or not! Thus the call to harvest fields is muffled, volunteers dwindle away, and the spirit of evangelism in the Great Commission is no longer one of urgency.

[3] cf. Beaver, R. Pierce, *Envoys of Peace*, p. 58ff.
[4] cf. Niles, D. T., *Upon the Earth*, p. 94.
[5] cf. Lawrence, David. A quotation in The *Readers Digest*, Oct., 1965, p. 19. Taken from The New York *Herald Tribune*, "Unifying Force."

JEWISH MISSIONS IN
RELATION TO UNIVERSALISM
Jakob Jocz

In the past, evangelization of the Jews was regarded as an extravagance peculiar to some pietistic groups. It was considered seriously at all only as part of the general task of missions. Not until quite recently was it realized that the Jewish people present a special problem to the Church. Some apologists for Jewish missions argued for lack of a better reason, that to exclude the Jews from the missionary outreach of the Church smacks of discrimination and is a clandestine form of anti-Semitism. There may be some truth in the allegation, but this is hardly sufficient ground for a theology of Jewish missions.

The purpose of this short paper is to show that the task of evangelism hinges on Jewish missions for the reason that it touches upon the question of universalism at the most vital point.

1. The Position of Historic Israel in Relation to the Church

To start with, we have to define the relationship of historic Israel to the Christian Church in order to establish our scale of priorities.

The Church has always believed that her faith is anchored in history in the sense that it centers upon definite historic events. If this is the case, then the Jewish people are forever linked to the story of revelation. It means that there is an unbroken link between Old Testament and New Testament, between Law and Gospel, between Hebrew history and Church history. This is historic fact and needs no elaboration. The difficulty arises when we are asked to define more closely what is meant by the historic link.

Usually, Jewish history is understood as *Vor-geschichte*, prehistory to the story of the Gospel. In this case, the Old Testament only serves as *praeparatio evangelica* and the history of Israel comes to an end with the advent of the Messiah. That the Jewish people have continued to our days is frequently felt as an anachronism. Israel's task once completed, his disappearance is almost a theological necessity. But the Jews have not disappeared; in fact, we are witnessing today a remarkable *renaissance* of the Jewish people. This means that the Church has misjudged the significance of historic Israel at a vital point. She has left out of account the meaning of the Covenant. Unless we allow the Jewish people their rightful place in the Covenant with Abraham, Jewish history remains an enigma.

DR. JOCZ is professor of systematic Theology at Wycliffe College in Toronto, Ontario, Canada.

2. Israel's Fall

Traditionally, the Church interpreted Israel's rejection of the Messiah as a unique case of faithlessness. In this respect two positions were held: some looked upon Israel's fall as final and absolute; others interpreted it as a temporary suspension of grace. The more lenient view was based upon Rom. 11:25 (RSV): "hardening has come upon part of Israel, until the full number of the Gentiles come in." This text has been frequently misunderstood. There are three points to be noticed here: a) hardening is applied to only part (meros) of Israel. There was in the Apostles' days, and there still is, another part responsive to the Gospel. b) In the context of the chapter, the text has eschatological implications. c) In the context of Pauline practice, the Jewish people always took first place in his missionary strategy. Even after he publically announced that from henceforth he was going to the Gentiles (Acts 18:6), we find the Apostle immediately afterwards preaching the Gospel in the Synagogue (Acts 19:8). The fact is that the Church has never been without Jews. The Hebrew Christian movement in modern times amply bears out this statement.

3. Israel's Fall in Relation to the Church

The theological misinterpretation regarding historic Israel has a hidden psychological reason. In approaching others we readily apply different standards than to ourselves. The result is a distorted assessment of our own position: the Jews have killed Christ, Christians are innocent of his death; the Synagogue has rejected Jesus, the Church has accepted him; the Jews are under judgment, the Christians are under grace. It is only when we look upon the situation in the perspective of history that these clear-cut divisions cease to make sense. Here the Master's words find their fullest application: "Not every one who says to me, 'Lord, Lord,' shall enter the kingdom of heaven, but he who does the will of my Father who is in heaven" (Matt. 7:21, RSV).

To understand Israel's fall we have to place it next to Church history. Once this is done a new situation arises: both Christians and Jews find themselves under the same condemnation. The Church has nothing to boast of against the Synagogue. What applies to Israel applies to the Church and *vice versa*.

In this respect we find ourselves in a typically biblical situation: Israel is both My-people and Not-my-people (Hos. 2:23); the Christian is both *peccator* and *iustus*; the Church is both the bride without spot or wrinkle (Eph. 5:27), and the Church of Corinth (I Cor. 5:1) and of Laodicea (Rev. 3:14ff.). Unless we allow for the dialectic — what we are in Christ, and what we are in ourselves — we are bound to falsify our position and become hypocrites in our judgment of others.

4. The Difference between Christians and Jews

With the historic facts before us we have to ask the question: what then is the difference between Christians and Jews, between the man *in* Christ and the man *without* Christ?

The question is susceptible of a simple and straightforward answer: the difference is Jesus Christ himself.

Viewed from the human side there is no difference: both are sinners and in need of grace. But seen from the Cross there is a difference: the Christian acknowledges his need and looks to Jesus for salvation; the Jew saves himself. These are two radically different attitudes and result in two utterly different perceptions of God.

We do not say that Israel is without God. In fact, we do not say that anyone is without God, not even the atheist. But we do say that the Jewish and the Christian knowledge of God is *different*. It is the difference which counts.

5. Universalism and Jesus Christ

To know God in Jesus Christ is to know oneself a sinner saved by grace. Such radical understanding of grace is peculiar to the Christian self-awareness. Anyone who fails to see the radical nature of God's grace in Jesus Christ has not yet discovered the meaning of the Cross. "Conversion" means exactly this, the humble acknowledgment of my utter helplessness. Man rebels against this fact and tries to mask it by taking refuge in his religion, his spirituality, his moral achievement, his intellectual profundity, his aesthetic refinement. It is only in confrontation with Jesus Christ that we drop the mask and acknowledge our bankruptcy.

Universalism abstracts from the radical condition of man as a sinner before God. Once this happens, anthropology takes the place of Christology and the Church becomes a Synagogue. In the center then stands man himself, and Jesus of Nazareth is understood as a specimen of heroic human achievement.

This is exactly what is happening today. The peculiarity of the Western Church is the displacement of Jesus Christ by cultural values. We have thus reached a position when we can have theology without God, Christianity without Christ, Church without faith. In such a situation, Jewish evangelism appears as sheer bigotry. Roy Eckardt speaks of the "nonsense of seeking to make Christians out of Jews" (*The Christian Century*, March 30, 1966, p. 395). This is only bettered by Frederick Grant, former president of a theological seminary, who regards Jewish conversion as in "bad taste." For him, there is no difference between the two faiths; a converted Jew, he tells us, only adds "some additional matters" to what he already believes (*Christianity Today*, Jan. 7, 1966, p. 47). It is obvious that Eckardt and Grant speak in purely cultural terms, and that for them Jesus Christ is not at the center of the Christian faith.

Here cultural Christianity faces cultural Judaism not in terms of faith but in terms of cultural values. In this case the difference between Church and Synagogue reduces itself to the difference between tradition and ethnicity. Whether one worships in Church or Synagogue is decided by the accident of birth. Personal conviction has given place to sociological factors. In the last resort, everyone is right because no one is wrong. Under such conditions the biblical situation is completely altered: here there is no clash between God and idols, between cultic religion and personal loyalty, between the letter of the Law and the commitment of the heart.

6. The Challenge of Jewish Missions

We must not underestimate the difficulty of the Christian position. Too much has happened for Christians to claim any advantage over historic Israel. If evangelism implies a display of superiority, then we would do well to heed Eckardt's advice and not preach the Gospel to Jews.

Those who take the negative position point to the distressing record of Christian history: anti-Semitism, persecution, legal discrimination, forced conversions, and so on. They ask: with such a record, how can one possibly preach the Gospel of God's love to the very victims of Christian hatred? But once we acknowledge the ambiguity of the human situation and the intertwining of Jewish and Christian history, the position appears in a different light. All preaching, both within the Church and outside, is primarily preaching *against* oneself. Preaching is always an embarrassment for it carries the indictment of the preacher. The only legitimate reason for preaching the Gospel is loyalty to Jesus Christ.

It is at the point of loyalty that our Christianity is tested. Commitment to Jesus Christ makes universalism impossible. The testing ground is the Jewish mission field. It is only when face to face with the Jewish people that the question regarding Jesus takes on proper proportions. At this point the New Testament issue becomes alive again: does man save himself by his religious and cultural achievements or does he *utterly* depend upon God's grace?

The answer to this question decides whether we take our refuge underneath the Cross or make our stand upon our self-sufficiency.

Once we have decided about Judaism we have decided about all other religions. If Judaism can manage without Jesus Christ, so can the Church and so can the world religions. This is the reason evangelism hinges upon our attitude to Jewish missions.

Report of Group Discussion

The discussion was opened by a delegate from Israel, a man concerned with the work of Hebrew Christian missions. He spoke of his father and mother who were strict Orthodox Jews. He said that they fasted and tithed and kept scrupulously all of the Commandments, that no evangelical witness was ever given to them, that the only Christian Church they ever saw was one in which idols were worshiped, a matter which would repel any Jew. He said his parents were put to death in the slaughter of the Jews by Hitler. He had himself come to faith in Jesus Christ as the Messiah and his Savior. He asked the question very movingly, "Is there no hope for my parents who died, as far as I know, without any faith in Jesus Christ?" The members of the panel said that such questions had to be dealt with not only from a theological standpoint but from a pastoral standpoint, that the Judge of all the world would do right, and that one must understand the hardship through which these people had passed, that some questions could not be completely answered in this life.

There were those present who immediately responded that we had no authority to go beyond what Scripture states, that there is no apparent hope for anyone except through faith in Jesus Christ.

Delegate James Kennedy of Fort Lauderdale, Florida, brought an especially moving statement at this point, stating that he loved his parents dearly, but that neither of them was a Christian nor showed any promise of becoming same, that he prayed for them every day but that the integrity of God's Word was at stake and he had no hope for them apart from their acceptance of Christ as their Savior and Lord.

Dr. Akbar Haqq, the former dean of the Henry Martin School of Islamic Studies, brought an interesting discussion regarding those who had had no opportunity to hear the Gospel. He said there were great men such as Socrates and Plato who doubtless would have responded to Christ had such an opportunity been given them, and that there were other gifted people, such as Karl Marx, who would not respond. Dr. Haqq stressed that it was commonly believed that Christ did preach to those of the Old Testament who died without faith or hope in the Messiah, because no light had come to them.

He cited I Peter 3:18-22 — "For Christ also hath once suffered for sins, the just for the unjust, that he might bring us to God, being put to death in the flesh, but quickened by the Spirit: By which also he went and preached unto the spirits in prison; Which sometime were disobedient, when once the long-suffering of God waited in the days of Noah, while the ark was a preparing, wherein few, that is, eight souls were saved by water. The like figure whereunto even baptism doth also now save us (not the putting away of the filth of the flesh, but the answer of a good conscience toward God,) by the resurrection of Jesus Christ: Who is gone into heaven, and is on the right hand of God; angels and authorities and powers being made subject unto him."

The discussion was marked with a lively and free exchange of ideas; courtesy prevailed at all times. The interest was at such a peak when the close of the discussion period came that many lingered afterwards to carry on the serious nature of these matters which had been brought to the attention of the delegates. There seemed complete unanimity at one point — that man has a soul, that it can be won or lost for eternity, that the greatest work man could ever do is to seek to win as many as possible to faith in Jesus Christ.

Reporter: *Calvin Thielman*

THE CHURCH AND THE WORLD
A. J. Dain

Dr. Walter Künneth's stimulating and thought-provoking paper raises at the outset the problem of defining our terms, and this becomes supremely important when we speak of the Church. The biblical concept of the Church has been, and is, constantly confused with a given denomination, a group of denominations, or even with the total mass of nominal Christians in a given country.

Dr. Künneth recognizes that our use of the word here in the conference is general, and not limited to the biblical context of the Church: the body of Christ, the company of true believers. Once we accept a more general definition, we face immediately the basic obstacle of "nominalism" which weakens both the life and evangelistic outreach of the Church in every continent of the world.

The subject of this panel, however — defined in different documents as parochialism, self-containment and isolation — suggests that we are to limit our examination to the aspects of Church life covered by these headings and which hinder the evangelistic program of the Church. We will direct this inquiry into three main areas: first, preoccupation with other interests; secondly, failure to communicate with the outside world; and thirdly, dependence upon the professional ministry.

1. Preoccupation with other interests

Perhaps the greatest hindrance to evangelism within the life of a particular parish is its preoccupation with other interests. While these interests may be good, and even essential, their sum total in terms of time, energy and finance can result in a minimal concern for evangelism.

I would be the first to recognize and applaud a comprehensive program of teaching and instruction in the life of the local Church. Similarly, the cultivation of spiritual maturity and cultivation of personal holiness are essential, but if such efforts fail to lead to a concern for and outreach among those who are lost, both at home and abroad, they are dangerous, and probably unbalanced.

A second area of probable hindrance to evangelism in the life of the parish lies in the multiplicity of its own organizations, each organization having its own highly developed program. Such a complexity of meetings inevitably makes the Church centripetal rather than centrifugal in its emphasis. Members tend then to come to the church and its buildings to receive, rather than to go out and meet the world in order to give their witness.

THE REV. MR. DAIN is Bishop Coadjutor of the Diocese of Sydney, Australia (Church of England in Australia).

A third area of preoccupation with other interests concerns the mundane problem of buildings — their erection, maintenance and financing. How much time in the regular meetings of the parish council or committee is spent in considering buildings, property, budgets, and how much on the Church's evangelistic responsibility and program?

2. Failure to communicate

The second major area of hindrance in the Church's evangelistic outreach is its failure to communicate the Gospel to the outside world.

Self-complacency is perhaps one of the most common reasons for this failure. It is tragically possible for even a mature congregation to settle down into the confortable rut and routine of parochial life and perhaps unconsciously become satisfied and complacent. This settling down process inevitably brings spiritual paralysis.

In such churches, aggressive programs of evangelism would be considered unwise and likely to cause misunderstanding. There is an unwillingness to accept the basic fact that the Gospel must divide, and that the proclamation of the Gospel will always arouse hostility among those who reject it.

A further reason for failure in communication is the mistaken belief that evangelism must take place in the church, or on church property. Such a mentality insists that people must be brought to the church, instead of allowing the congregation to take the Gospel to the people, to their homes or wherever they can be reached.

Yet a further cause for the failure to communicate is the sheer inability of many sincere Christians to establish rapport with those whom they wish to win. Far too many Christians have isolated themselves from the world of today; they do not understand the language and find it impossible to "sit where they sit." Their clichés and religious terminology constitute a foreign language to people outside the Church.

A final possible cause in the breakdown of communications is the lack of personal holiness. It is still true that "the heathen shall know that I am the Lord when I am sanctified in you before their eyes." The quality of personal holiness is still the most potent form of evangelistic witness, but the present pattern of much parochial life is hardly conducive to its development.

3. Dependence upon the professional ministry

Mention has already been made of certain factors which tend toward an "inward" rather than an "outward" looking church. An even more powerful deterrent to any major emphasis upon evangelism, however, lies in the unscriptural dependence by the congregation upon the ordained minister or ministers. In far too many churches the laity are unwilling to take an active part in many areas of church life and particularly in evangelism. Church members in general inevitably think of evangelism as a specialized function to be undertaken exclusively by ministers, or perhaps by a few laymen who have a special gift for it.

The problem of such "clericalism" is much more acute where the pattern of ministry within a large congregation is the "one man" ministry. If all ministry is centered in one man, and he is clearly a teacher and not an evangelist, the imbalance of that Church's total witness is obvious.

The rapid spread of the early Church was undoubtedly the result of spontaneous lay witness; the areas of most rapid growth in the life of the Church are those where lay witness has been most effectively organized. Bishop Azariah's work in the Dornakal diocese of South India, and more recent Evangelism-in-Depth campaigns are but two telling examples of this truth.

If there is one single solution to the problem of parochialism, self-containment and isolation, it is mobilization of the total membership of our churches for, and in, a program of dynamic evangelism. It will, first of all, however, require a new breath of the Spirit of God upon the dry bones of the churches, so that motivated by a passion for Christ, and by compassion for the lost, men and women will cry with the Apostle, "Woe is me, if I preach not the Gospel."

THE GREATEST ENEMY IS WITHIN
Samuel H. Moffett

The more obvious hindrances to the proclamation of the Gospel of Jesus Christ are not necessarily the most deadly. Perils of geography, difficulties of communication, opposition of false religions, persecution by unfriendly governments — while all of these are powerfully obstructive, the greatest enemy is within. Even in the heat of the Reformation, Luther had the honesty to say, "I am more afraid of my own self than of the Pope and all his cardinals. Because I have within me the great pope, Self."

It is easier, of course, and more self-satisfying to blame evangelistic set-backs on external enemies. But the more searching question is how much of the blame for failure we must share ourselves. What are the hindrances within the Church?

Some have been discussed elsewhere in the Congress: spiritual indifference, sacerdotalism, heresy. But another may be even more dangerous because it is so often unrecognized. This is the sin of self-containment. It may be defined as a lack of meaningful contact with the non-Christian world. It comes in many forms, but whether it is caused by willful indifference, or fear of contamination, or ignorance, or selfish pre-occupation with the Christian community itself, the result is what contemporary theologians call "the Christian ghetto complex."

Of all the internal obstacles mentioned above this is most nearly fatal, for it so closely partakes of the very essence of sin — that is, a love of self that crowds out love of God and love of neighbor. Self-containment is sub-Christian, or perhaps more accurately, pre-Christian, for the Christian life begins with the new birth; the very imagery of the language suggests a breaking-out from a self-containing womb into a world of awareness and contact and need. The pattern of the new life is the self-emptying Christ (Phil. 2:3-8), not the self-satisfied Pharisee (Luke 18:9-11). At no point is the Christian self-contained; he is either Christ-sustained or dead. As for Christian mission and evangelism, self-containment and outreach are mutually exclusive. The church that is turned in upon itself has turned its back on the world to which it was sent by Jesus Christ.

There is no need to labor the point further. Self-containment is a basic denial of all that is Christian. The problem is that few will admit to having this disease. It is always someone else's problem, some other church's crippling weakness.

There is the classic example of a "Christian ghetto," the fate of Eastern Christianity under the Moslem conquerors. While often compassionately

DR. MOFFETT is professor of Historical Theology at Presbyterian Theological Seminary in Seoul, Korea.

described as the inevitable result of persecution, this is not altogether true. It was, in the final analysis, the deliberate choice of the Church. What finally produced the withered ghettoes of the Nestorians and the Copts was not so much the sword of Islam as the law of Islam, which permitted conquered Christians to worship but forbade them to propagate the Christian faith. Faced with a choice between survival and witness, the Church chose survival. It turned in upon itself. It ceased to evangelize. It survived, but what survived was no longer a whole Church. It was a sick, ingrown community.

In Czarist Russia, Christian withdrawal was even less of an imposition from without than what the Eastern churches experienced. The Russian church made its own ghetto, but in the mind, not the body. Isolating themselves from the agony of the people, Orthodox priests argued about the color of their vestments and about how many fingers should be extended in the benediction, until the revolution broke in on them and brought them, too late, out of their never-never land of liturgy into the world as it really is.

It would be comforting to think that such crippling self-containment is safely buried in the Church's past. The saddening truth is that no church in the world is quite free from the taint of the same poison.

There is self-containment of race, for example, and self-containment of liturgy. Separatism is another form of self-containment. So also it its opposite, preoccupation with church union. There is also the self-containment of the great, state churches, too intent on national prestige, ceremonies and subsidies to notice that they no longer have worshipers. And there is the self-containment of the small, free churches, so busy protecting their freedom from the world that they have ceased to have any influence in the world. There is self-containment by creed, and self-containment by sacrament. There is the self-containment of old and tired churches who no longer want to send missionaries; and the self-containment of younger, nationalist churches who no longer want to receive them.

But no matter what form it takes nor how plausibly its forms may be justified, self-containment is always and inevitably a hindrance to evangelism.

Take, for example, racial self-containment. This is probably the single most explosive issue in the world today. When racial discrimination penetrates the Church, it becomes more than a crime against humanity, it is an act of defiance against God himself (I John 4:20). In America, eleven o'clock Sunday morning has been called the most segregated hour. I do not believe this is true, but that such a statement could be made at all is indictment enough. The fact that there is any racial discrimination in the Christian Church has already done irreparable damage to world evangelism. If present trends continue, future historians may some day single this out as the decisive factor that drove a whole continent, Africa, away from Christ and into the embrace of Islam.

Another form of this sin is self-containment by caste. Christians would like to pretend that this is limited to India and its Hinduism, but our own Western, Christian suburbs are riddled with it. It is more subtle in the West. When the Church of England in the nineteenth century could be described as the Conservative Party gathered for prayer, and when a recent study of American church unions can point out that they never really cross class lines but usually remain a high-caste denominational phenomenon (R. Lee, *The Social Sources of Church Unity*, 1960), it can hardly be claimed that Christians have bravely broken down the barriers of class. The Church's social structure has become so self-contained in America that some sociologists assert that it purposefully excludes the lowest classes of American society from its evangelistic efforts. "Church programs are not designed to appeal to them and ministers never visit them . . .", say Vidich and Bensman in *Small Town in Mass Society* (Quoted by P. Berger, in *The Noise of Solemn Assemblies*, 1961). "The ministers and laymen . . . either do not see the unchurched or they have no desire to pollute the church membership with socially undesirable types."

All unwittingly, Christians sometimes shut themselves behind a language barrier. Evangelical jargon can be as unintelligible outside the inner circle as military alphabetese is outside the Pentagon. In a world where "redemption" means green stamps, and "sin" means sex, the very words with which we try to proclaim the Gospel sometimes only obscure it. It can be dangerous therefore to read nothing but evangelical literature. The man who lives in a one-vocabulary world too long loses the ability to talk meaningfully to anyone but his fellow-believers; this is not evangelism.

Another kind of self-containment is separatism. It is as old as the Syrian desert where Anchorites chained themselves to rocks or walled themselves up in caves. It is also, alas, as new as the latest church split in Korea. As a search for purity, separatism may have a touch of justification, but its fatal flaw is self-containment. It faces inward, not outward. It leads to negativism and withdrawal and self-righteousness. It talks evangelism, but its Christian outreach has lost its winsome appeal and has built into it a self-defeating pattern of schism and isolation that aborts the evangelistic invitation by the grimly exclusive attitude with which it is extended. There is no such thing as evangelism by separation. Every Christian should belong actively to at least one non-Christian — that is, not specifically Christian — organization in his community. Moreover he should join not just to evangelize it, but to understand it.

This last point is important. We defined the sin of self-containment as lack of meaningful contact with the non-Christian world. Perhaps this should be qualified. It is possible to have contacts that are meaningful, but only to one side. That kind of outreach only soothes the conscience or feeds the ego, it does not really break through the self-containment barrier. The Christian who is willing to meet the world only on his own terms, who feels no need to understand any position but his own, is still in his "Christian ghetto," and living to himself. His so-called contact with the world is counterfeit and artificial. His approach to others is gingerly self-protective, and carefully encapsulated from contamination.

Its defensiveness precludes any real meeting of minds. Its self-interestedness prevents the meeting of hearts and breaks down the one indispensable approach for any evangelism worthy of the name Christian, that is, the way of love.

There may be worse sins than self-containment, but few can more quickly blunt the growing edge of the Church of Jesus Christ. The Bible counts it as the accursed sin. This is no light condemnation. Its sign is the barren fig tree (Mark 11:12-14), heavy with leaves for its own self-beautification, but sterile and without fruit. When Jesus saw it, he cursed it.

MAINTAINING A DELICATE BALANCE
Everett L. Cattell

Why does the Church so often succumb either to absorption by the world on the one hand or to walled-in isolation from the world on the other? The reason, which may seem shocking at first, is simply that the Church is trying to follow its Lord. That is to say, there is value and good in both these positions; only when they become distorted do they become evil and troublesome.

Jesus' life displayed a superb balance. He was no ascetic. He mingled with crowds. He socialized with sinners. He was equally at home with Galilean peasants and the sophisticates of Jerusalem. He cared for people. On the other hand, he frequently retired to a quiet place for prayer, meditation and renewal. In other words, he was neither a recluse, nor was he a worldling. He also displayed a unique awareness of timing. In the face of mounting opposition he sometimes avoided an issue by staying away from Jerusalem and saying his time had not yet come. When the proper time had come, however, he went directly to Jerusalem and to death. He fully exemplified in his own life what he meant in his prayer for his disciples: "I do not pray that thou shouldst take them out of the world, but that thou shouldst keep them from the evil one" (John 17:15, RSV).

The incarnation is the pattern for all evangelism. When Jesus Christ came into the world he mingled with and ate with sinners. Yet no one ever accused him of sin. In his ministry of forgiveness and healing, several women of evil character were transformed and became his followers. Yet never was there a word of scandal — even when false witnesses tried to make a case against him. He was totally in the world yet wholly uncontaminated by it. He touched all kinds of human evil with the same confidence. He touched lepers knowing that instead of succumbing to the disease, he would issue healing and help for the diseased.

As the Father sent Jesus into the world, so he sends us. We too, have a mission and a message to proclaim which must be given to the whole world. We too, must keep ourselves unspotted from the world, much like the lotus flower whose special waxy surface keeps it impervious to the water in which it floats.

Let us be clear about one thing. The desire to be pure, the desire to be holy, the desire to keep ourselves unspotted from the world, the desire to have victory over the world, the flesh and the devil is completely Christian! Anyone who tries to live by the Scriptures takes this matter very seriously. We cannot emphasize this too strongly! To be effective in evan-

DR. CATTELL is the president of Malone College in Canton, Ohio, USA.

gelism the Church must be pure! But how shall we, how can we, keep free from worldliness?

Too often we follow what Jerome said: "I retire to the desert . . . that the eyes of wantons may not lead me captive; that beauty may not engender lust. You answer, 'This is not to fight but to run away! . . .' I confess my weakness," said Jerome. "I dare not fight in the hope of victory, lest perchance I be overcome. . . . Flight makes it impossible for me to win the victory; but at least it ensures me against defeat."

Sometimes we pride ourselves in thinking that we have kept ourselves unspotted from the world and have kept the faith. But actually we have kept the faith imprisoned behind a wall of separation and fear, which is as ineffective as what the disciples did on the night they gathered behind locked doors and barred windows to save their lives and to enjoy each other's fellowship.

We must face the fact that often this withdrawal has been rationalized on the grounds of preserving the purity of the Church and of believers when actually the motivation is fear and unbelief. We simply do not trust God. We are protective of the Gospel. We lack confidence in the power of the Holy Spirit to preserve Christ's Church without our devices.

We need an enormous resurgence of confidence in God and the Gospel. We need to realize that God still holds the whole world in his own hand. He has placed boundaries around man's rebelliousness beyond which not even Communism can penetrate.

We need to realize that the Kingdom of God is still the answer to man's predicament and that the Gospel of God is still wiser than the wisdom of men. We need enough confidence in the power of the Gospel to carry it to our halls of learning, and to the underprivileged and needy everywhere. We need to believe in this power of the Gospel so deeply that we will forget our own safety and even the human protection of the Church and will release the Gospel to do its powerful transforming work.

This Gospel does not need protection — it needs proclamation. Its messengers do not need safety — they need sending. Its relevance for the world in which we live needs probing by the best minds we have, not because the issue is in doubt, but because our effectiveness should be unquestioned and of the very best!

SOME MODERN TEMPTATIONS
C. Stacey Woods

Dr. Künneth has emphasized basic causes of the failure of the Church to fulfill her commission of world evangelism. Perhaps the following points should be underlined or considered as additional elements of this problem.

1. Nominalism

Nominal Christianity, which tragically represents by far the greater part of baptized church membership within the churches of Christendom, is the basic reason for the Church's failure to evangelize. Christendom itself demands evangelization, let alone the non-Christian world. Not only, however, is there this mass of baptized unbelief within the Church, but our theological faculties are filled with speculative philosophers rather than Bible-believing teachers of God's Law. These unbelievers have adulterated the pure Gospel with their rationalistic imaginings. These men destroy what little faith theological students may have in God and in his Word; consequently, many of the pulpits of our churches are filled with pastors who themselves have never experienced the regeneration of God. Is the answer to this dreadful situation to be found in the Church of true believers within the structure of this false and anomalous thing called Christendom? Can we seriously consider the task of the Church — evangelism — without first of all honestly recognizing this situation?

2. The content of the Gospel

It must always be realized that the Gospel is God's and not man's message; therefore we dare not add to it, nor take away from it. Our task is to proclaim and explain this saving Word. The Gospel is not some truncated formula like, "Believe on the Lord Jesus Christ and thou shalt be saved." Such a statement is the truth, but not all the truth of the Gospel. These words were spoken to a man already partially informed and under deep conviction of sin. Furthermore, this was not all that Paul taught him that night.

If a study were made of the work of evangelism as recorded in the book of Acts and in the New Testament epistles, we would see that to evangelize includes impartation of the entire New Testament revelation. The Gospel is more than a syllogistic plan of salvation. As an example of this fact, one may note Paul's work of evangelism at Thessalonica where he instructed the newly-born Christians in the whole counsel of God, including the truth of the second advent of Christ.

MR. WOODS is the general secretary of the International Fellowship of Evangelical Students, with headquarters in Lausanne, Switzerland.

The task of evangelism is more than spiritual obstetrics. Paul, as an evangelist, likened himself to a mother giving birth. He refers to himself as "again in travail until Christ be formed" in them (Gal. 4:20 ASV). If the evangelist is an itinerant preacher, and cannot remain to impart this whole counsel of God, then it should be realized that those preached to have not been evangelized in the New Testament sense. If care goes into the preparation of an evangelistic campaign, surely equal — and even more — care should be given to ensure that those professing Christ are received by Bible-believing Churches, and not by apostate congregations that falsely bear the name of Christ. These New Testament Churches must instruct babes in Christ more fully. Therein lies the failure of many evangelistic campaigns and of many Churches involved in the task of evangelism. The root of this problem is doctrinal, not situational. There are those whose evangelistic activity betrays an essential pelagianism, and whose Augustinianism commences once a decision has been made. Those thus professing Christ are said to be eternally secure. Salvation is regarded as a fire-escape from hell to heaven, rather than the goal of presenting every man perfect in Christ Jesus.

3. Spiritual infantilism in the Church

A consequence of the failure of the Church to complete this work of evangelism, teaching converts to observe all that Christ and his apostles commanded, is spiritual infantilism — babes in Christ who never have grown into young men or fathers in the faith. Today in many of our churches we find believers who know almost nothing of the principles of Christ's kingdom and of the laws of the new life in Christ. They are ignorant of the Scriptures. They know next to nothing of the divine goals and of their salvation. In fact, they would be unable to explain the Gospel to a seeker. Carnality, ignorance, lack of love for Christ and lack of intelligent obedience to his Word have produced a condition which has rendered even most of the regenerate impotent for effectiveness in evangelism.

Another factor contributing to this spiritual infantilism is the practical denial of the priesthood of all believers; the pulpit dominates and the pew is spiritually inert. The Acts of the Apostles makes it clear that besides the apostles, the ordinary Christian of those days fulfilled a God-given ministry of witness and evangelism. Persecution only succeeded in scattering the Christian laymen who went everywhere preaching the Word. If we contrast that situation with ours today, one of the reasons for the Church's failure to be effective in evangelism becomes obvious: world evangelism cannot be considered seriously apart from mobilizing and instructing every Christian for this task.

4. The Church a distinct people

The loss of a clear distinction and separation between the Church and the world, between Christian and non-Christian, is another hindrance to evangelism. While it is true that the Christian, in terms of language, culture, environment and empathy, is to be one with the world, at the same time the Christian, the new man in Christ, is a new creation, and is different from, and other than, the natural, unregenerate man. The Christian thinks differently, reacts differently, has a different standard of values and a different perspective. Although in the world, he is not of it. Unless this distinction is maintained, effective evangelism becomes very difficult.

To alienate and separate evangelism from the totality of the life and ministry of the Church is likewise false. Evangelism must always be woven together with the worship, fellowship, instruction and discipline of the Church. In such a context, the glory of God and the proclamation of the church Evangel is paralleled. If we allow concern over human response to the message to overshadow the glory of God in the victory of Christ over the world, the flesh and the devil, we shall also, in a measure, fail to fulfill our evangelistic task.

5. False methodology

A modern phenomenon in evangelism is the attempt to induce decisions or professions of faith in Christ by employing the techniques of American salesmanship and psychology to bring about such commitment. Such practices are in disobedience to the teaching of I Cor., chapters 1 and 2. Special methods which are said to ensure results, formulas for the infilling of the Holy Spirit, short steps to becoming a Christian, easily can falsely simplify the divine message and attempt to confine the Holy Spirit to our own structures. The Gospel must always be proclaimed with a view to the salvation of men, but also with a view to the glory of God — not only in the salvation of men, but in the way the message is proclaimed, so that faith never rests in the wisdom of men, but in the power of God. Our Lord has said: "I will build My Church." This is God's Work; our work is to proclaim the Evangel. True evangelism by the Church will be hindered rather than advanced if human techniques are permitted to substitute for the sovereign work of God the Holy Spirit.

Report of Group Discussion

Racial self-containment as a hindrance to evangelism emerged as a lively issue. Many delegates felt that racial tension is today a major deterrent to the evangelistic enterprise.

The Rev. Louis Johnson (USA) was appalled that Dr. Walter Künneth overlooked the matter of race in the position paper. 'If evangelicals run from the whole concept of race, how can they ever evangelize the world?" Johnson asked. Howard Jones (USA and Africa) termed the racial issue "a serious problem, a burning issue, one that needs to be dealt with in the Congress."

The issue took on added urgency in view of the statement of Dr. Moffett that racial discrimination in the Christian Church may drive the whole continent of Africa away from Christ and into the arms of Islam. Some of the African delegates spoke of personal experiences of discrimination. Others called upon an expression of Christian love as the only means by which such breaches can be healed.

In subsequent discussion, Congress delegates spoke of other types of self-containment which also hinder evangelistic work: self-containment by age-groups, a Western self-containment which refuses to acknowledge non-Western concepts even on the mission field, an intellectual self-containment where the academic communities are concerned, and a spiritual self-containment which hinges upon a lack of prayer and Bible study by Christian workers.

C. Stacey Woods (Switzerland) proposed suggestions on the academic level by mentioning the opportunities for evangelicals in theological and secular institutions. Isaac Ababio (Nigeria) called for an increase of corporate prayer by delegates on these specific issues.

Reporter: *Kenneth L. Downing*

LOSING GOD AT THE CENTER
Festo Kivengere

The topic "Spiritual Indifference" is too embarrassingly close to each of us to be treated with intellectual detachment. To deal with such a problem means probing one's own as well as others' spiritual inadequacy. And so I, no less than you, stand in the searchlight of our risen Savior, the head of the Church.

Spiritual indifference is not in itself a cause but rather an effect. Insights regarding it may be gained by studying God's dealings with his people, and by permitting the Holy Spirit to teach us through the Scriptures. Only the Holy Spirit can lead us from speculations about our spiritual problems to humble, honest confession of need and willing submission to his work of correction. Spiritual indifference comes to light in many ways: in our sickly relationship to Jesus Christ, in our backsliding, in our lovelessness toward the world, in our indifference toward reconciling men to God in Christ. In fact, spiritual indifference makes us "see men as trees, walking" (Mark 8:24).

Spiritual indifference is a symptom of a deeper spiritual disease. The story of Lot (Gen. 19:15-20) presents a godly man who became insensitive to impending danger. You remember the story of God's indignation against the sin-sick cities of the plain, and of Lot's lack of alarm. How did Lot become so indifferent, so Laodicean in his attitude? Not even the thunder of God's judgment could seemingly shake him. Lot had become so like his environment and therefore so deafened to God's warnings that he barely escaped the destruction that befell his fellow citizens. Here was one whose life, although he had not lost his religion, had shifted from being God-centered to being Lot-centered and Sodom-tinted. Indifference was a symptom and result of this condition. Having become spiritually insensitive, Lot was blind both to his own needs and to those of his community.

Numbers 21:4-5 records the sad experience of the Israelites who turned their backs on the Land of Promise. Redeemed from Egyptian bondage, they were to go forth to possess the Land of Milk and Honey. Overcome, however, by the trials of the way they lost their vision of God's promises and became indifferent to what he had said. "There is no bread," they complained, "neither is there any water, and our soul LOATHETH THIS LIGHT BREAD" (v. 5). Within reach of God's heavenly provision, these anemic followers of the true God chose to starve. When they thus lost spiritual sustenance, their strength to press on deteriorated and their vision failed; they lost the reality of God's promises – they became indifferent

THE REV. MR. KIVENGERE has been a lay preacher in Uganda for many years, is presently a student at Pittsburgh Theological Seminary in Pittsburgh, USA.

to their redemption, their hope, their privileges, their responsibilities. Canaan seemed no better than Egypt. Indifference here was a symptom of spiritual starvation caused by turning aside from God's provision to something supposedly more satisfying and palatable.

The story of Samson (Judges 15) offers another warning. By concentrating on satisfying natural desires in his own way instead of concentrating on the Giver and Controller of those desires, Samson lost his spiritual, then his physical sight. When he turned away from God, Samson became indifferent to the very enemies he was called to fight and subdue. Spiritual values are kept alive only when God's Spirit is in control. God must touch us anew in order to restore in us the feeling of his holiness and the ability to discern his enemies.

Another lesson comes from post-exilic times during the rebuilding of the walls of Jerusalem. Despair had overtaken the leaders of Judah. "The strength of the bearers of burdens is decayed, and there is much rubbish; so that we are not able to build the wall" (Neh. 4:10). Indifference, we must remember, can come from despair, and despair may come from lost confidence in God's ability to act in power. Nehemiah therefore said: "Remember the Lord, which is great and terrible, and fight . . ." (4:14). Was weakened strength the result of forgetting the Lord? Did accumulated rubbish dim the vision of rebuilding the wall? By turning once again to the Almighty God, the builders saw despondency and indifference turn to determination, and rubbish became a challenge to renewed, united application to the task at hand.

Hosea 7:8-9 records Jehovah's complaint against Ephraim. "Ephraim," says the prophet, "hath mixed himself among the people; Ephraim is a cake not turned." Moreover, without his knowing it, "Strangers have devoured his strength;" without his knowing it, "Gray hairs are here and there upon him. . . ." Ephraim's problem is not one of inactivity, for he bustles about to gain the favor of neighboring countries. In the process he is indifferent to his spiritual downfall. Ephraim suffered from a kind of introversion in which he felt remorse — but only on a horizontal level — for what he seemed to be missing. God's people here had developed what Charles Spurgeon called "a marvelous skill in missing;" in this case they missed a proper focus upon God to solve spiritual and national problems. Indifference to spiritual decline was symptomatic of a broken relationship with the Lord and of only half-hearted measures to remedy the situation.

In Revelation 3:15-20 our risen Lord speaks of the church at Laodicea. Blind to her true condition and self-satisfied, this church considered herself in need of nothing, spiritually or physically. To her, coldness, backsliding, lack of zeal and spiritual commitment seemed no cause for alarm; she is comfortably stagnant, serenely lukewarm, totally indifferent to any spiritual feeling whatever. By keeping the Lord locked out of her life, she had become spiritually indifferent first to her condition, then to her relationship with her Savior and Lord who should be her first love, and then to the world to which she was called to minister.

These biblical examples indicate that spiritual indifference is always the result of losing God as the center and source of spiritual vitality. When Christians and churches turn to various social and religious remedies to fill the void they vaguely feel, they are but hobbling about on crutches in doing the Lord's work and become a laughingstock to the world.

Spiritual indifference today encounters us everywhere at close range; none of us is exempt from its inroads. When the Church, the body of Christ, no longer gives preeminence to its Head, it inevitably loses its capacity for spiritual sensitivity and becomes indifferent to its unique commission to spread the Gospel. Christ must be central, and the Church must be totally dependent upon him. All our elaborate programming and organization, all our discussion of faith and doctrine fall short as remedies for spiritual indifference.

Only a real relationship to Christ can give the Church the needed purifying fire of evangelism for a soul-saving ministry. Strict orthodoxy is not a sufficient answer, not even our evangelical heritage. Unless the Church is infused and empowered by the Spirit of God it will be dry and lifeless and apathetic. It is embarrassing for God's people to be caught in spiritual indifference; it is deeply heart-searching to admit this condition and to turn from it to the living God. Perhaps this fact is a major hindrance to spiritual refreshing in our time. Are we willing to come under God's searching, revealing light? Are we determined and willing to repent? If not, spiritual apathy will continue and worsen. The Lord who alone can heal his Church waits to bless us when we humbly confess our dire need. This will happen when one or another steps out — from whatever comfortable and secure position he occupies — to stand where his Lord stood and still stands. Only at the Cross are lives stripped of whatever breeds indifference toward Christ and toward his world. Here only will the Church experience the fresh liberation and vigor that stirs the attention of an indifferent world.

"For thus saith the high and lofty One that inhabiteth eternity, whose name is Holy; I dwell in the high and holy place, with him also that is of a contrite and humble spirit, to revive the spirit of the humble, and to revive the heart of the contrite ones" (Isa. 57:15).

May God save his people from spiritual indifference and set his Church on fire before it is too late.

AS THE WORLD SEES THE CHURCH
Robert E. Coleman

Nothing quite so contradicts evangelism as the church's indifference to it. An atheist expressed it well when he wrote: "Did I firmly believe, as millions say they do, that the knowledge and practice of religion in this life influences destiny in another, religion would mean to me everything. . . . I should labour in its cause alone. I would esteem one soul gained for heaven worth a life of suffering. Earthly consequences should never stay my hand, nor seal my lips. Earth, its joys and its griefs, would occupy no moment of my thoughts. I would strive to look upon Eternity alone and on the immortal souls around me, soon to be everlastingly happy or everlastingly miserable. I would go forth to the world and preach it in season and out of season, and my text would be, 'What shall it profit a man if he gain the whole world and lose his soul?'" (Quoted in Norman Grubb, *C. T. Studd*, Atlantic City, N.J., World Wide Revival Prayer Movement, 1935, p. 40. Reading this tract greatly influenced the decision of C. T. Studd to give up his fortune and to become a missionary).

Perhaps this unbeliever saw things more clearly than many in the Church. At least he honestly recognized that to believe on Christ commits one to proclaim his Gospel, and at any cost.

To this the Church would agree. We all know that a Christian must witness to his faith by word and by deed. The problem comes when our noble professions are spelled out in specific action. However sincere, mere affirmations of concern simply do not get the job done. Nor is a constant whirl of activity in the Church any assurance that souls are being born again. The Great Commission is fulfilled only as we set our hearts to practice it in a deliberate course of action. Making disciples for Christ simply does not happen by accident. One must aim at the target to hit it.

Dedication to this task costs something. It cost Jesus his life. Ironically, the worldly-minded priests stated the truth when in derision they said of Jesus on the Cross: "He saved others; himself he cannot save" (Mark 15: 31). What they failed to comprehend in their smugness, of course, was that Jesus had not come to save himself. He came to save them. He "came not to be ministered unto, but to minister, and to give his life a ransom for many" (Matt. 20:28). He "came to seek and to save the lost" (see Luke 19:10). This was the only reason for his earthly existence. Continuously dedicating himself to this mission, he went to the Cross.

Yet Jesus made it clear that those who followed him were called to

DR. COLEMAN is professor of evangelism at Asbury Theological Seminary in Wilmore, Kentucky, and president of *Christian Outreach* in Huntingdon Valley, Pennsylvania.

the same task for which he had come "into the world," and that it would demand the same dedication. The cross which every disciple must accept finds its most relevant meaning at this point (Mark 8:34). Moreover, the inward cleansing of his sanctification is to prepare us for this ministry. Without this giving of ourselves to serve those Christ loved and died to save, our spiritual experience is not likely to mean much to the world, or to the Church. (Further discussion of this point may be found in Robert E. Coleman's book, *The Master Plan of Evangelism*, Westwood, Revell, 1964).

Failure of the Church to apply this principle in practice is our greatest hindrance to evangelism. For the most part we are trying to live unto ourselves. The challenge of world evangelism is not denied; it is just ignored. Anyone who dares to take it seriously is looked upon in many quarters as a religious fanatic. The rugged obedience of the Cross may still be seen in our creeds, but it is hard to find in our lives. There are so many things more precious to us than the fulfillment of God's purposes, and we do not want to give them up. It would mean changing too much of our own easy-going pattern of living.

I am afraid that most of us are still like Peter at Caesarea Philippi when he rebuked his Lord for talking about being crucified (Mark 8:31, 32). The Big Fisherman did not want the Son of God to endure such suffering and death. Knowing how superficial was Peter's understanding of his redemptive mission, Jesus turned and said: "Get thee behind me, Satan: for thou savorest not the things that be of God, but the things that be of men" (Mark 8:33). This is a startling reprimand, especially when it is recalled that Jesus was speaking to the leader of the apostolic company who just a moment before had expressed so forcibly his faith in Christ (Mark 8:29). Yet it should serve to remind us all that there lurks within our hearts a natural reluctance to accept fully Christ's commitment to the Cross.

Here finally is where we must face the issue. It is well enough for us in the Church to talk about the Cross, but what is more to the point is for us to take up our cross ourselves. In practical terms, this means that we must offer our bodies in living sacrifice. Only as we lose ourselves for his sake and the Gospel's can we truly live with him in the fullness of his Spirit.

This is the answer to our spiritual indifference. When our hearts are filled with his Presence, evangelism is as inevitable as it is contagious. In his abiding, the Cross becomes the glory of our life, consuming us with the very love of Calvary.

I am convinced that the renewal which the Church is seeking will only be known as this truth is experienced. It may be necessary for us to focus the theological basis of our faith more clearly and to learn more relevant ways by which we can communicate it to our generation, but this in itself cannot alter the deadening blight of our spiritual impotency. We must know again the power of Pentecost. Nothing else will suffice if we are to meet the challenge before us. We may try to get by on less, and sometimes the makeshift form of religion may satisfy the normal standards of church respectability, but unless the Holy Spirit is allowed to flow unhindered through our lives, we cannot fulfill our high calling.

Evangelism is the way of the Cross. If we miss the Cross in its commitment and purpose, we will miss the reality of the Spirit-controlled life, and in so doing, we will miss the dynamic of evangelism. The sooner we recognize this fact, empty ourselves of those things known to be contrary to the mind of Christ, and lay hold upon the Power from on High, the sooner we can get on with the work of God.

THE POPE OF SELF

Robert P. Evans

In his paper on hindrances to evangelism within the Church, Professor Künneth has already enunciated the problem faced by this panel in his words, "Much more serious, probably, is the hindrance to the Gospel from the weak faith, the doubting faith, yes, even the unbelief of those who call themselves Christians." He goes on to remark that many professing Christians "appear so 'unredeemed' and act as if they have no faith."

In the Bible we note frequent allusion to this problem of spiritual non-expectation. Perhaps the classic statement of it is Jesus' rebuke to his disciples who tried to exorcise a demon from a child. When they asked why they failed, he said, "Because of your unbelief" (Matt. 17:20). A moment earlier he had called them a faithless and perverse generation, and had asked, "How long shall I suffer you?" (Matt. 17:17). It is obvious that Jesus expected miracle-performing faith from his disciples; when he did not find it he grew indignant with them. Then Jesus, in visiting his own neighborhood, ". . . did not many mighty works there because of their unbelief" (Matt. 13:58). At the tomb of Lazarus, Christ told Mary, "Said I not unto thee, that, if thou wouldest believe, thou shouldest see the glory of God?" (John 11:40). These sample verses from the New Testament show how unbelief inhibits the progress of God's cause.

Our concern here is not so much with those who have introduced doctrinal heresy and produced schism within the Church, since that lies more in the province of other panel groups. Rather, we are considering here the plight of those evangelical Christians whose faith somehow fails to appropriate the power of God in evangelistic fulfillment. Millions of regenerate Christians who heartily affirm the truth of the Bible and are active in corporate worship in their churches fail to engage in habitual personal witness to Jesus Christ. What is still more grave, their unbelief actively hinders men from faith in Jesus Christ as Savior and Lord.

The first step toward dealing with this condition of unbelief among evangelicals is to recognize it as a problem and a sin. That is not as simple as it sounds. Like the Israelites before the Jordan, we are more prone to point to the walled cities and frightful giants in front of us than to the unbelief in our own hearts. We tend to find our nemesis in liberal doctrine and other expressions of a godless age rather than in our own doubts. It is always easier to find a scapegoat upon which we can heap the blame of our failure. But if we are to help restore spiritual health to the evangelical community, we must first recognize that we evangelicals are sick. We must

DR. EVANS is the founder and European director of the Greater Europe Mission in LePecq, France.

agree with Martin Luther, who said he did not so much fear the Pope in Rome as the pope of self who reigned in his heart. Yet God would ask more of us than mere acquiescence that something is wrong. We evangelicals must face the dark truth: the unbelief which has cooled and dampened our evangelistic endeavor is sin. A first and unavoidable step is humiliation, repentance and God's forgiveness. Along with this comes quite naturally a rededication of life.

A second step toward the recovery of belief in God's power in effective evangelism lies in our use of the Scriptures. According to Rom. 10:17, "Faith cometh by hearing, and hearing by the word of God." Evangelism of any sort requires an utter dependence upon the revelation of God, not only for the content of the message, but as a guide to our methods of delievering it. It is not enough for evangelicals to affirm and defend the inerrancy of Scripture. We must learn more about wielding it as a sword of the Spirit. By this we do not minimize the role of apologists, of which evangelicals have a good number. But in evangelism we are concerned with communication of the message of Christ to the world. To that end we should resaturate ourselves in the Bible, increasing our reading, study and use of it; and thereby increasing faith. If faith feeds upon Scripture, and flourishes through hearing it, the use of the Bible is obviously a very important key to evangelism.

Thirdly, the complacent evangelical must have a perennially fresh experience of the Holy Spirit. The presence of the Holy Spirit in the Church, as described in Acts, is too well-known to deserve comment. But in a Church which is only 34 years away from the twenty-first century, the miracles of the Holy Spirit are no less needed than in the first. An evangelism adapted to modern man may be more sophisticated in expression, more technical in methodology, but can it be any less dependent on the third person of the Trinity? We remind ourselves that according to the Lord Jesus Christ, the one who sent him — the Holy Spirit — is God, and is the executor of the divine will in the Church on earth throughout this age. In a system which relies on the Holy Spirit, the evangelizers of men are dependent on his persuasion if they want to convince man of sin and the judgment to come. An evangelism deprived of the preeminence of the Holy Spirit, and consisting only of intellectual dialogue, is irreconcilable to the teaching of the Holy Spirit. Not only individual evangelizers are dependent on the Spirit for proclaiming reconciliation through Christ, but the Church bodies deputizing them need his vision, guidance and decision. A good expression of this is Acts 13:2: "As they ministered to the Lord, and fasted, the Holy Ghost said, Separate me Barnabas and Saul for the work whereunto I have called them."

Lastly, we know from experience that purposeful physical action in evangelism tends to dissipate doubt. The apostle Paul said to Timothy, "For God hath not given us the spirit of fear; but of power, and of love, and of a sound mind" (II Tim. 1:7). Modern psychology comes to our aid here. For all his denial of the supernatural, William James is helpful in showing how the use of the motor reflexes, over which we have firm control, facilitate the response of the will, which is less subject to control. Let a Christian, believing the promises of the Bible and trusting in the Holy Spirit, initiate evangelistic action and he will be surprised how his lagging faith will revive.

We might summarize this by recalling that faith is more indispensable to the Church militant than many of her other weapons, like organization, efficiency, or unity. This is why Paul insists to the Ephesians that "the shield of faith" is the peerless weapon, "above all" (Eph. 6:16) in value. With faith, the believer will be able to quench all of Satan's fiery darts and will likewise please God. "But without faith it is impossible to please him" (Hebrews 11:6).

SOME IMPORTANT FLAWS
Augustus B. Marwieh

When we consider the redeeming power of Christianity, we are puzzled by the indifference of Christians towards sinners that are dying outside the Church. This negligence towards men's souls is a matter of concern in every evangelical circle today. I shall therefore suggest some of the possible causes for this prevailing spiritual indifference.

1. Spiritual indifference results from failure of the Church to make Christianity relevant to the needs of modern man.

Salvation of the soul from hell after death has been overemphasized at the expense of salvation of the soul from hell on earth. There are believers in every congregation who are going through all kinds of personal crisis. But the majority of ministers today have no message for these people. They have only one message, namely, that men should repent of their sin and put their faith in Jesus Christ. Obviously, no born-again Christian will deny the fact that the primary mission of the Church is to get men and women to repent of their sins and to accept Jesus Christ as their Savior. But this vital message has been preached to disadvantage by preaching it indiscriminately every Sunday without regard for the personal problems of believers who have already repented of their sins and accepted Christ as Savior. In Hebrews we are told to "go on unto perfection; not laying again the foundation of repentance from dead works, and faith toward God." If after conversion believers are not led on to perfection, they will be like unwanted babes whose emotional and physical needs are unmet and uncared for. Such a condition is bound to create spiritual indifference. For how can a Christian be eager to tell a sinner about Christ when he himself is only a babe and experiences a frustrated and confused life?

2. Insufficient knowledge of the Scriptures leads to spiritual indifference.

When an individual accepts Christ, he must be fed by the Word of God if he is to grow. When such feeding ceases, spiritual growth will also cease and the person remains a babe in Christ. Consequently he remains indifferent to spiritual matters. We know that children are often completely lacking in interest in the constructive work of home and nation building that customarily absorbs the attention and energy of adults. Interest in mature activities comes through growth. A mature person will not only develop interest in a constructive program of activities but will also initiate other such programs. So Christians when they are spiritually mature will work naturally and actively in the building of the Kingdom of God.

THE REV. MR. MARWIEH is a Christian educator with the E.N.I. Mission in Sinoe County, Liberia, West Africa.

Moreover, children are often frustrated and extremely dependent. Were they to remain such children all their lives they would be a terrible liability to home and society. Similarly, Christians who have not been given the opportunity to grow through increasing knowledge of the Scriptures are not only indifferent to spiritual things, but are also a serious liability to the Church. Ministers must therefore teach the whole Bible, which speaks to the whole man.

3. Lack of missionary emphasis in our churches promotes spiritual indifference.

The minister's foremost duty is to enlist each of his members in soul winning. It is his duty to inspire each church member to obey the Great Commission. This is a far from simple task, for not everyone finds it easy to witness.

4. Another cause for spiritual indifference is the coercive urging of Christians to witness without considering the difficulties involved.

It is a known fact that repeated failure invites lack of interest. A Christian who repeatedly fails in attempts to witness will sooner or later dread even the thought of witnessing. There may be several reasons for his failure. A Christian may be overly shy, or perhaps he may not know just how to proceed or what to say. Or he may not know how to handle objections raised by the unsaved. Hampered by such difficulties members will become frustrated and ultimately hardened to the pastor's repeated appeals to witness. When the pastor in turn has repeatedly failed to get response from his members, he, too, becomes discouraged and subconsciously evades the subject. The result will be a spiritually indifferent pastor who has a spiritually lethargic congregation.

In order to be effective, church evangelism must be methodically and prayerfully planned. For instance, in promoting church evangelism, the entire membership could be divided into evangelistic departments with key members serving as departmental heads. These leaders could then be responsible for enlisting each member of their respective departments. But to operate such a highly organized evangelistic church program in addition to the regular program of the church is beyond the ability of any one man.

5. Many people are spiritually indifferent because their spiritual and emotional needs are not being met, inasmuch as one minister or worker must do the work of several persons and therefore cannot help everyone thoroughly or most effectively.

In these days when the whole world is rapidly becoming urbanized, we need to reconsider our present methods of church operation. Certainly today's church needs more than one minister. There is plenty of work for a pastor, a minister of Christian education, a minister of evangelism and missions, and a minister of counseling.

If we are to check the disease of spiritual indifference in our churches, we must consider taking the following steps:

1. We must begin where the disciples began when they set out to evangelize the world. We must pray. Each local pastor should spare no effort in organizing his Church into evangelistic prayer groups.

2. We must know what to pray for. The disciples prayed with a profound consciousness of a lost world completely abandoned to vice and barbarism.

3. We must pray and work with a goal. The disciples prayed and worked to evangelize the world in their generation. Each church member should be inspired to pray and work with a passion to win every soul in his community for Christ in his lifetime.

4. We must promote spiritual growth and maturity in our church members by the purposeful preaching and systematic teaching of God's Word.

5. We must be specific and specialized in our ministry, in order to meet the emotional and spiritual needs of our church members. To continue their special work of prayer and ministry of the Word, the apostles asked that another office be created in the Church to take care of those being "neglected in the daily ministration." Thus the office of deacons was created. If the apostles were living in this complex world, they would undoubtedly create new administrative offices to handle the problems of today's modern Church.

Report of Group Discussion

Schulte (Germany) objected to Dr. Künneth's assumption that a "Christian is planted into fellowship with Christ . . . through baptism and confirmation." "This is not biblical," Schulte said. "Moreover, the belief that sprinkling a child makes it a Christian is the greatest hindrance to evangelism in Germany."

Kivengere (Uganda) remarked that one initiates a convert into the Church by outward signs such as baptism, but it is afterwards, especially after a revival experience, that baptism and confirmation become a living reality.

Roy Hession (England) remarked that spiritual indifference exists not only in "the Church" but also in the hearts of leaders, whether pastor, evangelist or missionary.

Antidotes to such indifference were seen by various delegates to lie in: a fresh experience of the Holy Spirit, attention to the Word of God, the value of so-called "crisis situations" and the obligation to teach people to witness as well as asking them to do so.

Reporter: *I. Ben Wati*

PRESERVING THE TRUTH OF THE BIBLE
Hermann Sasse

1. "Evangelize" is the English translation of the Greek word "euangeli-zesthai" which means to proclaim the evangel, the Gospel, as in Romans 1:15, I Corinthians 15:1. Actually, the word appears also in the Old Testament — in Isaiah 61:1, for example. While the word "evangelize" can be used for any form of proclaiming the Gospel — to non-Christians, let us say, or in the Sunday sermon to Christian congregations (Acts 2:42) — the word today is used preferably for that special kind of preaching which is directed toward those who have either lost the Christian faith or are in danger of losing it.

2. Our age has been called the "Post-Christian Age" because one of its features is what has been called the "great divorce," the severing of that bond which in former centuries held together Western nations and Western culture on the one hand and Christian faith on the other. By a slow process that began in the Renaissance at the end of the Middle Ages, and that has accelerated since the eighteenth century, our Christian heritage of the past has been vanishing. Our society and its civilization have become secularized. Churches are losing their influence on people. Believing Christians are a minority in what we still call the "Christian" nations. A general breakdown seems to be taking place similar to what the churches of the Near East experienced during the rise of Islam. Perhaps the fate of Western Christianity will be like that of the Oriental churches which became small minorities. While they more or less preserved their heritage, they no longer progressed and had no impact upon the politics, society, and culture of their countries.

3. This possible dire future for Christianity was first sensed during the French Revolution when the Church and Christianity were abolished in one of the oldest Christian nations of Europe, and when the death of God was proclaimed. Subsequent revolutions up to the Russian Bolshevist Revolution of 1917 seemed to confirm the prophesied end of Christianity. Hence in the nineteenth and twentieth centuries we find the churches awakening to the new great task of winning back the lost and of preventing further apostasy. Home missions in Germany, and corresponding evangelistic enterprises in the Protestant churches of English-speaking nations are examples of Christians' efforts to counteract this ominous trend. Roman Catholicism has taken up the challenge also. The Second Vatican Council has inaugurated a new era in the history of Roman Catholicism, in which the largest church of Christendom is trying to mobilize all its spiritual resources and

DR. SASSE is a professor of Theology in Immanuel Theological Seminary, North Adelaide, Australia. He was formerly professor of Theology in the University of Erlangen, Germany.

to unite with the rest of Christendom for a great counter-attack against the powers of secularism with the purpose — in accordance with the Roman understanding of the Gospel — of winning all mankind for Christ and his Church.

4. The attempts we make at this Congress to define the task of evangelism in our time must be based on the evangelical understanding of the Gospel. Over against Protestant Modernism (under whatever flag it flies) which has lost the Christian, biblical concept of sin, and Roman Catholicism which minimizes the sin of mankind, we reaffirm the Gospel as it was rediscovered by the Reformers. The Gospel is not a new law, a message of what we can do or ought to do. It is the glad tidings of what God has done for us in Christ. We maintain the biblical doctrine of man which states that man has fallen away from his Creator and can do nothing to save himself or even to prepare himself for salvation. We maintain the doctrine of God who was in Christ reconciling the world unto himself; the doctrine of Christ who alone is the Savior of sinners and, therefore, the only hope of mankind (Acts 4:12); and we maintain the doctrine of the Holy Spirit, the Paraclete, whom Christ sends from his Father to accomplish his work in human souls and in the Church.

5. Christendom has learned that personal belief in the Savior can be lost. From the very beginning of the preaching of the Gospel we find that believers do indeed fall away. Even our Lord experienced this and not only in the case of Judas (John 6:66; 12:37 ff.). Moreover not only individual believers, but whole churches have apostasized. The riddle of unbelief and apostasy plays a great role in the Bible (Isa. 6:10 ff.). Jesus and the apostles made frequent use of the passage in Isa. 6:10 ff. (Mark 4:12; Acts 28:26 ff.). The divine mystery of him "(who) openeth and no man shutteth; and shutteth and no man openeth" (Rev. 3:7), should keep us from Pelagianism in our evangelistic work. On the other hand, we should joyfully deliver our message as the apostles did, following our Lord even to the way of the Cross. The true evangelist must *live* by grace alone, by faith alone, and not only preach about it.

6. Another lesson from history is that we cannot preserve a living faith in the Savior unless we preserve the doctrine of the Bible concerning his person and his work. Christology is not an invention of men. Jesus himself provoked it when he asked his disciples, "Whom say you that I am?" and asked his adversaries, "What think ye of Christ? Whose son is he?" Churches that lose faith in the true divinity of Christ are doomed. Churches that have lost faith in the true humanity of Christ have been unable to preserve faith in the merciful High Priest who is our brother (Heb. 2:17 ff.; 4:15 ff.). Here perhaps is the reason why the vast majority of Monophysites who could no longer forthrightly confess the true human nature of the Incarnate One gave up their Savior and became Muhammedans. Luther always stressed that no one can understand the "pro nobis"

of the Creed, the words "for us and for our salvation," "crucified for us," who does not believe in the true divinity and the true humanity of Christ.

Evangelism without solid doctrinal instruction may perhaps lead to an emotional conversion, but not to that conversion of the whole man of which we read in the story of Pentecost. "They continued steadfastly in the apostles' doctrine," it was reported. The greatest evangelists, Christ's apostles, were also the greatest teachers of the Church. The Lord of the Church had not been ashamed to be their "master," which means their teacher, not ashamed to be the great divine teacher of all mankind.

THE UNIQUE CONTENT OF THE GOSPEL
Jules-Marcel Nicole

While the word "evangelization" does not appear in the New Testament, the use made by sacred writers of the terms "Gospel," "evangelize" and "evangelist" enables us to see clearly what conditions are necessary to make our evangelization fruitful and to overcome the obstacles that would normally make it impossible.

We have three different constructions of the word Gospel. Reference may be made to:

a. the messenger, as when Paul speaks of *his* Gospel (Rom. 2:16);

b. those evangelized, as when the Gospel of the circumcision or the uncircumcision is referred to (Gal. 2:7);

c. the content of the message.

We read the phrases, Gospel of the kingdom of God (Matt. 4:23; 9:35; 24:14) of grace (Acts 20:24) of salvation (Eph. 1:13) and especially the Gospel of the Son or of Christ (Rom. 1:9; I Cor. 9:12; II Cor. 2:12; 9:13; Gal. 1:7; Phil. 1:27; I Thess. 3:2). The last expression may have two interpretations: the Gospel of which Christ is the theme or object (evangelium de Christo) or the Gospel of which Christ is the author or the subject (evangelium Christi). The first interpretation is preferable because of the comparison with scripture passages that emphasize the "good news of Christ." To these we will refer later. The second interpretation, however, is supported by the phrase, Gospel of God, where without doubt, God is understood to be the author of the message (Rom. 1.1; 15:16; II Cor. 11:7; I Thess. 2:2; 2:8, 9; I Pet. 4:17).

Similarly, the Greek verb *euangelizomai* may be applied either to the individuals to whom the Gospel is being preached or to the message that is given. This distinction is not as clear in our translations as in the original text. In the English only people are "evangelized," whereas in the Greek text it is the content of the message that is proclaimed. The apostles preached as the good news, *euangelizonto*, the Lord himself (Acts 5:42; 8:35; 11:20; 17:18; Gal. 1:16). This resulted in the preaching of the Word (Acts 8:4; 15:35; I Pet. 1:25); of the promise (Acts 13:32); of the kingdom (Luke 16:16); of peace (Acts 10:36; Rom. 10:15); of faith (Gal. 1:23); of conversion (Acts 14:15); of resurrection (Acts 17:18).

All this calls our attention to the content of the Gospel. The "Good News" is not just any message that might be preached but is unique and clearly defined in its content.

Even in the apostolic era, there were those who, using the name evan-

MR. NICOLE is professor and president of the Bible Institute in Nogent-sur-Marne, France.

gelist, preached "another" Gospel (II Cor. 11:4; Gal. 1:6, 7). Paul cursed them (Gal. 1:8, 9). To change the content of the Gospel is to destroy it. There is no substitute. It makes no difference how dignified the author of this counterfeit may be: "But though we, or an angel from heaven, preach any other gospel unto you than that which we have preached unto you, let him be accursed" (Gal. 1:8).

The temptation to change the content of the Gospel generally has its origin in a desire to make it more palatable. The Gospel has always been foolishness and a stumbling block to them that perish (I Cor. 1:18, 23). Those who think that the apostolic preaching was well adapted to the mentality of that generation, but that it is necessary to make it more acceptable to the man of the twentieth century have not carefully read the Epistle to the Corinthians. The Gospel will never be fashionable at any period of history or in any country. We note also that some have always sought to have a wider and more ready hearing. They have tried to improve the Gospel by rounding off its sharp angles, by sweetening some of its more bitter aspects, by removing some of its hindrances to the natural man.

But this approach has very serious consequences. First, it is a direct betrayal of the Lord who has sent us. What would we think of an ambassador who changed his instructions from his government to please those to whom he is sent? It is also unfair to those whom we are supposed to evangelize because it deprives them of the divine message they have a right to hear and which alone can bring them salvation.

Christianity "is not a religion that flatters the natural man; those of the world as they reject it testify that Christianity is a strange teaching; those who do not dare reject it, try to adapt it. They take away its unpleasant features or its *myths*, as they choose to call them. They make it almost reasonable; but, when it is made intellectually acceptable, it has lost its power. . . . Zeal, fervour, holiness and love disappear with these strange dogmas. The salt of the earth has lost its savour. . . . On the other hand, when you hear that revival has started somewhere, so that faith is quickened and zeal is flourishing, do not ask on what kind of ground, do not inquire concerning the system that has produced these precious plants. Before the question has been asked, you may be able to reply that it is on the rough and uneven soil of orthodoxy, in the shadow of these mysteries that transcend human reason and which the latter would like to avoid." (Vinet, *Discours, Un caractere du Christianisme*, ed. 1853, pp. 59, 60).

In view of what we have just seen, we conclude that effective evangelization is closely associated with a certain "form of doctrine"; this very expression is used by the apostle Paul (Rom. 6:17). Thus it is evident that unbelief and heresy constitute the greatest obstacles to evangelization.

Other panels will examine certain contemporary errors such as universalism and sacerdotalism, with its twin brother sacramentalism. But many other doctrinal deviations threaten the proclamation of the Gospel, and we will denounce them at this point.

First, since we are to preach *Jesus Christ*, any false teaching concerning the person of the Lord cuts at the root that enables us to evangelize in the right way. It is certainly true that "we know in part and that we prophesy in part." We must be modest in our presentation. But since the Lord has revealed himself to us, we must adhere to this revelation of himself. If Jesus is not at the same time God and man, there is no more Good News. God alone is able to save (Isa. 43:11) and it is only by his incarnation that the Son is able to be our Mediator (I Tim. 2:3, 5). The miracle that has confirmed this dual nature of Christ is the virgin birth (Isa. 7:14). As Karl Barth so well expresses it, "let us take two theologians who seem to show forth the same respect for the mystery of Noel. Can we say that they have the same idea in their heads, if one accepts the virgin birth as a confirmation of this mystery and the other rejects it as a useless form or refuses to preach it? Must not this negation or indifference with respect to the miracle of the virgin birth reveal a negative attitude with respect to the reality toward which this miracle points? Is not this reality only perceived by him who has firmly accepted the miracle as purposed by the Biblical witness?" (Karl Barth, *Dogmatique*, first volume, chapter 2, second section, 615:3, page 167 from the French translation, page 196 from the German text).

Jesus himself came to announce the Good News of *peace* which was by the blood of the Cross (Eph. 2:13, 17). This message of reconciliation which was committed to us is interwoven with the fact that he who was without sin was made sin for us (II Cor. 5:20, 21). We cannot explain the mystery of the atonement. But we must believe that Christ's death is a sacrifice for sin (Isa. 53:10). Surely it is also an example, an act of devotion, a way of reaching the heart. But when we see only this side of the atonement and neglect his vicarious suffering, there is no longer a message for the troubled conscience or the anguished heart. Evangelization has become impossible.

Paul sums up the Gospel in three points: Christ has died, he was buried, he rose again (I Cor. 15:3, 4). Then he recalls the various appearances of Christ. The objective reality of that resurrection is the only guarantee that we have of forgiveness and life (Acts 13:37-39; Rom. 4:23-25; 10:9). If the resurrection of Jesus is a myth, evangelization has become a fraud. "If Christ be not risen, then is our preaching vain, and your faith is also vain" (I Cor. 15:14, 17).

The New Testament speaks of it also as the gospel of the grace of God (Acts 20:24). Anything that tends to cloud the fact that this salvation is a free gift from God or that we are undeserving, destroys the Gospel. It is quite clear that by our own efforts we can never satisfactorily meet the holy requirements of God. One must be very superficial to imagine that eternal blessedness can be earned. "Who will say: I have purified my heart, and my sins are cleansed?" (cf. Prov. 20:9, Berkeley). The Gospel is simply this: God has consented not to consider our failures; he does not expect us to acquire a personal holiness that is forever beyond our possibilities, but he clothes us in his righteousness, a righteousness fully sufficient for time and eternity. It was this essential subject that the Judaizing teachers repudiated by insinuating that observance of the Mosaic law must be added to the redemption that is in Christ. We know with what spirit Paul refuted this doctrine in his epistle to the Galatians. Yet even today there are those who would make good works a requirement for salvation. Those who accept this error create a certain kind of propaganda which alas, is sometimes crowned with success. But they are not evangelists; they are more like messengers of bad news.

The Gospel call requires a reply from man. We find the expression "preach the *faith*" as the Good News (Gal. 1:23). Elsewhere the Gospel is presented as an invitation to conversion (Acts 14:15). We cannot stop at this point very long because it approaches the theory of universalism which is to be discussed in another panel. But it is certain that an invitation is of primary importance if there is to be real evangelization. Jesus called his disciples to follow him, and to do this immediately and visibly (Mk. 1:16-20; 2:14; Luke 9:59-62). In the Acts of the Apostles, we read again and again that the hearers accepted the Word, believed and committed themselves – and all this without delay (Acts 2:41; 4:4; 8:15; 11:21; 13:43; 16:34; 17:34; 18:8, etc.). Certain opponents of our methods are especially irritated by this aspect of our evangelization. It is quite apparent that we must be careful not to exert psychological or emotional pressures on the audience, and not to confuse a visible act which may be ambiguous with a true conversion which God alone is able to know with certainty. And we must not put our confidence in statistics which can often give the wrong impression. But it is not only biblical but also psychologically necessary to invite those who have been touched by the message of grace to manifest it in some visible way. Otherwise there is the risk of letting the ripe grain dry and rot rather than of harvesting it. We must not throw out the net of the kingdom of God and then neglect to draw it in.

All these obstacles in evangelization that we have mentioned have a common denominator: in one way or another, they have their source in unfaithfulness to the biblical standard. The apostles preached the Good News of the Word (Acts 8:4; 15:35; I Pet. 1:25). They were confident that they brought a message from God and confident that they must make it heard whatever the cost. They did not hesitate on certain occasions to enter into dialogue with their contemporary philosophers (Acts 17:17, 18), but they were fully persuaded that the Gospel was not of human origin and the trumpet that they put to their lips did not give forth an uncertain sound.

We must not be afraid to bring an authoritative word to our contemporaries. Some tell us that we must not speak like those who give the appearance of knowing and instructing others, but that we must listen to what the world has to say, and must seek to discover the voice of Christ in the accents of the world. That is, we should be engaged in a dialogue where we receive at least as much as we can give. This is not the way to evangelize.

Certainly, we must be unpretentious, and more than that, sincerely humble. We must show that our confidence does not come from ourselves (II Cor. 1:9). We must be ready to confess our sins and errors. We are only human vessels. But we have a treasure that those to whom we are preaching do not have (II Cor. 4:7). Let us not forget that the world by its wisdom did not know God (I Cor. 1:21), that the history of the most brilliant human civilization may also be considered a time of ignorance (Acts 17:30), and that we preach him whom men at their best ignorantly worship (Acts 17:23). Let us not be ashamed of the Gospel (Rom. 1:16), but proclaim it with boldness, as we ought to speak (Eph. 6:20)!

PREACHING AN AUTHORITATIVE MESSAGE

Wayne Dehoney

In this discussion I use evangelism in the sense of "bringing men to a saving knowledge of Jesus Christ."

I confine my generalizations about the Church to my church and my denomination, and speak from the perspective of a denomination that has been relatively effective in evangelism, doubling its membership in a quarter of a century to 11 million.

1. The secret of effectiveness

What are some primary factors that contribute to the effectiveness of Southern Baptist churches in evangelism?

a. Theology — a conservative biblical faith.

b. Motivation — a consuming concern for reaching people.

c. Practice — the use of the traditional methodology of revivalism. We have emphasized the techniques of mass evangelism, church and simultaneous revivals and city crusades.

But our "bread and butter" methodology in evangelism has been the Sunday-school for all ages with its week-by-week program of outreach. During the last generation, our multiple-unit and small unit Bible classes, through a continuous program of visitation, have brought literally millions of lost persons into our churches for Bible study. As the Sunday-school became saturated with lost souls, we simply reaped them through revivals and regular Sunday services.

We have discovered that 90 per cent of our baptisms came through the Sunday-school, having been enrolled, enlisted and cultivated first in the Bible class. We have discovered that in any given year, we have one-chance-out-of-243 of reaching the average lost person in our community through all the other activities of the Church. But if a Sunday-school class enrolls that lost person in Bible study, the chance then becomes one-in-three that he or she will be converted and baptized within the year. We have discovered that any Church enrolling 300 lost persons in Bible school can expect to baptize an average of 100 new converts each year for the next three years.

In the 1950s, the success of this "Sunday-school methodology" in evangelism produced for Southern Baptists net gains in Sunday-school enrollment approaching half a million annually, with baptisms matching this figure. But in this decade, Sunday-school enrollment has leveled off and baptisms have dropped proportionately.

DR. DEHONEY is president of The Southern Baptist Convention and pastor of the First Baptist Church in Jackson, Tennessee, USA.

2. Hindrances to evangelism in our churches today

It is against this background that I discuss the theological and practical heresies that retard our advance, and the revival that we need to offset them.

(a) *We need a revival of authoritative Gospel preaching in our pulpits.* Faced with moral collapse and futility, modern man does not want to hear "Thus saith Bultman" but "Thus saith the Lord."

We are asked to be relevant in our preaching. But what is more relevant than to deal with man at his deepest need – his estrangement and separation from God by sin? Truly relevant preaching, as Paul declared, proclaims the Good News that Christ in his own body on the Cross broke down the middle wall of partition to reconcile man to God. This makes absurd the argument over whether the Gospel is "to do good deeds" or "to preach Good News!"

(b) *We need a revival of preaching that pleads for a verdict and magnifies the miracle of instantaneous conversion.*

There are those to whom preaching for a verdict and for visible results is an anathema. They would preach "only to register truth," and consider an immediate response to be superficial or inadequate. Such a position is completely inconsistent with the New Testament example.

The keen edge of evangelism has been dulled also by those churches that require new converts to confer with a membership committee, and to go through a waiting period (presumably for the believer to "cool off") before being received into the Church. Who are we to sit in judgment upon another person's sincerity, motivation, and commitment? The Church must have faith in people and faith that the grace of God can immediately transform a repentant sinner.

(c) *We need a revival of experiential Christianity.* Historically, the blight of Christianity has been the substitution of traditional faith for experiential faith.

But scientism and intellectualism have brought a new challenge, namely, to substitute *propositional* faith for *experiential* faith. Some would reason their way to a certain theological or philosophical position and then identify the result as "an adequate faith."

But our faith is experiential. Jesus said, "Ye must be born again." To be saved, we must experience the living Christ as a person.

(d) *We need a revival of respect for and the use of methodology* in evangelism. Although Jesus said, "Ask, and it shall be given you," there is a sophisticated attitude that scorns anything so methodical as "cause and effect" when applied to the Gospel.

In the Church and in evangelism, if we do certain things, we can expect, within reason, certain results. This does not rule out the activity of the Holy Spirit. If there is any validity in the parable of the talents, then

God holds us responsible for using every honorable method within our power to achieve results for the kingdom.

We have no right to disdain results. We must be concerned about the results as well as the depth and quality of our witness. We are responsible to God to be effective in our evangelism! We must have a revival of appreciation for measurements, methodology, technique and program if we are to have a new day of evangelism in the churches.

(e) *We need a revival of compassion and concern for people.*

In our pluralistic society, syncretism as a theology is a subtle challenge to Christianity. Are we honestly convinced that it was imperative for Christ to die on the Cross, and that in order to be saved it is absolutely necessary for every individual in this world to accept personally what Christ has done for him on the Cross? I am afraid that some of us either have doubts about the total depravity and lostness of man, or we simply do not care that the person outside of Christ is "without God and without hope in the world."

(f) Finally, *we need a revival of spiritual optimism, expectancy and excitement.* Melancholy defeatism in the Church is nothing less than unadulterated heresy that repudiates the New Testament message of conquest and victory. God is not dead. This is no post-Christian era. God's Church has not lost its relevancy. The living God is at work in his world today. Personally, I believe that we are on the threshold of a great spiritual renaissance, if those of us who are at this Congress are willing to be God's instruments in bringing about this awakening.

SOME OVERLOOKED HINDRANCES
Pieter J. Mietes

We are dealing with hindrances within the Church! In this confused and needy world how humbling it is to see the Church being accused!

But this should not lead anyone to take the role of judge, for all of us are a part of, and are personally responsible for, this failing Church. It would be wrong if in our discussions we tried to cure the Church and forget our own guilt for its condition.

Perhaps a few questions can give direction to our thinking:

1. How does the Lord Jesus Christ see these hindrances? Is this Congress not ordained of him? Should we not, first of all, consider his instructions, his provisions, his return?

2. How does a world in unbelief see these hindrances? Are they a sign of weakness, of infirmity, of senility? Is the holy Church an issuer of high affirmations; does it point always to Calvary's Cross as the isle of safety; does it speak of a living Lord but keep its spiritual medicine from an ailing world?

3. How do we see these hindrances? Do we say: "What a pity? What a shame?" Or are we restless, until we find the answer? This situation ought to make us jump out of our traditional routine. It should so grieve our hearts that we kneel on the blood-pillow of Calvary. Someone has said: "We are not so much in need of theology as of knee-ology." The situation ought to stir all our reserves of love and service. Only a fresh new consecration will be acceptable to the Lord of Evangelism.

Internal hindrances to evangelism are the most dangerous ones. They suggest defeatism, Judas among the disciples. They bring to mind Peter who said, "I go a fishing," and took others with him. They may even suggest Demas who forsook the apostle Paul, because the present world stole his heart.

True evangelism is impossible without a personal acceptance of Scriptural truth, no matter how it clashes with man-made ideas. The Bible must be the guidebook.

Evangelism is one of the streams that flows from God's great river of love. "There is a river, the streams whereof shall make glad the city of God" (Ps. 46:4). "Thou visitest the earth, and waterest it; thou greatly enrichest it with the river of God, which is full of water . . ." (Ps. 65:9).

Evangelism may also be seen as the artillery that batters the bastions of the enemy of men's souls. All fighting against unbelief and heresy may prove useless without the cannonade of prayer, of testimony and of the

THE REV. MR. MIETES is the minister of the Free Evangelical Church in Zeist, The Netherlands.

fire of the Holy Spirit. Founder of the Navigators, Dawson Trotman, had this conviction: "I believe it is an army of soldiers, dedicated to Jesus Christ, who believe not only that he is God, but that he can fulfill every promise he has ever made, and that there isn't anything too hard for him." And again: "We are born to reproduce." The first order ever given to man was that he "be fruitful and multiply." God did not tell Adam and Eve to be spiritual. They were already perfect, made in his image. He just said: "Multiply. I want more just like you, more in my own image."

Among overlooked hindrances to evangelism are the following:

1. The self-satisfied attitude. Religion limited by spiritual shortsightedness. Religion with no vision.

2. Keeping one's faith private in the well-locked safe of the heart.

3. Fear of man. God is a dwarf while men are giants.

4. Total misconception as to life's true riches.

5. Indifference to strangers and outsiders (Matt. 5:46, 47).

6. Irrelevance of the Gospel to modern man (I Cor. 2).

7. Misapplication of the phrase "The Fatherhood of God," as if it applied to all men.

8. Placing the Lord's return in the far distant future.

9. Archaic language, religious jargon.

10. Beautiful church architecture that stimulates more awe than love, liturgy instead of evangelism.

Our goal, of course, is not so much to identify as many hindrances as we can but rather to find a way out of them.

The Bible gives us some helps for meeting these hindrances.

1. Is enough emphasis being laid on the unique name of Jesus? (Acts 4:12). Ludwig Hofacker (1798–1828) once said: "Brethren, pray until the name of Jesus becomes a power in your preaching."

2. Are we on the outlook for a harvest to reap as the fruit of Jesus' sacrifice? (Isa. 53).

3. Do we reckon with a God who will give us "all things" freely through the gift of his Son? (Rom. 8:32).

4. Are we the "salt" of the earth? Many seem to read instead, "You are the pepper of the earth." They attack the sinner in a bitter way. Or they say, "You are the vinegar of the earth." They are like sour pickles and preserve their griefs. They would frighten away any shy enquirer. Others would say, "You are the sugar of the earth." They are oversweet and fear to hurt anyone's feelings. But is this the way of the Gospel? Are they not forgetting the judgments and holiness of God?

No, we are the cheap, but indispensable, "salt" of the earth.

5. We might also ask, are some of us, like Jonah, asleep during the storm, while the life of the crew is in danger?

6. Is priority always given to the Kingdom of God? (Matt. 6:33).

7. Do we see that Christ's hands are still and continually outstretched? (Isa. 65:2).

8. Have some believers left their first love? D. L. Moody said in connection with I Cor. 13: "A man may be a good doctor, without loving his patients; a good lawyer, without loving his clients; a good geologist, without loving science; but he cannot be a good Christian without love. Love is greater than prophecy, greater than faith."

The Word of God is not bound. The Holy Spirit will empower the obedient. May we in this Congress not add to the Church's guilt. Worldwide evangelism may prove to be the best remedy for a sick and sinful world.

BAPTISM AS A GATEWAY
Richard Møller Petersen

About 95 per cent of the children born in my parish in Copenhagen are brought to the Church to be baptized. Before their baptism I explain to the parents what baptism is and what responsibilities it entails for them in bringing up their children in Christian nurture. Later in public school the children receive instruction in Bible history and in the Christian faith. Sometimes this instruction is very fine; sometimes it is mediocre. At the age of 13 or 14, practically all of these children then spend a winter in preparation for confirmation. They have two hours each week with the pastor. It is in this framework that baptism is performed in our Church. To be honest, one must admit that much is lacking in the kind of Christian instruction that the children generally receive.

Despite this fact, I think most pastors will agree that these observances are among their finest experiences. Here they feel they are on solid ground, believing the New Testament Church has placed central importance on baptism as an indispensable means of becoming a member of the Christian ecclesia.

We are all aware of the problems pertaining to the mode of baptism in Christian churches. Churches that perform infant baptism may ask: Is it right to baptize infants when we have no guarantee they will receive a truly responsible Christian education? This question goes also for those churches that perform baptism only upon personal proclamation of faith in Jesus Christ.

In spite of this situation, it is still a tremendous privilege to be used of the Lord of the Church to say to a little child: "Little one, from now on, as you grow up, you may know that the salvation which Christ won on his Cross also includes you." Baptism proclaims some of the deepest truths of the New Testament. "Herein is love, not that we loved God, but that he loved us, and sent his son to be the propitiation for our sins" (I John 4:10). We proclaim to the one who receives baptism: "If I take the wings of the morning, and dwell in the uttermost parts of the sea; Even there shall thy hand lead me, and thy right hand shall hold me" (Psalm 139:9, 10).

It is intellectually quite inconceivable that Christ should choose such simple means as baptism or the breaking of bread as instruments of his grace. It is just as incredible as the fact that God, in a small distant country on a definite day in history, let his son be born into this world of the virgin Mary and let him die on a Cross.

Whatever outward similarities may have existed between the practice

THE REV. MR. PETERSEN is pastor of Holy Cross Church in Copenhagen, Denmark.

of Christian baptism and the washing practices in Jewish sects like the Qumran group for instance, the doctrine of baptism in the New Testament is quite unique. And there is no parallel in any known religious movement to the concept of baptism into the death and resurrection of Christ, as St. Paul expressed it in Rom. 6:4, "Therefore we are buried with him by baptism into death: that like as Christ was raised up from the dead by the glory of the Father, even so we also should walk in newness of life"; or in Col. 2:12, "Buried with him in baptism, wherein also ye are risen with him through the faith of the operation of God, who hath raised him from the dead." Baptism is really a stumbling block to the intellect, whether it be administered as infant baptism or to adults upon confession of faith in Christ Jesus. But it gives us a tremendous resting place. My baptism, performed perhaps when I was but a little child, tells me that Christ Jesus has wrought salvation for all mankind, and that in that salvation he included me.

But it is also clear that baptism is a tremendous challenge, for it is evident that the New Testament Church did not contemplate the possibility of a saving faith apart from baptism. Nonetheless, we see how the New Testament Church began to digress from the dominant pattern according to which confession of faith preceded baptism. We read that Christians were baptized with their household and there is no indication that these people had the same religious experience as the head of the house (Acts 16:15; I Cor. 1:16). Has not the Holy Spirit so guided the Church — right from New Testament times — that we should refrain from over-emphasizing the hows and whens of baptism. Rather, we are to accept the basic challenge that baptism and a life of faith in Christ Jesus belong together.

Baptism is also regeneration. "According to his mercy he saved us, by the washing of regeneration, and renewing of the Holy Ghost; Which he shed on us abundantly through Jesus Christ our Savior . . ." (Titus 3:5, 6).

Does this not indicate that God has an important place in his household for the Christian congregation? One cannot but recall Jesus' words to Peter: "I will give unto thee the keys of the kingdom of heaven: and whatsoever thou shalt bind on earth shall be bound in heaven; and whatsoever thou shalt loose on earth shall be loosed in heaven" (Matt. 16:19).

God has so bound himself to his Church on earth, that he has given eternal promises to those that undertake to bring men into the Church by baptism. My own redemption is not the precondition for what God does for us in baptism but is the fruit of the regeneration which Christ has given to the people of God on earth and addressed to me, the individual Christian, in my baptism. That is why I dare hope for a true redemption. I am saved not because of my own works, but by the grace of God. By his grace there has been a witnessing Church, a Christian people that makes intercession for the world; by his grace there are Christian parents who prepare the hearts of their children to receive God's grace. It was by the grace of God that I came to see the light. I had to respond. But it was God who placed me within the sphere of redemption.

What a gift it is, that God has ordained baptism as the gateway into the Christian Church! Suppose this landmark were not there.

We would be groping in uncertainty as to where the Christian Church is. We would be constantly asking whether we as individuals were really Christians or not. But now God has set clear boundaries. There may be good Christians and bad Christians. There may be Christians who betray their Master consciously or Christians who yearn to be in the Lord's service. But this Church tells the world that God has placed his people in the midst of it.

But being baptized does not mean an automatic salvation. St. Paul knew this. "But I keep under my body, and bring it into subjection: lest that by any means, when I have preached to others, I myself should be a castaway" (I Cor. 9:27). He knew that each man must work out his salvation with fear and trembling (Phil. 2:12).

Just as Israel — although it was God's chosen people — did not escape judgment (cf. I Cor. 10:1-13), so we Christians who in baptism have participated in Christ's death and resurrection must live our lives under the judgment of Christ, and at the resurrection must appear before his judgment seat.

Our baptism reminds us that God has a plan for our lives. He wants us as his witnesses and partners in the world. "God wants man to be his creature. Furthermore, he wants him to be his partner. There is a causa Dei in the world. God wants light, not darkness. He wants cosmos, not chaos. He wants peace, not disorder. He wants man to administer and to receive justice rather than to inflict and to suffer injustice. He wants man to live according to the Spirit rather than according to the flesh. He wants man bound and pledged to him rather than to any other authority. He wants man to live and not to die" (Karl Barth).

Our baptism points toward a fulfillment of our lives — toward a conscious acceptance of Christ as Lord and Savior, to a committing of our lives to him and to a life of service for him and our fellowman. It points toward the day of fulfillment. "For now we see through a glass, darkly; but then face to face: now I know in part; but then shall I know even as also I am known" (I Cor. 13:12).

With our baptism we obtain the greatest promise anyone can receive: "Lo, I am with you always, even unto the end of the world." We become ". . . persuaded, that neither death, nor life . . . shall be able to separate us from the love of God, which is in Christ Jesus our Lord." Our baptism is God's seal upon us, our guarantee of Christ's presence in the Holy Spirit, so that as Christ "was raised up from the dead by the glory of the Father, even so we also should walk in newness of life" (Rom. 6:4).

Of course there are many questions concerning Christian baptism.

What about the millions of children who have been baptized only because this is the thing to do? What about the many people who seem never to experience a personal Christian faith? What about the many who never receive Christian baptism? What about those who were baptized, but turned away from God? Let us avoid supplying answers that the Bible does not give. Rather, let us open our hearts to God's Word as he speaks to us and draws us to himself.

A PLEA FOR BELIEVER'S BAPTISM

Duke K. McCall

No Christian theologian, it seems to me, defines his views of baptism in such a way as consciously to make baptism a barrier to evangelism. As he describes baptism, it is always an asset if not an instrument of evangelism. Unless each one of us clearly understands this point, we will think that others' views of baptism demand critical scrutiny and revision while our own baptismal practices are a channel of divine grace. What must concern us, therefore, is what baptism means to the non-Christian.

When baptism is administered only to those who have entered consciously into a saving relationship with Christ Jesus, it obviously is not a hindrance to evangelism. On the other hand, there are some who contend that to withhold baptism until after such a conscious experience is to deny the effectiveness of a means of grace to those who should be saved. Let me review briefly, therefore, the two perspectives from which a case for indiscriminate baptism is most commonly presented.

The Augustinian doctrine of mankind as *massa damnata* leads to the conclusion that every child is born with the intolerable burden of Adam's sin and has no hope of eternal life except for baptismal entry into the realm of grace. This doctrine is vividly portrayed in a woodcut that appears in the introduction to the 1700 A.D. Benedictine edition of Augustine's works. The interior of a church depicts a baptistry on the right where a bishop is plunging a naked infant into the font. Over on the left is another christening party; its members show expressions of horror, for the infant being brought for baptism has died unexpectedly. The picture carries the inscription in Latin, "One is taken and another is left; because great is the grace of God, and true is the justice of God." This Augustinian interpretation of divine justice brought about a purely mechanical view of the efficacy of baptism. The ancient baptismal formula *ex opere operato* becomes a powerful incentive for parents who themselves may or may not be Christian to "get the baby done," as the English say. It has none of the strengths of covenant theology which assumes that faith will be joined to the baptismal act as a result of Christian nurture. The forces of evangelism are effectively dammed up in the hearts of others who hold this view because what is needed has been done; we find, too, that in this scientific era some non-Christians are repelled by this "magical" baptismal practice.

In other quarters, indiscriminate baptism gains support because of the theology represented by F. D. Maurice.

DR. McCALL is president of The Southern Baptist Theological Seminary in Louisville, Kentucky.

This views holds that the world, although infected by evil and marred by man's sin, is still God's world. In Christ, God reclaimed the universe that belongs to him. Consequently every baby is God's child whether faith discerns the fact or not. The Cross and resurrection of Christ claim and save every human being whether or not the fact is recognized. In this system, "The Church is that part of the world which has discerned and seeks to live by the truth." Maurice says, "We tell all men, those who are most incredulous of my message, most hostile to it, that this Name is about them, that they are living, moving, and having their being in it. They do not acquire this privilege by baptism; we baptize them because they have it."

We might comment that if baptism signifies only the recognition that the world as it is belongs to God, modern secular man may be pardoned for having other more important, pressing concerns.

Indiscriminate baptism which affirms that regeneration has already been accomplished is contradicted for the man in the street by the morning's newspaper headlines and by his daily contacts with business associates and neighbors. The Church as the chaplain of the *status quo* will not do. The Church as the messenger of the Gospel of regeneration for every generation of men is something quite different and what is required.

Moreover, John Calvin reminds us: "The sacraments properly fulfill their office only when the Spirit, that inward teacher, comes to them, by whose power alone ears are penetrated and affections moved and our souls opened for the sacraments to enter in. If the Spirit be lacking, the sacraments can accomplish nothing more in our minds than the splendor of the sun shining upon blind eyes, or a voice sounding in deaf ears."

Martin Luther pointed both to a radical eschatalogical implication of baptism which stems from baptism as the gift of God and to the human acceptance of the gift. "You pledge yourself to continue in this desire," he said, "and to slay your sin more and more as long as you live, even until your dying day. This, too, God accepts. He trains and tests you all your life long, with many good works and with all kinds of suffering. Thereby he accomplishes in you what you in baptism have desired, namely, that you may become free from sin, die, and rise again at the Lord's day, and so fulfill your baptism." The focus of baptism is therefore not on being, but on becoming. The apostle Paul has clearly set forth an understanding of baptism which, in spite of any other misunderstandings we may bring to baptism, will make the baptismal experience not a barrier to but a powerful instrument of evangelism.

"What shall we say then?" asked Paul. "Shall we continue in sin, that grace may abound? God forbid. We who died to sin, how shall we any longer live therein? Or are ye ignorant that all we who were baptized into Christ Jesus were baptized into his death? We were buried therefore with him through baptism into death: that like as Christ was raised from the dead through the glory of the Father, so we also might walk in newness of life. For if we have become united with him in the likeness of his death, we shall be also in the likeness of his resurrection; knowing this, that our old man was crucified with him, that the body of sin might be done away, that so we should no longer be in bondage to sin; for he that hath died is justified from sin" (Rom. 6:1-7, ASV).

BAPTISM AS A RITE OF INITIATION
A.W. Goodwin Hudson

Perhaps no other subject has so tantalized the Christian Church or called forth such difference of opinion. This paper will simply try to state that scriptural argument in this matter is not, as many would suppose, all on one side.

The ordinance of baptism – named some eighty times in the New Testament – is important by virtue of our Lord's command. Yet, according to Scripture, a person can receive without deriving any benefit from it. Each generation of church members has had its Judas Iscariots, its Ananias and Sapphira, etc., who were undoubtedly baptized persons, but "all that be washed with water be not washed with The Holy Spirit" (Archbishop Cranmer, 1553).

Nor can it be proved from Scripture that baptism is absolutely essential to salvation, for it is an ordinance which a person may never receive, and yet be a Christian. The classic example is the repentant thief who received neither of the two sacraments, yet received the blessing of a place with Christ in paradise when he died. Contemporary examples are members of the Salvation Army, or of the Society of Friends who normally are not baptized yet who, it cannot be denied, give evidence of true grace.

We must also consider the different practices of the various Christian denominations, and the doctrinal emphases these practices involve.

The Nature or Meaning of Baptism

There are three main interpretations:

Adult, or *"Believers' Baptism,"* emphasized a personal profession of repentance and faith that only a person who has come to the age of discretion can make.

Infant Baptism, (or the Hypothetical Theory), the primary consideration is the Godward side of the sacrament, rather than the candidate's attitude toward him.

Baptismal Regeneration, means that regeneration depends upon baptism; when baptism takes place, regeneration also occurs.

All three positions agree in *one* point – that baptism has to do with what God has done for the person in Christ. Beyond this main premise, however, they part company.

In *Baptismal Regeneration* it is claimed that grace is bestowed potentially. It is the implanting of the seed, which may or may not develop, rather than a moral or spiritual revolution taking place upon, or only after, the exercise of faith by the individual.

THE RT. REV. BISHOP HUDSON is rector of St. Paul's (Anglican) Church, Portsmouth Square, England.

In *Believers' Baptism*, baptism is regarded more as a sign or symbol of regeneration – a public witness to the fact that regeneration has already occurred in the true believer.

The Hypothetical Theory is so-called, because baptism in the New Testament is always expressed as "unto," that is, with a "view to," or "for the purpose of" spiritual blessing, and is therefore not by itself, and alone, the act of conveyance of that blessing. That is, it gives "as a deed gives," and not "as an electrical wire gives."

The *Jewish Baptism* was "with a view to" temple membership and worship. *The Baptism of John the Baptist* was "with a view to" repentance and the coming of the Messiah. *Christian Baptism* was "with a view to" relationship with God, in Christ. In other words, baptism always looks forward, not backward.

This third position is linked with Infant Baptism, and assumes that the baptismal service is not complete in itself, but anticipates the time of personal repentance and faith when the child comes of age to ratify the promises made on his behalf by sincere godparents. The practice of baptizing infants must never be considered apart from the ordinance of confirmation, of which one important aspect is the act of consecration to God, and the ratifying of promises made on the person's behalf at baptism.

Infant baptism is an act of faith on the part of the officiating minister, the parents and the godparents who believe that Christ has already done a saving work on the child's behalf, a work that in later years must be appropriated by repentance and faith. Such baptism is the divine pledge that salvation shall come to the person who fulfills the proper requirements. All God's promises are conditional. Baptism, either of an adult or of an infant, does not actually regenerate. Article 25 of the Anglican Church's 39 Articles declares, "In such only as *worthily* receive the same, they (the Sacraments) have a wholesome effect or operation;" no mere mechanical act can save a person.

In Adult Baptism, the ordinance is the seal of an already existing regeneration. In Infant Baptism it is a sign or seal that God's promises will be effectual if the promises of the godparents are faithfully carried out in the life of the child; it is similar to a contract requiring two signatures to make it valid. God has given us his signature (in Christ) as if by a legal deed, and the contract awaits the signature of the person to whom the conveyance is made.

The question, "What then does baptism do?", involves a most complicated answer if we are to do justice to the articles of faith of all the various denominations. Chiefly, we can say that baptism is regarded as an initiation rite into the Christian Church; that is, a person is not admitted into a church that he might be converted, but because he is converted. And in the case of the infant, he is identified with all the blessings obtained by

Christ through his death and resurrection on that child's behalf, with a view to his own acceptance of these benefits in years of discretion.

The greatest cleavage between these three main doctrinal positions may be that between Baptismal Regeneration, (ex opere operato) and the so-called "Hypothetical Theory." The difference between these two is one of a "different kind." And the difference between "The Hypothetical Theory" and "Believers' Baptism" concerns "to whom ought baptism to be administered?"

The gulf is wide indeed, if Baptismal Regeneration, by virtue of a formula, or performance of a particular action, (assuming it is done in good faith), requires no spiritual re-birth, and the spiritual result of that act is absolute.

And if "Hypothetical Theory" maintains that the result cannot be made absolute until the baptized member voluntarily exercises faith in Christ as Savior and Lord, then the difference between the two positions is fundamental. The points of difference between the "Hypothetical Theory" and "Believers' Baptism," although acute, are simple, and deal with (a) how baptism is to be administered, and (b) to whom.

Some assert that no person is truly baptized unless he is entirely covered with water; others with equal firmness maintain that pouring a small quantity of water on the head of the person to be baptized is sufficient to fulfill the requirements of the sacrament. It could be said that Scripture does not prove either method to be exclusively right or essentially wrong. The Early Church seems to have practiced both immersion and sprinkling, as seen in the Didache, as well as in some early paintings in the catacombs. The Anglican Church, by its present rubrics, allows for either immersion or sprinkling. New Testament references generally do not suggest immersion.

In two particular cases of baptism described in the New Testament, one of 3,000 converts in one day (Acts 2:41), and the other of the jailer at Philippi, baptized with his household at midnight (Acts 16:33) — immersion might be thought to have been highly improbable. The question could be raised, too, about practicing immersion where extreme temperatures obtain or where there is a scarcity of water. Should baptism then be forbidden? Or what about a person who is in delicate health?

The customs of countries must also be considered, especially where the immersion of women would be practically impossible due to the strictness of social etiquette. A major argument for immersion leans heavily upon the Greek word in the New Testament which is translated "to baptize." Some contend that the word "baptize" can mean only "to dip." But whether the word "baptize" means to immerse or not, must be decided entirely by the context, as in Luke 11:38. And to say that only immersion is a true figure of Christ's burial and resurrection (Col. 2:12; Rom. 6:4, "buried with Christ in baptism") is likewise to be questioned. It is more probable that his grave was a cave in the side of a rock, rather than a grave, (or bath), into which one is lowered.

a. To whom baptism should be administered forms so great a part of the divisions in the Christian Church, that I once again state the problem. Some assert that no one should be baptized who does not make a personal profession of repentance and faith, and that since infants cannot do this they ought not to be baptized. Others say this is a mistaken view.

b. Children were admitted into the Old Testament Church by circumcision, an ordinance appointed by God, and the neglect of which was a sin (Gen. 17:13, 14). St. Paul calls it a "seal of the righteousness of the faith" (Rom. 4:11). No doubt all Christians would agree that baptism in the New Testament is also the mode of entry into the Christian Church. And it could be argued that the Gospel of Jesus Christ does not diminish, but increases our privileges, and no child of Christian parents should be denied the "signs" of the promises we have in Christ. The absence of any direct command in the New Testament to baptize little children might be considered no argument at all. That infants were admitted into the church by an outward ordinance for 1800 years before Christ came, cannot be denied; it might be said that if Christ meant to exclude infants from this new initiation sign he would have given some plain directive about it. The text, "He that believeth and is baptized shall be saved" (Mark 16:16; Acts 2:38), applies by context to adults, and is not the same as if it read, "and nobody shall be baptized except he repents and believes." Such a text would have been conclusive, but it does not exist.

Of one thing we must beware, and that is to weaken the importance of baptism. And we must beware of excesses, the excess of making baptism the all-saving act without any need for the recipient's making a conscious act of faith in Christ and his atoning work and acknowledging Jesus Christ as Lord (Rom. 10:9 and 10). This excess cuts the nerve of evangelism, negates the imperative *must* of the Gospel, and, at worst, destroys the uniqueness of the Christian revelation, reducing it to the level of religious magic, a mere mechanical rite, that takes no account of the candidate's moral position. It robs the ambassador of the urgency of his message: "Now then we are ambassadors . . . in Christ's stead, be ye reconciled to God" (II Cor. 5:20). God does not need to be reconciled to man, but God sends his Son, and his Son sends his ministers to entreat them to be reconciled to him, to accept the pardon which is freely offered.

It is to this end that some *were* baptized; it is to this end that some *are* baptized; but *all* must receive Christ themselves, that they "might be made the righteousness of God in him."

BAPTISM IN
REFORMATION PERSPECTIVE
C. Darby Fulton

The special context of this discussion should not be allowed to suggest any basic conflict between baptism and evangelism. Indeed, there is a natural and reasonable compatibility between the two, for baptism as a sealing ordinance is the appropriate sequel to the act of faith. It is administered to those who have accepted the Gospel in response to its proclamation. The New Testament associates baptism and evangelism closely. The Great Commission joins them inseparably in the mandate to preach and to baptize. How else could it be? The same authority instituted them both; and it is the same Lord and Savior who is offered to the world, whether by the proclamation of the Word or by the signs of visible ordinances.

The problem we are to discuss is, partly, a legacy of the Reformation. It concerns the relative importance of the sacraments and of evangelism in communicating the Gospel. The medieval Church emphasized the paramount place of the sacraments. They were regarded as preeminently the means of grace. And this view was enhanced by the sacerdotal theory of the priesthood, at its highest for three centuries before the Reformation. With its powers of remitting or retaining, the priesthood was believed to hold in its hands the destiny of the soul, and there developed a widespread traffic in masses. Those in high places in the Church sought to repress these abuses, but it was commonly believed that a sufficient number of masses said for a man's soul would atone for a life of evil.

A corollary of this emphasis on the priestly office was the increasingly ritualistic character of the Church's worship. Religion became more and more stylized in ceremonial phrases and forms; and the repetition of these, often in words and imagery not understood by the people, enhanced the sense of mystery and reverence. The net result of the development of thought and practice in this period was to lay stress on the ritual act as itself conferring spiritual blessings. The sacraments were more than symbols; they were in some sense vehicles which *conveyed* saving grace and without which, ordinarily, such grace could not be received. Some insisted that baptism availed for the remission of sins and the regeneration of the subject, and the reception of grace was not dependent on the faith of the recipient. Infant baptism wiped out original sin even though the infant was wholly unaware of what was being done on its behalf.

It would seem self-evident that such a near-mechanical view of the

DR. FULTON is the Past Executive Secretary, Board of World Missions, of the Presbyterian Church in the United States.

efficacy of baptism would, indeed, present a hindrance to evangelism. If by this physical rite salvation can be insured for men apart from any apprehension of its meaning, the incentive for the preaching of the Gospel and the calling of men to repentance and faith would largely be lost. The main concern of the Church might then be simply to administer the rite to as many as possible, as was actually done in the mass baptisms that history records, involving thousands who were not prepared either by discernment or faith to receive it.

The Reformation made its protest against this ceremonialism that had produced a form of Christianity hardly recognizable as the simple faith of New Testament times. The reformers insisted that the preaching of the Word is the great means of grace. They recognized the sacraments, too, but as only *one* means of grace among others, and not necessarily the chief one. Indeed, it is the Word that is paramount. The necessity of the Word is absolute; without it there is no salvation. Thus, in the Reformers' view the proclamation of the Gospel, that is, *evangelism*, becomes the supreme duty and commitment of the Church.

Specifically with reference to baptism, the Reformation speaks with a remarkable degree of agreement, and out of varying interpretations presents a general consensus that might be summarized as follows:

Baptism is for believers, for those who profess their faith in Christ.

It becomes a means of grace, not from any virtue in the rite itself, or in him that administers it; but only by the working of the Holy Spirit in them that by faith receive it.

Baptism is a sign and seal of our ingrafting into Christ. It makes visible and confirms to our senses the reality of the divine grace that is represented.

It is, on the believer's part, a testimony of his fealty to Christ, and confirms his engagement to be the Lord's.

The practice of infant baptism in some communions today must be interpreted in the light of the covenant theology which recognizes the children of believers as heirs of the promises. It is not to be confused with baptismal regeneration. The administering of the rite to infants does not secure their salvation. Rather, it signifies an acknowledgment of parental responsibility for the spiritual training of the child, the dedication of the child to the service and glory of God, and an acceptance of the solemn duty to bring him up in the nurture and admonition of the Lord, in the hope that when he has come to years of discretion he will by his own act of faith lay hold upon eternal life. Nothing here sets aside the necessity of personal faith for salvation.

There has been a trend toward formalism during the past two decades within some communions in my country, a wider use of ritualistic and liturgical elements in our worship — candles, crosses, chants and responses, "worship centers," formal prayers, incense, signs and symbols. This is partly a reaction against bareness, and reflects a feeling that our worship would be enriched by appropriate use of form and beauty. These influences have brought some dignity and order to the haphazardness existing where each minister has practiced his originality in services aptly described as "without form and void." But there have been baneful effects also in the tendency to place less emphasis on the sermon, to think more of beauty than of witness, and to exalt the priestly role of the man in the pulpit. Here history sounds a warning and reminds us that the trappings of religion have sometimes obscured the reality, and aids to worship have themselves become the objects of veneration.

With this emphasis on ritual there has been a decline in evangelism, and the spiritual birthrate has dropped rather sharply. Is there a causal connection here? The forces working against evangelism are varied and complex, ranging from simple indifference, to naturalistic ideas of conversion as a pedagogical or psychological result rather than as a radical work of the Holy Spirit through the Gospel. But it is quite likely that religious formalism, too, is having its adverse effect, prone as it is to look with disfavor on methods of Gospel proclamation that it regards as sensational or charged with undue pressure.

Once again the Church is in crisis, groping in theological confusion, preoccupied with matters of organization, obsessed with social activism, concerned with phrase and form, while spiritual vitality languishes and the trumpet gives forth a muffled sound. No need is more critical in this day than to bolster the fundamental affirmations of the Christian faith and to reflect these in a New Testament call to evangelism.

Report of Group Discussion

Delegates discussing sacerdotalism concentrated exclusively on the problems connected with baptism. On a topic in itself controversial, they expressed a remarkable measure of agreement. All speakers tended to recognize the importance of baptism as a handmaid of evangelism — a means of grace, a sign and a seal of the rebirth in Christ, and as a testimony to the non-Christian world. They were also united in a clear recognition that baptism is often a hindrance when practiced too mechanically or when unaccompanied by a clear statement of its fullest Christian meaning.

Bishop Gibson (Jamaica) expressed a theological approach to baptism which was warmly greeted by the delegates. Basing his comments on a covenant theology, Gibson differentiated between infant baptism as a change of status which is correct and a change of nature which is more properly the result of the new birth alone. "The grace of salvation is not tied to the sacrament, nor can the new birth be bound to one type of conversion either sudden or progressive," the bishop said.

A measure of unity also appeared in response to the opinion of Dr. McCall (USA) that the most significant problems lie at the point where baptism as a practice is either understood or misunderstood by people inside and outside the Church. Delegates from Anglican, Baptist, Lutheran and other confessions provided examples of such misunderstanding within their own communions. What we emphasize in baptism must be geared to the understanding of the people, many felt.

There was no clear answer to the question why the sacraments have so often tended toward sacerdotalism and have thereby hindered the proclamation of the gospel.

Reporter: *Hans Büerki-Fillenz*

SECTION IV

OBSTACLES TO
EVANGELISM IN THE WORLD •
Harold B. Kuhn   251

Materialism, Prosperity and Social Standing

ACHIEVING GREAT THINGS FOR GOD • *W. Maxey Jarman* 263

THE IMPACT OF MATERIALISM IN AFRICA • *Howard Jones* 268

THE GRIP OF MATERIAL COMFORTS • *Florentino Santana*   272

REPORT OF GROUP DISCUSSION • *C. Ralston Smith*   272

Renascent World Religions

ATTITUDES TOWARD NON-CHRISTIAN
RELIGIONS • *Hideo Aoki*   273

MAN'S UPREACH AND
GOD'S REVELATION • *Akbar Abdul-Haqq, Jr.*   276

OBSTACLES IN THE MUSLIM WORLD • *J. N. D. Anderson*   281

THE RELIGIONS OF ASIA • *Chandu Ray*   285

REPORT OF GROUP DISCUSSION • *Warren Webster*   286

Totalitarianism and Collectivism

THE TOTALITARIAN CLIMATE • *Samuel Escobar*   288

COMMUNIST OPPOSITION TO EVANGELISM • *Helen Kim*   291

COMMUNISM AND CHRISTIANITY • *Andrew Ben Loo*   294

THE U.S.S.R. AND EASTERN EUROPE • *Arthur F. Glasser* 298

REPORT OF GROUP DISCUSSION • *Duke K. McCall*   301

Political Nationalism

NATIONALISM AND EVANGELISM • *Hudson T. Armerding* 302

NATIONALISM AND THE GOSPEL • *Heini Germann-Edey*   305

BREAKING THE BARRIER
OF NATIONALISM • *Augustine G. Jebaraj*   309

THE ETHICS OF POLITICAL
NATIONALISM • *Michael Cassidy*   312

PAGE

REPORT OF GROUP DISCUSSION • *Samuel H. Moffett*   316

Religious Cults

CONFRONTING THE CULTS • *William Culbertson*   318

MODERN RELIGIONS AND
PERSONAL NEEDS • *J. Stafford Wright*   321

REPORT OF GROUP DISCUSSION • *Arthur M. Climenhaga*   323

THE ZEAL OF THE CULTS • *Stephen Slocum, Jr.*   324

STRANGE AFRICAN CULTS • *Ernest K. Martin*   327

Discriminations and Intolerance

TRUTH BY FORCE • *Ernest H. Trenchard*   330

ECCLESIASTICAL TOTALITARIANISM • *Argos Zodhiates*   333

RELIGIOUS PERSECUTION • *Benjamin E. Fernando*   336

REPORT OF GROUP DISCUSSION • *J. Graham Miller*   338

OBSTACLES TO EVANGELISM
IN THE WORLD
Harold B. Kuhn

Opposition to forthright and vigorous evangelism is as old as the proclamation of the Christian Gospel. As in Apostolic times, so today "the natural
man receiveth not the things of the Spirit of God." Realism requires that the
Church Evangelical recognize man's built-in resistance to forthright assertion of the demands of Jesus Christ as a constant element in the sinful human
situation. Its presence should not surprise us, and the sensitive evangelist
should be prepared to cope lovingly with its manifestations.

Realism demands keen awareness, also, that at given periods in history
the factors in human experience which resist proclamation of the Good
News frequently gain additional force and supporting rationale by appearing in some new form. We propose to identify and discuss those elements
and movements that are especially and typically characteristic of our day,
and that constitute a special obstacle to projecting the message of *Christus
Redemptor* upon modern society. While most, if not all, of these elements
are not entirely new, they seem to exert their force in new and formidable
combinations as we move into the last third of the twentieth century. They
find vigorous implementation in the dynamics of our time — a time whose
developments we witness, not with fear, but with a sense of challenge and a
spirit of faith. This issue should and must be considered in terms of a
"realism of faith."

1. Nationalism as an Obstacle

The Christian finds himself perplexed by some of the problems posed
by patriotism and especially by nationalism, its distorted syndrome. Love of
locale (and with it, love of country) are a part of God's endowment to man,
and are significant factors in shaping man's everyday life. Like all of God's
Ordnungen, they are open to distortion, and to implementation that may
be humanly disadvantageous, even disastrous. It may be noted, parentheti-
cally, that a part of the paradox of human freedom is that God permits the
Ordnungen through which he is at work providentially in the world to be distorted by human error and human sin.

In its extreme form, nationalism is a distortion of that normal love
of country, and normal pride which men and women take in their country's
group achievement. It is foolish to denounce nationalism without trying to

DR. HAROLD B. KUHN is professor of Philosophy of Religion and chairman of the Department of Doctrine and Philosophy of Religion at Asbury
Theological Seminary, Wilmore, Kentucky.

understand its dynamics. In a very real sense, today's growing nationalism is a reaction to the older colonialism by peoples who seek "a place in the sun." It takes no political radicalism to suggest that God's providence may be working in those movements whereby peoples historically disadvantaged by cultural, economic or religious factors try to share the freedoms and comforts achieved by the more prosperous societies.

There are movements, for example, as expressions of God's providential order in the world, through which men and women heretofore limited by predetermined social structures are demanding and receiving the opportunity to participate creatively in a far broader society. Likewise, Christians can applaud movements that erase the feeling of fatalism from the under-privileged and that recognize such infusion or restoration of a sense of self-worth as "the Lord's doing." At the same time, the rising tide of human aspiration may adopt shortsighted methods, and thereby thwart its own best interests. Seen in some contexts at least, nationalism may be one of these myopic techniques.

Nationalism may appeal too largely to past grievances; by holding these so prominently in memory, it may jeopardize their proper evaluation and thus encourage an unwarranted and unfortunate clinging to obsolete cultural patterns. That is to say, people under the pressures of nationalism may adhere to outmoded and deleterious social forms simply as a symbol of resistance to something else that is disliked or not wanted. Nationalistic feeling may thus result in perpetuating institutions and practices that are actually harmful to a given society, and may implement resistance to forces that would be beneficial, that would offer new horizons and fresh opportunities. This resistance and rejection may stem from lack of understanding or perspective. Sometimes, for example, even when the contributions of Christian missions are acknowledged and used, a proud people may reject their source on the ground that they represent something alien and foreign.

Such nationalism may identify the presence of an evangelistic agency or movement with colonialism, and, as a reflex, advocate policies that are emotionally charged and that offer no positive and far-reaching benefits. Strong nationalistic feeling may lead, for example, to denial of visas to evangelistic missionaries, perhaps on the ground that "they would duplicate the work that nationals can do." Although this is an understandable attitude, it may overlook the fact that the national may desperately need and want outside assistance and sympathetic support.

The Christian Church will need to live for a long time with the accumulated results of exploitive practices and condescendingly humiliating attitudes that secular agencies of the Western nations have exercised during the past two or three centuries among the underdeveloped peoples of the world. Or, to turn for a moment to the Church overseas, it may even be that in some places the paternalistic attitude of certain mission leaders has generated its own brand of reflex nationalism. In any case, no person interested in vital evangelism can afford to overlook or underestimate the dynamics of nationalism within the rising and aspiring nations. If nationalism contains elements that frustrate him, it may nonetheless also offer the fore-gleams of promise. Nationalism has a way of running its course, and better counsel often prevails after a period of fumbling national experimentation.

2. *Totalitarianism as an Obstacle*

Viewed pragmatically, the questions posed by totalitarian systems for Christian evangelism seem to resolve themselves into simple black and white terms: where totalitarian systems prevail, mission fields close and evangelism, of the public variety at least, ceases. The question comes immediately, however: should the Christian Church accept this pattern as a final and foregone conclusion? While it is difficult to project the "world of the future," yet there is reason to suspect that while they grope for viable political and social systems, many of the slowly developing lands will experiment with some form or other of totalitarian or quasi-totalitarian governmental forms. In some cases this fact may lead to temporarily closed mission areas. It is also possible, however, that the processes by which totalitarian systems modify themselves from within may so continue to work in some lands formerly closed to evangelism that opportunities for the Gospel may present themselves sooner than we think. In other words, if, for example, citizens under dictatorships move increasingly toward stability and away from disruptive revolution, some of the developing lands now not open to public evangelism may in the foreseeable future become lands of promise for evangelistic endeavor. At the same time, we must reconcile ourselves to the probability that some countries formerly regarded most suitable for missionary and evangelistic endeavor may not be capable of penetration for several decades.

Those of us who are vitally interested in evangelism are perplexed by the fact that, as a rule, churches in totalitarian lands cease to be prophetic in several important senses. First, they seldom speak with a prophetic voice, for example, concerning the corruption of their youth by doctrinaire antireligious teaching. Second, they tend to develop a protective mentality — to remain as inconspicuous as possible lest they be drawn into conflict with official policy. As a consequence, evangelism tends to be eliminated altogether, or to be confined to groups in the church's immediate orbit. In short, churches under totalitarian governments tend to become priestly, ritualistic and cloistered, and fall prey to more or less subtle forms of nationalism.

Today s evangelistic Church needs to be keenly alert to possible small opportunities in totalitarian lands. It must be recognized that some countries wholly closed to evangelistic endeavor five or ten years ago manifest a "crack in the door" for operation of a free-church form of evangelization. Openings need to be explored and potential opportunities seized — always with the Holy Spirit's guidance. There must be no place in the mentality of men and women of faith for a theological fatalism that accepts as final the slamming of a door by revolutionary movements. Not despair, but cautious exploration, should be the mood of the Christian who seeks by all means to "become all things to all men." It is helpful to recall that originally Christianity was projected into a world that was under a sophisticated totalitarian system. No doubt St. Paul and the other Apostles, no less than the Fathers, felt frustrated and limited in many aspects of their work. But they never allowed forbidding external circumstances to paralyze them into inaction. Then as now, those who view things with eyes of faith see God working providentially also in human governmental structures, however imperfect as media they may seem for expressing God's activity.

3. Modern Materialism as an Obstacle

The charge of "materialism" is frequently leveled indiscriminately against all who are concerned with the material and temporal aspects of human life and society. Some of the unstructured thinking on this question, in the West no less than in the East, has failed to remember that God is Creator of the material order, and uses it to channel and accomplish both his providential and redemptive purposes. To be thoroughly and characteristically Christian in perspective, one must give proper recognition to the Divine ordination of the material structures of our world; one must see how the New Testament emphasizes the placement of Christians as stewards within them.

We readily grant that concern with the temporal and the material may very easily degenerate into a form of idolatry, into an absolutizing of visible finites. We recognize also that at this point certain thinkers tend rather uncritically to posit false antitheses. For example, it was once fashionable for representatives of Eastern cultures to say to the West, "You have refrigerators, but we have spiritual values." Obviously this is a radical oversimplification, for people of Eastern lands desire to participate in technological progress no less than do men and women of the West. Modern advertising has seen to that!

There is, of course, a legitimate place for recognizing and criticizing the wave of materialism that has swept over our world, that has gone hand in hand with the industrial revolution, and more recently with the technological revolution. It is an oversimplification to say that the factory — the assembly line if you wish — causes materialism. It is more correct to say that materialism is a distortion of something that is divinely implanted – a drive that impels man to greater heights of human comfort and human dignity. It must be acknowledged, after all, that while the advent of the machine placed heavy loads upon mankind at some points, it also relieved men of certain heavy and degrading burdens. No critique of current materialism is thoroughly penetrating unless it comes to grips with this fact.

The real heart of the matter is, of course, that the precise meaning of materialism is found in an outlook, an attitude toward life, which measures the meaning and goals of man's life in terms of visible and tangible things, and which dogmatically casts aside all values which cannot be resolved into these terms or harnessed to the acquisition of goods. In other words, materialism may exist not only at the level of ideology, but may also become a total philosophy of life. At the ideological level, materialism may exist quite independent of the presence or absence of the actual symbols of material existence. The mere availability of material objects (although this very availability or non-availability may complicate the problem) is not what generates materialism as a *Weltanschauung*; rather, it is a basic attitude toward the structures of the universe and toward the nature of human existence that determines this point of view. Our divine Lord had this in mind when he said, "Take heed, and beware of covetousness: for a man's life consisteth not in the abundance of the things which he possesseth" (Luke 12:15).

It must be said here that while today's materialism is often covert and unarticulated, it is at the same time constitutive. At the most obvious level, and in the closest meaning of the term, few persons will openly profess materialism. Even in Marxist lands, professed materialism is the articulate creed of the few. Wherever even the most superficial acknowledgment is given to doctrines of human worth and dignity, materialism becomes unpalatable. This reaction answers to something deep within man — something which we gratefully acknowledge has survived the Fall. However, while it is possible to disavow the materialist creed, it is possible at the same time to manifest its consequences and expressions to a disturbing degree. Such practical materialism, which uncritically measures all values in terms of visible and tangible things, can produce a climate of indifference which, in the long run, may be less responsive to the Christian Evangel than the climate of active resistance and articulate rejection that stems from avowed materialism. Certainly the latter is less difficult to recognize than the former; and certainly anyone who professes materialism as an overt creed is more self-conscious of his position, and therefore more susceptible to direct confrontation by the claims of the Living Christ.

We are simply saying that covert materialism may offer an oblique form of opposition to Christian evangelism that has far more frustrating aspects than does creedal and dogmatic materialism. Outspoken and articulate opposition is frequently less difficult to measure and to penetrate than is the mildly curious and bland type, which tends simply to bypass the claims of our Lord as irrelevant. A message that emphasizes the unseen and the eternal frequently appears quaintly antique and colorless to the materialist mentality which uncritically but persistently measures life in terms of visible achievement, in terms of acquiring the symbols of power and status. True Christian evangelism summons men and women to a vital commitment to the unseen — to a Person who in this life must be "seen with the eyes of faith." It is tragic that a genial, practical form of materialism can decisively dismiss Christ and his claims with a shrug or smile no less than can the hard, dogmatic type.

It would be a grave error to suppose that today's materialism is seen only in its attitude of commitment to tangible and marketable items. On the contrary, the materialism so evident in our affluent civilization is a way of thinking which stresses its own "invisibilities." These are frequently such factors as leisure, entertainment, modes of "escape." We would unhesitatingly call "materialistic" those mental attitudes which, for example, make the mere attainment of retirement age a value, and which seek the earliest possible opportunity to withdraw from creative effort, in order to "enjoy life" at the beaches and pass simply as spectators on the world scene.

For all its stress upon how *things* are to be secured, the spirit of modern materialism rejects the Christian view of work as something God-given, and returns to the "classical" view which regards work as a necessary but unwelcome intruder into the life of man. As Carl F. H. Henry rightly observes, the materialistic mood of modern man tries to solve the qualitative problem posed by the biblical mandate to work in narrow quantitative terms. The qualitative approach regards work as a stewardship, to be pursued under the recognition that some day the Lord of the harvest will call the laborers to a reckoning. The quantitative approach tends to view and evaluate life in terms of how men and women are released from grinding toil in order to engage in a narrowly-construed "pursuit of happiness."

Certainly no Christian can deny that there are forms of work and exploitation by ruthless employers which violate human dignity and reduce men and women to something less than persons. The evangelical cannot reflect the heart of his Lord without not only sympathizing with those thus bound, but also identifying himself as a Christian citizen with movements that offer genuine promise of remedying social and economic wrongs. It must be remembered, however, that if exploitation by an unjust employer has served to dull the worker's ears to the Good News, the tyranny of uncreative leisure is scarcely much better for opening the heart to the Lord's "Follow me."

As a member of the Christian task force, the evangelist must therefore bear in mind that today's materialism has a two-pronged thrust: on the one hand, it encourages and underwrites high (and frequently inordinate and unrealistic) forms of temporal aspiration; on the other, it tends to make a man a prisoner of his own leisure, of his own quest for entertainment, of his own pursuit of spectatorism, of those "escapes" now sought the world over. The result in either case is a shrinking of what is meaningful in human life – of what gives relevance to life. The most vicious aspect of the tyranny of materialism is its ability to produce merely earth-bound aspirations, to produce a climate in which the transcendent and otherworldly seems strangely antiquated and dull. It is against this kind of materialism that Christian evangelism must do its work, and into the mood created by materialism that evangelism must project its message.

For all the contemporary stress upon individuality and individualism, current materialism nevertheless tends to be anti-individualistic in a particularly invidious sense, in that it affords a wider variety of ways to evade moral accountability. There are trends in our materialistically oriented society which erode the sense of individual self-reliance and foster "great expectation" quite apart from either personal endeavor or personal worth. Without assuming a spirit of uncritical and wholesale opposition to programs that try to increase people's security within a technological society, the Christian must nonetheless recognize that the welfare state, by assuming responsibility for ever more areas of human life that were once considered the legitimate realm for exercising human initiative, undermines the sense of individual responsibility.

This fact has inevitable repercussions in the area of personal evangelism, where proclamation of the Good News is considered to have a basically individual appeal, and in which the proclaimer, through the power of the Divine Spirit, seeks to bring about the confession that "against thee, thee only, have I sinned, and done this evil in thy sight!" (Psalm 51:4). The calls of our Lord are, after all, intensely and persistently personal and individual. A constituent part of evangelism is the isolating of an individual from the crowd, and confronting him with the issues between him and his Maker. Loss of the sense of individual responsibility, chargeable in significant part to a materialistic outlook, tends to cause modern man to relegate high ethical and spiritual decisions to the limbo of "matters that are of concern only to the aged, the infirmed and the life-evaders." The mood is a powerful enemy to the projections of the Christian Evangel.

In summary, let it be said that materialism, insofar as it objectifies the aspirations of long disadvantaged groups, is a factor with which we must reckon permanently, until there come "a new heaven and a new earth." Nor will it suffice for the Evangelical to take refuge in any simple and acquiescent misapplication of the Scripture, "the poor ye have always with you." There are, obviously, grave and subtle perils in the contemporary and unstructured demand for "involvement", which has come to mean the identification of great ecclesiastical structures with some specific program of social and economic betterment. At the same time, there are equally grave perils implicit in the danger of restricting the cutting edge of the Christian Evangel solely to the matter of personal redemption, and of neglecting the manner in which the Christian mandate includes bringing the claims of the sovereign Lord of all life to bear upon the structures of society.

But at whatever level materialism asserts its claims within the movements and structures of modern life, it will pose both problems and temptations to the evangelical Christian. Nothing will be gained by an indiscriminate attack upon technology, or by any proposal for some artificial simplification of today's life. Clarification of vision and Christianization of our value judgments: Yes. Return to an allegedly simple agrarian form of existence: No. Evangelism must take a realistic measure of its opponents:

it must seek to examine and to evaluate as highly determinative the issue of man's involvement with materialism in an increasingly complex society. The emphasis must be, not upon a mere denunciation of trends, but upon skillful application of the weapons at our disposal to the task of breaching the walls behind which material-minded modern man has entrenched himself — the walls of exclusive preoccupation with one-level existence, of cultural and ethical relativity, and of collectivistic evasion of responsibility and ethical accountability.

4. Today's Intellectual Climate as an Obstacle

The Christian cannot dismiss current intellectual trends with a sweep of the hand as being either basically friendly or unqualifiedly hostile to the proclamation of the Christian message. At the same time, it is unrealistic to fail to recognize that the general *Zeitgeist* of the 1960s tends to operate in a manner that is anti-evangelistic in several important senses. A brand of intellectualism is abroad which associated itself all to easily with a cavalier attitude toward public, mass evangelism. In some allegedly sophisticated circles, it is regarded as "in" to take the stance of downgrading evangelistic institutions. It is to this mood that dramatist Bertolt Brecht appealed in his *Heilige Johanna der Schlachthöfe* (*St. Joan of the Stockyards*) with its brutal caricature of the Salvation Army.

With predictable and almost boring frequency one hears the typical "liberal" verdict: "the day of mass evangelism is past." This sentiment had so filtered into the thinking of non-religious circles, that until events of the past two decades called it into serious question it was accepted almost as an axiom. Happily, God in his providence has brought movements to the fore which have challenged this assumption in wide and significant circles.

Too, scientific naturalism — enjoying tremendous prestige — has been an articulate foe of the major premises underlying Christian evangelism. The honest Christian cannot but admit a certain ambivalence in his attitude toward contemporary naturalistic science. On the one hand, science has discovered techniques and released procedural resources that have revolutionized his way of living and greatly increased his comforts. On the other hand, the overall impact of naturalistic science upon the intellectual and spiritual climate of our age has meant the undercutting of many factors that are indispensable to vigorous propagation of the Good News. It tends to reduce the force of the Gospel's appeal to the individual sinner to turn to the supernatural. It tends to crowd out from modern man's perspective any compelling glimpse of the life to come, and to exclude from his concern those issues which would make the pursuit of that future life an urgent issue.

Again, the intellectual climate of the day frequently caricatures Christianity's role in the world. This may be done at a number of levels. The modern secularist spirit abstracts the unfortunate elements in the total impact of Christianity in history — these have indeed existed and have done their work — and makes them a gauge for evaluating Christianity as a whole. Or, modern intellectualism may implement its objections to the Christian revelation by appealing to the alleged claim by other religious systems to exclusive authority. Those who argue thus overlook the fact that what is genuine inevitably calls forth its counterfeit; moreover, it is one thing to lay claim to an exclusive authority, and quite another to proclaim a Person who has come into man's daily life, and who in his own Person has come to grips with life's most persistent and staggering problem and has emerged triumphant from the conflict.

Realism demands the recognition also that today's intellectual climate is shaped by a hedonistic spirit, a spirit that regards pleasure (often understood very superficially) as the highest good. This spirit is articulated in life philosophies that parade as "new"; adherence to them, accordingly, whether in theory or in practice, is regarded as "in" and thus culturally acceptable. Among these none has greater appeal, it seems, than the so-called "new morality." Regrettably some theologians, seeking to be *avant-garde*, are lending the support of their scholarship and reputation to the so-called "situational ethic," which ranges itself against all forms of principal morality, and insists that every behavioral situation is unique and *sui generis*, and should therefore, be met, not by any appeal to principles or revealed mandates, but by applying an unstructured form of *agape,* which allegedly is sufficient, even in volatile and emotionally-charged situations, to tell persons what to do.

We do not intend to give a detailed critique here of this system. It must be said, however, that it caricatures the ethical demands of the Christian Evangel, and leaves the inexperienced person with the overwhelming task of navigating the seas of a precariously balanced moral world without chart or compass. Moreover, its net result is the weakening of the sense of moral obligation to which the Christian evangelistic message addresses itself. When the ethical norm is rendered nebulous, when the individual himself becomes the ultimate source of ethical judgment, it is no wonder that a person's awareness of God's claims upon him is weakened and diluted.

A parallel trend is that precipitated by certain superficial psychological systems which seem determined to undercut man's understanding of the problems of sin and guilt. Accounting for human behavior on the basis of environmental pressure upon "normal and neutral response-patterns," they reduce or eliminate the sense of personal responsibility for those types of behavior which Christianity considers sinful. In many intellectual circles it is fashionable to insist upon a radical appraisal of all that has historically been called "sin" or "sinful" and to do so within a context that tries to cope with what are termed "feelings of guilt" rather than to point men and women to him who gave himself to destroy sin and to lift the crushing burden of man's guilt through genuine forgiveness.

The implications of this for Christian evangelism are evident enough. Projection of the claims of the Lord Christ, in terms of the message which by the help of the Holy Spirit seeks to precipitate a sense of guilt in keeping with the realities of man's sin-predicament, and to produce evangelical repentance, must face the fact (in today's intellectual climate) of sophisticated and highly articulate ideological foes. False intellectualism unceasingly insists that man is somehow "captain of his soul" and haughtily suggests that to press upon him the claims of supernatural assistance is to downgrade him. This spirit creates a formidable barrier in appealing to the Gospel to meet man's distressed and helpless plight, and his need for supernatural rescue. St. Paul may have referred to just such elements in the intellectual climate of his day when he reminded the Church at Ephesus (and the Church of our day with them) that "we wrestle not against flesh and blood, but against principalities, against powers, against the rulers of the darkness of this world, against spiritual wickedness in high places" (Ephesians 6:12).

5. Obstacles Created by the Influence of Alien Elements Impinging Upon the Church

To a degree sometimes unrecognized, the Church finds that the thinking of both her members and her leaders is subtly shaped by outside forces which are uncongenial, at times even hostile, to her evangelistic thrust. Interaction between the thinking of the Christian and the thought-climate of his world is inevitable. It is likewise to be noted that the mid-twentieth century Church has been singularly unaware of the massive, if not glacial, incursion of paganism into the contemporary world. Far too long, multitudes of Christians have assumed a sort of "inverted Constantinianism" in this respect — inverted in that the Church has not assumed responsibility for the thought modes of the world, but instead has tended to assume the world to be essentially Christian in its ideology.

It is not easy for an organization or for individuals to be keenly aware of the essentially alien quality of much of the surrounding world-climate, on the one hand, and, on the other, to operate affirmatively and creatively within that climate. A certain peril besets anyone who does indeed possess an awareness of the crucial and crisis nature of the Christian's position in an alien thought-world, a peril, namely, of assuming defensive attitudes that will alienate the non-Christian. A greater danger, however, seems to lie in uncritically accepting the ideals and norms of the world and, in doing so, becoming their prisoner. To be specific, it is possible for well-meaning Christians to become immersed in the materialistic *Weltanschauung* to a degree which they do not realize; an experience which leaves them really unimpressed with the urgent claims of the Christian Evangel with its strong insistence upon the reality of the unseen. After all, materialism is materialism whether it creeps or gallops!

Further, the Church too often finds her self-image, the vision of her mission, and the understanding of her destiny to be subtly shaped by the essentially pagan nature of her environment. After all, it is not pleasant to realize and acknowledge that the civilization of the so-called Christian West has been erected upon principles which very largely omit God from their reckoning. But it is this that lies at the heart of paganism; and seen in this light, our culture can scarcely be judged in any other terms. In such a situation only a prophetic Church can retain her "vision glorious" and her "hope eternal"; without these, her evangelistic task inevitably loses meaning and dynamic.

Moreover, the Church needs always to be aware of the peril that she may be paralyzed into inaction by the sheer weight of the forces ranged against her. The statistical trends of the day are not encouraging, for it is evident that growth in world population is greatest in those areas where the Christian witness, so far as one can see, is the weakest; nor has missionary endeavor by any reckoning been able to keep pace with the population increase. Perhaps here the Church needs to listen to those whose world vision entitles them to speak, and who say that never has there been a time when so many persons from "every nation, kindred and tongue" are lifting their voices in a sincere "Our Father." At the same time, the vast forces ranged against the Christian Gospel and the Christian Church may cut the nerve of evangelistic endeavor, unless they are counterbalanced by a strong assurance that it is "the Father's good pleasure to give you the kingdom."

The foregoing obstacles suggest the imperative need for a renewed spirit of discernment, no less than a spirit of dedication, by the Church — a renewal which takes realistic account of the alien and paganizing forces ranged against her, and which at every level and front threaten to penetrate her own thinking. The Church needs to become acutely aware that the creeping paganism of the time bears no friendship for the essential facts that underlie aggressive evangelism, such as: the universal sinfulness and consequent lostness of men apart from Christ the Redeemer, the imperatives of repentance and faith in him, the certainty of a final day of reckoning, and the overwhelming sterility of life lived apart from the living Christ. Insofar as the world impinges upon the thinking of the Church, to that degree the presence of built-in opposition to the Evangel at these levels constitutes a potentially hostile base of operation against a vital evangelism, especially if this opposition conceals its objectives by subtle invasion of the intellect.

This constellation of obstacles to Evangelism in the world and in the intellectual climate of the world points up several imperative needs within the Church as she faces her task of proclaiming the Gospel. There is need for a renewal of vision. There is need for a realistic assessment of the magnitude and organization of the forces ranged against her. There is need for a renewed appraisal of her mandate to world evangelism in terms of her "marching orders," parallelled by a realistic reassessment of the inner dynamic of her message.

Christian realism will dictate an awareness that the crucial and decisive phases of the Church's struggle cannot be won by any vast holding-operation, however well this might be planned and articulated. This struggle is a conflict that can be met only by a vigorous and affirmative thrust of the Evangel into the age. For such a thrust, our age must have a highly skillful and deeply discerning evangelistic task force.

ACHIEVING GREAT THINGS FOR GOD
W. Maxey Jarman

What is the business of Christians? Do we clearly see the picture of God's purpose for us? Every business, every organization, every group that wants to achieve must first be clear as to the nature of its business and its objectives. It is surprising how much confusion exists at this primary point in various endeavors of all kinds. It is natural and right for every Christian to want to accomplish great things for God. When a person comes to a saving knowledge of Christ, one of the first things he wants to do is to tell others the Good News. Not only is this due to a sense of joy and gratitude for having been saved from sin and from having a new life opened up, but this new attitude is also one of the results of this new life that has been created within the individual. This is God's love at work in the person. "We know that we have passed from death unto life, because we love the brethren" (I John 3:14). Loving others as God has loved us is one way of expressing the real business of Christians — as individuals, or as fellow associates in churches, or groups of churches.

While Christians will agree on this as a general premise, there is considerable difference of opinion on the method and approach of accomplishing great things for God and of loving and helping others. This difference of opinion results in a great deal of lost motion in attempting to achieve results. How can Christians be most effective? How can they reach people in these days and times? How can they be worthwhile instruments of God's design for the world and show his love for the world? How can they be most effective in helping others and in achieving great things for God?

Looking at this from a human standpoint, what chance do Christians have to accomplish great things for God? We live in a world full of trouble, wickedness and distress. Christians are a relatively small part of the total population of the world. We are divided and scattered all over the world. Most professing Christians are weak and relatively ignorant of what they really believe. Most individual Christians are without the necessary elements that are usually considered important for achieving great things in this world.

What elements does the modern secular world consider necessary for power to achieve? How do influential people reach and guide people, or at least how do they *attempt* to do it? While we examine these factors let us bear in mind that these elements of power have usually turned out to be an illusion and without lasting value. The history of the world is full of failures.

MR. JARMAN is chairman of the Genesco Corporation in New York City, New York.

Wealth has always been considered a means of power. A worldly minded person, a cynic, assumes that with money he can buy anything or anybody and achieve anything. But money has been a source of much evil and misery and the love of money has cost many people more than they have ever realized. Money has the power to destroy, not really to achieve. It is a fearful thing. As a tool it can be used in various ways, but it is a tool with a double cutting edge. As a business man who has lived in a world that concerns itself with money, I have been in a position to judge and observe the effect that money has on people. I have seen much more achievement without dependence upon money than I have seen achievement where money was the ruling influence, and I have seen the evil that money can do to individuals.

Organization is another approach that is supposed to be strong. As a businessman, I have also been concerned with organization. Organizations can develop a kind of power. Business organization is the kind of power that is necessary to survive in a competitive world and it achieves economic results by putting together in a useful way the human abilities of individuals. But it cannot change human nature, nor does it try. Organization takes human nature as it is and caters to its physical needs.

Military power has been a tool of mankind throughout history. But has war ever settled anything? It has done nothing but destroy. As military people develop even more potent weapons, such as the nuclear bombs, military power seems to have even less influence to accomplish anything worthwhile. A military organization must be so designed that elements of the military group can continue to function in battle even when the key people are killed. For that reason military organization is rigid and subordinates the individual to the needs of the organization as a whole. Business organization stresses flexibility, while military organization stresses conformity; but in either case, the organization uses the individual and does not produce any change for the better in the individual. Military power has show its futility from the time of Alexander the Great with his collapse at an early age, to the present ineffective power of the United States in Southeast Asia.

There is another kind of power that is worshiped in this world and that is political position, political power. Centuries ago, political leadership and power were acquired by physical strength and force; then it gradually developed into a hereditary procedure, and from this has gone into a kind of popularity contest. Those with the most pleasing personality, best appearance, a facility to make all kinds of promises, are put into office by votes of the masses. A popularity contest does not necessarily do a better job of selecting the right person than did the hereditary process or the brute force process. Political position is one of the worst deceivers in the world. Men and groups subject themselves to untold sacrifices of time, money, and reputation in order to achieve political power. They will make trades, commitments, associate with all kinds of people, sacrifice their health, their time, their principles. If and when they acquire position, they then find that they must deal with all kinds of factions, good and bad, in order to get one good thing accomplished, they must agree to go along with something they do not believe in and find themselves involved with associates of whom they cannot be proud. The history of the governments of this world has nearly always been one of corruption, stupidity, and futility, in spite of those who have had high motivation to serve properly. It was concerning political power that Lord Acton said: "Power corrupts, and absolute power absolutely corrupts."

Because individual Christians feel their own individual weakness, they are greatly tempted by the seeming strength of political power to try to force reforms and improvements upon people. Thus, there are those in influential places in the religious community who feel that Christians must join together to achieve political influence in order to accomplish great things. A careful study of history must convince us not only of the danger of political power with all of its corruption but also of the futility of trying to change human nature through legislation or political influence. And it is only by changing human nature that we are going to make this world a better place. Superficial surface effects can be achieved; but in spite of all the legislation of the centuries, there is just as much evil among men as ever, if not more. There is injustice, greed, lust, unhappiness, misery. Crime increases, mental hospitals are filled, divorce is rampant, hate abounds, illegitimacy increases, drunkenness and drug addiction spread, immorality is defended, and the affluent society ignores religion and denies God. It is evident that modern civilization and political power have been unable to achieve stability in the world, much less bring integrity and intelligence into the affairs of men. It is tempting to think of the possibilities of political power; but when we remind ourselves of the actualities that exist, we are naïve if we think that we can achieve great things for God through the use of such political power. The problems of racial integration demonstrate the inability of legislation, of military force, of money to produce the right kind of relationship. It is all too evident that if results are to be achieved, there must be some change in the hearts of people. How can this be done? What elements are available that can influence and change human nature? Here are some that are used, sometimes for good, sometimes for evil.

The spoken word has perhaps been one of the most influential things in the history of the world. Words spoken in private or public by orators and dedicated people have inspired others to action in various directions. Cicero said that when he spoke to the people they all applauded but that when Demosthenes had spoken to the people they got up and went out and fought for their country. So through the history of the world there have been people who have had the ability to stimulate people to action through the spoken word. With radio, with television, with tape recordings, the spoken word can be more influential than ever before. Moreover, the written word is a most important way to reach people, again either for good or evil. With more people able to read today then ever before, the written word becomes even more significant. In general, however, ten times as many people will listen to the spoken word as will read the written word.

The power of ideas and the power of personal example are strong influences that can be used for both good and evil. Combined with other factors they become effective in guiding people's actions and behavior.

But Christians, in achieving great things for God, have other resources besides those that the secular world thinks of. "God hath not given us the spirit of fear; but of power, and of love, and of a sound mind" (II Tim. 1:7). Christians have powers to accomplish great things for God which we do not use as well as we should. Preaching, the spoken word in public, and the private testimony; the power of writing; the power of example; all these, under the guidance of the Holy Spirit, offer powerful avenues of reaching people for good. But in addition, God has given us the instrument of prayer, with its mysterious power to accomplish great things. He has given us the Holy Scriptures, with their amazing power to influence people far beyond any human writing. The worship service of the Church, guided by the Holy Spirit, is also a powerful influence, an influence that will change the lives of people and uplift those who already believe. With these, we can begin to see the possibilities of doing great things for God that go far beyond the puny influence that human approaches can bring to bear.

Perhaps most important of all are the three great spiritual gifts: faith, hope, love — the gifts that will result in great spiritual fruit as they apply in the individual life. First of all, there is faith and trust in God. Then the hope or the expectation and the assurance of eternal life. And above all, there is the love of God which possesses us, motivates us, directs us, fills us with individual power beyond anything we can conceive of. Here we have the means to change human nature, to reach people more effectively than any other possible approach, to accomplish lasting, worthwhile results.

God tells us that he uses the weak things of the world to accomplish his purposes. It is not the things that seem strong to us but rather the divine power that produces results far greater than anything we can arrange, finance, organize, force, or influence in a human way. The world, in general, considers love as weakness, not strength. But to reach people, it is by far the strongest element of all. It can be done only on an individual basis. Love on a mass basis is never meaningful. Love is a shared relationship between God and me, and passed on to another individual through me as a channel. The psychologists tell us that every individual must have love to survive. This is the way to reach people — not through something we generate ourselves but through serving as channels of God's love for each individual whom we meet.

So then how do we accomplish great things for God? How do we as Christians achieve and effect the burning desires that we have within us because we have been born anew? Let us not count on human power. Let us not count on money. God supplies whatever money is needed for his purposes. Long ago we gave up military power when we abandoned the crusades and the holy wars as a means of doing good things for God. Let us not count on the strength of organization. That type of power fails when we are dealing with the souls of men. And above all, let's avoid political power, with its corruption, its evil influence, and its alliance with Satan. Worldly power produces counterfeit results. Political power to accomplish good things is just as false, just as counterfeit as military power proved to be. We must have real, enduring, genuine results that glorify God.

Let us then count on spiritual power . . . the spiritual power of faith and hope and above all of love, the love that comes from God, that is of God, that can take full possession of us and make us more influential than anything else that we could possibly do. Let's count on it, preach it, publish it, and exercise it in every possible way.

What then is the business and purpose of Christians as individuals and in churches? It is to reach individuals one by one. That is the only way we can be effective. As individuals and through our churches we can accomplish great things for God by spreading the news of God's love for every person. People are hungry for love, they respond to it. Our mission, and the mission of the Church is so to spread this Good News and the Word of God that more individuals will be brought to a saving knowledge of Jesus Christ and will have access to that love that changes lives and accomplishes great deeds. Through the spoken word of preaching, through the distribution of the written Word of God, through being living examples of what God's love does for us as individuals, we can reach more people and accomplish far more results than any other way. Our business is to do this and through love to help those who have already believed to grow in grace, and in the knowledge of God's love, and in the power of Christ as it works through us. One person with a heart full of God's love, counting on prayer and the guidance of the Holy Spirit, can accomplish more than a whole season of legislation, appropriations, and public demonstrations.

The people of this world have many needs. Our hearts ache for them. Since God has so loved us that we have been changed into new kinds of people, we are filled with desire to help others, to witness, to serve.

There is only one real genuine way to get genuine results. We cannot get results in an artificial way. Counterfeit results through the power tools of the world all fail when put to the test.

Above all, every individual needs God's love; this we cannot give them by legislation, reform movements, or mass influence. Love must be given to people one by one, by using God's spiritual power working in us and through us. Praise God for the opportunity that he has given each of us to be a channel of his love and grace.

THE IMPACT OF MATERIALISM IN AFRICA
Howard Jones

Materialism is making a great impact today, especially upon the new African nations. Long known as the dark continent, Africa is now fully involved in social, economic, technological and industrial changes.

Many people are unaware of Africa's amazing progress and still envision it as a pagan, underdeveloped continent. The new Africa, growing in materialism, affluence and social aspirations, has great hopes for the future.

A visitor to Africa today sees modern government buildings, hospitals, educational institutions and business establishments. In many countries, networks of modern roads link interior areas with large cities. Radio and television keep Africans well informed on world events. Expensive stereo sets play Bach and Beethoven as well as jazz and rock and roll.

Many Africans are financially able to dress fashionably, live in beautiful well-furnished homes, drive the latest cars, and educate their children abroad.

The question soon arises, how can we effectively evangelize these Africans whose lives are being affected by such multitudinous changes? Surely it would be inadvisable to oppose wholesome trends of progress. Therefore, we must accept the fact of the new and emerging Africa and must adjust ourselves and our ministries accordingly.

Unfortunately, some foreign missionaries have been unable to make this adjustment. They feel that Africans should not possess too much of this world's goods or be given major responsibilities because they are "not ready yet." Some missionaries fear that if the African abounds economically, socially and educationally, he will become proud, lose his spirituality, and consider himself on an equal with the missionary.

Serious problems sometimes arise when African Christians return home after studying abroad. I think of one fine Christian couple whom some of the white missionaries discouraged from going to the United States for advanced degrees. When the couple returned to Africa, the husband with a doctorate and the wife with a master's degree, they experienced resentment on the part of the missionaries who were now eclipsed in training and qualifications for leadership.

Certain factors are helping whet the appetite of African Christians for more of the material things of life. There is, for example, the impact

THE REV. MR. JONES is an associate evangelist with the Billy Graham Evangelistic Association. He conducts crusades in many countries, but primarily in Liberia, where he has an active radio ministry over Radio Station ELWA in Monrovia.

of other wealthy countries. Africans who travel to Europe and the United States see how well other people live; Africans also come in contact with the many who visit their continent.

I also believe that the way white missionaries live stimulates materialistic ideas among African Christians. Our African brethren know that large sums of money come from supporters at home for establishing, developing and maintaining the mission stations. Africans become accustomed to seeing the missionaries' homes, cars and expensive equipment. It is no wonder then, that they say: "Oh, the missionaries are rich because they come from America and Europe." Many Africans equate the missionary's spirituality, dedication and service with wealth, affluence, prestige and power. They observe that the missionary gets answers to his prayers, not only in terms of spiritual blessings but also in regard to financial and material matters. Knowing that God is no respecter of persons, African Christians believe they, too, have the right to prove the power of God as the Provider of all things, both spiritual and temporal.

Foreign missionaries must realize that simply converting Africans to Jesus Christ is not enough. To the ministry of evangelism must be added efforts to improve the social conditions of those to whom we minister. The Gospel we preach must penetrate every area of life. This Gospel emancipates, lifts people from the depths of sin, and transforms them from sinners into the children of God. Foreign Christian workers cannot keep the African Christian in a "bush boy state" and deprive him of the material blessings of life. He will not be satisfied with such a state, nor will he respect the missionaries for keeping him there. Missionaries must so labor that they challenge and inspire national Christians to help themselves to be better witnesses for Christ and outstanding citizens of their country.

Though aware of the many blessings associated with materialism, we dare not overlook its dangers. The desire for material things may cause departure from God and his Word. History speaks often of nations that worshiped the idols of materialism and pleasure.

Africa's thirst for prosperity is beginning to stifle the spiritual life and power of its people. One detects a growing indifference on the part of certain political leaders toward spiritual things. We often forget that many of Africa's leaders, both past and present, are products of Christian missions. In their feverish search for greater wealth and political power, however, their love for Jesus Christ, for the Christian Church and the Bible often waxes cold. The philosophy of many of these heads of state might well be summed up in the words of Kwame Nkrumah, former President of the Republic of Ghana: "Seek ye first the political kingdom, and all other things shall be added unto you."

There is no doubt that the Christian churches in African are being affected by the modern spirit of materialism, secularism and hedonism. Far too many churches in Africa are losing instead of gaining members. Church attendance is on the decrease. Many people no longer consider Sunday as the Lord's Day for worship and rest: Sunday has become the popular day of the week for sport, sin and pleasure.

There is also a growing contempt among African young people toward the Christian ministry in cases where churches do not support their ministers adequately and ministers must therefore find other means of livelihood. They become the victims of scorn and ridicule. This situation accounts in part for the shortage of trained and consecrated young men in the Christian ministry. One young woman told me, "Oh, I would never marry a minister. Ministers are too poor. They don't have anything."

Currently there are thousands of Africans in Europe and the United States studying medicine, law, engineering, political science and so on. If asked why they have chosen their particular profession, they say, "There is more money in this profession for me. When I return to my country I want to become a leader in my field. I want to be a great success, make a lot of money and live well."

The number of those preparing for the Christian ministry is almost nil. And no doubt mission organizations have not always had happy experiences in sending Christian young people abroad to receive further education. The hope was that these young people would eventually return to Africa for Christian service. When once abroad, some lost their sense of Christian values, were overcome by material things and by laxity of living. They forsook God and broke their promises to him.

The snares and pitfalls of materialism, therefore, can be serious indeed. What are we to do?

As Christians we are to accept what the Bible says about our material needs. God, not materialism, must control our thinking and living. We are to trust him to supply all our needs, both spiritual and temporal. It was our Lord who said, "Take no thought for your life, what ye shall eat, or what ye shall drink; nor yet for your body, what ye shall put on . . . your heavenly Father knoweth that ye have need of all these things. *But seek ye first the kingdom of God, and his righteousness; and all these things shall be added unto you"* (Matt. 6:25-33).

Let us remember, too, Christ's penetrating message to the Church at Laodicea, a church that had lost its spiritual life and vitality through pride, and by trusting in its material wealth rather than in the riches of Christ.

In this time of crisis Africa needs a mighty moral and spiritual awakening that begins in the Church and then reaches throughout the length and breadth of the land. This divine visitation will give direction and hope to African leaders as they face an uncertain future. The Church also will receive fresh vision and necessary motivation to fulfill the unfinished task of evangelism and missions before Christ returns. Time is running out. What we do in Africa must be done quickly.

Foreign missionaries cannot do this job alone. With its rising tide of nationalism and expanding development and prosperity, the new Africa needs African Christians who will fulfill their responsibilities to God in soul-winning. The key to evangelizing Africa with the Gospel of the Cross is the African himself. We desperately need more dedicated Africans whose vigorous faith in Jesus Christ and bold and forthright Christian witness will not succumb to the onslaughts of materialism, self-indulgence, and political power. God give us saved, consecrated, sanctified, selfless servants to win and secure a restive Africa for Jesus Christ!

THE GRIP OF MATERIAL COMFORTS
Florentino Santana

In 1933, the Disciples of Christ had a revival in Puerto Rico that changed the whole panorama of our own denomination and even of other groups.

After 35 years we are again in need of a spiritual renewal of the same kind. Many are praying for a refreshing outpouring of the Holy Ghost. As we have not yet had such experience after much prayer, the reason may be that prayer must be accompanied by confession and commitment.

There is, first of all, a prosperity which tends to some kind of materialism. Prosperity is a blessing of God but it is spiritually very dangerous. Sometimes it is difficult to seek the face of the Lord when we are steeped in comfort.

Another temptation that comes from prosperity is the desire to use it as a means of social elevation.

We need to heed the voice of God in the present world.

As the people of the world proclaim their worldly products, we must know the power of the Lord in order to preach the Gospel effectively.

Pentecost changed everything for the early believers. It activated a chorus of praise to the God of heaven by adding new joy to the Christian life. The "push" of preaching was "agape."

We have not been diligent in transmitting the old experience to the new generation. We need to be prophets even to death. If we let the Spirit of the Lord work in us, we ourselves can be victorious over materialism.

THE REV. MR. SANTANA is pastor of Sequnda Iglesia Cristiana (Disciples of Christ) in Bayamon, Puerto Rico.

Report of Group Discussion

The consensus was that materialism is amoral or evil only when an end and not a means. The problem of the Church as an institution entering the area of political, social and economic affairs was raised. Many agreed that every part of life must be invaded by and influenced by the Gospel, but that this influence is ideally accomplished by Christians as individuals rather than by a lobbying group.

Reporter: *C. Ralston Smith*

ATTITUDES TOWARD NON-CHRISTIAN RELIGIONS
Hideo Aoki

There are cultural barriers to the proclamation of the Christian Gospel. If the core value of a culture is synonymous with the religious values then the various world religions have become the basis of the mode of behavior, attitude and thinking whenever they have taken root. This non-Christian psychological set created within the cultural context has set up resistance to the demands of Jesus Christ. The task of evangelization of the world requires a realistic view of the cultural-religious competitive forces. First, Christianity which is regarded as a Western religion must be compared with the Eastern thought as being diametrically opposite on several points.

1. The concept of time

To the East, time is not a constantly flowing river into the future, but a wheel. It always revolves a full circle. No moment is ever totally lost because it will be repeated. There is always another chance, for what I should have done at this time, month and year, I can do again when I once more arrive at this time and month next year. Thus the Orient is without haste. This moment is not of essential importance, because it is not thought to be irretrievable. Remorse is therefore singularly absent, and sin either of omission or commission is not absolute. This is still another reason why the sensitive evangelists find difficulty in presenting the message of Christian salvation to the East. They have felt that the East has no feeling of sin, or guilt. The East in return, has felt that the Western concept of sin and guilt was rather narrow and limited. The East is dominated by the concept of the wheel. The Occident, by that of the straight line and the two seem to each other irrational and incompatible. The circular concept of time of the East and the linear concept of the West leads to a further incompatibility, namely, the concept of salvation.

2. The concept of salvation

To the Westerner, time is a one-way street leading to some definite terminal point in the future that we cannot identify but which we are sure is there. He asks the same question which was uttered by Job: "If a man die, will he live again?" To the Easterner, particularly the one who embraces the doctrine of *samsara* or reincarnation, this question is meaningless for he believes in the endless chain of life and death and there is no

DR. AOKI is a lecturer at the University of Maryland's Far East Division in Tokyo, Japan.

end to the misery of being tied to the external wheel of *samsara*. The Westerners' desire is to extend this earthly life beyond the grave.

3. The idea of progress

Although historic Christianity denies the concept of relativism, it has felt the subtle effects of Western thought which has embraced a belief in progress. This optimistic belief in progress implies that nothing is as good as it could be, and that it will never be so good as it is capable of becoming.

The foregoing incompatibilities represent a few of the areas where obstacles to evangelism exist.

In spite of the long history of East-West interaction, the penetration of Western culture into the East has usually affected the material rather than the immaterial or spiritual aspect of culture.

There is at present in the oriental world, quite clearly, a kind of revulsion from the impact of Western civilization and a serious re-study of its own roots and heritage.

Taking into account the political tensions and resentments against Western dominance in the colonial past, and the present crisis in Vietnam, this revulsion against the Occident does not diminish the desire in the Orient to acquire those Western skills and achievements, especially in the field of technology and social technique.

4. What should be the attitude of the Church in the face of these obstacles?

In the first place it must set all parochialism and regionalism aside and ascend to a yet unknown dimension of world-embracing thinking.

Secondly, it must recognize the central issues involved. The central issue in the coming confrontation with the Eastern system of humanist thinking will, it seems, be to vindicate the personal conception of the living God as manifest in Jesus Christ, and the meaning and purpose of man and the world in the light of God's revelation.

The key word of Oriental humanistic philosophies is "harmony." In contrast to Christianity, the tendency is to gloss over the glaring disharmonies in man's inner and outer life. The peculiar trait of biblical Christianity is to face disharmony or sin in man realistically.

Part of the success of the evangelistic efforts of the early church was its willingness to enter the stream of Judaism and other dominant philosophical systems without compromise. The Apostle Paul confronted the Stoics and the Epicureans with the message of the living God.

There are several possible attitudes that a Christian Evangel may take.

One is that all other religions except Christianity are without a single truth.

The second attitude is that all religions including Christianity have some truth. Perhaps Christianity contains a greater degree of truth, and its insights are to some degree superior to any of the other world religions.

This view regards all religions as being equally valid and tends to obliterate the distinction between historic Christianity and non-Christian religions.

The third attitude is that the ethical teachings of other religions have elements of truth and may in some cases become the basis for the propagation of the Christian message. This position does not surrender the uniqueness of biblical Christianity.

A superficial knowledge of the alien religious ideas has been a detriment to the advance of the Gospel in a non-Christian society. Evangelical Christianity must attempt to seek a deeper and sympathetic understanding of world religions. At the same time the uniqueness of the Gospel, namely the living Christ who is "the way, the truth and the life" must be reemphasized. In the midst of the confusion and conflict of ideologies, a clarion call must declare that "neither is there salvation in any other: for there is none other name under heaven given among men, whereby we must be saved."

MAN'S UPREACH AND GOD'S REVELATION

Akbar Abdul-Haqq, Jr.

A living experience of the ultimate reality is the crucial issue involved in the religious aspirations of mankind. From the very dawn of history, man has been groping after God in a thousand and one ways. The contemporary religions of the world are a culmination of this basic drive of humanity. But they remain essentially man's attempt to find God.

The Gospel of the Lord Jesus Christ connotes God's outreach in history to rescue the lost. The difference between the two is as distant as the Tower of Babel from Pentecost. Hence, apart from the common denominator of man's innate hunger for God, there is bound to be a conflict and tension between the confusion of tongues and the gift of tongues. The former is clearly indicative of the endless disillusionment of a soul in search of its God. The latter is possible only when God has whispered the secret of his presence in the secret chamber of the heart to be proclaimed to the world from roofs and housetops. Apart from this basic difference of orientation, the Gospel is also opposed by the religions of the world insofar as they remain under the sway of the god of this world. In this regard some types of theology are essentially opposed to the Gospel. These mere forms of godliness which deny the power thereof are one with the religions of the world in keeping man a captor of the categories of sense, experience and life here and now alone. The Gospel seeks to enable man to live in the world but save him from being of the world, because the supernatural kingdom of God has invaded history in and through the Lord Jesus Christ. This fundamental difference of outlook is also bound to create obstacles between religions of the world and the Gospel in the world.

In our time, there has been a great renaissance of the major religions of the world. Since the end of the last war this renewal has been hastened by the drawn of political freedom in those large sections of the world which erstwhile were under the colonial sway of the Western nations. As this paper deals with renascent religions alone, the politico-religious phenomena of Communism and its like have been excluded from our study.

It is noteworthy that there are two major outside factors which are responsible for precipitating the movement leading to the renaissance of religions of the world. The first cause, political independence, has already been referred to above. The second significant factor, strangely enough, is the modern impact of the Bible and Christian witness on these religions

DR. ABDUL-HAQQ, JR., is an associate evangelist with the Billy Graham Evangelistic Association.

which otherwise had been given to age-long sleep. The Bible brought sweetness and light to the non-Christian heart directly or indirectly. As a result there appeared mounting concern within these religions to reform themselves and assert their identity in the light of the new day of political freedom. Thus this phenomenon of renaissance is marked by a lot of imitation of Christian methods of propagation and modes of worship and service. With this brief background we must now turn to a consideration of some major hindrances to evangelism raised by the newly revived major religions of the world.

Persecution

The Lord's warning as to persecution following in the wake of the Gospel is as true today, if not more true, than it ever was. In practically any country where a non-Christian religion is predominant, a convert to the Gospel exposes himself to physical, social and economic persecution. Even in the case of those religions which proclaim their tolerance from public platforms in the world, great pressures are brought to bear against a convert joining the Christian fold. Pertinent facts to substantiate this could easily be had from any one of the countries under consideration. Despite this, some of the countries where such a state of affairs prevails try to keep a facade of a separation between church and state. Burma, Ceylon and Pakistan are right in the midst of a fluid sort of religious nationalism. India is experiencing similar birth pangs in terms of the great drive of Hinduism for linguistic, cultural and even political supremacy in the country.

In the contest with such a religious nationalism, the message of the Lord Jesus Christ appears to a hearer to be an alien intrusion. The presence of Christians in many of the non-Christian lands is looked upon with suspicion. In the case of two such countries going to war the minority groups of churches dare not express freeely their "agape" and universal sense of communion for fellow Christians across the border. For example, in the recent war between India and Pakistan many Christians living in the states directly affected had a tough time due to an atmosphere of morbid suspicion.

In these former colonies of the Western powers, which are now free, Christianity is considered an Occidental religion. Moreover, in their thinking, it is closely linked with colonialism and white supremacy. Therefore a missionary from the West comes under particular suspicion and this hurts the religious and national pride of the people. Those enlightened people who can rise above religious fanaticism still wonder honestly as to why the business of Christian missions happens to be a one-way traffic from West to East. The chance presence of a Christian national in the foreign missions structure is an evident eye-wash to them. In the face of the evident moral and spiritual decay in the West, they often wonder why missionaries from the Occident still have to come to the Orient. All this reflects on the Gospel that the missionary and national Christian are trying to preach. The answer to this hindrance is not just an indigenization of the church and its instruments of propagation of the Gospel. Part of the answer will come only through a universalization of the foreign missionary enterprise. Then the whole world will be considered a mission field where Christians from East and West will be able to serve hand in hand under God.

It needs to be pointed out that in a way religious nationalism is not peculiar to the lands of the renascent non-Christian religions. It is to be found also in the so-called Christian West. Thus the concern of many Christians and churchmen to save Western civilization through preaching the Gospel and combating Communism in the name of God in order to project political democracy, is an expression of a brand of religious nationalism. This type of pseudo-evangelism is bound to stir up a hornet's nest when it is exported to the lands under the sway of non-Christian religious nationalism. The only antidote to this obstacle is a proclamation of the Good News under the honest burden of the Great Commission and by the power of the Holy Spirit.

Religious nationalism is bound soon to dissipate itself. There are sure indications that such a process has started already. A renascent religion is put to the test under the conditions of the new-found freedom of a given country. One can see evidence of the increasing failure of the renascent religions to bear the burden of a nation on its own. Their own adherents show signs of growing disillusionment in what they once considered to be a possible panacea for all ills. This is more true of the youth and the intelligentsia of the society. In view of this, there are great doors of opportunity being opened up for the evangelization of the non-Christian world.

Proselytism

One of the distinguishing features of a renascent non-Christian religion is its proseltyzing zeal. Some of the religions, strangely enough, have received the original impetus in this direction from Christian missionary and evangelistic activity. Thus, Hinduism has no doctrinal basis whatsoever for missions. Its fundamental doctrines of Karma, transmigration and caste system go against it. However, the renascent Hinduism has come to the scene not only with a sense of mission to win all Indians to Hinduism, but also to claim the whole world. The real encounter between the evangelistic outreach of the Church and the world missionary activity of non-Christian religions raises the vital issue of a distinction between proselytism and evangelism. According to the Bible, true evangelism always means that we are co-workers with God. Proselytism, on the other hand, is an all too human attempt to win adherents to a given ideology. This fine but crucial distinction between the two approaches to a world mission should cause serious self-examination on the part of the bearer of the Gospel. We have to watch out lest like the Pharisees of old we may find ourselves touring land and sea to win one proselyte only to make him doubly condemnable in our misguided zeal. This is why tarrying in Jerusalem and receiving the power from on high is the inalienable prerequisite to being witnesses of the Lord to Judea, Samaria and the uttermost parts of the world.

Religious tolerance based on religious neutralism

The Gospel of Christ is most tolerant to a race in rebellion against God in so far as it is rooted in his love, grace and long-suffering. But it has an appearance of intolerance and narrowness when it proclaims that there is only one way provided by God out of the besetting predicaments of man.

The ultimate justification of the intolerance which invariably accompanies truth is to be found in the fruit borne in living situations. A brand of tolerance is abroad whereby all religions are equally good because all lead to the same God. This philosophy is a peculiar contribution of Hinduism. It is based on the orthodox Hindu agnosticism. The SANATAN DHARMA — orthodox Hinduism — believes that the ultimate reality is essentially unknowable. All the religions of the world are mere guesses at truth. They are like several blind men attempting to guess at the shape of an elephant on the basis of their limited contact with the trunk, an ear, or a leg. Being essentially ignorant of the ultimate nature of God, all religions are equally good. They may be right according to their particular approach to God but none dare claim ultimate validity. Now agnosticism is right as far as man's unaided search after God is concerned. But the Bible declares that God has taken the initiative to reveal this nature in Christ for men to behold and share. Thus Saint Paul went about proclaiming the Gospel, "God was in Christ, reconciling the world to himself."

Those who preach religious neutralism are usually those who have not taken even their own religion seriously. This is a pet rationalization that the secular man indulges in to avoid the challenge of God. If it were true that all religions are equally good, how do we explain their sharp divergence from each other in their concepts of salvation and its attainment? Again, the problem with all ultimate agnosticism is that it is self-contradictory. If God is unknowable, then it should be impossible even to say that he is unknowable. The knowledge that he is beyond knowing is a piece of knowledge itself.

The Lord Jesus Christ said, "I am the way, the truth, and the life: no man cometh unto the Father, but by me." A Christian becoming a victim of religious neutralism and tolerance of untruth is bound to become intolerant toward Christ. Therefore, sooner or later he may find himself engaged in toning down the unique claims of Christ so that in the end he may find himself to be a Christian without Christ — a Christian in a post-Christian predicament. A post-Christian is one born after his time. He may be a living being but he is bound to be a dead Christian — salt which has lost its savor and is being trodden under the foot of men.

The Hindu brand of tolerance, apart from its philosophic presuppositions, is based also on the psychological urge to get along with people avoiding intellectual confrontation. It amounts to seeking the honor which comes from men and turning one's back upon the honor which comes from God. Moreover, this tolerance remains very tolerant so long as one agrees with its point of view. But the moment one begins to differ, and affirm the uniqueness of the revealed truth of God, all such tolerance turns into bigotry and intolerance. One may be called names or even persecuted.

The kind of religious tolerance a bearer of the Gospel can exercise freely was demonstrated by Paul in the city of Athens. In his speech to the Athenians he acknowledged the function of non-Christian religions which is to prepare man for the Gospel — the Good News — a living encounter with God who otherwise remains unknown and unknowable. Such an outlook would lead a Christian sympathetically to study living religions of the world and their positive contribution to keeping the human heart restless till it finds its rest in God. Such a student will discover an altar to the unknown God in the temple of every religion as they talk about the ultimate reality.

OBSTACLES IN THE MUSLIM WORLD
J. N. D. Anderson

Basing my remarks on Dr. Kuhn's paper on "The Obstacles to Evangelism in the World," I add a few observations about the obstacles to evangelism encountered distinctively among Muslims.

1. The Obstacles of the "Natural Man" and Nationalism

This consideration is highly relevant to our subject, since Islam appeals strongly to the natural man.

According to the strictest school of Muslim orthodoxy, man has no real liberty of choice whatever; the movements of his body, even the thoughts and impulses of his mind, are dependent upon an omnipotent Creator's continual creation and recreation of the atoms from which that body and mind are made. This dependency should certainly humble any temptation to pride.

Why, then, it may be asked is Islam spreading so rapidly today in a number of different countries? For the most part this development is at the expense of primitive animism, and is not very difficult to explain. The animist normally finds his horizons severely limited, for animism varies locally almost from one village to the next. As soon, therefore, as roads, education and progress penetrate, the animist is apt to become unsettled. At this point he may meet a Muslim merchant or holy man, for such persons are scattered throughout Africa and Asia. He sees the Muslim pray five times a day, and asks questions. He learns, among other things, that the Muslim worships one God. This probably appeals to him, for animists almost always acknowledge one creator God, although they ignore him in practice in order to spend their lives propitiating other far more immanent and malignant spirits.

By embracing Islam moreover, the animist becomes part of a world-wide brotherhood, and this is exceedingly helpful if he goes to a big city to look for work. He finds, too, that Islam for the most part consists of clear-cut rules about what he should and should not do. These rules, moreover, are not too exacting, for he may still indulge in polygamy and divorce. So he feels that Islam provides not only a higher theology and many social advantages, but a religion in which he may hope to earn salvation in a way which is not really beyond his power. Muslims commonly boast that their religion is not nearly so costly or "extreme" as Christianity. Not only so, but where nationalism is strong, Christianity is apt to be

PROFESSOR ANDERSON is director of the Institute of Advanced Legal Studies in the University of London, England.

rejected because it so often presents itself in foreign dress. Islam, on the other hand, equally foreign though it is in historical fact, comes in indigenous apparel. It is in no sense tinged with "colonialism" but savors of Middle Eastern independence.

2. The Obstacles of Totalitarianism and of Materialism

In this context, many would say that Islam is on our side, for does it not stand in stark opposition to atheistic Communism and in unequivocal favor of transcendental values? This is perfectly true; but we need to remember that Islam itself represents a monolithic ideology that claims men's total allegiance. Supposing, therefore, this system should cease to command the intellectual conviction of those who have received a Western education, what then? Would it not be exceedingly easy for such persons to transfer their loyalty to another monolithic ideology, and one which may seem to be economically effective? For in most Muslim countries materialism is, in fact, strongly entrenched today, however much people talk about the "spiritual East" and the "materialistic West." And in such localities Communists are clever enough to slant and level their propaganda at the gross maldistribution of wealth which usually exists, and at obviously and urgently needed reforms, rather than at the inherent atheism of Communist ideology.

3. The Obstacle of the Intellectual Climate

Here, in one sense, the orthodox Muslim stands in much the same position as the conservative evangelical, for he believes in a revealed religion which runs counter, at many points, to modern thought. True, the Muslim always maintains that his religion makes ample provision for reason and science; but it is exceedingly difficult for an educated man to believe that every verse in the Quran was written from eternity in Arabic in heaven, or that Muhammad was the perfect exemplar of humanity. Here the evangelical Christian has an enormous advantage, but one which it is by no means easy to exploit.

When we turn to psychology — and, in particular, to sin and guilt — the position is rather different. The Muslim does not believe in original sin; he emphasizes orthodoxy of belief much more than ethical conduct; and his ultimate response to moral lapses too often is simply that God made him that way. He therefore has little consciousness of sin. Despite the voluptuous imagery of the Muslim paradise and the ample provision on earth for polygamy, continual divorce and remarriage, and — in the past, at least — for slave concubinage, it would be unfair to depict the Muslim as a hedonist. But it is axiomatic that the Muslim — like the Christian, but unlike the Hindu — cannot consistently indulge in syncretism, for he has clear-cut beliefs which run directly counter to those of other religions.

4. The Obstacle Posed by Basic Islamic Teaching

This brings us to the heart of the opposition of Islam to evangelism — and, indeed the Evangel. For the Muslim is still fanatically opposed to the belief that Christ was the Son of God, and he usually reacts strongly to any use of that title. This is so partly because Muhammad believed the Christian trinity to consist of the Father, the Virgin Mary and Christ, the implication being that God married a human woman and produced a son. Modern Muslims know better; but they find it hard to avoid the conclusion that we really worship three Gods, and that we have taken a mortal man — prophet though he was — and committed the unpardonable sin of putting him on an equality with God. They find it desperately hard to realize that we do precisely the opposite; for we worship a God who in his love and condescension became man. The movement is down, not up.

Also, the Muslim still denies that Christ ever died on the Cross. Instead, the orthodox believe that when the Jewish leaders came upon him to crucify him, God could not allow this to happen to his chosen messenger, mere man though he was, and caught him up alive to heaven. Then, by what we could only describe as a piece of divine deception, they believe God threw his likeness on someone else, who was crucified by mistake in Christ's place. Muslims regard the Christian doctrine of the atonement as both blasphemous and unnecessary: blasphemous, because it postulates not only the incarnation but what they regard as weakness; unnecessary, because the Omnipotent can forgive or retain sins just as he chooses.

As for the Ahmadiya, they believe that Christ was indeed nailed to the Cross, but never died, and follow an adapted form of Venturini's theory regarding the stories of the resurrection.

It is obvious what a stupendous barrier to evangelism these beliefs represent. Moreover, the Muslim believes that the Old and New Testament Scriptures, though originally inspired, have been corrupted by Jews and Christians, and that they have in any case been superseded by the Quran. Not only so, but if a Muslim renounces Islam it means that he should, in the orthodox view, be executed for apostasy, and he loses wives and children and by operation of law any right of inheritance from Muslim relatives. He frequently also loses his job, and is regarded as a traitor to his culture and community. For a woman, the path of baptism and open discipleship may be even more difficult, if not almost impossible.

This is perhaps enough to show that *mass* evangelism, in the sense of premature appeals for decision, is not desirable in the Muslim world. False attitudes need to be broken down, deep-rooted misunderstandings smoothed away, and both the heart and mind of the individual won, before we can expect a Muslim to step out on the thorny path of total discipleship. In my experience it is not only the proclamation of the Gospel, but also its authentication by something unmistakably Christlike in the life of some

Christian — together, not infrequently, with some dream in which Christ himself appears — which prompts such costly obedience.

We must also sadly confess that throughout the greater part of the Muslim world there are very few churches into which the lonely convert will be welcomed, and where he will find the warmth of fellowship and understanding he so greatly needs.

THE RELIGIONS OF ASIA
Chandu Ray

The hindrances mentioned in Professor Kuhn's presentation of national-ism, totalitarianism, materialism, resurgence of other faiths and so on, are indeed true hindrances to the spread of the Gospel. I believe, however, that the greatest hindrance is the age-old one, namely, that man still tries to prove his own righteousness and does not submit to God's righteousness (Rom. 10:3).

Four hundred million Hindus believe in the theory of "Karma" — what you sow you reap — and in the transmigration of the soul. Six hundred million Muslims believe that their good works will be weighed against their evil ones and that their reward will be accordingly. Two hundred million Buddhists believe that by renunciation they will achieve salvation. And, alas, three fourths of those who call themselves Christians also believe that good works have merit.

The pride of man does not allow him to accept the finished work of Christ on the Cross for mankind, and the Christian Church is yielding to the pressures and is not insisting that the Gospel gives no hope to man in himself "with men this is impossible" (Matt. 19:26). No amount of prayers, alms, fastings, pilgrimages, strivings and labor will save man from his sin and his conscience. Thus the need is to study the biblical theology of evangelism afresh, and to know that when men come to us in their midnight darkness we have nothing to set before them except God's grace revealed to us in Jesus Christ (Luke 11:6).

When I became a Christian, what most hurt my people was that I was leaving such a "moral" society and sheltered home and family for an im-moral, selfish, and self-seeking community. The image of Western Christian-ity is that of a life of licentiousness where sex relationships are no longer sacred. It is said that nearly 90% of the men and women have experienced sex relations before marriage. The social pattern allows the drinking of alcohol. Respect for parents and elders does not exist, for everyone thinks only of himself. Where money is the motive for everything, the sacredness of life has disappeared. I do not say that this is necessarily a true picture, but this is the image projected by many who call themselves Christians. For evangelism in Asia, we need a fresh understanding of the Christian calling of holiness of life. There is no greater incentive to evangelism than the changed lives of the Christians — a "growing conformity unto his death" — unto the social and ethical standards set by our Lord Jesus Christ, and not to those of America or the West.

The feet of those who preach good tidings of joy (Rom. 10:15) are

THE RT. REV. DR. RAY is the Bishop (Anglican) of Karachi, Pakistan.

not the beautiful changed lives of believers but instead we are aware of big cars and expensive equipment, large salaries and beautiful houses. "But the Son of man [had] not where to lay his head" (Matt. 8:20). We need to ask ourselves why Islam spreads so fast and captures so many adherents without a professional ministry. It depends almost entirely on the life and witness of the rank and file of its adherents. We need to recapture the vision of the Thessalonians who were an example to all and through whom the Word of the Lord sounded forth not only in Macedonia and Achaia, but whose faith in God went forth everywhere (I Thess. 1:8). Our display of wealth is also a hindrance to the Gospel in Asia.

And what can we say of our bickerings and squabbles, of the disunity even among evangelicals? What an ugly picture we give to the world that is hungry for a community of love, for the family of God. When we get together our talk seems to be, not a sharing of "the greatness of his loving heart," his sterling righteousness and matchless mercy, his magnetic tenderness and lofty courage, the example of his patience at Nazareth and passion at Gethsemane, his pity and compassion for the lost. Instead we talk about fellow Christians and pick holes in their worship and ways. We make tradition the truth, forgetting that we are not justified by our beginnings but by the end to which we move, even our hope of the Bridegroom's return for his Bride.

We need therefore to give thought to:

1. the true meaning of evangelism in terms of biblical theology

2. internationalization of our mission, so that the image is true

3. a survey that shows how fast we are becoming a minute minority (we are not even catching up with population explosion)

4. a deeper sense of unity as evangelicals who are committed to our task of bringing many sons into glory.

Report of Group Discussion

Delegates went on record as recommending to the Congress the following resolutions:

1. Resolved that consideration be given by the Congress or its Executive Committee to appointing a body to investigate and report on practical and effective means of internationalizing the Christian world missionary outreach in today's world.

2. Resolved that consideration also be given to setting up one or more Institutes for Advanced Study of World Religions with a view to the more effective evangelization of their adherents to the glory of God.

The resolutions grew out of numerous expressions of need in the

Asian-African world, most expressing a concern for greater understanding by evangelists and church workers of particular Afro-Asian problems and thought patterns.

The delegates expressed a particular concern for a sympathetic ministry among foreign nationals studying in the United States or Europe and for the preparation of Christian laymen going abroad in business or government service for effective lay evangelism.

Reporter: *Warren Webster*

THE TOTALITARIAN CLIMATE
Samuel Escobar

The rise of totalitarian states, due to different reasons, has become a sign of our time. Though totalitarianism is disappearing or waning in some regions of the world there is nevertheless, a constant threat of totalitarian upsurge from the left or the right.

1. The nature of totalitarianism.

We can consider as totalitarian any state which having assumed the whole political and technical control of a nation, seeks also to rule the mind and conscience of its citizens to gain their absolute loyalty. The most dangerous totalitarianism is that whose ideology becomes an official religion (state religion) and opposes any doctrine or teaching that does not conform to it.

Communism and Nazism are the two typical examples in our century. Both show totalitarian ideologies that are a world-life view and have given evidence of their militant opposition to the Gospel.

Other totalitarian states, even though they have not clearly formulated an ideology, intend to rule even the conscience of their citizens for political expediency. Some of them use an existing religion to justify their political behavior. Even some Christian groups have made themselves available for this purpose.

The two totalitarianisms of our century (here we consider Nazism as a form of Fascism), hold collectivistic notions about the nature of man which go so far as to deny the basic freedom of individuals.

2. Evangelism.

The Church of Jesus Christ lives in a society that is under the rule of human governments, but Christians are to be witnesses of Jesus Christ and his absolute Lordship over those who have committed themselves to him. The Church is expressly commanded to announce the message of salvation to the world; she must live as an evangelizing force.

The Christian way of life, with its basic loyalty and obedience to Christ, finds a specially hostile environment under a totalitarian regime because it clashes with the totalitarian demands of the state or of the dominant élite. The proclamation of the Gospel of Christ becomes unbearable for totalitarianisms which are usually built upon concepts of man, life, morality and society that are radically opposed to those of the Gospel.

Christians in our time should be aware of the possibility that a govern-

MR. ESCOBAR is a staff member of the International Fellowship of Evangelical Students and traveling secretary for the Inter-Varsity Christian Fellowship of Argentina in Cordoba, Argentina.

ment which allows some degree of freedom for ecclesiastical activity is opposed nevertheless to fundamental aspects of Christian witness in areas where such a government makes totalitarian claims.

3. Ways of opposing evangelism.

There are several major ways in which totalitarianism opposes evangelism.

(a) Totalitarianism creates an anti-Christian ideological atmosphere. All means of mass communication and persuasion are used to indoctrinate people in the essentials of the official ideology. Christianity is attacked both in its doctrine and in its practical application and usually has no way of defending itself. Thus, ideological barriers are established in the minds of the citizens and they become closed to the Gospel.

(b) It isolates the Christian community within a country. Adducing many and different reasons, believers are separated from their brethren inside. There is an effort to establish racial, national, or class barriers; these are a denial of the universal appeal of the Gospel.

(c) It perverts Christian witness. When violent efforts to eradicate faith in Christ prove a failure, then attempts are made subtly to infiltrate the Christian community, to have the Gospel conform to the totalitarian ideology. The examples of Communist China and Nazi Germany show that a Church which is not prepared or has ceased to be faithful to the Word of God, can easily be trapped.

(d) It eliminates trained leaders. Efforts to "re-educate" pastors and leading laymen will reveal those who resist and who are faithful. These are then eliminated for political, moral or social but never religious reasons. Such strategy is evidently an attempt to cut the evangelizing advance which such persons carry on, and leaves believers without spiritual help and guidance.

(e) Totalitarianism rigidly controls the life of the Church. By using police laws, it tries to control carefully the corporate life of the Church and the individual lives of believers. By a similar control of education, the state tries to capture the minds of the younger generation, and prevents the Church from fulfilling her evangelistic and educational work.

What has happened in countries dominated by Fascism, Nazism and Communism abundantly illustrates how totalitarian opposition operates.

4. What can we do about it?

(a) We must detect it in time. Evangelical leaders must have their eyes opened before the imminent appearance of totalitarian regimes. We cannot surrender the loyalty of the Church to totalitarianism out of a fear of Communism. In young nations there are threats of totalitarianism that smack of Communism, or Nazism or even Shintoism and Islamism.

(b) We must keep a Christian perspective. God is Lord and it is he who has the final word in history. Sometimes the Church is called to suffer under oppression, but if she is faithful to God, he will give ways of witness. Let us not think that evangelism can be accomplished only within the framework of public activities such as we enjoy in the so-called "free" societies.

(c) We must be concerned for our oppressed brethren. We should maintain regular, persistent and faithful prayer for them. As far as possible we should keep in contact with them; this will encourage them and edify us. Let us not forget the universal, supra-national character of Christian fellowship. The Church cannot commit herself to any socio-political system, no matter how "free and democratic" it appears to be.

(d) Our Congress should issue an urgent call to Evangelicals all over the world, especially to those living in freedom, and ask them to:

Pray unceasingly for the oppressed believers under totalitarian rule.

Evangelize with a sense of urgency while it is yet day.

Teach "all the counsel of God" and especially those biblical truths about the claims of God, his sovereignty and the witness of the Church in society, that is in the world but not of it.

Proclaim the presence and meaning of suffering, discipline and trial in the Christian life, so that those who think they live "in freedom" will not fall under Mammon or any of the modern false gods of the West.

We should also issue a call to all missionary organizations working in areas of the "Third World" where totalitarianism is imminent. We should ask them to accomplish their task as missionaries, remembering "the lessons of China," working in faithfulness to the New Testament and overcoming the paternalistic, imperialistic and colonialistic mentality so that indigenous churches will rise that are well established in the faith, have a well-trained national leadership, and structures flexible enough to face the trial of any totalitarian persecution.

COMMUNIST OPPOSITION TO EVANGELISM

Helen Kim

1. Introduction

One of the greatest obstacles to evangelizing the world for Christ has been an unswerving opposition to Christianity by Communism. The method used to block successfully the advance of Christianity in Communist countries has been both subtle and direct. Freedom of religion is guaranteed, at first; but quietly and systematically, church work in welfare agencies, hospitals and educational institutions is banned. Church literature is restricted, and finally only worship is left and this is usually scheduled when attendance is demanded elsewhere. The policy of the Communists outside of Communist countries has been equally defeating. By classifying religion as "an opiate of the people" used by "capitalists" to keep the "workers happy while exploited," or by making missionaries out to be puppets of the "imperialists," the Communists have tried to make Christian belief as unattractive outside their immediate spheres of influence as they have within.

To document the above statements we shall present a few historical facts concerning the Christian Church in Communist countries. Next, we will point out some overall obstacles which Communism has used in its cold war on Christianity. Then, because the Communists believe in evangelization to advance their cause, particularly among young people, we will emphasize some basic Christian beliefs which declare where we stand, and which we teach our young people. Finally, we suggest some practical ways of sending Christ's message into Communist countries.

2. What Has Happened to Christianity in Communist Countries?

a. The Church in the Soviet Union

The pattern in all Communist countries is clear: first, oppression of religion; second, divisiveness, and a militant movement of atheism; and third, use of what religion and Christianity remains for Communist ends. Communist leaders firmly believe that education can eradicate religion, something which they consider to be a form of ignorant superstition.

In the Soviet Union, in direct competition with the Christian young people, there has been a "League of Militant Godless," which was disbanded in 1941, but was revived in 1957. In the same year at Odessa the government established the "House of the Atheist," devoted to atheistic

DR. KIM is president emeritus of Ewha Woman's University in Seoul, Korea, and president of the Upper Room Evangelistic Association. For many years she was the Korean delegate to the United Nations, and since 1965 has been Roving Ambassador of Korea.

indoctrination. Some 10,765,000 persons were reached in one year through the 239,000 meetings held in this house. While Christian literature was banned or restricted, the League published a total of 14,200,000 pieces in one year. Through persecution, death, and various indirect means, the former 80 percent of Christian believers in Russia was cut to 30 percent by 1960. This encourages Communist leaders in their belief that "religion will gradually die out."

b. Communist China and Christianity

Either every man, woman, and child must fit into the mold of what the Communist Chinese consider a good Chinese citizen to be, or they must pay the penalty. Atheism is taught with the same enthusiasm as in the Soviet Union. Though a church is in existence it has been forced into a nationalistic mold called the Three-Self Movement: Self-support, self-management, and self-propagation. God in China is a "benevolent" God who approves of the Communist program. Christian teachings have been changed into Communist dogma. The few churches that remain are in metropolitan centers and are showpieces for the Communists and their propaganda to indicate that freedom of religion is allowed.

c. The Church in North Korea

Similar patterns of oppression are found in North Korea. Between 1959 and 1960 seven thousand party leaders carried on a concentrated program of examination and censorship of all the people. In this process three million persons were liquidated, including all Christians. Present indications are that there is no surviving church in North Korea.

3. The Obstacles which Communism Presents to Evangelism

Not only are there past and present but also future obstacles to evangelism. Among them are:

1. Lack of contact with the outside world because of the iron and bamboo curtains.
2. Indoctrination with Communist ideology so that Christian beliefs are "educated" away.
3. The use of fear to confiscate personal freedom so that people cannot learn about basic world facts; people are drilled in the idea that individuals exist only for the state and not for themselves.
4. The use of tyranny that makes people dependent on and expendable to the state.
5. Direct suppression of religion, or the use of it as a propaganda device.
6. Subversion of young people all over the world who have no real knowledge of Communism.

4. Ways of Meeting These Obstacles

a. Since we believe that Christianity offers something that transcends one's material, political and nationalistic needs, we here list some basic Christian affirmations that can be taught to our own young people.

1. We believe in an all-righteous, all-loving God who is the source of man's existence and his only final deliverance from sin and death. Service to Him should be man's primary motivation in continuing personal and social reconstruction of life.
2. We believe in moral and spiritual values founded in the character of God.
3. We believe in the supreme worth and dignity of persons.
4. We believe in a universal and eternal Christian fellowship.
5. We believe in the Kingdom of God. If men will obey the will of God, justice and peace will increasingly prevail in history.
6. We believe in Jesus Christ, the son of God, as our Savior and Lord. Through his life and death he completed God's plan of salvation and he alone reconciles all men to God and to one another.
7. We believe in the Holy Spirit who guides and empowers man to work for the achievement of the Kingdom of God.
8. We believe the Holy Bible to be the record of God's revelation to men.
9. We believe in the Church as "the body of Christ" in which we carry on universal and eternal fellowship with God and with one another.

b. We offer the following concrete ways of sending Christ's message to Communist countries.

1. We can use radio as a means of evangelism and to reach Communist countries.
2. We must find ways of sending the written message. Can we use other literature than our own to get this message across?
3. Balloons can be used to carry the message.
4. Water kegs can be used to send the message.
5. Where they are free to visit or live in Communist countries, we can use people as living witnesses.
6. We must depend on prayer and the witness of Christian living. Only with God's help can we surmount our many obstacles and find ways of taking his message. Only by righteous Christian lives can we overcome the economic and political problems that make men susceptible to Communist offers.

COMMUNISM AND CHRISTIANITY

Andrew Ben Loo

1. Introduction

The greatest obstacle to evangelism today is the international conspiracy of Communism. It is not what it appears to be — a social, economic and political reform. It is a satanic religion which endeavors to enslave not only man's body but also his soul. Communism is a devilish system of totalitarianism and collectivism that has spread around the world and subjugated a third of its population. In Red China alone, the figure of 25,000,000 people liquidated is considered conservative. Churches, hospitals, schools, orphanages and other institutions have been seized and confiscated. Recent escapees give blood-curdling accounts of Communist atrocities. One thing is sure, these people who risked their lives to reach a better world will never understand why anyone, especially those who are Christian leaders, can say a good word for Communism.

Its atheistic, materialistic and idealistic views have deceived the youth of many new nations. Its misleading propaganda promises a perfect world. Despite their failure to achieve a Utopia, people in Communist countries cannot shake off the cruel yoke that controls them.

Today Communism has penetrated into high levels of the Christian Church in the Free World. Through infiltration, agents direct policymakers of church councils and their subsidiaries to positions of compromise and appeasement. And while Christians smile upon such policies or accept them complacently or indifferently, Communism looks upon Christianity as its archenemy. In all her history, the Church of Christ has never encountered so great and subtle an opponent. For the last forty years, I have witnessed at close range the coming into power and expansion of Communism in the Far East. I believe evangelical Church leaders must warn the people of God to stand fast on the solid foundation of his Word. We must wield this sword of the Holy Spirit to war against the prince of power in the heavenlies. We must show God's people that a minority block of present-day church leaders are either blind, as President Johnson put it, or thoroughly infiltrated by Communism. These leaders first departed from the faithful Word of God, then lost sight of the Great Commission. In their pro-Communist political views, they never pause long enough to realize that if Communism actually descends upon their various countries they will lose their present ecclesiastical positions.

DR. LOO is the South-East Asia representative of The Pocket Testament League, Inc., in Taipei, Taiwan.

2. Conditions in Red China today

If ecumenism is what the Christian church wants today, then Communist China has it. What is left of the Church of God on the mainland of China is like that in Moscow and Leningrad; it is a mere exhibit for foreign visitors and a pretext of religious tolerance. This controlled situation is the remnant of the purge in which church members were methodically eliminated and brainwashed. Reckoning the Church as its greatest foe, Communism has tried to change her into a tool for Communist ends. The true believers on the China mainland today are literally underground. Due to intimidation, ridicule and murder, no half-hearted Christian would risk appearing in a place of worship. Furthermore, work schedules are purposely set at church meeting hours. And whatever sermons the brainwashed preachers can preach are along Communist lines. Young people are made to participate in various discussion or purge meetings; consequently no young people are in the churches. Attendance is drastically reduced and the small congregations have been forced to combine their meetings in one church in a given area.

The latest news that has leaked out of the mainland of China reveals a sad state of affairs. The so-called church leader there is the one who cooperates best with the Communists. For his loyalty to Communism in surrendering the whole church, he is made a member of the Central Committee. Foreign funds are strictly forbidden to reach the churches or individual preachers, a regulation that was reinstated in 1965 by a church council. Two elderly evangelists who managed to roam the countryside and lead church services, were recently purged and the congregations forced to accuse them of ugly crimes.

From the Republic of China and Hong Kong we get information from escapees and travelers concerning Red China. Chinese who have escaped from the mainland, like ourselves, number two to three million. Thousands who failed to get out in time were murdered.

January 23 is Freedom Day in the Republic of China, and elsewhere in Asia. It commemorates the day eight years ago when 14,000 prisoners of the Allied Forces in Korea turned their backs on the Chinese Communists and came to Taiwan of their own volition. They are 14,000 living witnesses to the nature and wickedness of Communist totalitarianism and collectivism.

3. The nature of this twentieth century peril

No mortal can deal directly with the devil, and so it is with Communism. After his experiences in dealing with the Communists for almost two years on the Chinese POW issue, General Harrison said: "We could not talk with the Communists. It was like talking to the devil himself. We Americans seemed to be children in front of them. They swayed the issues

again and again, and trapped us with our own words. They were filled with
the devil himself; therefore, we cannot deal with Communists, except as
we are filled with the Holy Spirit."

President Chiang Kai-shek knows the Communists better than anyone because he has dealt with them the longest. He knows that force is the
only persuasion that the Communists can understand. He knows, as no one
else, that cooperation and coalition with the Communists is a waste of time.
A Chinese adage says, "You cannot bargain with a tiger for its skin."
Communists want all or nothing. If it were not for the determined efforts
of the United States government in South Vietnam, these disciples of
Satan would be achieving their goal to take over all of Asia by 1970.

4. Why Christians should oppose Communism

One of Communism's techniques is to persuade church council leaders
that for Christians to oppose Communism is to engage in politics. Yet if
Christians do not oppose this totalitarianism, Communism has won half
its battle.

Communism is not merely a social, economic or political reformation
or revolution; it tries to control not only the bodies and souls of men, but
also the spirit. It invades man's will and determination, a realm originally
reserved for knowing and worshiping God. Christians must oppose Communism because it hinders the carrying out of the Great Commission.

Communism is an enemy of God. It attacks and denies him who
created heaven and earth. Christians are to protect and uphold the name of
God, as well as the Bible.

Communism, while denying that man has a soul, yet tries to bind it
with lies, distortion and brainwashing. Communism, like liberalism denies
the deity of Christ and tends to make him a mortal man. Communism is
totalitarian and collectivistic, the absolute enemy of freedom. It promises everything but gives nothing.

5. The Church appeasement movement and Communism

Along with the current One-Church movement go pressures by various
church councils to admit Communist China to U.N. membership. They
also encourage the United States to re-think its relationship with Red
China in regard to business and aid programs, and exchange of scholars
and correspondents. Investigation shows that such proposals have come
directly or indirectly from Communist-inspired sources, or from persons —
clergymen among them — who are sympathetic to Communism. Such persons claim that the 600,000,000 people of Red China should not be left
outside of the family of nations, because the destiny of so great a people
affects the world as a whole. The truth is, however, that fraternization with
Red China involves only the Communist cadres or about 5% of the population. The other 95% are slaves who have no right to speak for themselves.

There is no freedom of the press in Red China; the Geneva Red Cross regulations regarding POWs are disregarded.

Sympathizers claim that membership of Communist China in the U.N. will make the country easier to deal with. But Red China would be ten times more troublesome in the U.N. than the U.S.S.R.! And the delegates from Red China would actually represent only 5% of the 600,000,000 people. The rulers of Red China today, and the delegates they would send to the U.N. are the same people who created the slave state. Moreover, Red China demands that if she joins the family of nations, the Republic of China and perhaps even the United States must withdraw! And yet certain church leaders are pressuring the United States to beg Red China to come in!

6. The Vietnam war issue

For so-called Christian leaders to propose the withdrawal of United States forces from South Vietnam is utterly ridiculous. They are either blind to the facts, or being misled. If they are pacifists, they should remember what Winston Churchill once said: "War is most terrible, but slavery is worse than war." We must not forget that what the Communists want is to enslave people. If this can be done without war, so much the better. Pacifists often play right into the hands of the Communists.

7. In opposing Communism, what comes first, faith or politics?

We oppose Communism not becaue of politics but primarily because of faith in God, in Christ, in his Word the Bible, and in his Church. As already said, Communism is a religion that brings body, soul and spirit under its ruthless control and abuse. It aims to destroy everything we count precious: God, Christ, the Bible, and the Church. The ultimate question, then, that even church leaders must answer is: Are we for God, or are we for Communism?

THE U.S.S.R. AND EASTERN EUROPE
Arthur F. Glasser

The Communist world is determined to prevent all Christians from "outside" crossing its borders to evangelize its peoples. Here is no minor issue. One third of the world's population is involved. Never has the Church faced so baffling a problem — at least, not since the rise of Islam in the seventh century. General De Gaulle may order French diplomats to strike the phrase "Iron Curtain" from their vocabularies, but Christians in the West cannot but agonize over the barriers that separate them from the Communist world.

Their sense of agony arises from an awareness of the infinite value of every man, demonstrated by Christ's redemptive concern for every man. They reason: "He has commanded that the Gospel be brought within the reach of every creature. This means that this generation of Christians must reach this people if they are to be evangelized at all." And yet, Communist barriers make the task impossible. Decade follows decade; the situation remains unchanged. Here at this Congress we are being called upon to face this staggering problem. What are we going to do about the billion souls behind totalitarian walls?

1. The Church exists in the Communist world.

Before iron curtains clanked down, the Gospel had already been preached to the major peoples now within the Communist world. Today, the Church exists in every nation they control. This fact is of tremendous importance. Don't underrate its congregations because of their smallness, their poverty, their limited freedom, and their harrassment by the atheists. God is watching over his people.

We believe this Berlin Congress demonstrates that God has given his believing Church in the West a sense of urgency to complete its evangelistic task. Let us also believe that he is as concerned to impart evangelistic passion to his Church in the Communist world. But don't expect him to follow the same patterns in the East that he is using in the West.

2. But the Church in Communist lands is different.

The totalitarian world is different from the one we know in the West. We should therefore expect that, under God, its Church would be essentially different from the believing Churches we know. We should expect them to go about their evangelistic task in their own distinct way.

Actually, we almost pity these churches because our missionaries, our

DR. GLASSER is Home Director for USA and Canada of the Overseas Missionary Fellowship in Philadelphia, Pennsylvania, USA.

money, our evangelistic know-how, and our promotional literature are not available to them. They have neither property nor financial resources. All have been taken away. Perhaps God has overruled this so that his people might be more free to display their spiritual wealth. These churches have been denied the right to social and political action. Perhaps God has overruled this so that his people might be pressed to concentrate the more on evangelism. The State's hostility and slander have long since driven away all nominal members. Perhaps God has overruled this, so that despite their numerical insignificance, they might display significantly the presence of God in the midst of those who are truly his.

Frankly, the more I ponder the life, worship, and service of these Churches in the Communist world, the more I find myself wishing our evangelical Churches in the West had their wholeness and vigor. As a result, I cannot but challenge the rightness of comparing them unfavorably with our evangelical Churches. This Congress should not speak critically of their "priestly, ritualistic, cloistered and nationalistic" limitations, their lack of our "free-church form of evangelization" methods, their silence as a "prophetic" voice in society. One could make the same negative generalizations about evangelical Churches in the West.

3. How the Church regards the State.

In all Communist countries, government scales are weighted heavily against the Church. Freedom of worship is harshly restricted. Christian dogma is officially attacked as unscientific, and individual Christians are slandered as "rogues," as "un-Soviet" people. And yet, these same Christians are grateful for the privilege of living in a land that demands clearcut faith. They admire the Soviet social system. In short, as with Christians from earliest times and in all types of societies, the Church has come to terms with the Communist State, and is loyal to it.

4. Evangelistic advance despite the State.

Everywhere the Church is on the offensive. (Can you say this about the Church in your country?) "Scarcely a city in the USSR now lacks a Baptist prayer-house." They number between five and six thousand congregations, and are multiplying more rapidly in industrial districts than in rural areas. Congregations of working people are increasingly winning the intelligentsia to Christ. Indeed, the significance of the Church in the USSR today is its vivid demonstration that "an instructed, spiritually virile laity can mean an expanding Church even in an unsympathetic environment" (Pollock).

Evangelism is pursued by friendship. Concern for one's neighbor is paramount. By conversation at the workbench or in the field the Gospel goes forward. All Christian activity centers in the local Church. Its fellowship is the key to spiritual survival and service. Its dominant characteristic is a tremendous sense of the presence of God in the midst of his people. We need not sound any note of despair over God's missionary purpose in the Communist world. He is calling from its nations "a people for his name."

5. Our responsibility.

What can Christians in the West do to help their brethren in the Communist world? A good deal.

First: This *Congress* should issue a call to Christians everywhere to remember them daily in prayer. That they will preserve inviolate the deposit of "the Faith once delivered to the saints." That they will "walk as Christ walked" in the service of God *and* Caesar. That they will proclaim the Gospel "in season and out of season" to non-Christians "beseeching them to be reconciled unto God." That they will meet persecution by loving their enemies, blessing those who curse them, doing good to those who hate them, and praying for those who despitefully use them.

The word "Remember" might be made into a slogan to remind us of this obligation to pray. "*Remember* those who are in prison, as though in prison with them; and those who are ill-treated, since you also are in the body" (Heb. 13:3, RSV). The *Congress* should prepare and disseminate materials to insure that this intercession shall be both intelligent and importunate.

Second: This *Congress* should explore all means for reaching the peoples of the Communist world via the use of such mass media as radio, and eventually TV. There is absolutely no doubt that radio broadcasts are already reaching people in all parts of the Communist world. They are making a significant contribution to the nurturing of believers, whether Orthodox or Protestant. They are also confronting non-Christians with the Gospel.

And yet, how tragic that at this time when religious persecution is again sweeping the Communist world, Christians in the West are cutting back the number of radio broadcasts because of an acute shortage of funds. In addition, Radio Luxembourg has terminated its broadcasting of Protestant programs to the Communist world. All this is serious beyond words to describe. This *Congress* should do something about it.

Finally: This *Congress* should interpret to the world-wide Church, both within and without the Communist world, the place of suffering in the missionary purpose of God. In the Scriptures, the dimension of suffering is central, even crucial, to the evangelization of the nations. The Gospel demonstrates its truthfulness and resurrection power when it is accepted in the encounter of repentance and faith, death to self and life to God. God's *Truth* demonstrated that he was unconquerable when he "steadfastly set his face to go to Jerusalem" and there embraced the Cross. This is a strange word for Christians in the West, but it is a familiar word for Christians in the East. Actually, it is God's Word for all Christians in these days when man is manifesting with increasing boldness his age-long rebellion against the living God.

What lies ahead? What if the Communist movement climaxes in the emergence of the final Antichrist? Will God lose? No, on some dark day, his trumpet will sound and his Son shall return. And then it will be demonstrated that the Gospel was indeed published among all nations and the elect won to Christ.

Report of Group Discussion

Delegates observed that totalitarian philosophies and governments — whether on the right or on the left — pose problems, obstacles and challenges to Christian evangelism. But the focus of their discussion fell on Communism.

Three different sets of relationships between Christians and Communism were distinguishable in different parts of the world.

1. In Latin America, with the exception of Cuba, Communism is confronted only as a competing ideology, delegates reported. Many individuals have made a commitment to it and are therefore difficult to reach with the Gospel.

2. Communism in eastern Europe is in control of political, social and economic structures; however room has been left for the operation of the Christian churches. Despite severe limitations the Church continues its life, including its worship and its witness.

3. Delegates in contact with Chinese and Oriental Communism could accept no possibility of a relationship except open hostility and warfare unto death in view of the ruthless hostility of Communism to Christians.

Many stressed that the Kingdom of God transcends all relative human achievements. Thus all forms of government, all economic and social systems, lie under the judgment of God. Despite the wide differences in the environment for evangelism in various social structures, the greatest caution should be exercised in identifying any one of them as *the* Christian structure.

Christians throughout the world were warned to anticipate the possibility that they or their children might be called upon to live in a hostile environment. Delegates believed that Christians are called to out-think, out-live and out-die the advocates of all anti-Christian or sub-Christian systems.

The ties of Christian fellowship with those who must serve God under totalitarian regimes must be kept alive in every way possible, delegates believed.   Reporter: *Duke K. McCall*

NATIONALISM AND EVANGELISM
Hudson T. Armerding

Nationalism has been described as "one of the most significant forces of our times" (Louis L. Snyder, *The Meaning of Nationalism*, New Brunswick: Rutgers University Press, 1954, p. 3). A complex historical phenomenon, it has become a dominant characteristic of the modern nation-state. Like so many other societal forces, nationalism, as broadly defined, may have a legitimate and productive function when properly located within a larger context, but when not informed by divine imperatives may become predatory and destructive of the moral and spiritual.

One thing is certain. In the foreseeable future of man's history nationalism is here to stay. To affirm otherwise is to fly in the face of a mounting body of evidence including that accumulated during the last decade. Gone is the optimism which prompted Woodrow Wilson's proposals for a League of Nations. Fading also are the hopes voiced in San Francisco in 1945 for a United Nations. The concessions to national sovereignty made at that time in the expectation that the experiences of peaceful intercourse would generate progress toward a true unity proved almost at once to be futile. The inherent competitiveness – not to say combativeness – of the nations of the world forced them into blocs which were quickly aligned in the traditional balance of power so characteristic of previous eras.

To some, these developments seem paradoxical in the light of vastly improved means of communication and transportation. The grim fact is, however, that the technological revolution in communications has been matched by a similar one in the techniques of mass destruction. Furthermore, the almost miraculous developments in communication have been exploited by the unscrupulous in order to propagandize others and create fear of reprisal or destruction.

The use of technology in such ways clearly reveals the problem which underlies the perversion of a legitimate nationalistic spirit. It is not only the understandable but sometimes misdirected ambition of newly liberated peoples for "a place in the sun," but also the practice of some who already have that place to extend their dominance even further. Nor is this to be refuted by citing the current practices of some of the great nations (e.g. Britain or the United States) who in their use of power seem content with a policy of self-restraint. Generally, the root causes of such restraint more often than not may be found in the juxtaposition of military power rather than purely and simply in the altruism so eloquently protested by the politicians. Moreover, the growing urbanization of the nations of the world

DR. ARMERDING is president of Wheaton College, Wheaton, Illinois.

has produced an inevitable domestic interdependence; this, in turn, has generated circumstances that demand a concentration of power if the nation is to function effectively or defend itself. This localizing of power has tended to supplant the traditional "checks and balances" so characteristic of constitutional democracies and has therefore made possible the concentration of authority and influence in the hands of one, or a few, strategically placed officials. It is here that the biblical declarations about the sinfulness of man are of immediate significance in any consideration of the punitive aspects of nationalism. The natural man, ambitious and self-seeking as he is, cannot but be attracted to prospects for the exercise of power, whether domestically or in international affairs. The geometric expansion of such power today, however, outruns the ability of contemporary leaders to control it. Hence, the emotional compulsiveness of the nationalistic spirit, when combined with the ambitions of sinful men, trap mankind in a cruel dilemma. Small wonder that the prospects for a world at peace through human efforts seem bleak indeed. To the biblically oriented observer no other conclusions about world peace seem possible. The Scriptures give no justification for the view that men will, through various associations or alliances, sufficiently sublimate nationalistic tendencies so as to permit the realignment of interests and loyalties toward the human community at large. Rather, in describing the end of the age, the Lord Jesus spoke of nation rising against nation and kingdom against kingdom (Matt. 24:7), a clear indication of their continued existence up to that point in history.

If it is granted, then, that the phenomenon of nationalism will continue to characterize modern civilization, what immediate significance does this have for world evangelism? Assuming that there are beneficial factors even in situations fraught with deleterious possibilities, consider as an illustration the nineteenth century, a period of imperialistic expansion by the western nations, yet an era described by an eminent historian of world missions as "The Great Century." Despite policies and practices which today are adjudged by some to have caused the anti-Christian feeling to be found among newly independent peoples, it is a fact that scores of thousands during this era were won to Christ because these same western nations were cordial to the ministry of the Church at home and generally sympathetic to its outreach abroad. Had there been the militant opposition so characteristic of today's totalitarian regimes, the history of the expansion of Christianity might have been markedly different. This extension of Christian witness occurred despite manifestations of nationalistic superiority displayed by some missionaries and public servants. Fortunately these manifestations were balanced by demonstrations of remarkable concern exhibited by sympathetic government officials as well as by many missionaries.

These inferences drawn from the recent history of Christianity and imperialism support the observation that nationalism need not necessarily thwart an evangelistic outreach and can quite possibly provide conditions under which the preaching of the Gospel may prosper. On the other hand, it would be fanciful to conclude that such a situation is a normal by-product of a strong nationalism *per se*, for contemporary examples would refute this.

The key to the difference may well be the kind of leadership to be found in a particular nation. Here the strategy of evangelism needs careful structuring, taking into account the realities of today's politics. Reaching national leadership with the Gospel can have consequences of the greatest significance in forwarding the cause of Christ, particularly in the newer nations where changing political fortunes often result in strategic modifications of national policy.

The evangelizing of political leaders must be so planned that it includes a discipling ministry as well as a convicting and convincing one. As these individuals are taught in the Holy Scriptures and commit themselves in obedience to biblical commandments, the results, it may be expected, will be favorable to the work of evangelism within the country.

Such immediate, direct action is imperative, but will be incomplete or futile unless there is also the preparation of other Christians for eventual leadership in public affairs. Such preparation is many-faceted. It includes the development of a rigorous faith that is articulate and informed on biblical truth and its relationship to the contemporary scene. It involves an understanding of political life and experience in it. Above all, it demands a sense of being called of God to this area of service, so that the stress of public office will not deter the individual or blunt his enthusiasm for the task.

As a fact of contemporary life, nationalism therefore, need not necessarily be a deterrent to evangelism; it may well be one of God's means for helping Christians make the Savior known to this generation. Let this be our prayer to the Lord of the harvest.

NATIONALISM AND THE GOSPEL
Heini Germann-Edey

It is unquestionably not just a case of luck or accident that we should today focus our attention on this theme, while commemorating the day of the Reformation. Martin Luther's daring declaration and spirited proclamation of the 95 theses just about 500 years ago in Wittenberg, at an hour of complete crisis, proved to be God's will and way to break victoriously through the "religious-iron-like curtain" of that day.

A simple A-B-C order will direct our thoughts to the heart of our subject, political nationalism: A. Advantages; B. Evils; C. Conceptions.

1. Advantages

It is expedient to observe, and important to realize, the fact that our God is actually using this current type of "new nationalism" worldwide, positively to mold and manipulate all world ferments to his own ends, just as he did at Calvary. History provides innumerable proofs of God's amazing activities in and through political nationalism. One excellent example of this is the United States in its revolutionary break from Britain in 1776, thus producing the greatest missionary Church in history, out of the independence it fought for.

A striking illustration of a later date is the world's fifth largest nation, Indonesia. Living since 1949 in that country, I personally followed from an unbiased standpoint the unforseen, tremendous revolutionary transformation, with its various dilemmas and deliverances. The practical advantage, however, of the challenge of that newly emerged nation, inspired with a glowing, vehement nationalism, forced the hitherto "colonial" and "westernized" churches to recognize and to accept their independence, and with it their new responsibilities before God as the national churches of Indonesia. The new impulse coming to the indigenous believers resulted in an hitherto unheard of rate of response to the Gospel nationwide. Within the short span of just a few years, these churches, once stagnant for so many years, have now, since the liberation, experienced an unparalleled growth, with increase in some cases of 100 to 1000%.

With few exceptions, new nationalism has stimulated and speeded the proclamation of the Gospel, and broken down old racial and religious barriers. It has provoked us to new thinking, confronted us with new challenges. By it, new and various forms of missionary activity, before unknown and undiscovered, have contributed to the enrichment of his Church and advantages for the Evangel.

THE REV. MR. GERMANN-EDEY is director of World Vision of Canada, in Toronto, Ontario, Canada.

Think of the one-sided, selfish and limited way some of our old and often fanatical political systems of the western world would be racing toward more power and glory, were they not reversed and replaced by the counter-action of nationalism. It is simply amazing to see how God performs his work and accomplishes his purposes even through this disturbing political channel. Nationalism is a specific pioneer and promoter. It is well to remember that this present prevailing nationalism was largely created and fostered through the oppressive controls and "apartheid" attitude of older nations, thus forcing with open opposition the desire of the human heart for freedom and justice. In the modern sense, nationalism to many younger nations is an assertion of a desire by a people for full freedom from all external domination, that is, it asserts its own national identity and aspirations over against outside influences. Would it not be a right and God-pleasing response not to criticize, but to accept this new challenge and even cooperate with it, until it becomes a "sanctified-nationalism" for the help and healing of many nations?

2. Evils

We need to distinguish between "new" nationalism as a legitimate expression of a people's desire for freedom from external forces, and "old" nationalism, more cultivated and established among the older nations, which assumes the proportions of glorifying and worship of the state, so that it becomes a form of idolatry.

Little needs to be mentioned about the deplorable excesses of immature, distorted and uncontrolled nationalism, which has caused harm to many nations, and hurt many respectable leaders. These destructive elements found in older nations just as frequently as in younger countries, should be considered exceptional rather than normal. And these often serve as a needul thorn-in-the-flesh ministry to Christ's body!

Far weightier problems of resistance to the Gospel are unfortunately often found "within" the camp. The impact of petty western church organizations has produced synthetic shadowy churches. It often appears as if these benevolent missionary societies had come to set up their own kingdom and to seek their own interest, and this in the name of Christ. What a tragedy and shame it is, when a country-to-be-evangelized has to request their missionary guests to adjust and adapt themselves better to the life and law of the land! Frequently the sticky and stubborn attitude of the "white" man has caused unnecessary tension, squabble and even battles. Not a few have been expelled. However high and holy the aims might have been, if generated and operated by the flesh they produce utter resistance to the Gospel.

Our western know-it-all attitudes confuse and divert what God has blessed in the humble beginnings of a ministry in the Christian cause. The appearance of this false superiority is possibly one of the greatest obstacles in the service of our Lord. The very methods of much of our modern religious and theological education seem to produce an obscure mist in the mind of the trainee. The sharp edge once wrought by the Holy Ghost has been blunted and dulled. Much of this green-house-produced, often vague academic stuff leaves the hearts of the people-to-be-won, empty and disillusioned!

On a recent visit to the Orient, I stayed in one country where a Missionary Society with over 100 foreign workers held a 10-day missionary conference. Not one single national pastor was invited. How can God's work actually be done with such an outlook, ignoring or neglecting indigenous voices and authorities? It will not be surprising that we reap the harvest of reaction. A good motive cannot excuse a wrong attitude in the work of God. We need to learn that God may already have his Church where we imagine we have to build it.

A shocking surprise is the fact that some of the super-fundamentalist groups have shown the longest resistance and opposition to the signs of what God is doing through the national Christians. On some fields the "internationals" face the "nationals" like two competitive football clubs! A few organizations have come to a compromise in now accepting national workers on an equal status with the "foreigners." Viewing this from the standpoint of the indigenous Christians, such deals somehow do not ring the bell! Has the time not yet come where we should be willing not to seek our own? Why then are we not willing to be absolutely absorbed into the national churches? Would that not be the highway of missionary endeavor?

3. Conceptions

From the above observations, it is obvious that there are some constructive bridges as well as some destructive barriers found in political nationalism. The existing and growing tensions should be speedily dissolved or overcome with a common concern, not in competition, but by coalition and collaboration, based upon spiritual consanguinity. God's salvation for, and emancipation of, men has not a purpose and is not a goal in itself. It is simply the basic provision for the actual and positive fulfillment of God's eternal projected plan, which is the main subject of this World Congress on Evangelism. It is on us to seek and to know his desired and dignified design, resulting hereafter in definite, tangible deeds.

The present challenge is to give absolute priority to the Holy Spirit in our work and witness for Christ, and to find out what, where and how he is working, so as to be flexible and adjustable in this drastically changing world system. Spirit-disciplined and Scripture-principled men are all God needs and wants to speed and spread the redemptive message worldwide. The color, creed and culture problem will be satisfactorily solved by him who is God's perfect answer to men.

Traditional professionalism in our ministry should give place to the untapped potential of the unpaid laity until evangelism becomes again the principal concern of the whole body of Christ. Let us forsake our personal conception and performance of men-invented tactics and techniques on evangelism and missions, which have hindered so long the achieving of God's goal.

To the human mind the Great Commission is an impossible, gigantic task. However, faith knows and appropriates him, who is the divine executive. The closer our fellowship with God, the clearer the spiritual conception of his plan and availability of his power to execute it. The Holy Spirit alone can teach and will lead us experimentally into what Christ already has abundantly accomplished for our lost world. "Hereby perceive we the love of God, because he laid down his life for us: and we ought to lay down our lives for the brethren" (I John 3:16).

BREAKING THE BARRIER OF NATIONALISM

Augustine G. Jebaraj

In the past we have encountered several obstacles in presenting the Gospel message. One such obstacle has been *Political Nationalism*. As Eric Fife and Arthur Glasser say in *Missions in Crisis:* "It can be characterized as a revolt against foreign domination, . . . against poverty, . . . against social inequality and oppression, . . . against conformity to customs and functions of the traditional groups, such as, family, tribe, clan, caste and creed. Nationalism also has the patriotic feeling of the people to take upon themselves the responsibility for self-government, economic development, industrial progress, educational schemes and other social welfare projects."

During the twentieth century numerous new nations have come into being, especially in Latin America, Africa and Southeast Asia. Political nationalism has taken on new and powerful dimensions.

Fife and Glasser classify the major types of nationalism as self-expressive, self-satisfied and self-assertive. Self-expressive nationalism is found mainly among formerly subjugated people who are awakened to an awareness of themselves. They desire to express themselves, achieve self-respect and determine their own destinies. "Self-satisfied nationalism," says Fife and Glasser, "is found mainly among the long established nations of Western Europe and North America. They have a sense of cultural superiority." The Soviet Union and China are cited as examples of self-assertive nationalism. Nationalism, moreover, is not static, it may change from one type to another and for many different reasons. It is something that yearns and burns in the hearts and minds of men. Because nationalism is so emotionally deep-seated, it is not necessarily related either to facts or reason. This makes it potentially troublesome, as leaders try to direct its energies into constructive channels.

Christians have expressed different attitudes toward nationalism. Some Christians withdraw completely from national activities saying that any participation in politics would corrupt their spiritual life. They feel they must remain aloof from politics. Some Christians use Romans 13:1-7 as their basis. They defend the status quo, for, they say, to resist the governing authorities is to resist what God has appointed. They take the attitude that the ruling party must always be supported. Then there are the Christians who participate actively in politics. They go so far as to say

THE RT. REV. MR. JEBARAJ is the Bishop in Tirunelveli, India, for the Church of India.

that indifference to political matters is sin. One must make political choices; not to participate or to be merely fatalistic about things is wrong.

We do not intend to discuss whether or not a Christian should involve himself in political nationalism. Our task, rather, is to learn whether political nationalism is a hindrance to evangelism.

The Constitution of India (Article 25 (i)) makes the following provision: "Subject to public order, morality and health and to the other provision of this Part, all persons are equally entitled to freedom of conscience and the right freely to profess, practice and propagate religion." Although several amendments were proposed to remove the word "propagate" from the constitution, we thank God that the word has not been deleted. In the Dominion of India, therefore, Christians have not only the liberty to profess and practice Christianity, but also to propagate it.

The same is not true in all countries. India has declared itself a secular state; other countries have declared themselves to be theocratic states. Whatever religion has the support of the majority of the people is the religion that provides the general principles for the government. Understandably then, Christianity the minority religion is experiencing numerous problems and hardships. Distribution of religious literature, for example, and preaching in public places are forbidden by law.

Political nationalism is a great hindrance to evangelism when Christians are called upon to give supreme loyalty to the state or nation and not to God. The pressure of circumstances forces them to decide whether their Christian beliefs will be determined by their nationalism or whether their nationalism will be fashioned by their Christian beliefs. In some countries this is a very real issue.

When it becomes "party politics," then nationalism is a hindrance to evangelism. Too many people identify themselves and their interests with but part, rather than the whole, of their nation and give their first loyalty to that section. They want to consolidate their own party even at the expense of the national interest. Consequently they fall prey to such evils as bribery, corruption, nepotism, abuse of public trust and unfair discrimination. Moreover, people who do not belong to their parties are considered enemies.

How can a zealous Christian identify himself with a government that indulges in such malpractice? When he boldly condemns its evil actions, he is considered an enemy of the state, and is denied the freedom to exercise his religious liberty as a free citizen of the state.

Political nationalism becomes the greatest foe of evangelism when it is anti-international in its outlook and activities. Nations should have friendly relationships with one another. They must work not only for their own welfare, but also for that of other nations. If a powerful nation wants to subjugate its weaker neighbor, Christians must protest. But when their protest becomes articulate they are often considered enemies of the nation.

By its very nature the Christian Church is a supranational organism. Every Christian needs every other Christian. No Christian can afford to be permanently isolated from any other fellow believer.

Christ is the head and believers are the body of the Church. We need one another's fellowship. We cannot be at war with one another, for war disrupts fellowship.

Can evangelism break through this barrier of nationalism?

1. Evangelists whether national or non-national should divest themselves of anti-national feelings. They should have a sympathetic understanding of the national aspirations of the people among whom they serve. They should be able to distinguish between what is good and what is bad for the country in relationship to other countries. They should also be able to instruct and warn fellow Christians both at home and abroad concerning the distinctive aspects of nationalism.

2. Evangelists should work in teams comprised of persons belonging to different nationalities. Such teams should be international and interracial in composition and leadership, so that they reflect the supranational character of the Christian Church. An Indian and a Japanese evangelistic team for instance should minister in Africa. Similarly a European and African team should work in India.

3. Each national church should send out and support its own missionaries in other lands. Each local congregation should have an opportunity to share in this missionary outreach. National barriers are already being broken in this respect: Korean and Indian Christians are laboring in Thailand, Japanese evangelists in Okinawa, and Filipino teachers in Indonesia.

God wills that all men should find salvation and come to know the truth. Let us therefore so present Christ Jesus the Savior that people shall come to God through him, accept him as their Redeemer and serve him as their Lord and King in the Church.

THE ETHICS OF POLITICAL NATIONALISM

Michael Cassidy

It has been suggested by a South African who reviewed this paper that it is one-sided. This may be true, for total objectivity and perfect clarity of vision *vis-à-vis* the most complex social situation in the world is far from easy. What follows is admittedly a personal view on the assigned topic of "Political Nationalism as an Obstacle to Evangelism," with particular reference to the South African context.

A word of definition about terms. The reference to white nationalism is not specifically to the nationalism of the government — which does quite a lot to encourage Christian outreach — but to the extreme forms of nationalism which has its devotees in both Afrikaans and English-speaking Europeans. Likewise black nationalism refers to African nationalism in its extreme forms.

One aspect of nationalism, white and black, concerns me here — its ethics.

In South Africa, as in other parts of the continent, political nationalism creates a number of problems and obstacles for evangelism. In this part of the world one does not see the neat contained nationalism of a neutral Switzerland, a renascent France or an independent Ghana. Rather one sees a clash of two nationalisms, white and black, both struggling for predominance within one geographical area.

Of course black nationalism in Southern Africa is a comparatively new phenomenon, some 50 years old at the most. Its struggle since Union in 1910 has focused mainly on franchise questions, with the whole *apartheid* controversy coming to the fore as a burning issue since 1948. The Second World War, increased travel and overseas study, plus the stimulus of other African independence movements have all contributed to firing African nationalism to its modern intensity. As of this moment, black nationalism in Southern Africa is a somewhat frustrated movement under radical leadership.

White nationalism on the other hand is a much older force. It is the product of some three hundred years of pioneer history. To the Afrikaners, as the guardians of this nationalism, no other country except South Africa is home. This is a land they have pioneered and developed. They won it from hostile tribes and British imperialists, and at a price. Small wonder

THE REV. MR. CASSIDY is team director of Africa Enterprise, operating in South Africa, with headquarters in Pietermaritzburg, Natal.

then that Afrikaans nationalists are determined this land will not be relinquished to anyone.

English-speaking South Africans, on the other hand, have traditionally felt both apart from, and hostile to, the Boers' fierce nationalism. But external attacks on the country and fear of the so-called "black menace" to the north, are slowly driving all whites together in a new kind of white nationalism, which is more unitedly South African than anything the country has known before. Boer and Briton are starting to feel that they must either swim together or sink apart.

The basic problem, of course, in South Africa revolves around the race question and the matter of rule. The extreme black nationalist, with time and numbers on his side, says that majority rule must come now, as in Africa's other former colonial territories. The white nationalist denies the colonial comparison, choosing comparison rather with America's manner of "settlement" by Europeans at much the same period in history. He also insists on responsible, rather than majority, rule. Majority rule is for 30 to 40 years hence. However, this political gradualism is totally anathema to African nationalists who view it with grave, and sometimes valid, suspicion.

Now if the emotions generated by nationalism within one ethnic group are complex, they are much more complex when two nationalistically motivated ethnic groups stand face to face within one country as in South Africa. The agony of complexity and ambiguity must be appreciated by outside observers, and the temptation to reduce the problems to the oversimplified categories of literally black and white issues has to be resisted. Oversimplification has the appeal of neatness, but it lacks realism, objectivity and often truth itself.

However, it is within this acknowledged context of nationalistic complexity that South African Christians, of all races, have to live and witness. What really creates the problem for Christian witness and evangelism is that powerful race feelings among both black and white tend to foster what one might call the *group ethic* — an ethic developed by group-thinking along racial lines. The temptation on both sides of the racial fence is to subordinate Christian principle to political expediency.

This leads to what is perhaps the greatest problem which South African nationalisms raise for evangelism, namely the clash between the relative ethic of nationalism and the absolute ethic of Christianity. The call to Christian commitment is a call among other things to an *absolute ethic* — an ethic which embraces means as well as ends. But some African nationalisms, assuming a semi-religious dimension and defining their own ethical absolutes, begin to equate their own political progress with the divine will. Thus legitimacy is often defined in terms of the pragmatic. What the majority agree to be the most rapid and efficient way of achieving a desired end becomes *ipso facto* morally valid.

When nationalism operates like this, it becomes idolatrous and anti-Christian. When intentionally or otherwise it attempts in addition to meet in any measure the religious needs of man for purpose, significance or security, then it has overstepped its bounds. The Christian at this point must preach and show that Christian commitment involves a superior allegiance that does not permit the confusion of Christ and Caesar. The Church dare not permit itself to be aligned with the corporate self-interest of any state or race group within it. Consequently, a difficult part of the evangelistic task in South Africa is to woo people from the idea that God is concerned primarily with the promotion of the interests of their group, whether black, white or brown.

This idea though popular, is particularly devastating in South Africa, because it has the effect of reducing ethical vision in the body politic and pushing people toward a kind of collectivist or corporate selfishness, whose moral justification is established on the strange and precarious grounds that it has the majority blessing. Thus corporate selfishness is made to appear more legitimate than individual selfishness simply because of corporate blessing. But the cold fact remains that the nature of selfishness is not altered by being dignified with majority assent.

In the face of this insidious and dangerous philosophy of *vox populi vox Dei*, the Church has a task to remind the body politic that the ideal is not simply self-government or majority rule, but good government and responsible rule. Power is to be used in the service of justice and truth, and no dichotomy should be permitted between what is legal in the technical sense and what is right in the ethical sense.

It was surely to avoid just this sort of dichotomy that Plato in his "Republic" required that the ruling class be made up of good men — men of character and integrity, who were the least likely to be corrupted by the exercise of power. Such men would ensure that law and right were properly wedded. This is still a worthy ideal. The Christian, however, believes this to be an impossible ideal apart from Christ; and he therefore calls on men both individually and corporately to bring their lives under the judgment of the Word of God. Nationalism remains a legitimate force only as long as it operates within the ethical limits prescribed by the New Testament. It is never to become its own master. It is always to be under the authority of the Word.

And, of course, if we start to say this, we find ourselves in collision with both the white philosophy of self-preservation without reference to the African, and the African philosophy of self-realization without reference to the European. True evangelism must confront both these philosophies, modifying both and being seduced by neither.

At the same time, the Christian seeks to understand that which has produced these outlooks. He cannot condemn without entering into the agonizing ambiguities on both sides of the fence. The Christian tries to understand what has produced each force. He recognizes first that Africa's militant — and some times unreasonable — nationalisms have their roots in long bitternesses engendered by the indignities of the slave trade and some of the less happy aspects of white rule. The African's desire to fight back and assert his value and dignity is natural enough; but the Church has to stand in firm condemnation of the nationalistic force when it serves causes beyond its original causes and when it reduces all life and value to a narrow equation with the so-called liberation struggle. Evangelism finds another obstacle arising out of the equation just mentioned — namely, nationalism's obsession with the temporal and the material. To remind those who are intoxicated with the furthering of political and economic ends that man does not live by bread alone is both difficult and unpopular, but it must be done if we are to be true to our Christian commission.

Equally difficult but equally necessary is a condemnation of that sort of nationalism that blinds its devotees to human sacrosanctity and value. This was seen in the Congo atrocities when the world waited, largely in vain, for any condemnation from African governments of the bestialities perpetrated by the rebels in the name of nationalism. "My country right or wrong" is never a valid watchword, and when pressed into the service of any nationalistic group it must incur proper condemnation. Besides, for the African to be anti-white is no more morally defensible than for the white to be anti-black. A double standard may not be permitted at this point. Moral objectivity must be the order of the day.

If the black philosophy of self-realization is understandable, even more so is the white philosophy of self-preservation. Of all instincts, that of self-preservation is the most powerful, and it is in fact just this force that lies at the heart of white, particularly Afrikaner, nationalism. Before condemning white nationalism, at least one must recognize the understandable emotion that inspires it. White fear of annihilation by an overwhelming black majority may be exaggerated at points, but extravagant statements by some leaders on the African continent have lent some substance to it.

Again the Christian must call on the white nationalist for charity in spite of dangers, unselfishness in spite of risks, faith in spite of fear. White nationalism has to be reminded that the Christian ethic is to "lose one's life in order to save it," whereas it is the very reverse of this — save your life in order not to lose it — which stands as the ethical heart of some white thinking.

Here one sees a partial obstacle to the evangelization of Africa's whites. The fact is that the injunction to love, carrying with it, as it does, the injunction to unselfish promotion of African interests, appears to involve just that kind of political action which will lead to racial suicide for the whites. Evangelism's task is thus to help people, through Christian commitment, to work through the dilemma of whether they can in fact dare to love and leave the consequences with God, whether they can dare to lose their lives in order to save them. This is no easy task when politics seem to advise realism about human nature and a selfish protection of the life, so as not to lose it.

The challenge to faith is, at any rate, the starting point for the solution, but to be meaningful it must also be accompanied by both the proclamation and the demonstration of the supranational nature of Christian allegiance. The body of Christ is not a pretty idea, but an authentic spiritual reality uniting all kinds and conditions of people. The church in Southern Africa must therefore beware of national identifications. In crossing racial boundaries, it must also demonstrate within itself that sort of society which it desires to see in the body politic. Guarding not what is old, but what is ageless must be our pressing concern. In this capacity we must speak bi-directionally to both white and black nationalisms, promoting what is good in both, tolerating what is evil in neither. Patience, faith, love and the New Testament ethic must be preached as basic ingredients of all policies and the essential prerequisites of all national progress.

The following appendage was submitted by other participants from South Africa and is included with the approval and consent of Mr. Cassidy:

The Republic of South Africa has to deal with a complex problem that is created through its multi-national population. The policy of parallel development has grown out of the historical background as stated above, and for generations it has been generally accepted by all the various racial groups and applied in the country.

It can be regarded as an honest endeavor to create harmonious coexistence. The task of the Church to promote evangelism is encouraged and practiced in an atmosphere of peace.

Report of Group Discussion

Discussion of the explosive subject of political nationalism provided some tense, frank and open disagreement and a sharp clash of opposing opinions. Afrikaans delegates were quick to take issue with Anglican panelist Michael Cassidy's analysis of white and black nationalism in his own South Africa. The Rev. R. J. N. Van Tonder of the Dutch Reformed Church in Transvaal rose to ask that Cassidy's paper be withdrawn as "representing only the English-speaking view and as damaging to evangelism in South Africa." It was ruled that the freedom of panelists must be protected, that their papers were not necessarily intended to represent a group consensus, and that the paper ought therefore not to be withdrawn.

Mr. Cassidy was gracious enough to admit that any report of South Africa's exceedingly delicate situation was liable to error. He offered to correct any one-sidedness in his paper by tribute to the South African government's protection of complete freedom of evangelism.

"What about nations where the national government has been identified with Christianity?" asked the Rev. Angel B. Taglucop (Philippines). "Is this good or bad for evangelism?"

"If the identification of the government has been with Protestant Christianity, in general this has not endangered freedom of evangelism, for it has been accompanied by the development of a religious pluralism which has permitted freedom of religion," replied panelist Dr. Hudson Armerding (USA). The discussion suggested by implication that this has not always been true where nationalism has been identified with Roman Catholic Christianity.

In spite of differences, the hour closed with an African tribute to the power of Christian love to break through all and any barriers that rampant nationalism can erect against the free flow of the Gospel "Love sees no color, no national barriers," declared Samuel Obaker (Cameroun). "Where there is no Christian love there is no unity. Foreigner and national are divided, but where there is true love in Christ there is unity."

Reporter: *Samuel H. Moffett*

CONFRONTING THE CULTS
William Culbertson

To clarify the use of the term *cults* the following definition may be of help: *Cult* may refer to either (1) the group which differs from orthodoxy in "externals or ceremonies of religion as distinguished from its inner meaning or truth," or (2) the group which differs doctrinally as well as in practice. Far more often than not, both areas of difference are involved. The term "sect" is used synonymously with cult.

The cults differ greatly in the amount of deviation from the historic Christian faith. Frequently their denial is of cardinal Christian tenets. Certain of the cults are closer to the historic faith than others, but all are characterized by some deviation.

Major deviations are those having to do with the Holy Trinity, the deity and humanity of the Son, the deity and the personality of the Holy Spirit, the suffering and the atonement of our Lord and Savior, the reality of the resurrection and other miracles, and the doctrine of grace. From the ethical standpoint, Antinomianism is the greatest divergence from orthodoxy.

Some deviations are the result of the omission of a vital doctrine or its submergence by another emphasis. A heresy may be correct as far as it goes, but becomes erroneous because it omits a qualifying or correlative truth.

Minor defections may have serious logical implications.

1. The Need to Oppose the Teaching of the Cults

a. Let us admit at once that a merely negative approach is not enough. It is readily confessed that there is always need for a positive presentation of the truth plus the endorsement of a truly Christian life. But this does not mean that we should only be positive. As a matter of fact, one of the problems of current ecumenicity is its broad tolerance — anything is acceptable. An article in the *National Review* (Jan. 11, 1966) observes:

"The skeptic has some excuse for suspecting that what is bringing the churches together is an increasing doubt about the doctrines which divide them." The enervating force of such lack of conviction is pointedly emphasized by the statement of the author's father, "My dear boy, there was a great deal more life in Methodism when the Primitive Methodists doubted the salvation of all other Methodists than there is today." Of course, we are not pleading for suspicious narrowness, but we are observ-

DR. CULBERTSON is president of the Moody Bible Institute in Chicago, Illinois.

ing that there is a boundary over which more is lost than gained. Let us not hesitate to brand heresy as heresy.

   b. The need for discernment of error is attested by *six* considerations.

   There is *the warning of Scripture concerning error*. Interestingly enough many passages have eschatological significance:

   ". . . In later times some shall fall away from the faith, giving heed to seducing spirits and doctrines of demons" (I Tim. 4:1, ASV).

   ". . . There shall be false teachers, who shall privily bring in destructive heresies" (II Pet. 2:1, ASV).

   "Beloved, believe not every spirit, but prove the spirits, whether they are of God; because many false prophets are gone out into the world" (I John 4:1, ASV).

   The enemy of our souls is a subtle foe, who will do all in his power to destroy or at least negate the Christian witness. Insofar as the beliefs and practices of a cult deviate from the truth of the Holy Scriptures, the devil is successful. But it is not necessarily true that the greater the deviation, the greater the victory, for far more are deceived by slight but significant deviations than by wholesale negation. Note Scripture's descriptions of the devil's strategy such as craftiness (II Cor. 11:3), corrupting (II Cor. 11:3), deceiving (II Cor. 11:13; II Tim. 3:13; Rev. 12:9), wiliness (Eph 6:11), working of error (II Thess. 2:11), snaring (II Tim. 2:26), seducing (I Tim. 4:1). In his work he has his doctrine (I Tim. 4:1), his ministers (II Cor. 11:15) and his congregations (Rev. 2:9; 3:9).

   The viciousness of error is itself an impelling reason we should be aware of it. Granted, there are some deviations which in themselves seem of small significance. But there are others which logically lead to further unbelief and/or to viciousness of life. Remember, it is not always the error in itself that is so devastating; its logical consequences and complications are what need to be feared.

   There is *attractiveness of error to the sin-twisted mind of man* apart from the truth of God's Word as taught by God's Spirit. Some delight to be martyrs and take the position which entails persecution. Some are proud to be different. It is probably true, however, that heresy depends more on surrounding influences than on its own vital force. Therefore, some advocate the cult because of dissatisfaction with the current brand of orthodoxy they have seen or experienced.

   The *aggressiveness of error* compels that attention be given to it. Utter devotion and loyalty on the part of cult converts is phenomenal. Sacrifices are gladly borne. Desire for others to experience "the liberating forces of the new doctrine" or to enjoy the newly found fellowship is at peak height. Undoubtedly even the sects have their troubles with "second generation faith," but it would seem that their minority position and their "special revelation" combine to keep them aggressive. Unless the Christian church is alert it could lose wide areas by default.

The *proselyting activity of cults* is normally centered in the area of Christian profession. There are exceptions. But traditionally, the area of missionary activity on the part of cults is where the Christian church is already working. Our concern is not only for the heretic, but also for those whose faith may be overthrown (II Tim. 2:18). "Men who concerning the truth have erred . . . and overthrow the faith of some. Howbeit the firm foundation of God standeth, having this seal, The Lord knoweth them that are his: and, Let everyone that nameth the name of the Lord depart from unrighteousness" (II Tim. 2:18, 19, ASV).

2. What should the Christian Church do toward meeting this challenge?

a. It should exercise firm faith, relying upon God for its strength and its wisdom.

b. It should speak the truth in love (Eph. 4:15). It is never either/or. It is always both.

c. It should aggressively engage in the proclamation of the Gospel in evangelistic thrust, supported by the resistless witness of a life full of the Holy Spirit. This proclamation includes denunciation of unbelief, whether it is manifest in false doctrine or ungodly life or both. Indeed, in convincing of sinfulness, this may well be the first note sounded.

". . . In meekness correcting them that oppose themselves" (II Tim. 2:25, ASV) ". . . on some have mercy . . . and some save, snatching them out of the fire; and on some have mercy with fear; hating even the garment spotted by the flesh" (Jude 22, 23, ASV).

"But be thou sober in all things, suffer hardship, do the work of an evangelist, fulfill thy ministry" (II Tim. 4:5, ASV).

MODERN RELIGIONS AND PERSONAL NEEDS

J. Stafford Wright

We evangelicals do not find it easy to think of other religious people as human beings with deep human needs. They appear to us more like personifications of erroneous doctrines, and we approach them as figures who need adjustment and correction, not as persons with whom we can talk at a personal level. Certainly we must know how their doctrines differ from those of the Bible, but we must realize that the forms of the doctrines are one expression of their personalities, and meet certain inner needs. This paper discusses several types of modern religions in the light of some inner needs, beginning with those cults that are dogmatic and authoritarian, and working through to those that are largely experiential.

If the Church is uncertain about its beliefs, then dogmatic sects, like Jehovah's Witnesses, will step in. Jehovah's Witnesses form one of the tightest and most intolerant groups. They express their needs through depersonalization, attracting those who are group-addicted, and who find relief in having their thinking and action prescribed by the group as a whole, or (as with Jehovah's Witnesses) by a nucleus within the group. There are two ways of approaching them: (1) by matching authoritative text with authoritative text, but letting the Bible as a whole be the authority (Evangelicals who accept the whole Bible as the Word of God are in a good position to do this); (2) by personal testimony to the reality of Jesus Christ in the life (Jehovah's Witnesses are starved of this, and we may have an ally in the shadow side of their personality).

Mormons are authoritarian, and have their own allegedly inspired book and inspired prophecies. Their doctrine of God and gods is polytheistic, yet their published statement of belief sounds reasonably orthodox to the unwary. The convert is drawn into Mormon differences gradually. Mormonism attracts more balanced personalities, with its positive attitude toward art and culture, with basic discipline, tithing, many opportunities for service, and a challenge for good living. We must meet them at the theological level, concentrating on the doctrine of God and on Christ's finished work for our justification. But we must also demonstrate by example that our Christian way of life is better, since the Mormon already has much of the fellowship and joy and discipline that should mark the Christian.

Christian Science is another dogmatic sect, though the dogmas are less specifically stated. Mrs. Eddy's book, *Science and Health with Key to the*

THE REV. MR. WRIGHT is principal of Tyndale Hall in Bristol, England.

Scriptures, gives this sect's only permissible interpretation of the Bible. At a Christian Science service only the Bible and this book are read, and preaching is not allowed. Accredited teachers give instruction privately from Mrs. Eddy's book. Members are to abstain from alcohol and tobacco, and live a good moral life, but, like the Mormons, they have a full social life, and are concerned with world affairs. Here they differ from Jehovah's Witnesses who have a tendency to withdraw. Christian Scientists are also less hostile to other churches.

Christian Science Churches and Societies are not found in poor areas. They attract people who have a comfortable life, and who need some mystery in their thinking. They may not have mastered the philosophical intricacies of *Science and Health*, but they benefit from positive thinking, and know something about inner experiences. They relate all this to God, but God is more readily conceived of as Infinite Spirit than as our personal God and Father. We need the theological approach to show that Mrs. Eddy's book is not a reasonable expression of all that the Bible says about God and man. We have a point of contact with the doctrine of God's immanence, but must present God as personal, since otherwise there is a deficient sense of sin. It is helpful to have a biblically-based Christian philosophy, and some understanding of mental and psychic forces.

Finally there are the cults that appeal to the seeker of inner experiences related to cosmic realities. These include Theosophy, Anthroposophy (Steiner), Vedanta, Buddhism, Zen, and Higher Spiritualism (professing to teach cosmic truths). These may accept Jesus as one appearance of the Christ-Spirit, but God, if he exists, is the all-pervading Unknowable Absolute. There is the quest for merging into the Oneness of all life, usually with a belief in reincarnation. These people are not content to argue from the Bible, except from isolated texts and these out of their contexts. They speak of the esoteric teachings of Jesus and the early Church, which orthodoxy has neglected and which they themselves claim to hold.

Few evangelicals have explored these inner world experiences, and this type of investigation should be done only by those who are firmly anchored in the Bible and who have some understanding of psychic forces and of so-called cosmic consciousness. If there is an experience of the universal immanence of God, God nevertheless still remains unknown at this level; he has revealed himself as Savior in the Person of Christ, as Paul showed at Athens in Acts 17. We must show the complete supremacy of the Lord Jesus Christ.

This paper has considered the evangelization of certain groups, each of which has a religion which it believes to be the true one. Each system may contain some truth, and this truth with its perversions gives satisfaction to personalities of different types. While we should appreciate sympathetically their feelings, we must point them to Christ and his Gospel as God's only answer to the intellectual, emotional, and other inner needs, and above all as the only answer to man's total need as a sinner before God.

Report of Group Discussion

The following is a summary report of the main points of emphasis as they were developed both in presentation of the papers and in the discussion afterwards.

1. The cults are varied and represent wide and distinct areas of need. Certain cults attract those seeking an extreme authoritarianism or those of an extroverted character (e.g. Jehovah's Witnesses). Others attract persons introverted in character (e.g. Christian Science and Bahaism). No single cult answers on the broadest basis such varied needs.

2. The cults are noted for their zeal in propagating their point of view. Such zeal must be recognized as a serious aspect of the cultic thought and practice.

3. The cults should be recognized as demonic. This term does not necessarily connote demonism or demonic possession although in some cases demonism may actually be present.

4. The Bible and the message of redemptive grace in Jesus Christ is gloriously wide. It can meet every religious need, that of the extrovert and that of the introvert.

5. The best evangelism in reference to the cults is the teaching of the Bible. Since the cultist zeal is often expressed in distribution of the writings of a man or woman and in a fragmented usage of Scripture, the Christian must be careful not to fall into the same pit by the use of annotated Bibles in an untoward or particularistic way. However, by the test of time and experience the great creeds of the Church will still play a part in witness.

6. Where any ministry to the demonic in cults is envisaged, sound procedures are necessary. Exorcism, as such, is an area needing the greatest care, spiritual insight and understanding.

Reporter: *Arthur M. Climenhaga*

THE ZEAL OF THE CULTS
Stephen Slocum, Jr.

The remarkable evangelistic zeal of certain of the cults is a puzzling fact. How is it possible for those who follow a false gospel to drive forward with such intense zeal, while Christians show such lethargy in their obedience to the Lord's command to evangelize the world? The general reference to "cults" is restricted to those noteworthy groups which display a remarkable zealousness in the propagation of a counterfeit gospel. The sharp disparity in zeal between such cults and evangelical Christianity raises some practical obstacles to effective world evangelism.

1. The effects of such zeal

Such zeal is a widely admired characteristic that tends to sweep aside all other questions, and acts as superficial confirmation of cultist teachings. Furthermore, the cults' contagious enthusiasm not only communicates but also breeds excitement, thus providing a powerful sustaining force for the life of the cult.

Conversely, there are some disturbing consequences for Christians. The most serious consequence is the confusion wrought among uninformed Protestants and Catholics by the zealous witness of cultist groups.

Such zealousness also provides a basis for damaging criticism of the evangelistic fervor of the Church, and tends to create a discouraging atmosphere as well as a defensive attitude for Christian witness.

It is essential, therefore, for Christians to recognize the source of and understand the reasons for such "damnable" zeal (II Pet. 2:1) in order completely to disengage the cults from any connection with true Christianity.

2. The underlying reason

Basic to any understanding is the recognition that the zeal of the cults involves a false gospel fabricated by Satan from a deliberate distortion of Bible truth. Although the majority of the cultists may be sincerely deluded (Eph. 4:14, II Cor. 4:2), the origin and sustaining strength of their zeal can be traced directly to satanic influence.

Satan has always adapted his methods to fit the times and conditions, and the use of a counterfeit is Satan's most natural method of resisting the purposes of God. In these days, there is a general realization that man's highest ideals have already been stated in the Bible and exemplified in the life of Christ. This has opened the way for counterfeit systems of

MR. SLOCUM is executive secretary of the American Tract Society, Inc., in Oradell, New Jersey.

truth which, according to prophecy, are the last and most-to-be dreaded methods of the satanic warfare.

Furthermore, the Scriptures teach that the militant activity of Satan against God is to increase sharply (I Tim. 4:1-2). The recent vigor of the cults indicates that they are a special antichrist force promoted by satanic strategy to attack the person and work of Christ (II Cor. 4:3-4). Proof rests in the fact that their thrust is aimed solely at the Church. The cults manifest a complete lack of pioneer missionary outreach and concern. Instead they "feed" as parasites entirely within and upon the life and influence of Christianity.

3. How accomplished

There are certain practical avenues through which Satan produces zeal.

The cults' principle of *an active membership* generates individual responsibilities for personal evangelism. Thus a biblical methodology is used to propagate a false message.

Historical Christianity, however, has fostered a distinction between clergy and laity. Despite the scriptural teaching of the priesthood of believers, the average Christian believes that it is his pastor's task and not his to reach the lost.

There is also *an induced aggressiveness* in the cults' doctrine of salvation by works. In contrast to Roman Catholicism and Judaism with their inward liturgical demands, the cults require outward zealousness.

Satan also is able to insinuate his influence through *psychological responses*. One such key psychological drive is reinforcement of faith. Where elements of uncertainty threaten established convictions the immediate psychological reaction is to seek a reinforcement of "faith." Persuading others to believe as he does offers the cultist such reinforcement.

In a revealing study of a small sect faced with a disconfirmation of belief, it was discovered that "if more and more people can be persuaded that the system of belief is correct then clearly it must, after all, be correct" (Festinger, Riecken and Schacter, *When Prophecy Fails*, Mpls: University of Minnesota Press, 1956). By surrounding himself with supporters, the "believer" reduces the uncertainty in his own heart to a point where he can live with it.

Another deep-seated psychological stimulus is the reaction against change. Where a person has made a personal commitment and has taken irrevocable actions because of it, the behavioral commitment is so strong it produces evangelistic fervor as a defense mechanism.

Although there are superficial similarities between the zeal of the cults and the dynamic witness desired by God for the Christian, the two are not comparable. The cults display a counterfeit zeal based on a false gospel and arising out of deep-seated psychological needs. Such zeal is in stark contrast with true Christian motivation.

4. True zeal described

True Christian zeal is the outward expression of an individual's inward motivation. It is produced by a moving of the Holy Spirit on the believer's heart in response to an understanding of the Word of God.

But even where Christians are established in the faith, some of the glorious truths that accompany new life in Christ also tend to tranquilize the Christian's witness. Conversion to Christ brings a fulfillment (Heb. 4:9) which often tends to relax one's evangelistic fervor.

True motivation for a zealous witness is defined as "knowing therefore the terror of the Lord, we persuade men" (II Cor. 5:11). Therefore Christians urgently need a strong teaching ministry which emphasizes redemption and coming judgment.

The Christian also needs a renewed emphasis on total commitment so that he no longer lives unto himself but unto his Lord (II Cor. 5:15).

Finally, he needs to be reminded of God's purposes to reveal himself through his children (I Pet. 2:9). "Every Christian a missionary" is a fundamental necessity for true Christian zeal.

5. A true zeal stimulated

Although true zeal is the result of a Spirit-filled life, the Church should provide *an initiating framework* through biblical teaching accompanied by scriptural challenge.

The Church also should provide *a sustaining atmosphere* whereby the motivated Christian can be nourished and strengthened in his witness for the Lord.

Finally, the Church should serve as *a reinforcing encouragement* with *all* members engaged in a dynamic witness so that individual ardor will not wither.

Despite the travesty of zeal offered by the cults, true zeal is a key factor in the effectiveness of Christianity's endeavor to call men everywhere to repentance. It is fitting that it begin here at this Congress by the individual heart commitment of each delegate to a fervent, zealous personal witness for our Lord Jesus Christ.

STRANGE AFRICAN CULTS
Ernest K. Martin

Prior to the coming of the first missionaries to Cameroon, the inhabitants had their own beliefs concerning life, sickness and death. These beliefs controlled their respective clans from one generation to the other; the responsibility of each succeeding generation was to guard these beliefs strictly and to pass them on.

In this paper I shall describe the Bakweri, the Isubu and the Wovea tribes and the numerous sub-tribes that occupy the Forest and Coastal regions of Cameroon. In the main, these beliefs concerning sickness, birth and death have very deep roots in the minds of the inhabitants and constitute the chief obstacles to evangelism among them.

The various cults that have developed in attempts to allay the fears of the members of the clans and to give hope to the sick, the suffering and the bereaved, have tended to lend much credence to the practices of sorcerers and medicine men.

1. The Fertility Cults

a. Because expectant mothers often die, the onset of puberty brings great anxiety and concern for the safety of the girls who will be future mothers.

b. Founding of the Jengu or Liengu (Mermaid) Cult was the outcome of the search for a solution.

c. The ceremonies that accompany the treatment of illnesses associated with conception create a religious atmosphere and encourage belief in a supernatural being.

d. What takes place in the Jengu or Liengu house and in the initiation of the adolescent plays a vital role in the lives of the people.

e. While the Jengu or Liengu Cult is mainly concerned with initiating young women into the art of motherhood, the MESUMA Cult deals essentially with the treatment and care of pregnant women.

f. It is compulsory that the expectant mother consult the medicine man for protective treatment. There is great fear in the family if this is not done.

g. Everything that the medicine man demands must be carried out in order to continue uniformity of tradition.

h. All rules must be strictly obeyed in order to avoid dire consequences.

i. The significance of the bangle cannot be dismissed easily or explained away so long as belief in and fear of witchery exist.

MR. MARTIN is education secretary of the Cameroon Baptist Mission schools in Buea, West Cameroon, Federal Republic of Cameroon, Africa.

2. Healing Cults

a. Belief in the existence of witches and wizards is as old as the Bantu race.

b. Fear of their power to destroy life has resulted in the development of sorcery and juju practices by medicine men.

c. The Veongo (Bangle) Cult exists to protect unfortunate victims from the influence of evil spirits and witchcraft.

d. Wearing of the special copper bangles which the medicine man claims have come from the spirit world is of vital importance.

e. Where the preservation of life is concerned, it is not easy to remove the importance attached to the bangle.

f. The Abasinjong Cult claims to have the power to eradicate witchery and evil spirits.

g. It attracts adherents by the masquerade dance and by singing accompanied by drumming and clapping of hands.

h. Confidence in this cult is established when the place where a juju has been buried is located and the hidden fetish is exposed to the view of all the villagers.

i. The Prayer Cult attracts weak Christians who do not believe they can pray effectively by themselves.

3. Ancestor Worship

a. Reverence for ancestors springs from the belief that, though invisible, the dead continue to exist. The spirits of the dead can be summoned in times of need.

b. The solemnity of the libation ceremony creates an atmosphere of reverence, and hence is associated with worship.

c. It is believed that departure from the libation tradition will bring misfortune and bad luck to the family, since the dead will no longer be interested in the affairs of the living.

4. The Cults as Obstacles to Evangelism

a. The African is tied to the traditions that have been handed down from generation to generation.

b. Although some of the traditions are termed mere superstition, they nevertheless have great significance as far as life, sickness and death are concerned.

c. It is no simple matter to dismiss as unimportant what a people accept as the basis of their existence.

d. Usually there is great fear that abandoning old beliefs will arouse the anger of other members of the clan who may seek ways of revenge.

e. The influence of the sorcerers and of the medicine men is extremely strong since they jealously guard their art as professionals.

f. Christian teachings must be presented in a way that the African can understand. The Old Testament contains much that can help him change his beliefs concerning the power that controls life and death.

g. It is important to impress upon would-be converts that the unseen Power — God — came to earth in the form of man — Jesus Christ — in order that Christians should no longer look to the past but should fix their trust, their faith completely in God through Jesus Christ.

h. In order to eradicate unscientific ideas that enslave the gullible minds of the untutored, evangelism must be accompanied by thorough education.

i. When people begin to appreciate God's wonderful power through education that is built on the Christian religion and on an understanding of the Bible, they can no longer be deceived by superstitious practices.

j. Since Africans regard reproduction and prolongation of life as the principal functions of mankind, education in the care of pregnant women, both before and after childbirth, in the care of babies, and in healthful living must also accompany evangelism.

k. Good Christian leadership of the young must be a basic responsibility of the Church.

TRUTH BY FORCE

Ernest H. Trenchard

The Gospel is the power of God to all who believe; sometimes this is especially evident in times of persecution. The Gospel, however, cannot exercise its divine power unless it reaches the ears of men and women; and when intolerance and discrimination hinder the penetration of the Message, "How shall they believe in him of whom they have not heard, and how shall they hear without a preacher?"

While *legal* conditions may soon change in Spain, it will continue to be true that the spread of the Gospel is tragically hindered by intolerance and discrimination; these problems will not be automatically eliminated by more favorable legislation. *Intolerance* is the spirit which refuses to admit the practice of more than one set of religious or philosophical postulates. It is more or less recognized that external pressure cannot change personal convictions, but it is lamented that this should be so. Moreover, the dominant party seeks to monopolize all the usual means of communication (the press, wireless, television, etc.), refusing the right of the minority to "proselytize," which really means, to witness. Obviously, intolerance tends to disappear in democratic societies, but comes into its own with the limitation of personal liberties.

Even while this paper is being written, we are expecting that legalized intolerance in Spain will disappear under a new law based on the Declaration of Religious Freedom promulgated by Vatican Council II. This declaration was much more explicit than was anticipated, and indeed, marks the reversal of the "truth by force" policy that has prevailed for nearly 1,500 years in countries dominated by the Roman Catholic system.

Legalized intolerance. From 1939 to 1945, evangelicals in Spain were left with no rights whatsoever and almost all of their churches, chapels and halls were closed down. The Constitution of 1945 maintained the absolute preeminence of the Roman Catholic church as an integral part of the regime. It indicated, however, that no one should be molested for his religious beliefs or in the *private* exercise of his faith. In "bad" times this meant that no manifestation of non-Catholic belief was permitted at all, apart from meetings in a few authorized places of worship; much of the persecution arose from this strict official definition of *private worship*, which evangelicals could not accept, for it would have meant the death of active witness. On a more intimate plane, official intolerance was shown by putting almost insuperable obstacles in the path of couples wanting to get married by civil law, if one of the two had been baptized as an infant into

MR. TRENCHARD is the founder and director of "Literatura Biblica" in Madrid, Spain.

Rome, for by the accepted canon law, the baptized person belongs to Rome forever. Even now the *modus vivendi* is very objectionable in such cases, as "apostasy" from Rome must be proved to the satisfaction of judicial and ecclesiastical authorities. Interested friends were bound to conclude: "If I become an evangelical I shall not even be able to get married properly" – a most serious obstacle to evangelism! Muzzling the media of communication meant that evangelicals not only were excluded from national broadcasts and television programs, but also were unable legally to publish any book or tract. Only recently – and that through censorship – has it become possible to get evangelical books officially authorized for sale. This enforced silence has hindered many thousands from considering biblical truth.

Discrimination means the withdrawal of benefits and privileges – due all citizens, but unjustly withheld because of intolerance. In a regime of legalized intolerance, such discrimination may be *legal, social* or *economic*. *Legal discrimination* may be promoted directly by means of laws, decrees or regulations. During the period of Spanish history referred to – and the regulation still continues – non-Catholics were excluded from public office, for they could not declare unlimited allegiance to all the principles of a Roman Catholic state. In fact, an evangelical is a kind of second-class citizen.

Even if our hopes for a reversal of legal intolerance are realized, *social intolerance* will persist in nearly every sphere, especially in the middle and upper classes. Rome's *religious* impact in Spain is not nearly as strong as supposed, and according to Catholic bishops themselves, only 15-20 per cent of the Spaniards are practising Catholics. But at his baptism an individual enters a closed social system. Anything but a Catholic marriage seems incomplete, almost immoral; to bury a loved one in the despised, unconsecrated civil cemetery constitutes a note of shame for the ordinary Spanish family. Not to comply with the dominant system in these great moments of life and death is to be a social outcast. I remember long conversations with an intelligent middle-class person who was emphatically anti-clerical, quite out of sympathy with Roman dogma and who expressed great appreciation of the Scriptures and of our presentation of the Gospel. But he always finished by saying, "But you realize that I speak as a Roman Catholic!" This shield was a social necessity and would not be thrown away.

Economic discrimination. During the Republic a small group of evangelicals moved into a new chapel at Arenas de San Pedro, in the province of Avila. Those were days of complete religious freedom as far as the laws of the land were concerned, and the new chapel was filled to capacity night after night. But then one of the parish priests stationed himself opposite the chapel entrance and recorded the names of all who were not known to be evangelicals. Then he would visit the homes concerned and indicate that if members of the family persisted in entering the Protestant chapel, he would see to it that the men were dismissed from their employment; as a result, chapel attendance dropped from 150 to 15 within a few days. Local influence was much stronger than legislation from Madrid. Such economic discrimination is especially true in the smaller provincial centers. In the larger cities, workers have little to fear, for the individual is just a name on a list as far as the employers are concerned, and nobody knows or cares where he goes on Sundays.

But in strong Catholic areas such as Navarre the means of livelihood are still controlled by a few local bosses who can be influenced by the priest. If the priest is a "new" type and understands "conciliar" Catholicism — as it is now called — he will not use his influence to the detriment of a "separated brother," but if he is a "Council of Trent" type, or just ignorantly despotic, he can force an evangelical to leave the district by causing him to lose his employment. Such tactics may close the door of a whole district to the Gospel.

Where so much depends on the fluctuation of public opinion, no statistics can possibly be given. The illustrations I have cited are not the most dramatic or tragic, but are known to me personally. Spain will continue to be a difficult field because of intolerance and discrimination, but if we have reasonable laws to which to appeal, the problem will be lessened. The best way to evangelize Spain will *not* be to flood the country with foreign-looking propaganda that is interpreted as opposition to a way of life forged over centuries of constant clerical and official pressure. What we need is a courteous offer of the Gospel, clearly presented, that on the one hand avoids mere official dialogue, and on the other, bad-tempered attacks on Rome.

ECCLESIASTICAL TOTALITARIANISM

Argos Zodhiates

Greek wisdom has sometimes been acclaimed as an ally of the Gospel. Attributing to philosophy the role of the Hebrew Scriptures, Clement in the second century A.D. makes this astounding statement: "Philosophy educated the Greek world as the Law did the Hebrews – to bring them to Christ; so philosophy is a preparation making the way ready for the man who is made perfect in Christ" (*Stromateis* 1, 5, 28 quoted by Stewart Perowne in *Caesars & Saints*, London 1962).

It is against this historical background of an attempted interplay between Greek philosophy and the *Evangelion* preached by Paul that the Greek evangelist today must interpret whatever antagonism he encounters. Indeed, so great is the pride of Greece that she has taken credit for whatever good the West may have derived from Luther's Reformation (Constantine Paparrigopoulos, *History of the Greek Nation* (in Greek), vol. II, pp. xi, xiii). One can understand the joy with which Metropolitan Panteleimon of Thessaloniki quotes a Lutheran professor in Oslo as saying: "What a pity that Luther did not appreciate the Greek Orthodox church enough to turn to the East and that he plunged us instead into the present Protestant chaos" (*Oikoumenika* (in Greek), Thessaloniki, 1959, p. 42).

Such boasting can be interpreted as "normal pride which men and women take in their country's group achievement" (Harold B. Kuhn, "The Obstacles to Evangelism in the World"), and is perfectly harmless until it becomes so distorted that it jeopardizes a people's prerogative to come under the sound of the Gospel. A case in point is the controversy over the second article in the Greek constitution which forbids the use of the Scriptures in any other language than that of the original text. Commenting on what made it necessary in the seventeenth century for Patriarch Dositheos to safeguard his flock from the Protestants by banning the reading of the Scriptures, one writer has said it would be nothing short of national heresy to sever the strong bond that unites Greeks everywhere by allowing the Bible to be translated into modern Greek! (Constantine Callinikos, *The Greek Orthodox Church*, Longmans & Green, London, 1918, p. 53ff.).

This kind of nationalistic outlook permits an ecclesiastical totalitarianism that places severe restrictions upon evangelical witness. In view of such restrictions one must be all the more grateful for enterprising evangelistic agencies such as the American Mission to Greeks of Ridgefield,

THE REV. MR. ZODHIATES is pastor "in absentia" of The Greek Evangelical Church in Katerini, Macedonia, Greece, now associated with the American Mission to Greeks, Inc., in Ridgefield, New Jersey, as a radio evangelist.

N.J., and Trans World Radio, both of which God has raised up to fill the gap, the latter through a regular fifteen minute Greek program aired twice a week from Monte Carlo, and the former through newspaper evangelism (*Decision Magazine*, July, 1964, p. 42. Evangelical Radio Alliance, *News Bulletin*, No. 2, 1966). A considerable reader and listener response reveals the spiritual restlessness that today characterizes many Greek intellectuals. George Seferis, former Ambassador to London and winner of the 1963 Nobel prize, voiced the complaint of many a thinking Greek when he said before the Swedish Academy: "We cannot help feeling some bitterness against those in the past who prevented the re-translation of the Gospels and who even today insist on putting the stigma of illegality on the translation of the words of Christ."

Criticism of the church is growing at all levels and is becoming less inhibited. King Constantine expressed the complaint of the whole nation when he described the Greek Orthodox church as "wrapped in a cocoon of self-defensive formalism," losing contact with its flock, and failing to keep abreast of changing times ("King Constantine Urges Greek Church to Reform," London *Times*, May 4, 1965). It was this same religious chauvinisn that a leading Greek news commentator attacked when he wrote: "The Church of Greece has proved to be the most reactionary and blind church in Orthodoxy. It cowers before the slightest innovation. It shivers at the prospect of a dialogue. It does not desire purification. It cannot capture the spirit of our times, but displays inordinate ability in protesting material interests. It has confronted the great issues with monkish obstinacy and sterile negation and has come in conflict with the overwhelming majority of its own flock" (Greek Clergy Dig in Their Heels," London *Times*, February 28, 1964).

One becomes all the more concerned about the totalitarian claims of the Greek Orthodox church when one is aware of the low spiritual state of the church and its utter inability to understand and communicate the Gospel. This ecclesiastical totalitarianism attacks not only Protestants of all kinds, but also other branches of the Christian Church including the Roman Catholics and even other sections of the Eastern Orthodox church, Patriarch Athinagoras being a special target of criticism for his moderate and tolerant spirit (*Letter of the Primate of Greece*, August 16, 1963 to the Metropolitan of Meloe. See also, *Hellinikos Vorras*, Thessaloniki, August 18, 1963).

In an editorial, "Russian Calls on Pope but Greek Snubs Him," the *Christian Century* of October 2, 1963, quotes Archbishop Chrysostomos as saying, on the eve of the Pan-Orthodox meeting in Rhodes: "As the first step toward beginning talks with the West, the Greek Catholic community should be immediately abolished." That Pope Paul's friendly overtures should be received with an ultimatum is not hard to explain.

Rome was once again under fire. The octogenarian Archbishop was directly accusing it of proselytizing.

The intolerance inculcated by such attitudes and by unliberal decrees such as Article 4 of Emergency Law 1363 which, under the cloak of forbidding proselytism, tends to ban all evangelism, is evidenced by a recent encyclical read from every Greek Orthodox pulpit in the country: "Protestant belief is a disease in the nation worse than leprosy and cholera! Have nothing to do with Protestants! Sell them nothing, buy nothing from them!" Seltsame Okumene (Strange Ecumenicity), in *Licht Und Leben* (German), January, 1965).

Would to God that the church which so uncharitably blocks the path of the evangelist had the answer to the Greek people's spiritual hunger (John 12:20)! But has it? The testimony of such men as the present moderator of the Greek Evangelical church would certainly indicate quite the contrary. Said the Rev. Michael Kyriakakis, pastor of Athens' First Evangelical church, when he was still a young divinity student in Edinburgh: "The church in which I was brought up was the Eastern Greek Orthodox church; and, apart from the mass, there is nothing in the Greek Orthodox church to instruct you and to bring you into the knowledge of God" A bank clerk from Athens in *How I Found Christ* – a Church of Scotland Publication, D. P. Thompson, Editor). In spite of some signs of spiritual awakening which one is grateful to note, as well as a more tolerant and moderate spirit by certain individuals in the Greek Orthodox church, the same, unfortunately, must be said today.

In avoiding Scylla do not let us head toward Charybdis! We need to avoid not only the totalitarian outlook but also that other outlook which empties the Gospel of all its saving content. Under the terms of the Great Commission we are obliged to preach to all the world the Good News that Christ died on Calvary's Cross and rose again to save man from his sins. This we are bound to proclaim in season and out of season, whether free or in bonds!

RELIGIOUS PERSECUTION
Benjamin E. Fernando

Almost 12 million adherents of the four great world religions are concentrated within the 25,000 square miles of Ceylon. Indeed, immediately adjoining my own Christian home is a Muslim household; this, in turn, is next to a Buddhist Temple beside which, on the other side, lives a Hindu family. The Buddhists of Ceylon (64% of the population) are Sinhala-speaking, the Hindus (20% of the population) are Tamil-speaking, the Muslims (7%) are mostly Tamil-speaking, while of the Christians (9%) some speak Sinhala and others speak Tamil. How religions interact under such conditions becomes a useful study.

Buddhism and Hinduism existed side by side in Ceylon for many centuries and although there were many conflicts between the language groups (Sinhala and Tamil) there was never a serious clash between the religious groups. With the conquest of the coast by Roman-Catholic Portugese in the early sixteenth century, however, and their replacement by the Protestant Dutch in the mid-seventeenth century, the concept of religious intolerance emerged. Some Buddhists, it is recorded, even gave refuge to certain Christians who were being persecuted by fellow Christians! This obviously was not the best advertisement for Christianity. Of the Christians in Ceylon today, 85% are Roman Catholic.

By the Treaty of 1815 the British promised to safeguard Buddhism but, actually, there was no hindrance to the practice, profession or propagation of any religion. In time, Christianity came to replace Buddhism as the favored religion. With the granting of universal franchise in 1931 and independence in 1947 the Buddhist majority looked upon Christians with disfavor, however, and for the following reasons:

1. Christianity was introduced into Ceylon by the conquering Western powers. Now that Ceylon was independent, all vestiges of foreign domination (including Christianity) were to cease.

2. The language and culture of Ceylon prior to the foreign conquests were not encouraged by these "Christian" powers. Rather, these were preserved with great difficulty by the Buddhist priests. It was thus felt that to be a true Ceylonese one had to be a Buddhist. At most, Christians were second class citizens.

3. It was almost an obsession to think of Ceylon as the place where Buddhism should be preserved in all its pristine glory and purity.

In view of this background, it was not surprising that the following developments came about:

a) Holidays for Christian festivals were curtailed drastically; in fact,

MR. FERNANDO is director of the YMCA and president of the Gideons in Colombo, Ceylon. He is a writer and religious broadcaster.

the weekly holiday now is not the Christian Sunday but the Buddhist Poya Day (Holy Day).

b) The Education Code provided that every child should be instructed in the religion of his father, even if both parents should wish otherwise.

c) Christian broadcasts on the commercial service were discontinued and radio-time on the national service restricted.

d) Foreign missionaries were restricted and replacements were allowed only if made within a year.

e) On all state occasions Buddhist ceremonies were practiced.

f) Almost all schools (previously assisted by the state) were taken over. The property was vested in the state without compensation and the management transferred. Although exactly the same treatment was given to Buddhist, Hindu and Muslim schools, the Christians were most affected as they had the largest number of schools and had originally entered the field of education at the request of the government.

The Constitution of Ceylon

When the constitution of Ceylon was framed, the possibility of religious discrimination was never anticipated. Therefore no Bill of Rights was incorporated. The only provision made is Sec. 29(2) by which the Parliament of Ceylon shall have no power to make laws that "shall (a) prohibit or restrict the free exercise of any religion; or (b) make persons of any community liable to disabilities or restrictions to which persons of other communities and religions are not made liable; or (c) confer on persons of any community or religion any privilege or advantage which is not conferred on persons of other communities or religions; or (d) alter the constitution of any religious body except with the consent of the governing authority of that body, so however, that in any case where a religious body is incorporated by law, no such alteration shall be made except at the request of the governing authority of that body." This is a negative statement and may perhaps not be a sufficient safeguard against acts of administrative discrimination. Moreover, any disabling could be introduced so long as it applies to every citizen. While the taking over of religious schools therefore does not strictly contravene these provisions, to Christians a religious education may be much more important than to Buddhists and Hindus, and thus Christians are in fact more affected than other groups. A proposal is now pending to have a Bill of Rights introduced into the Constitution.

Obviously a Bill of Rights is not the full answer. Opposition to conversions to Christianity would be automatically reduced if it were quite obvious that no economic and social advantages are attached.

The Inevitability of Persecution

Persecution and intolerance are found everywhere, not merely in the religious realm. There is discrimination because of color, of race, of community, of caste, of language, of social status etc. Many Christians are persecuted for these reasons and not because of their faith. Others suffer because of their own foolishness or ignorance or because of others' fanaticism. But even apart from these considerations and even in a reasonably tolerant society a committed Christian will, must, suffer. The Cross will never completely cease to be a symbol of derision and division. Jesus himself gave the promise in John 15:20, "If they have persecuted me, they will also persecute you"; and in II Tim. 3:12 we read, "Yea, and all that will live godly in Christ Jesus shall suffer persecution." There is no room for exceptions. For the many of us who come from countries where there is no official persecution of Christians, the relevant question to ask ourselves is not "Why are Christians persecuted?" but "Why are Christians not persecuted?" How many of us qualify for the blessings promised in Matt. 5:10, "Blessed are they which are persecuted for righteousness' sake, for theirs is the kingdom of heaven"? Moreover, when we are privileged to suffer for Christ's sake we have no scriptural authority to frame a Bill of Rights, or otherwise to agitate for constitutional amendments, etc. But the Bible does say, and in unmistakable language, "Pray for them which persecute you" (Matt. 5:44) and "Bless them that persecute you" (Rom. 12:14). What other action we must take in our different situations, the Holy Spirit will disclose to obedient Christians at the right time and in the right way. Persecution is one of the surest signs of the genuineness of our Christianity. Persecution must drive us to our knees. Even more so, should absence of persecution drive us to our knees. For crushing the Church is like smashing the atom: divine energy of high quality is released in enormous quantity and with miraculous effects. The blood of the martyrs is still the seed of the Church.

Report of Group Discussion

Christians in countries where discrimination and intolerance are most apparent are reluctant to invoke the intervention of international agencies to secure the aid of world public opinion according to delegates convened to discuss discrimination.

The question had been raised whether the Congress should express itself on the problem of religious discrimination and intolerance in certain lands or seek the intervention of international ecclesiastical organizations. Several speakers voiced warnings that such action could rebound unhelpfully upon their local situation and expressed a preference to work through such local Church councils as exist in their respective countries.

It was agreed however that appropriate action might well be taken to bring any such cases to the attention of governments through existing national councils. Where such national coordinating councils do not exist, the Congress could strongly encourage their formation.

In many cases delegates felt that God is overruling the difficult situations highlighted in the printed reports. Mr. Trenchard (Spain) said that Protestants in Spain had doubled in the last twenty-five years. Mr. Fernando (Ceylon) said that more conversions had taken place in Ceylon in the past three years than in the previous thirty. Mr. Trenchard also called attention to the fact that the declarations of the Vatican Council on religious liberty are remarkably explicit and could prove of substantial help to evangelicals in Spain if conscientiously applied. "The Roman Catholic Church should adapt itself to this changed situation," Trenchard said.

Reporter: *J. Graham Miller*

SECTION V

METHODS OF PERSONAL EVANGELISM •
Richard C. Halverson   343

DISCIPLE MAKERS: KEY TO EVANGELISM • Lorne C. Sanny   354

REACHING THE ADOLESCENT • Winnie Bonner   357

THE "PHILIPPIAN METHOD" • John W. Alexander   359

FRANCE AS A MISSION FIELD • Marcel Saltzmann   362

REPORT OF GROUP DISCUSSION • James M. Boice   363

THE CONFRONTATION OF IDEOLOGY • Hans Bürki-Fillenz   364

AN HOUR FOR MOBILIZATION • Muri Thompson   367

TRAINING IN PERSONAL EVANGELISM • William R. Bright   370

WORKERS TOGETHER WITH GOD • W. F. Batt   373

REPORT OF GROUP DISCUSSION • Sergio Garcia   375

SPIRITUAL NEEDS OF THE NEGRO • William E. Pannell   376

NO STEREOTYPED APPROACHES • Daniel Bakhsh   381

CAUTION IN THE USE OF TECHNIQUES • Ross F. Hidy   384

MAN-TO-MAN EVANGELISM
BY BUSINESSMEN • Dirk van Katwijk   388

REPORT OF GROUP DISCUSSION • Michael Cassidy   390

COMPASSION IN PERSONAL
EVANGELISM • Isaac H. A. Ababio   391

EVANGELISM AND THE HOME • Mogens Larsen   394

FISHING PATIENTLY WITH A ROD • Josip Horak   397

THE MINISTRY OF LETTERS AND TRACTS • Doan van Mieng   399

REPORT OF GROUP DISCUSSION • Samuel Wolgemuth   402

WIN THEM BY FAMILIES • Roy N. Oshiro   403

EMPOWERED BY THE HOLY SPIRIT • Thomas Cosmades   406

THE SOUL-WINNER'S PRAYER LIFE • Peter van Woerden   409

FOREIGN MISSIONS EVANGELISM • James R. Graham   412

REPORT OF GROUP DISCUSSION • David Foster   414

PAGE

PHILOSOPHY AND METHODS
OF EVANGELISM • *Samuel K. Arai*   416

NOT METHOD, BUT MESSAGE • *Hisashi Ariga*   418

VISITATION EVANGELISM IN JAPAN • *Shuichi Matsumura*   421

THE WORLD OF A SINGLE SOUL •*Takesaburo Uzaki*   424

REPORT OF GROUP DISCUSSION • *Akira Hatori*   426

METHODS OF PERSONAL EVANGELISM
Richard C. Halverson

Evangelism never seemed to be an "issue" in the New Testament. That is to say, one does not find the apostles urging, exhorting, scolding, planning, and organizing for evangelistic programs. In the apostolic Church, evangelism was somehow "assumed," and it functioned without special techniques or special programs. Evangelism happened! Issuing effortlessly from the community of believers as light from the sun, it was automatic, spontaneous, continuous, contagious.

Roland Allen, Anglican missionary to China (1895–1903), parish pastor in England, and missionary author, contrasts the contemporary with the New Testament evangelistic approach as follows: "When we turn from the restless entreaties and exhortations which fill the pages of our modern missionary magazines to the pages of the New Testament, we are astonished at the change in the atmosphere. St. Paul does not repeatedly exhort his churches to subscribe money for the propagation of the faith; he is far more concerned to explain to them what the faith is, and how they ought to practice and keep it. The same is true of St. Peter and St. John, and of all the apostolic writers; they do not seem to feel any necessity to repeat the Great Commission, and to urge that it is the duty of their converts to make disciples of all nations. What we read in the New Testament is not anxious appeal to Christians to spread the Gospel, but a note here and there which suggests how the Gospel was being spread abroad . . . for centuries the Christian Church continued to expand *by its own inherent grace* (italics ours), and threw up an unceasing supply of missionaries without any direct exhortation" (Roland Allen, *The Spontaneous Expansion of the Church*, Grand Rapids, Michigan: William B. Eerdmans Publishing Company, 1962, p. 6).

Four statements recorded by Luke show this spontaneous expansion of the apostolic Church by virtue of its inner health. "And they, continuing daily with one accord in the temple, and breaking bread from house to house, did eat their meat with gladness and singleness of heart, Praising God, and having favor with all the people. And the Lord added to the church daily such as should be saved" (Acts 2:46-47). "And the word of God increased; and the number of the disciples multiplied in Jerusalem greatly; and a great company of the priests were obedient to the faith" (Acts 6:7). "Then had the churches rest throughout all Judea and Galilee and Samaria, and were edified; and walking in the fear of the Lord, and in the comfort of the Holy Ghost, were multiplied" (Acts 9:31). "And so

DR. HALVERSON is executive director of International Christian Leadership and minister of Fourth Presbyterian Church, Washington, D.C.

were the churches established in the faith, and increased in number daily (Acts 16:5).

The sense of spontaneity and of effortlessness is inescapable in these accounts of additions to the primitive Church. As the "word of God increased," as believers in fellowship "were edified" and "walked in the fear of the Lord, and in the comfort of the Holy Ghost," as they were "established in the faith," converts were "added daily." Because of its spiritual health, the apostolic Church experienced exciting and effective evangelistic results with monotonous regularity. It is a safe assumption that evangelism is inevitable in a spiritually robust congregation. Failure to be evangelistic or "mission minded" in the New Testament sense betrays a poor spiritual condition. The way to evangelistic vigor is not some special emphasis or program, but rather repentance and healing and nurture. The very necessity for organizing special evangelistic efforts betrays the deep need of the Church for renewal. One might as well exhort a woman with a barren womb to have children as to exhort a sterile church to evangelize or respond to missions.

Evangelism was not optional in the New Testament; Jesus did not say ". . . ye *may* be witnesses unto me after that the Holy Ghost is come upon you." Nor on the other hand was evangelism coercive. Jesus did not say ". . . ye *must* be witnesses unto me . . ." Rather, evangelism was inescapable! Jesus said, "But ye *shall* receive power, after that the Holy Ghost is come upon you: and ye *shall* be witnesses unto me both in Jerusalem, and in all Judea, and in Samaria, and unto the uttermost part of the earth" (Acts 1:8). That is to say, the Spirit-empowered Christian was a witness, not because he elected to be or was compelled to be, but because the divine witness indwelt him and worked through him. They did not witness because they had to but because they could not help it. "We cannot [help] but speak the things which we have seen and heard" (Acts 4:20). "Verily, verily, I say unto you," Jesus promised with absolute certainty, "he that believeth on me, the works that I do shall he do also; and greater works than these shall he do; because I go unto my Father" (John 14:12). What Jesus had done in the world, those who believed on him would do also, not because they chose to, nor because it was required of them, but because they would be embodied by the same Spirit who had done the work in and through the incarnate Christ. Through Spirit-empowered disciples the world would be convicted of "sin, and of righteousness, and of judgment" (John 16:8).

Those early disciples were no less human than we, no less subject to temptation, no less dogged by human weakness and inadequacy. They had none of the so-called advantages we enjoy in our contemporary churches because of nineteen centuries of history and tradition; their world was certainly no less hostile to the Gospel of Christ than ours; yet with their witness they "turned the world upside down." They were of one mind. Their witness was unanimous because their infilling with the Holy Spirit was unanimous. Their witness was unanimous because they "continued steadfastly in the apostles' doctrine and fellowship, and in breaking of bread, and in prayers" (Acts 2:42).

The Anglican commentator, W. H. Griffith Thomas, has said, "It is a fact, perhaps a significant fact, that throughout the epistles of the New Testament, where naturally, we find full instruction for Christians, there is only one exhortation to do the work of evangelism (II Timothy 4:5); while appeals to carry out the duty of foreign missions are equally conspicuous by their absence. On the other hand, the Christian life, its provisions and possibilities, its secrets and methods, its duties and responsibilities, will be found emphasized everywhere. Is there any connection between the silence and the emphasis? May it not be a reminder that when the Christian life is what it should be, the duty of evangelization at home and abroad will be the natural and necessary outcome, as effect to cause, as stream to source?"

The New Testament clearly shows that Jesus expected every disciple to be an evangelist in the sense of being a witness; this expectation was certain of fulfillment moreover, because of the promised Holy Spirit who filled all the disciples waiting in the upper room and apparently all who were subsequently added to the fellowship. It is likewise abundantly clear in the New Testament that despite their weak and sinful humanity, those early Christians were often found exhorting and encouraging one another, confessing their faults one to another, praying for one another and bearing one another's burdens, honoring and esteeming one another better than self. Whatever they did individually in their witness for Christ, they shared with others who prayed for them and studied the apostles' doctrine with them. In short, fellowship was essential to their witness. Indeed, authentic Christian fellowship was the matrix of New Testament evangelism. Witnessing proceeded out of fellowship, forward and into fellowship. "That which we have seen and heard declare we unto you, that ye also may have fellowship with us: and truly our fellowship is with the Father, and with his Son Jesus Christ" (I John 1:3). J. B. Phillips translates the verse following (4) ". . . the more that fellowship extends, the greater the joy it brings to us who are already in it." Commenting on this particular verse in his exposition of I John, G. G. Findlay says, "We have a great secret in common — we and the Apostles. The Father told it to Jesus, Jesus to them, they to us, and we to others. Those who have seen and heard such things cannot keep the knowledge to themselves" (George G. Findlay, *Fellowship in the Life Eternal*, an exposition of the Epistles of John, London: Hodder and Stoughton, 1919, p. 89). "Evangelism in its pure form simply means to tell men what God has done for them in Christ" (author unknown).

The world has nothing to offer that is comparable to authentic Christian fellowship, no social structure or unit or function which corresponds even remotely. Lodges, clubs, fraternities, secret societies, taverns, bars, and so on, are the best that secularism can provide, and surely they fall infinitely short of the satisfaction and fulfillment brought by Christian fellowship. Exposed to this unique spiritual relationship, contemporary, sophisticated, pagan man finds a quality therein completely lacking in any other associations. In and of itself, fellowship in the New Testament sense is a testimony to the world, a demonstration of the efficacy of redemption. The unregenerate man finds it attractive, compelling, fulfilling. This explains, partially at least, Luke's observation that the early disciples "[had] favor with all the people" (Acts 2:47).

Whatever evangelistic impact the individual Christian may have on the world where Christ "sows" him, much depends upon his relationship with other Christians. Fellowship is fundamental to effective personal evangelism. Evangelistic methods can never be a substitute for it. However thoughtfully propagated and cleverly applied, methods will be ultimately fruitful or futile depending upon the quality of the Christian community into and out from which those who use them move. In this context the significance of Jesus' remarkable promise in Matthew 18:19-20 and his sending forth of the disciples two by two can be most deeply appreciated. It is hardly accidental that at this point Matthew should record Peter's question concerning forgiveness and our Lord's penetrating answer (Matthew 18:21-35). "Then," we read, "came Peter to him, and said, Lord, how oft shall my brother sin against me, and I forgive him? till seven times? Jesus saith unto him, I say not unto thee, Until seven times: but, Until seventy times seven."

Reconciliation between Christians is an absolute requisite to fellowship. In the opening words of his first epistle, the Apostle John establishes the centrality of fellowship as the evangelistic goal and motive. He then instructs his readers concerning the nature of that fellowship – a matter of basic honesty about oneself (I John 1:5-10). To "walk in darkness," that is, to say "that we have no sin," is to be self-deceived and to frustrate fellowship. To "walk in the light," which means to acknowledge or "confess our sins," is to be forgiven and cleansed and to "have fellowship one with another."

In the apostolic Church, the relationship between believers and God and between fellow believers was paramount. The light and warmth and love, the forgiveness and acceptance that emanated from that unique community penetrated a jaded, bored, loveless, weary culture and awakened the spiritual hunger of both Jew and pagan. "Lo, how they love one another!" it was said of them; sinsick, fed-up men tried to understand the strange and inviting quality of life that marked the disciples. In such an appealing atmosphere, lost men were ready to hear those who could not "help but speak of the things which they had seen and heard."

Today in personal evangelism the tendency is to ignore the relationships within the Christian community and to be preoccupied instead with the individual Christian's relationship to those outside of the Church. As a consequence, one of the greatest stumblingblocks to the world outside the Church is the way Christians treat each other. It is not inconceivable that today's world might be inclined to say with some justification as it views the Church, "lo, how they dislike one another!" The faithful work of zealous Christians in personal evangelism is often neutralized by the attitudes and actions within the Christian family. The corporate image of the Church often nullifies the faithful witness of individual members. And there is that peculiar phenomenon, the zealous Christian, who in his desire to do personal work, walks a guarded, careful way among unbelievers, but who within the Christian community acts like the devil himself.

Jesus said, "By this shall all men know that ye are my disciples, if ye have love one to another" (John 13:35). In his lesson on prayer (Matthew 6:6-15) Jesus underscored one petition in the model prayer, as if to cite it as essential to Christian conduct: "For if ye forgive men their trespasses, your heavenly Father will also forgive you: But if ye forgive not men their trespasses, neither will your Father forgive your trespasses." In regard to an offering as a part of worship (Matthew 5:23, 24) Jesus cautioned, "Therefore if thou bring thy gift to the altar, and there rememberest that thy brother hath aught against thee; Leave there thy gift before the altar, and go thy way; first be reconciled to thy brother, and then come and offer thy gift." Paul's description of the delicate balance that God in his sovereignty has achieved in placing each member of the body (I Corinthians 12:18-26) suggests the gentlest, tenderest of relationships among Christians: ". . . the members should have the same care one for another. And whether one member suffer, all the members suffer with it; or one member be honored, all the members rejoice with it." Roland Allen describes the spontaneous expansion of the Church as something which "follows the irresistible attraction of the Christian church for men who see its ordered life, and are drawn to it by desire to discover the secret of a life which they instinctively desire to share" (*op. cit.*, p. 7).

All evangelism is born out of such a relationship, and personal evangelism in the true New Testament sense will be the inevitable and abundant fruit of such renewal in the Church. Outside of this context, methods of personal evangelism can be perilous indeed. Methods wrongly born may attract, indoctrinate, and regiment certain zealous persons in a way that produces self-conscious "spiritually elite" individuals preoccupied with "results," who tend to think of themselves as superior to those not so inclined. This kind of situation militates against the fellowship and hence defeats witness; moreover, it tends also to suggest to the rest of the Christian community the false view that apart from a special course in personal work and in mastering evangelistic methods, one is not qualified to bear witness to an outsider. We do not discredit methods properly taught and practiced (the Holy Spirit uses means); we insist, rather that they always be kept in the context of the total life of the Christian community and subordinate to the ministry of the Spirit of God within believers as individuals and as a body.

Evangelism in the finest New Testament tradition is the vocation of every believer; for this calling, the Holy Spirit of God will equip him through "the apostles' doctrine, fellowship, breaking of bread and prayers." Any methodology which produces a kind of semi-professional class of evangelist within the Christian community, implying that personal evangelism is limited to those who have the time and/or inclination to take special courses and learn special methods, militates against total involvement, justifies those who default and discourages those unable to enroll for and master certain evangelistic techniques. In such a situation, the distinctive feature is not one's relationship to Jesus Christ, to the Holy Spirit and to others in the Christian family, but rather an artificial "system" which, however effectively used by its proponents, tends to make all others, voluntarily or involuntarily, feel useless so far as evangelism is concerned.

It is important at this point to distinguish between the general Christian community and those independent organziations founded for specific evangelistic thrust in a specialized way to a particular group or groups. This paper is to be understood in the context of the Christian congregation as it exists in its natural form, a microcosm of the universal Church, a heterogenous community bound together in a particular fellowship. It does not apply to organizations of specialists, homogenous in nature, drawn out of many congregations, uniform in methods, dedicated and trained for a clearly defined and limited evangelistic purpose. As far as the writer can tell, the New Testament does not contain specific instructions for such groups, but rather addresses itself to the total Christian family: the strong and the weak, the attractive and the unattractive, the gifted and the not so gifted, the brilliant and the humble. The Church of Christ is made up of all kinds of sheep. "One sows, another waters, but God gives the increase." The Church has its Pauls and its Barnabases, its Peters and its Andrews, its Stephens and its Simons, its Marys and its Marthas.

This suggests another grave danger in a methodology that does not take into account the ministry of the Holy Spirit in the total Christian community. That is the tendency to regimentation which hinders a Christian from being himself in the fullness of the Holy Spirit and the fellowship. Under these conditions his Christian influence becomes something else than it might be if he were really himself, unique among other Christians in bearing his personal influence for Christ to those among whom he is placed and to whom he is peculiarly fitted. Instead, under the pressure of the system, he tends to become like the one whose methods he is learning; the implication is, of course, that what works for one person will work for everyone in the same way. Within limits, this generalization may be true, but if it prohibits a Christian from finding himself with the endowment given at birth or by the Holy Spirit, then such a system is sub-Christian and perilous.

The one completely safe and dependable manual on personal evangelism and witness is the New Testament; yet the fact remains that the more one studies the New Testament the less one can deduce from it a system of personal evangelistic methods. Jesus employed a different approach with each person. He reminded Nicodemus that he "must be born again;" so far as we know, Jesus never said these words to any other. He spoke quite differently to the Samaritan woman at the well. And with the rich young ruler or the questioning lawyer he again used entirely different techniques. His dealing with the man born blind was different, not only from the approach used with others in general, but even that used with other blind men. Jesus dealt with no two seekers alike. His ways with men were as diverse as those to whom he spoke and with whom he reasoned. One factor alone remained constant in Jesus' contacts with men and that was his personal presence. This self-same fact of his presence, incidentally, is guaranteed every personal evangelist who labors in the fullness of the Holy Spirit (II Cor. 2:14, 15).

Andrew's approach was different from Peter's and both men in turn were unlike Paul, this one who determined to be "all things to all men, that he might by all means save some." Neither Peter nor Paul lays down systems or methods, except in the most general sense, whereby their disciples might propagate the Gospel. "The things that thou hast heard of me among many witnesses, the same commit thou to faithful men, who shall be able to teach others also," Paul had exhorted his young disciple Timothy, and that was the extent to which he passed on his methods to his disciples. They were to transmit a message to men who in turn would transmit it to still others; just how this message would be propagated was left to the personality and gifts of each messenger. No one, in fact, was so emphatic in insisting on the diversity of each Christian's witness as was Paul. "For I say, through the grace given unto me, to every man that is among you, not to think of himself more highly than he ought to think; but to think soberly, according as God hath dealt to every man the measure of faith. For . . . we have many members in one body, and all members have not the same office . . ." (Romans 12:3-4). He besought every Christian to "walk worthy of the vocation wherewith ye are called." He wrote, "But unto every one of us is given grace according to the measure of the gift of Christ." He portrayed "the whole body fitly joined together and compacted by that which every joint supplieth, according to the effectual working in the measure of every part . . ." (Ephesians 4:16).

Paul comprehended the marvelous diversity in the body and the interdependence of each part: "If the foot shall say, Because I am not the hand, I am not of the body; is it therefore not of the body? And if the ear shall say, Because I am not the eye, I am not of the body; is it therefore not of the body?" Then Paul asks with irresistible logic, "If the whole body were an eye, where were the hearing? If the whole were hearing, where were the smelling? . . . And if they were all one member, where were the body?" (I Corinthians 12:15-19). Diversity is of the essence in the unity of the Church, and to destroy this diversity is to destroy the unity! However noble their purpose, we must beware of institutionalized methods that indoctrinate and regiment and fashion every Christian into a common mold or a carbon copy.

Paul's understanding of the mission of the Church is most clearly given in his letter to the Ephesians where he describes Christ's giving of gifts to men: ". . . he gave some, apostles; . . . and some, pastors and teachers; For the perfecting of the saints, for the work of the ministry, for the edifying of the body of Christ" (Ephesians 4:11-12). Each Christian is "equipped for the work of ministry" as he is empowered by the Holy Spirit and instructed in the apostles' doctrine, in fellowship, in breaking of bread and in prayer with other disciples. He becomes able to testify to the reality and relevance of Jesus Christ on the basis of personal experience. He becomes able to communicate to others the facts concerning Jesus Christ upon which this personal relationship is based. Taught in the Scriptures, he has a defensible faith and is able "to give answer to him that asks, the reason of the hope that is within him." He does this in his own distinctive way and with his own choice of words among those with whom he is associated wherever the Lord "sows" him in the world. "Spontaneous expansion begins with the individual effort of the individual Christian to assist his fellow, when common experience, common difficulties, common toils have first brought the two together. It is this equality and community of experience which makes the one deliver his message in terms which the other can understand, and makes the hearer approach the subject with sympathy and confidence — with sympathy because the common experience makes approach easy and natural, with confidence, because the one is accustomed to understand what the other says and expects to understand him now" (Roland Allen, op. cit., p. 10).

Now empowered by the Holy Spirit, the Christian becomes a witness for Christ in everything he does, wherever he may be, twenty-four hours a day, seven days a week. He recognizes he has been "apprehended by Christ" for a purpose and like Paul seeks to "apprehend" that purpose. All he does, even the trivial, mundane things of life, he does to the glory of God. He believes that he is where he is, not by the accident of circumstance, but by the sovereign placement of God. His witness begins where he is, in what he is doing, among those with whom he associates. Spontaneous expansion is "the expansion which follows the unexhorted and unorganized activity of individual members of the Church explaining the Gospel which they have found for themselves . . ." (Roland Allen, *op. cit.*, p. 7).

What must be done to bring Christians to this place of positive, effective witness? What means are to be used to guarantee that each Christian will fulfill his vocation as Christ intended, using the methods which are peculiar to him in the Spirit and suited to those among whom Christ plants him and to whom Christ sends him?

(1) Each Christian must be made to realize that the work of the ministry belongs to every Christian. It is not reserved for a relatively few professionals peculiarly equipped and educated to evangelize; nor can it be delegated to a group of semi-professionals who have been given a special indoctrination in evangelistic techniques. The empowering of the Holy Spirit qualifies the Christian for witness and Jesus Christ promised him to every believer. As the Holy Spirit worked through Christ in his incarnation, so the Holy Spirit will work through all who believe in him now. Actually, there is only one Evangelist, one Preacher, one Missionary, one Witness; and that One is the Holy Spirit who will do his work in and through all who take Christ and his mission seriously. The Great Commission is the personal, inescapable obligation of every Christian, no exceptions!

(2) Keeping this vision of total involvement in constant view, Christians must be instructed in the Scriptures in order to know Christ's person and mission in history, the reason for his death by crucifixion and the significance of his resurrection.

(3) They must know that the warfare in which they are engaged in evangelism is "spiritual" warfare and that the only weapon provided by God for this conflict is the "sword of the Spirit, which is the word of God" (Ephesians 6:17). Their main discipline therefore is to study the Scriptures that they may become increasingly proficient in using them (II Timothy 3:14-17).

(4) Christians must be encouraged to "lead from weakness" as Paul did (I Corinthians 2:3); they must learn to depend upon the efficacy of their weapon and upon the presence and power of the Holy Spirit. Here again the inclination to lean upon methods rather than upon the Holy Spirit can be a peril; propagating methods of personal evangelism, if not carefully guarded, may imply that one must "lead from strength" or somehow be stronger than those to whom he speaks. It is almost as if the potential convert must be "conquered," an outcome which demands superior strength on the part of the evangelist. If this idea is not guarded against, the trainee gets the impression that not to get a decision constitutes failure, an outcome which the methods are intended to preclude. Under such compulsion the arguments must be strengthened, the approach refined, the tactics perfected for the sake of maximum results. It is so easy to overlook the fact that Jesus often did not get a positive response. The rich young ruler, for example, "went away sorrowful." This strategy is the way of the world, but

it is not the way of the Spirit lest a man's faith "stand in the wisdom of men, [rather than] in the power of God" (I Corinthians 2:5). Weakness is a positive asset to the Christian! (II Corinthians 12:10).

(5) Christians must be joined with others in authentic fellowship in order to share their experiences, burdens, victories and defeats, weaknesses and faults, hopes and aspirations. They must have opportunity to pray for one another, to bear one another's burdens, to exhort, to rebuke and admonish one another "in psalms and hymns and spiritual songs." They must study the Scriptures together and learn from each other as the Spirit illuminates. They must learn to take seriously the Lord's profound promises as given in Matthew 18:19-20; Luke 11:13; John 14:12; Acts 1:8; and elsewhere.

(6) Christians must conceive of their lives as constituting a plan of God and must consider what they do as a sacred vocation, and where they are as God's place for them. They must believe that their ordinary tasks, fulfilled as unto the Lord, are as productive for eternity as are those of their pastor. They must know God has placed them where they are as his contact, his distribution center, his agent or ambassador by and through whom he speaks and loves and works. They must believe that if the world where they live and work and socialize is to be evangelized, they are the means the Spirit of God will use.

(7) Christians must be encouraged to be themselves as God has gifted them; to give themselves (Romans 12:1-2) to Christ as living sacrifices in and through which his will may be demonstrated. They must learn to depend implicitly upon the indwelling Spirit to do the work of Christ by them and to witness to Christ through them. And they must learn to walk by faith insofar as results are concerned, realizing that there are no adequate criteria by which any Christian may measure his effectiveness. They must realize that to desire such criteria in order to ascertain how successful they are is a kind of lust that is unbecoming, indeed may be a pious indulgence which is in direct contradiction to our Lord's exhortation to self-denial (Luke 9:23; cf. Luke 10:20). Success as such is an illusion, "it is required in stewards that a man be found faithful (I Corinthians 4:2). They must learn to "walk by faith" in this also and to leave the results of their walk and witness with the Lord.

(8) Christians should recall continually the lesson of John 15 that the one who "abides" in Christ and in whom his "word abides" will bring forth "much fruit" as Christ promised. The basic strategy for maximum Christian effectiveness is the abiding life. When we abide in him and his Word abides in us, we can be sure that fruit is abounding. Not because we see the fruit, but because we are abiding!

The above eight suggestions, incidentally, place a tremendous obligation upon, and opportunity before, the "some" who are prophets, evangelists, pastors and teachers. These "some" whom Christ has given to the

Church have their work clearly cut out for them. Whatever it takes in preaching and teaching, fellowship, counseling and guidance "to equip God's people for work in his service, to the building up of the body of Christ" (Ephesians 4:12 NEB) is their mandate.

The methods of evangelism are legion. They are as numerous and diverse as the vast number of persons to be reached plus those who are to reach them. The worldwide task of evangelism will be realized, not by organizing for evangelism as though it were a department of church life requiring increased emphasis and effort; but by the renewal of the Church with a fresh infusion of the life of the Spirit. In his introduction to *Letters to Young Churches*, J. B. Phillips has expressed it vividly. "There is one other point that should be made before the letters are read. Without going into wearisome historical details, we need to remember that these letters were written, and the lives they indicate were led, against a background of paganism. There were no churches, no Sundays, no books about the Faith. Slavery, sexual immorality, cruelty, callousness to human suffering, and a low standard of public opinion, were universal; travelling and communications were chancy, and perilous; most people were illiterate. Many Christians today talk about the difficulties of our times as though we should have to wait for better ones before the Christian religion can take root. It is heartening to remember that this faith took root and flourished amazingly in conditions that would have killed anything less vital in a matter of weeks. These early Christians were on fire with the conviction that they had become, through Christ, literally sons of God, they were pioneers of a new humanity, founders of a new Kingdom. They still speak to us across the centuries. Perhaps if we believed what they believed, we might achieve what they achieved" (J. B. Phillips, *Introduction to Letters to Young Churches*).

DISCIPLE MAKERS:
KEY TO EVANGELISM

Lorne C. Sanny

For world evangelism in 1966, our resources are tremendous. One of every three persons in the world is a *nominal* Christian. Further, every major language group has a body of *evangelical* Christians.

Yet how many of these persons are helping the cause of world evangelism? How many church members *ever* lead someone to Christ? In America, at least, certainly less than two per cent.

World evangelism is not forwarded by nominal Christians, nor necessarily by evangelical Christians, but by a certain kind whom Jesus called disciples.

Only the disciple has a *message*. He takes time to look at Jesus and listen to him, hence can witness to what he has seen and heard (Acts 22:14, 15). He has a *motivation*: "For we cannot but speak of what we have seen and heard" (Acts 4:20). He has a *method* — Jesus said, ". . . Follow me, and I will make you fishers of men" (Matthew 4:19). Following Christ, the disciple learns how to catch men.

Making disciples was central in Jesus' ministry.

This is where he told us to begin. "Go therefore and make disciples of all nations . . ." (Matthew 28:19, 20, RSV). The command is not merely to go, but to make disciples. Further, we must make disciple-makers. Jesus said, ". . . make disciples . . . teaching them to observe all that I have commanded you . . ." The "all" includes making more disciples, who will in turn multiply.

This emphasis, prominent in the early church, has been largely obscured in later centuries. Therefore we again approach world evangelism with the task of multiplying disciples — beginning with those we have and teaching *them* to make disciples.

But to do this we must first have a pattern, a picture of what a disciple is. The Scriptures give us this pattern.

First, a disciple is *identified with the Person of Christ*. He openly confesses Christ before men (Romans 10:9, 10), is baptized (Matthew 28:19, 20), and takes up his cross (Luke 9:23). He is publicly identified with Christ whether this is popular or unpopular.

Second, a disciple is *obedient to the Word of Christ*. Jesus said, ". . . If you continue in my word, you are truly my disciples" (John 8:31, RSV). The disciple seeks to obey the Scriptures in every area of life.

THE REV. MR. SANNY is President of The Navigators in Colorado Springs, Colorado, USA.

Third, he *bears fruit in the work of Christ*. One fruit is love. "By this all men will know that you are my disciples, if you have love for one another" (John 13:35, RSV). Another fruit is lives influenced towards Christ. ". . . Go and bear fruit" (John 15:16, RSV).

But how do we make disciples — those who are identified with, obedient to, and bearing fruit for Christ?

One effective method is that of the disciple-maker's gathering a few potential disciples into a "koinonia" fellowship group. Canon Samuel Shoemaker said, "Every congregation needs two things — the formal service for worship, the informal gatherings for fellowship." Robert Raines says, "A small group is necessary for . . . personal and mutual encouragement. The strategy for our time is the *small-group* approach."

Such small groups of two or three, at most ten or twelve, are at the heart of disciple-making. The Church has largely failed to encourage such groups, but they are beginning to spring up around the world, and we should recognize their value and potential.

Unless the groups center around testimony, Scripture, and prayer, however, they become mere social gatherings, without disciple-making dynamic.

Giving *testimony* in the group, the disciple identifies himself with Christ and commits himself further. Bible-based testimony is a powerful spiritual weapon (Revelation 12:11).

In order to obey the *Scriptures* the disciple must know them. "He who has my commandments and keeps them . . ." (John 14:21, RSV). Bishop Stephen Neill says, "Competent knowledge of the Bible is the only basis for effective Christian witness."

No one bears fruit without *prayer*. "If you abide in me, and my words abide in you, ask whatever you will, and it shall be done for you" (John 15:7, RSV).

The disciple-maker acts as leader, not lecturer, helping members individually and in the group. The group member learns to give testimony among sympathetic Christians before testifying outside. He shares with others his own study and meditation in the Scriptures. He learns to pray, claiming the promise of Matthew 18:19.

Thus prepared by the koinonia group in testimony, the Scriptures, and prayer, he now comes to the critical matter of learning to do evangelism. He should be trained on the job or in the battle. "Learning the art of Christian service," says Bishop Newbigin, "must largely be by doing."

The Twelve watched Jesus as he did evangelism. Then he sent them out, training them through guided experience. The disciple-maker, who is a veteran of the battles for which he is training new recruits, should show them how to do evangelism, then help them actually begin to do it on their own.

He should first give them a tool, a method, some simple outline which incorporates the basic Gospel message concerning the Person and work of Christ. Having an outline to follow gives the disciple confidence and liberty. He learns, of course, to use whatever method or tool fits the opportunity.

The disciple may be guided into formally structured evangelistic endeavors, such as counseling at a Billy Graham Crusade or helping inquirers after a church service. Or he may join in informally structured activities, learning to talk with people personally after the Gospel is presented at a luncheon or tea by testimony, message or film. The koinonia group itself may plan evangelistic events in which its members can participate.

The best training in creative evangelism, however, is through everyday, unstructured channels of witness in office, neighborhood, among family and friends.

From these experiences the disciple learns he *can* talk with people about Christ, that friendship opens opportunities, that the Holy Spirit gives power, and that he needs more answers. He goes back to his Church, his koinonia group, for answers and encouragement. He is not theorizing now; he is practicing.

Thus he continues to come in for fellowship and instruction and to go out for evangelism. He has his Cave of Adullam and Valley of Rephaim.

When in due time he reaps, he must help disciple his converts, getting them into a Church, into koinonia fellowships, and eventually into doing their part in evangelism. He will have become a disciple, will be making disciples, and at length will make disciple-makers, following Paul's method of entrusting what he has heard and learned to faithful men able to teach others (II Timothy 2:2).

"And the word of God increased; and the number of the disciples multiplied . . ." (Acts 6:7).

REACHING THE ADOLESCENT
Winnie Bonner

The particular aspect of personal evangelism I wish to present is how to reach the adolescent for Jesus Christ. First of all, what is adolescence? It is a period of transition from childhood to adulthood, from dependency to independency. Life patterns crystalize. Adolescents look through the eyes of an idealist. They are capable, but have limited experience. They mature rapidly. They respond to a challenge. It is an age of curiosity. Adolescents crave activity, yet need self-control. The adolescent period — a most impressionable age — ranges from approximately 12 to 22 years of age.

An adolescent must make adjustments in certain difficult areas. 1. He has an uncertain status — he is expected to act as an adult at one time, but reminded at other times that he is only a child. 2. He moves from dependency to independency, from parent control to making his own decisions. 3. He undergoes bodily changes. 4. He expands his social relationships; he moves into high school or college, meets new friends, new teachers. Fearful of being different, he feels a dreadful need to conform. He becomes alert to sexual interests. 5. Life values are being formulated. Conflict of double standards is being felt; he senses, however, values that go beyond fleshly satisfaction. 6. He contemplates the matter of a life work, and thinks beyond material gain.

Our problem is how to reach this world's overwhelming number of adolescents. Of India's 470 million people, fifty per cent are below the age of 21. Other Asian and African countries also have large numbers of adolescents who face rapid changes in politics, economics, society and education. Unable to adjust properly to these quick changes, they find themselves restless and perhaps purposeless.

Several years ago, the President of my country, Dr. Radhakrishnan, said to a large gathering of students: "The manifold ills of the youth are a lack of poise, balance, and that discernment which makes us distinguish right from wrong." He also said that youth have no goals in life. These statements properly describe the youth of today. As I have observed them, the modern youth of India, Pakistan and Ceylon have no faith — they are empty; bound by social ties, they fight the old deep-seated religious social culture — they hunger for reality and truth.

What can we do to meet their needs? First, we must try to understand them and their problems. Second, we must be intensely interested in them as individuals, for God is intensely interested in the individual. Jesus Christ, who gave much time to the individual, is our great example.

MISS BONNER is an evangelist with Central Asia Youth for Christ and the Evangelical Fellowship of India in Hyderabad, India.

358 ONE RACE, ONE GOSPEL, ONE TASK

Third, we know that while mass communication is a powerful instrument in the hands of an evangelist, spiritual decision is individual and personal. Every adolescent must know God in his or her own experience. We evangelical leaders need to be convinced that every unsaved adolescent in this world is a sinner and lost. God's Word says, ". . . all have sinned and come short of the glory of God" (Rom. 3:23). "[Every] soul that sinneth it shall die" (Ezek. 18:4). We need to be convinced that every adolescent in this world needs the salvation that God offers in Jesus Christ. We also need to be convinced that salvation is an individual matter.

In many countries mass communication is not possible. In some countries, like India, mass communication does not reach the millions of adolescents. How then shall we reach them? Personal evangelism is the only answer. The best and only method of reaching them is person to person.

Here are some methods I have found very effective in reaching the adolescent for Christ. 1. Challenge the adolescent directly with the claims of Jesus Christ. Doing this usually opens the way for further discussion and counsel. 2. Provide literature. In these days of rapidly growing literacy, as in India, adolescents are avid readers. They will read anything. It is a day of great opportunity to contact them with literature. This approach, too, opens the way for further contacts. 3. Teens reaching teens has been the most effective method in the last decade or so. The challenge of an adolescent who knows Christ as personal Savior, and who lives a balanced and consistent life on a school campus, has been the greatest instrument in reaching other adolescents. An adolescent who has a glowing testimony and is dedicated to Jesus Christ breaks through all social, religious, and political barriers. No law of any country can legislate against the effectiveness of such a personal witness. This is our only hope of ever reaching the millions of adolescents in India. I think of a Hindu Brahmin girl of 18, for example, who was challenged by the consistent witness and daily dedicated life of a 15-year-old girl and was won to Christ. This is no isolated case.

The greatest venture in adolescent evangelism is having teens of one country reach teens of another country. We have seen the effectiveness of this method in India and would encourage people at this Congress to send teens to evangelize teens in other countries. Teen-agers will open their hearts to those of their own age. Teen-agers break through all barriers of color and race.

In conclusion let me say that the most important person in a community or a country is the adolescent, for adolescents are dynamite in the hands of a political leader or trouble-maker. Let us be convinced that adolescents can also be dynamite in the hands of God. Therefore let us reach them now before it is too late. Let us remember the words of our Lord Jesus Christ, "and other sheep I have, which are not of this fold: them also I must bring, and they shall hear my voice; and there shall be one fold, and one shepherd" (John 10:16).

THE "PHILIPPIAN METHOD"
John W. Alexander

I have chosen to speak on what might be called "the Philippian method" of personal evangelism.

The scriptural setting is found in Acts 8:26-38. Here we read about Philip's meeting with the Ethiopian. Three points can be emphasized.

First of all, the Holy Spirit had planned this contact and had guided the two men so that their pathways crossed. Secondly, Philip opened the conversation with a question. Thirdly, Philip made certain that his evangelistic effort was rooted in Scripture.

1. The Holy Spirit's Planning and Guidance.

We can begin by observing that this Ethiopian was a man whose heart was truly hungry to know God. Hundreds of years before, through the prophet Jeremiah, God had revealed this basic principle: "If with all your heart you truly seek me, ye shall surely find me."

Still another principle which was certainly in force is that which the Lord Jesus expressed in John 6:44, "No one can come to me unless the Father who sent me draws him" (RSV).

Here, then is a good example of how the Lord had set the stage for a classic demonstration of personal evangelism: he had fostered within a man's heart a yearning to know God; and he had turned on the divine magnet to draw that man toward himself.

The Lord had been equally at work in preparing the other side of the contact. The Holy Spirit moved on Philip and told him where to go and what to do. God's guidance was perfect. The pathways of the two men intersected exactly, and a new member was born into the body of Christ.

In applying this first principle to our lives today, I think we can say (a) that it is our job to yield ourselves so completely to the Holy Spirit that we respond promptly to his directives to contact individuals, and (b) that he is at work in hungry hearts, drawing them toward us and preparing their minds for what we have to say.

2. Philip Began With a Question

One of the difficult aspects of personal evangelism for most of us is how to open the conversation. Or, if the conversation is already underway on some other topic, the problem becomes how to direct the discussion to the person of Jesus Christ. Philip's example is a good one: he opened

DR. ALEXANDER is the general director of Inter-Varsity Christian Fellowship in Chicago, Illinois.

with a question. Philip struck right at the target by asking, "Do you understand what you are reading?" which was a thoroughly timely and natural question to ask. The man's negative answer opened wide the opportunity for Philip to explain the passage.

In applying this second principle to ourselves I believe we would be quite in order in asking the Holy Spirit to help us develop the facility for asking questions as a part of our method in personal evangelism.

In this connection I would like to recommend an article written by Paul Little and Waldron Scott entitled, "Witness With Questions."

May the Lord make us as alert as Philip to ask the right question at the right time in our man-to-man contacts with people who are outside the fold.

3. Rooted in the Scripture

Philip's conversation with the Ethiopian was rooted in Scripture. Verse 35 of Acts 8 is particularly significant, "And beginning with this Scripture, he told him the good news of Jesus." I think this is a basic principle in all evangelism, yet one which is easy to forget in personal evangelism. To be sure, there is a place too, for answering the non-Christian's questions. And there is a place for urging him to receive Christ. But there can be the temptation to do these other things and fail to get the inquirer really into the Scriptures. In my opinion, it is possible to get "decisions" without getting people deeply enough into the Word. (Too many of these "decisions" can be less than genuine regenerations.) Our friends are more likely to count the cost accurately if, like this Ethiopian, they are taken through a substantial portion of Scripture.

In this connection let me report briefly on an effort some of us made to reach college professors at the University of Wisconsin when I was on the faculty there. We realized that most of our professorial colleagues would not go to Church to hear about Christ. So we decided to go to them. We launched a Bible study, held for one hour each Friday noon. Those who attended brought their lunches. Our strategy was to emphasize five basic questions and go straight to the Bible for the answers:

1. What did Jesus say?
2. Why did he say it?
3. What did Jesus do?
4. Why did he do it?
5. What might be the significance of all this to us as college professors and as members of society?

We started with just two men and began slowly but steadily to invite our colleagues, one by one. Response varied. Of those I invited to investigate the above questions with us, about 5% said they were not interested; 65% said they thought the study to be a good idea but they were too busy to get involved; about 25% attended once or twice and then quit. About

5% became regulars. Once 25 were in attendance. One of the lessons we learned was this: when someone in a group Bible study manifests hunger to know Christ personally, it is essential that one of the believers take him aside, as Philip did the Ethiopian, to concentrate on his questions and needs.

To sum up, "the Philippian method" of personal evangelism highlights three principles which can help us today: one, we need to function as instruments of the Holy Spirit who will lead us to individuals whom he is drawing to Christ; two, we need to develop the skill of witnessing with questions; and three, we need to get our friends into the written Word as we endeavor to introduce them to the Living Word.

FRANCE AS A MISSION FIELD

Marcel Saltzmann

What will be the future of France, this young and vital country, brilliant in its culture and in international influence? There will soon be 50 million inhabitants, 25 million of them under 25 years of age. Will they be atheists, deists, or Christians? What is the so-called Christian Church doing in the face of this population explosion? The traditional Catholic Church affirms that only 7 to 11 per cent of the people attend its services. Protestants number less than 2 per cent and evangelicals less than 0.2 per cent.

On the other hand, cults like the Jehovah's Witnesses, Mormons and others are flourishing and are a hindrance to Bible colportage work.

Nine-tenths of the French people (about 44 million) are completely detached from all religious life.

There have been noble Christians filled with faith, however, men like Calvin, Farel, Coligny, Neff and others born in this country, who spread the light of the Gospel through the darkness of France and far out into the entire world. For decades, even for hundreds of years, our Christians have truly suffered for their faith; they have been persecuted, expelled, martyred, put in prison and even put to death. Their blood is crying out to God. As in the time of Joshua by the sin of Achan (Josh. 7:11-12), a great curse holds this country in its grip and hinders the Word of God from penetrating people's hearts, while it opens wide the door to liberalism, worldliness, superficiality, and to ecumenism which is moving ahead with giant steps. In addition to witchcraft, white and black magic and healers (about 40,000 of these as against 38,000 doctors), astrology, idolatry, and spiritism flourish in all their forms and are increasingly at work in Europe.

Because of these facts, France is showing more and more non-religious and materialistic tendencies. There is a vague religious tradition associated with baptism, marriage, and funerals. But 34,000 villages out of 37,000 have not Christian evangelical witness. For that matter, someone has said that France is the second country in the world after India for missionary needs.

Who will win? Will a convenient paganism with perhaps a vague deism in an ecumenical kind of religion or will the Cross of Christ?

Among the different evangelistic methods, is that of extended campaigns — used also by the apostle Paul. In certain villages and in small cities, young men or young ladies in teams of two or three live in trailers and put up a tent or a portable hall that accommodates 80 to 100 people. Much prayer surrounds this work. One by one all homes are visited in

MR. SALTZMANN is a lay preacher and director of his own electrical firm in Mulhouse, France.

order to make a contact and to win the confidence of the people who, in general, are very warm, but ignorant or indifferent to the 'Good News of the Gospel. Television, which has become a passion and a trap also for many Christians, is hindering interest in the Gospel, paralyzing the spirit of prayer, and is serving the cause of the Anti-Christ. There is also a hidden and fanatical kind of opposition. As soon as a person reads his Bible, is converted and begins to witness to the truth, he is sought out, beleaguered, and sometimes even threatened to prevent him from going to the Christian meetings. One might say that the entire population of an area gets excited when someone is converted. "For we wrestle not against flesh and blood, but against principalities . . . against spiritual wickedness in high places" (Eph. 6:12.)

Despite all these struggles, however, precious souls are being saved. We try to bring them together in small prayer groups, where they continue to be taught by older brothers and are delivered from the chains which hold them back in their spiritual life. The Word of God is all that matters: all read it and become interested and seek to put it into practice. Joy fills the hearts of the young converts who, in spite of their difficulties, very often are no longer afraid to witness, but desire to win souls for Jesus. In the Early Church each Christian was an evangelist (I Thess. 1:8).

Report of Group Discussion

Delegates speaking to the subject of personal evangelistic methods agreed almost overwhelmingly on the need for personal encounter between individuals as the basis for all lasting commitment to Jesus Christ. At the same time, many expressed an acute need for the systematic and pointed training of the mass of Christians to do such man-to-man evangelism.

Many shared methods which they themselves had found to be effective. Lorne Sanny (USA) spoke extensively of cell-group methods used by the Navigators to train disciples. By disciples Sanny meant effective witnesses. Bellman (England) shared the successes of a new "Coffee-bar Evangelism" which has won many of the youth to Jesus Christ by means of meeting places, questionnaires and counseling rooms. Paul Little (USA) spoke of a three question approach to individuals which he felt seldom missed its mark: Have you ever personally trusted Christ or are you still on the way? How far along are you? And if the person is responsive, Would you like personally to receive Christ and be sure of it?

Final comments dealt with the motivation to evangelism, many feeling that the best motivation follows from engaging in the work.

Reporter: *James M. Boice*

THE CONFRONTATION OF IDEOLOGY
Hans Bürki-Fillenz

Corporate and personal evangelism is, according to Richard Halverson's exposition, an inevitable expression of virile spirituality and genuine fellowship. It is our common concern to ask why there is so little spiritual maturity and love-arousing togetherness.

Many churches and missions appear to move in a vicious circle, giving birth to children according to their own likeness. Christians with low standards of faith-life will exemplify low standards for entering the Christian way. And a poorly structured pattern of fellowship will give rise to new believers with little readiness towards relevant communication.

One cannot ignore the observation that much of the evangelistic endeavor contributes directly towards the emergence of a new type of a nominal Christian. He may not produce an infant baptism certificate, nor may he rest his faith on the sacraments, yet he has "answered the altar call," he has come forward, he did raise his hand, he signed a decision card, he said a prayer in the presence of a counselor, he has had an experience. And since he is immediately accepted into the low standard group, neither he nor they may ever discover that his conversion has been a psychological brainwashing process and not the regenerating work of the Spirit of God in the soul of man.

The important question to ask is: Why does the practice of evangelism (corporate and individual) increasingly distort the doctrine of evangelism? The answer that is put forward here for discussion and evaluation can be summarized in the following sentence: The observed aberration in action is caused by an ideological alteration of the Christian faith. The motives mold the methods.

An ideology is a total system of thought and action, erected to justify and consolidate the position of a political party, a social class, a cultural group, or a religious institution. Typical signs of ideology at work are: The emphasis on public opinion, propaganda, prestige, name, title, relationship, efficiency, result, modernity, actuality, statistics, money, influence; and most easily detected — the oversimplification of the complexities of life by means of rigidly stereotyped language patterns.

Now, Dr. Halverson maintains that the only safeguard against these tendencies lies in the Christian congregation, the Church. For him the Christian congregation is a heterogeneous community in contrast to the homogeneous groups of specialized organizations.

However, seen in a wider perspective, churches are also homogeneous groups, e.g. many have a typical middle-class constituency with its cor-

DR. BÜRKI is general secretary of the Swiss Inter-Varsity Christian Fellowship (Vereinigte Bibelgruppen), Lenzburg, Switzerland.

responding mentality. On the other side, organizations do not per se exclude the possibility of a heterogeneous composition of their members.

The Church congregations are not spared by the ideological indoctrination. The quantifying of church life (statistics of attendance, conversions, offerings, etc.), or the prevalence of church activity centered around the gifts of one man can be as persistent as the distorted management of an independent organization. It would be ideological thinking, if the constituted churches and the independent organizations were to blame each other for the present state of affairs.

Dr. Halverson mentions that "the New Testament does not contain specific instructions for such groups." Negative conclusions cannot be drawn from this statement. The New Testament likewise has no reference to special church buildings, to printed Bibles, to mission societies, etc. While the geographical expansion of the missionary activity has reached its climax, new patterns and areas of evangelistic pioneer activity emerge.

The most significant developments of our century should here be mentioned: the unprecedented and universal rise of city population and the equally incomparable growth of the number of universities and students all around the world. While until 50 years ago university education was an economic luxury, it has now become an economic and national necessity.

And just as according to the New Testament, evangelists have been called to open new geographical areas for the Gospel of Jesus Christ, so the same Spirit can "set apart for him" pioneers in new sociological areas.

Such individuals and organizations need to be safeguarded from their specific pitfall by the loving concern of all the local congregations around the world, while these pioneering movements have to provoke the existing Churches to imaginative love and good works in regard to these new areas of evangelism.

While the established Churches tend to lead to stagnation and legalistic formalism, the independent movements are in grave danger of confusing their dynamic outreach — suspiciously enough often called "aggressive evangelism" — with the working of the Spirit of God. Both aberrations, however, further the vulnerability of Christians with regard to the pervading ideological distortion of the Christian faith.

A great portion of the present world population becomes increasingly suspicious of any slightest hint of indoctrinating practices. Many of the so-called follow-up problems reveal a lack of true concern for the total life of other persons. If the object of one's effort is converted, then the intended result is accomplished, and therefore continued care is no longer needed. If he did not yield to the persuasion, then it is his own mistake. He has heard the Gospel, the Christian's duty is fulfilled. This attitude proves that the personal interest in the conversion of others is ideologically motivated.

Artificially-originated interest and adherence will have to be maintained by artificial means of continued indoctrination and control.

Another great section of the world population (intellectuals also in-

366 ONE RACE, ONE GOSPEL, ONE TASK

cluded) becomes increasingly liable to ideological indoctrination. Great is the latent temptation to intrude a "Christian ideology" upon such persons. Whenever the "Christian way of life" is presented as superior to another way of life, a subtle misunderstanding is already creeping along. To state it flatly: The Christian way of life is primarily a way of death. Salvation is not a means for the "pursuit of happiness," nor for success and psychological equilibrium, rather it is salvation from death and judgment. Not that life and peace and joy are excluded from Christian experience, but the basis of all this is an eternal and not a temporal issue. It is exactly this denial and loss of the eternal reality that marks the ideological thinking most significantly.

The Christian is not spared from suffering, hunger, persecution, war, bodily and mental sickness, failure and darkness, even unto the edge of despair. His identification with the totality of the groaning creation, "the victim of frustration" (Romans 8:20, NEB) is not weakened, but is intensified by his salvation.

Man is not merely asked to face Jesus Christ as his Savior, who saves him personally from total loss. This aspect taken alone leads inevitably to a narrow and selfish understanding and experience of salvation. Christ has also to be presented and received as the Head of the body of his Church. To stop here can still lead to an ideological misuse. (You have to be saved in order to join our church or our group.) The Church is not an end in itself. Christ is to be honored as the Lord and Mediator of the whole universe. The redemption he offers carries eternal consequences for the totality of the created universe.

The personal Christ of the individual, the corporate Christ of the Church, the cosmic Christ of the universe, he is the one Mediator of creation and salvation through whom the divine counsel will be completed. This fullness of Christ will restore a believing sinner into the fullness of his original mandate: to become king of the earth under the sovereign rule of the Lord of all.

Therefore, genuine Christian evangelism will never, as all ideologies necessarily do, make of man a means for an end (Mark 2:27-28). The contrary is true: All motives and methods, all institutions and organizations will have to be made and kept subservient to man, who is honored to stand or fall before his own master.

AN HOUR FOR MOBILIZATION
Muri Thompson

The twentieth century's exploding population is in sharp contrast to Christianity's desperate manpower shortage. Can Christianity survive the crisis of being hopelessly outnumbered? Is it able to make any appreciable impact upon the multiplying masses? Or is the gap between the masses and the Christian minority too vast to span?

The task is frightening and formidable. The question arises, "Can the forces of righteousness shrug off the deepening sense of frustration and despair that stares them in the face?" The whole situation brings into sharper focus the relevance of Christianity to this present age.

This is not a lament — this is a challenge! No one truly Christian with an implicit faith in his God can afford the luxury of doubt or pessimism in this gripping situation. This is not the first time that the Church of God has had to face overwhelming odds. It has happened before . . . it is happening again. History is repeating itself. The Church once more enters the crucible of testing to face the greatest trial by fire it has ever known. How does it stand in this crisis?

Is God too severely handicapped with only Gideon and his guerrillas? Is he in danger of being disgraced by the unequal odds between David, the youth who champions God, and Goliath? Is our pity wasted upon Jonah, the lone reluctant prophet and patriot, confronting an alien city with his denunciations? What of the incongruity of the "battle of the giants" — Elijah versus the State? Or of the naïve optimism of an insignificant minority of equally insignificant provincials from Galilee commissioned by their Carpenter King to evangelize a sophisticated society and civilization?

This is no time for morbidity; this is an hour for mobilization. Our greatest problem is not manpower shortage — and we certainly need men — our problem is manpower wastage. Our churches are packed with worshipers whose energies are being dissipated through lack of effective employment in the service of God. A vast majority are far from extending themselves to capacity for God. Before this legion of nonaligned can be channeled effectively, certain common attitudes will have to be demythologized.

Many Christians entertain the delusion that they are exempt from responsibility to God and to their fellowmen. They are not aware of any personal accountability to reach others for Christ. They disqualify themselves because they feel that this is the privilege of a select minority who are specialists in the field. Winston Churchill's wartime eulogy, "Never has

MR. THOMPSON is the founder of and evangelist for the Muri Thompson Crusade in Auckland, New Zealand.

so much been owed by so many to so few" is particularly relevant in the conflict for souls outside of Christ.

A sense of duty is never easy to impose but Christians must face their obligations through their sense of loyalty and devotion; love, moreover, places the highest premium on our missionary relationship to others. The Christian has no choice. Jesus said, "Ye have not chosen me, but I have chosen you that you should bring forth fruit."

We need to harness the great manpower resources lying idle in our ranks, mainly the casual or occasionally involved and uninvolved Christians. Otherwise they shall remain in the limbo of statistical ballast. Some have a measure of preparation and practical experience, but only in periodic special services, which is ideal for launching into personal evangellism. Few, however, become sufficiently airborne to remain in orbit regularly winning others. A time and motion study on productivity and conservation would reveal an excessive loss of time, energy and experience.

Our problem lies in training for short term objectives rather than for long range activity, for an event rather than a lifetime of service. With fresh undertakings the whole training program needs repetition. Some churches keep their members regularly engaged but this is not the general condition. Most Christians have difficulty in relating campaign experience to daily circumstances; very little training seems to cover this aspect.

Others depend upon traditional patterns of evangelism to execute their responsibilities. In an extremely healthy congregation this seldom escalates beyond a routine of one hour, of one day, of one week, in one location, by one individual, to one small section of the community. Seen in the context of the total church life per week and per annum the minimal annual total amounts to 52 evangelistic hours; this composes the ordinary working week for the average individual. The tragedy is that parishioners rely on so-called professionals and semi-skilled assistants to do the work. They little realize the strategic placement for service that they have in their secular situations. Unless they grasp this, the Gospel will remain imprisoned in ecclesiastical cells.

Jesus left no doubt as to our responsibilities. He said, "The servant is not greater than his Master . . . the works that I do shall he do also. The pattern had long been established when he said this. His Church and ministry was founded on personal evangelism. Despite new methods and media of communication it will never be outmoded or abandoned. It is fundamental and indispensable to all evangelism. As such, therefore, it absolutely and unqualifiedly places a common obligation upon all believers.

The Lord Jesus sought people right where they were. Those who came to him had varying motives, some to criticize, some to be cured, some out of curiosity. He often took the initiative. He found Peter and Andrew, James and John in the fishing industry. He took Matthew Levi from a customs office, challenged the scholar Nicodemus in the privacy of a home, invited himself to the home of Zaccheus.

Jesus contacted the notorious woman of Samaria, showed compassion to the woman of the street weeping at his feet, turned tragedy to triumph at his own execution and pardoned a dying criminal hanging beside him. No situation however discomforting, inconvenient or embarrassing dissuaded him from winning others.

Jesus' inner compulsion and urgency projected him right into the heart of the community. Peter sustained this attitude and declared before the Sanhedrin, "We cannot help but speak the things we have seen and heard." This kind of dynamic is lacking in our members, and thus often disqualifies them from any participation in personal outreach.

Although the Christian experiences eternal life, many a one is not enjoying it more abundantly. Jesus taught that this abundant life was to flow in a constant stream of blessing to others. But how soon following conversion are we shown this? Can we be too premature in entering a life of continual power and fruitfulness? Is maturity — of long standing presumably — a prerequisite to effective witnessing and soul winning? Was God arbitrary in equipping the Early Church with phenomenal power while we in our era stumble blindly on? Or were their handicaps, educational lack, and immaturity so pronounced that special dispensation was a peculiar essential for their time?

Facing every conceivable difficulty the Early Church seemed invincible, its attitude toward life almost irresponsible in the light of the resurrection. Its energy, enterprise and dynamic power, with crowds or individuals — some even hostile — challenges the Church in this century. Unless we experience something of this same dynamic we shall remain victims of our sanctified slave labor, serving under tyranny of self effort and speculative outreach.

If every member is a soulwinner, not just a statistic, any impression upon the masses may not be immediate, but one thing will certainly follow. Deficiencies will be corrected which have plagued the Church and hindered it from exercising a vital and authoritative influence in the world today.

TRAINING IN PERSONAL EVANGELISM
William R. Bright

If the Great Commission is to be fulfilled in our generation, there must be a dramatic new emphasis on personal evangelism.

Most every Christian leader will agree with this statement. In practice, however, very little is being done about personal evangelism. Why?

1. The Problem.

From a special project on personal evangelism involving thousands of counseling sessions, four basic reasons for this lack of personal evangelism have become apparent.

a. Christian leaders are not setting an example in the area of personal evangelism, because most of them have not been trained, are not fruitful themselves, are "afraid of man," and are too busy.

b. It is estimated that approximately ninety-five percent of all Christians are living defeated, fruitless, carnal lives. How can a defeated, carnal Christian who is living in the experience of Romans 7, present a witness for Christ?

c. Most Christians do not know how to share their faith effectively with others. In the United States, it has been estimated, one thousand laymen and six pastors are required to introduce one person to the Lord Jesus Christ in an entire year. In one major denomination there were two thousand individual churches without a single salvation decision reported during the year of 1961. Of the few Christians who have the courage to share their faith, most see little response because they do not know what to say or how to present the Gospel.

d. There is unbelief. Our Lord could do "not many mighty works in Nazareth because of their unbelief" (Matt. 13:58). This same "spirit of Nazareth," the spirit of unbelief, also renders the twentieth-century Christian impotent. Most Christians have believed the "big lie" of the centuries, namely, that "men don't want to know God." The Christian has been brainwashed into presupposing a negative response to a personal witness for Christ. The Christian knows that he should and wants to witness, but is afraid to try.

This failure on the part of the Christian to witness is all the more tragic when one discovers that the average non-believer wants to become a Christian, but does not know how.

In a "Collegiate Challenge Magazine" survey of 10,500 students from scores of campuses throughout the United States that covered a period of

DR. BRIGHT is President of Campus Crusade for Christ, International, in San Bernardino, California.

three years, it was discovered that 89.1 percent of all those interviewed did not know how to become a Christian. Yet the majority were looking for a faith.

2. *The Solution.*

What then is the solution to this problem of the fruitless witness and the impotent church? If most Christians want to introduce others to Christ and many non-believers want to become Christians, what can be done to satisfy the desires of both?

a. First, the Christian must understand how to abide in Christ, how to appropriate the power of the Holy Spirit in his life moment by moment by faith. Personal evangelism apart from a conscious moment by moment abiding in Christ, or "walk" in the Spirit, leads to legalism, spiritual pride and ultimate frustration. No Christian can be used of God consistently to introduce others to Christ unless there is an understanding of and personal experience with the person of the Holy Spirit as our source of power for witnessing.

b. Second, training in personal evangelism is imperative.

Jesus trained his disciples – the three, the twelve, the seventy, and then one-hundred-twenty.

Paul emphasized the value of training when he admonished Timothy to teach others the things which he had learned (II Timothy 2:2). Even though Timothy was a third-generation Christian and his trained helper, Paul still found it necessary to admonish Timothy to be more bold and aggressive in his witness for Christ. He said, "Stir up the gift of God that is in you," "Do not be ashamed to testify to and for our Lord" (II Timothy 1:6-8 ANT).

Paul depended upon the men whom he had trained to communicate his methods and procedures (I Cor. 4:16-18 ANT).

Those trained by Paul's methods in Thessalonica became disciples and were greatly used of God (I Thess. 1:4-10).

If Paul in the first century found it necessary to say: "Recall to your minds my methods of proceedings, course of conduct and way of life in Christ, such as I teach everywhere in each of the churches," how much more must we give attention to training, to methods, to procedures.

Through training in personal evangelism the Christian learns how to communicate his faith. He learns how to share the basic facts of the Gospel in a logical, clear, brief and precise way, free of offensive religious jargon.

Hundreds of Student and Lay Institutes of Evangelism conducted by Campus Crusade for Christ, Inc. have shown us the validity of training in personal evangelism. In thousands of cases carnal fruitless Christians have become effective fruitful witnesses for Christ with only a few hours of instruction.

A word of caution should be given regarding the use of "canned approaches" or definite methods and procedures: the trainee should be carefully instructed to avoid using techniques, methods and materials without complete reliance upon the person and ministry of the Holy Spirit.

It should be made emphatically clear that the Christian is only an instrument, a channel of God's love. Salvation is a gift of God made known through the ministry of the Holy Spirit, as Jesus explained to Nicodemus (John 3:1-8).

No amount of argument, logic, high pressure, techniques, methods or materials are adequate to bring someone to Christ. Jesus said, "No man can come to me, except the Father which hath sent me draw him . . ." (John 6:44).

A proper understanding of the Christian's role in the witnessing experience and of the Holy Spirit's role helps to remove the tendency to fear man, to become discouraged when there are no results, or to become spiritually proud when God blesses with "much fruit."

The importance of training in personal evangelism is demonstrated from Scripture, from history and from experience. Renewal cannot come to the Church of Jesus Christ until a renewed emphasis is given to the person and ministry of the Holy Spirit and Christians are trained to share their faith in the Lord Jesus Christ in a more effective way.

c. Third, Christian "leaders" must place greater emphasis on personal evangelism. The pastor must assume leadership by personal example as well as by exhorting his people about the importance of personal evangelism. To produce pastors with a vital concern for personal evangelism, Christian schools and seminaries must restore personal evangelism to its rightful emphasis in the classroom.

The Great Commission can and by God's grace shall be fulfilled only through a renewed emphasis on personal evangelism.

WORKERS TOGETHER WITH GOD
W. F. Batt

In personal evangelism we are workers together with God, and need to know the division of responsibility between God and us. God has promised that the Holy Spirit will bring men under conviction; it is our job to believe he will do so. Although the Holy Spirit often works quite unaided in bringing people under conviction, yet God has promised to use us in this work also. We are the light of the world. Light reveals the truth, discloses guilty secrets, shows the way. We are to expect that this will continue to happen as we move among men and women.

These clear promises of God imply at least two things. First, as the light of the world we are to be in the world, and not withdrawn from it. If men are to see the light, they can do so only as they meet us. We are the link between Christ and them. For this reason Christ prayed that the Father should not take us out of the world, but that he should keep us from the evil one. A Christian life which is lived primarily within the Church, and removed from contact with unconverted people, is a light hidden under a bushel and useless for the purpose for which it was lit.

Second, if we claim these promises of God, it is reasonable to expect that people will indeed come under conviction. In fact, not to do so is to deny our faith. It is here that our responsibility in personal evangelism comes in. We must always be moving among unbelievers, and, sensitive to those coming under conviction, must befriend them and lead them to Christ. We should be all things to all men that we might by all means save some.

Seeking and winning lost souls is the work to which every Christian is called, and to which he should devote his life. Only a tiny fraction of those who are under conviction will be found in our churches; the majority are encountered only outside. Perhaps it is the shop assistant, petrol pump attendant, a business or club associate who is under conviction and who is one's responsibility for today. Yet how often we simply use the services of such people, instead of determining if they have some conscious need, and instead of making it easy for them to confide in us. We need to practice spiritual diagnosis and to become proficient at it. This is what is involved in yielding one's members — eyes, ears, and so on, — as instruments of righteousness unto God. If the detective can train himself to be observant, and the doctor to notice every symptom, how much more should the Christian. Every meeting with an unconverted person, be it social, business or casual, may bring one face to face with someone under conviction. For this reason we must learn to recognize the symptoms of convic-

MAJOR BATT is active in local civil affairs in Norwich, England, and in church and university evangelism in the British Isles.

tion of sin which usually reveal themselves in some sense of personal need. Only as we study to show ourselves approved unto God, workmen that need not to be ashamed, rightly dividing the Word of God, will we begin to be effective in personal evangelism. As we study and practice, we shall learn that some are converted through the intellect, like the Ethiopian of whom the evangelist asked, "Understandest thou what thou readest?" Or there are those like Paul, whose conversion involves a dramatic surrender of the will to the Lord; or those like the Philippian jailer whose conscience is pricked, and who in fear of death and judgment cry out, "What must I do to be saved?" And there are the Lydias whose emotions draw them to Christ, and whose hearts the Lord opens. The personal evangelist needs to be a well-instructed theologian, but his theology must always be applied theology, that is, theology rightly applied to the problem and circumstances of the particular person to whom he is speaking. Therefore he must be always sensitive and alert, not only to diagnose the person's case aright, but also to use the particular theological aspect of the Gospel which best meets that one's conscious need.

We might well cry with the apostle, "Who is sufficient for these things?" did we not know, like Paul, that our sufficiency is of God, who has qualified us to be ministers of this new covenant. Yet many Christians have drifted into the habit of unbelief. They apparently do not expect God to use their lives as the means by which the Spirit will bring others under conviction, and rationalize this lack by claiming that they do not have the gift of an evangelist, and therefore should not expect to be soul winners. But this position is most untenable, for our Lord himself said, "If *any one* thirst, let him come to me and drink; he who believes in me, as the Scripture has said, out of his heart shall flow rivers of living water. This he said about the Spirit which those who believed in him were to receive."

The secret of personal evangelism lies not in withdrawing from the world; lies not in undertaking so-called "full time Christian service"; lies not in some particular method of communication or in some special evangelistic agency. It lies in using all our God-given opportunities to move among unbelievers, in expecting the Spirit to bring them under conviction, in allowing rivers of living water to flow constantly through us in lives devoted to the service of men and women and to studying how to lead them to Christ.

People may flock to churches during times of revival. But in view of the circumstances in which many persons live today, it is neither practical nor scriptural for ministers to think in terms of getting very many unbelievers to church. To do so would be to invite failure, for if scores of unbelievers came, the ministers could not deal with all of the numbers, nor would the buildings hold them. It is essential, then, that every Christian be a fisher of men, and go where the fish are. Our church policy must be,

"Every Christian a soul-winner, and every Christian home a mission station."

Report of Group Discussion

Living a victorious, Spirit-filled Christian life does not exclude the need of a proper training in personal evangelism, delegates agreed. Similarly, no amount of training or material can succeed without the ministry of the Holy Spirit in the life of the evangelist and in his converts, many said.

Several delegates expressed the danger of making "numbers" a criterion of success in personal evangelism. It was recognized at the same time, however, that God is not uninterested in numbers (the 3,000 and 5,000 in Acts) and that numbers of committed Christians encourage the evangelist's faith.

There seemed to be a consensus in open discussion that "results" mean "changed lives" as a result of personal acceptance of Jesus Christ.

Reporter: *Sergio Garcia*

SPIRITUAL NEEDS OF THE NEGRO
William E. Pannell

I am an evangelical. For fifteen years I have been an evangelist. I am also a Negro. My remarks grow out of the contemporary social issues of my culture, and my deep concern for the nearly twenty million Negroes in America.

To be a Negro evangelical today is considerably more difficult than it was fifteen years ago. Something has happened to the dream of the "inalienable rights" of "life, liberty, and the pursuit of happiness." Something also has happened to that more fundamental vision about men being "all one in Christ." Being a Negro means involvement in the destiny of people — not merely one's own, but admittedly with a peculiar concern for one's own. Like most non-whites, I want "to loose and shake off the confining coils of race and the racial experience so that my integration — my personal integration and commitment — can be made to something bigger than race, and more enduring and truer" (J. Saunders Redding, *On Being Negro in America*, Charter Books). That something must be more than one's family or ethnic institution, it must be "a people and all their topless strivings; a nation and its million destinies" (*ibid.*).

But being an evangelical on the other hand, has meant, at least in my lifetime, not only passivity in social matters, but also, by default, a tacit support of the status quo. There has always been a contradiction in this stance, and we have now been forced to see it. We have been forced into the open — black and white alike, pagan and Christian alike — to rethink our historic assumptions. ". . . what confronts us today is no speedy change of scenery, flag, costume, posture or facial expression," says Harold R. Isaacs, "no frantic flashing of news pictures on the propaganda screens. It is the beginning of a change in the under-pinning of the total relationship between Western and Asian men. For nearly three hundred years this under-pinning was the assumption of Western superiority; a whole vast political, military, social-economic, social-personal complex was built upon it. . . . The whole structure based upon it is being revised. All the power relations that went with it are being changed. This is history in the large, a great continental rearrangement, bringing with it a great and wrenching shift in the juxtapositions of cultures and peoples" ("Scratches On Our Minds," quoted in *World Vision*, June 1965, p. 3).

This "shift" affects the evangelical church. Whether she responds affirmatively is another thing, but she can never be the same. As LeRone T. Bennett Jr., Senior editor of *Ebony* magazine, says:

MR. PANNELL is an evangelist, and a member of the executive staff of Youth for Christ International in Detroit, Michigan.

"We are heading now for a land no American has traversed. For perhaps the first time . . . we have a thoroughly restive minority population on our hands. So far we have done our best to bring out the worst in urban Negroes who are strategically placed to cause social chaos. Negroes, for the most part, inhabit the inner cores of America's largest cities, and they hold the key to the future of the city and the future of American democracy.

"This is an important moment in the history of the Commonwealth. There stretch out before us two roads and two roads only. America must now become America or something else, a Fourth Reich perhaps, or a Fourth Reich of the spirit. To put the matter bluntly, we must become what we say we are, or give in to the secret dream that blights our hearts." (*The Negro Mood*, Ballentine Books, New York, pgs. 47, 48)

What then are some of the issues bearing upon an effective witness in this explosive context? Initially, there is the spectacle of a racially divided church. Ralph McGill, Pulitzer Prize winning editor of the *Atlanta Constitution*, asserts:

"Every minister with any shred of sensitiveness understands that just as the racial issue is the paramount political issue before the world today, so it is for Christianity. If the first commandment, and the second which is like unto it, have no validity in the minds of church members, then their churches are finished, or eventually will be."

Yet it was the peculiar genius of the early Church that she solved "the race problem." Both in precept and practice, she spoke to a divided world (Eph. 2:13-16).

The appeal of the early disciples was the quality of life they knew among themselves (Acts 4:32-35). In a real sense theirs was not personal evangelism, it was community evangelism – the new society speaking to the old, from which it had been born by the Spirit of God.

This is the crucial point. If "the good seed are the children of the kingdom" then we need to notice the plurality of this concept. Christ stated and demonstrated a team approach to evangelism – the Gospel was being demonstrated even as it was being preached. This is not true today. Even our language accuses us: we speak of white and black churches; of white and black Christians.

As a first step to evangelism in a racially torn society, we need then a wholesome evangelical fellowship with the courage and humility to confront fellow-believers honestly about the attitudes that divide them. It will be painful for there is suspicion and resentment in both black and white churches. This must be faced, but it can only be faced together. This will not just happen; it must be structured, pushed and prayed for. Leaders must be found who, like Paul, jealous for the uniqueness of the Gospel, can speak a word of correction to Peter.

We must also try to involve ourselves in our world. Traditionally we have conceived of evangelism as the personal task of individual believers to individual non-believers. We have felt that the only way to change society was to change individuals in that society. Ideally and scripturally this is true. But this traditional view is being used as an excuse for almost complete non-involvement at any level. Man today is found in crowds. He is not only "lonely" there but also lost. He is worldly, secularized, urbanized and collectivized. To find him we must penetrate his social order.

I am well aware of the pitfalls here and of the justifiable criticism aimed at those whose only gospel is social activism. But the other image of a conservatism that is pro-status quo is equally regrettable. It seems reasonable to expect that those who decry the methods employed by those seeking human rights would offer a suitable alternative. To declare that morality cannot be legislated is worse than spitting into the wind. Apparently it cannot be experienced in the Church either. I am speaking now as a Negro, and frankly I am a bit weary of hearing that Lord Shaftsbury and Wilberforce effected social change in England. Have we no more contemporary evidence of evangelical social involvement and influence? What does "Involvement In A World In Crisis" really mean?

Dr. Elton Trueblood has said: "Standard Protestantism is characteristically urbane and well-mannered, but it is sadly deficient in driving power and the ability to imagine new and fresh ways of penetrating the world."

But the future moral health of the Church — and the re-birth of a scandalous respectability — may not be completely ours to decide. We live in a young society; an army of young people is loose in the land, and they are concerned about moral issues. Dr. Arthur M. Ross of the University of California has observed of many students: "Rather than aiming to be successful men in an achievement-oriented society, they want to be moral men in a moral society. They want to lead lives less tied to a financial return than to social awareness and responsibility. Our educational plans should recognize these values."

So also must the Church. But the Church is not yet alert enough. Many young people realize that the Church has often been on the wrong side of moral issues. Said one teen-ager, "Religion is getting to be like a vending machine. You put in a nickle and you get a reward. It doesn't lead the people, it only reflects their values." Given a choice by the emergence of dramatic social and political issues, many of today's youth are addressing themselves to these as a means of finding personal significance. They seem to agree that the world needs changing, but they have no program nor "piper" to call the tune. But they are waiting. For the most part they remain uncommitted.

The black youngster agrees. But he is showing signs of impatience. He is not waiting. While white youth try to out-grunion the grunions at farflung beaches, black youth are in the streets agitating for "rights." But they too, are lost. But for them there is a crisis in religion as well as race. A vacuum is being created that cannot be filled by hamburgers at an integrated lunch counter. The Negro young person at both the high school and college levels represents one of the most critical areas for evangelistic effort in the world. From an evangelical standpoint, this field is virgin.

In the light of these insights, we must structure a more vital fellowship among Christian young people. Possibly an effective thrust could be made by — integrated — teams of young people who witness in colored and white churches and on college campuses. This should be an integrated venture to be both Christian and contemporary. Successful efforts of this kind have been used in overseas ministries, but have yet to be tried with the same diligence at home.

Speaking of diligence, I was impressed by something Dr. Donald McGavran said recently in *Christianity Today*. Addressing himself to the continuing challenge of world missions, he said:

". . . (We should) take full advantage of insights now available from the sciences concerned with man. . . . An army of scientists are discovering detailed information about the social structures of classes, tribes and castes everywhere; and the processes by which it pleased Almighty God to change societies are becoming known. Servants of Christ have the privilege of using the now known dynamics of culture change to mediate Christ to men. Missionaries regard these insights from the social sciences as particularly important in the propagation of the Gospel."

Good. Now if we are prepared to be scientific in overseas ventures, why not in Chicago, New York and Los Angeles?

We must also take the cloak of silence from this issue on every Bible college and seminary campus in America. We must expose to biblical truth and scientific knowledge every myth and fantasy that hinders communication with minority groups. We must dare to inform Christian students and workers that the Negro is a needy man, that he is fair game for the Gospel, and that he can be reached with the same dedication needed to penetrate Africa, Asia or Latin America.

We need seminars at these institutions to acquaint young people with Negro needs and views. These should include both Christian and non-Christian non-whites in lecture capacities.

There must also be greater attempts to recruit Negro youth for Christian colleges. No doubt this will involve scholarship aid. These institutions must update their publications and propaganda. Christian publications as a whole perpetuate the image of an all white world, unless the subject is missions, entertainment or juvenile delinquency.

There are Christian youth who happen to be Negro. Their world is narrow and confined. Their involvement and interest in world missions, understandably, is negligible. We must find these young people, their churches and pastors, and recruit them for Christian training and evangelism responsibilities.

I know I have given little attention to personal techniques in evangelism here. To me this is almost irrelevant. We talk of strategy for overseas because we have the commitment to do that job. Meanwhile, back at the ranch, we have yet to engage our wills for a determined assault on the spiritual needs of this invisible man called the Negro.

As Paul S. Rees has said: "The reshaping of our images across the lines of race and color will not take place without resistance. It is conceivable that it will not take place at all, with disaster as a consequence. In this event what will be supremely calamitous will be the failure of the Christian community in the hour when it had its chance to lead the way, to set the pace, to incarnate the truth."

NO STEREOTYPED APPROACHES
Daniel Bakhsh

One of the mightiest weapons in the hands of the Christian Church is that of personal evangelism. It not only can bring about revival, it can also sustain the spirit of revival. Winning souls keeps a Christian closer to Christ in his own daily living. Witnessing is the normal expression of the abundant life. Through personal evangelism the free world could be evangelized in this generation.

Soul winning begets soul winners. Andrew led his brother Peter to Christ, and Peter on Pentecost preached a sermon that led to the conversion of 3,000 people. Where would all Mr. Moody's wonderful work for Christ have been if he himself had not been led to the Savior through the personal work of Mr. Edward Kimball? The same experience is true of Wesley, Finney and Billy Graham who, in turn, became instruments for leading thousands of people to the Lord. The Gospels record more instances of our Savior's personal work than of his preaching.

When a teen-ager inquired of his athletic coach how to ask a girl for a date, he got this reply, "Son, there is no wrong way to do it." The same could be reverently said about methods of personal evangelism. G. Campbell Morgan is supposed to have said, "If you have a little book that tells you how to lead people to Christ, go home and burn it." The great Bible scholar took this way of underscoring the idea that no stereotyped approach can be used in leading men into fellowship with Christ. There are, however, certain principles based upon an understanding of human nature that should govern our approach. It is basically the goodness of God that leadeth to repentance, for no human effort can be effectual apart from the work of the Holy Spirit. So we must humbly admit that our methods in seeking and saving the lost are mere instruments in the hands of God.

Let us examine the methods employed by the Great Shepherd of the lost sheep in his earthly ministry, using, as a model, Christ's dealing with the woman of Samaria. Notice, in the first place, that you can do nothing until you have a person's attention. *Jesus attracted the woman's attention* (John 4:7). Jesus used non-directive therapy in dealing with her. His attitude was not judgmental. He did not start by saying, "Woman, you are a harlot and bound for hell." Instead he said, "Give me a drink," for the woman had come to draw water. Jesus often began with the present interest of the persons he met. He showed friendliness and acceptance toward a social outcast and lonely woman. We also remember Paul's statement that he became everything to everybody for the sake of the Good News.

PROFESSOR BAKHSH is the chairman, Psychology Department, Gordon College in Rawalpindi, West Pakistan.

There is the illustration of a Christian young man who shared a room in a college hostel with a delinquent student. He shared the student's shame and disgrace but won him over to Christ. We must begin by being a friend. While in the armed forces, I used to work in the slums. I was not ashamed of greeting the people who lived there. Many responded to the Good News.

Henry Wright's approach to personal evangelism through "Expert Friendship" was tested and proved in his relationships with college students and men in the army. Recent psychological research studies in counseling have proved that the procedures and techniques of a counselor are less important than is his acceptant attitude toward his counselees. The same is true in our personal work. Of course we ought not compromise in friendship to the extent of evading the real issue.

Jesus arrested her mind (John 4:9-12). To a thirsty soul, Jesus talked about "living water." This aroused the woman's curiosity so that she wanted to know what it was and how to get it. Jesus probed her mind to secure active mental participation. He established psychological "rapport," a necessary step in soul winning.

An unregenerate person is a diseased person who needs the therapy of the Gospel to heal his soul. We should remember that if action results purely from emotional arousal without any mental or intellectual support, an individual may reject or reverse whatever decision he makes. Gaining consent of the mind is an indispensible step in personal work. The Gospel makes sense; that is why we read, "Paul reasoned." Our big concern must be to find a common ground for a meeting of minds.

Jesus appealed to her restlessness (John 4:13-14). Notice the Master's method. Jesus appealed to the woman's basic need. She desperately needed inward peace. She had tried to fill the void of her soul through worldly pleasure but this had made her all the more miserable. A sense of guilt weighed heavily upon her. Jesus offered her eternal life and abiding peace of mind. A ship without an anchor tosses like a cork on the angry waves. We must discover the basic need of our counselees and cater to that need. We have seen, then, that Jesus' method in dealing with the woman of Samaria was to attract her attention, arrest her mind and appeal to her restlessness. But something deeper needed to be done so *Jesus aroused her conscience* (John 4:15-18). One of the effects of sin is to harden or deaden the conscience toward spiritual things. Jesus said, "Go, call thy husband." The dialogue made her see her wicked past and moral laxity. Jesus invariably put his finger on the root of a malady. To the rich young ruler he said, "Do you know the commandments?" To Nicodemus his abrupt reply was, "Ye must be born again," and to Zaccheus, "Come down, for today I must abide at thy house." These phrases have diagnostic value. The conscience of man is the candle of the Lord. We need to awaken it and set it aglow with the Word of God and let people look within.

An old college mate came to my city on business and stayed at my home. I availed myself of the opportunity and started praising God for how he brought me out of the miry clay. I noticed tears rolling down my friend's cheeks and he cried, "But I am still rolling in the mire of sin. How can I be delivered?"

I led him to the Lord, and he left me rejoicing in the joy of salvation. As I related my past life, my friend saw his own vicariously. His conscience was awakened to his basic need.

Jesus gave her soul assurance (John 4:19-26). The woman was looking for the Messiah who could tell them all things. Jesus' words, "I am He" gave her full assurance. In the person of Jesus Christ the woman found the answer to her longing and weary soul. She ran to the city to share the good news, "Come, see a man who told me all things that ever I did: is not this the Christ?" The twentieth century is an age of insecurity, perplexity, and anxiety and the modern man needs assurance. Bring him face to face with Jesus Christ, our Blessed Assurance.

Personal work includes four steps: contact, cultivation, commitment and conservation. It is a developmental process which must be built step by step as Jesus did, in order to involve the total man — his awareness, his mental processes, his conflicts and complexes, his moral and spiritual insight.

What far-reaching consequences issued from this simple talk with the woman at the well! In the first place, a local revival came to her village. Many believed that Christ was the Savior of the world; later after the Lord had shed his blood and had poured out his Holy Spirit and had formed the infant Church, we read of revival in Samaria. The ground had been prepared, for we read that the Lord "must needs go through Samaria." Why? To reach the one seemingly unlikely person who would be the key to the whole situation that resulted in many believers at that time and in revival later in the whole area (Acts 8:5, 6). Dear brethren, each day we rub shoulders with similar key lives. Let us be awake to our responsibility and set off what may become far reaching movements for bringing others into the kingdom of God.

Personal evangelism is extremely delicate work. It is the most strategic and important task in the world. It can hasten the second coming of Christ by helping fulfill the Great Commission. If each believer takes personal evangelism seriously, we can revolutionize the entire world. The early Church took this responsibility seriously; let us not be found lagging behind.

CAUTION IN THE USE OF TECHNIQUES
Ross F. Hidy

First, let me offer a word of caution about methods or techniques. Any study of methods runs the risk of viewing the winning of souls to faith in Christ as something man achieves by his cleverness or by his skill in evangelistic procedures. Evangelism is God's work, the mysterious working of the Holy Spirit. We witness; God wins! Luther expressed this so very well in his explanation of the Apostles' Creed; "I believe that I cannot by my own reason or strength believe in Jesus Christ my Lord or come to him; but the Holy Ghost has called me through the gospel, enlightened me by his gifts, and sanctified and preserved me in the true faith; in like manner as he calls, gathers, enlightens, and sanctifies the whole Christian Church on earth, and preserves it in union with Jesus Christ in the true faith; in which Christian Church he daily forgives me abundantly all my sins and the sins of all believers, and will raise up me and all the dead at the last day, and will grant everlasting life to me and to all who believe in Christ." (You will pardon my reading this classic quotation from Martin Luther, but for a Congress on Evangelism in Berlin this gem of distilled Scripture brings into focus much that I wish to emphasize.)

Notice that this testimony reminds us that the fruit of evangelism — the coming of a person to faith upon hearing the Gospel and being led by the Spirit — is the work of God. Scripture evidence for this abounds (cf. John 15:26 or II Timothy 1:8, 9, "but take your share of suffering for the gospel in the power of God, who saved us and called us with a holy calling, not in virtue of our works but in virtue of his own purpose and the grace which he gave us in Christ Jesus ages ago . . ."). Again and again let us remind each other to trust in the promises of God and to be faithful in preaching the Word . . . by every means to every man everywhere, in our time and in his strength.

Christians knew well what they were doing when the classic outline of Scripture truths took form in the Apostles' Creed, a summary of Bible teaching to instruct new believers in God's Word and God's work as Creator, Redeemer and Sanctifier: God the Father and Creator, Christ the Son, Savior and Lord, and God the Spirit, Sanctifier and Strengthener. In this little cluster of words a new believer may praise and thank God and find comfort and hope in this Scriptural shorthand which quickly spans the pages of Scripture — all with the wondrous words of confession, "I believe!" If much of the difficulty in evangelism is in our work of guiding new believers to know the promises of God's Word, perhaps we have failed at times

THE REV. MR. HIDY is pastor of St. Mark's Lutheran Church in San Francisco, California.

to use these historic resources to give them a running start on the key promises of God's Word.

My major concern about evangelism today is that kind of evangelism which leads people to the altar of decision but does not follow through. What tragedy! Remember the classic sermon about the lost sheep in Luke 15 — four wonderful words of action and concern! What to do about the lost soul? "Find him! Fetch him! Feed him! Fold him!" If genuine love motivates the evangelist, he will be as fully concerned with the new believer's growth in grace as with his coming to know that wondrous grace of God in Christ.

We deal with *people*, not statistics. We dare not become mechanical. In one congregation a successful automobile salesman became interested in evangelism. He felt I needed guidance and organization to win more people to the faith and into the Church. He outlined a procedure, a kind of Christian sales campaign. After listening to his plan I had to remind him of one simple fact. When people bought his cars he had no further contact with them, for the service department then took over. But when a person believes in Christ, often that is the time when more and more demands are made upon a minister for guidance and counseling. As Christians we cannot compartmentalize our Christian work; we deal in sales *and* service. We work with burdened, fearful, weak people, not with automobiles.

Mechanical training in evangelism will prove fruitless. Non-believers want to see Christ's people filled with love. I remember a specific example from the follow-up to the Graham Crusade in San Francisco. Hundreds of Churches were cooperating in a follow-up visitation of those who had come forward. We had morning meetings of ministers, and at night lay people made calls. One minister shared a perplexing problem. His people had been very well-trained in the Scriptures for calling on those who visited their Church. They were taught how to enter homes and how to use the Bible to describe the way of salvation. They visited diligently and followed "the plan." But for some reason those who were visited did not attend the church services. What could be wrong? Eventually one thing changed the results for these callers. As a part of their training for post-Crusade visitation, they were encouraged not only to bear their witness, but also to show genuine interest in the people being visited. They were taught to listen, to become acquainted with the people and their needs, their work and their children. In each home each caller was encouraged to ask specifically, "Is there anything we may do for you? " This change of approach brought a great change in response. Perhaps earlier visits had been "preachy" or super-pious. Perhaps some had not been trained to express their sincere concern. It is not enough to be "saved from sin"; we must be "saved to love." We must emphasize I John as well as John 3:16.

My second major concern may seem controversial, but when understood, it is truly an endorsement of evangelism. Evangelism is always in danger of being given a place out of proportion to the total concerns of Christian faith. Evangelism is the first work of the Church but not its only work. And seen properly, everything that a congregation does has a relationship to evangelism.

Let us come back to those four phrases of evangelism found in Luke 15: *"Find* that lost sheep!" *"Fetch* him!" *"Feed* him!" *"Fold* him!" This is our task as under-shepherds of the Good Shepherd, and no single one of the four commands is enough. What implication each word has for our task! The worst tragedy that can befall a child of God is to lose love for his brother — like the pitiful elder brother in the story of the prodigal son. The fellowship of the faith must ever be the fellowship of sacrifice. The Christian faith is confessed not only with words but with a life. Pressures will always come. There are those who may suggest modifying the Gospel to fit the situation. Actually when the Gospel truly transforms people, it can also change the situation. Does the Gospel speak to situations or to people? All of us here represent different continents but one Christ. Christ binds us into a spiritual brotherhood. Unfortunately, there are those in this world who would divide this family of God. When that happens we must boldly speak the will of the Father as shown in his Word. Tension may swell the roll of martyrs and add new names to the saints in glory. Each tradition reveres those of its members who spilled their blood for the faith. In certain tragic chapters of history when men glorified man and not God, and debased their brothers by not claiming them as brothers, there were godly men who did great things for God. Let us not present a weak Christ whose people can hear anything, believe anything, watch anything, accept anything and be silent. To be called to Christ is to be called to discipleship. As Dietrich Bonhoeffer said so well, "Salvation without discipleship is 'cheap grace.'" Perhaps the Christian Church has invited people to believe without telling them the price of faith and the necessity of service. If this is so, it is no wonder that the world does not always respect the Christian Church. When the Church loses the deepest meaning of discipleship as a part of its confession of faith, perhaps this confession is not really the faith of the Christ who said, "take up your cross and follow me."

An effective secret of evangelism that we Lutherans in America have found to be important is planning special seasons of evangelistic outreach. No one can do everything all of the time. We have found that some seasons are wisely used to reach out in personal concern for those not a part of the Christian faith. In those times we seek, and often with very careful organization, to reach the unreached — the unbeliever, the unbaptized, the inactive. (To reach the inactive Christian who is not coming to worship, studying God's Word or receiving communion is no less a concern than to reach the one who has never been a part of the Church). We seek out these people, encourage them to come to study the Word of God, then to make a decision for Christian discipleship within the family of the Christian Church. By setting aside specific times for this the entire year becomes organized. Other seasons — for us periods like Advent and Christmas, and especially Lent — become times to let the devotional life of the believer find new strength in the love of God which sent the Savior. Or we may review the life of Christ, a study that becomes an effective call to renewal and can easily become a call to renewed concern for those outside the faith.

Evangelism ought to be natural for the Christian. I wish I could say that evangelism is natural for Lutherans, but in truth it often has not been so. Lutherans are often more active in sanctifying the saints than in winning people outside the Church and outside the faith. This is all the more reason for having periodic times of evangelism that are specifically directed to winning those outside the Christian faith. Such a challenge often warms the heart of the believer and rekindles the devotion or deepens the faith of Christians.

Each week we ought to challenge each Christian in our pastoral care to rededicate himself to Christ; in fact, this is asked in the confessional service that opens each worship service. Does our lack of evangelistic concern indicate that we are forgetting that each of us needs the daily grace of God's forgiveness, that as sinning believers we ever need the forgiving love of God? In the mystery of Scripture we are at once forgiven yet in need of forgiveness. As Luther said we are "simul iustus et peccator," at once justified and sinning, so that we may avoid the deep pit of pride.

Only the forgiven sinner will speak of the joy of being forgiven. Perhaps the lack of this awareness may be the lost note in the Christian's song. Is this why the Church is not an evangelizing Church? Let us sing the joyful songs of salvation! Our infectious enthusiasm will once again rouse the people of God to their most sacred Christ-given task, to win others to the joy of serving him who is the Lord and Savior of the world!

MAN-TO-MAN EVANGELISM BY BUSINESSMEN

Dirk van Katwijk

My experience across the years in man-to-man evangelism can be summarized by a few very important spiritual considerations. There must be: preparation, a sense of adventure, expectation, and obedient action.

1. Preparation

To succeed in business requires sound and careful preparation in every detail. As businessmen we usually have in mind a specific goal, namely, *profit*. To reach this goal requires a great deal of planning. And we invest our time and money as well. Certainly as Christians, as evangelists, as soulwinners for the Lord Jesus Christ, we ought to give as much preparation, time and spiritual sacrifice to reach our holy objective of fruit bearing, more particularly, of winning souls for Jesus Christ.

Preparation for this venture involves:

a. Realization of who and what we are: Sons of God, the body of Christ, powerful and almighty instruments in and through Christ. Again and again I have experienced the encouragement of knowing who I am. There is no reason for us to live and to act like poor, weak, deserted creatures. I often quote from Joshua 1: "Every place that the sole of your foot shall tread upon, that have I given you . . . I will not fail thee, nor forsake thee. . . . Have not I commanded thee? Be strong and of good courage; be not afraid, neither be thou dismayed: for the Lord thy God is with thee whithersoever thou goest."

Another significant passage is Ephesians 1:3: "Blessed be the God and Father of our Lord Jesus Christ, who hath blessed us with all spiritual blessings in heavenly places in Christ."

A part of daily preparation is to realize that these promises of a Holy God, who is still the same God and will be in all eternity, are really true for me and can be accepted in faith for that particular day.

b. Prayer. Every Monday morning for at least 6 years a group of business friends have gathered in my home at 7 o'clock. After a short meditation from the Word of God we spend an hour in prayer; regularly, the subject of soulwinning is brought before the throne of God.

If one of the men is going on a business trip, the group prays that God will provide opportunities to witness to people even on trains and planes. Private prayer is also necessary preparation for each day.

MR. VAN KATWIJK resides in Velp-Gelderland, Holland, and is president of van Katwijk's Industries N.V. in Aalten, Holland.

We need to pray for cleansing by the blood of the Lamb, for protection from evil (John 17:15), for willingness to yield more fully to the Holy Spirit instead of asking for more of the Holy Spirit; this is a very important spiritual secret. We need to pray for open eyes and ears for Spirit-given, not self-made, opportunities. We need to pray for love, that is for patience in listening, for understanding, for open-ness of heart. We need to pray for the glory of Jesus and for the enlargement of his kingdom.

Our prayers should be in the name of Jesus, according to his will, in faith, and persistent.

2. A sense of adventure

Each day we live, I think we must realize that as the body of Christ we are our heavenly King's representatives and ambassadors here on earth. We have been included in his plan of liberation. We have been armed for that purpose. This is a tremendous holy adventure that is new and thrilling every day. Am I willing to present myself to the Lord as a participant in this spiritual adventure?

3. Expectation

When we hunt or fish or do business, we are in a tension of expectation all the time. We are ready to shoot, ready to cast, ready to book an order. Results would be poor if we did not believe there were rabbits in the fields, or fish in the lakes, or customers in need of our products. And results would be poor, if we did not give full attention to the matter at hand.

The same is true in man-to-man evangelism. After proper preparation for my spiritual adventure, I must be assured that Christ has indeed chosen me to be a *fisher of men*, and I must believe there are many people around who are in need of Christ. I must believe that Christ is seeking the lost, that he loves them and died for them. If I believe this, then I can enter upon his adventure with a holy expectation that "the fish" may appear and be caught and that they will come because of his Grace. The constant question for me is: Am I ready and attentive? Do I expect them?

4. Obedient action

As a businessman I must always be aware of my competitors, just as a soldier must be aware of his enemy. Both situations require alertness and prompt decision. Lack of attention, indecision, or hesitation can be fatal. The same is true in man-to-man evangelism.

If I understand what it means to walk with the Lord even as Enoch did and as Paul recommends in Col. 2:6, then I will not walk nor run ahead of him nor lag behind. I will walk step by step at his side.

Because it is he who saves and who uses me as an instrument, I must be very attentive to his commands and concerned about the opportunities he gives me. We are aware that a battle is raging in high places against spiritual wickedness and against the rulers of the darkness of this world (Eph. 6:12-17). Much effort will be exerted by these powers to keep souls in darkness and to prevent their turning to Christ the light. So I must *stand*, having my loins girded with truth and having on the breastplate and other parts of defensive armor mentioned by Paul, realizing that as long as I *stand* there may be joy in heaven for a sinner who turns to Christ. On the other hand, the regions of the demons will roar over one believer whose knees buckled because of inattention or lack of discipline.

Prompt response to the opportunities given by God means immediate use of the only offensive weapon God has given us, the Sword of the Spirit which is the Word of God.

For this reason I never go on a business trip or to foreign countries without taking this sword with me, not only in my own language but also in the language of the country to which I am going. If the Lord brings me in contact with someone there and gives me the opportunity to discuss the Bible, I can then give this person a Bible and minister to him in his own language.

Report of Group Discussion

Ross Hidy (USA) was emphatic that no rigid techniques or methods can be laid down, because every situation is different and calls for an approach or technique geared accordingly. He perceived a real danger in hunting for the "neat answer" or the "fixed technique."

Some discussion followed on the place of the mind in a conversion experience. How far should we make a mental appeal in personal evangelism? Bakhsh (India) pointed out that Jesus seemed to appeal to all the human faculties.

Later in the discussion David Clark (Jamaica) asked Bill Pannell, a Negro panelist, if he felt a barrier to exist when he tried to witness to whites. Pannell (USA) said that this was often true but that he found it could be overcome when he made the attempt to win the other man's respect as the first stepping stone to winning his affection.

Moomaw (USA) asked Pannell what he thought of the view that you can't legislate morality or abolish prejudice by rules and regulations. Pannell considered this type of outlook an evasion of the issue by those who do not wish to face the effects of discriminating laws. "People must be released from corrupt forms, and often only law can do this," he said. Bob Harrison (USA) pointed out that laws and legislation are necessary because of human nature and should be in line with Christian principles.

Reporter: *Michael Cassidy*

COMPASSION IN PERSONAL EVANGELISM

Isaac H. A. Ababio

Compassion is the very expression of God's love toward a dying world. It is that which drew salvation's plan and brought Christ down to die to save this wicked, sinful world.

To the soul-winner, compassion means sowing the Word "in tears." For "They that sow in tears shall reap in joy" (Ps. 126:5). It makes him wish even to die for the lost. By it Moses could plead, "Oh, this people have sinned a great sin and have made them gods of gold. Yet now, if thou wilt forgive their sin —; if not, blot me, I pray thee, out of thy book which thou has written" (Exodus 32:32). By it Jeremiah could cry, "Oh that my head were waters, and mine eyes a fountain of tears, that I might weep . . . for the slain . . . of my people!" (Jeremiah 9:1). Then he turns to his own people and pleads, "Hear ye, and give ear; be not proud: for the Lord hath spoken. . . . But if you will not hear it, my soul shall weep in secret places for your pride; and mine eye shall weep sore, and run down with tears, because the Lord's flock is carried away captive" (Jeremiah 13:15, 17).

How amazing it is that we have so few tears these days when there is so much to weep about. It was not so with Jesus. He saw the people as sheep having no shepherd and "had compassion on them." His compassionate heart would not let him sleep, for he must needs go into a mountain and pray all night or rise a great while before day to pray for the lost. Oh, how he wept over Christ-rejecting Jerusalem!

Of his own burden for lost sinners Paul says, "Remember, that by the space of three years I ceased not to warn every one night and day with tears" (Acts 20:31). And again, "Brethren, my heart's desire and prayer to God for Israel is, that they might be saved" (Romans 10:1). "For I could wish that myself were accursed from Christ for my brethren, my kinsmen according to the flesh" (Romans 9:3).

The personal soul-winner needs a broken heart. It is not hard to believe that "God so loved the world that he gave his Son," if those of us who tell about it have some of the same love to transform our appeal and give urgency to our message. May God give us tears! I am often amazed at the callousness of my own heart.

A noted, gifted infidel had this to say of soul-winning: "Were I a religionist, did I truly, firmly, consciously believe, as millions SAY they do,

MR. ABABIO is a student of physics at the University of Science and Technology in Kumasi, Ghana.

that the knowledge and practice of religion in this life influences destiny in another, religion should be to me everything. I would esteem one soul gained for heaven worth a life of suffering. There should be neither worldly prudence nor calculating circumspection in my engrossing zeal. Earthly consequences should never stay my hand nor seal my lips. I would strive to look but on Eternity and on the immortal souls around me, soon to be everlastingly miserable or everlastingly happy."

Even the devil knows that there is wisdom in soul-winning. Yet Christians of our time can live with their wives and children, friends and co-workers for many years and never so much as dare face them with the invitation to come to Christ.

Dear Christian friend, how concerned are you for the salvation of the unsaved souls around you?

"Would you care if some friend
You had met day by day
Should never be told about Jesus?
Are you willing that he
In the judgment should say,
'No one ever told me of Jesus'?"

If we could but estimate the worth of one human soul, we would give up all of self to save it. Christ conceived the human soul to be of such transcendent value that he gladly exchanged the shining courts of glory for a life of poverty, suffering, shame and death, rather than let it perish. Placing the world and all it could offer in one scale and the human soul in the other, he declared that the scale bore far greater weight on the side of the soul. His verdict was, "For what shall it profit a man, if he shall gain the whole world, and lose his own soul? Or what shall a man give in exchange for his soul?" (Mark 8:36, 37). Yes, so costly is the soul of man that it requires not gold or silver to redeem it, but crimson drops of precious blood from the broken body of the Son of God. If then, a soul is of such surpassing value, no expense is too large, no pain too agonizing, no trouble too great, to save it, no labor too hard and no tear too costly.

The Fact of Hell

If we believe in an eternal Hell, could our eyes be dry and our hearts undisturbed, when we see so many sinners blindly drifting to an eternal doom?

Jesus said that "The worm does not die and the fire is not quenched" in Hell. Hell is a place, men are conscious there, men remember there, they cry out and beg for water, they long to warn their loved ones, "lest they come to this place of torment." The most awful fact in the world is the fact of Hell, and that some of our dearest relations and friends with whom we have lived, worked, and worshiped, will spend an eternity of anguish, away from God, eternally unforgiven, eternally doomed. If we are not wicked men, the fact of Hell should drive us to follow the Master's footsteps in "Saving, redeeming at measureless cost."

Oh, for tear-filled eyes! Oh, for sleepless eyes, because of the imminent danger and doom of the lost! Preaching sometimes fails and so does the singing, but individual concern never fails, for "He that goeth forth and weepeth, bearing precious seed, shall doubtless come again with rejoicing, bringing his sheaves with him" (Psalm 126:6). What we need is a holy compassion, given of God, and wrought in the heart by the Holy Spirit. If ever there was a time to weep over sinners, if ever there was a need to shed tears for the unsaved — pleading with broken hearts before God for their salvation — it is now. The Lord is at hand. "Let the priests, the ministers of the Lord, weep between the porch and the altar, and let them say, Spare thy people, O Lord . . ." (Joel 2:17).

EVANGELISM AND THE HOME
Mogens Larsen

Our subject is one of the most wonderful in the life and activity of the Church of Jesus Christ, for personal evangelism is for all believers, irrespective of culture, nationality, church background, education and personal talents and abilities.

If you read the Bible you will see that the home was important in evangelism. Yes, we might consider Christianity a home religion. Think of the publican Matthew (Luke 5), or Priscilla and Aquila (Acts 18), and Cornelius, the Roman centurion (Acts 10).

Today, too, the home can be used for personal evangelism. In fact, the home is the best place for presenting the Gospel of Jesus Christ to nonbelievers. There are no fixed hours to keep, and people are relaxed and removed from the worries and burdens of the day. These facts, together with hospitality, kindness, and friendliness, are advantages that make the home an effective tool in personal evangelism.

1. How to get people to visit

It might seem that this is the heart of the problem. Often, however, the reason for not doing home evangelism is that we have not taken seriously the commission Christ gave us.

The first step in visitation is to contact people. Ordinary points of contact are many. Wives talk with other wives about children, collectors share collections and use that as an entry for presenting the Gospel. Think of Philip; he used the Ethiopian eunuch's interest in the Scriptures as a point of contact.

Other contacts are more difficult, perhaps. One young couple invited their neighbors to discuss how to answer Jehovah's Witnesses when they came. What the couple actually had in mind was to present the Gospel to their friends.

In Denmark we say that love makes a person clever. This proved to be true for a young fellow who wanted to introduce Christ to other young men. He took his motor-scooter and drove past the military camp where it was easy for him to get back seat hitch-hikers. By this offer of a ride, coffee and pastry in a home, which a couple from his church put at his disposal, and by conversation about Christianity, he made the desired contacts.

Two families who knew the joy of salvation were very much concerned over the little interest people showed in going to Church. So they decided to invite everyone they knew and came in contact with to a coffee party, as coffee was hard to get after World War II, and for a talk about the

MR. LARSEN is director of Youth For Christ in Copenhagen, Denmark.

Bible. What a success! Through the years, the two families have continued these effective nights of Bible conversation and through the converts get still more new contacts.

A newly-wed young wife wanted to win the young couple at the dairy where she shopped. Using her wedding gifts as a point of contact, she soon had the young lady in her home, and a prospect for the Gospel.

Very often some of the best contacts come through casual conversation. If there is interest, the people can be invited to a home for further discussion. After selling a boat a salesman said: "Aren't you afraid to go out in the boat?" "No," said the customer, "my Father watches over me." That was the beginning. The salesman later trusted Christ in the customer's home.

These examples are very straightforward and simple, but they show that it is necessary to use natural points of contact or to create them as a point of beginning.

2. How shall we present the Gospel?

If it is hard to get people into a home for Bible talks, it is equally hard to present the Gospel so that it suits the occasion or gathering. Either a layman or pastor can give a presentation. Since this is not an ordinary meeting, the presentation should be a kind of introduction to further conversation. Often a testimony is good, something especially suitable for a layman. Visitors often feel more at home with laymen.

Another method is group discussion or conversation. This is even better because several visitors are active and take part. However, it requires Christians who can lead such a discussion and work as a team. It is good to read together from the Gospels. Then let everyone who wishes say something but under the control of the team. If it is hard to get the conversation going, then ask questions and let another member of the team answer with a further question.

These methods normally end up in person-to-person evangelism, where problems and doubts may be answered. Proper matching of visitors is important as well as being a good listener. Simple explanations can often remove the biggest questions and open hearts to the Gospel.

3. Special things to watch

It is dangerous to get sidetracked. The purpose is to present the Gospel, not just to have a social evening.

People expect the conversation to center around what the Bible teaches. Avoid arguing. It is better to lose the argument than to lose the chance of presenting the Gospel.

Use honest approbation instead of criticism and harsh judgment. Most of all, see that what you say is not merely routine. Your personal confidence in Christ should be what impresses people.

The Gospel presentation should lead to getting a personal commitment to Jesus Christ. This will follow under the Holy Spirit's working.

Door-to-door visitation is a very effective way to contact people whom you would have no possibility of reaching and is also a part of evangelism and the home.

It helps a great deal to go two-by-two. It is good to invite people to special programs and to ask questions of them. Well-written tracts are good to leave behind.

Where home visitation is a part of the Church program, it is important to record not only the name of the prospect but also the result of the visit, so that the Church can further its contact.

Evangelism and the home involves another very important factor, the matter of personal spiritual preparation. We must be saturated with the Word and in much prayer. When dealing with people face-to-face, we must remember what the Old Testament prophet said: "Not by might nor by power, but by my Spirit, saith the Lord" (Zech. 4).

FISHING PATIENTLY WITH A ROD
Josip Horak

When the disciples asked their Master about the time of his second coming, he rebuked them saying: "It is not for you to know the time. . . . But you shall receive power . . . and you shall be my witnesses. . . ." It is not our duty to calculate the time but to use the time as his witnesses. We should not use our so precious time for propagating or fighting political ideas. Our job is to proclaim the Gospel of salvation and so to hasten our Lord's return.

How grateful we are to our heavenly Master that he gave to his servants everywhere open doors of opportunity to witness for him, even as he did to the Philadelphia church. He will give us the power if we are obedient, if we are faithful in keeping his Word and do not deny his name. So in every country real believers have their opportunities even if perhaps their methods differ.

The first Christians also had their opportunities: in Jerusalem at Pentecost they held the first evangelistic crusade with the great evangelist Peter. They were unable to have many evangelistic crusades in that day, for enemies soon scattered them. But they did not cease to evangelize: they simply continued with the other kind of evangelism, namely, personal evangelism!

Evangelistic mass meetings and crusades are very useful for encouraging believers for further personal evangelism. In other words, evangelistic crusades and personal evangelism are to complement each other. While in many countries believers cannot conduct mass meetings, they are able to use certain methods of personal evangelism. In today's world, Christians in almost every country have more opportunity to witness than they had in Rome in apostolic times. The most important thing for Christians today is not merely to talk about the opportunities but to use them properly.

Many times we dispute at length about freedom of religion. We should remember that dead men do not need this freedom or other human rights. Dead Christians, nominal Christians, do not need to be given freedom of religion; many never use the wonderful privileges they have — their freedom to evangelize, their open door to witnessing.

It is true, of course, that we do not have the same opportunities for evangelism as some others of you. But we pray that God will give us wisdom to use for his glory what talents we do have!

Protestants in our country of Yugoslavia, most of them just nominal Christians, represent only one per cent of the population. A very small

DR. HORAK is a pastor and president of the Yugoslavian Baptist Convention in Zagreb, Yugoslavia.

number of real believers has far greater influence than their number would suggest.

Certainly, methods of evangelism must vary. When people have never heard the Gospel, have never seen the Bible, they must first be introduced to the basic terms in some specific way. Many methods that are highly useful in Western countries are not adequate for the present situation in many Eastern lands.

If distribution of tracts is forbidden, surely there are other opportunities for personal evangelism. If there are no opportunities to preach in the streets, we can preach in our Churches and invite our friends. If we cannot witness from house to house, we can give our testimony in the houses of our friends or in friendly everyday conversation with someone who will listen to our experience with the Lord or who asks us about our hope. If we are willing to witness, we can find an open door anywhere. If it is impossible to fish for men's souls with large nets of mass evangelism, we still have the privilege of fishing patiently with a rod! We have freedom to converse after Church services or evangelistic appeals in the Church and can talk with children in the Sunday School.

Now, thank God, we have the special opportunity of using radio for evangelism. Radio preaching offers wonderful opportunities: it is really an open door that no man can shut, an open door from the outside. We are also tremendously grateful for the generous help of Trans World Radio which sends out six weekly broadcasts in our language from Monte Carlo and Bonaire. Thus many can be reached who never heard the Gospel and who without radio could not be reached at all for various reasons: believers may be few in number, for example, or unbelievers may be afraid to contact believers directly. But by means of radio such persons are able to hear the Good News in the privacy of their homes. Radio preaching, in fact, is a kind of personal evangelism. Speaking by radio one does not speak to crowds, but—perhaps with some exceptions—speaks heart-to-heart to individual souls.

Many letters we receive from radio listeners tell of their personal experience with the Lord.

Another wonderful opportunity for personal evangelism is through records. Sometimes believers who lack courage to witness will invite friends to their homes to hear Gospel messages and songs on records. We have had some wonderful experiences in our country with records, records made with the kind help of Gospel Recordings, Incorporated, of Los Angeles and distributed by H. Schulte of Wetzlar, Germany.

Let us remember then, that when our Lord sends us out to witness for him, he does not send us out against a wall. Rather, he gives us an open door for personal evangelism, an open door that no man can shut.

THE MINISTRY OF LETTERS AND TRACTS

Doan van Mieng

In every age and every place personal evangelism is the Church's most effective means of bringing sinners to the Lord. Every Christian should know the methods of personal evangelism and should employ them thoroughly throughout his lifetime.

The Lord Jesus was very zealous in practicing personal evangelism. As he walked on the shores of Galilee he called Peter and Andrew, John and James; he dealt by the hour with Nicodemus and the woman of Samaria.

The disciples followed the Lord's example and also practiced personal evangelism. Philip dealt with the Ethiopian eunuch, Peter with the family of Cornelius, Ananias with Saul; the scattered Christians went everywhere bringing the Gospel to many people.

No Christian is exempt from the responsibility of personal evangelism. Anyone who is truly saved cannot sit quietly with lips sealed and let sinners around him go to the place of everlasting destruction. Practicing personal evangelism will bring blessing to the believer, salvation to the sinner, and glory to the name of the Lord.

Let me present several methods of personal evangelism:

Writing Letters. Everyone of us has relatives and friends, many of whom live far away and whom we seldom see. We can use the method of letter-writing to bring the Gospel to them. By skillful letter-writing we can gain their affection; they will then be willing to read what we have to say about the Lord, and we can thus lead them to the Savior. In the past and even today, many people have been saved by reading letters from relatives and friends.

I think of a Christian whose work took him to a distant country. Once a month he wrote a letter to his relatives and friends at home, every letter being a short sermon that urged them to believe on the Lord. As a result, some of these people were saved.

We can also write to people in our city letters that speak of the Lord and that invite them to come to Church to hear the preaching.

Paul certainly used letters as a method of personal evangelism, and reaped great results. Sinners were saved and Churches were established through his letters. Moreover, these letters were effective not only in Paul's day, but are helpful to readers even today, after almost twenty centuries.

THE REV. MR. VAN MIENG is president of The Evangelical Church of Vietnam in Saigon, South Vietnam.

Tract Distribution. Distributing tracts to those who have not yet believed in Christ is not hard and is something that everyone can do.

Many people have no time to attend Church, or if they do, perhaps they nonetheless stay away for one reason or another, even though they want to know about the Lord. There are not enough people nor is there enough time to deal with such persons individually. But we can give them a well-chosen tract to read. This method of personal evangelism is convenient for both the worker and his prospects. Practical experience in Vietnam as well as in many other countries has shown that the distribution of tracts brings excellent results.

A certain preacher went down to the docks to distribute tracts. Just as one of the ships was about to pull away, a passenger ran down the gangplank. The preacher had just enough time to hand him a tract. Three years later the minister met this same passenger, who was a zealous Christian. Because of the tract he sought out a Church and was lead to believe on the Lord.

One day while driving his car, a missionary saw a group of people standing at the side of the road. He stopped his car and handed every one a tract. Among those people was a young man who read the tract, was moved by it, went to the pastor of the Church in his area, and found the Lord. Today that young man is a pastor of the Evangelical Church of Vietnam.

A man walking along the road noticed a little pamphlet someone had dropped. Not knowing what it was he picked it up and discovered it was a Gospel tract. After reading it he was so moved that he went to a Church and asked to follow the Lord. There are hundreds of similar incidents that attest to the value of tract distribution. Obviously we need many, many religious books, but we also need tracts for those who have not yet believed on Christ. Tracts have been instrumental in saving many souls.

Personal Contact. Working with individuals is not an easy but rather a very difficult task. For this reason only a few persons seem to engage in this method, and among the few who do, even less see results.

Let me suggest a few requirements for dealing with individuals.

One must be keen-minded. If we want to evangelize someone we must carefully study that person — note if he is young or old, to what strata of society he belongs, how educated he is. Although our estimate may not be one hundred per cent correct, at least it will be partly so and will help us use the right approach in speaking to him about the Lord. A fisherman, for instance, does not use just one kind of fishhook and one kind of bait for every kind of fish. Rather, he selects the hook and suitable bait for each different kind of fish.

There is only one way of salvation, but to bring that salvation to every person, each with different standards, different personalities, and different positions, requires the use of different approaches. When Philip met the Ethiopian eunuch who was reading Isaiah 53, Philip simply asked, "Do you understand what you are reading?" When Jesus began dealing with the woman of Samaria who had come to the well to draw water, he said, "Give me to drink." When Paul presented the Gospel to the Jew, he did so differently than when he presented it to the Greek. To the Church at Corinth he said, "I used guile to catch you" (cf. 2 Cor. 12:16).

One must use the Bible. When Philip met the Ethiopian eunuch he "opened his mouth, and beginning at the place in the Scriptures, preached to him about the Lord Jesus."

There are those who think that the witness of a good life is enough, that no further witness is necessary. This point of view is wrong, for no matter how good a person's conduct may be, the spoken word of witness is still needed to lead a soul to Christ. The Christian who says, "If I have good conduct I don't need to add my word of witness," is simply trying to run away from responsibility to witness. Surely our Lord lived a better life than anyone, but even he added to it the word of grace of God's love to all men. To rely only on good behavior without speaking about the Lord may unintentionally cause others to think that our good behavior is of ourselves and not of the grace of the Lord working in us; thus they will praise us and will not glorify the Lord.

We have the responsibility for telling everyone about the beauty and work of Jesus Christ. We are not to urge people to believe a religious dogma, receive a theological concept or join a church; our message is an invitation to leave their sins and return to the living God and receive Jesus Christ as Savior.

If we want to speak to others about Christ then we must know who Christ is. If we do not know him then we cannot introduce him to others. In Christ's day the disciples introduced Christ to everyone for they had lived with him and knew him. Therefore those who heard them believed their words of witness.

We must also know the Bible and believe the Bible. We must believe that God will use his Word to convict, teach and move the sinner and we must use the Bible in personal evangelism. In dealing with people we must ask questions that encourage them to think and talk. And we must be ready to listen, for by listening we learn a great deal about personality, ways of thinking, and so on. Listening is as important as speaking when we witness. For if we have not listened sufficiently, our witnessing may not meet a person's particular need or situation, and we may not be able to lead him to the Lord. If we take time to listen to our prospect, then he will listen to us; our conversation will be intimate and one of mutual understanding. This makes the matter of leading him to the Lord far easier.

We must have a heart of love, for this may determine our success or failure in evangelism. Moses, Jeremiah, and Paul wept out of love for their fellowmen. Jesus wept over Jerusalem; when he saw the multitudes he was moved with compassion.

We must also have a heart of patience. We seldom achieve results after but one or two times of witnessing: sometimes we must witness a hundred times! Nor should we witness only occasionally or at one period of our lives; all our lives through we must be engaged in personal evangelism. Coupled always with intercession, our labors must never cease; we must continue in perseverance and patience in the work of bringing lost souls to Christ.

Report of Group Discussion

Speakers on the methods of evangelism pointed to the opportunities of group literacy classes for reaching the masses of people in underdeveloped countries. Half of the world is hungry, and people are largely hungry because they are illiterate, delegates observed. To assist people in this way is to create a receptivity to the Gospel which can never be presupposed as a background for mass campaign evangelism.

Delegates also expressed concern for an evident lack of evangelical zeal within the churches. People need to be motivated. Many felt that this situation could be helped by teaching believers the mechanics of witnessing, how to witness. The pamphlet "Four Spiritual Laws" published by Campus Crusade was pointed out as helpful. Dr. Halverson drew attention to the fact that it is the nature of the Church to witness.

Too often Christians hide behind political, economic and social problems as an excuse not to witness, said one delegate. "If there is a willingness in our hearts, it can be done," he said.

Reporter: *Samuel Wolgemuth*

WIN THEM BY FAMILIES
Roy N. Oshiro

How much impact do the Church and Christians make upon our communities? When we have preached, "Come ye out from among them and be ye separate," some have indeed come out. They have come only a few at a time, but they have come out. This has often meant separation to such an extent, however, that many of these Christians have been unable to exert an effective, positive witness for Christ. Many have become negativistic Christians, withdrawing from society, and passive in their participation. Families often look upon Christians as a group of misguided, queer, uncertain, lone individuals who shirk their responsibilities in the family and who contribute nothing vital to their society. It was Christ who said, you remember, "I pray not that thou shouldest take them out of the world, but that thou shouldest keep them from evil."

In the Orient, an individual exists not for himself but for the family. He thinks of himself, not as a solitary, independent unit, but as an integral part of a system in which he plays an important part. He is part of the group and has a definite position in it. He is recognized for what he is and is expected to fulfill his role. For him to make his own decisions – such as the selection of a school, an occupation, or a wife – is practically unheard of. In many cases he would not even want to. The family's approval is important, for without it, he would lose his position, his place, his rights, his security. Since childhood he has been taught to consult the family; decisions were made together with the members of the family and with their backing. He was secure in the knowledge that they would stand by him no matter what happened. In other words, these family members think together, they suffer together, they even die together.

The family in the Orient consists not only of the immediate family, but also of persons so distantly related that other cultures would not consider them relatives at all. This leads to the clan system in which a common ancestor holds together relatives who may actually be several generations apart. Underlying this whole rigid structure of the family system, or closely interwoven with it, is ancestor worship which regulates many of the family's activities, and also its socio-economic pattern. The worship of ancestors is a cementing force that holds many relatives together. In every line the oldest son becomes a much respected person in the household inasmuch as he is responsible for carrying on the family line. Second sons, third sons, and so on, even though they will initiate new family lines of their own, are nonetheless still responsible to the oldest son because they must go to

THE REV. MR. OSHIRO is a missionary with the Far Eastern Gospel Crusade on Okinawa.

his home to worship the deceased father. This father, however, might have been a second son; in this case he and his children, grandchildren and so on down the line will go to the house of his oldest brother to worship his father. Take this pattern, say, for five generations, and you begin to see the structure of the Okinawan family. It is the relatives who steer and control individuals within a family. The individual family members find security in this, they would not want to be outside this system. They take their places willingly and do not begrudge the oldest son his favorable position.

It is almost impossible for the Church to penetrate this closely knit family system; Satan and his hosts have a definite foothold therein and control every possible entrance. Aware, in our spiritual warfare, that the battle is not ours but the Lord's, we suggest the following concrete methods of operation.

1. Pray for the new converts! The salvation of an individual, a miracle in itself, has already gained for us an entrance into the family and into Satan's territory. While we are not in very far, we have at least managed to get our foot in!

2. Pray for the individual's family and pray with the individual Christian for his family. He will be deeply grateful and will be strengthened.

3. Place the family on a specific prospect list. This is important in order to know what one is doing. Too often we expect to win the families but our thinking is so vague that we are not too sure which ones we are trying to reach. Without a prospect list, our work and our effort will not be as definite as it should be. Much of our haphazard work results from indefiniteness and also explains much of our hit or miss approach.

4. These families should be visited from time to time; any occasion for a visit — illness, birth, death, etc. — should be utilized to show sincere interest and concern. Very few families will object to special prayer in their behalf.

5. These families should be prayed for by name in the Church prayer meetings. This remembrance will give a feeling of kinship to other family groups. It also provides a substitute family for the one who has become socially orphaned because of his faith in Christ and makes him a vital part of a spiritual family. How often, however, our Churches fail to provide a warm, spiritual and friendly family atmosphere!

6. Church members should call upon different families. In this the missionary must take the initiative, for how else can he direct the laymen?

7. Perhaps the most difficult person to win is a second person in a given family. When such a person is won, it becomes relatively easy to win others. Too often our Churches include only one member from a family. We must do everything possible to win a second and then even more members.

8. Although it is not primarily a place for social gatherings, the Church has a special opportunity on such occasions to invite entire families to the Church.

9. Sunday School work must not be a separate entity in itself. Most of our spiritual teaching will be uprooted by heathen customs and festivals unless Sunday School teachers establish some contact with the families and make definite efforts to win them.

10. If we are to win individuals and their families, then the cottage meeting is perhaps the best method for reaching them next to visitation. Relatives and neighborhood friends who might not come to a church will come to a meeting in a home. Not only does the cottage meeting make it possible for the Church to reach new people, but it also gives families definite responsibilities "to go and seek that which was lost."

Most of us have tried all these methods in one form or another. Why then have we not seen more fruit? As far as we ourselves are concerned, we realize that we were not specific in our goals or prospects. We were haphazard in our methods, and we did not persevere. Definiteness, perseverance and persistence are essential if we are to see the Lord win the families and build his Church.

EMPOWERED BY THE HOLY SPIRIT

Thomas Cosmades

In approaching the topic of personal evangelism, we must consider our *Great Advocate* and our *great adversary*. Our Advocate is the Holy Spirit of the Living God (Acts 1:8). Our adversary is that old serpent, the devil (I Peter 5:8).

The Scriptures state very clearly that the Spirit gives life (John 6:63), whereas Satan binds (Luke 13:16, Acts 10:38). The Spirit is the source of all truth (John 15:26, 16:13); Satan is the father of all lies (John 8:44, Acts 5:3). The Spirit conveys the Word of God (I Thess. 1:5); Satan takes away the Word of God (Mark 4:15). The Spirit desires to set apart the messengers for himself (Acts 13:2); Satan desires to sift the messengers like wheat (Luke 22:31). The Spirit sends forth (Acts 13:4); Satan hinders the outreach of the workers (I Thess. 2:18). The Spirit gives utterance (Acts 2:4); Satan contends against the messenger (Jude 9). The Spirit illumines (John 16:8); Satan blinds the hearts and minds of unbelievers (II Cor. 4:4). The Spirit liberates from the power of sin and death (Romans 8:2); Satan had the power of death (Heb. 2:14).

Ever since the Church of Jesus Christ started spreading abroad in the world, all that has been accomplished has been done in the power and energy of the Holy Spirit. All that has fallen short of accomplishment has been caused in one way or in another by the intervention of Satan.

The Method of the Advocate. In our efforts of personal evangelism, we need to experience personally the Person and power of the Holy Spirit. For the early Christians witnessing was the normal course; no particular pressure was placed upon them. The Holy Spirit alone induced them to witness, whereas many of us today expect to be persuaded through a course on evangelism or by exhortation or by persuasive preaching. Even then, many today remain unconvinced and unmoved about witnessing.

The Strategy of the Adversary. We have a vicious adversary who is constantly on the alert to counteract the work of evangelism. The Scriptures state very plainly the fact of Satan's existence and inform us that he opposes all evangelical witness about the Lord Jesus Christ. It should be borne in mind that anyone who witnesses to the grace of God revealed in Christ is undertaking a direct assault against Satan's dominion. Therefore both he and the recipient of his testimony will be special targets of the devil's onslaught. Satan does not work haphazardly but attacks systematically. He can be crushed only in the power of the Holy Spirit. And blessed be God, the Holy Spirit is aware of Satan's techniques.

THE REV. MR. COSMADES is a missionary to Turkey, living in Athens, Greece.

The Secret of the Evangelist. A pure life, a life beyond reproach, is an absolute must in evangelism. As David states in Psalm 51:13: "Then will I teach transgressors thy ways; and sinners shall be converted unto thee." Possessing these heavenly qualities, the early Christian went out to conquer in the ministry of evangelism.

We must also bear in mind that in carrying the testimony of Christ to people *we need Holy Spirit inspired sound doctrine.* Evangelism permeated with scriptural theology is right and necessary. If, in the course of our witness, we fail clearly to include, even briefly, such subjects as God, Christ, the Holy Spirit, the condition and doom of man, and plenty of soteriology, our work has been incomplete. Only sound theology can make sound converts. Shallow believers are often the product of superficial witnessing.

Evangelism is not a spare time activity. It often requires many hours, time which should be given without complaint. The farmer spends long hours on his farm. We can do no less.

We must not apologize for our motive to win converts and to establish churches for Jesus Christ — a motive that is unpopular in many countries, and that is opposed by Satan and his servants. Our very activity is considered to be against certain national interests. In some places Satan is concentrating his opposition to evangelism through this unwarranted accusation. Those of us who deal with people that harbor preconceived notions against the Christian witness often sense the need to be extremely cautious in carrying out our work. We must be tactful in stating our message.

We need a strong faith to counteract men's misconceived notions about the purpose of our witness. Paul won converts in Caesar's palace. No doubt, he first of all was sure to remove from the minds of his hearers any erroneous thoughts they might have had about his personal motivation and the nature of his message. People who hear the witness of Christ today often wonder what our incentive could possibly be, to give our time, energy, and even financial support as we do in order to convey the message of Christ to them in spoken or written form. They imagine that we have economic, political, religious, and other motivations for doing our work.

These are certainly significant barriers that hinder the effectiveness of evangelism. One of our prime aims should be to remove these misconceptions. First we must establish personal trust and a common ground of confidence with the hearer. This can be done only in the power and sufficiency of the Holy Spirit.

An even greater struggle is initiated when a person is convinced of the validity of the Gospel and trusts Christ as his Savior. If the chief concern of Satan is to keep lives from responding to our Gospel, his next important desire is to discourage, disillusion and destroy the new believer.

Proclaiming the message and leading a person to the Savior is considerably easier than nourishing him in the faith and devotion of Jesus Christ. It certainly requires greater effort, fuller understanding, and more time. Evangelism carried on without this part of the commission is no evangelism at all. Christ reminded his disciples that after baptism they should teach the new believers to observe all that he had commanded them (Matthew 28:20). Converts in the early Church were immediately ushered into the instruction and absolute requirement of discipleship. This, too, was done in the power and wisdom of the Holy Spirit.

It would be unwise to end this paper without reference to a most vital factor in evangelism. No person should even contemplate this work without realizing the necessity of unfailing love toward every recipient of his message. Love that bears the imprint of total devotion and commitment constitutes the touchstone for effective evangelism. Anyone who is truly interested in this ministry must pass through a heavenly baptism of love.

Besides all these factors there must be a constant appeal to a Sovereign God through unfailing prayer; for all that is being carried on represents the sound biblical teaching concerning evangelism. Thus the ministry will be kept from all mechanical and methodical weight and heaviness. God has a method for every man. Only by yielding to the full authority of the Holy Spirit can one find God's method for his own life and carry it on successfully. The desired results should then be rightfully anticipated. Each of us needs to put his heart and soul as well as his whole body into this vital undertaking. The guarantee for success is given by Christ himself.

THE SOUL-WINNER'S PRAYER LIFE

Peter van Woerden

While preparing this message, my thoughts went back many years ago to one of my first experiences in personal evangelism. I was traveling along the West Coast of America and had become acquainted with a group of soul-winners there. Impressed with the courage of these people, I was humbled by my own timidity and decided to do something about it. I told myself I would go to the park near my hotel in Seattle and witness to the very first person I met. It so happened that that first person was a young lady sitting on a bench all by herself. Rather awkwardly I started telling her I had something very important to talk to her about. She gave me one furious look and then shouted: "If you don't scram, I'll call the police!" Well, that's just what I did: I scrammed!

I felt very much discouraged and thought I would never make a real soul-winner. Later I discovered, however, that there is no need for such tension in a Christian's life. As Dr. Halverson brought out in his message, what really counts is our personal relationship to the Lord Jesus Christ. When our cup runs over, some drops will naturally fall on others. When the Holy Spirit fills and directs the heart of a believer, he will lead him into natural contact with others for witnessing. I am sure that the Holy Spirit has as many methods as the personalities he creates. So, rather than stop at the methods, we must get back to the original pattern for evangelism as laid down by the Lord Jesus Christ himself before he left this earth: "Ye shall receive power," he said, "after the Holy Ghost has come upon you and ye shall be my witnesses. . . ."

I feel it should be stressed that personal evangelism is one of the most important means of spreading the Gospel because it is biblical. During the time of the early Christian Church it was the man-to-man witness which accounted for the rapid spread of the Gospel. A personal contact between Philip and the Ethiopian eunuch, for example, meant the beginning of evangelism for Ethiopia. And an informal talk to women gathered for prayer at the riverside in Philippi was the setting for a personal contact with Lydia and marked the entrance of the Gospel on European soil.

It is interesting that the apostles did not hold evangelistic campaigns in places where a Church was established. When passing through such a city, they "went to the brethren" where the meetings consisted of exhortation, of deepening the spiritual life of the Church members. Evangelism as such was the responsibility of every individual member of the body of Christ and not the object of a specialized ministry.

MR. VAN WOERDEN is a children's evangelist and a composer of sacred music in Geneva, Switzerland.

Perhaps one of the most important aspects of personal evangelism is that it permits the unbeliever to see for himself what the power of the Gospel can do in an individual. Since the development of modern technical means like printing and radio, however mightily used by the Lord, there has been the danger of losing personal contact with the outsider. Nothing can ever replace the "personal touch" of a person-to-person witness which gives that certain special impetus to the message to be transmitted. Our world is becoming more and more materialistic and materialism makes man want to "see." The question becomes: Can the world see God's presence and power in our individual lives, in our home-life, in our attitude at work, on the street?

I am sure that God still wants to confirm his Word by visible miracles. But by this I do not mean only miracles of healing and deliverance. I think that to the unbeliever in today's world a happy home life, based on the love of God, can represent as much of a miracle as anything else. I find it easy to witness to people when I can invite them over to my home and have them attend that precious moment of the day when we put our children to bed with song and story. A Christian rejoicing in the midst of suffering and sickness may speak as clearly today to the unbeliever as a miracle of healing, for which the science of medicine tries to claim some glory. Only by personal contacts can such miracles be seen by the unbeliever. Also, only through person-to-person contact can Christian love be shown, friendship given, and help be administered in time of need. These features make personal evangelism more than ever the effective means for spreading the Gospel message.

Our main subject is methods of personal evangelism. However, we find it difficult to speak about methods, since, as spiritual conditions are met, the Holy Spirit himself will guide every Christian into that method for which he is individually suited. I once heard a preacher say that the best example of an effective soul-winner is represented by the fish in the story of Jonah. First, the fish was where it should be to receive the sinner; second, once he got hold of the sinner, he did not let him go until he repented; and third, once the sinner repented, he sent him on his way to evangelize others. This is a rather unique approach to the subject, but a very good one, I think.

Instead of outlining methods, we will recall some guiding principles that are foundational to all personal evangelism. Let me mention the one I consider most important. Of greatest importance, I think, is the intercessory prayer life of the soul-winner. Whenever we confront someone with the Gospel, we launch an attack on the kingdom of darkness, on Satan's domain. This inevitably provokes a battle in the spiritual realm that centers around this person. Intercessory prayer is one of the most important weapons with which to fight and win this battle. The Apostle Paul, that great soul-winner, had a vital and unique prayer life. Throughout his letters we find expressions that reveal this phase of his life: "for this cause we do not cease to pray for you," we read, or "always in every prayer of mine for you all making request with joy," or "without ceasing making mention of you always in my prayers," and so on.

I am deeply convinced that the quality of our fruit in personal evangelism is in direct relationship to our intercessory prayer life. To all who are concerned about this aspect of their lives I suggest the reading and study of Norman Grubb's biography of Rees Howells. I personally have received great blessing from this book and have experienced for myself the truth of the principles laid down in it. I think it contains the secret underlying the effectiveness of Paul's witness. For Paul, leading people to Christ meant bringing spiritual children to birth. In I Corinthians 4:15 he says: "in Christ Jesus I have begotten you through the gospel."

There is nothing "easy" about this type of personal evangelism, and it is costly. It demands willingness to suffer, to throw one's entire concentration into this greatest of all occupations. But, oh, what reward awaits us, when we see Jesus and gather around the throne of God surrounded by those whom we have led to the Savior in our life here on earth!

FOREIGN MISSIONS EVANGELISM

James R. Graham

From the time that our Savior gave the Great Commission to his disciples, ascended to heaven, and sent the Holy Spirit, he intended that the central thrust of the message concerning him should be outward to those that have not heard.

Priority for hearing his Gospel rested not upon wealth, position, power, influence or education. Rather, it was preached to the cross-section of society wherever the message had not penetrated: "Jerusalem . . . all Judea . . . . Samaria . . . the uttermost part. . . ." The mandate of the Master as recorded in the Synoptic Gospels emphasizes "all nations" (Matt. 28:19; Luke 24:47) and "all the world" (Mark 16:15).

The clarity of the King's command was attested by the implicit obedience of the members of his cabinet; by the impulse of the Holy Spirit they were even more devoted in his absence than in his presence.

We have come to Berlin from many countries of the world to re-examine the great subject of evangelism – the proclamation of the Good News of forgiveness of sins and eternal life granted by our heavenly Father to all who put their trust in his incarnate, crucified, buried, risen, ascended and returning Son. This concern is nearest to the heart of God. Unfortunately a multitude of gimmicks and projects, for which there is tremendous promotion and vast expenditure of Christian money, are side-tracks from this main line. It would almost seem that biblical evangelism, the central job to which Christ has called us, has in many places well-nigh perished from the earth.

What the work of evangelism pre-eminently needs is men sent from God. My own concern was transmitted from missionary parents whose combined service in old China, during troublous and dangerous times, totalled more than a century. I myself have ministered in Asia almost half a century. Christ himself gave transformed lives that "remain" as the standard of evaluation of our work. The quality and/or quantity is largely determined by the messenger's personal commitment to Christ, giving due allowance, of course, to the differential of "talents" or "pounds" given by the Master (Matt. 25:14-30, Luke 19:11-26).

In former days missionaries were all evangelists, and doctors were as much evangelists in their sphere of service as were the "evangelists." Concurrent with their evangelism some of the latter operated primary and secondary schools largely for the children of converts, and training schools for national workers. There were no "specialists," no "short-term workers."

DR. GRAHAM is President of the Free China Christian College Association in Taipei, Taiwan, China.

Absent from homes and families for weeks at a time, all were directly preaching the Gospel far and wide, seeking the lost, planting Churches and instructing believers. Like the early disciples they went forth expecting danger and hardship. They had a great *sense of mission.* Going forth from many nations to many nations, they bore the precious seed of the Gospel and often, after long periods of seeming failure, returned with their sheaves, having planted Churches of believers.

Today the quality of evangelists, and consequently of evangelism, is deteriorating. This is no mere observation of a senile pessimism that delights to disparage present people and conditions over against "the good old days." Indeed, we older workers ought probably to accept our share of the blame for the deterioration, even as Daniel and Nehemiah in their prayers included themselves in the guilt of Israel's apostasy and decay (Dan. 9:3-19, Neh. 1:4-11). The fact that a World Congress on Evangelism has been called and delegates have come to Berlin from all over the world at great expense of time and money indicates a sense of need, and awareness of lack, in today's worldwide outreach of evangelism. This is true despite the fact that God has raised up in a "world that is aflame" someone whose voice has resounded with the Gospel in more countries and to more people than has that of any other evangelist in history.

Promotion, publicity, personality, politics, popularity, and even prosperity, we have in abundance. But there is a dearth of God-empowered men and women with a deep love for the Savior, unconditional commitment to him and complete indifference to their own well-being. Those who in time past have wrought great things for God have possessed a sanctified energy totally devoid of sloth. Because the "night cometh when no man can work," they utilized each full day to the limit. Of all these qualities, William Carey, who was said to have been conversant in thirty-three Indian languages, was a glowing example. "God make us such men: God give us such men!" must be our collective prayer in this Congress.

The quality and content of the message almost invariably reflect the character and texture of the messenger. If the messenger has experienced deeply the holiness of God and the exceeding sinfulness of sin, the awesomeness of eternity and the fearful destiny of unrepentant sinners, he will have little time or use for fanciful tales, philosophical flights, or human speculation. He knows that in the retrospections of eternity, either of joy or torment, such things will seem contemptible twaddle, useless at best and vicious at worst. No, the true messenger will give himself rather to things of eternal importance. He will be mindful of Solomon's words: "He that saith unto the wicked, Thou art righteous; him shall the people curse" (Prov. 24:24).

The God-sent evangelist is more concerned with pricking the consciences of the few who listen than with gaining the praise of many for his preaching. He has nothing in common with the political vote-seeker or entertainer. Nothing is more contemptible than a religious clown who cavorts between serious truth and levity.

Efficient missionary evangelism must be carried on by those who are so closely identified with the language and thought forms of the nationals that without altering the message of the Gospel they can convey it by speech and illustrations that are drawn from their hearers' way of life and are thus completely intelligible to them. In every land this has been the proven method of pioneer missionaries. The modern shortcut approach of preaching through interpreters is largely abortive of the main purpose. (World-travelers visiting the mission fields must of course address native audiences through interpreters.) To the natives the preacher or professor who speaks in his own tongue, however famous in his homeland, is just another white-faced foreigner who knows neither their language nor them.

When the old and the new methods are compared pragmatically, the old are found to be consistently better. In this Congress, called to re-examine the principles and methods of evangelism, we can only counsel a return to the old paths.

There is no mystery about the effectiveness of the Gospel message and its results. The old message of redemptive truth — God's remedy for sin in the Cross of his son, his offer of forgiveness and eternal life to all who receive him, his warning of eternal penalty to all who reject him — this message of unequivocal affirmations the Holy Spirit freights with convicting power. This is our message and hope in a hopeless world. Let us work, for the night is coming. "Behold I come quickly," said our Lord, "and my reward is with me to give to every man according as his work shall be!"

Report of Group Discussion

The Rev. R. Oshiro (Okinawa) and the Rev. T. Cosmades (Greece) presented their papers as published. Mr. Peter van Woerden (Switzerland) gave personal testimony concerning God's dealings with him during the Congress. And Dr. James R. Graham (Taiwan) dispensed with his paper as well, pleading for *alertness* to the need, *ingenuity* in establishing personal contacts, and *adaptation* to circumstances in personal evangelism.

Subsequent discussion began at the point of Oshiro's paper on evangelism through the family and was originally little more than an attempt by Westerners to appreciate a situation more or less peculiar to the Orient.

The Rev. Homer Payne (Belgium) spotlighted the place of initiative in personal evangelism. "Taking the initiative is often the means of opening the door to this type of contact," he said. He also affirmed that there are situations in Scripture that speak to the whole of human need.

The entire Greek delegation was present in this section and fully discussed the problems of family pressure following the conversion of someone in Greece. Also aired was the problem of legal action following anything interpreted as proselytism and the grave consequences when this concerns a child.

Miss Corrie ten Boom pleaded for an honest presentation of the price of discipleship in contrast to encouraging an easy Christianity. The chairman endorsed this by underscoring the need to emphasize "instant discipleship" rather than implying that this begins later with maturity in the Christian faith.

Reporter: *David Foster*

PHILOSOPHY AND METHODS OF EVANGELISM

Samuel K. Arai

In order to clarify the philosophy and methods of personal evangelism, it is advisable to define terms.

Evangelism, as I understand it, is the communication of the Gospel to non-Christians that they may receive Jesus Christ as their personal Savior and Lord. Personal evangelism deals particularly with this communication on a "person-to-person" basis. What we are to communicate is set forth by Paul in Colossians 1:27, 28. He preached Christ himself who is the hope of glory. If we preach theological dogma and doctrines rather than Christ, we are likely to create problems rather than present solutions.

That evangelism should be practiced — through various mass media, or by personal contact — is clearly indicated in the Bible. It is necessary because Christ is the author of our salvation (Matt. 28:18-20, Acts 1:8); the world is lost without Christ (John 14:6, Acts 4:12, Acts 16:9); and Christian conscience knows that this is the only way of salvation (I Cor. 9:16).

Personal evangelism is especially important because the increased population is far too great a responsibility for ministers alone. Moreover, people need to have personal dealings and relationships. Group instruction is not enough. Personal evangelism is significant also for the edification of Christians as they share in this ministry.

While there seems to be no question about the need for personal evangelism, it is sadly true that very little has been done in this area. A line seems to separate clergy and laity, and gives the impression that the ministry of evangelism is exclusively the task of the clergy. Even then, ministers are often found to be unfruitful or ineffective in this task. And since the average Christian layman is not trained in personal evangelism, the total picture in this work is not a happy one.

What can be done? To meet the demand for evangelism and to deliver the Church from its dilemma, a definite emphasis must be given to personal evangelism. This emphasis should include a realization of and reliance upon the dynamics for evangelism, namely, the power of the Person of the Holy Spirit. Moreover, Christians must be recruited for training in personal evangelism. This training should include instruction in what to present, how to present the Gospel truth, how to understand the people ministered to and finally, actual practice of personal evangelism.

THE REV. MR. ARAI is National Director of the Japan Campus Crusade for Christ in Tokyo, Japan.

In Japan it has been said that college students need a highly intellectual approach and a great many explanations of a formal kind. We dared to differ from this way of thinking and followed a method that Jesus himself preached and taught. We trained Christian students to be effective in personal evangelism and urged them to minister to their friends on campus. We have seen that students are ready to listen to the Gospel message on a personal basis. Scores have responded to Christ.

We must once again discover the necessity for personal evangelism which is so beautifully and amply recorded by John the apostle in his Gospel and was so effectively demonstrated by Jesus Christ himself.

NOT METHOD BUT MESSAGE
Hisashi Ariga

Methods of personal evangelism! Everytime I hear these words I recall a famous saying by Samuel Zwemer: "Not method but message!" This was spoken originally to warn against the social "gospel" of liberalism, but I feel that evangelicals today would do well to heed this word also. I say this not because I minimize the value of "methods," but because human technique is often overemphasized to the neglect of biblical methodology, i.e. to the neglect of the message that the Bible presents when we seek a solution to the matter.

Dr. Halverson's position paper also seems to focus on this point. I especially echo his remark, that in the early Church personal evangelism "happened" spontaneously, and that the presence of the Lord was the recurring factor in all personal evangelism.

In regard to Dr. Halverson's claim that it is "authentic Christian fellowship" that causes spontaneous evangelism, I would say that this matter of fellowship is only a part and that the Bible suggests something more comprehensive, namely, the concept of "holiness."

Needless to say, the significance of "holy living" is that it accomplishes God's purpose of evangelism on this earth. In other words, when a non-Christian sees someone living a holy life, he wonders and begins to ask questions. In this way "holy living" becomes a means of speaking God's Word to non-Christians and re-enforces it. However, much as "holy living" witnesses to the Word, it in itself cannot accomplish the task of evangelism. It is important to distinguish between witness and evangelism, and in evangelism we must press for a positive decision for Christ. Therefore, where there is "holy living," there is God's presence and also a spontaneous evangelistic attitude.

The above is what may be called a theoretical premise of personal evangelism. Actually, however, Christians expect more definite direction. Especially do they want to know what method should be adopted in this present complex age. Here the words of Roland Allen on spontaneous expansion are relevant: "Spontaneous expansion begins with the individual effort of the individual Christian to assist his fellow, when common experience, common difficulties, common toil have first brought the two together. It is this equality and community of experience which makes the one deliver his message in terms which the other can understand, and makes the hearer approach the subject with sympathy and confidence — with sympa-

MR. ARIGA is general secretary of Inter-Varsity Christian Fellowship of Japan in Tokyo.

thy because the common experience makes approach easy and natural, with confidence, because the one is accustomed to understand what the other says and expects to understand him now."

What we must learn from Allen is that method varies according to the difference in position and circumstances of each individual. Until recently such methodology was described by the term "comprehensive approach." We must remember, however, that this is what Zwemer was warning against when he said "not method but message." As Boer says, "The Gospel of which we read in the New Testament does not come to men in the form of a comprehensive approach, but in the form of a comprehensive message. The Gospel is Good News for the whole of life. The Spirit renews humanity and the natural world. He renews the life that he gave at creation. The result of his work is a new creation flowing in a new humanity, a new heavens and earth. The renewal of the Spirit is cosmic. This is the message of the Gospel."

When we realize the nature and scope of the Bible message in this sense, we realize that the weak point of personal evangelism on the part of evangelicals today lies in the incompleteness of the Church's teaching ministry. Although the Church points out the necessity of personal evangelism to lay Christians, it says almost nothing about the Bible message regarding the life situations in which we find ourselves. It may even be said that the Church is the cause of today's laxity in personal evangelism. When one realizes this, three other points in regard to Allen's comments can be stated. The founder of the Nameless Movement, Dr. M. Toyotome, calls these three "Evangelism of the heart," "Evangelism of the lips," and "Evangelism of the ears."

"Evangelism of the heart" teaches that evangelism in actual, practical life must first begin from each individual's prayer life.

"Evangelism of the lips" means the activity of sharing the Gospel and leading individuals to a personal decision for Christ. Here simple systems such as the Navigators, Campus Crusade, Robbet, etc., are helpful and good.

"Evangelism of the ears" means evangelism by disciplined listening. In many cases evangelism tends to end with just the above two stages; the personal worker does most of the talking and although he presses for a decision, yet he often does not give his listener an opportunity to make a decision. The purpose of "Evangelism of the ears" is to remedy this defect; disciplined listening to open the non-Christian's heart encourages him to reveal his fundamental problems and to realize the necessity of making a positive decision for Christ – a decision made in gratitude and joy.

For the second stage, each Church should prepare materials that are in keeping with its teachings. The third stage has not yet been taken up by evangelicals in general, and I feel a thorough study should be made of it immediately. To my mind these are the things that lay personal workers want to know. In summary, therefore, I propose that instead of trying to train proficient and to an extent semi-professional workers in these methods, churches should try so to ingrain a deeper and more basic understanding of the Bible message that congregations as a whole, and whole congregations, will take a more evangelistic attitude.

VISITATION EVANGELISM IN JAPAN
Shuichi Matsumura

When we evangelize in Japan, people do not oppose us as long as we talk about God. They even hear us sympathetically. But when the message comes around to "Jesus is Lord," many people go away. This is the same experience Paul had at Athens, an experience I believe is common to both past and present, both East and West.

Let us analyze the hindrances to Christian evangelism in Japan.

The first factor to consider is that the Japanese people, because of the influence of Buddhism, think of God pantheistically. According to pantheism, God is the "Great Life of the Universe," and the whole world, including mankind and each individual, is a phenomenon of that Great Life.

As stated in the *Shakubuku Kyoten*, the "Conversion Manual" of Soka Gakkai, "Life after death merges into the Great Life of the Universe; it cannot be found anywhere." This is the general essence of Buddhism.

According to this view, an individual has no existence, and thus death's sorrow is overcome. And there is no Almighty God to confront me, for God and I are one. Moreover, since there is no concept of sin, the Japanese people are cheerful and optimistic.

The heaven that the Japanese envision is not "this world minus sin" but "this world minus suffering." In other words, what must be absent from Paradise is not sin but suffering.

The Japanese have combined the solution to suffering with humanitarianism. In Japan, what characterizes the Communist Party, the peace movement, relief for the poor, and even evangelism is that all of them are motivated by humanitarianism.

This humanitarianism is based upon godless humanism, and like a religion, strikes a responsive chord in men's hearts and gives them a sense of peace.

Christianity is God-centered, however. It points out man's sin and does not allow him to be intoxicated with humanitarianism. Christianity teaches that man is saved only by Christ's atonement.

The second factor that hinders evangelism in Japan is the mental framework of the people. Someone has said that they live in a two-story house. On the first floor they think and feel like Japanese. On the second floor they have neatly lined up the learning of Europe from Plato to Heidegger. No stairs connect the two floors, however. New learning and ideas are constantly entering Japan, but they remain purely intellectual concerns and do

THE REV. MR. MATSUMURA is Vice President of the Baptist World Alliance and Pastor of the Tokiwadai Baptist Church in Tokyo, Japan.

not relate to real life. Consequently, the daily life of the Japanese is lived on the first floor, in conformity with old traditions and customs.

This holds true even when Christianity enters. What people learn at church exerts almost no influence on their daily lives. They are double-structured: their life in the Church and their life in society are unrelated. They study evangelism and read classic books on prayer, but they neither witness nor pray.

The third hindrance to evangelism in Japan is the factor of foreign culture and custom. Church buildings erected in Japan have foreign shapes, and are used, first, for worship services, second, for Sunday School, and third, for Wednesday prayer meetings. Evangelism centered in these church buildings has served to call people out of a pagan society (in accordance with the term *ecclesia*) and to teach and train them. A building-centered Christianity has developed, however, and in connection with this, a clergy-centered church.

Hendrik Kraemer wrote that there has been in "the doctrine of the 'universal priesthood of believers' a tendency . . . towards disinterestedness in the Church as the 'household of God'" (Eph. 2:19) (*A Theology of the Laity*, p. 95). But in Japan the tendency has been for the Church to become pastor-centered. The pastor gathers a handful of people around himself, and the Gospel is thus circumscribed by the pastor's ability; the Gospel is monopolized by a few.

A high level of seminary training and the rite of ordination have been useful for maintaining the ideal of purity of the Gospel, but they cannot produce that purity of the Gospel which is based upon God's dealing directly with souls through the Holy Spirit. Clergy-centeredness has been the result.

The fourth factor that hinders evangelism is the historical situation in the nineteenth century, when Christianity knocked on Japan's doors for the second time. Christianity brought with it Western civilization which spread among the upper, ruling class of people who were able to accept the new technical culture. This has been an important factor in Christianity's falling into a two-storied hyper-intellectualism.

Since Christianity moved from the upper class to the lower, and not vice versa, it could not really demonstrate its power. Received by only the few in the apex of the social triangle, Christianity missed the general population.

Having presented four factors that hinder the Gospel in Japan, I nevertheless believe there is a way of overcoming them. That way is through personal evangelism by visitation. Although visitation evangelism is the most difficult method for Japan, it is the answer to the needs of the Christian Church there.

First, through visitation evangelism the Church becomes believer-centered rather than pastor-centered; believers face situations in which they must answer questions personally and explain the Bible. When this happens, the help that ministers can give becomes truly relevant.

Second, the division between Church life and daily life—the so-called double structure—breaks down. When believers set out to visit in their neighborhoods and witness for Christ, they come to understand the meaning of their faith in relationship to daily life. Knowing and living become one.

There has been a tendency in Japan to choose a Church that is somewhat removed from one's own neighborhood. This is probably due to an escapist attitude; it is an effort to avoid the Church's influence in personal life. But visitation evangelism in one's own neighborhood is gradually breaking down the wall in this double structure.

Third, by visitation we can move from the upper class of the social triangle into the base; we can evangelize the masses.

Fourth, through visitation the center of evangelism shifts from the church building to the family living room. Thus the Gospel is received, not in a special mood or in a controlled atmosphere that is isolated from life, but in a setting and with the feeling of normal living.

Methods for personal evangelism are many. We must choose the method to suit the time and circumstances. But we need to remember three things for effective evangelism. First, there must be proper guidance and training. Second, there must be organization suitable for this purpose. Third, we must do away with optimistic thinking such as prevailed in the old mystery religions, and think seriously of God and eternal judgment. We must consider it an honor that the Gospel of salvation has been committed to the Church. We must set out to evangelize with deep feeling and joy.

When this is accomplished, when our awareness of God's salvation stirs us up to visitation evangelism, then the hindrances we have mentioned will be overcome, and the Church will be a strong and healthy body, fit for Christ the Head of the Church.

THE WORTH OF A SINGLE SOUL
Takesaburo Uzaki

Mass evangelism adapted to today's needs is extremely necessary. But mass evangelism without effective personal evangelism and follow-up seldom brings lasting spiritual results.

In the past twenty years God has sent a number of good evangelists to Japan and crusades have been sponsored. The harvest of souls has been comparatively small, however, the reason being, I believe, that personal work after the crusades was not adequate.

We should remember that the first work in our Lord's public ministry was personal work — personal evangelism. Jesus spent a night talking to Nicodemus, for example. And through personal work he brought the Samaritan woman to the joy of salvation. Talking to people on their level, getting to the core of their problems is an important part of personal evangelism. God's Spirit works in the heart of each person individually and in response to individual faith; only thus can God's miracle of salvation be accomplished. The more extensive mass evangelism becomes, the greater becomes the need for personal work.

Ephesians 4:11-13 points out the minister's responsibility for the souls in his charge. Calling on people in their homes is an effective and important phase of a pastor's work. Since his time and strength for home visitation are limited, however, would not the training of lay members as personal workers or soul winners help extend this ministry?

The pastor and his Church members are like a baseball team, the pastor being the coach and the members the team. The coach's responsibility is to develop a fine team, to organize, discipline, and train the members to move from one victory to another. This is the task of the pastor on the field of Gospel evangelism.

Protestants believe in the "priesthood of believers." The spirit of Methodism is that each member be a soul winner or "each one win one." All Churches need to put this idea into practice. Believers in the Early Church were filled with the Spirit and could not but witness (Acts 4:20). Today, too, those who are being used of God as his witnesses are filled with the Spirit.

Water flows from higher to lower levels. If Church members are to be filled with the Spirit, then we ministers must first receive a fresh infilling before we can lead them into this blessing. This blessing must be received by prayer and passed on in prayer. The Pentecost experience of the early Church must be repeated today if the Church is to be vigorous and win souls for Christ.

THE REV. MR. UZAKI is a bishop in the Japan Free Methodist Church, and president of Osaka Christian College and Theological School in Osaka, Japan.

In organizing Spirit-prepared volunteers for personal evangelism and house visitation, a pastor can perhaps follow some of these suggestions.

1. One evening a week volunteers can meet to study the Bible and an appropriate textbook on personal evangelism and home visitation. Then comes a time of prayer and testimony for mutual encouragement.

2. Volunteers can receive actual experience in personal work at Church. Every service can offer opportunities to put personal work into practice. Close guidance may be needed at first. From time to time the workers may meet to give a report, and the pastor may offer helpful comments.

3. Volunteers may be given responsibility for one specific seeker and his family. After being led to Christ, the young believer needs much guidance and prayer and encouragement in his newly found faith.

4. Volunteers may be asked to fill out forms regarding converts and their families. Together with the pastor, they work to lead the family members to Christ.

Volunteers for personal work should have some very specific qualifications. First and foremost they must have a personal experience of salvation. To lead another person into the joy of salvation, one must oneself have had the experience. Unfortunately, there are some people in the Church who know nothing of this experience and if the blind lead the blind, both shall surely fall into disaster.

The new birth alone is insufficient, however; the worker must be Spirit-filled. To lead someone to Christ, he must also be Spirit-cleansed and filled. While he may be able to lead a soul to Christ, he cannot love that soul nor persevere properly in working with him without the love which only the Spirit imparts. To lead a soul to Christ often requires much love and patience. Only if the soul-winner is cleansed and filled will his personality, his being, reflect the Spirit of Christ; only then can God use him fully (2 Tim. 2:20-21).

We must be so spiritually prepared that God can truly depend upon us to do his work. I am reminded of what happened seventy years ago in a little fishing village on the island of Awaji. Full of love and the Spirit, Teikichi Kawabe was doing street evangelism. Seeing a drunken gambler huddled in a blanket on this cold January night, Pastor Kawabe went to him, loved him and led him to the Lord. This drunkard fisherman became the first convert of the Japan Free Methodist Church. Through this first convert many who did not know the Lord were saved.

The Lord needs prayer warriors, those who love men's souls and will bear the burden of prayer (Rom. 9:1-3). It is through the work of the Spirit that souls are born again. All human efforts and zeal are in vain unless the Spirit causes a sinner to open his heart and mind to accept the Gospel. Intercessory prayer is therefore very essential, for the Spirit works where prayer prevails. Work and prayer go hand in hand.

In Japan out of every 1,000 believers there ought to be at least ten per cent who would dedicate themselves as personal workers. If we could get such a percentage to participate in personal evangelism, the Church would thrive and many would be added. Unfortunately not many, but a few Churches in Japan have succeeded in attaining this percentage of personal workers. Perhaps the situation in Europe and America is different from that of a heathen country like Japan.

The most effective and direct means of enlarging and revitalizing the Church is personal evangelism. For this there must be members who will dedicate themselves to earnest prayer. These prayer warriors must ask God to raise up many personal workers who will be enabled to do effective, lasting work (Matt. 9:36-38).

Effective work also requires good Christian literature. Personal workers should have appropriate tracts and pamphlets — ten or more kinds suitable for their work.

Most important of all in personal evangelism is the worker himself. He must be convinced of the importance and sacredness of his task.

Someone has noted that if we carve on marble too long, we may carve it away. If we cast a bronze mold, it may crumble in time. Unlike marble or bronze, the soul that is shaped into the image of Christ will remain forever. Moreover, if even just one soul makes a decision for Christ, he may be instrumental in bringing hundreds, thousands, yea, millions of souls to salvation.

The Church needs to awaken to the importance and urgency of personal evangelism. When believers' prayers, efforts and resources are consecrated and concentrated for this task, then revival will come to the Church and through the revived Church countless souls will come to Christ. We have a mission to fulfill. Let us be found faithful until Jesus comes.

Report of Group Discussion

The fundamental need in personal evangelism in Japan is the Christian who has a strong conviction of the forgiveness of sin and the experience of the new birth, Japanese delegates said. Two areas of particularized need are the obligation to recapture for the Church the so-called "retired" Christians (those who have drifted from the Christian community) and the imperative of breaking down an excessively minister-centered activity. At the same time the status and leadership of the pastors must be retained, said delegates.

Evangelist Honda (Japan) made two suggestions for stimulating personal evangelism in the Japanese Church. He suggested the establishment of regular seekers' instruction classes and of training courses for believers during the winter season.

Campus Crusade staff-man Arai explained the seven-step training course of Campus Crusade designed to educate believers in personal evangelism, and Pastor Chin of Taiwan spoke of similar programs used successfully in campaigns in Formosa.

Reporter: *Akira Hatori*

SECTION VI

PAGE

THE METHODS OF GROUP EVANGELISM •
A. W. Goodwin Hudson   431

AVOID CANONIZING ANY METHOD • Oswald C. J. Hoffman 441

PLANNING A GRAHAM CRUSADE • Walter H. Smyth   445

GROUP EVANGELISM IN ASIA • Gregorio Tingson   448

REPORT OF GROUP DISCUSSION • Roy Fish   450

THE PRACTICE OF TRUTH • Francis A. Schaeffer   452

THE EVANGELIST TODAY • Stephen F. Olford   456

LIKE A MIGHTY ARMY • Horace L. Fenton, Jr.   459

LESSONS FROM MASS EVANGELISM • John Wesley White   462

REPORT OF GROUP DISCUSSION • Enos Zimmerman   465

THE GIFT OF THE EVANGELIST • Leighton F. S. Ford   466

ASPECTS OF GROUP EVANGELISM • Anton Schulte   469

SOUTHERN BAPTIST EVANGELISM • C. E. Autrey   472

REPORT OF GROUP DISCUSSION • Carl Lundquist   474

TWENTIETH CENTURY EVANGELISM • Oral Roberts   475

NEW CONCEPTS OF EVANGELISM • Harold John Ockenga   478

A TIME FOR ACTION • Efrain Santiago   481

PREPARATION, PRESENTATION,
PRESERVATION • Leo E. Janz   485

REPORT OF GROUP DISCUSSION • James M. Boice   488

THE LOCAL CHURCH AND EVANGELISM • José M. Martínez 489

EVANGELIZATION BY GROUPS • José Maria Rico   492

EVANGELISM-IN-DEPTH • Ruben Lores   495

THE SOCIAL PROGRAM OF THE CHURCH • José D. Fajardo 498

REPORT OF GROUP DISCUSSION • Herbert Money   501

EVANGELISM IN FRENCH-SPEAKING LANDS • Maurice Ray 503

MASS EVANGELISM IN THE
IVORY COAST • Joseph Diéké Koffi   506

REPORT OF GROUP DISCUSSION • David Barnes   508

THE METHODS OF GROUP EVANGELISM
A. W. Goodwin Hudson

It is difficult to speak on a subject which can never be mastered, and about which one is always trying to learn. While professions like medicine, engineering, and law, are subject to long training in the theoretical and practical nature of their jobs, ministers of the Christian Church, and especially, the members of that Church, launch upon the most important work in all the world — evangelism — with but a shadow of preparation. At best, with little help, a few spend their lives trying to learn how to do this work, while the majority persuade themselves it is the exclusive work of the few. Most never learn, neither do they bend their spiritual, intellectual, social, and artistic knowledge to this task. Even ministers blunder along as best they can, and all too often die amateurs.

No training can do for a minister what experience and a spiritual life alone can do. But he, and every Christian, can be helped to begin on the right lines some form of evangelism within a group. The present evangelistic poverty of the Church causes many to look back to the rich traditions of the past for inspiration and guidance. But if we do this, we must emerge with the principles, not necessarily with the methods, of former days; we must not attempt our service for God and man as if we lived in a pretelevision, pre-radio, pre-electronic era.

1. Evangelism

The future of your nation and mine depends on evangelism; and evangelism depends on skilled, trained, and equipped groups within their Churches, who, strong in Christ, and confident of the Good News they proclaim, look on their task without misgiving in a world in which truth has disappeared. Many of the godliest men and women — many of the most effective evangelists, have been outside the stream of the ordained ministry.

I personally acknowledge my deep indebtedness to a laywoman who prayed me into the kingdom — my mother; and to godly laymen who have encouraged me in the things of God. No Christian is outside our Lord's last command — all Christians carry this obligation. Much of the future of evangelism depends upon laymen and women. But we must also hope for a skilled clergy, specialized in certain aspects, who not only can offer their experience for group evangelism, but also can train others in the same fields.

It might be thought that evangelism is the normal work of the Church, and that it exists for the conversion of sinners. But this does not detract

THE RT. REV. DR. GOODWIN HUDSON is a bishop in the Church of England and is rector of St. Paul's Church, Portman Square, London, England.

from the need of specialists and methods, and the need to make special efforts from time to time. While we are commanded to "pray without ceasing," there are also times for *special* prayer. The Christian life must be one of unbroken fellowship with God, but who of us does not need to be renewed and strengthened by someone (specially gifted, maybe) who comes and challenges us to some new spiritual crisis? Just as the soul makes progress by a series of crises, so, too, may the local Church. A mission can be a turning point, a time of crisis, of decision, of awakening.

This paper on *The Methods of Group Evangelism* is not to be concerned with the "what" or the "who" of the evangelist's message, but with the "how." And *how* shall we present Christ to a constantly changing world is a question which should engage us to the end of our ministry.

Evangelism is not the conversion of every individual. You could say a city was evangelized when everyone in that city has been faced with the challenge of Christ, and made aware of his invitation. The old Roman principles of teaching – to win people's interest, to impart information, and to incite to action – might well be serviceable to our methods and techniques in evangelism. Group evangelism is a special effort to convert people to God. It is a concentration of spiritual effort upon one place for a brief period.

The method by which God has educated our race, and guided its moral and spiritual welfare, has been by special missions. The mission of the prophets, the dispatch of Moses to deliver and restore a race of slaves, the challenge of Elijah, the warnings of Jonah, the voice of John the Baptist, the going out of apostles to conquer the world for Christ – each emphasized a different phase of the prophetic message, but all made the claim of God absolute upon each person. The sacred fire has been handed down by one Christian to another Christian, although not by all Christians in all generations. For there are those who will not pray, will not study, who will avoid their Gethsemanes of concern for others. There are those who will not take up their cross, who never go through the agony of giving spiritual birth to a single living soul by being the one to bring the lost to the Lord Jesus.

The purpose of group evangelism is not to feed the ninety and nine in the fold. It is not to build up the Christians; its purpose is to convert the unconverted. Edification and conversion are entirely different, and generally call for entirely different qualities in a preacher. Few speakers can successfully fulfill both of these ministries with power. One task is the work of the family doctor, the other, of the surgeon. One aims at building up the soul in the things of God. Conversion aims at securing the definite turning of the will, the entire surrender of the life to God.

If a Church is content with the ministry of edification alone, it will settle down to over-feeding (at best) a little clique of church-goers who fatally forget the lost. Further, in all probability, even the ones right outside the fold will not be touched by ordinary parochial methods; special methods must be tried, therefore, and a specialist may be called who has studied methods to reach and win that which was lost.

If the purpose of a mission is lost, then the methods used will suffer, and more harm than good will be done by the unreal atmosphere created by the absence of the unconverted and the failure to contact them. The misuse of missions or campaigns has done a great deal to destroy their force. Often they are used to express, through a visiting missioner, some doctrines which timidity has feared to teach. Or they may be used merely to increase the membership of a church.

The first purpose of evangelism is to seek and save that which is lost. We must proclaim, in new tones, the two-fold vision of the love of God, and the loss of God; of eternal life and eternal separation; we must win from the individual that decision on which his salvation now depends. There is no room for shallow universalism, for some vague belief in heaven and hell, which is a product, not of love, but of the self-indulgent morality of our times, and of the invasion of hedonism into the affluent society of the West.

No such religious trivialities will invoke the blessing of God. Modern prophets have been described as "mild-mannered men standing before a mild-mannered congregation, asking them to be more mild." "Wherefore," said St. Paul to the Ephesian elders, "I take you to record this day, that I am pure from the blood of all men. For I have not shunned to declare unto you all the counsel of God" (Acts 20:26-27).

The faithful will always be in need of spiritual stimulation, to "come alive," as the Psalmist so often prays. The Christian needs times of renewal to save him from the peril of lukewarmness. A special mission provides opportunities for sacrifice, for working for others, for confessing Christ; all these experiences rescue him from spiritual selfishness, and nerve the life with that touch of pain and concern without which there is no progress.

There is such movement in the world today that by the time the local Church catches up on a situation it no longer exists! There is the movement amongst youth towards delinquency and crime, in society towards immorality and divorce, in organized religion towards liberalism or ritualism. And the Church should be in movement too, moving society toward Christ, putting thought above the conflict, putting conversion by Christ above all other plans for improvement.

On the grave of a missionary, it is written:
"When he came, there was no light.
When he died, there was no darkness."

2. Methods of Group Evangelism

By group evangelism we mean evangelism other than a personal, one-win-one evangelism. The latter is basic evangelism. Group evangelism is a special effort to convert men and women to God. It is a concentration of spiritual effort in one place for a brief period of time.

"To the Jews I was a Jew that I might win the Jews. To those who were under the Law I put myself in the position of being under the Law (although in fact I stand free of it), that I might win those who are under the Law . . . To the weak, I became a weak man, that I might win the weak. I have, in short, been all things to all sorts of men that by every possible means I might win some to God. I do all this for the sake of the Gospel; I want to play my part in it properly" (I Cor. 9:20-23, Phillips).

Today there are two types of group, or mass, evangelism. There is the *Direct Method*, and the *Indirect Method*. The Preaching (Direct) Method includes every variety of group evangelism where a person meets people face-to-face, whether in a specialized way, or in the traditional environment of the Church. In the *Mediated (Indirect) Method*, the message is communicated through the printed page, radio, TV, film, or other mechanical media.

(a) *The Direct Method*. There is much in the present state and condition of Western society that closely parallels Old Testament times. And each generation of prophets must find the prophetic approach, as they are chosen men and women sent and suited to the task for which they are gifted. Some will have the touch of a Jeremiah, who with yearning love tries to woo people back to God. Others will have the double approach of an Isaiah, and will reveal God as unapproachably holy, but full of forgiving love. Another will be like John the Baptist; piercing the conscience like steel, he will stress the need to repent because of certain judgment. Someone else, overwhelmed by a personal experience of the love of God, will seek to win men like Hosea of old. The expression of the message will differ with different temperaments. It is the prophet's experience of God which is of primary importance. He must make the ways of God essential and a reality. He must bring religious phraseology into the language of ordinary un-theological men and women. This will mark the difference between that bigger body of men and women who are truly disciples, and that infinitely smaller group who have the prophetic touch and can speak to people in terms they understand.

The other great problem in communicating the message — more apparent in the person-to-person method than in any other — is the problem of contact. This is not only our problem, but our peculiar obligation. Conversion is God's work alone; our work is to contact the unconverted. For this we shall need all the consecrated imagination of which we are capable. Both the environment and the character of the people with whom we want to make contact will largely determine the methods we use. Climate, culture, and economics will also be variables in the formula of success. Many methods would be meaningless or impractical in certain areas. The basic facts of the Gospel of our Lord Jesus Christ have universal appeal. (Christ died for our sins — Christ rose for our justification — Christ lives as our Intercessor.)

The person-to-person, or Direct Method will not vary in respect to the message. But the methods used to make contact are influenced by climate, culture, and character of the audience. Safeguarded by the Scripture — "for the Jews ask for miraculous proofs, and the Greeks an intellectual panacea, but all we preach is Christ crucified. . . . Christ the power of God and the wisdom of God" (I Cor. 1:22, 25, Phillips) — techniques or methods must vary in order to reach the unsaved.

In the New Testament, *open air evangelism* would seem to have been the ready "harvest field." In some countries this may still be the natural place for group evangelism. But in the West, this setting would appear to have lost all effectiveness and drawing power, unless it occurs in a place where the crowd is ready-made. At the time John Wesley and George Whitefield addressed thousands in the open air, it was a novelty for a gentleman to appear in such a situation; the results, moreover, would indicate these men to have been spiritually dynamic. Since then, churches that have followed this good example by treating the open-air service as a training ground for would-be preachers and amateurs have been most unwise. Passers-by may well have thought what they observed was a sample of the Church's normal performance — and reacted accordingly!

(b) *The Visitation Method.* Whether the sending of the "seventy" by our Lord "to every city and place where he himself would come" included house-to-house visitation, we do not know (St. Luke 10).

This visitation method has been used most successfully in North America in recent years and also in Britain, although with less success. The method is by no means new, however, and under the Parish System of the Church of England, generations of clergy have documented each home in their parish with information on every family, their work and interests. Pastoral concern was basically the purpose of this house-to-house visitation.

The London City Mission, since 1835, has made a feature of financing full-time lay missionaries. Men specially trained for this work spend their time in allocated areas in working-class districts, going from home to home. A daily journal is kept that records their visits, details of all contacts, and the results of each contact. A copy of this record is always at headquarters.

The skill required by commercial firms of their salesmen should be an example to us whose task is to commend the most valuable treasure this earth affords. Churches in the West have organized men and women into teams of two to visit thousands of homes; trained to engage in conversation those who are courteous enough to give them a hearing, these teams make the transition to spiritual things comfortably, if not easily!

Team evangelism can be carried into factories and business houses, or to cinemas — wherever there are stationary groups of people to be evangelized, and wherever opportunity permits.

(c) *Film Evangelism*. Apart from the Lutheran Church, the great Protestant denominations do relatively little in this important area of visual aids. The work has been left largely to private individuals and in-independent organizations, who have had to bear the burden with little or no support from the churches. With this method perhaps more than any other, the object of the exercise must be kept constantly in view. We so often design an occasion that is supposed to reach the unconverted, but which in fact is arranged to suit the Christian. In film evangelism, we are trying to create a situation that reaches the unconverted, a situation where the non-church-goer will find it easy to cross over to our ground, or at least to familiar ground. While this method has been fully exploited in sophisticated communities, its usefulness is not exhausted. In areas where the film as a method of evangelism is not over-used, the method should be one of the most successful for making contact with the non-Christian.

There are two types of films:

1. The religious film, if produced for evangelism, should be able to do the whole work, and convey the message, and produce a verdict. The human "agent" is still required with the film to provide counseling or any other help for the persons responding to the appeal of the film message. However, it is increasingly difficult for the obviously religious film to attract an audience of unconverted people unless they are brought by converted friends to see the film.

2. The alternative to the religious film is the selective professional (secular) film. A film with a good story and an obvious moral can "lift" the viewer several stages in his mental attitude toward life; after the film an evangelist can commence immediately at that level to apply the Gospel. The right secular film, in the right setting, can still be an effective incentive to the "outsider" to attend. The evangelist can generally be relied upon to remember that he is a "fisher of men"; he needs imagination and enterprise in the choice of his "bait," however. All too often we blame the "fish," when results are not forthcoming. To change the metaphor, it is possible for a business man to be sincere, honest, and faithful, and yet be bankrupt. We tend to turn all our evangelistic efforts into just another religious service that is geared to the converted, who quite properly want to sing hymns and open and close the meeting with prayer. It could be said of one or another leader that he was —

"A man in whom men could find no fault, but in whom God could find no fruit."

Our failure to reach the lost is not so much a lack of love as a lack of imagination and desperation to reach the unchurched at all costs. "I have, in short, been all things to all sorts of men," said Paul, "that by *every possible means* I might win some to God" (I Cor. 9:22, Phillips).

My personal experience has been that wherever it is possible to get a sufficient number of unconverted people together, some have always found Christ irresistible. To preach the Gospel in the traditional setting of a church service is not necessarily the total discharge of our obligation to the outsider. We must find ways and means to contact him wherever he is, and so fulfill the command of Christ.

The present use of the films produced by the Billy Graham Association is an example of what the film can do as an evangelistic method. These films are used throughout the world, and although their greatest ministry is in the United States, through their use in Britain alone, a conservative reading of the statistics reveals that some 240 people every week (12,480 per year) are making open decisions for Christ.

The potential in *newspaper evangelism*, especially in areas where no other mass means of communication is available, should challenge the thinking of all Christians. If a group of Christians sponsored a regular column in a national newspaper, they would reach millions of readers and embark on a spiritual adventure that might well discover new areas of prayer support and release new blessing in the Churches or participating groups. The larger the space taken, the better. In England, for example, seven hundred pounds would buy a whole page in a newspaper that has three and a half million readers.

As long as four hundred years ago Martin Luther said, "We must throw the printer's inkpot at the Devil."

The Christian Church has exploited meetings, clubs, and organizations of every shape and form. It has turned the pen and the press to brilliant account, has utilized the Magic Lantern, and to some extent the cinema. In this generation, Christians have the challenge to buy up the opportunities presented by radio and television. We are faced with one of the greatest problems of all time, namely, the "population explosion." Between 1900 and 1962 the world population doubled; between 1962 and 1980 (i.e. 18 years) it is expected to redouble. Surely this phenomenon has not caught God unawares, and he has allowed it to coincide with the two electric miracles of radio and TV. How else will we perform the task of causing everyone to hear (and/or see) and believe? I regard the following words of our Lord as the greatest comfort and challenge: "He that heareth my word, and believeth on him that sent me, hath everlasting life" (John 5:24). How can we expect people to hear unless we use the media to which they listen? According to certain experts in this field of broadcasting, "both place and space" may be running out for any new Christian broadcasting project.

Whatever overseas missionary broadcasting there is, we owe almost entirely to North American Christian enterprise. Undoubtedly, St. Paul would have made magnificent use of the microphone and of the television camera, for both vehicles convey the passion and message of the user to both sinner and saint in an all-penetrating medium which knows no barrier.

How effectively the radio, and/or television, can move and mold a whole nation was demonstrated by Hitler's destructive propaganda. Similarly, Sir Winston Churchill proved how mightily a nation could be stirred to fight for freedom though it meant "blood, sweat, and tears." For good or evil, hundreds of transmitters now saturate the atmosphere with their communications.

Radio today is not the radio of the early thirties, for when television came, radio lost its place as the only means of home entertainment. The radio set or loudspeaker is no longer the centerpiece in the living room.

Although radio has vacated the family room, it has taken up new and important positions in the kitchen, the bedroom, the car, the factory, the barber shop, the out-of-doors, and even in the pocket. The transistor radio has revolutionized radio broadcasting, and has become woven into the daily fabric of our lives. More radio sets are being sold today than ever before, both in developed and underdeveloped areas of the world. In countries enjoying a high standard of living there are approximately two radios in each home, with 96 percent of the population listening to radio some time during every day. Radio has developed a vast personal audience of individual listeners, the largest congregation ever mustered.

In less affluent areas where few own radio receivers, a unique opportunity exists for Christians to provide these "mechanical missionaries."

In a certain area of the United States, a Protestant group sponsored a radio test campaign. For a period of nine weeks it used 110, 30-second radio "spots" each week over three stations. The objective of the "spots" was to promote the basic truth that "when a man accepts Christ as sin-forgiver and leader, he gets a whole new outlook on life." Effectiveness of the broadcast was to be measured among men between 18 and 40 years of age. Interviews took place prior to the test, and 43 percent of those interviewed were unaware of the basic Christian truth the radio messages were to promote. After the trial period of nine weeks, it was found that 32.9 percent, that is, approximately one out of every four, had some form of recall of the "Gospel Spots." The progress was from continued unawareness among some listeners, to awareness among others, to understanding, and on to a rewarding number who took action.

To be saved, a man must hear and believe, and call upon the name of the Lord (Romans 10:13–15). The "chain" that accomplishes this work has five links: sending, proclaiming (that is our task), hearing, believing, calling (these are the listener's responsibility). Over all, of course, is the Holy Spirit of God to bless the effort and the response.

For best results, radio ministry must be coupled with literature follow-up. But where literature is not possible, radio must "go it alone." While we may not build mature Christians, at least we shall bring men and women into communion with him, who is the Light and Hope of the world, the source of eternal life.

In more and more countries, television is becoming available. Dr. Billy Graham himself has said, "Experience has shown that more people will respond to the Gospel message on television than to any other means of communication." Although television has been with us for about 29 years, for most Christians it would be a strange new medium in which to work, inasmuch as there are few Christians experienced therein to guide or help. It would seem better to use films with a message, rather than not have a Christian program on TV at all; or rather than use a preacher who does not "come over" well on a TV screen, or who lacks the conversational style essential to this intimate instrument that brings the speaker right into the living room.

There are many books on "know-how," and training schools in some capital cities, where at least the basic "do's and don'ts" can be learned, and scriptwriters discovered and encouraged. It is important to develop someone as a TV personality. This can be achieved only by a long term of broadcasting experience. Generally speaking, religion has been so badly represented on television that a religious program gets poor ratings. Confidence in the religious message, and in the man who gives it, can only be built up over many broadcast appearances.

But the rewards are worth any expense and trouble, in a medium which does more than any other means of communication to shape the social and moral life of the people. Television is the greatest single influence on the minds and lives of people today, far exceeding the power of radio, film, and press. The aim in religious telecasting should be to give the viewer what *you* want him to have of your faith, *but* packaged as he likes it.

Regrettably, some countries do not allow time to be purchased on television; this fact is a grievous handicap to the cause of Christ. It might be debated whether any revival of true religion has ever come without the use of modern means of communication. Certainly we cannot think of the Great Reformation without the use of the printing press. And the first use given to this invention was the printing of the Bible. When a man had a Bible of his own, he was a modern.

We now live in a mechanized and electronic environment that in large measure exerts a materialistic influence on people. Unless churches realize this fact, and approach communication of the Gospel with new energy and action, the decay of the Church will increase. Television has become the modern market place, where news and views are communicated with terrifying speed and cleverness. The Christian Church must be in that market place.

Every major denomination should have its own broadcasting house and film studio, which need not lose money if rightly and efficiently operated.

Whatever the method of outreach, evangelism should involve the individual in both aspects of conversion: in that of personal acceptance of Christ, and in that of open confession. Right from the beginning the intellect has been involved, and man has had to make a mental assent. "Whom do men say that I am?" (Mark 8:27) was addressed to a group, but the response to the question was individual: said Peter, "Thou are the Christ." Much harm is done by those who shirk the stern duty of winning others through conviction and confession. And this failure often robs a person for life of the opportunity of a thorough conversion.

Anyone who is content to say "peace, peace," when there is no peace, and who fails to emphasize the urgency of a decision for Christ *now*, is but a spiritual "quack." No one can love more truly nor more deeply than our blessed Lord, and it was he who unveiled the terrible consequences of unrepented sin in a final judgment. The refusal to echo his teaching generally springs from some sin, or weakness, in the evangelist — love of popularity, or failure to realize the extreme holiness of God.

So often we lack the courage to press home conviction, and thus miss the first step in a true conversion. This point in evangelistic work is most delicate, and not even our Lord attempts to "force the door" to any man's soul. But we must, nevertheless, move on from preaching to dealing personally with individuals. The methods used to help people make this great decision vary, and are presented in other discussions.

AVOID CANONIZING ANY METHOD
Oswald C. J. Hoffmann

Proclamation of the Gospel is the responsible *activity* of a Church committed to Jesus Christ its Lord, and responsive to his atoning work for the whole world.

The *primary* task of the Church is proclamation of the *Gospel*. Law convicts, Gospel forgives. Law condemns, Gospel saves. Law kills, Gospel gives life.

The Holy Spirit of God does his work through the Gospel of Christ, proclaiming Christ and testifying to Jesus Christ, Savior of the world.

The Spirit of God also proclaims Christ and testifies to Jesus Christ through the Word of God, given to the world through inspiration of prophets, apostles, and evangelists by the Holy Spirit himself.

The testimony of the Spirit comes to the world today through the people of God, empowered by the Spirit himself to give witness not merely *about* Christ as he is described in the Scriptures but *to* Christ, as he is embraced and held fast in personal faith, which is also the gift of the Holy Spirit.

Anchored solidly on the Word of God and responsive in personal faith toward the Lord Jesus Christ, evangelism is the full-throated expression of the people of God at their Spirit-filled best.

Faith works by love. The evangelistic work of the Church and of its people bears the stamp of the Holy Spirit when the proclamation of Christ and the witness to Christ are recognizably, noticeably, obviously moved by love — by kindness toward people and understanding of their problems, by sympathy toward people in their weaknesses and even in their degradation, by willingness to give of oneself, as the Lord gave himself — putting himself in our place.

Evangelism is confident proclamation — certain that the whole world needs the forgiveness and life Christ gives and certain that Christ has answered the need of the world with his innocent death for all men, his resurrection to life for the life of the world, his resumption of the full use of his powers as the Lord of life, and his intercession at the court of divine judgment and grace.

Evangelism is positive witness to Jesus Christ, not an attempt to prove oneself right and someone else wrong. The wrongness of the world and of individual people in the world is put before all men by Christ himself, and put right for all men by Christ himself.

Methods suitable for effective evangelism of individual persons or

DR. HOFFMANN is the speaker on The Lutheran Hour broadcasts heard around the world from Saint Louis, Missouri.

of large numbers of people can be and must be *developed* by the people of God in every age to proclaim the Gospel to people in the language and circumstances of that age, that men and women, boys and girls, may know, understand, believe, and be saved.

Methods

The Holy Spirit has always called people of varying abilities and temperaments to testify to Christ, and has exerted his divine power through many methods for reaching people with the Good News of the Gospel. Care should be taken, therefore, not to canonize any one method of evangelism or any one point of view regarding the mode of carrying out the mission of the Church to those who do not yet know Christ as their Savior or even to those who have gathered in congregations to worship and serve him.

No worthy method of evangelism can ignore the basic historic and theological fact that people who have come to know Christ as their Savior are called to fellowship in faith nurtured by preaching and teaching of the Word of God, faithful use of the Sacraments, and worship with other believers in prayer and praise.

Person-to-person evangelism has an effectiveness all its own, resulting quite naturally and almost automatically in the establishment of a certain fellowship in the faith. For this reason, it may be advanced by some as the only worthy or effective method for proclaiming of the Good News in Christ and for effective witness to Christ. The example of the Early Church, however, from the first Christian Pentecost onward, and the experience of the Church today are evidence of the effectiveness of various methods of mass evangelism to accomplish the purpose of the Spirit of God in the hearts of people.

The best methods of mass evangelism are those which adhere most closely to the purpose of the Holy Spirit — to witness to Jesus Christ as the world's Savior, Redeemer, and Lord — with the closest attention to bringing those who are won to faith in Christ into active fellowship with others in the faith.

The media of mass communication peculiar to the modern world offer effective tools for direct evangelism and also for the preliminary approaches some call "pre-evangelism" (preparing the way for person-to-person testimony of various kinds by Christian pastors and people in the community). The mass media deserve to be employed with Christian intelligence, avoiding concealment of the truth and overstatement of the truth, each of which serves only to insult the listener and to demean his worth as a human being redeemed by Christ.

Whatever methods are employed to bring the Gospel to people through mass media, to be worthy tools of the Holy Spirit they ought to make it clear that:

a. Man is called to faith in Christ, not to faith in some theological concept or position, in some church and its tradition, or in some man or group of men, though they may possess certain charismata of proclamation or witness.

b. Man makes his decision for Christ only through the power of the Holy Spirit exerted through the Good News of Christ. No man speaking by the Spirit of God abjures Christ, and no man calls him Lord except by the Spirit of God working in him through the Gospel.

c. Man is saved from his folly and futility by God alone, not by what a man has done, still does, or can do. God's action of salvation is in Christ, and in no one else, ruling out every form of universalism apart from the universal redemption of the world through acceptance of Christ, crucified and risen again from the dead.

d. Man is justified — put right with God and with himself — only by the goodness and grace of God received in trust and faith; that is, faith in Christ, faith in the Good News of Christ, faith in the Word of God bringing the Good News of Christ through proclamation of the truth.

e. Man is justified by faith, which is the gift of God's Holy Spirit, not a good work of man by which he wins the favor of God. Christ is the gift of God, received by the gift of faith.

Christ's statement, "He that heareth you, heareth me," made to those who witness to his saving Name, is not an invitation to personal pride or professional license on the part of preachers, teachers, and evangelists; but an encouragement, a divine order, to proclaim the Good News with divine authority that is an inducement to faith and a call to the assurance of faith.

The Spirit confers life. There can be no manifestation of the fruits of the Spirit apart from prior acceptance of the Gospel with genuine faith in Christ, however small, weak, or uninformed that faith may be. Once the Spirit of God has brought a person or a group of people to new life through faith in Christ, the varied manifestations of the new life must and will follow as day follows night.

Since all is accomplished by the kerygma of Christ, the Church must be first, last, and always a witnessing community, proclaiming the Good News in Christ as the good news it really is.

Witness to Christ through mass media, by its very nature, must be personal witness of a personal witnesser, himself a forgiven sinner sharing in the new life through faith in Christ.

Evangelistic witness often has a dual thrust of laying foundations for faith and building up those who have come to faith in Christ.

Witnessing to Christ through the means of mass communication places upon the witnesser an obligation, a responsibility, to build audience and to develop listenership in appropriate ways.

In an age of developing dialogue where none existed before, new doors seem to be opening for genuine dialogue with people through the use of mass media.

Methods arising out of the imperatives of the Spirit, which are always Gospel imperatives, must be so devised, ordered, arranged, and employed as to reach out winsomely to men where they are with the message of Christ, his Cross and his resurrection. In Christ alone can forgiveness, life, and salvation be found for modern men and by modern man.

PLANNING A GRAHAM CRUSADE
Walter H. Smyth

As Vice President of the Billy Graham Evangelistic Association in charge of Crusade Organization and Team Activities of the Association, I thought it might be helpful to tell how a Billy Graham Crusade is planned and organized. A Crusade is divided into four phases: (1) preliminaries, (2) preparation, (3) penetration, and (4) preservation. Actually any evangelistic activity, however large or small, or wherever held, might be similarly planned. Hence, I hope my comments will help all who take seriously our Lord's commission: "Go ye into all the world and preach the Gospel."

The *preliminary* stage involves that period — perhaps years — during which the Lord has been laying upon the hearts of local believers in a metropolitan area the burden for a Billy Graham Crusade. Eventually this compulsion is expressed by extending an invitation to Mr. Graham. If the invitation comes from a city where the need is sufficiently great, where most of the churches join in issuing the invitation, and where a suitable and large enough meeting place can be secured, Mr. Graham will accept the invitation. Then, of course, the burden to go to that place at a time and for a period agreeable to both evangelist and those who invite him must be placed upon Mr. Graham's heart by God, the Holy Spirit. It will interest you to know if he accepted the entire backlog of invitations he has at any one given time, it would take Mr. Graham perhaps 200 years to get to all these places. However, when convinced he should go to a particular place, he will accept the invitation to come, generally between one and two years hence.

After such an affirmation by Mr. Graham, the stage of *preparation* begins. Somone from the Team Office in Atlanta then goes to the community, and at a meeting of local pastors assists in selecting a General Committee. The next step is to form an Executive Committee made up of a Chairman, Vice Chairman, Secretary, and Treasurer: these persons become the duly constituted officers of the corporation which is immediately incorporated as a non-profit organization. This Executive Committee, which, together with representatives of the Billy Graham team, does the real ground work in a campaign, is soon enlarged to include the chairmen of the working committees: i.e. of the Prayer, Finance, Counseling and Follow-up, Visitation, Operation Andrew, Youth, Publicity, Arrangements, Ushering, and Choir committees. An adequate and centrally located Crusade Office is procured, someone from the crusade team is put in charge, and a budget is set up. At this initial stage, an Arrangements Chairman takes

DR. SMYTH is director of crusades and team activities for the Billy Graham Evangelistic Association, with offices in Atlanta, Georgia.

the lead in seeing that the proposed meeting place for the crusade is provided with adequate seating, lighting, ventilation, acoustical equipment, platform facilities, medical requirements, policing, et cetera.

At this point the preparation stage for a crusade merges with the *penetration* stage. The Prayer Chairman undertakes to divide the prescribed crusade area into, perhaps, 5,000 prayer cells. In the United States this is done according to our postal organization. Therefore, there will be Zone Chairwomen (the women, like Lydia of Philippi, take the initiative in this matter of prayer), and under them division captains, district lieutenants and finally neighborhood hostesses, who open their homes for weekly prayer meetings. If there are 5,000 such homes there will probably soon be 25,000 to 50,000 women gathering regularly for prayer.

Then, several months before the crusade, a number of our Associate Evangelists are sent out to conduct ministers' meetings in all the districts of the crusade area. In London, for example, Dr. Bob Ferm and the Reverend Lane Adams met with nearly 5,000 different clergymen and pastors. Finally, a feature of every crusade just before the public services begin, is Mr. Graham's personal meeting with the ministers.

Two or three months before a crusade, the Christian Life and Witness classes are conducted. These are intended not only to train counselors, but also to provide a nucleus from which many different workers can be recruited and for leading people to Jesus Christ. In a place like London, or Los Angeles, five such classes will enroll up to 22,000 church members, all of whom have been invited by their pastors to participate. About one fourth of these will serve as regular or reserve counselors; about five per cent, preferably pastors or full-time Christian workers, will be advisers.

Operation Andrew, based on the example of Andrew's bringing his brother, Simon Peter, to Jesus, is our sytem for mobilizing Christians to bring their relatives, neighbors, school companions, social and business associates to the crusade. Buses are chartered by churches and other organizations for this purpose. Group bookings are made for reserved seating at the crusade. Through Operation Andrew, one nursing sister in Sydney, Australia, witnessed 1,100 nurses make decisions for Christ. About two weeks before a crusade, visitation campaign is launched. Its purpose is not only to apprise the public of the crusade but also to invite and sign up on behalf of a cooperating neighborhood Church those who are responsive to the Operation Andrew program. The Youth Committee also works on the basis of Operation Andrew, as do the Choir (which may have a membership of several thousand) and the Ushers (there may be 1,000 or more). Helping this penetration is the Publicity Committee which distributes perhaps a quarter of a million car stickers, gets out posters, leaflets, notices in public transportation, and makes use of the mass-communication media of newspaper, radio, and television.

Thus everything is ready, when, after the proclamation of the Gospel,

Mr. Graham calls inquirers to respond to the call of Christ. Beside each inquirer is a counselor, who seeks to lead that person into a decision for Christ, assurance of salvation, or re-dedication. It is here that the *preservation* stage of a crusade is undertaken in earnest. Advisers interview the counselees and decision cards are filled out in triplicate. That very night of decision, one copy of the card is sent by the colaborer staff to the place of worship designated by the inquirer. The pastor of that Church is asked to visit the inquirer and report this fact to the Crusade Office within ten days. If he is uncooperative, a Designation Committee assigns the inquirer to some other pastor. Meanwhile, the original counselor will have telephoned, written or visited the inquirer within forty-eight hours of the decision.

When the crusade is over, Mr. Graham is concerned about two things. First, he is eager that the converts be integrated into local Churches; to this end, where it seems necessary, seminars for inquirers and Bible study groups are sometimes held immediately after the crusade. Second, as soon as all bills are paid and crusade business completed, preferably within a month or two, Mr. Graham is anxious that the crusade office close, the committee organization be dissolved, and all Billy Graham staff withdrawn. As everyone returns to his designated place and Church, the prayer continues that God, the Holy Spirit, will consummate what he has been doing.

GROUP EVANGELISM IN ASIA
Gregorio Tingson

Group Evangelism has been defined as the presentation of the person and claims of Jesus Christ in his death and resurrection to a group of people. One of the most effective methods of disseminating the Gospel message, group evangelism has been mightily used of God in our specific area of ministry in Asia to bring many souls to Christ.

Besides its singular effectiveness in spreading God's redemptive plan for man, group evangelism has proved immensely fruitful in welding a more cohesive evangelical testimony which, in turn, enlarges the evangelistic vision of the cooperating evangelical groups.

My experience demonstrates the unique value of group evangelism in presenting the Gospel to the millions of Asia. It also confirms the sublime truth that Christians everywhere yearn to fellowship with believers in other denominations. Paul expressed this same yearning in his letter to the Christians at Rome (Romans 1:10-13).

Group evangelism has given local evangelical communities a sphere of fellowship in their common task of presenting the Gospel. It has given local evangelical Churches vast opportunities to emerge from denominational seclusion into a larger partnership with Churches of like persuasion in propagating the Christian message. The coming together of these Churches not only enlarges their sense of fellowship, it also develops a deeper understanding among the brethren. Without this mutual understanding it would be difficult, if not impossible, to develop and maintain unified and consistent Christian witness in a given community.

This feeling of togetherness among Christian groups generated by group evangelism reminds the cooperating believers of their basic union in and with the whole body of Christ. It gives them wider opportunities to express their love for the brethren, whom perhaps they may never learn to love outside of the cooperative evangelistic endeavor that has brought them together.

Working as one group in presenting the common message of salvation in Christ, the cooperating churches guarantee a greater impact for the evangelical voice than would be possible if each acted separately and independently. Cooperative witness gives an evangelical image of unity and strength; this is especially important in places like Asia where Christianity has but a very small following. The need for a more sturdy and unified voice of biblical Christianity must be met if evangelicalism in Asia is to be more than just a "voice crying in the wilderness."

MR. TINGSON is chairman of the Asian Evangelists Commission in Manila, Philippine Islands.

These facts have impressed us time and time again in our crusades with the Asian Evangelists Commission. As evangelists from different countries and denominations in Asia gather to pray, plan, and propose evangelistic programs for the teeming millions of Asia, we have felt more than ever before in the history of the Christian Church in our part of the world that evangelism is indeed the most unifying factor among Christians of many different national, denominational, and other backgrounds. While the Asian Evangelists Commission has as its motto, "Winning Asia to Christ by Asians," it also cooperates with evangelical and missionary groups from outside Asia. Beyond the boundaries of our Asian unity in Christ is the reality of Christian love and fellowship extended by Christian workers of other lands. We have seen therefore that while the Asian Evangelists Commission emphasizes indigenous evangelism for winning Asia to Christ, it does not reject or preclude the participation of sympathetic evangelists from non-Asian countries. In other words, far from being just an Asian enterprise, the AEC welcomes the fellowship of non-Asian brethren. In this way, while maintaining the Asian denominator in order to insure greater effectiveness in evangelizing Asia, the AEC invites non-Asian Christian workers into its fellowship and cooperates with them in their respective missionary and evangelistic endeavors.

This is the basic meaning and purpose of the Asian Evangelists Commission. As Asian evangelists we feel we have a specific responsibility to our fellow Asians. While the Great Commission to the Church is to spread the Gospel throughout the world, we feel it is our duty to God and to our fellow Asians to carry out the Great Commission in the manner that the AEC is doing. To this end, we Asian evangelists have agreed to pool our resources not as an organization, but as fellow evangelists who are in full agreement concerning our common duty to fulfill God's commission for the Church in Asia.

There are many reasons why, in projecting an Asian approach to group evangelism in Asia, the AEC feels it is moving in the right direction. The AEC believes that to have effective and lasting results, group evangelism in Asia today must take into consideration the pressing tensions of Asian countries as well as the customs and culture of the people, their institutions and governments, their cares and problems, their associations and relationships, the life they live. In other words, there are many and complex social, cultural, economic, political, and religious tensions to consider.

One need not be reminded that Asia today is a vast picture of unrest because of resistance against what has been described by new emerging leftist nations as neo-colonialism or an attempt of so-called western imperialism to perpetuate its colonial designs in Asia. We Asians therefore feel that amid the strong wave of nationalism sweeping across our continent anything that presents an entirely western or non-Asian approach to the people would be exposed to unnecessary problems. Under these circumstances the AEC fits in as perhaps no other group could do. We are convinced that the time has come for Asian Christians themselves to continue the ministry which many years ago was introduced to Asia by missionaries from other lands.

Group evangelism by Asians with the prayerful support and fellowship of Christians from all over the world is what the Asian Evangelists Commission believes to be the answer for the spiritual needs of Asia's unsaved millions. In pursuing its primary objective of winning Asia for Christ, the AEC follows this program:

1. It sponsors gospel campaigns and conferences on Asian evangelism every two years.

2. It conducts and promotes city-wide evangelistic crusades in key Asian cities.

3. It encourages the formation and sponsorship of international teams for evangelistic thrusts into prayerfully selected countries of Asia and other parts of the world, as the Holy Spirit leads.

As popularly defined, group evangelism relates primarily to the group of people to whom the Gospel is presented. In the AEC we have given group evangelism a further dimension; we relate group evangelism to the group of messengers who carry out the specific program of evangelistic activity. This approach has proved efficient and fruitful in Asia.

This concept of group evangelism in no way replaces group evangelism under a single evangelist. It does, however, follow a specific strategy that must be used to the full in order to advance the cause of evangelism. Together with all other methods of group evangelism effectively used by various agencies of the Christian churches in Asia, presenting an Asian challenge like that of the AEC may yet, we believe, bring about the evangelization of Asia's two billion people in our generation.

Report of Group Discussion

The methods, merits and limitations of group evangelism constituted the main body of material presented and discussed. Delegates listed basic principles for every evangelistic campaign. The most important factor in such campaigns is preparation, and the most important factor in preparation is involvement. Spiritual preparation should have priority, but it is not to serve as a substitute for preparation of a more practical nature.

Many agreed that group evangelism is usually an effective mode of spreading the Gospel. The advantages of having natives of particular areas serving in the capacity of group evangelists was pointed out.

Delegates also pointed to the limitations of group evangelism. In certain sections of the world, only a very small number of non-Christians attend mass meetings. For these areas person to person evangelism was recommended. In countries lacking radio and television the use of the telephone was suggested.

Reporter: *Roy Fish*

"I would rather speak exclusively on evangelism among the twentieth century people the Church is not generally reaching, and concerning helping the Christians' children who get into difficulties because it has not been clearly shown to them how the Bible answers their honest questions. However, something must be said before that and thus my paper is entitled:"

THE PRACTICE OF TRUTH
Francis A. Schaeffer

The central problem of evangelicalism and evangelism in the second half of the twentieth century is the problem of the *practice* of principles, especially taking into account a spiritual and intellectual comprehension of that which is the dominant mentality of our century. If consistent Christian principles are not practiced, "success" in evangelism can, in the flow of history, result in weakening Christianity in the next generation. Any consideration of methods and programs is secondary to a consideration of this central problem.

The mark of our century is the victory of the Hegelian concept of synthesis, instead of a recognition of truth in the sense of antithesis and absolutes. Prior to Hegel, non-Christians generally acted upon the classical concept of truth. While they had no sufficient foundation for their optimism in regard to absolutes, yet in general they acted upon the concept that if a thing was true, the opposite was false. In morals likewise, if a thought or action was viewed as right, the opposite was considered wrong. Thus if the Church in that day, including the evangelist, said that Christianity was true, or that a thing was right, this had meaning and was understood. If one said "be a good girl", for example, the statement was meaningful to those who heard it.

Since the influence of Hegel's dialectic and Kierkegaard's "leap", this is no longer the case. We are increasingly surrounded by a culture in which a concept of truth in the sense of antithesis, and of moral right and wrong, does not exist. Thus "be a good girl" is today a nonsense statement to an increasing number of twentieth century people.

This concept spread in three different ways. It spread geographically from Germany in the aftermath of Hegel. Thus, continental Europe felt its force before England, and England before the United States, and the United States before the so-called missionary countries. Secondly, it spread

DR. SCHAEFFER is president of L'Abri Fellowship Foundation in Huémoz sur Ollon, Switzerland.

academically through the different disciplines. It was expressed first in philosophy, and later in art, music, and so on, including theology, down through the general culture. Thirdly, it spread socially by classes. Intellectuals and creative people were the first to think in this way. Through the arts and later the common media they then carried this concept of relativistic thinking to the masses. What remains unaffected by this modern way of thinking today is what we may call (for want of a better term) the middle-class people of a certain age group. However, as the children of these people are educated a step away from their parents, a gap opens between parent and child which is greater than the gap between the parent and the Renaissance man or even between the parent and the Greek. Among these then are those children of Christians who became known as the rebels and whom we often lose. This follows because the present gap is total, inasmuch as it rests upon a completely different concept of truth. The process which brings about this change is not only formal education by educators who think in relativistic terms, but also by the art forms — the novel, the play, poetry, the serious cinema and television, far-out jazz. These things today educate men in this direction in an almost monolithic voice.

By contrast, historic Christianity rests upon truth — not truth as an abstract concept, nor even what the twentieth century man regards as "religious truth", but objective truth. (The contrary to this is then an antithesis to the truth of what is.) Part of this truth is the emphasis that certain things happened in history. There were, for example, the manifestations at Sinai and Christ's propositional communication to Saul in the Hebrew tongue on the Damascus road, as well as Christ's open tomb. Historic Christianity rests upon the truth of what today is called the "brute facts" and not just upon an unknown experience of men in past ages of which we have only a faulty hermeneutical interpretation. Behind the truth of such history is the great truth that the personal, infinite God is objectively "there". He actually exists (in contrast to his not being there); and Christ's redemptive and finished work actually took place at a point of time in real space-time history (in contrast to this not being the case). Historic Christianity rests upon the truth of these things in absolute antithesis to their not being true. This carries with it the possibility and the validity of that personal antithesis which occurs at the new birth, wherein the individual passes from death to life. To weaken the historic Christian concept of antithesis is eventually to make meaningless the personal antithesis of the new birth.

If a clear and unmistakable emphasis of truth, in the sense of antithesis, is removed, two things occur: first, Christianity in the next generation as true Christianity is weakened; and second, we will be communicating — in any real sense of communication — with only that diminishing portion of the community that still thinks in terms of the older concept of truth. We are not minimizing the work of the Holy Spirit; we would remember, however, that our responsibility is to communicate so that those who hear the Gospel will understand it. If we do not communicate clearly, then those who respond will not really understand the Christian answer clearly. If we do not communicate clearly on the basis of antithesis, they will respond to their own interpretation of the Gospel in their own relativistic thought-forms — including a concept of psychological guilt-feelings rather than of true moral guilt before the holy living God. If they do respond thus, they have not understood the Gospel; they are still lost, and we have defaulted in our task of preaching and of communicating the Gospel to our generation.

Thus, in the Conference's theme: "One Race, One Gospel, One Task", one might ask whether perhaps the most important thing has been omitted, namely, "One Truth".

The unity of orthodox or evangelical Christianity should be centered around an emphasis on *truth* and not on evangelism as such. This emphasis on *truth* is always important, but doubly so when we are surrounded by a generation for whom the concept of truth in the sense of antithesis is not so much denied as it is considered to be totally untenable. In such a setting, the Christian with his emphasis on *true truth* is the real radical on both sides of the Iron Curtain, because today the unifying factor on both sides of the Iron Curtain is the general acceptance of dialectical thinking.

In such a setting the problem of communication is serious; it can only be overcome by negative statements that clearly say what we do *not* mean, so that the twentieth century man understands our positive statements of what we do mean. Moreover, in an age of synthesis men will not take our protestations of truth seriously unless they see by our actions that we seriously *practice* truth and antithesis in the unity we try to establish and in the evangelism we practice. Without this, in an age of relativity, we cannot expect the evangelical, orthodox Church to mean much to the surrounding culture or even to the Church's own children, for what we try to say in our teaching and in evangelism will be understood in the twentieth century thought-form of synthesis. Both a clear comprehension of the importance of truth and a clear *practice* of truth, even when it is costly to us to practice truth, are imperative if our witness, our evangelism, and such a Congress as this are to be significant, or even useful, in our own generation and in the flow of history.

We being here in Berlin in front of this horrible wall must ask a very serious question, and the question is this: Whose fault is it that that wall is there? Whose fault is it that those people are shut away on the other side with the machine guns trained on them as they work near the wall?

The guide on our western tour of Berlin told us clearly whose fault it is. He pointed out that the wall is there because twenty years ago some of our own men did not understand the enmity of the enemy. Twenty years later those people on the other side of the wall have a right to say very hard things against those men, because they are now caught in the historic results of what the men of twenty years ago allowed and produced.

Let us never forget that we who stand in the historic stream of Christianity really believe that false doctrine, at those crucial points where false doctrine is heresy, is not a small thing, but is an enemy. If we do not make clear by word and by practice our position *for* truth and *against* false doctrine, we are building a wall between the next generation and the Gospel. And twenty years from now, men will point their finger back and say of us, "This is the result in the flow of history."

If we do not make plain by word and practice that false doctrine is really an enemy, in the flow of history we cut the ground from under the next generation of the Church. And even those who respond in this generation, are in danger of responding to their own thought forms and not to what we are sincerely saying. Thus — because of our commitment to evangelism on the basis of the holiness of God and for the sake of truth — I can visualize times when the only way to make plain the seriousness of what is involved in regard to a campaign where the Gospel is going to be preached, but where men (*whose doctrine* is known to be an enemy) are going to be invited to pray, etc., is with tears not to accept an official part in that campaign. Evangelism that does not lead to purity of life and purity of doctrine is just as faulty and incomplete as an orthodoxy which does not lead to a concern for, and communication with, the lost.

And let us not deceive ourselves, we will not really touch the tough fiber, far-out twentieth century young people unless we show *at a cost* that we take truth seriously, and on that basis give honest answers to honest questions.

THE EVANGELIST TODAY
Stephen F. Olford

There was a time — and that not so long ago — when evangelism, in the words of Principal James Denney was "the disinterested interest of the comparative few." In other words, it was regarded simply as a hobby for cranks and fanatics. But, thank God, today there is a rising responsiveness in the Church to the challenge of evangelism, and those of us who have any share in this field of the Church's ministry ought to study afresh what the New Testament has to say about the evangelist and the world in which he serves.

Perhaps the most comprehensive treatment of this subject is found in Ephesians 4:7-13. Consider, first of all:

1. The Ministry of the Evangelist

". . . (Christ) ascended up on high, he led captivity captive, and gave gifts unto men. . . . And he gave some, apostles; and some, prophets; and some, evangelists; and some, pastors and teachers" (vv. 8, 11).

To understand the true nature of the evangelist's ministry, we need to think first of his gift and then of his task. To begin with, the New Testament reveals that there is indeed such a thing as *the evangelistic gift.* The ascended Lord ". . . gave gifts unto men . . . some, evangelists . . ." (vv. 8, 11). The risen Lord has so positioned this gift among those enumerated that it holds together what is fundamental and what is developmental in the life of the Church.

Alongside the evangelistic gift is what the New Testament calls *the evangelistic task.* Writing to his son in the faith, Paul exhorted Timothy ". . . do the *work* of an evangelist . . ." (II Timothy 4:5). The noun, "evangelist" comes from the verb "to announce the good news"; in simple terms, therefore, an evangelist is the herald, or announcer of the Good News of the Gospel. Whether in public preaching or in personal counseling, the task of the evangelist is "so to present Christ, in the power of the Holy Spirit, that 'men and women' shall come to put their trust in God through him, and confessing Christ as Lord seek to serve him in the fellowship of the church" (William Temple).

Along with the ministry of the evangelist, Paul speaks of:

2. The Message of the Evangelist

If one phrase could sum up the message of the evangelist, we could select no better word than "the knowledge of the Son of God" (Eph. 4:13).

DR. OLFORD is minister of Calvary Baptist Church in New York City, New York, and has been active in evangelism around the world.

This preaching of "the knowledge of the Son of God," says Paul, has two essentials.

The first is *the Proclamation*. ". . . I declare unto you the gospel which I preached unto you. . . ." (I Corinthians 15:1). Central to every aspect of the Gospel must be the proclamation of the person of the Lord Jesus Christ. Sin and grace, repentance and faith, judgment and salvation, hell and heaven, must all be seen as related to him.

The second essential is *the Invitation*. No message is complete without *beseeching* men to be reconciled to God (II Corinthians 5:20). As Dr. J. Packer puts it: "Evangelizing includes the endeavor to elicit a response to the truth taught."

This brings us to our third consideration:

3. The Method of the Evangelist

"And he gave some, . . . evangelists, . . . for the equipping of the saints for the work of service. . ." (Eph. 4:11, 12, N.A.S.B.). These words indicate that the evangelist must first *stir the saints*. He must "equip the saints for the work of service." No one can stir up Christians to their evangelistic responsibility like the man with the evangelistic gift. Indeed, any evangelistic endeavor which fails to stir up believers in the local Church to see their duty to bear witness to the lost has failed in one of its essential objectives.

In the second place, he must *seek the sinners*. The "equipping of the saints" is "for the work of service" (v. 12); such service is seeking the lost to bring them to repentance toward God and faith in our Lord Jesus Christ.

The last thought in this study is:

4. The Motive of the Evangelist

". . . he gave some, . . . evangelists; . . . for the perfecting of the saints for the work of the ministry, for the edifying of the body of Christ: till we all come in the unity of the faith, and of the knowledge of the Son of God, unto a perfect man, unto the measure of the stature of the fulness of Christ" (vv. 11–13).

Paul tells us in no unmistakable terms that the motive and objective of the evangelist is to effect, by the power of the Holy Spirit, true *spiritual unity* in Christ. "Till we all come in the unity of the faith . . ." (v. 13). Through his witness and preaching, men must come to know God as Father through faith in one Lord, one baptism, by one Spirit. Only thus can there be one Body and one hope of our calling.

Then believers must be led on to true *spiritual maturity*. "Till we all come . . . unto the measure of the stature of the fulness of Christ" (v. 13). In other words, the evangelist's task is not so much that of securing decisions as of making disciples. As Dietrich Bonhoeffer put it, we must shun the preaching of "cheap grace" until men come to be involved in this costly business of discipleship. The Cross must be presented not only as an objective truth in which we can glory, but as a subjective power which slays self and sin in order that the life may be wholly dedicated to God and his service. Such discipleship will mean steadfast continuance in Christian teaching, in Christian fellowship, in Christian ordinances, and in Christian worship (Acts 2:42).

We have seen, then, that the evangelist is Christ's gift to the Church. We must accept him together with apostles, prophets, pastors and teachers, and prayerfully support his work. The time is short and we must win the lost. Let us join hands with the evangelist as all of us seek to meet our evangelistic responsibility to our generation.

LIKE A MIGHTY ARMY
Horace L. Fenton, Jr.

Too often in our day we consider the methods of group evangelism individually, as though each were completely isolated from all the rest. We defend the virtues of one particular method, often at the expense of someone else's favorite approach. We form groups to promote and to exploit our own program.

Occasionally this sort of rivalry and competition may be helpful, but there comes a time when this type of approach is not good enough. A government may tolerate, for a time, a certain amount of rivalry between its army, air force, and navy. But when global victory is at stake, any kind of uncoordinated activity is a luxury that no nation can afford.

If, in group evangelism, we want only to carry on "business as usual," we can indulge in endless claims and counter-claims concerning the virtues and limitations of various methods. But if we take our task as Christians seriously, we cannot be satisfied with anything less than a thorough survey of the media available to us, a careful evaluation of their relative effectiveness, and a prayerfully devised program for their coordinated use.

In the countries where Evangelism-in-Depth has been carried on during the past seven years, there has been just such an earnest attempt to match resources to needs. Behind all this has been the conviction that in order to evangelize the world we need the maximum number of evangelists (but not in the narrow sense of that term), the maximum number of effective means of evangelization, and the simultaneous, coordinated, fruitful employment of these men and methods. Too often in the past we have not mobilized our manpower nor our other resources.

To do a better job demands the training of a host of lay witnesses for Christ. Our need is not so much to multiply our audiences as to multiply the propagators of the message.

But even this is not enough. We must also learn as evangelicals to coordinate all available media. If we can bring the concentrated firepower of evangelism to bear on any given area, the possibilities of effectively evangelizing it will be immeasurably increased. If, instead of utilizing the weapons of evangelization in a haphazard manner, we can tie these things together in a synchronized attack, we shall be much more likely to evangelize the world in our generation.

Such a program will do much for the believers who are involved in it:

1. It will give each Christian a place in the program of evangelism. Many a believer gifted by the Lord never recognizes his gift because he is

DR. FENTON is the general director of the Latin America Mission in Bogota, New Jersey.

unaware of the great variety of ways in which he may fit into the divine plan for world evangelization. It is little use to challenge him or even to train him unless we can also show him a number of channels through which he can find his place in some form of soul-winning witness. This we *must* do; Scripture demands it, and so do the times in which we live. A coordinated program offers every believer just such an opportunity.

2. It will remind him that he and his local Church are not working alone. Perhaps for the first time in his experience, he comes to see that the Church is "like a mighty army" — in something more than a poetic way!

3. He will quickly learn that God's armory has unlimited resources. His God has anticipated the diversified strategies of Satan, the population explosion, and the complexity of twentieth century life. Even in such difficult times he has provided his Church with all that is needed for victory. The believer sees this, thanks God, and takes courage.

4. The Christian is driven to a new understanding of the unity of the body of Christ. This great truth becomes to him a visible, functional element to be used for the glory of God and for the spread of the Gospel. He sees cooperation and coordination as the very will of God for his Church.

But such a program has an equally great impact on unbelievers, and we do well to note its effect on them:

1. It multiplies the ways in which unbelievers may come to know Christ. After all, no fisherman would think of using the *same* kind of bait for *all* kinds of fish! Some non-Christians will be reached through prayer groups, where they see faith in action at close range. Others, trying to lose themselves in the anonymity offered by a mass campaign, will find Christ there. Still others will respond to a Gospel film or, safely hidden in their homes, will seek the truth through radio or television. There are many ways to reach men for Christ, and a coordinated effort greatly increases the possibility of exposing them to the Gospel.

2. Moreover, through these many ways the unbeliever feels the cumulative effect of a many-pronged Gospel offensive. In a year-long effort he is confronted by the Gospel on every hand: at the theater he attends, in his daily newspaper, on the commercial radio and television outlets, from the lips of his children who have heard the Gospel in a newly organized club, on the university campus, and in the sports arena where bullfights and soccer have been temporarily replaced by Gospel services. Everywhere the unbeliever is confronted by a message which he confessedly knows little about, but which he comes to think just might be the answer to his troublesome and pressing problems. Without realizing it, he has been conditioned to hear the Good News of God by the cumulative effect of a coordinated program of evangelism.

These effects are not imaginary, nor the product of wishful thinging. We have seen them in Latin America; the facts are on file. These things happen when believers coordinate the many effective media at their disposal and bring them to bear on a whole nation at a crucial moment in history.

There is no reason why the same should not happen all over the world in the days just ahead.

LESSONS FROM MASS EVANGELISM
John Wesley White

Let us take a telescopic look at Anglo-American mass evangelism of the last two and a third centuries, refraining from more than just an occasional allusion to the past generation. Rather than chronologically, I shall deal with it analytically, examining ten types of evangelists who have been in evidence. Perhaps these lessons from the past will assist us in meeting the challenge of the future.

First, there were the *Incumbents*, pastors who in the course of their ministries applied themselves intensely to prayer and then earnestly exhorted their people on the great Gospel themes. As they did so, "suddenly there came a sound from heaven, as of a mighty rushing wind," and the Spirit of God moved sovereignly and powerfully in their congregations; multitudes of people were converted.

The Colonial Revival of 1734-41 broke out in such a manner under the ministry of Jonathan Edwards in Northampton, in New England. Edwards itinerated his message from God up and down the Connecticut Valley, never, however, becoming a professional evangelist. It might be said, however, that modern revivalism began with his ministry. Eventually he became president of Princeton. Similar fruitful ministries of evangelism were also effected by Robert Murray McCheyne, Thomas Chalmers, Charles Spurgeon, and Dewitt Talmage, men who never left their settled churches except to take up others. They provide a precedent for the pastor of today to "do the work of an evangelist."

Then there were the *Inflamers*, George Whitefield providing the precedent for these. Coming into unusual blessing only a short time after Jonathan Edwards, his future trans-Atlantic friend, Whitefield was as peripatetic as Edwards was stationary. An Anglican clergyman who always noted on the title pages of his publications that he was "late of Pembroke College, Oxford," Whitefield was a sort of spirtual ignitionist. Wherever he went, his cohorts observed that "the Holy Ghost fell on them, as on us at the beginning." This was true, whether he was addressing 20,000 colliers near Bristol, or 200 lords, ladies and actors in Lady Huntingdon's chapel in Bath. As he roved about the Old and New worlds, multitudes were turned to the Lord through him. He has had many emulators over the last two centuries.

On the other hand, Whitefield's senior in the Oxford Holy Club, John Wesley, was an *Institutionalist*. He did not easily break with tradition, and while having a heart as "strangely warmed" as Whitefield's, he never

DR. WHITE is an associate evangelist with the Billy Graham Evangelistic Association in Toronto, Ontario, Canada.

worshiped outside the Anglican fold, even though he did most of his evangelistic preaching in fields, market places, and wherever else people would gather. He was a "Methodist," and evangelized within the framework of the societies he founded, all kept in the Church of England during his lifetime, despite the opposition he incurred.

William Booth, with his Salvation Army and its extreme methods but rigid regimentation, was another institutionalist. So were George Williams with his Y.M.C.A., Wilson Carlile with his Church Army, and Francis Clark with his Christian Endeavour. Perhaps you today are evangelizing within the framework of a society, denomination, or association. You have a great work to do.

Fourthly, there were the *Individualists*, isolationists often, whose call to evangelize was undoubted, but who, perhaps with a zeal outsized to their brethren, took the apostolic exhortation, "We ought to obey God rather than men," as the basis for their efforts. The Primitive Methodists of England sprang largely from the camp meeting innovation of Lorenzo Dow, who dressed quite literally like John the Baptist. With his exotic frontier vernacular he called multitudes to Christ who perhaps came to his meetings first out of curiosity, and then to seek the Lord. He has had many imitators, occasionally awkward, if not idiocentric and not infrequently disruptive characters who do "some things hard to be understood." But recognize them in history we must; and ignore them we cannot. "God forbid that I should touch the Lord's anointed," said David of Saul.

Easier to appreciate have been the *Intercessionists*. David Brainerd, who, had he lived, was about to marry Jonathan Edward's daughter, was such a man. He evangelized the Indians by kneeling in the snow and praying for them. His biography has provided missionary motivation for thousands; prayer was his secret.

Charles Finney, while he might fit into several of these types, was launched into his vocational orbit from a prayer pad. As the sturdy lawyer knelt in the woods of Upper New York in 1821, he recalled vividly a half-century later: "The Holy Spirit descended upon me in a manner that seemed to go through and through me." Other intercessionists, who being dead, yet speak, were the Reformed pastor in New York and the three young men at Kills in Ulster who prayed during the 1850s for a revival, which indeed swept the world when it came.

Rushing to the scene of spiritual revivals have always been the *Ingatherers*, who move into the harvest fields rendered white by a sovereign God in answer to the intercessions of his people. Payson Hammond, a Presbyterian ordinand, newly graduated from Union Theological Seminary in New York, went to Edinburgh to do research in 1859, when the revival broke out in Scotland. Caught up in its movement, Hammond was the means of bringing thousands to Christ. Returning to the United States, he was for a decade the greatest evangelist in the country. Great revivals like harvest time on the farm, require readily recruited help. Any evangelist does his best work in a revival.

Dwight L. Moody might be considered the first evangelist among the eminent *Interdenominationalists*, a tradition which includes Wilbur Chapman, Billy Sunday, and Billy Graham of our day. From many groups and denominations, believers in Christ as God the Son and only Savior of the world gather in a prescribed area, after prayerful and careful planning, to present a united witness for Christ in that community. Converts are encouraged to unite with the Church of their choice, seeking through worship and fellowship in that Church to serve God acceptably. The interdenominationalist relies on team effort.

The *Indoctrinator*, Reuben A. Torrey being the first in this succession, emerged at the beginning of the present century. He stressed the basics of the Christian Gospel and enunciated them with clarity, depth, and yet with simplicity. He undertook to confirm doubting Thomases in their faith, and to lead many to Christ who as a result of the industrial revolution and the often audacious claims of science, had lost all confidence in Revelation. Wittingly or unwittingly, he often alienated disbelievers even further from the churches from which they had already drifted a long way. In some circles, extremely zealous Indoctrinators later became known as "fundamentalists," men of varying effectiveness and power.

Nineteenth century evangelism eloquently confirmed that social action and scriptural doctrine are closely related. The *Interactionist* was one who wedded his particular social concern to the Gospel he preached. Besides Booth, Carlile, and Williams, there were John Woolman, the Beechers, and Finney concerned with the abolition of slavery; Keir Hardie, Moody convert and evangelist, who founded Britain's Labour Party; Finney, the Beechers, John Gough, and Billy Sunday who fought alcoholism; Asa Mahon, Finney's collaborator, and Elihu Burritt, active in the matter of World Peace congresses; and Henry Dunant, the Swiss founder of the International Red Cross.

Finally, there was the *Internationalist*. It was Edwards' work that largely inspired William Carey to launch the modern foreign missionaries outreach after 1792. And out of the Moody-Sankey Revival sprang the Student Volunteers, who, between 1886 and 1914, inspired 11,000 recruits to become Internationalist evangelists and to take the Gospel to the ends of the earth under the leadership of the Studds of England and of the Americans John R. Mott, Robert Wilder, and Robert Speer. As we fan out from this World Congress on Evangelism, may each of us realize afresh the significance of our Lord's words, "The field is the world."

Report of Group Discussion

Highlights of the discussion fell on the role of the ordinary layman in witnessing. Many felt that the fulltime witness of the entire Church is the proper conception in evangelism, and that in this conception the role of the layman is as important as that of the clergy. "He is a link in the chain," said Dr. Olford (USA). Dr. Fenton (USA) pointed out that all are to share their faith, many laymen discovering in their witness a gift for evangelism they never knew they had.

Earlier in the discussion Dr. Schaeffer (Switzerland) suggested that the conference theme could include "One Truth" in addition to the themes "One Race, One Gospel, One Task." His observation was based on the conviction that evangelical Christianity should be grounded upon an emphasis on truth and not upon evangelism as such.

Reporter: *Enos Zimmerman*

THE GIFT OF THE EVANGELIST
Leighton F. S. Ford

Preaching the Gospel to the masses has been a basic method of evangelism since biblical times. It is still an essential approach in our day of population explosion.

The evangelistic campaign and the ministry of the evangelist are inseparable: man and method stand together.

1. The Gift of the Evangelist

While the noun "evangelist" occurs only three times in the New Testament, the verb "euaggelizomai" occurs over fifty times. Jesus Christ, Paul, and ordinary disciples all evangelized; Philip, the deacon, and Timothy, a settled pastor, were "evangelists."

But there was also a distinct "charisma" of the evangelist. Ephesians 4:11 states that "evangelists" are a gift from Christ to his Church. We conclude then that while all Christians are called to evangelism, some are specially called and equipped for the task.

The evangelist's relationship to other Church ministries is complementary, not competitive. Said Paul, "I planted the seed, Apollos watered it, but God made it grow." Neither evangelist nor pastor can say to each other "I have no need of you!"

The Church has a responsibility to the evangelist. It must recognize those whom God separates for this task, commission them for the work, support them by prayers and gifts, and rejoice with them in all that God does through them.

When a Church has no place for the evangelist, it denies itself a blessing God wishes to bestow. It also drives the evangelistically gifted into independent channels of expression. Unhappily, too many Churches have no doctrine of the evangelist, and no practical structure to support his work. Could strong evangelical congregations call gifted men to be ministers-of-evangelism-at-large? Could evangelical fellowships be formed to encourage and support promising evangelists? Could an evangelistic institute be formed to conduct brief courses and to provide "on-the-job" training by inviting potential evangelists to participate in actual campaigns?

Let the Churches find men who will seek the gift of evangelism! Let these men be sent where they must have the gift! Let them face their own inadequacies! Let them cry out to God for divine endowment! Then let

DR. FORD is an associate evangelist with the Billy Graham Evangelistic Association, and lives in Charlotte, North Carolina. He heads his own evangelistic team and conducts world-wide crusades, many in his native Canada.

them exercise the gift in faith, for just as evangelistic urgency comes in evangelizing, so the gift is realized and developed in using it.

The evangelist also has a responsibility to the Church. He must recognize that Christ is the source of his ministry, that his gift is intended to build up Christ's body. His gift is not from *himself* but from *Christ*, not for *himself*, but for the *Church*.

The evangelist must avoid spiritual isolation and independence. Even while promoting evangelism, he must also wait on his brethren. If God guides him to a certain place, Christians in that place will usually share that guidance.

The evangelist serves the body of Christ by adding new converts to that body. Moreover, Paul teaches that the gifts are to be used "to equip God's people for work in his service" (Eph. 4:12 NEB). The evangelist is to evangelize and also to equip others to evangelize. As he evangelizes, he communicates something of his own passion and "know-how" to his co-workers. The whole Church is strengthened in its evangelistic task by the presence of those who have the special charisma of evangelism.

2. The Role of the Evangelistic Campaign

Preaching God's Word to large crowds is nothing new. Moses and Joshua did it; so did Ezra and Ezekiel, John and the Lord Jesus, Peter and Paul. Through the centuries faithful men have given Christ to the masses. In the last century and a half, under Finney, Moody, Sunday, Graham and their colleagues, large evangelistic campaigns have become a rather standard technique.

Critics have attacked evangelistic campaigns as lacking in permanent results, but scholars like Timothy Smith, J. Edwin Orr, Kenneth Latourette, and John Wesley White have amply documented the impact of such evangelism on social reform, world missions, Church growth, and Christian unity.

Proponents of "mass evangelism" point to certain good results, critics point to alleged weaknesses. Both friend and foe, however, are often unaware that today's evangelistic campaign is playing a fresh role. New dimensions of breadth and depth are stimulating many evangelistic responses.

Today's campaign is a united witness by many Churches. Through the preaching of a gifted evangelist and mobilization of many Christians, it penetrates a whole area with the Gospel in many ways, as part of a continuing strategy of evangelism.

a. It is a *"united witness."* Does not the Holy Spirit seem to bless in a special way when all that believe are together (Acts 2:44)? Evangelistic campaigns give opportunity to witness together; a true, scriptural ecumenism is often a by-product.

b. It is a witness *"by many churches."* Large united crusades are sometimes opposed by those who say "Evangelism should be the work of the Church." But what is the Church? Wherever Christians meet in Jesus' name, there is he and there is the Church.

The united campaign thus combines rather than by-passes local fellowships.

c. It uses "the *preaching of a gifted evangelist.*" Proclamation remains central, for "faith comes from what is heard, and what is heard comes by the preaching of Christ."

d. It aims at the "*mobilization of many Christians.*" The evangelistic campaign provides excellent opportunity to stir average Christians to evangelism. Public interest makes it easier for Christians to talk of their faith. Personal counseling offers invaluable training for personal evangelism.

e. It seeks to "*penetrate a whole area in many ways.*" Mass meetings in themselves may not be penetration, for, at worst, they may represent the "convinced convincing the convinced." A public mass meeting, however, creates a spiritual beachhead through which the infantry can infiltrate.

To utilize this beachhead the campaign must be extended beyond the mass meetings by every possible means — house meetings, TV and radio, visitation. Often these auxiliary efforts produce more fruit than the large rallies.

In depth, the campaign must be planned to penetrate people's little "worlds" — their homes, schools, businesses. Key laymen must be gathered in cells, with responsibility to penetrate their areas of influence for Christ.

f. Finally, the campaign operates as "*part of the continuing strategy of evangelism.*" A weakness in many campaigns is their "hit-and-run" nature. Too often the evangelist has had no sense of his relationship to the continuing witness of the Churches. And, too often, some Churches take part in the campaign in desperation, hoping it will remedy or cover their evangelistic deficiencies. The campaign then becomes merely an episode, or even an interruption, instead of a catalyst to further and continuing witness.

The timing of united campaigns is extremely important. Evangelical Churches in each area need to coordinate evangelistic plans so that campaigns are strategically timed to link with other facets of evangelism, to gather in harvests when the time is ripe, and to avoid duplication of ministry.

The old evangelistic campaign pattern of inviting a visiting preacher, renting a hall, putting up a poster and expecting the unconverted to pour in is not feasible today. Under God's direction, we need united Church involvement, proclamation, mobilization of believers, penetration, and continuing strategy to carry out our unfinished task.

ASPECTS OF GROUP EVANGELISM
Anton Schulte

Evangelization of the world is related to the calling of evangelists. It is true that all persons who have received the Holy Spirit have also been commanded by God to be witnesses. The ministry of an evangelist however, is dependent upon a special God-given gift. We find this ministry mentioned in Eph. 4:11 in conjunction with reference to apostles, prophets, pastors, and teachers. Many people and much activity are no substitute for this gift. As ten Christians without a talent for teaching cannot replace a teacher, so ten witnesses are no substitute for an evangelist. Paul writes in I Tim. 4:14 that Timothy was given this gift through prophecy and by the laying on of hands by the elders. Evangelization of the world, therefore, depends upon a mighty working of the Spirit in the Churches. Only thus can there be prophesying and clear recognition of a call. We have far too few evangelists in the world. Only a revival in the Church can lead to awareness of this need. Then there will be those who are called, those whom an alert congregation will acknowledge: Whom God calls he will also grant the gift to carry out the task. A gift must be quickened however and for this, in my opinion, the following are necessary:

A God-given conviction that this world is lost.

A person who does not know the desperate condition of a patient, cannot tell him the good news of his healing. Anyone who does not fully realize that man without Christ is totally lost will not find his propagation of the Gospel to be Good News. Jesus Christ came to this earth because there was no other possible way to redeem man. And so we have been sent to impart the message of redeeming grace to mankind because there is no other possible way for people to be saved. The evangelist must obtain this realization from the Bible over and over again. This realization must also be imparted to the Church. When I see that something is absolutely necessary, then I also know that the task must be accomplished without fail.

Purposeful prayer and expectation that God will act.

If I know that only the Good News of Jesus Christ can help this world, that only the Gospel can deliver a man from his misery, yes, and in addition to this, fully comprehend that only God can redeem man, then I, too, will begin to pray. What's more, true prayer is contagious. It is like an epidemic, but a healing one. God grant that we will pray purposefully, with the expectation that God will redeem men in our day.

EVANGELIST SCHULTE is director of the New Life Missionwork (Missionswerk Neues Leben) in Alterkirchen, Germany.

This produces a ministry that is free of tradition.

Love stimulates creativity, and what more do we need in the task of evangelism than to see new possibilities in every new situation. The paralyzing thing today is that we so often say, "We used to do it that way, too," or "Things used to be so and so." But the fact is that we always have a new situation before us and therefore need an untraditional, tradition-free way of working in evangelism.

1. *Organization.* The place where we preach can be as different as people themselves are different. It must not be limited only to a church, to a church hall or assembly room. Many people can be reached more easily at some neutral gathering place. Even the gospel tent still has its attraction, and in Germany, where open-air meetings are still permitted, this avenue provides a good opportunity to preach during the summer months, especially at beaches and health resorts.

2. *The question of time* must be considered carefully. The fact that a hundred years ago three o'clock Sunday afternoon was an ideal time for an evangelistic meeting does not mean that today we can pull young people from the swimming pool for a meeting at this same hour.

3. *The advertising methods* of our grandfathers are no longer adequate. Amidst the jumble of posters and advertising in newspapers and movies, we must think of new ways to stimulate people's interest in our message. Naturally, someone will argue that this costs entirely too much. But this again raises the question as to what is the most important thing in this world. If the Gospel is the only answer for man's problems, then the method we use to bring the Gospel to people cannot be considered too costly.

4. Above all, in the matter of organization we need new orientation in respect to coordinating various mass media such as radio, television and the press. Properly directed reports can turn people's attention to the Gospel. In other words, *one must publicize the person who is to proclaim.*

5. As a part of the evangelistic effort one should begin *a literature crusade* so that every residence in the city receives a brochure with an attached coupon. Such a literature crusade carried out by hundreds of volunteer distributors is excellent help to an evangelistic crusade.

6. Even *the telephone* can be used as a part of the total advertising, perhaps in the following manner. Before the beginning of the crusade a telephone set up can be arranged so that people can listen in day or night to a taped sermonette by the evangelist.

7. Church members can conduct a *visitation program* to invite especially the people of the neighborhood and to bring them to the meetings.

8. *Newspaper articles* also pay special dividends if, for example, instead of inserting an advertisement, the evangelist inserts a short message each day for the entire week before the crusade begins.

Procedure of the evangelistic crusade.

Procedures in evangelism have changed frequently in the course of Church history. Ever since Moody's day we have had evangelists working with their soloists and have known choirs as an instrument of proclamation. Both are good supplements and supports to preaching. Our Lord said: "Go," and if people wander farther away, then we too must go further in order to reach them. This past summer on a youth night in a tent at Hagen we allowed a rock and roll band to perform. It wasn't the Beatles, of course, but a group of young people from the congregation who had set Gospel texts to beat music. Will jazz music determine the form of the worship service in the future? It is possible, but one thing must be clear. Whether a soloist sings, a choir assists, a beat band or a jazz orchestra plays, the motive for our action is always primary and not the form. The motive must always be to save souls.

The choice of themes for the messages.

Two world wars, automation and mass media have greatly changed people's thinking. If we want to reach them with our evangelistic message — and the Lord has said: "Go" — then our emphasis must begin with people's problems. Man's greatest problem today is loneliness. He longs for companionship, he hopes for security.

In selecting our topics and in planning our messages we must meet man on his own level. But we must also be careful that our contemporary themes are genuine and true, and that in our advertising we announce only what we actually intend to proclaim.

The language of the evangelist is today probably the biggest hindrance in proclaiming the Good News. The use of religious terms — without explaining their meaning — drives the people away, for they do not understand the language of Canaan. We may think we are speaking the language of the day, often because we ourselves came to Christ out of a godless world only 15 or 20 years ago, but we soon adapt to our environment, even in respect to speech. And because thinking precedes speaking, we ourselves fail to realize this. Jesus Christ left the pious isolation of the synagogue. He was found among tax collectors and women of the street. The Pharisees turned up their noses at this, but Jesus spoke the everyday language of the people of his time. He actually spoke Aramaic, the dialect spoken in the streets. The apostles did not write their epistles in classical Greek but in Koine. Can we still speak like an ordinary worker? Are we at home in the businessman's world? Can we talk informally with a miner? This is a part of exercising the evangelistic gift within us. It is part of being "a Jew to the Jews and a Greek to the Greeks," yes, to be all things to all men. But we are not to do this to gain recognition or to have godless men like us, but rather "that we may be able to win some for Christ."

SOUTHERN BAPTIST EVANGELISM
C. E. Autrey

Several types of group evangelism are being used in America. I shall present three of them briefly and discuss but one. They are: 1. The individual church revival; 2. Area crusades or city-wide crusades; 3. The simultaneous crusade.

Preparation is vital to all of these group efforts. While preparation is a bit different for each type, in the main it consists of spiritual and organizational preparation. The success of any kind of group evangelism is determined largely by preparation.

Spiritual preparation is essential. Lead people to pray, for results will come only to those who pray. Have people write on a card the names of those for whom they pledge to pray. Pledge them also to pray daily for the revival as a whole. Have them pray in groups. For this the neighborhood prayer meeting is effective. Have all day and all night prayer meetings. Assign prayer partners to young people. Have each praying person enlist five or more Christians outside of the area where the revival is being held to join in prayer for that particular revival.

Create a deep spiritual concern. This is vital (Isa. 66:8).

Promote complete surrender. If we would see revival we must first of all surrender ourselves to God. We must be open to promptings of the Holy Spirit. We must place everything on the altar, including our life, our talents, our money (Matt. 19:21).

Promote daily Bible reading. Wherever and whenever the Bible is read and studied, revival fires will burn. The Bible is a book of life and reveals God to be the source of life. The Bible was given to us by God and tells us about his relationship to man and about man's proper relationship to man.

Organizational preparation is vital also. Take a census wherever possible, for we must know who and where the people are. Publicity is also essential for all types of revival meetings. It creates expectancy. It advertises the great spiritual values of the crusade. If the average business used the same kind and amount of publicity as the average church, it would soon be bankrupt. Publicity has always been necessary. John Wesley believed in and practiced thorough advertising and that in a day when publicity was little known and used.

It is essential to conduct large rallies in preparation for the coming revival services, whether the revival is to be a city-wide effort or whether it is to be a simultaneous crusade.

DR. AUTREY is director of the Division of Evangelism of the Southern Baptist Convention in Atlanta, Georgia.

At least one other general item of preparation and performance should be mentioned. Evangelistic singing is an essential part in revival, and not a preliminary part of the service. It is not an effort to prepare people for the main feature. Evangelistic singing is an actual part of the worship experience. The purpose of revival singing is to prepare people's hearts to hear God speak, and very often he speaks to them during the song service. A stirring song service brightens the atmosphere and assimilates the crowd into a congregation of worshipers. When an evangelistic team first comes before an audience, it is never a congregation. It is always a crowd, and it remains a crowd until it is integrated by the singing into a worshiping congregation, if the singing is spiritual and worshipful.

A simultaneous crusade is a cooperative effort in a given area in which all churches conduct revivals at the same time, each individual church conducting its own meetings. If there are fifty churches in the area, each church will conduct revival services simultaneously for two weeks or more. This method has some distinct advantages.

1. The publicity is effective. All churches pool their money and a central committee plans and purchases the publicity. This procedure helps small and financially weak churches to have the same publicity as larger and more wealthy churches.

2. If fifty churches are involved, it provides fifty reaching places instead of one and thus makes more meeting places accessible to more people.

3. This method guarantees a better overall attendance. In America 100 churches will have a total attendance of 10,000 to 17,000 persons each week night and 40,000 or more on Sunday. These figures might obtain any place in the world where Protestant churches are strong and will obtain anywhere proportionately. The total number of first-time decisions at a simultaneous crusade will often exceed those at an area crusade in the same community. Between 1954 and 1964, Southern Baptists won to Christ and baptized 4,334,000; the major group method employed was the simultaneous crusade. Southern Baptists are now promoting the Billy Graham type of area crusades — in many places they combine the two with great effect.

4. This method is suited to the average preacher. Only a few hundred preachers at present are capable of conducting an area crusade, but almost any evangelist and pastor may effectively conduct a simultaneous crusade. In the Southern Baptist Convention most simultaneous crusades are conducted by pastor-evangelists.

In September of 1965 two staff members of the Division of Evangelism of the Southern Baptist Convention took 102 preachers to New Zealand to conduct a simultaneous crusade with the Baptist Union of New Zealand. This crusade resulted in 1,969 conversions and 2,118 other decisions. The same method was used in Australia in 1964 with equally good results, and in 1965 in Brazil.

The daily clinic on evangelism held for participating pastors, evangelists, and song leaders during the simultaneous crusade is one of the fine features of this type of revival. There is discussion of some vital phase of evangelism each day at the luncheon period followed by a time of prayer for the crusade. Instruction and encouragement are given daily.

In my opinion, all Protestants should use all the various group methods and should do so in cooperation with each other. Billy Graham has shown us that Protestant groups can indeed cooperate in evangelism with great advantage to all, and without surrendering any of their vital convictions. Such cooperation helps eliminate prejudice and jealousy, the archenemies of evangelism.

Report of Group Discussion

In the discussion which followed, the focus fell on five basic areas:

1. *Follow-up.* Mr. Bradley (South Africa) affirmed that follow-up presents the major problem of mass evangelism. After a recent campaign in his area, for example, he found it necessary to begin a business men's Bible Class in Capetown. Mr. Bhengu (South Africa) indicated that he felt the converts themselves must do the follow-up. However, the African campaigns often run for as long as six months, and the campaigns themselves provide some training and opportunities for growth.

2. *Child evangelism.* A delegate from Ireland inquired if children need special methods and, if so, why they are employed so little. Mr. Ford (USA) acknowledged that he was concerned about more effective counseling for children. Mr. Schulte (Germany) warned of pressing children too far and beyond the call of the Holy Spirit, reminding the panel that German theologians have often expressed the view that no one under fourteen should be approached about accepting Christ as Savior. Mr. Pontemannes (Mexico) told the delegates that in his area the biggest concern was following up children of non-Protestant parents, for these are often adversely affected through their home environment.

3. *Publicity.* Some sounded a warning against slick publicity campaigns which play up the evangelist.

4. *Semantics.* Mr. Fuchs (Germany) objected to Schulte's endorsement of updating the words of Scripture. He felt that the Holy Spirit is "tied" to certain expressions and certain types of theological language. Schulte contended that we must constantly interpret the words of Scripture so that the common man will understand their meaning.

5. *Pastor-evangelists.* A number of delegates supported Mr. Autrey's (USA) endorsement of using pastors as evangelists in simultaneous campaigns.   Reporter: *Carl Lundquist*

TWENTIETH CENTURY EVANGELISM
Oral Roberts

Our Lord Jesus Christ clearly set forth guide lines concerning the manner in which the Gospel was to be communicated to every creature in each generation. He instructed his followers to *preach*, to *teach*, and to *heal*.

His first followers were eye witnesses of him as a person — in his life, death, resurrection and ascension. Their evangelistic endeavors, so powerful and productive, rested upon a miracle, the greatest miracle of all — the person of the Lord Jesus Christ. In the lives of these men we observe a divine-human reciprocity, an interaction of the Holy Spirit and the human spirit. The Holy Spirit made Jesus the theme of their utterances. In his name they healed the sick, cast out demons, won souls, and established churches.

The sweep of their ministry was irresistible. How were they able to do this? The ministry of Jesus continued without interruption because the person of the Holy Spirit, the Paraclete, had come alongside to endue these ordinary men with the dynamics of the baptism made possible by Jesus.

The Spirit-filled men freely used the nine gifts of the Paraclete which enabled them to display the wisdom and works of Jesus himself to those who were in need of deliverance. The apostle Paul enumerated these gifts in I Corinthians 12, verses 8 to 10: "For to one is given by the Spirit the word of wisdom; to another the word of knowledge by the same Spirit; to another faith by the same Spirit; to another the gifts of healing by the same Spirit; to another the working of miracles; to another prophecy; to another discerning of spirits; to another divers kinds of tongues; to another the interpretation of tongues."

At any moment of need, the Holy Spirit manifested one or more of the nine gifts of the Spirit through an apostle, a prophet, a pastor, a teacher, an evangelist, or a layman.

The Holy Spirit manifested the gift of the *word of wisdom* and the inspired utterance cost the deacon Stephen his life in cruel martyrdom; this, however, was crowned by the subsequent salvation of Saul of Tarsus.

The *word of knowledge* imparted divine perception and insight into events and people. Through it the lying deeds of Ananias and Sapphira were exposed and instantly judged. (Acts 5:1-11.)

The *gift of faith* supernaturally emptied believers of all doubt and brought them to a state of knowing that God would act. (Acts 27:22-25.)

A compulsive urge to bring Christ's healing power to the sick and

DR. ROBERTS is president of Oral Roberts University in Tulsa, Oklahoma, and has held large evangelistic crusades in many parts of the world.

afflicted came from hearts stirred with compassion and hands empowered with a *gift of healing*. (Acts 9:17, Acts 3:6-8.)

The *gift of divers kinds of tongues* was followed by the companion *gift of interpretation of tongues* which brought edification to the Church. (I Cor. 14:12, 13.)

When error concerning the gifts of the Spirit crept into the Corinthian Church, there was no dispute as to the value and validity of these gifts. Paul simply clarified their use by defining the proper relationship of each gift to other gifts and the meaningful manifestation of the gifts in public assembly so that the entire congregation might continue to be edified.

The first Christian witnesses were positive people, set afire to do exploits in the dimension of the gifts of the Holy Spirit. They were natural men quickened by the supernatural.

They were willing to go anywhere, face anyone, endure any privation, stand up to any situation in order to preach, teach and heal in the name of the Lord Jesus Christ.

No aspect of man was ignored as they ministered to man's inner yearning to be made a whole person. They were satisfied with nothing less than seeing men made whole in body, mind, and soul.

The physician Luke faithfully recorded the miracles of healing which were wrought through faith. Nowhere does Paul refute the good work of medical science. Here was a union of the natural and the supernatural that fulfilled God's desire to have people made whole.

The early believers were person-centered. They were absolutely Christ-centered and therefore could not fail to be people-centered in their approach. They had a concern for sound doctrine, but their greater concern was to recognize each person as an immortal individual for whom Christ died. The lost sinner could become a new creation, a whole being.

In the early Church the life of Jesus was reproduced, his ministry was expanded to "greater things" as multitudes experienced deliverance at the hands of clergy and laymen.

The manifestation of the nine gifts was so frequent and of such great power that it became evident that the possible misuse of these gifts had to be governed by proper teaching. In this manner the charismatic power of God would continue to meet adequately the needs of the people.

Although the Christians spoke out against adultery, fornication, homosexuality, books of sorcery, demon possession, and other sins of their age, they were never problem-centered. Instead they offered the answers that are found in Christ Jesus the Lord.

They took the offensive and went to the people instead of waiting for the people to come to them. They witnessed in jails, in courtrooms, in open fields, along the river banks, and on boats. Not only did they preach and teach, they also healed wherever there was opportunity.

Today the person of the Lord Jesus Christ is alive in us through the

Holy Spirit, manifesting his gifts through us in order to minister to this present generation.

It is my conviction that the only way to evangelize this generation is to be absolutely Christ-centered, Spirit-filled and charismatically equipped to serve effectively God and man in selfless abandonment.

I am deeply aware of the outstanding ministry of other men and value them very highly as God-ordained and God-sent. In the final analysis, each one of us must function as an individual, yet all of us are members of the same body of Christ. We are one body with one mission: to press the revolutionary claims of Jesus Christ upon every human being on our planet, so that every person has opportunity to be saved and healed and transformed into a witness of the Lord Jesus Christ.

NEW CONCEPTS OF EVANGELISM
Harold John Ockenga

Evangelism, like every Christian doctrine, is under attack by the enemies of Christianity and is suffering from uncertainty among its friends. The need of evangelism is denied and the nature of evangelism is misunderstood. Small wonder that "ersatz" evangelism is found in some areas of the church today.

The biblical definition of evangelism is demanded at the inception of this discussion. This I take to be the proclamation under the anointing of the Spirit (I Cor. 2:4) of the Good News of the death and resurrection of Jesus Christ (I Cor. 15:1-4) for man's salvation (I Cor. 1:21) with the purpose of gaining conversions (II Cor. 5:20). As J. I. Packer says, "It is the preaching of the evangel with a summons to conversion" (*Evangelism and the Sovereignty of God*, p. 41, IVF).

This definition avoids the two pitfalls of neutralism, that is, the preaching of the Gospel with a take it or leave it attitude, and activism, that is, the attitude that it is our persuasion which converts a person. The former produces a sterile church with few additions of the "being-saved ones" and the latter produces false converts who fall away under persecution and trial. True evangelism depends upon the agency of the Holy Spirit, but is accompanied by fervent persuasion. It is measured not by the effects achieved, but by the faithful devotion to the Evangel.

Much which passes for evangelism today is not compatible with the biblical concept. In *Time* for May 14, 1965, is an article on Evangelism. It says: "The new approach to evangelism – visible in such ministries as coffee-homes, industrial missions and missions to drag strips, ski resorts and 'night people' – is primarily interested not in selling Christianity but in sympathetically expressing a human concern for others."

Biblical evangelism is a prerogative not confined to the ordained ministry of the Church but, as Roland Allen says, should be the spontaneous activity of the people of God. The witness of the radiance, joy and freedom of Christian life, causes others to seek the reason and results in the communication of the message. "What carried conviction is the manifest interestedness of the speaker. He speaks from the heart because he is too eager to be able to refrain from speaking. His subject has gripped him. He speaks of what he knows, and knows by experience. The truth which he imparts is his own truth. He knows its force. He is speaking almost as much to relieve his own mind as to convert his hearer, and yet he is as eager to convert his hearer as to relieve his own mind; for his mind can only be relieved by sharing his new truth, and his truth is not shared until

DR. OCKENGA is minister of Park Street Church in Boston, Massachusetts.

another has received it. This his hearer realizes. Inevitably he is moved
by it. Before he has experienced the truth himself he has shared the
speaker's experience "(*The Spontaneous Expansion of the Church*, p. 10).

This sharing of the Evangel may be on many levels, that of a nation-
evangelism-in-depth; that of a city or region — an evangelistic crusade; that
of a congregation — calling campaign; that of a group — a Koinonia
prayer meeting; that of an individual — personal witnessing; that of a
tract-printed evangelism. On whatever level, it is evangelism if it fulfills
the above definition. The object in view, as Dr. L. S. Chafer clearly
pointed out, is to reach those who have never heard with the message.

As pastor of an inner city Church in a great metropolitan area, I
embrace the validity of all types of biblical evangelism, and have used all
of them.

Mass evangelism may be understood as the proclamation of the
Evangel by mass media, in large assemblies, by amplification, by radio, by
television, by movies, by printing. Twenty years ago leaders of the Church
declared that the days of mass evangelism were over. Then God raised
up Billy Graham, who has preached to more living persons than any
other preacher in history, and who uses all of the mass media.

Group evangelism is very popular today. Bible study and prayer
groups often called Koinonia groups have spontaneously risen in many
areas, through which large numbers of moribund Christians have been re-
vitalized and numberless individuals have been introduced to vital Christian
faith and life.

Personal evangelism depends upon involvement with individuals rather
than upon promiscuous witnessing. Time for friendships, service, ministry
must precede the sharing of the message. This may be done at luncheons
with business men, where pointed questions are asked, such as, What
kind of Bible study do you pursue? What work are you doing for God?
Have you witnessed to anyone lately? This may be the entire ministry of one
member of a church staff, but should be practiced by us all.

Visitation evangelism may be of a campaign type, may be a sustained ministry of deacons, or may be a general church responsibility and
is most fruitful. The high-rise apartment has sealed off thousands from this
means of contact, but in suburban areas it cannot be surpassed in value.
Face to face confrontation with the claims of Christ will always bring fruit.

Tract evangelism is a method within the reach of every Christian. A
doctor with a wide practice in Boston was impressed by a sermon on this
topic a number of years ago and ever since has set aside his Sunday
afternoons to place tracts in hotels, railroad stations, telephone booths,
airports and other public places. This ministry supplements his personal
witness to his patients.

Evangelism means involvement with persons, interaction and instruction. The chairman of a former united evangelistic campaign in St. John

introduced me to the Atlantic Provinces Baptist Ministers' Conference of Canada with this statement: "Following a meeting in the St. John campaign a fellow-minister said, 'He is not an evangelist, he is a teacher.' And yet God gave us the greatest campaign in one hundred years." Teaching the Word with a passion for commitment to Christ is evangelism.

Evangelism must take account of the biblical emphasis on human responsibility to decide, to choose, to convert. Faith is erroneously ascribed to God as a gift (see Eph. 2:8 where "gift" is neuter and "faith" is feminine. Salvation is the antecedent of gift). Man is commanded to repent, to believe, to convert. The Bible places these acts within the ability of man. Let us not diminish the biblical emphasis by stressing divine sovereignty. Salvation is of God; reprobation is of man.

Hence we proclaim the Gospel; in seeking conversions we also entreat, exhort and persuade. If we expect these conversions we shall see them.

A TIME FOR ACTION
Efrain Santiago

This is a time for action rather than words. Today more souls are headed for hell than at any other time in history. During the time it takes to give this talk, over 2,000 souls will pass eternally into the abyss. Most of these have never heard one invitation to accept Jesus Christ. Yet we are the ones "He is sending out around the world to tell all people everywhere the great things God has done for them, so that they too will believe and obey him!" Yes, our conflict is world-wide. However, I am going to speak primarily about Latin America, the area and the people I know best.

Latin America today has only two choices: either atheistic Communism or biblical Christianity! Yes, spiritual war is under way in Latin America to a degree never before experienced. We must remember that in war there is no substitute for victory, and this spiritual warfare we must win!

The first step to victory in Latin America is saturation evangelization, the second, follow-up. "No evangelism is complete until the evangelized become evangelists." Evangelism involves harvest preparation and harvest reaping. Two instances where the Lord calls a group of souls a "harvest" are found in Matthew 9:36-38, and John 4:35.

But to have a harvest there must first be harvest preparation. There are three major steps in preparing for a harvest: 1) preparing the ground, 2) planting the seed, and 3) cultivating. Clearing the trees and under-brush, blasting and clearing the stumps, plowing, disking, harrowing, fertilizing, and other problems of preparing "new ground" are a farmer's most difficult jobs. Likewise, clearing the obstacles, bridging the prejudices, and finding personnel and methods to cross the geographic, religious, social, and political barriers, in order to have contact with lost souls — are the most difficult jobs in evangelism.

Seed must be planted in exactly the right place. In evangelism that place is man's heart. Much evangelism today misses God's plan by about twelve inches. We aim at men's heads and completely miss their hearts. Romans 10:10 says, ". . . it is by believing in his heart that a man becomes right with God . . ." (Living Letters). Paul said in I Corinthians 2:4, "And my preaching was very plain, not with a lot of oratory and human wisdom. . ." (Living Letters).

Cultivating is necessary to develop a ripened harvest. A man seldom comes to Christ after the first contact. Most of us heard God's plan of salvation over and over again before we came to a decision. Most great

THE REV. MR. SANTIAGO is a Latin American staff evangelist with the Billy Graham Evangelistic Association and pastor of the Wesleyan Methodist Church of Puerto Rico in San Juan, Puerto Rico.

evangelistic crusades today actually start years before the evangelist arrives on the scene. To reap a great harvest we must pay the price of preparation.

"Remember this, that if you give little you will get little. A farmer who plants just a few seeds will get only a small crop, but if he plants much, he will reap much" (II Cor. 9:6, Living Letters). Evangelism involves both preparation and reaping!

Latin America is an area of 8,000,000 square miles, and 170,000,000 people. The races are mixed more than in any other part of the world, and the population of South America is growing faster than that of any other continent. Seventy-five percent of the people work on farms, plantations, and ranches controlled by rich landowners. Life in Latin America is not like it was twenty years ago; we have changed completely both economically and politically, and have advanced intellectually. Spiritual progress, however, has not kept pace with other developments.

We cannot understand the basic problem of evangelism in Latin America without considering the Roman religious system which claims over 90% of the population. This system holds its power over people by fear and leaves their lives completely empty. It threatens to cut them off from God for eternity, if they do not bow to the hierarchy.

Latin America is tired of an empty religious system and people are rebelling at a religion of fear. This rebellion creates a vacuum that is open either to atheistic Communism or biblical Christianity. The victory of Christianity and the true Church of Jesus Christ depend on aggressive evangelism. We must fight boldly! Now is the time to fight and to conquer with all-out evangelism.

As we anticipate the battles that lie ahead we must first examine our warriors, the evangelists. Besides the categories of laymen and clergymen I would like to add that of the technician, since our modern warfare depends so much on him. We soldiers may be expendable but we are indispensable. We are God's tools for bringing his Word to those he loves. God does not speak to the lost directly from heaven, but he speaks through the faith of one heart to stir faith in another. One man preaches and another believes. No one is ever saved apart from the instrumentality of another believer. If you know someone who was saved in the loneliness of his room, I would say that the bud bloomed when he was alone, but that others planted and watered the seed. In fact, one person is seldom alone responsible for the salvation of a soul. Some sow the seed, some water and cultivate, and still others reap the harvest. It usually takes the combined faith of a team of believers to bring saving faith to the lost. The salvation of a soul in Latin America is the combined result of those who pray, those who organize and prepare, those who promote, those who send, and those who make direct contact. Saving faith comes to the heart of an individual through the teamwork of faith.

We must also have proper weapons. A United States general once said, "It's not the number of men that wins the battle, but rather, it's the firepower." The spiritual power needed for victory will first come when God's people pray earnestly and fervently. The prayer cells which are organized months, sometimes years, before a campaign are the heart of any great evangelistic crusade. It is God's power that brings spiritual victory. The most important part of successful evangelism is prayer!

Soldiers also need the weapons of modern equipment and methods. With radio, television, public address systems, fast transporation, printing presses, all kinds of office equipment, etc. not known to evangelists a few years ago, the ministry of one man can now be felt around the world. These weapons must be backed by faithful fervent prayer or they will be abused and misused.

In spiritual warfare one of the hardest tasks is to make effective contact with the lost. Paul says in Colossians 4:5, "Make the most of your chances to tell others the Good News. Be wise in all your contacts with them" (Living Letters). We must Go. "We have been ringing church bells when we should have been ringing doorbells; we have been doing by proxy what we should have been doing by proximity; and we have been doing by purse what we should be doing in person."

We must also balance the various phases of our warfare. We will be no more effective than our weakest link in the chain of operations. We must balance promotion and equipment with program and people. We must balance preparation, reaping, and follow-up.

The local Church is vital in mass evangelism. The Church is responsible for strengthening, and training new soldiers. It is the agency through which the evangelized are transformed into evangelists. More often than not, however, the Church fails in this very important phase of its work and often for two basic reasons. In II Timothy 2:2, we are told to commit the things we have heard to faithful men. Most efforts of the Church are directed toward unfaithful men. We call on absentees who were too lazy to attend church or preferred to play golf. We nurse them along to get them back. Meantime we do little or nothing to help the faithful who attended the services. The faithful who should have our attention and help are neglected and never develop into their full spiritual potential. The unfaithful do not want to be developed, so we end up with a church full of spiritual infants and no mature soldiers. God says we are to concentrate on the faithful. When we do, we will see spiritual giants springing up whom God can use to reach and teach others.

The second reason for the Church's failure to transform the evangelized into evangelists is given in II Timothy 2:15: "Study to show thyself approved unto God, a workman that needeth not to be ashamed, rightly dividing the word of truth." Most of our Bible teaching does not produce workmen. Suppose two carpenters apply for work, but I need only one. I interview the first man and he says, "I know all about the saw. It has ten teeth to every inch. It is rolled thirty times to give it just the right temper and strength. I know the exact alloy to make the best hammer and the kind of wood used in the handle." Then I ask the second man about his qualifications. "I don't know all the technical details about the saw," he says, "but I do know how to cut a straight line in the right place. With the hammer, I know how to hit the nail on the head and drive it in the right place." Obviously I will hire the man who knows how to use the tools. Today too much of our Bible study and teaching in the churches is aimed at seeking what kind of metal the Bible is made out of, rather than learning how to use it to hit the nail on the head! God help us to produce workmen who will not need to be ashamed when God examines the work. God help us to produce soldiers who will satisfy the One who enlisted them in his army!

To be free from the blood of all men we must pray, we must send, we must go, we must mobilize every soldier, we must use every modern method, and we must win! In spiritual warfare there can be no compromise! We must have victory! It is either heaven or hell for the ninety and nine that are lost. They must hear God's Word!

PREPARATION, PRESENTATION, PRESERVATION
Leo E. Janz

The most effective method of evangelism is that done at a personal level. Its importance is reflected in the fact that every other method of evangelistic approach must eventually culminate in individuals having a personal encounter with Jesus Christ by making a personal response to a personal challenge.

But only 5% of all Christians ever directly lead another person to Christ. It is small wonder, then, that our generation has not seen every home in every community, even in our Western world, penetrated with the challenge of the Christian Gospel.

Christ's command, "Go ye into all the world . . ." is usually thought of in geographic terms, but it implies vocational responsibilities as well. His witnesses are to proclaim the Gospel to their contemporaries in every vocation. To do this requires total mobilization of every Christian for man-to-man evangelism.

Group evangelism, in addition to its own direct approach, can also ignite a chain-reaction of personal evangelism. In fact, crusades which do not actively involve many local Christians before, during and after the evangelistic meetings fall short of their full potential. In our crusades we stress the idea that the evangelistic team is not limited to a group of "professionals" but should be as large as the body of born-again believers in that particular area.

From our experience of crusade evangelism we feel there are three main aspects to be considered: the *preparation* of the place and the people, the *presentation* of the Gospel during the period of advertised public meetings, and the *preservation* of the results that God gives.

Preparation is extremely important. In political campaigns that promote men-made programs, endless hours are sacrificed, vast sums of money invested and boundless energy is expended. The presentation of God's plan of salvation surely merits equally enthusiastic preparation. An evangelistic crusade will reflect the dedicated effort of many people who participate in prayer groups, and as counselors, musicians, ushers and many other kinds of workers.

The *presentation* of the Gospel is the heart and core of the effort. The crusade platform is no place to display oratory, provide entertainment

THE REV. MR. JANZ is president and director of the Janz Brothers Gospel Association in Basel, Switzerland.

or even parade the gifts of the Spirit. The Word of God should be proclaimed simply, seriously and sincerely.

Music has its ministry of preparing hearts for the preaching of the Word. Judiciously used music can be of invaluable help in evangelism.

Preaching must be well-balanced, presenting the whole counsel of God concerning salvation. The first truth to proclaim is man's lost and sinful condition. Secondly, man must hear God's judgment on sin, and thirdly, he must see his complete and utter inability to save himself. Fourthly, the proclamation must declare the sacrificial and substitutionary death of Christ as God's remedy for sin, emphasizing in this provision the revelation of God's love. The urgency of making a decision for Christ must also be stressed as well as the danger of rejecting the divine offer of salvation. Finally, the glorious possibility of living for God through the power of the resurrected Christ should be declared.

In short, a clear presentation must be given of sin and righteousness, repentance and faith, heaven and hell, God's wrath and God's love. Difficulty in maintaining this standard, lack of courage, and fear of unpopularity sometimes cause preachers and evangelists to dilute their presentation of the Gospel.

Simplicity is a hallmark of good evangelistic preaching. Ernst Modersohn, one of Germany's most effective evangelists admitted: "It has taken me ten years to learn to preach simply, so simply that not only every professor but also every household maid can understand."

Most Germans never attend college or university, yet much of the preaching is on the level of the less than 10% who do. Even the average intellectual, though perhaps a genius in his particular field, is largely ignorant of simple Gospel truths.

Extending an invitation to make a clear decision for Christ is an important part of our task. Peter and Paul, Stephen and even Jesus, in their preaching confronted listeners with a choice. *"Brethren, what shall we do?"* was the response to Peter's preaching, as recorded in Acts 2. Sometimes where there has been a clear preaching of the Gospel, but no invitation to make a decision for Christ, hundreds will respond as soon as an opportunity is extended to accept Christ and to confess him publicly.

A fine Gospel minister in Switzerland who increased his congregation ten-fold questioned new members to learn what attracted them to his church. It was his clear explanation of how salvation is to be personally appropriated, they said, that met their spiritual need. Elsewhere they had been shown Christ as the door, but were never told how to enter, neither encouraged to do so.

Since there are various ways of "drawing in the net," dogmatism on this point should be avoided. God will direct in how to do it, but opportunity *must* be given to take a definite step of faith. The urgency of the Gospel demands this.

Preservation of the results God gives us is the most difficult phase of evangelism. Usually there are two distinct groups of people to be dealt with — those who want counseling but make no clear decision, and those who definitely trust Christ. It is unfair to label mass evangelism as merely an emotional upheaval, because all who come for counseling do not immediately become true and steadfast followers of Christ. We must remember that many who come for counseling but do not make a clear decision are candidates for follow-up work. And those who make clear-cut decisions for Christ likewise need further help, need to be taught how to grow in their new-found faith.

Even in Paul's day the most obvious follow-up center was the local church. If new believers can be channeled into Bible-believing churches, their chances for growth are that much better.

More than half of our crusade converts receive little help or encouragement from their pastors. Converts entrusted to an indifferent or hostile pastor find it difficult to remain true to their commitment; less than 10% survive. Conversely, where converts are under the spiritual care of a faithful counselor, up to 90% have showed themselves to be true followers of Christ as long as six years after their decision.

Laymen are invaluable in the after-care of converts. While such helpers need instruction for their responsibilities, they are probably motivated and prepared best of all by their experience and blessing in actually dealing with inquirers during a crusade and helping them grow in the faith. Where crusade counselors keep in personal touch with their counselees, up to 60% of the converts remain faithful to Christ.

Follow-up programs can be summarized briefly as follows: get converts into the Word of God; encourage them to witness and work for Christ; establish them in Christian fellowship, worship and prayer; and bring them into Christ-centered social spheres.

Always the whole Gospel must be made relevant for the whole person — his mind, his emotions and his will. The Bible reminds us: *"Thou shalt love the Lord thy God with all thy heart, and with all thy soul, and with all thy strength, and with all thy mind; and thy neighbor as thyself* (Luke 10:27).

Our task, then, is to preach the Word of God in the manner indicated by the Apostle Paul when he wrote to the Thessalonians: *"For we speak as messengers from God, trusted by Him to tell the truth; we change his message not one whit to suit the taste of those who hear it; for we serve God alone, Who examines our hearts' deepest thoughts"* (I Thess. 2:4, Living Letters).

Report of Group Discussion

An overflow crowd packed the conference room for a discussion of faith healing which revealed a remarkable measure of agreement among the panelists. All recognized the reality of divine healing, acknowledged that it is but one part of the gospel presentation, and openly repudiated the errors and excesses so often connected with it in popular campaigns.

The largest degree of disagreement was in terms of emphasis. Dispensing with his paper early in the discussion, Oral Roberts (USA) called for a greater use of the gifts of the Spirit, especially healing, to reach those outside the Church, those who will not respond to a mere preaching or teaching of the Word. On his part Dr. Harold Ockenga (USA) stressed what he termed a scriptural formula for genuine revival and genuine conversion. The latter involved repentance, confession of sin and a turning to Christ, a turning away from sin, and a personal commitment to Christ as Savior. "Such formulas are valuable," said Ockenga, "because they work." Ockenga felt that healing has always been practiced in the Church, but he tended to identify it in our day with medical missions and Christian social programs.

Several panelists spoke to questions dealing with faith healing.

"What is the reason for failures in faith healing?" asked an American delegate. Ockenga felt that the answer lay in the entire theology of faith healing, stressing that biblical healing is in the atonement and therefore in its fullest measure for the end of time. In the present age, however, God may heal and he may not. And the reason may not be traced to either a lack of faith or a lack of prayer. Roberts stressed that Christ did no miracles in Nazareth (where "he could not . . ."), but in these cases the reason was due to lack of faith on the part of the people.

Hession (England) wondered whether healing could be divorced from faith in Christ. There was general agreement that one cannot eliminate the possibility of psychic or demonic healing, and Leo Janz (Germany) spoke of an emergence of demonic power in German-speaking Europe.

Reporter: *James M. Boice*

THE LOCAL CHURCH AND EVANGELISM
José M. Martínez

To speak of methods of evangelism is to expose ourselves to the temptation of giving them a disproportionate importance, as if the ultimate success of the proclamation of the Gospel depended upon them. A Christian or group of Christians filled with the Holy Spirit will always find an effective way to evangelize. On the other hand, the best systems will be a failure if they lack the power of the Holy Spirit.

Nonetheless, proper consideration of methods and their application can be of inestimable help in propagating the Gospel. Let us first indicate what we mean by "group evangelism." While in personal evangelism only one believer is the instrument of witness, in group evangelism more than one unite in the work. The New Testament abounds in examples of this joint and cooperative endeavor. Its more simple form is exemplified by the disciples whom Jesus sent out to preach two by two. The preaching of the Gospel with the subsequent spiritual harvests in Jerusalem, in Samaria, in Antioch, in Asia Minor and Europe were usually carried out through the work of a group or number of people.

1. The local Church as the unexcelled nucleus for evangelism

The apostolic era has very few examples of Christian activity whose origin, growth and purpose were not intimately related to the local Church. The evangelizing witness issued from the local Church. When this witness resulted in conversions, converts either were added to an established Church or were joined together in order to form one.

Perhaps one of the greatest needs today is to awaken churches as a whole to their responsibility in witnessing, so that evangelism stops being what James Denney called "the disinterested interest" of a few. Mobilizing all the members of a Church for the task of witness is perhaps the only method for carrying out a thorough work of evangelism in breadth and depth.

2. The need for adequate instruction

Such important work as proclaiming the Gospel requires training. It would be well if churches had special courses in evangelism for their members in which, in addition to thorough Bible training, guidance would be given on the conditions and circumstances for presenting the Gospel. Clear comprehension of the cultural, sociological, political and religious

THE REV. MR. MARTÍNEZ is pastor of the Gracia Baptist Church in Barcelona, Spain.

factors of the area in which the Word is to be sown helps greatly in presenting the Gospel in an effective way.

3. Christian fellowship in evangelism

Every age has been difficult for messengers of the Gospel, but our times are perhaps particularly adverse. The seeming powerlessness of the Church's witness before the world brings a feeling of frustration to many Christians and not a few leaders. But in Christian fellowship, such as Paul and his colaborers portrayed so magnificently, the believer's witness for Christ receives new strength to continue the task.

4. Methods of evangelism

It would be foolish to think that all methods apply equally well everywhere. It might be said of evangelism what Bishop Stephen Neill declared in regard to missionary strategy: "It is good to have one or two principles, and no theory." Each situation and place will determine in large measure what procedures and methods to use.

Only by way of example, however, let me mention a few procedures that lend themselves to wide application, even in places where complete religious freedom is absent.

a. Surveys. Members of the evangelizing group prepare a survey that includes questions of a religious nature. This questionnaire can be used in personal contact in parks, squares, on the street, or in visits to homes.

b. Correspondence. Securing names from a good source of information — a telephone book, for example, — workers send letters containing one or two well-selected Gospel tracts to as many people as they are then prepared to follow-up if there is some response. In addition to the tracts, the letters enclose a card which offers: (1) further evangelical literature, (2) a copy of the New Testament, (3) the address of an evangelical church, (4) a personal visit.

c. Meetings in homes. Here a tape recorder and especially-made tapes of a brief service could be valuable.

d. Special campaigns. These are usually fruitful provided there is good spiritual preparation and wide collaboration on the part of the members of the churches.

5. The evangelization of new fields

The evangelizing efforts of a Church should reach out in ever widening circles, even "to the very ends of the earth" (Acts 1:8, Phillips). When such effort reaches new fields, the work should be conscientiously planned for the best use of time, energy and resources. Prolonged, concentrated efforts are particularly advisable in strategically important cities; here participants should be especially selected for their aptitudes, in order that solid foundations may be laid for churches that in time will themselves become new centers of evangelism and the source of new churches.

6. Evangelism in relation to the world-wide work of the Gospel

We cannot make evangelism an end in itself. It is only the beginning of a much more extensive work that includes the edification and growth of the Church in the world. If it is fruitful, evangelization opens the door to great pastoral and educational opportunities; unless the evangelistic thrust makes adequate provision for meeting these opportunities, it may result in failure.

In this aspect of its divergent facets, evangelism is closely related to missionary work and demands good coordination and implementation of efforts in order to realize the same goals. A missionary superstructure that controls all initiative is probably not advisable. It is most unfortunate, however, that in some cases unrelated missionary efforts that have no awareness of the true needs of a country are often multiplied on the same field, and accomplish nothing that could be considered important either in basic evangelism or in consolidation of the work. Perhaps this great Congress on Evangelism ought some day to be supplemented with another of the same magnitude on missionary work. May the Holy Spirit guide and control the Church so that in the glorious work it has been given to do in the world, it may act with the harmony and power proper to the body of Christ.

EVANGELISM BY GROUPS
José Maria Rico

We must begin by recognizing that there is no way of evangelizing the world without the Gospel. To evangelize with the Gospel means simply to accept the Word of God as our standard for every message that we preach. Consequently, this divine Word will inspire the practical procedures that lend greater efficacy to our preaching. Our compass is the familiar challenge: "Go ye into all the world and preach the Gospel to every creature. He that believeth (in the Gospel—not the person) shall be saved: But he that believeth not shall be damned." In other words, salvation of the world is directly related to exact and effective preaching of the Gospel. For this reason Paul urged Timothy to "rightly divide the word of truth." And Peter rests proper growth of believers and the Church upon the "sincere milk of the word." If we sincerely want to save the world, we must dedicate ourselves to in-season and out-of-season propagation of the Gospel which is the "power of God unto salvation to everyone that believeth." This was Paul's only motivation. "For Christ sent me not to baptize, but to preach the gospel" (I Cor. 1:17). Therefore he asked the Thessalonians to pray "that the word of the Lord may have free course, and be glorified, even as it is with you" (II Thessalonians 3:1), for saving faith comes by hearing and hearing by the Word of God. The earnestness and sense of responsibility of the early Church in carrying out this solemn commission given by the Lord was indeed admirable. In Jerusalem these first Christians began the preaching of the Gospel that continued to Samaria and should eventually reach the uttermost parts of the earth. In the first generation of Christians the Gospel spread throughout the ancient world of that day.

In discussing how to get today's Church into action Dr. Melvin H. Hodges says: "God wants all men to be saved (I Tim. 2:4); however, the population of the world increases in greater proportions than the persons that accept Christ, so while time marches on, the number of non-believers increases and the church gets farther and farther behind in the fulfillment of its mission." Dr. Hodges continues, "It isn't lack of consecration or sacrifice on the part of the pastors, but a lack of a sufficient amount of workers. The souls that need Christ total millions upon millions while the workers number in the twenties and hundreds. There is only one solution to this problem, enlist every believer in Jesus Christ and delegate a task that requires personal responsibility. . . ."

This alarming situation forces us to find and analyze the best methods for propagating the Gospel. While each Christian should be a light and the

DR. RICO is an international evangelist for the Foreign Missions Department of the Assemblies of God in Springfield, Missouri, USA, and for the Bolivian Indian Mission in Cochabamba, Bolivia, South America.

salt of the earth, yet it is also urgent that Christians unite to promote a general offensive against the unbelieving world. Who should comprise these groups? The most important group in this task is the local Church. A look at the mission field in Latin America, for example, will verify this statement. Here the Gospel has been diffused because of direct and opportune witness by the Church in the United States, Canada and Great Britain. These non-ethnic groups have carried the burden and responsibility of sending missionaries and sufficient financial aid to preach the Gospel. Without the work of these churches, our beautiful continent of Latin America would still be in death's darkness. It is no exaggeration to say, I think, that the key group in the evangelization of our present age is the local Church. It is here that God seeks out those whom he needs in his work. Were not Paul and Barnabas selected in this way at Antioch? (Acts 13). We must give the local Church a missionary vision that it often lacks. What shall we do, however, when the task becomes too great for the limited resources of the local Church? In my opinion the only remedy then is the united participation of other Christian churches. Such collaboration of churches can be denominational or interdenominational. Let us examine both approaches.

Denominational Collaboration

Suppose the preaching is at some designated part of the city or suburbs. Several churches then unite to plan the spiritual invasion of the predetermined area. These churches pray together and together plan the methods to be used in carrying out the evangelistic project.

Going by trucks and buses to designated locations, united church groups then distribute literature door to door, speak to people on the streets, meet in homes to preach, and continue working in various ways to strengthen the local witness. Other times churches have felt a responsibility toward those who use public trains and buses. Then various churches of the same denomination have trained believers to travel in the conveyances and to hold what are called lightning services.

Assemblies of God organizations like Christ's Ambassadors (for young people) and Fishers of Men (for adults) have but one purpose—namely to recruit forces in the denomination that will realize objectives that cannot be met in any other way.

The same united approach has been used in spreading the Word of God by radio and television. In such cases, the various talents found in several churches unite to present a shared witness.

All such activities come under the one banner of Christian Brotherhood for Gospel Propagation.

Interdenominational Collaboration

In Latin America a new procedure is in operation called Evangelism-in-Depth. It works under the auspices of the Latin American Mission and has met with great success in various countries. The Rev. Ruben Lores, a member of this panel, will have more to say about the structural ideology of this movement.

Total Evangelism, which is the method used by the Assemblies of God, has no regard to the number of people that can be reached but places its emphasis on the total power of the Gospel, in every phase mentioned in the Word of God, i.e., salvation, healing, and the baptism of the believer in the Holy Spirit.

The So-Called Social Gospel

In any social system, whatever benefits are granted are for society as a whole; individuals are really quite anonymous and lost. In spite of the social efforts made by governments and private enterprise, therefore, many individuals do not share in the so-called social benefits.

While we commend efforts that result in benefit to society, we in no way consider them efficacious in the salvation of men. The Gospel does not consider man to be just one of many cells in a collective social group; indeed it focuses on the individual as the direct object of the entire divine plan. For this reason the Word of God says: "Therefore if any man be in Christ, he is a new creature: old things are passed away; behold, all things are become new" (II Cor. 5:17).

In other words, every time an individual makes a personal decision to belong to Christ, a definite change takes place in the person who is experiencing the birth of the new creature in his own life where old things are left behind. What society needs, therefore, is the multiplication of these new creatures in its fold. When these take control of society, society will experience total and natural renewal.

It is worthy of mention that Jesus never mentioned social reforms in the usual popular sense. Rather he projected an evangelical principle that he desired should become the social principle. "Seek ye first the kingdom of God and his righteousness," he said, "and all these other things shall be added unto you."

Let us be faithful administrators of the Word of God; let us fulfill faithfully the commission that the Lord of the Harvest has entrusted to us. Let us not use this holy and blessed Gospel as a pedestal to promote our own viewpoints. Our goal is to reach individuals so that they will turn their eyes on the author and finisher of our faith, Jesus Christ. Thus we will be effective co-laborers with God in the salvation of the world and in the renewal of society.

EVANGELISM-IN-DEPTH
Ruben Lores

Since 1960 seven Latin American countries have felt the impact of Evangelism-in-Depth. This movement originated in the mind and heart of the late director of the Latin America Mission, Dr. R. Kenneth Strachan, a man of deep theological insight concerning the task of evangelization, and widely experienced in great evangelistic endeavors throughout Latin America. Therefore, biblical principles and sound strategy are at the heart of the movement.

The expression "in-depth" indicates the opposite of superficial, passing and limited. While the Evangelism-in-Depth movement is multi-dimensional, the dimension of depth is basic to all the others. "Depth" has to do both with the believer's spiritual life and with the theological understanding of the foundations of evangelization. It refers also to the extent or breadth of the program and to the use of all available methods and resources to accomplish the task.

The first experiment in Evangelism-in-Depth occurred in Nicaragua in 1960. In subsequent years similar programs took place in Costa Rica, Guatemala, Honduras, Venezuela, Bolivia and the Dominican Republic. This last effort ended in April, 1966. Evangelism-in-Depth will begin in Peru early in 1967, and Colombia is making preparations for 1968. The story of the early movements is described in the book, EVANGELISM IN DEPTH. This book has kindled the evangelistic flame in more than 30 countries outside of Latin America. No doubt this is just the beginning, for Evangelism-in-Depth has all the characteristics of a living organism that has just begun to develop.

Evangelism-in-Depth is not just a program nor is it limited to certain methods. It is an all-inclusive strategy whereby all Churches use all available resources to reach an entire country with the whole Gospel of Christ.

Evangelism-in-Depth is a philosophy of evangelism that correlates all propositions, principles, objectives, etc. into a logical relationship. This philosophy is implemented by a program of evangelistic activities based on previous experiments, and under local leadership tries to match all available resources with the needs and opportunities of the local situation. Moreover, Evangelism-in-Depth creates an atmosphere of optimism, a positive attitude that stimulates creativity, courage, and enthusiasm. This attitude becomes the collective experience of all God's people, an experience that must be shared to be fully appreciated.

THE REV. MR. LORES is international coordinator of Evangelism-in-Depth for the Latin America Mission in San Jose, Costa Rica.

The Program of Evangelism-in-Depth

The program of Evangelism-in-Depth is a series of continuous, successive and alternative phases of evangelistic and teaching activities held simultaneously in all the cooperating Churches. Everything centers around the local Church but within the framework of its denominational structure and in full recognition of its responsibility toward the total body of Christ. The program is *united* inasmuch as all the Churches work together; it is also *simultaneous* because each Church works in its own territory at the same time as the others. The formal program generally lasts a year.

The main phases of the program are as follows:

1. *Organization of prayer cells throughout the country*

Since the objective is to engage every believer in a prayer cell, a goal is set to have a prayer cell for every five believers in the total evangelical community. Each Church organizes its own prayer cells; these continue throughout the year's effort and even beyond.

2. *Training every believer in soul winning*

The idea is to train not just a few key laymen but to mobilize the entire Church: children, young people, adults. Usually the pastor himself teaches the basic course of twelve lessons at whatever service has the largest attendance. Sometimes the training classes alternate with house-to-house visitation.

3. *House-to-house visitation in the church's immediate and adjacent areas as designated by the coordinators*

The purpose of this visitation is not simply to give out literature or even to invite people to the Church. The main purpose is to give an evangelistic witness in every home. Results depend on the receptivity of the neighborhood, and on the number and perseverance of the callers. In one city, the members of a small Church visited over 9,000 homes and found hundreds of people interested in the Gospel. In every such effort thousands of people accept the Lord right in their homes.

4. *Special efforts*

The objective during this phase is to reach every person within his own social structure: in jails, hospitals, military barracks, universities, schools, factories, public places, etc. Special activities are planned to reach children, young people, women, professional and business men, government employees, industrial workers, etc. Every available means is utilized: literature, moving pictures, clubs, suppers, contests, congresses, conferences, literacy programs, etc.

5. *Evangelistic meetings*

Usually there are four types of special evangelistic meetings during the year: (a) a congregational campaign held simultaneously in each participating Church; (b) a united city-wide campaign, usually in a public place; (c) a regional or state campaign, conducted in the country's chief cities; and finally, (d) a national campaign in the capital city, with people coming from all over the country, that culminates with a colorful, impressive parade. Other meetings such as the Youth Congress, the Women's Congress and children's rallies are not primarily for evangelistic purposes but nonetheless produce a tremendous evangelistic impact.

6. *Continuation*

This phase does not begin at the end of the program but accompanies all aspects of the movement. It handles follow-up and related work. New believers are incorporated into the program immediately. Churches and denominations receive advice about applying the principles and strategy of Evangelism-in-Depth in continuous and long-range programs.

Projections of Evangelism-in-Depth

Although the statistical results of this movement may be quite impressive, its importance is measured by other criteria which usually are not evident in a statistical analysis, and which affect the life and work of a Church for many years. I shall mention only a few.

1. A Church gains a new vitality because during this year of Evangelism-in-Depth more conversions occur than in any other year in the entire history of Christian work in that country.

2. Evangelism-in-Depth provides a framework in which foreign missionary societies can use their resources in a partnership program that contributes directly to the growth and development of the national Church.

3. Local leaders emerge in and from the coordinated evangelistic efforts.

4. In its responsibility for mobilizing believers, the local Church gains experience and retains the tools to continue in-depth evangelism.

5. Denominational leaders experience deeper understanding of their function and responsibility concerning needs, objectives, and long-range planning.

In short, Evangelism-in-Depth, as a philosophy of evangelism, affirms that the responsibility for evangelization rests upon the whole Church; that the objective of evangelization takes in every person of an entire nation; and that in order to fulfill this mission, we must use all the resources God has given his Church. But remember that Evangelism-in-Depth is not just a theory: it is a very real part of the history of Christian churches in seven Latin American nations and in other parts of the world. To God be the glory!

THE SOCIAL PROGRAM OF THE CHURCH
José D. Fajardo

"Let your light so shine before men, that they may see your good works and give glory to your Father who is in heaven" (Matt. 5:16 RSV).

For more than a century and a half, Protestant missions have been struggling to give the people of Latin America a knowledge of the living Christ, and through him to bring them to a new life. In most countries this great effort has attained almost negligible results. In some countries, gains have been recorded only within the last twenty years. Mass evangelism has been almost unknown, and people have tended to respond better to person-to-person contact. We must seek to understand how conditions long prevailing in Latin America have affected the acceptance of the Gospel message.

The conquest of Latin America was both political and religious. The Indians became Christian either willingly or by force; the colonists and explorers were imported Christians of the Catholic tradition and for three centuries the people knew no other religious thought except that of the Catholic church. The people became accustomed to the notion that Church and State are almost the same thing. As the population in the colonies grew, people saw that there was little help for them either from the State or the Church. A kind of feudal system prevailed, in which a few large landowners dominated the economic and political life of the country. In many places the church was also a large landowner and therefore was considered one with the rich and the mighty. As a consequence, when people rebel in Latin America and ask for changes, they ask for changes also within the established church. The peasants, the working people and uneducated classes consider the Church not as their defender and redeemer, but rather as a force which cooperates with the governments or strong political parties to subdue them.

As a result, many Latin Americans viewed religion as a social and political necessity, impinging neither upon their spiritual life nor upon their moral conduct. Since religious beliefs could not be questioned or examined, the people did not worry about the rightness or wrongness of these beliefs. Gradually they became indifferent to anything that was called religion. If they identified themselves with some religious belief it was for the sake of being accepted into the society in which they lived. But most people have lost confidence that the Church can contribute to their well-being. For this

DR. FAJARDO is principal of Colegio Americano of Cali, and an ordained minister missionary in Cali, Colombia, South America.

reason they are very skeptical, and even suspicious, about taking a new religious stand. Could it result in just another form of church which, once they help it to gain power, will forget about their many needs?

We Protestant leaders should be very realistic about this and try to avoid the pitfalls of an institutionalized church. Perhaps people have been slow to accept the Reformation message because they want more than just "good preaching;" they want "good preaching and good deeds." They seem to be saying: "They preach as good or better than the church we are used to, but what are they doing to change our condition?"

I have heard many missionaries say: "Do not preach a social gospel, because that will not save or change the people." But social *service* need not be the "social gospel." A social gospel might be preaching about the needs of the people and even denouncing their oppressors, presenting a picture of what a good Christian society could be, indicating the good things that good Christians could do. But social service really means actually doing things for people right where they are and where they need it. It means serving those that do not belong to our own denomination, or creed, or language or race. It means doing something about their pain and suffering, for the sake of Christian love, and not insinuating at every turn that we do what we do in order to get them into our churches and to take up our form of creed.

What I am about to say may sound heretical and even offensive, but I feel that this has been the western philosophy of social service in the Church. I have always felt that when we help the needy or do something for a group or community, we usually think: "We are doing this for this group or person in the hope that they will follow us to our church." This kind of charity reminds me of what I used to do as a child, when I was sent out into the pasture to get a horse. I would carry a banana in one hand in front of me and the halter in the other hand behind me. This "banana-halter" type of charity has greatly disillusioned us because the people whom we thus serve are usually the last ones to take up our faith and become militant Christians. But when others outside of this circle see what the Christian Church is doing, they want to join in and carry on the work we are doing. I believe this is what Jesus meant when he said: "Let your light so shine before men, that they may see your good works and glorify your Father who is in heaven." Naturally we want eventually to bring everyone to the feet of our Lord in order that they be saved, but even if those whom we serve should not accept him as their Savior, we should still continue to serve them, if they need our help.

I should like to analyze briefly the general nature and scope of the methods used up to the present in Latin American evangelism.

With few exceptions, evangelism and service in Latin America have been limited to the preaching of the Word and the establishment of "mission schools." We could say then, that apart from preaching, the only significant form of social service which we have given during the past century has been in education, and that purely on the academic level; we have left almost untouched the arts, crafts, agriculture, medicine, building, animal husbandry, the conservation and utilization of natural resources, preparation for political service, and so on.

Schools generally start as very small institutions, and are usually supported by a mission board or local Church. While these schools are small and dependent, they tend to be more evangelistic, but as they grow and acquire status, they tend to become more like any other educational institution in the country, with very little concern for the evangelization of students. Many times students who have been through our mission schools go on to higher institutions and eventually reach government positions, but without being dedicated Christians, so that their service to the country and to the evangelical cause is very insignificant. This means that the only significant service being given by the Protestant church in Latin America is not being used as a means of evangelism.

The Bible tells us that when Jesus gave his disciples the Great Commission to preach the Gospel, he also added: "Heal the sick, raise the dead, cleanse lepers, cast out demons." As already stated, the ministry of the Protestant church in Latin America has been limited almost wholly to preaching and teaching, while it has done almost nothing about the physical needs of millions of people in every country.

The needs of each country are so many that I could not enumerate them all. Thousands of people live in the large cities in very crowded conditions; they have little or no sanitation, little or no drinking water, few or no health centers. Where some form of public health service exists, the time and trouble involved in getting attention is so excessive that many people prefer not to go. Many people cannot afford a doctor, so it is common for men, women and children to die without medical attention. In the rural areas, medical services are almost negligible.

In many cities thousands of people are homeless, especially women and children who sleep under park benches, under the awnings of downtown buildings, or under bridge abutments. In all the large cities of Colombia, children as young as three years of age go from door to door with tin cans begging for leftover food for themselves and for their parents.

In Lima, Peru, one of the most beautiful cities of Latin America, more than 50,000 people live on top of the city's garbage dumps and exist from day to day as scavengers. Men, women, children, dogs, and hogs all live here together and grub together.

Despite the fact that the Protestant church has been working there for over a century, Colombia still has about 500,000 Indians who can neither read nor write, who live and die in extreme poverty, hunger, sickness, ignorance and superstition. In northern Colombia a tribe of some 40,000 souls live in hunger and misery because of the lack of water. No church or mission group has thought of going to this area and digging some wells for drinking water and for irrigating the fields. Yet we say we would be very happy for an open door to preach the Gospel among these Indians.

People in the rural areas need help in learning how to make their land more productive, to raise better farm animals, to build better and more sanitary houses. In some places the peasants' greatest need is someone who will take up their cause and protect them from the landowners who still rule them under a kind of feudal system.

Orphanages, widows' homes, and homes for the aged operated by Protestant agencies are either unknown or operated on a very small scale. We need nurseries where the children of unwed mothers can be kept during the day, while the mothers try to earn a decent living. We need a program to help rehabilitate drug-addicts, alcoholics and prostitutes.

The Latin American people, despite the fact that about 75 per cent have become indifferent to the Catholic religion, have been very slow as a rule to take a stand with the Protestant church. Many Latin Americans think that we are just another church that, in the end, may let them down just like the one they supported for so many years. Since they see no great difference in our actions, they decide to stay outside. Millions of people in Latin America today may be waiting to see what the Protestant church has in its program to redeem the multitudes who are crying for help, but who do not see from where it is to come.

Could we not show these people that we are concerned not only for the salvation of their souls but also for all areas of their lives, a concern that may determine their attitude toward God?

When they see our good works and begin glorifying our heavenly Father, then the people of Latin America will be ready for mass evangelism.

Report of Group Discussion

It is the duty of the Church to maintain a continuous and vigorous evangelistic witness, not limiting itself to sporadic and occasional campaigns, delegates emphasized. Many observed that Bible studies, prayer and worship services and meetings for Christians make up the bulk of normal Church programs and that so-called evangelism seldom goes beyond the walls of the church buildings.

The program of the Church requires restudy in order adequately to bring its witness into line with the Great Commission of the Lord.

Earlier in the section discussion, exception was taken to the view that the "social gospel" approach is the proper way to conduct evangelism. Many believed that this approach fails to take into account that the individual is the primary unit which needs to be transformed. In Scripture the gospel is directed to the individual rather than to society in general. It is the converted individuals that change society.

Evangelism should not be reduced to a rule of thumb however. Many points of contact have proved useful: the questionnaire method which provides a good opening for conversation with students and intellectuals, well-conducted Bible studies in private homes, and other methods. At the same time a warning was sounded against the duplication of efforts by denominational groups, the escalation of personal or denominational interests to the detriment of evangelistic outreach, and the tendency to forget that evangelism is a never ending task.

Reporter: *Herbert Money*

EVANGELISM IN FRENCH-SPEAKING LANDS

Maurice Ray

Since we are to answer the question: "How may we present Christ to a world which is constantly changing?", it seems necessary first to characterize "the spiritual climate" of the French-speaking countries of Europe if we wish to evangelize in a fruitful way.

Whether it be in France, Belgium or Switzerland, the population as a whole is either of Catholic or Protestant tradition. This means that the great majority of the people have had or still have a contact with the Church, and therefore with the Gospel — by baptism, by catechism, or by a faithful or an occasional attendance at religious services.

A minority know Christ as a personal Savior and living Lord. Another minority, which is growing, has broken all regular contact with the Church. Between these two poles, there is the mass of those who know the Gospel in greater or lesser degree, holding it above all as a moral and religious law offered to those who wish to put it into practice. For those, the Church is a traditional institution which contributes to the safeguard of public morality and brings together "those who still believe in something."

All forms of evangelism meet both indifference and suspicion. So much greater suspicion when the organizers do not belong to the official church. This opposition to evangelism is even found among the officials of this church, who reproach the evangelist at the time he calls for a decision because he makes no distinction between pagans and baptized people.

The church also is unhappy about the fact that in a time of ecumenical activity and at a time when we should be creating "a church for the others," evangelism would be accompanied by proselytizing or contributing to the strengthening of "closed communities," in which the "converts" demonstrate more spiritual pride than love for the world.

We could reasonably ask ourselves if these criticisms made against evangelism really concern evangelism. But this is not our present question, which is limited simply to giving an acquaintance with the situation and the conditions in which the evangelist works.

The indirect methods

The general climate of unconcern on the part of the Church concerning evangelism has not especially favored the development of indirect methods.

Film — A great deal more can be done in this area.

Television — The programs given over to evangelical expression are

MR. RAY is director of the Scripture Union in Switzerland.

limited, at this time, to a kind of "Protestant presence" by the televised worship service, and religious news.

Press — Except for rare instances, the religious papers are related toward news or toward the discussion of questions about inner problems which have specially to do with the life of the Church. In the secular press, evangelism messages seldom appear. Very rare are those men or women who will deal with problems about evangelical witness. The only papers speaking about evangelism come from churches not bound to the federation of official churches; they are considered (wrongly) as sects, and are not read outside of the membership of those communities.

Radio — What has just been said concerning the press can also be applied to radio, where the message of evangelism is regularly and intentionally the work of the evangelical communities independent of the official church. And even here we ought to specify that the stations only allow these broadcasts to come on between 5:30 and 6:30 in the morning.

In other words, indirect evangelism in French-speaking countries is yet very little developed and offers a field of activity for which workers are being sought.

The direct method

This method is practiced very often in evangelical groups and occasionally by the official church. Cooperation with the official church should always be sought because all evangelism carried out independently of the church would be considered a sectarian enterprise, from which those that the organizers would like to reach would turn away immediately.

This evangelism is practiced in three ways:

1. In the Camping Grounds, if the team leader and those accompanying him have received a calling for evangelism, otherwise this work takes the form of a worship service, with the liturgy suitable to open air.

2. In the parishes of the cities.

a. Indispensable conditions: get the agreement and cooperation of the church by preliminary contacts with the authorities and Christians in the parish, and if possible, with the leaders of the other local Christian groups.

b. Evangelism is not to be confused with edification. It is necessary, however, to think carefully about what will happen on the local level to those that evangelism will have reached and to provide for their integration to the churches and communities. Experience shows that if this aspect of the follow-up is not very concretely formulated, many of those who have responded will become discouraged and will turn away from the road of faith.

c. In the same way, in the countries which are mostly Catholic, all evangelistic efforts should seek the agreement and cooperation of the local communities and local churches, or if not, that of the Christians in that area. It is necessary to get them to work with us.

d. In evangelism, children are a special public which should never be neglected. The message illustrated by flannelgraph will make them listen and through them, the family can be won.

e. The contact with the audience will be facilitated if the message finds a special point of insertion into the reality which preoccupies many of our contemporaries — sexual and conjugal ethics; the problems of social justice; of health, physical, mental and psychiatric; the anguish one may feel about the future of the world, facing the enslavement of men to science, etc.

3. Camps for young people and adults, "retreats" for couples, for different trades or professions, for single people, etc., offer opportunities for direct evangelism to develop.

The criticism of our methods

1. It is necessary to discern if the criticism, very often addressed to the *form* of evangelism, does not hide criticism of the *principle* of evangelism.

2. Evangelism has its weaknesses and sometimes its bad fruits. While it is right to recognize this, it is also right not to decry evangelism because of some of these failures. The pastoral ministry also knows unfruitful times!

3. Many of the objections show up as being without a foundation when one looks at them in the light of the Scripture.

a. The difference which must be made between those who are baptized and those who are pagan, in the light of Matthew 13:4-9.

b. The fact of taking Holy Communion.

4. The evangelist should not allow himself to be stopped by objections or even by opposition which might come to him. He knows that in conjunction with the ministry of the Church, his own ministry prepares for and hastens the coming of the Lord, who will take out only his living and sanctified Church.

For more than forty years in our French-speaking countries, the evangelism of children, young people and adults has found its framework of ministry and a very large number of workers especially in the work of the Scripture Union.

MASS EVANGELISM
IN THE IVORY COAST
Joseph Diéké Koffi

"Go ye into all the world, and preach the gospel to every creature. He who believes and is baptized will be saved, but he who does not believe will be condemned." This passage is an imperative command of the Lord (Go) and is spoken to every believing child of God. It is not something that depends upon your will, but upon the necessity of obeying an order. We must act on these words from the Lord whatever the cost may be. According to the word of the angels to the women in Matthew 28:6, 7, "Go and see and tell," we are witnesses of that which we know. And also that which has been sealed in our hearts by the Holy Spirit through what we have learned in the Scriptures: this state of affairs makes of us disciples of Jesus. And he said in Acts 1:8, "and ye shall be witnesses unto me . . . unto the uttermost part of the earth." It is to us as witnesses that this mission has been committed, and we have the formal promise from the Lord that we will not be alone (Matthew 28:20): "I am with you . . . unto the end of the world." In John 14:12 he adds that he who believes in Christ will do greater works than those he did. We are witnesses who wish to obey this imperative order from the Lord.

Here are some of the methods that we use in the Ivory Coast for mass evangelism and by which many souls have been converted to God.

First method: Evangelism by group and music

In I Corinthians 9:13, the Apostle Paul says, "I do all things for the gospel's sake, that I may be a joint partaker thereof" (ASV). We must be aware of the fact that the Africans are innate musicians. Even in the face of death, the African sings and dances. Because of this, very often the Christian men and women go in a group (about 20 to 30) from a single village, and with the permission of the local chief they make a sort of procession through the village singing and playing the band; then they go and take their place on the public square. Great crowds are thus drawn together by the singing. Then the preaching begins and such a meeting can bring together at one time 400–500 people and can terminate generally with numerous conversions. This method is the oldest and the most often used in our country. By this method with the help of the Holy Spirit, we have been able to establish most of the local churches.

MR. DIÉKÉ KOFFI is president of the Protestant Evangelical Church CMA in Bouake, Ivory Coast, Africa.

Second method: Scholastic education

In the Gospel of Luke, in the sixteenth verse of chapter 18, the Lord Jesus said: "Suffer little children to come unto me, and forbid them not." Scholastic education is a means of evangelism. It reaches the youth in a straightforward way. We are conscious that in order to have the best success in an underdeveloped country like ours, the Ivory Coast, the youth must not be neglected. We have, consequently, created primary and secondary schools which make it possible to bring together a number of children at a time. While teaching them the sciences of this world, we teach them to know our Lord as their personal Savior. This message is very important because we know that the young boys and girls we are training today will be the Church of tomorrow.

Third method: Bible camps and school chaplains

In I Corinthians 10:31, we read these words: "Whether therefore ye eat, or drink, . . . do all to the glory of God." With this in mind, we organize evangelistic Bible Camps at the end of each school year; bringing together the young people of both sexes, coming from the primary and secondary schools. This plan is very efficient. It allows us to reach a small number of young people with whom we can do a deep work in leading them to Christ. To this work we must add the school chaplain. In full agreement with the heads of the schools, missionaries or pastors are appointed as chaplains, and several times each week visit the secondary schools and colleges in order to preach to the students.

Fourth method: The radio

With its development, radio has become a universal means of evangelism, especially Radio ELWA of Monrovia in Liberia, which sends out our messages in all the vernacular languages as well as in French, the official language of the country. With the full cooperation of the Head of State, the President Felix Houphouet Boigny, the government of the Ivory Coast puts at our disposal the radio and television of our country, thus making it possible to send out weekly messages.

Fifth method: Diffusion of Christian literature

At this period of time, when the educated love to read many novels and magazines in order to be well informed on news from the entire world, biblical literature plays an important role in evangelism.

Sixth method: Religious films

Religious films are also the means of easily reaching considerable numbers of people in a very fruitful way.

Seventh method: Prison visitation

A wonderful work has also been undertaken among the prisoners. With the authorization of the administrative authorities, we go into the prisons and we freely preach Christ; numerous conversions take place through the help of the Lord among these prisoners.

Eighth method: Evangelism through medical care

The experience already gained in this domain proves that one of the most favorable moments for a man to be easily reached with the Gospel is when he is seriously ill. Thus at a number of places, dispensaries and hospitals have been created where the Gospel is announced with success among those who are suffering in their bodies. If I might give a personal testimony, I would say that the Lord called me to a knowledge of himself through illness. With the help of God these methods give satisfactory results. I ask you to pray that God will continue to bless these methods with a view to the advancement of the evangelization of the Ivory Coast.

Report of Group Discussion

Discussion centered on two questions. First, "What can the French-speaking peoples of Europe do to help French-speaking people in other parts of the world?" Second, "How can they bridge the gap between evangelicals and the authorities of the large Protestant Churches in French-speaking Europe? How can they share with them the content and spirit of what has been received at the World Congress?"

Replying to the first question, delegates requested help from French-speaking Europe to meet the following needs elsewhere:

1. Editors and secretaries for *Champion*, a French evangelical magazine for French Africa.

2. Qualified people to train Africans in writing and publishing techniques.

3. Films in French. The discussion revealed a great need for training and help in the production of French Gospel films for the whole French-speaking world.

4. A closer contact between mission sponsored churches and missionaries and indigenous evangelical movements.

The following conclusions were reached concerning question two:

1. In order to study the problems raised in the paper by Maurice Ray, a meeting of French-speaking evangelists will be convened in the Spring of 1967 in Switzerland under the guidance of M. Ray.

2. It was suggested that those present prayerfully seek opportunities

to contact personally fellow ministers (even those who are not necessarily sympathetic) in order to share the burden and message of the Congress and recall them to the main mission of the Church.

3. The French report of the Congress papers should be prepared as soon as possible. Releases to the secular and religious press should be issued stressing the broad ecclesiastical support of the Congress in order to demonstrate to the large Protestant denominations in French-speaking Europe that the forces for evangelism are considerable and will not be stopped.

4. Evangelicals must admit that some of their methods have justified the criticism that they are sectarian, and they must therefore avoid these methods.

Reporter: *David Barnes*

SECTION VII

Supplementary Discussion Groups

LITERATURE EVANGELISM • *Jack McAlister*   513

REPORT OF GROUP DISCUSSION • *Kenneth McVety*   516

STUDENT EVANGELISM • *David Adeney*   518

REPORT OF GROUP DISCUSSION • *Isaac Ababio*   521

REPORT OF GROUP DISCUSSION ON EDUCATION
IN RELATION TO EVANGELISM • *James M. Boice*   522

REPORT OF GROUP DISCUSSION ON
MASS EVANGELISM • *Werner Bürklin*   523

REPORT OF GROUP DISCUSSION ON
EVANGELISM AND RACE • *Dana Minnaar*   523

REPORT OF GROUP DISCUSSION ON
EVANGELISM-IN-DEPTH • *Roger J. Voke*   524

REPORT OF GROUP DISCUSSION
ON YOUTH EVANGELISM • *Bill Yoder*   525

REPORT OF GROUP DISCUSSION
ON MISSIONS AND TECHNOLOGY • *David A. Hubbard*   525

REPORT OF GROUP DISCUSSION ON
FOLLOW-UP TECHNIQUES • *Angel B. Taglucop*   526

REPORT OF GROUP DISCUSSION ON
THE ETHICS OF THE EVANGELIST • *Gregorio Tingson*   526

REPORT OF GROUP DISCUSSION ON
EVANGELISM AND REVIVAL • *Norman Cook*   527

LITERATURE EVANGELISM

Jack McAlister

One of the most probing questions we can ask ourselves is, "What will this World Congress on Evangelism mean to the unevangelized?" One year from now, will the unevangelized be more numerous than today?

Because of the "population explosion," the answer will probably depend upon how effectively and how extensively we use the printed page. Martin Luther said, "God's supreme gift to Christendom to aid the spread of the Gospel is the printing press."

We urge all men at this Congress to unite the flame of evangelism with the almost limitless outreach of the printed page.

Billy Graham has challenged Christendom to think about World Evangelism in terms of 10 years, rather than "in our generation." This is an attainable goal if Christian leaders are willing to harness the vast potential of Literature Evangelism to the extent of giving one million people the Gospel every day.

Population facts force us to use the mass media of literature if we are honestly to face the "every creature" command.

If we think of primarily using the spoken word we are doomed to disappointment. Few evangelists in history will preach to such large crowds as Billy Graham. Since 1949 he has preached to an average of 5,620 people every day. If we estimate that this represents about 2,000 different people daily, it would still require 500 evangelists with the phenomenal ministry of a Billy Graham to reach 1,000,000 new people every day.

However, if God can find 500 key leaders who will mobilize enough literature distributors to reach 2,000 people daily, we will introduce 1,000,000 people to Christ every 24 hours (365,000,000 a year). In 10 years (or slightly longer) the entire world can receive a witness as to who Christ is, what he did when he came, and what he will do now for "every one that believeth." And remember, for properly prepared "paper missionaries" there is no "cultural barrier."

If the printed page is to be used of God to a maximum in this late hour of history and if we are to face successfully the challenge of a world that is largely unevangelized, we must give priority to three major considerations.

The *literature thrust must be evangelistic.* Dayton Roberts of Latin America Mission says, "Only 4 per cent of our literature is directed to the non-Christians." This fact reveals the heart of a major tragedy. "Gen-

DR. JACK McALISTER is president of World Literature Crusade, North Hollywood, Calif.

erally speaking, literature men are not evangelistic and evangelists are not literature men."

Continental surveys have revealed that 80 per cent of evangelical literature produced has been for pastors! Sixteen per cent has been for Christian laymen and 4 per cent for the unevangelized masses of millions!

The most meaningful sentence in the pre-Congress pronouncements was a statement by Dr. Carl Henry, "The decline of evangelistic compassion is the most crucial matter facing Christendom today." The naked truth is, only divine compassion in our hearts will ever cause us to use the printed page to evangelize the billion people in our world who will never be contacted by pulpit or stadium preaching. Compassion compels you to "find a way" to evangelize.

We must *conserve the results* of literature evangelism (and all other forms of evangelism) and nurture "babes in Christ" through effective "follow-up" literature. Dr. Clyde Taylor says, "There is a tragedy I see all over the world regarding the distribution of gospels, testaments and tracts. The seed is sown but usually there is no follow-up or plan to gather the harvest."

Last week I phoned the international headquarters of the Seventh Day Adventist organization. They told me that they have sent their correspondence course follow-up literature to 22,126,978 people!

How many people does your denomination or organization have who are studying in a literature follow-up program?

Hundreds of millions of hungry minds in our world reach out for truth. Will we as Protestant leaders of this Congress accept the challenge of allocating a proper proportion of funds to this ministry which can instruct millions in scriptural truth? Hundreds of millions of dollars pass through our hands annually. If one single religious organization can reach 22,000,000 people, what could be the global impact of the more than one hundred organizations and denominations represented in this Congress, if they would act within their own sphere of influence and engage in large scale literature follow-up ministries?

A high official of a major evangelistic broadcasting ministry in the USA told me, "We wouldn't dare offer a Bible correspondence course. We'd be swamped with requests." We believe that the potential of literature follow-up of new contacts and new converts has never been fully explored. This is also the case of literature evangelism. Evangelical Christendom has not yet given the emphasis to the printed page which would allow the world to evaluate the true potential of literature evangelism.

Our best opportunity to evaluate the potential of literature would be to examine the phenomenal literature success of the cults and the Communists. Even this comparison would not be adequate because a global evangelistic thrust via literature would have the active assistance of the Holy Spirit, which the cults and the Communists do not have.

To be dynamic and effective, an evangelistic literature effort must be *saturated with prayer*. Because of the fact that World Literature Crusade has invested more than one million dollars in radio time to mobilize prayer partners, we speak from experience and with enthusiasm on this subject.

We have special prayer for the literature distributed by our Pioneer Crusaders in remote, totally unevangelized areas. This "specially prayed for literature" brings one response for every 100 messages distributed.

It is true of verbal preaching that "it is not by might nor by power, but by my Spirit saith the Lord." It is of maximum importance to remember that this applies equally to preaching by print.

We have been encouraged by Congress leaders to come to Berlin and ruthlessly examine our deficiencies. Let us do it! By and large, Protestants have not used the printed page on a mass scale for evangelism. While church membership increased 65 per cent in the last 25 years in the U.S., the Jehovah's Witnesses increased 2,000 per cent. Literature was their key weapon. We were thrilled when people filled Yankee Stadium to hear Billy Graham. That summer the Jehovah's Witnesses filled both Yankee Stadium and the Polo Grounds on the same day – 180,291 people! They baptized 7,136 people in a single service! They don't have one full-time paid preacher in the entire U.S.A. – but they do have the largest privately owned printing press in the world! One press produced more than 4,000 tons of literature last year.

What about a million towns in the free world where Clyde Taylor reports there is no gospel witness? What about 484 million in India who will number 1,234 million in 34 years?

T. E. Lloyd, the British Home Secretary of the Africa Inland Missions says, "Christian literature is today's absolute number one priority in all missionary planning." The late Kenneth Strachan said, "Eighty-five per cent of all Latins won to Christ are converted as a result of a Christian book, paper, tract, or Bible, and were convicted of sin because of it."

Dr. Guy Playfair of the Sudan Interior Mission said, "After much thought, I believe that the influence of our Africa Challenge literature would be worth more than 5,000 new missionaries going to Africa at this time."

Dr. Harold Cook, Missions Department Chairman of Moody Bible Institute says, "Literature can be our most efficient medium of mass communication of the gospel. In terms of the price paid for it, the number of people reached, and the fact that the message can be read over and over again until it is understood, there is no other method that can compare with literature." No other agency can penetrate so deeply, abide so persistently, witness so daringly and influence so irresistibly as the printed page.

Missionary statesman, Dr. Oswald J. Smith, said, "After studying the challenge of World Evangelism for more than 50 years – the only plan I have heard of that could result in the fulfillment of the Great Commission is a literature distribution ministry."

One of the great German Christians of the 15th century was Johann Gutenberg, the father of modern printing. Five hundred and sixty years ago he wrote, "God suffers because of the great multitudes whom his sacred Word cannot reach. Religious truth is captive in a small number of manuscript books which guard the treasures. Let us break the seal which holds the holy things; give wings to the truth that by a means no longer written at great expense by the hand that wearies itself, but multiplied by an unwearied machine it may fly to every soul born into the world." The God-given purpose and vision of the man who invented the first printing press was World Evangelism!

If God trusted the revelation of the living Word to the written word — so can we! There is no reason to believe that God's Word is more powerful when it is spoken than when it is written.

We have one task. It is to evangelize the human race with the only Gospel God ever gave. The size and urgency of our task demands the use of the mass media of literature.

Report of Group Discussion

It was agreed, both in Dr. McAlister's presentation and in the discussion which followed, that the wise and widespread use of printed material is of supreme and strategic importance in evangelism today. The world's exploding population, the astounding rise in literacy, and the universal availability of printing facilities all combine to underscore the need to re-evaluate the use of literature evangelism.

Evangelistic literature appeals across all cultural lines if the basic Gospel is faithfully presented, many stated. However, it is always essential to observe the cultural context of the people to whom the literature is distributed, for unfortunately it is possible fatally to alienate a society by using literature which does not take national and racial peculiarities into account.

To be effective, Christian literature must be carefully designed, both as to writing and appearance, not only for the specific country in question but also for the cultural and educational level of the reader. Much literature is written at too difficult a level.

Illustrations from Central America arose to highlight the need for a carefully planned distribution of material. Much effort is wasted by the use of literature produced in a foreign country, raising unnecessary negative reactions, and by repeated distribution in easily accessible areas while other parts of the country are left untouched.

Beyond question, Christian literature is one of the great evangelistic tools of this day, delegates believed. In the hands of a witnessing Church and as an expression of a deep compassion for the world's billions, it is a facet of today's evangelistic task, calling clearly for new attention and fresh concern and planning.

Reporter: *Kenneth McVety*

STUDENT EVANGELISM
David Adeney

The population explosion of which we have been hearing in this Congress is most clearly seen in the student world. A few weeks ago I was speaking in a mission in the University of Malaya which in 1958 had only 100 students. Today there are 3,600 and by the end of this decade they expect the number will have doubled.

In many countries students are exerting an important influence in the field of politics. During recent weeks the newspapers in India, where I have been during the last few weeks, have been full of reports of student riots and strikes. I was reminded of the day when I was caught up in the great student demonstrations in Seoul, Korea which brought down the Sygman Rhee government. In the midst of the troubles one student said, "Our fellow-students have shed their blood today for a political cause. What have we done for Jesus Christ?"

The Church of Jesus Christ must recognize the great potential for good or evil to be found in the universities of the world. If the students of this generation are not won for Jesus Christ and challenged to serve him in his Kingdom, the church in the future will suffer. Some of the great missionary movements of the past have been spearheaded by students. Great missionary watchwords such as "The Evangelization of the World in this Generation" (S.V.M.) and "Evangelize to a Finish to Bring Back the King" (I.V.F.) have inspired many in the western world to give their lives for missionary service.

Today we are realizing that "the missionary call is not the exclusive privilege of the Anglo-Saxon world, it belongs to all the people of God" (Dr. R. Padilla, IFES Lima, Peru). We should therefore look for a new movement of the Spirit of God calling out from this generation of students in Africa, Asia and Latin America those who will give themselves sacrificially for the work of the Gospel. This will only be possible if Christian students are actively engaged in evangelism in their own universities, for only those who manifest a real zeal for winning others on campus are likely to respond to God's call to missionary service.

In spite of the materialistic outlook of many students there are those who share the perplexity of a Muslim engineering student who asked "Materialism is encroaching on every side, why does not God speak to man?" Students in Asia, Africa and Latin America are hungry for the truth. A Hindu wrote to me saying, "I am like a blind person seeking a piece of God, lying afar off and I cannot find the way to search for it. Is to know the preaching

MR. ADENEY is associate general secretary for the Far East International Fellowship of Christian Students, Kowloon, Hong Kong.

the way or is there some other process of seeking God and realizing him? Tell me the way. How can we realize God, and realize that we are the sons of God?" Another student asked, "Why does God seem so much nearer in Christianity than in other religions?" God has given us a wide open door for evangelism among students. Let us consider therefore certain principles which we must keep in mind if we are to be effective in our witness.

1. "The object of our work must be to proclaim Christ, warning every man and teaching every man in all wisdom, that we may present every man mature in Christ" (cf. Col. 1:28, Berkeley). We cannot be content with superficial results. Students may "make decisions" but unless they are built up, established in the faith, and introduced to the local church, the work will have no lasting value. In Asian countries, conversion is often accompanied by severe conflict. A student may "accept Christ" at an evangelistic campaign, but then he may run into intense opposition at home, or his friends belonging to his old religion may come with strong arguments to overthrow his faith. Only the Christian fellowship can provide the teaching and fellowship he needs to keep him true to his Lord. Student workers must therefore insist on spiritual depth and seek only to glorify the Lord Jesus. To publicize statistics of conversion at evangelistic campaigns and then later to find that most of them have disappeared is to bring dishonor to the name of Christ.

2. It is most important that the leadership should be in the hands of national workers. If western leadership is prominent and the work is dependent upon foreign financial resources, the foundations will be insecure. Whenever the apostle Paul established a new group of believers, he always appointed local leaders and encouraged the Christians to give for the support not only of their own work but also to help needy members of the body of Christ in other places. National Evangelical Unions should produce staff workers from their own ranks, and the Christian graduates who have benefited spiritually from the student work must provide the financial support. Non-Christians will only respect a movement which is rooted in their country and gives evidence of sacrificial living. This does not mean no help can be accepted from outside. The testimony of teams made up of Christians from different countries, both from the East and from the West can be very valuable. Christians from other lands must be free to share the financial burdens of their brothers and sisters in need. But to receive occasional gifts for special projects as the Lord leads his servants to give is very different from being dependent upon a regular income from abroad.

3. The witness must, wherever possible, be within the university. The object must always be to make the Christian fellowship a part of the life of the university or college. In many Asian universities there are Buddhist, Muslim, and Catholic action societies. Evangelicals should make sure that the true witness is maintained right on the campus to the crucified and risen Savior and Lord. While Christians may invite their friends to visit local churches, they will find that there are those who would attend a

student meeting on campus but would never go inside a church building. A Christian professor now active in the Church told me that he would not have been converted if he had had to go to an outside church, but at a Christian fellowship meeting in a lecture hall he came to know Christ. At recent Varsity Christian Missions in Singapore and Malaysia, where hundreds attended lectures on campus each night, many were coming to Christian meetings for the first time. This was only possible because the VCF was recognized by the University. They could publish thousands of copies of the mission newspaper, visit from door to door in the hostels, display attractive posters and maintain a mission book-table staffed by students right on the campus. Such an effort required a high degree of student initiative. Outside Christian workers would not have had the privileges possessed by these students. Funds to cover the very considerable expenses of these missions were provided locally. Non-Christian students realized that the message of Jesus Christ as Lord and Savior was being proclaimed by their fellow students. On the last night of the mission in Singapore, the university Buddhist Society put on a meeting in the next door lecture theatre, but only a very few attended it. Students who have been responsible for organizing such a mission and have taken part in the personal evangelism and follow-up work have gained experience which will be of great value to them as they seek to serve in the Church of our Lord Jesus Christ.

4. The Christian Fellowship in the university must maintain close links with the local churches and build up in their members a deep sense of missionary responsibility.

Many of the student leaders in University Christian Fellowship hold responsible positions within the youth organizations of their local Churches. Among the graduates and staff workers are to be found many who are serving as Church officers. In Asian countries it has been encouraging to see a good number of graduates serving God in a non-professional capacity. Christian doctors and dentists have been used to pioneer new Churches. One young dentist in Malaysia is now in the happy position of seeing the Church that he started seeking for a full time pastor. But it is not enough to encourage Christians to witness within their professions. The work of the Church requires university graduates who will give their full time to the service of the Lord Jesus, both in their own countries and overseas. We thank God for over forty young Asian graduates who have become staff workers of their National Evangelical Unions. Some have given up well-paid teaching positions and even medical practice to accept salaries which are often far too low, though the financial situation is improving as more graduates give sacrificially to the work. A few Christian graduates have become pastors of Churches or are now taking training in seminaries. But it is here that we find the greatest weakness in the work, for the number of Christian Asian graduates who have responded to God's call to the ministry of the Church of Jesus Christ is still very small. Missionary vision is increasing and some are now preparing to preach the Gospel in other lands. Many of the evangelical unions have a missionary fund and missionary conferences are being held to enable Church and missionary leaders to challenge Christian students with the needs of unevangelized fields.

Report of Group Discussion

The founding and development of student-led and student-attended Bible studies on the campus emerged as the number one method of student evangelism. Participants called for close liaison between the campus and the Churches, and emphasized the value of lay witness to interested students as well as the opportunity to invite students to private Christian homes. Christian lecturers should be careful to match their academic work with their Christian witness, many said.

Reporter: *Isaac Ababio*

Report of Group Discussions

EDUCATION IN RELATION TO EVANGELISM

Speaking briefly to educators at a special luncheon in the Kongresshalle, Dr. Carl F. H. Henry (USA) called for reactions to proposals for a world student congress to be held in London in 1970, to provide the focus for an evangelical thrust toward the student campus in the final generation of the twentieth century. The year set for the congress would coincide with the target date of the Apollo moon program and the date which Khrushchev's Russia had set to overcome the West. "The Congress would do much to impress, engage and challenge the student world," Henry said.

Also included in the remarks by the editor of *Christianity Today* was a criterion for evaluating the effectiveness of Christian education in its indirect task of evangelism. "We must ask how many of the graduates from Christian schools are teaching now on *secular* campuses," Henry stated. "This should be a major goal." Earlier in his remarks Henry had disclaimed active evangelism as the *primary* task of evangelical educational institutions. Their primary task is academic, Henry contended.

The need for placing evangelical PhDs on the secular campus was an imperative which impressed most of the delegates. Myron Augsburger (USA) called for a two-pronged thrust toward the secular academic world. There must be an emphasis upon the redemptive aspect of truth, and there must be a new emphasis upon the cosmic significance of Christ and of the Christian faith. Dr. W. Stanford Reid (Canada) called upon the Christian school to train men for secular positions. Dr. Hudson Armerding (USA) broadened the plea to include leadership positions in all levels of society. "It is also necessary to evangelize the existing national leadership," said Armerding.

Armerding, president of Wheaton College, also announced proposals to establish a new chair of evangelism at the Wheaton Graduate School. It would be named "The Billy Graham Chair of Evangelism." Only three other schools among those represented claimed to have similar chairs. A British observer voiced his belief that there is no chair of evangelism in any British institution.

Considerable attention was given to the task of preparing the secularly trained PhD for the evangelical task envisioned for him on the secular campus. Emphasizing the theological illiteracy of many Christian graduates in secular fields, Dr. Kenneth Kantzer (USA) suggested that such men be given opportunities for at least a year of theological training prior to assuming their secular positions. Such training would have to include the biblical disciplines in the Old and New Testament areas as well as theology, Kantzer believed.

Reacting somewhat to statements regarding the value of a PhD gained at a secular university, Oral Roberts (USA) proposed an extensive effort to supply graduate programs in Christian institutions, terming the exodus of Christian students to secular universities a lamentable retreat. Despite the mammoth cost of 100 million dollars for a Christian university, Roberts felt that the evangelical Church could well stand such an emphasis. In a less dramatic appeal, L. Gough (USA) called for informal agreements among Christian institutions to prevent the duplication of graduate programs and to implement the direction of interested students.

In an opening statement at the luncheon, Rabbi Gilbert (USA) of B'nai B'rith spoke of a new climate in Jewish-Christian relations and called for new opportunities for Jewish-Christian dialogue especially between Jewish scholars and the evangelical community.

Reporter: *James M. Boice*

MASS EVANGELISM

Delegates meeting in afternoon discussion sections to consider mass evangelism spent much time contrasting mass evangelism with personal evangelism and arguing the merits of one or the other of these approaches. The most enlightened remarks pointed to their mutual interdependence.

Reporter: *Werner Bürklin*

EVANGELISM AND RACE

"I have seen and heard much about our Congress motto — One Gospel and One Task — but I have not heard so much about 'One Race'," observed Felix Dias-Abeyesinghe (Ceylon) in the midst of the discussion of evangelism and race. He seemed to speak for many who were hopeful that the Congress would take a clear cut racial position. Many more agreed that the racial problem, especially as it exists in the United States, presents grave hindrances to the preaching of the gospel in Negro-dominated lands.

"The racial problem is the number one stumbling block to the proclamation of the Gospel," observed R. E. Harrison (USA).

Not all agreed that the race issue should receive such prominence, however, and two delegates spoke to that effect on the basis of their experience in South Africa.

R. J. M. van Tonder (South Africa) expressed the view that the racial question has taken our attention off the main issue: to proclaim Christ. "If that is done, 'race' takes care of itself by bringing us together in a new 'oneness' that will also be seen in new attitudes toward each other."

A colored South African delegate, N. Bengu, spoke at considerable length to enlighten the Congress on the situation in his country. "I think we are progressing toward a real solution," he said. "Only the people in the country can solve the country's problems, and we are doing well. Prayer helps and does change things, but excessive talk only aggravates the situation.

"The racial position is no impediment to the proclamation of the Gospel in South Africa. Our situation is different from that in the United States where people from Africa had been uprooted and been forced into a new situation on a new continent. Our position is even different from that of the other nations in Africa. From the beginning in 1652, the races were never integrated, and they never wanted to be until the world began writing about it. Since 1948 we have had a clearly defined policy of parallel development. We have our own areas, our own schools, hospitals and parliament.

"The desire for integration is a waste of time at present and for this generation at least. We want two highly developed cultures to decide the issues in the coming generations. There is no hatred between Christian people in South Africa. I can go eat, sleep or preach wherever I am invited. There is no legislation to prohibit this, and I often preach to whites. Pray with us. But allow us to decide on this issue ourselves. We are satisfied with the present situation. 'Solutions' forced on us will only bring disaster."

Reporter: *Dana Minnaar*

EVANGELISM-IN-DEPTH

The concept of "Evangelism-in-Depth" has resulted in seven nationwide movements in South Africa and has operated in thirty other places around the world, delegates to the World Congress on Evangelism were told.

The Evangelism-in-Depth program is based upon the mobilization of every Christian witness within the framework of the Church using local leadership with global objectives. It is based upon the convictions that: abundant reaping requires abundant sowing, Christians can and must work together in evangelism, when Christians pool their resources God multiplies them, and a minority can make an impact on the whole nation.

Comments on the presentation disclosed the general feeling that while Evangelism-in-Depth has proved itself in countries still being pioneered by missionaries, it would be much more difficult to implement in the so-called Christian countries such as Britain.

Evangelism-in-Depth has engaged all churches of all shades of theological interpretation. In Nigeria the "new life for all" movement safeguarded itself with a statement of belief coupled with the invitation to participate. The outcome was no loss to the evangelicals, but in many cases a reviving of the liberals occurred, some felt.

Reporter: *Roger J. Voke*

YOUTH EVANGELISM

Delegates meeting to discuss youth evangelism confined themselves to three key issues: 1) the problem involved in communicating to and involving oneself with young people, 2) the apparent "second place" which youth leadership takes in Christian activity, and 3) the use of special literature for youth.

It was the general consensus in the discussion of the first issue that some degree of identification with young people is necessary to communicate to them, but care should be taken and good taste observed in how far one goes in following the patterns set by "teen jargon" and by teen-age dress. The youth worker must be able to adjust quickly and rapidly since jargon, dress and the values of youth change rapidly.

Not only the youth leader but also the young person himself must be recognized as important in our modern world. Many emphasized the importance of closely integrating all youth evangelism with the local Church.

The importance of using a good, accurate, modern translation of the Scriptures was emphasized as a partial answer to the problems of literature for youth. Such translations as *Living Letters* (in special teen-age editions) and the translations of J. B. Phillips were mentioned.

Reporter: *Bill Yoder*

MISSIONS AND TECHNOLOGY

Delegates attending the discussion of missions and technology pointed to the need for research into means and methods of evangelism, marshaling of missionary information, and continuous analysis of the results of evangelism if the Christian outreach is to reach maximum effectiveness in our time.

A key result of information sharing and research will be long range planning. Technological breakthroughs in science will enable us to solve major problems in evangelism.

Ted Engstrom (USA) of World Vision International gave the background of his interest in technology and missions, calling for a concentration on means and methods in evangelism. D. A. McGavran (USA) protested the fact that much missionary information is sealed in compartments, tucked away in annual reports, and appealed for ways to share this knowledge with the world. "We need ways of finding out how and where the Church is growing," McGavran said.

Dr. Bob Pierce (USA) stressed the possibility that modern techniques of research and planning may be used for evil purposes with devastating results if Christians do not use them. He issued a call for those present to put these approaches to work for Christian causes.

Reporter: *David A. Hubbard*

FOLLOW-UP TECHNIQUES

"Follow-up is a process of making disciples out of new converts to the end that they may grow into the full stature of the manhood of Christ in the fellowship of the Church," agreed delegates drafting a definition of this aspect of evangelism.

Most delegates agreed that the implementation of this task should be a primary responsibility of every believer. The Church through the guidance of the minister should be organized and trained for this type of work.

In the final period of discussion, attention turned to specific types of follow-up — Bible studies, literacy classes, cell groups, conferences and the availability of Christian homes being listed in this category.

Reporter: *Angel B. Taglucop*

THE ETHICS OF THE EVANGELIST

Why is there antagonism against evangelists in some quarters? Why are pastors who become too evangelistic at times suspect in the eyes of parish members? The very fact that this section grappled with such questions presupposes that there are problems connected with the ethics and practice of the evangelist in too many cases.

A delegate from Florida remarked that an evangelist who is interested in "shekels rather than souls" would be met with much antagonism. A Canadian delegate observed that evangelists are sometimes tempted to get responses by fair means or foul, decisions often being used as a gauge of one's effectiveness and consequently of one's reputation.

Questions from the viewpoint of the evangelist also entered the discussion. Is it ethical for the evangelist to be away from his family for great lengths of time? A delegate from Australia suggested that there are occupational hazards for every vocation and the evangelist is not exempt. This occupational hazard should be accepted by the family, he felt.

At one point in the discussion, a Mexican delegate called for re-examination of the motivation behind altar calls.

Reporter: *Gregorio Tingson*

EVANGELISM AND REVIVAL

What is revival? Can we create it? Can we create the circumstances in which God will send revival? How is revival related to evangelism? These questions occupied delegates discussing "evangelism and revival."

"Revival and evangelism are distinct but related," suggested A. Skevington Wood. "Evangelism has to do with the Evangel — the Gospel. Revival has to do with renewing life which is already there. If this is so, then revival exclusively concerns the people of God." Evangelism should be the natural product of revival.

The same general point of view was taken by Richard Roberts (USA) who proposed five theories as to why God does not send revival: 1) people do not meet God's requirements, 2) revival is a phenomenon of less sophisticated people, 3) revival is not supposed to characterize "the last days," 4) God does not send revival because the Church is unprepared for it, and 5) God does not send revival because the Church would not recognize it if it should come. Roberts rejected the first four explanations in favor of the last one.

"Some have said that revival comes when hearts are prepared," objected Dave McKee (India). "But I have seen revival come where there was hatred, immorality, lying and so on." McKee felt that genuine revival must express a union of a sovereign act of God and man's response to Him. "Only as these two work together can true revival fire fall," he said.

Reporter: *Norman Cook*